Terrorism, Intelligence, and Homeland Security

To the one person in this world that greets me every morning with a smile, is my constant and steady companion during the day, and keeps me warm at night ... my wife, Mary. With love and affection always.

Bob

My wife is the light that helps sustain me with her faith, compassion, caring, wisdom, and quick wit. Our journey through this life is an adventure. Paige, for these and so many other reasons, this book is lovingly dedicated to you.

Mike

Terrorism, Intelligence, and Homeland Security

Second Edition

Robert W. Taylor
The University of Texas at Dallas

Charles R. Swanson
The University of Georgia

 Pearson

330 Hudson Street, NY NY 10013

Vice President, Portfolio Management: Andrew Gilfillan
Portfolio Manager: Gary Bauer
Editorial Assistant: Lynda Cramer
Senior Vice President, Marketing: David Gesell
Field Marketing Manager: Bob Nisbett
Product Marketing Manager: Heather Taylor
Senior Marketing Coordinator: Les Roberts
Director, Digital Studio and Content Production: Brian Hyland
Managing Producer: Cynthia Zonneveld
Manager, Rights Management: Johanna Burke
Operations Specialist: Deidra Smith
Creative Digital Lead: Mary Siener

Managing Producer, Digital Studio: Autumn Benson
Content Producer, Digital Studio: Maura Barclay
Full-Service Management and Composition:
  Integra Software Services, Ltd.
Full-Service Project Managers: Ranjith Rajaram
Cover Design: Studio Montage
Cover Image: Piotr Krzeslak/Shutterstock; Aradaphotography/
  Shutterstock; Getmilitaryphotos/Shutterstock
Printer/Binder: LSC Communications, Inc.
Cover Printer: Phoenix Color/Hagerstown
Text Font: ITC Century Std Light 9.5/12

Acknowledgments of third-party content appear on the appropriate page within the text.

Library of Congress Cataloging-in-Publication Data

Names: Taylor, Robert W., 1951- author. | Swanson, Charles R., 1942- author.
Title: Terrorism, intelligence and homeland security / Robert W. Taylor, The
  University of Texas at Dallas, Charles R. Swanson, The University of Georgia.
Description: 2nd edition. | New York : Pearson Education, Inc., [2019] |
  Includes bibliographical references and index.
Identifiers: LCCN 2017057448 | ISBN 9780134818146 (alk. paper) | ISBN 0134818148
Subjects: LCSH: United States. Department of Homeland Security. |
  Terrorism—United States—Prevention. | National security—United States. |
  Intelligence service—United States.
Classification: LCC HV6432.4 .T39 2019 | DDC 363.325/1630973—dc23
LC record available at https://lccn.loc.gov/2017057448

Student Edition:
ISBN 10:   0-13-4818148
ISBN 13: 978-0-13-4818146

Student Value Edition:
ISBN 10:   0-13-4818202
ISBN 13: 978-0-13-4818207

Brief Contents

Contents

PART II *Typologies, Organizational Structures, Tactics, and Critical Processes of Terrorism*

CHAPTER 5 **Terrorist Organizations and Structures** 119

PART IV *Combatting Terrorism and the Future*

CHAPTER 14 **Combatting Terrorism** 387

Preface

Terrorism—Intelligence—Homeland Security are three subjects that often dominate today's news events. No other issues are so prominent, so compelling, or so critically important to our communities and our nation than these three separate but interconnected topics. Nothing is more contemporary.

We are still dealing with the lingering effects of the attacks on September 11, 2001, an event that clearly changed our world forever. On that day, our security weaknesses were exploited, our vulnerability was exposed, and our fear became real. Approaching two decades after 9/11, we continue working to improve the security of our homeland from attack, whether these attacks are from aircraft hijackings, the use of biological agents, or more sophisticated cyber attempts to infiltrate crucial infrastructures. In this effort, we have sent special operations troops to quell threats and train countries in responding to terrorism. These countries include Iraq, Afghanistan, Syria, Yemen, Algeria, Somalia, Albania, Uruguay, Uzbekistan, and the Philippines. More broadly, during 2017, special operations troops were active in 138 countries.

We have expanded our intelligence-gathering and analysis capabilities to filter even our largest social media sites. We have also developed entirely new departments of government to protect us, and to respond to emergencies whether they be caused by man-made terrorist events or natural disasters. Billions of dollars have been spent in this effort to make us safer. More important, our zeal to be safer and more secure has tested the limits of our government and the basic democratic values of "life, liberty and the pursuit of happiness" that underscore our country. Nothing is more important.

Hence, the decision to write this book was an easy one, inasmuch as we had previously collaborated for years on other coauthored books (*Criminal Investigation* and *Police Administration: Structures: Processes, and Behavior*). It was also an opportunity to contribute to the discussion of some of the most important issues of our times. More important, we thought there was room for a new book. In looking at the existing works, they seemed somewhat disproportionately concentrated on historical aspects of terrorism without discussing it sufficiently in a modern context. Other volumes focused on terrorism without addressing homeland security or didn't give enough attention to the basics, such as "How did we get here?" Although interesting, edited volumes were typically too narrow in scope.

We have written a book that is historical, contemporary, and exciting while also interrelating terrorism, intelligence, and homeland security. Our goal was to write a book that focused on students—one that serves as an introductory textbook to this complex set of topics. In doing that, we also produced a book that instructors will find easy to use.

This book has four elements that are of the utmost importance:

1. *The book is written in a clear and concise manner, aimed at piquing student interest and learning.* We stay focused on our readers, providing them with both interesting content and thought-provoking features. Embedded in the content are *Information Links* to Internet sites that contain extended insights on important topics. We wrote many case studies to illustrate chapter content and make it come alive; and we filled each chapter with interesting pieces of information that were directly aimed at sparking discussion. For instance, each *Box* ends with a compelling question, and forces students to think about and discuss critical issues presented in each chapter, while *Quick Facts* provide short doses of information that spark interest in the subject under discussion.

2. *The book is compelling.* This book is carefully researched and presents content from the latest findings in the literature. As important, interviews with key leaders in the

intelligence field, heads of departments, agents within the FBI and members of local task forces, as well as friends returning from battlefields in Iraq and Afghanistan provided keen insight into issues addressing the reality of combatting terrorism. Hence, the book represents not only a strong scholarly approach to the study of terrorism, but also incorporates the real-world experience of federal agents, police officers, and soldiers tasked with preventing the next terrorist attack on our country. In addition, the photographs in each chapter were personally selected by the authors after careful attention to detailed research. To the best of our knowledge, none of these images have previously been used in a college textbook. The pictures command attention and are accompanied by carefully written captions that tell a story, adding value to each image.

3. *The book is simultaneously historical and contemporary.* We believed it was essential for readers to understand the background of people, ideas, organizations, and movements. At the same time, readers are provided with current information about new issues in the field. This approach provides readers with a unified and cutting-edge understanding of terrorism, intelligence, and homeland security and their interrelationship. For instance, readers learn not only about the Islamic State, a newly emerged terrorist organization in the Middle East, but also about the historical factors that led to its development and how the international community is responding to this new international threat.

4. *The book is well organized and has unique chapters.* The book is divided into four separate parts. Part One provides a solid framework in which to understand terrorism. Because some significant threats originate in the Middle East, we provide strong chapters that explain the geography, history, culture, and religion of this complex area. We give significant time to understanding the complexities of Islam and the rise of radicalization in chapters that are well written and easy to read. Part Two focuses on terrorist groups, their organization, and their critical processes. These are important foundational chapters that provide unique interdisciplinary discussions on terrorist structures and strategies such as recruitment and retention of members, lone wolf strategies, and suicide bombing attacks. We provide strong chapters that differentiate among state-involved terrorism, single-issue terrorism, separatist or nationalist movements, and terrorism from the left and right wings. In Part Three, we discuss America's vulnerabilities to terrorism and present the governmental agencies that are tasked with preventing terrorism. We discuss the intelligence community and the myriad Constitutional issues that have sparked controversy in our country through the USA PATRIOT Act (e.g., clandestine spying on U.S. citizens, the use of drones, "enhanced" interrogation techniques and the abuse or torture of prisoners, and use of the military in preventing terrorism domestically). In every case, we tried to provide a *balanced* approach to understanding the issues that we face as a nation, providing security from real threats while still safeguarding civil and personal liberties. And finally, in Part Four, we define the forces that combat terrorism on a daily basis. In a one-of-a-kind chapter, we focus on those agencies that have anti-terrorism or counterterrorism as part of their primary missions. Again, the emphasis here is on clarity and the provision of pinpoint information in an easy-to-read format.

New to the Second Edition

- The design has been updated with a number of enhanced learner experiences to include new box items, Quick Facts, key terms, web links, chapter review questions, and critical thinking exercises.
- New interactive videos, point-counterpoint videos, and reader-based survey questions via interactive learning environment software that accompany the second edition highlight new student learning methodologies.
- Numerous additions have been made throughout the book to reflect significant changes in the Middle East and other geographic areas where terrorism has been a continual issue and problem.

- An expanded and updated introduction to Chapter 1 sets the tone for the entire book, with a special focus on the War in Syria and the emergence of the Islamic State.

- New Quick Facts on the decline of al-Qaeda and the rise of the Islamic State highlight Chapter 3.

- Chapter 4 reveals a new and focused section on the Islamic State today.

- Chapter 5 has new and updated material on the Lone Wolf Organizational Model and carnage resulting from such attacks in recent years.

- New box items on Islamic State recruiting videos via the Internet, and training of IS fighters highlights the new additions in Chapter 6.

- Better understanding the philosophical, ideological goals and meteoric rise of a worldwide caliphate presented by the Islamic State marks an interesting new section in Chapter 7.

- New material on the emergences of the Hammerskin Nation, the rise of the Neo-Nazi movement in the United States, a discussion of new incidents involving Sovereign Citizen groups, and a new right wing alliance are reflected in Chapter 8.

- Two new box items discussing the impact of the election of President Donald Trump on the intelligence community, and the new potential for cyberterrorism present by the Islamic State highlight Chapter 9.

- Chapter 12 provides new discussion on the organization of the Department of Homeland Security (DHS), the five core mission of DHS, and the impact of the Quadrennial Homeland Security Review.

- Introduction of the THIRA Model (Threat and Hazard Identification and Risk Assessment) and the Recovery Continuum marks new material on emergency management in Chapter 13.

- A completely new introduction on national security policy and strategies, expanded discussion on the role of the military in both antiterrorism and counterterrorism missions, and the introduction of hostage and crisis negotiations as a tool to managed critical terrorist incidents spotlight new additions to Chapter 14.

- Chapter 15 highlights include updated material on the START Study, a new Quick Facts on terrorism data in the United States, two new box items focusing on the media, social media, fake news, and terrorism, and a focused discussion on recent low-tech, unsophisticated terrorist attacks aimed at mass carnage in the international and domestic communities.

Organization

This section is not a table of contents, but rather an informative dialogue highlighting each chapter of the book.

We did not write a comprehensive history of terrorism chapter, although the first and second chapters have an overview of some of its milestones. It seemed more useful to write shorter history sections in the context of the content of chapters, linking the past and the present together to bring meaning to contemporary issues. This second edition has many new and updated sections, photographs, informational links, box items, quick facts, and case histories. A number of learning objectives and related features have been rewritten to reflect these changes.

Chapter 1: Defining, Conceptualizing, and Understanding Terrorism

This chapter introduces the subject of terrorism and some of the topics and issues that are explored in more detail in later chapters. In the introduction section, reasons why it is important or perhaps essential to understand terrorism are identified, for example, challenges such as the emerging tactic of system disruption and Black Swan events that are so different they will be difficult to predict, but will impact us nonetheless.

There was terrorism before we had a name for it. To this day scholars, governments, and international organizations, such as the United Nations, struggle to find a common definition of terrorism. One barrier to understanding terrorism is the surplus of competing and conflicting definitions. The chapter also addresses how our individual and cultural perspectives affect how we think about terrorism and create barriers to understanding it. The chapter concludes by contrasting war and war crimes, irregular war, and terrorism.

Chapter 2: Political Ideology and the Historical Roots of Terrorism

Chapter 2 is a foundational chapter for the entire book. It represents a significant work on the historical development of terrorist ideology. The chapter begins with a discussion of political ideology as the general belief system on which society is based and the mechanisms people undertake to achieve this perspective. Terrorism has a direct effect on the social structure of society. People depend on a framework of informal and formal rules that foster mutual respect and trust. Terrorism substitutes this trust with insecurity and fear. Essentially, terrorism attacks the very bases of social order, culture, and government. Chapter 2 explores the political and social theory that motivates certain groups—from the genesis of revolutionary ideology and terror to contemporary hate crime and radical Islamic movements. We start with the historic left-wing ideologies of socialism and communism as expressed by Karl Marx, Friedrich Engels, Pierre-Joseph Proudhon, and Vladimir Lenin in Europe and Russia at the end of the 19th century and trace ideological ties to more contemporary perspectives of revolution in South America and the Middle East as expressed by Che Guevara, Carlos Marighella, and Sayyid Qutb. A focus on the development of Latin American leftist groups like FARC and ELN in Colombia, the Tupamaros in Uruguay, and Sendero Luminoso (Shining Path) in Peru brings our discussion to the concept of a "guerrilla war" as part of a revolutionary strategy in some cases, and as terrorism in others. We also explore the development of the "new left" in Europe during the 1960s, including the Red Brigades, the Red Army Faction (also known as the Baader-Meinhof Gang), the Revolutionary Cells, and its feminist-leaning auxiliary group, the Red Zora, bringing us full circle from the inception of left-wing, political revolutionary thought to more contemporary anti-imperialist and anticolonial ideology.

The final part of this chapter focuses on the historical roots of terrorism in the Middle East, from early anticolonial ideology and the mandate system developed at the end of World War I to the establishment of Israel and the beginning of the Palestinian Resistance movement. The chapter sets up Chapter 3 by exploring the early tenets of oil, politics, and radical Islam in the modern era.

Chapter 3: Understanding the Middle East and Islam

This book has five sets of chapters that are so closely intertwined we think of them as "twin chapters." Chapters 3 and 4 are the first set of the "twins." In Chapter 3, we start with the assertion that knowing some history of the Middle East, a few laws, and a handful of definitions is not sufficient grounding to assert one has a grasp on the Middle East and Islam. The chapter provides a basic understanding of Islam, but there is more to be learned. To fully understand the Middle East, you must also fully understand Islam. Illustratively, some critics maintain that the "problem" with Islam is that it has never undergone a reformation, as has Christianity. The Muslim view is there has never been a need for it. In their view, the Archangel Gabriel revealed the Word of God to Muhammad and he, in turn, faithfully recorded it. While ideological change in Islam has not been an historical issue, certainly leadership after the death of the Prophet has been. Understanding the emergence of two Muslim traditions, Sunni and Shi'a, provides a basis for comprehending not only the historical differences between these two groups, but also sets a foundation on which to grasp more contemporary concepts of radical Islam and the Islamic State caliphate that now threaten the entire Middle East.

The vast majority of Muslims in America are good and decent people who practice their religion peacefully. Some Islamic religious leaders have twisted the meanings of Islamic concepts. For instance, "jihad" actually refers to an individual's struggle to overcome adversity and submit to the will of God. Jihad addresses an inner, spiritual struggle against evil, not a war against others. The twisted definition of jihad fuels hatred, violence, and grisly actions, such as the recent beheadings and executions of American journalists, English aid workers, and others by members of the Islamic State.

The concluding section of the chapter ends with an explanation of Islam's five pillars of faith: (1) Shahada (testimony of faith); (2) Salat (prayer); (3) Zakat (giving a portion of your annual income to those in need and to support Islam); (4) Sawm (fasting); and (5) Hajj (pilgrimage to Mecca).

Chapter 4: The Rise of Radical Islam

Islam is one of the world's great religions. Like Judaism and Christianity, it is one of the three primary monotheistic religions, meaning it is a religion that believes in one all-loving and powerful God. The histories of these three great religions are inseparably intertwined. So what events took place within Islam that led to such a vast radicalization of basic principles within the religion? This chapter explores that change and focuses on the political dimension of Islamic fundamentalism. It analyzes the radicalization of Islam in both traditions, Sunni and Shia (Shiite). Much of the discussion is centered on the Arab Revolution beginning after World War I and culminating in the Arab Spring of 2010, the ideologies that form major radical movements in today's Sunni tradition—the Wahhabi movement, the Muslim Brotherhood, the Salafi movement, and the Jihadist-Salafi movement. Each is discussed in terms of their primary philosophical leader and the contemporary evolution of the movement today as visible throughout the Middle East.

The radicalization of Sunni Islam has been an historic process, led by a number of key individuals. The chapter is laced with boxed items and commentary that provide a basic understanding of the historical complexities associated with radical Islam as proscribed by philosophical leaders such as Muhammad ibn Abd al-Wahhab, Hassan al-Banna, Sayyid Qutb, Ahmed Yassin, Abdul Rahman, Ahman al-Zawahiri, Usama bin Laden, Abu Musab al-Zarqawi, and Abu Bakr al-Baghdadi, as well as active Sunni groups, such as the Palestinian Islamic Resistance Movement (Hamas), al-Qaeda, al-Qaeda in the Arabian Peninsula (AQAP), Abu Sayyaf, and the Islamic State. The latter group, the Islamic State, is given additional attention in this chapter, particularly focusing on the ruthless violence stemming from extremist interpretations of early Muslim ideology originating from Wahhabi and Salafi doctrine. Known as *Takfiri Practices*, or the excommunication from Islam, the radical Islamic State claims the right to label other Muslims to whom they object as "unbelievers," justifying the violent torture and execution (beheadings, crucifixions, rape, burning, hanging, and shooting) of innocent individuals throughout the Middle East.

The final part of the chapter addresses the radicalization of the Shia (or Shiite) tradition within Islam, concentrating on the ideologies expressed by Ayatollah Ruhollah Khomeini during the Iranian Revolution of 1979. His thoughts provide the ideological foundation for today's Islamic Republic of Iran. The other primary Shia group discussed in this chapter is that of Hezbollah, under the leadership of Hassan Nasrallah, a group active throughout the world but centered in Lebanon.

Chapter 5: Terrorist Organizations and Structures

Chapters 5 and 6 are the second set of "twin chapters" in that they are interrelated: Both focus on terrorist organizations. Chapter 5 largely deals with how these groups are arranged and Chapter 6 scrutinizes the processes with which terrorist organizations operate. Organizational theory is a tool that explains how formal organizations are structured and relate to their environment. It can be applied to such disparate entities as General Motors, the *New York Times*, Girl Scouts, concentration camps, Red Cross, Hamas, and the Department of Defense. In Chapter 5, organizational theory is the lens by which we examine and explain the structure of terrorist organizations. We do so without requiring readers to learn, or be conversant with, organizational theory because this book is on a different subject.

The application of organizational theory to terrorist structures can provide important information about them. It reveals how authority is distributed, how work will be accomplished, and some indication of their relative importance of leaders.

Other topics in Chapter 5 include dilemmas of terrorist organizations, types of terrorist cells, organizational structures used by terrorists (such as hierarchical, umbrella, and virtual), the selection of targets, suicide bombing attacks, and how terrorist organizations end. The literature on how terrorist organizations end does not contemplate a movement that ends in a caliphate, despite the Islamic State's aspirations.

Chapter 6: Critical Processes of Terrorist Organizations

In this chapter we shift our analysis from how terrorist organizations are organized to essentially asking the question, "What does it take for a terrorist organization to be successful administratively and operationally?"

Like many other types of organizations, terrorists need administrative or organizational tools, which are the things they must accomplish to foster the organization's viability. To be operationally successful terrorists must have command of these operational tools. Chapter 6 covers these topics with examples and case studies. One of the organizational tools discussed is the financing of the group, with special attention given to funding via hawalas, narcotics trafficking, and other criminal activities, sponsorships and donations, charities, and even the trading of Bitcoins.

Chapter 7: Typologies of Terrorism: State-Involved and Single or Special Issue Movements

Chapters 7 and 8 are another set of "twin chapters," both dealing with typologies of terrorism. To avoid having one very long chapter we wrote two shorter chapters. We logically grouped movements in those chapters not by geography, but by their ideologies. Typologies logically group things, such as terrorist movements. In contrast, taxonomies create groups based on statistical analysis. We used typologies because there is insufficient data to create full taxonomies of terrorism. The history of each identified terrorist group is covered, and Chapters 7 and 8 are replete with examples and case studies to provide concrete meaning.

Chapter 7 scrutinizes four types of terrorism in which the political state is involved: state terrorism, state-enabled terrorism, state-sponsored terrorism, and state-perpetrated/international terrorism. By and large, single/special-issue terrorism is still a concern, but toward the lower end of the threat scale. "Fading" may be a reasonable description of these movements, which include the Animal Liberation Front (ALF), Earth Liberation Front (ALF), and Anti-Genetically Modified Organisms (GMO) groups, which oppose "frankenfood."

Chapter 8: Typologies of Terrorism: The Right and Left Wings and Separatist or Nationalist Movements

A large portion of this chapter covers right-wing groups, which envision having a homogenous "racially pure" country. All right-wing groups have in common "enemies" such as the "Zionist Occupied Government" (ZOG); illegal immigrants; people of color; and lesbians, gay, bisexual, transgender people, and those questioning their sexual identity (LGBTQ). Having a group to oppose promotes in-group solidarity, which helps to perpetuate the existence of right-wing movements (e.g., Hitler used the Jews for this purpose and the English Defence League targets Muslims). Right-wing movements in America include the Ku Klux Klan, neo-Nazis, and the anti-federalist/Christian Patriot groups.

Left-wing groups identified globally in the chapter include Sendero Luminoso (Shining Path) in Peru; the Red Army Faction (RAF) that operated mainly in Germany, but also in France, Switzerland, and the Netherlands; the Red Brigades in Italy; Revolutionary Armed Forces of Colombia (FARC); the Seung Fein in China; and the Weather Underground in the United States. The left wing historically has been unsuccessful in achieving its goal: replacing existing governments with ones that are based on Marxist-Leninist principles.

Separatist/nationalist movements are typically subnational groups who want a homeland. The groups often share a common culture, language, and history. Examples include the Kurdistan Workers Party, the Tamil Tigers, the Eritrean Liberation Front, and the Second Vermont Republic. Ireland's drive to become an independent country is discussed, as are the similarities between the Anglo-Irish War and the American Revolution.

Chapter 9: Intelligence and Terrorism

Chapters 9 and 10 represent yet another set of "twins." In Chapter 9, we define intelligence and counterintelligence and, more important, we define plaguing questions that continue to impede our ability to prevent terrorism. For instance, the final report of a Congressional Advisory Panel after 9/11, commonly known as the Gilmore Commission, identified several issues relating to the failure of the intelligence community to prevent terrorism. These included a failure to provide timely, accurate, and specific intelligence information to law enforcement, security, and military agencies, as well as an overly bureaucratic and decentralized structure (particularly within the FBI) that hindered a unified and coordinated effort between federal and local agencies to address the terrorist threat. While some of these issues continue, the intelligence community has worked hard to overcome many of these obstacles. More recent controversies involving the uneasy alliance between President Donald Trump and the intelligence community are also discussed in this chapter, with special attention given to the replacement (firing) of NSA Director Michael Flynn and FBI Director James Comey.

We address the complexity of the intelligence community in Chapter 9, defining the agencies involved in the intelligence community, including the Federal Bureau of Investigation (FBI), the Central Intelligence Agency (CIA), the National Security Agency (NSA), and the relatively new roles of the Office of National Intelligence and the National Counterterrorism Center. We also present an overview of other agencies within the intelligence community and explore "fusion centers," which have become common entities at the state and local level aimed at better coordinating the intelligence efforts among all divisions of government—federal, state, tribal, county, and city.

Chapter 10: Intelligence, Terrorism, and the U.S. Constitution

In Chapter 10, we address head-on the issues that surround the use of intelligence and intelligence gathering as a tool to prevent terrorism that seem to dot our newspapers on a near weekly basis. We closely examine the USA PATRIOT Act and discuss specific incidents that question and, in some cases, answer how far our government should go to protect our citizens. Specifically, we discuss the conflicts between the PATRIOT Act, the Freedom Act, and the Foreign Intelligence Surveillance Act (FISA) and the First, Fourth, and Fifth Amendments to the U.S. Constitution as related to the practice of extraordinary rendition, "enhanced" interview techniques and torture of suspected terrorist prisoners, the use of the military to supplement civilian police in conflict to the Posse Comitatus Act, police agencies that infiltrate political and religious groups that clearly blurs the line between policing and intelligence gathering, and the use of drones as both an offensive weapon in the Middle East and as a spying tool domestically. These issues and others are discussed in light of current events and the highlighted cases involving Bradley/Chelsea Manning, WikiLeaks, and Edward Snowden.

Chapter 11: Homeland Security

Eleven days after the 9/11 attacks, Pennsylvania Governor Tom Ridge was appointed as the first director of the Office of Homeland Security by President George W. Bush. His job was to develop, oversee, and coordinate a new, comprehensive national strategy to safeguard the country against terrorism and respond to any future attacks. Over a year later, on November 25, 2002, the U.S. Department of Homeland Security (DHS) was created as a stand-alone agency, composed of 22 different preexisting federal agencies. It was the largest reorganization of the federal bureaucracy since the National Security Act of 1947. Chapter 11 provides an overview of the key agencies assigned to DHS, such as the U.S. Coast Guard (USCG), U.S. Citizenship and Immigration Services (USCIS), Immigration and Customs Enforcement (ICE), Customs and Border Protection (CBP), Transportation Security Administration (TSA), U.S. Secret Service, and the Federal Emergency Management Agency (FEMA). The chapter explores each agency's role in fulfilling the core homeland security mission of preventing terrorism and enhancing the security of the United States.

Chapter 12: America's Vulnerability to Terrorism

Chapters 12 and 13 represent our final set of "twin" chapters. They are slightly different from the other sets as they are not extensions of the same subject matter, but rather complements to each other. In Chapter 12, we discuss openly America's vulnerability to terrorism. We define "critical infrastructure" and focus our work around the National Infrastructure Protection Plan (NIPP) that provides a framework in which to discuss potential target sites and give a reasonable risk assessment for each of the 16 sectors identified in NIPP. The discussion in Chapter 12 is all about "prevention" *now*, before an event, and providing an "all-hazard" plan that protects critical resources and human life from any kind of catastrophe, disease, or disaster regardless of causation, natural (e.g., flood, fire, hurricane, tornado, or earthquake) or man-made (e.g., terrorist strike; large cyber attack; mass shooting at a school, mall, or sporting event; or surprise attack from a foreign government). In Chapter 13, our discussion moves from prevention to response and mitigation—the effort to reduce loss of life and property by lessening the impact of such an event.

Chapter 13: Emergency Management

While FEMA is the key federal agency for the emergency management of a terrorist attack or natural disaster *after* the event, a myriad of other agencies have specific roles in responding to and recovering from a disaster. For instance, the coordination of local relief agencies, food banks, shelters, and the like fall within the FEMA management guidelines, while specific responses to public health issues from open sewage lines, biological agents, or even radiation may be more appropriately handled by another agency such as the Center for Disease Control (CDC), the Environmental Protection Agency (EPA), or the Nuclear Regulatory Commission (NRC)—all of which are discussed in Chapter 13.

The chapter provides a strong historical piece on the evolution of emergency management culminating in an in-depth discussion on our current National Preparedness System. We address the possibilities of significant attack from weapons of mass destruction and CBRNE-borne weapons, and more important, the formal mechanisms of the Incident Command System that are currently in place to address such an unspeakable event—from local and state perspectives to specific federal roles. Chapters 12 and 13 discuss America's defensive posture (i.e., planning, preventing, mitigating, and responding to a critical terrorist strike or disaster), setting up Chapter 14: Combatting Terrorism.

Chapter 14: Combatting Terrorism

There is an important distinction between anti-terrorism (AT) and counterterrorism (CT). At the risk of oversimplification, the former is largely composed of defensive actions, while the latter centers on offensive operations. Chapter 14 addresses AT and CT on the basis of a cross-section of the organizations that are executing those respective kinds of missions, although it must be noted that some of them perform both AT and CT activities. With respect to these activities, the military, federal agencies, state and local governments, and law enforcement agencies are covered. The role of the military is given substantial attention because of the array of units involved and their important contributions to America's national security. The chapter also examines types of action that can be taken against terrorists, including raids and direct action. Military deployments are determined by national strategy, security policy, and the determination of whether they fit into the ways, ends, and means that have been established.

Chapter 15: Terrorism, Intelligence, and Homeland Security: The Future

This concluding chapter of the book ties the subject matters of terrorism, intelligence, and homeland security together and identifies recent trends in terrorist activities. Many of the past attacks in the United States have been carried out by homegrown terrorists using lone wolf terrorist tactics. These events have been mostly bombings or spree shootings using very crude and nonsophisticated weapons. Internationally, while al-Qaeda appears to be weakening and fractionalizing as a single group, radical Islamic ideology appears to be dramatically increasing throughout the Middle East and the rest of the world with the emergence of the Islamic State in Syria and Iraq. While America has been victimized repeatedly by attacks on our transportation sector (particularly the airline industry), attacks that are cyber in nature pose a much more significant threat in the future. Much of our critical infrastructure—including water systems, power grids, gas pipelines, nuclear power functions, and financial and communication networks—were built long before the specter of terrorism was a consideration and contain weak defenses against potential attacks by terrorists, rogue nations, or even sophisticated criminals. Indeed, rather than focusing on attacks that raise the public hysteria, such as attacks from weapons of mass destruction (WMD), it might be more prudent to assume that the next major terrorist attack may be cyber in nature.

The final chapter also includes an important segment on the role of the media during terrorist events and the impact of such events on the mind of the general public. Our concluding remarks in Chapter 15 focus not on the significant dangers and potential threats that lurk in an unstable world, but rather on the richness, strength, diversity, and resilience of America as we confront the future together, no different than generations before us.

Pedagogical Features

Each chapter includes the following pedagogical features to aid students and instructors:

Learning Objectives at the beginning of each chapter identify the core elements students need to learn.

Learning Objectives

After completing this chapter, you should be able to:

1. State six reasons why it is important to understand terrorism.
2. Trace the history of key events in terrorism from the nineteenth century to 9/11/2001.
3. Contrast individual and cultural perspectives of terrorism.
4. Explain why there are so many definitions of terrorism.
5. Identify six acts punishable as war crimes.
6. Summarize the event that led to the Syrian War.

Key Terms in the margins define each term where it is first used in the text. At the back of the text is a comprehensive glossary of all the key terms.

Introduction

The subject of "politics" often provokes intense emotion, generates passionate discussion, and can frequently create extreme resistance to considering another person's point of view—this is obvious even during political discussions at the dinner table or seeing friends on Facebook tear into each other because of deeply held political convictions. Indeed, politics are sometimes so interwoven into people's psyches that it affects nearly every facet of their belief system.

And, as we learned in the previous chapter, the way that people think about or perceive their environment, government, and society—and the way they feel those entities should be structured—springs from a host of factors, including genetics,[1] family tradition, educational background, socioeconomic status, religious affiliation, and geographical location (individual perspective and culture). These factors are not mutually exclusive, they are not simple, and they have wide-ranging effects on a person's belief system. **Political ideology,** then, is (on an individual level) "the set of beliefs about the proper order of society and how it can be achieved."[2] On a group level, political ideology is the "shared framework of mental models that groups of individuals possess that provide both an interpretation of the environment and a prescription as to how that environment should be structured."[3]

> **Political ideology**
> The set of beliefs about the proper order of society and how that order can be achieved.

Boxes throughout the chapters highlight interesting topics that are relevant to the chapter subject matter. Each box concludes with challenging questions aimed at sparking class discussion.

Box 2-1
Characteristics of the Far Left and the Right

On the ideological spectrum, leftist groups like the ones discussed here are at the very extreme—located far from moderate or centrist ideologies and even more distantly from fringe right-wing counterparts. What really sets leftist terror groups apart—and, in fact, distinguishes all ideological groups from each other—is the types of groups that they "advocate," their techniques, and their endgame. For example, most moderate or centrist groups tend to advocate for society in general, not focusing on one group, but rather seeing a society as a "whole." Their process for advancing causes is via a group consensus—generally as part of a partisan democratic event such as voting—and the outcome is generally a balance between a gradual change with a nod to tradition or status quo. This is a good characterization of traditional American political groups.

However, on the far-right fringe of the spectrum, groups advocate for a specific race or ethnicity, religion, or nationality. Their endgame is a change based on a reaction to a perceived threat—that is, a changing values system or a new and pervasive culture that is upending a long-standing social order. Their methodology for achieving their endgame involves a retreat or return to the "good old days"—a social movement that seeks to restore a cherished social order. These are characterized by the neo-fascist, neo-Nazi, and skinhead hate groups, such as the Ku Klux Klan, Aryan Nations, and the Christian Identity Church.

Far-left groups, by contrast, are more future-oriented; they look to radical change, hoping to topple the social order of the past

on behalf of certain societal classes (e.g., the working class or proletariats). Their movements are often based in a complex theoretical groundwork that describes those that have wealth and those that are oppressed (e.g., anticolonialism, anticapitalism, Marxism). The ultimate goal is liberation from a real or perceived oppressive government. This designation contains groups that often self-identify as communist, socialist, or anarchist, such as the Black Blocs, Earth Liberation Front, Weather Underground, and Popular Front for the Liberation of Palestine (PFLP).

Far-right and far-left groups tend to hold sharply contrasting views on racial equality, law and order, patriotism, labor, economic issues, and religion; however, they do share some common ground. Both camps tend to be very alienated from mainstream society, mostly due to their zealousness and inflexible belief systems. They are also equally likely to embrace conspiracy theories and stereotypical views of social and political affairs.

Extremist groups on both sides of the spectrum are also similar in their pursuit of their goals: both sides will censor opponents and deal harshly with adversaries. Furthermore, both sides view civil liberties through an extremely partisan lens—calling for unyielding support of civil liberties when doing so supports their agenda, or completely eschewing them when they aid rival points of view.

What other similarities and differences can you think of between left and right extremist groups?

Information Links direct readers to Internet sites that provide more information on chapter topics.

---

had "usurped the authority of God," Qutb knew that those in the ruling class would certainly not be inclined to surrender without a fight. This vanguard of violence and terrorism is the foundation for the modern concept of jihadism.[24] Refer to Chapter 4, "The Rise of Radical Islam," for a more detailed discussion of Sayyid Qutb and his radical Islamic philosophies.

Leftist groups, then, with their roots in mid-nineteenth-century Europe, have demonstrably influenced modern terrorism philosophically and tactically. Elements of Marxism and Leninism—particularly the concept of the vanguard—have made their way into different factions of terrorism, from leftist to Islamic terror, as have anarchist principles of "propaganda by the deed." Historically, terrorism (widespread killing, assassinations, and bombings) was a major part of the violent cultural and social changes in Russia, France, Cuba, and elsewhere, and has always been part of an accepted strategy among the revolutionary left.

> **Information Link**
> Visit bio.truestory at www.biography.com. Search the site for the biography of Che Guevara. Listen to his biography, and watch the popular 2004 film entitled *The Motorcycle Diaries*, chronicling the written memoir of a twenty-three-year-old Che Guevara as he rode his motorcycle throughout Latin America.

Quick Facts boxes provide unique tidbits of information related to the chapter topics.

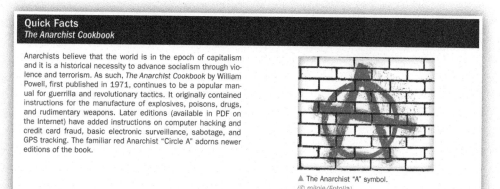

Summaries are organized around Learning Objectives that highlight the main points of each chapter.

Chapter Summary

SUMMARY BY LEARNING OBJECTIVE

1. **Describe the concept of political terrorism.**

   Political terrorism can be defined as "a symbolic act designed to influence political behavior based on extra-normal means, entailing the use or threat of violence." Recall that political terror is based on a set of ingrained beliefs that stem from the way people think about their environment, government, and society—and that those beliefs are often inflexible.

2. **Provide an overview of leftist terror cells, including Latin American and European groups.**

   Groups that espouse Marxist ideologies include the Revolutionary Armed Forces of Colombia, or FARC, which purports to represent the rural, agrarian poor in Colombia by protecting their land interests against the wealthier classes of Colombia, the influence of the imperialist United States, the privatization of resources, and the influence of global corporations. The National Liberation Army, or ELN, also a pro-Marxist group that operates in the Colombian countryside, seeks to replace the Colombian government with an egalitarian democracy that represents the rural peasant class. Tupac Amaru Revolutionary Movement (or MRTA) exists in Peru, and was founded in Marxist ideology to reform the Peruvian government, removing all imperialist elements, and create a society in which power, prop-

Review Questions at the end of each chapter pose a series of questions to test students' recall of the chapter information.

REVIEW QUESTIONS

1. What are the basic tenets of Marxism, and how do you see its effects in modern Middle Eastern terror?
2. How do you think Latin American and European terror organizations inspired present-day Arab terror organizations?
3. What was the mandate system and how do we see its lasting effects in Middle Eastern conflict?
4. Although the *Palestinian Liberation Organization (PLO)* fractured into over a hundred separate groups, identify the three primary groups and their respective leaders that gained worldwide notoriety for conducting terrorist attacks in the international arena.
5. How is the United States perceived by the Arab world, and why? How does this influence terrorist ideology?

Critical Thinking Exercises at the end of each chapter require students to go further and think on the analytical level. Most of the exercises involve web research.

CRITICAL THINKING EXERCISES

1. **The Impact of Oil in the Middle East.** Visit the homepage for Saudi Aramco at www .saudiaramco.com/en/home.html and *Life-Time Magazine* at http://life.time.com. Search these sites for stories on the discovery of oil in the Middle East. Learn about the history and culture of the Middle East in 1945 when the oil industry just began in that region. Notice the photos of the region and compare them to more modern times. How much has the landscaped really changed in half a century? Visit the home pages of some of the wealthiest Middle East countries like Saudi Arabia, Bahrain, Qatar, Kuwait, and the United Arab Emirates. Notice the significant improvements in health, education, and welfare of the individuals in those countries. Notice also that each of these countries is a royal monarchy. How do you think the form of government and the pervasive religion of Islam in the region have impacted the economic development of the Middle East—both negatively and positively?

In addition to these pedagogical features, we devoted careful attention to the maps, tables, figures, and photographs, researching and selecting them ourselves, striving for a blend of informative historical images and also more current ones, many of which are compelling and tell a story by themselves.

Instructor Supplements

Instructor's Manual with Test Bank.

Includes content outlines for classroom discussion, teaching suggestions, and answers to selected end-of-chapter questions from the text. This also contains a Word document version of the test bank.

TestGen

This computerized test generation system gives you maximum flexibility in creating and administering tests on paper, electronically, or online. It provides state-of-the-art features for viewing and editing test bank questions, dragging a selected question into a test you are creating, and printing sleek, formatted tests in a variety of layouts. Select test items from test banks included with TestGen for quick test creation, or write your own questions from scratch. TestGen's random generator provides the option to display different text or calculated number values each time questions are used.

PowerPoint Presentations

Our presentations are clear and straightforward. Photos, illustrations, charts, and tables from the book are included in the presentations when applicable.

To access supplementary materials online, instructors need to request an instructor access code. Go to www.pearsonhighered.com/irc, where you can register for an instructor access code. Within 48 hours after registering, you will receive a confirmation email, including an instructor access code. Once you have received your code, go to the site and log on for full instructions on downloading the materials you wish to use.

Alternate Versions

eBooks

This text is also available in multiple eBook formats. These are an exciting new choice for students looking to save money. As an alternative to purchasing the printed textbook, students can purchase an electronic version of the same content. With an eTextbook, students can search the text, make notes online, print out reading assignments that incorporate lecture notes, and bookmark important passages for later review. For more information, visit your favorite online eBook reseller or visit **www.mypearsonstore.com**.

REVEL for Terrorism, Intelligence and Homeland Security, Second Edition by Robert W. Taylor and Charles R. Swanson

Designed for the Way Today's Criminal Justice Students Read, Think, and Learn

REVEL offers an immersive learning experience that engages students deeply, while giving them the flexibility to learn their way. Media interactives and assessments integrated directly within the narrative enable students to delve into key concepts and reflect on their learning without breaking stride.

- **REVEL** seamlessly combines the full content of Pearson's bestselling criminal justice titles with multimedia learning tools. You assign the topics your students cover. Author Explanatory Videos, application exercises, and short quizzes engage students and enhance their understanding of core topics as they progress through the content.

- Instead of simply reading about criminal justice topics, REVEL empowers students to think critically about important concepts by completing application exercises, watching Point/CounterPoint videos, and participating in shared writing (discussion board) assignments.

Track Time-on-Task throughout the Course

The Performance Dashboard allows you to see how much time the class or individual students have spent reading a section or doing an assignment, as well as points earned per assignment. This data helps correlate study time with performance and provides a window into where students may be having difficulty with the material.

Learning Management System Integration

Pearson provides both Blackboard Learn™ and Canvas™ integration, giving institutions, instructors, and students easy access to Revel. Our Revel integration delivers streamlined access to everything your students need for the course in the Blackboard Learn and Canvas environments.

The REVEL App

The REVEL App further empowers students to access their course materials wherever and whenever they want. With the REVEL App, students can access REVEL directly from their tablet or mobile device, offline and online. Reminders and notifications can be set so you never miss a deadline. Work done on the REVEL app syncs up to the browser version, ensuring that no one misses a beat. Visit **www.pearsonhighered.com/revel/**

Acknowledgments

Although it is insufficient compensation for their gracious assistance, we would like to recognize here the individuals who helped make this book a reality. Many good friends at "three letter agencies" and the military, all of whom wish to remain unnamed, read several chapters and made cogent comments, for which we are grateful. Several provided up-to-date information on issues relating to the Middle East as the chapters were being written.

Ms. Jennifer Davis-Lamm provided ongoing research and contribution to several chapters. We are forever indebted for her services. Mr. Jason Lane greatly assisted with research on Chapter 12: America's Vulnerability to Terrorism and Chapter 13: Emergency Management. Dr. Kelley Stone contributed to Chapter 13 as well, and allowed us to draw upon his excellent knowledge of fusion centers in Chapter 9: Intelligence and Terrorism. A special "thank you" to our good friend and Bob's former graduate student, Dr. Ahmet Yayla, former Chief of Counterterrorism and Operations Division for the Turkish National Police (TNP) and the coauthor of a new exciting book entitled *ISIS Defectors: Inside Stories of the Terrorist Caliphate* (Washington, D.C.: Advances Press, July 2016), with Dr. Anne Speckhard. Ahmet and Anne graciously provided several photos for this book as well as their keen insight into the Islamic State. Dr. Suleyman Ozeren, Dr. Samih Teymur, and Dr. Mustafa Ozguler, again from the Turkish National Police, assisted in writing and developing Chapters 3 and 4. Their knowledge and patience greatly helped us understand the foundations as well as the historical evolution of Islam as presented in Chapter 3: Understanding the Middle East and Islam and Chapter 4: The Rise of Radical Islam. Mr. Zeeshan Syed proofread Chapters 3 and 4 for accuracy, and Ms. Amy Kryzak proofed the entire first edition through Grammarly. Last, but certainly not least, Bob's close friend and colleague, Dr. Galia Cohen, edited the entire manuscript for Pearson, providing a solid foundation and wonderful direction for the book. Her suggestions were invaluable to this edition.

Paige Cummings, Traci Swanson, and Kellie Pless also read and commented on the chapters, improving them. Our longstanding friend, Leonard Territo, went through materials very carefully, catching lapses. The Federal Bureau of Investigation provided photos, and we are appreciative of the speed with which they responded to our requests.

We would like to thank the following reviewers for their comments and suggestions: Salih Hakan Can, Penn State University – Schuylkill Campus; Brian LeBlanc, Rivier University; Deborah Louis, Eastern Kentucky University; Pamela Mertens, Northeastern State University; James O'Sullivan, Pace University; John Padgett, Capella University; Carlos Parker, Cumberland County College; Jennifer Estis-Sumerel, Itawamba Community College; and Lisa Ann Zanglin, Auburn University – Montgomery.

Lastly, we would like to thank our editors. Ms. Elisa Rogers, our developmental editor, has just been wonderful during this entire project. Thank you, Elisa, for your time, energy, and patience. And, thank you to our managing editor, Mr. Gary Bauer, for his continued guidance and support. He was willing to "go to bat" for us on numerous occasions. We truly hope this book realizes his expectations. It has been a pleasure working with him, as well as the entire Pearson team.

Robert W. Taylor is currently a tenured full Professor in the Department of Criminology and Criminal Justice at The University of Texas at Dallas. The Department was recently ranked fifth in the world in academic excellence based on the strength of its Ph.D. program. Previous to this position, he was the Director of the Executive Masters in Justice Administration and Leadership Program and the former program Head for the Public Affairs Program at UT-Dallas. Both are academic programs integrating the traditions of management, governmental affairs, policy analysis, and decision science in the public sector. The Public Affairs Program hosted one of the largest graduate degree programs on campus, including Doctoral (Ph.D.) and Master's Degrees in Public Affairs and Public Administration.

From January 2008 through 2010, Bob was the Executive Director of the W.W. Caruth Jr. Police Institute at Dallas (CPI). The Institute was established through a $9.5 million grant from the Communities Foundation of Texas. Bob was a principal party to the development of the Institute and was appointed the founding director by the University of North Texas System. The primary mission of the Institute is to provide direction and coordination of major training and research projects for the Dallas Police Department. The Institute represents a national "think tank" on policing strategies focused on major urban cities in the United States. He remains a "Scholar-in-Residence" at the Institute. From 1996 to 2008, Bob was professor and chair of the Department of Criminal Justice at the University of North Texas. He served in this capacity for thirteen years, and under his direction the Department gained national prominence, especially with the establishment of the Caruth Police Institute.

In 1995, Dr. Taylor took a leave of absence from university administration and teaching to join Emergency Resources International, Inc., the parent company of the famed "Red Adair" firefighters. His duties as Senior Vice-President, Crisis Management Division, included liaison with foreign governments and authorities, extensive contract negotiations, and the strategic development of a worldwide communication and information system. Bob's major project was acting as team leader on the largest oil spill in history (3 million barrels), located in the remote Nenets District of Russia, over 200 miles north of the Arctic Circle.

For the past forty years, Dr. Taylor has studied criminal justice administration and specifically police responses to crime and terrorism, focusing on issues in the Middle East. He has traveled extensively throughout the Middle East, meeting several heads of state in that region. He has acted as a consultant to numerous federal, state, and local agencies, and since September 11, 2001, Bob has been a consultant to the U.S. Department of Justice working with the Institute for Intergovernmental Research (IIR) as a lead instructor in the State and Local Anti-Terrorism Training Program (SLATT). Bob has also worked extensively throughout the Middle East, especially in the country of Turkey. He has been an instructor for the U.S. Department of State, Anti-Terrorism Assistance (ATA) Program (2001–2006) and taught internationally in the Executive Seminar on Cyber Terrorism presented to executives of foreign governments. Dr. Taylor holds appropriate *top secret* national security clearances through the JPASS system (archived).

Dr. Taylor has authored or coauthored over 200 articles, books, and manuscripts. Most of his publications focus on police administration and management, police procedures, international and domestic terrorism, drug trafficking, and criminal justice policy. His articles appear in numerous journals, including *Defense Analysis* (University of Oxford, England Press), the *ANNALS* (American Academy of Political and Social Sciences), *Police Quarterly, Crime and Delinquency*, and the *Police Chief* (International Association of Chiefs of Police). Dr. Taylor is coauthor of two leading textbooks, *Police Administration: Structures, Processes, and Behavior* (Upper Saddle River, NJ: Pearson Publishing, 2017), currently in its 9th edition, and *Criminal Investigation* (New York: McGraw-Hill, 2018), currently in its

12th edition. These texts are used in over 500 universities, colleges, and police departments throughout the United States. He is also the senior author of *Juvenile Justice: Policies, Practices, and Programs* (McGraw-Hill, 2014) in its 4th edition, *Digital Crime and Digital Terrorism* (Pearson, 2018) in its 4th edition, and *Police Patrol Allocation and Deployment* (Pearson, 2011).

Dr. Taylor has an extensive background in academic and professional criminal justice, having taught at four major universities and serving as a sworn police officer and major crimes detective (lateral rank of sergeant) in Portland, Oregon, for over six years.

In 1984, Bob was appointed as a Research Fellow at the International Center for the Study of Violence at the University of South Florida, Tampa, Florida, conducting various studies involving international and domestic terrorism, police training and management, public violence and homicide, computerized mapping, and international drug trafficking. He continues to conduct research in these areas and is the recipient of numerous grants and contracts (over $18 million in funded projects). His latest work is concentrated in four areas: (1) quality improvement in police agencies through advanced leadership and management practices; (2) international terrorism, especially Middle-Eastern groups, and the spread of radical Islam; (3) evaluation of community policing, CompStat, and intelligence-led policing strategies in the United States; and (4) intelligence analysis, fusion centers, and decision making, particularly during protracted conflict or crisis situations.

In 2004, the International Justice Mission in Washington, D.C., asked Bob to assist in the training of the Cambodian National Police on child sex slavery and human trafficking as part of a large project funded through the U.S. Department of State ($1 million). His interest and research in this area have led to a leadership role in designing and developing training efforts in the United States aimed at raising awareness of the human trafficking tragedy for American law enforcement officers, funded in part through the U.S. Department of Justice. Dr. Taylor focuses on the nexus between human trafficking, drug trafficking, and the financing of terrorist incidents internationally and domestically. He continues this important work as a guest lecturer, speaking at conferences internationally on these subjects.

In 2003, Dr. Taylor was awarded the *University of North Texas, Regent's Lecture Award* for his work in the Middle East. In March 2008, the Academy of Criminal Justice Sciences presented Bob with the prestigious *O.W. Wilson Award* "in recognition of his outstanding contribution to police education, research and practice."

Dr. Taylor has been a consultant to the U.S. Army, the U.S. Marine Corps, the U.S. Department of Homeland Security, the U.S. Department of Treasury, Federal Law Enforcement Training Center, the U.S. Secret Service, the Bureau of Alcohol, Tobacco, and Firearms, the U.S. Department of Justice, the Federal Bureau of Investigation, the Drug Enforcement Administration, the Police Foundation, the Police Executive Research Forum (PERF), the International Association of Chiefs of Police (IACP), and numerous state and local municipalities and private corporations. He has also conducted significant training in the United States protectorates of the U.S. Virgin Islands, Guam, and Saipan, and the countries of Canada, England, France, Switzerland, Thailand, Cambodia, Barbados, Northern Cyprus, Bahrain, Venezuela, Russia, Finland, United Arab Emirates, Kenya, Singapore, and Turkey. He is an active member of the Academy of Criminal Justice Sciences (elected National Chair of the ACJS Police Section – 2002), the American Society for Public Administration, and the American Society of Criminology.

Dr. Taylor is a graduate of Michigan State University (Master of Science, 1973) and Portland State University (Doctor of Philosophy, 1981).

Charles R. "Mike" Swanson enlisted in the Marine Corps when he was 17 years old, subsequently working as Patrol Officer and Detective with the Tampa Police Department. He joined Florida Governor Claude Kirk's staff as a Senior Police Planner and later as Deputy Director of the Governor's Council on Law Enforcement and Criminal Justice. Mike taught criminal justice courses at East Carolina University before becoming a faculty member at the Institute of Government (IOG) at the University of Georgia. Faculty members in the IOG are charged with carrying out programs of research, training, and technical assistance for Georgia units of state and local government. Mike specialized in reorganization of police departments to achieve enhanced performance.

For much of his 29 years in the IOG, Mike focused on three efforts:

1. *Designing promotional systems for police and fire departments.* Notably, he led a large city police department and a state patrol agency out of federal court, creating promotional systems that are still used and have not been successfully challenged. Mike has designed hundreds of valid and reliable written promotional tests and assessment center exercises. He has trained hundreds of assessors and directed more than 50 assessment centers.

2. *Training.* As Director of the IOG's Southeastern Law Enforcement Programs, he created and led advanced training programs for more than 10,000 officers from 46 states and 4 foreign countries.

3. *Partnering with police departments to foster improvements.* Virtually on a daily basis for 29 years, Mike worked with police departments to resolve smaller to large-scale problems, often acting as a change agent. On a larger scale, he conducted analyses that were the basis of his reorganization of units or entire police agencies, as well as the consolidation of a large city police department with a county police agency. Many of Mike's more than 100 technical reports were written to support his work in this area.

Mike advanced through the administrative ranks of the IOG, Program Director, Division Director, Deputy Director, and retired as the Acting Director. His home is in Athens, Georgia, a musical hot spot with several internationally known bands residing there. One of his more unusual consulting jobs was advising a major touring band on how to recover a member's stolen guitar.

In addition to conference papers, refereed articles, and chapters in books, Mike has co-authored several books, including *The Police Personnel Selection Process, Introduction to Criminal Justice, Court Administration, Police Administration: Structures, Processes, and Behavior* (9th edition, 2017), and *Criminal Investigation* (12th edition, 2018).

Mike has received an array of recognitions, including a Distinguished Service Award and the Walter Bernard Hill Award from the University of Georgia, commendations from the governors of three states for contributions to public service, the O.W. Wilson Award for Distinguished Scholarship, a Service Award from the Georgia Association of Chiefs of Police, as well as receiving their First Honorary Chief of Police Award for service to that organization. As a consultant, Mike has worked with police agencies as far apart as the Elizabeth, New Jersey, Police Department, the Dallas Police Department, and the Multnomah County (Oregon) Department of Public Safety. He has also taught abroad in the Shanghai Municipal Institute. In 2016, Mike was honored as a Distinguished Alumni of Florida State University's College of Criminology and Criminal Justice.

He received bachelor and masters degrees in criminology from Florida State University and a Ph.D. in Political Science, with a concentration in public administration, from the University of Georgia.

Defining, Conceptualizing, and Understanding Terrorism

1

Learning Objectives

After completing this chapter, you should be able to:

1. State six reasons why it is important to understand terrorism.

2. Trace the history of key events in terrorism from the nineteenth century to 9/11/2001.

3. Contrast individual and cultural perspectives of terrorism.

4. Explain why there are so many definitions of terrorism.

5. Identify any six of the ten acts punishable as war crimes.

6. Summarize the event that led to the Syrian War.

Members of the American National Socialist Movement (NSM) march against illegal immigration in Lansing, Michigan. Founded in 1974, it is a right-wing, Neo-Nazi, racist, and anti-immigration organization.

(ZUMA Press, Inc./Alamy Stock Photo)

Introduction

Terrorism – Intelligence – Homeland Security are three words that consume today's news events. No other issues are so prominent, so compelling, or so critically important to our communities and our nation than these three separate, but interconnected topics.

Some argue that as a nation, we are still suffering from the lingering effects of the attacks on September 11, 2001, an event that clearly changed our world forever. On that day, our security weaknesses were exploited, our vulnerability was exposed, and our fear became real. For the last decade and a half, we have struggled to dramatically improve the security of our homeland from attack, whether these attacks are from aircraft hijackings, indiscriminate bombings and shootings, the use of nuclear-biological-chemical-radioactive agents, or more sophisticated attempts to infiltrate critical infrastructures or deny services through the use of advanced cyber attacks. In this effort, we have not only been defensive in strengthening the homeland, but also offensive (taking the war to the terrorists abroad) by sending troops to the Middle East to quell international threats in Iraq, Afghanistan, and Syria. We have expanded our intelligence-gathering and analysis capabilities to filter even our largest social media technologies, and we have developed entirely new departments of government to protect us and to respond to emergencies, whether they be caused by man-made terrorist events or natural disasters. Billions of dollars have been spent in this effort to make us safer. More important, our zeal to be safer and more secure has tested the limits of our government and the basic democratic values of "life, liberty and the pursuit of happiness" that underscores our country and our Constitution.

In this first chapter, we discuss the reasons why it is important to understand terrorism, how to define it, and how to conceptualize it from an historical as well as contemporary viewpoint. More important, we discuss the problems and issues involved in understanding such an evocative and political term, and the role that individual perspective, culture, and religion plays in conceptualizing terrorism.

Understanding Terrorism

It is important, perhaps essential, to understand terrorism. There are a number of reasons why:

1. For most of its long history, terrorism's impact was subnational, national, or regional. In the American psyche, the subject did not loom large. In 2000, a Gallup Poll showed 4 percent of Americans were "very worried" about terrorism, while another 20 percent reported being "somewhat worried."[1] People around the globe who have lived with terrorism are wary about how they live their lives. Following the 9/11 attacks in 2001 on New York City and Washington, D.C., our vulnerability was exposed and our sense of security shaken. The attacks could have been even worse had the fourth hijacked plane, United Flight 93, reached its target, possibly the White House or the Congress. The passengers aboard it had learned how the other three planes hijacked that day had been used. They were determined to not let that happen and heroically fought to take Flight 93 back, but all aboard died as it crashed in the Pennsylvania countryside.

    In the wake of the 9/11 attacks, Americans changed how they lived: 33 percent of respondents in a national survey reduced their air travel and 25 percent reported avoiding certain cities and crowded places that might be targets of a terrorist attack.[2] In prudent anticipation of future attacks, some businesses now provide their employees with emergency kits,[3] an unknown number of families have created emergency plans, and confidence in the ability of governments to protect people has been damaged.[4] The threat of terrorism is associated with the proliferation of "preppers" and "survivalists." Who are acquiring the skills, goods, and remote homesites they will need to provide for their families and groups if our government falters.

    The 9/11 attacks precipitated the largest and most expensive reorganization in our history. Among the changes was creation of the U.S. Department of Homeland Security. In two full-fledged ground wars and numerous other actions, we have spilled the blood of our men and women in the military and spent what is estimated as $1 trillion. Still, a 2016 poll revealed 42 percent of Americans say they are less safe than before 9/11.[5] The attacks also prompted the United Nations (UN) Security Council to form a Counter Terrorism Committee (CTC).

2. Terrorism can be adapted with frightening speed to the needs of many causes. It is the violent equivalent of a Swiss Army knife because it can be used in so many ways and from come from many different directions. Faced with a loss of territory in Iraq and Syria while fighting an international force, the Islamic State (IS) adapted. During 2015–2017, it spread fear cheaply, gained publicity, inspired others to attack, and gained recruits by launching a series of attacks in Western Europe by small, but deadly, teams of terrorists. Only a very small number of refugees from the Middle East were involved in such attacks, but there was a strong backlash in several European countries against admitting them and some calls for the deportation of all such refugees.

Those attacks produced one to hundreds of casualties. Illustratively, in Northern France during 2016, two men claiming to be IS affiliated burst into a mass, forced the eighty-five-year-old Catholic priest to his knees, and filmed the cutting of his throat. One of the killers was wearing a police monitoring bracelet for twice traveling to Syria under false names. The conditions of bail for the nineteen-year-old allowed him to turn his monitoring bracelet off for a few hours every morning.[6] That time coincided with the murder of the priest. In Brussels, Belgium on August 24, 2017, a Belgium national of Somalian heritage shouting Allahu akbar (God is Great) attacked two soldiers with a knife, wounding both before being shot and killed.[7] Armed soldiers are not a "soft" target." Yet, there have been other attacks on soldiers which may reflect an IS decision to include targets that represent authority to reduce confidence in government's ability to protect the people. Counterterrorism has been a governmental focus for several years. More so than any other European Union country, Belgium has more citizens who joined IS or another terrorist group, fought in Iraq and/or Syria, and returned to their country of origin.[8]

While continuing to attack the West, IS, however, has not abandoned its ground warfare in Iraq, Syria, or elsewhere. By late 2017, IS had substantially been reduced or driven out of most of Iraq and much of Syria. Some experts believe they will attempt to established their sought-after caliphate there. IS is covered in more detail in Chapter 3, "Understanding the Middle East and **Islam**."

Some attacks can be thought of and carried out fairly quickly by a lone person or a handful of people with limited resources. Although a great deal of attention is focused on radicalized **Muslims** from abroad, "homegrown terrorists" may live next door to you. In the decade after 9/11, nine American Muslims a year have produced an average of six terrorist plots per year, most of which were disrupted, resulting in a total of fifty deaths.[9] The comparable annual average figures for right-wing extremist groups are 337 attacks and a total of 254 dead. In a survey of 383 law enforcement agencies, 74 percent saw homegrown anti-government extremists as the most severe threat.[10]

Homegrown terrorists have no formal connection to, or receive material support from a terrorist movement, but may have some psychological affinity with one, or have their own particular cause, such as calling attention to deforestation in Brazil. We all have a responsibility to be aware of possible terrorist threats and should, as suggested by DHS, "report something if we see something."[11]

3. The American preoccupation with protecting the homeland, as well as citizens, interests, and facilities abroad, can lead us into thinking that terrorism is a uniquely American problem. The data reveals a different picture. The top-ten countries most affected by terrorism, in rank order, are: Iraq, Afghanistan. Nigeria, Pakistan, Syria, Yemen, India, Egypt, Libya, and the Philippines. The United States ranks 36th on that list.[12]

In one recent year, there were 12,089 terrorist attacks with 29,376 deaths around the world.[13] World deaths due to terrorism began rapidly escalating in late 2010, when the "**Arab Spring**" pro-democracy movement started in Tunisia and in 2011 rolled into other countries, including Yemen Syria, and Libya. While other countries also saw violence, elsewhere things went no further than demonstrations. In Syria, the pro-democracy movement demanded the ousting of President Bashar al-Assad. Moreover, the movement was energized by years of government repression, corruption, and an unemployment rate that bounced from 8.3 percent to 14.9 in a single year. In 2011, the Syrian War

Islam
The religion of Muslims, referred to earlier in history as Moslems, who believe there is no God but Allah and Muhammad is his prophet. It is Allah that founded Islam through Muhammad. Islam's religious book is the Qur'an (Anglicized as the Koran).

Muslim
One who adheres to the Islamic faith. See Islamic.

Homegrown terrorists
Although it may send encouraging messages, homegrown terrorists have no real support from a terrorist movement. There may be a psychological identification with one, or homegrown terrorists may act on their own special interests, for example, "government spying" or protecting the whales.

Arab Spring
The **Arab Spring** began in December 2010, when people in Tunisia demonstrated in cities across their country for social, political, and economic reforms. They also demanded the resignation of their president, which he did in January 2011. The example excited people in countries in that region, and soon demonstrations seemed to be occurring everywhere. In Syria, it led to open warfare to remove the president and implement reforms.

Quick Facts
The Beginning of the Arab Spring

On December 17, 2010, a twenty-six-year-old man had a college degree, but no job. He began selling fruits and vegetables in an open-air market. A local official seized his goods and humiliated him. In reaction to the incident, he set himself on fire. Rioting broke out and government forces responded. Several days later, another jobless man climbed an electric pole, yelled, "No, for misery!" and "No, for unemployment." He touched the wires and electrocuted himself.

The President of Tunisia had held office for nearly twenty-four years. Among the ills the country was experiencing was high unemployment. Nearly 25 percent of male graduates and 44 percent of women graduates are unemployed. Their education prepared them for jobs that simply didn't exist.[14]

After weeks of rioting across the country, the president resigned and the Arab Spring was launched. Refer to the discussion in Chapter 4, "The Rise of Radical Islam," relating to "how" the Arab Spring impacted the development of radical Islam.

Taliban
Pashto, "student." The Taliban largely consists of members of the Pashtun tribes occupying parts of the border between Afghanistan and Pakistan. It is a fundamentalist Islamic movement that insists on strict enforcement of Sharia law.

al Qaeda
Arabic, "The Base." Foreign terrorist organization (FTO) led by Usama bin Laden until his death in 2011; currently led by Ayman al-Zawahiri. He avows continued jihad against Crusader America and its supporters.

Abu Sayyaf
Abu Sayyaf is the most violent of the separatist groups operating in the Philippines. They use terror as fundraising tool and to promote their jihadist movement.[22] Their most common money-producing tactic may be kidnapping and collecting ransom.

broke and is well beyond a simple pro-democracy versus the existing government and has interveners on both sides, including Russia, the United States, opposing terrorist groups, Kurds, and others. The Syrian War gets additional attention in the last section of this chapter.

Terrorists are active around the world. In a single year, the **Taliban's** Islamic terrorists launched 1,093 separate attacks, creating 4,512 fatalities. In doing so, it became that year's chief perpetrator of such actions.[15] The Taliban straddles the Pakistan–Afghanistan border.

In Pakistan, Christians make up 2 percent of the population and are a constant target of terrorists like the Taliban, which insists on strict interpretation of Islamic law. On an Easter Sunday in 2016, predominately Christian women and children were in a park when a suicide bomber struck. At least 69 were killed and another 341 suffered injuries. The attack was claimed by the Taliban splinter group,[16] Jamaat-ul-Ahrar/Jamaatul Ahrar, formed in 2015.

The Taliban came to power in Afghanistan during 1996 and lost it in 2001, when the Americans invaded following 9/11. The invasion was precipitated by the Taliban's government's refusal to: (1) extradite Usama bin Laden[17] for his role in 9/11 and (2) expel his terrorist group, **al Qaeda** (The Base). Currently, the Taliban is an insurgency seeking to regain control of Afghanistan. It is very active in executing terror attacks in Pakistan and Afghanistan. In 2014, seven gunmen, affiliated with Tehrik-i-Taliban, wearing suicide vests scaled the wall of an Army run school in Peshawar, Pakistani. They killed nine staff members and 132 children between eight and eighteen years old. All attackers were killed by Pakistani special forces. The attack was in response to Pakistani military operations against the terrorists. The brutal attack illustrates one problem President Trump has in trying to get Pakistan in doing more against the Taliban, which has been surging in Afghanistan, during 2016 into 2017, where more Americans will soon be deployed. Pakistan faces an ugly choice: do more and experience additional heinous attacks by terrorists or do little or nothing and lose important American support.

In 2014, IS entered Khorasan, an old name for Afghanistan, and had more setbacks than successes, battling the government, the Taliban, and U.S.-led coalition forces. By the Spring of 2017, the U.S. military believed IS had been reduced to 700 fighters.[18] However, Taliban strength increased and by the end of 2016, it controlled 15 percent more territory as compared to 2015.[19]

As a result, General Nicholson, leader of coalition forces in Afghanistan, told Congress on February 9, 2017, that his forces were in a stalemate with the Taliban and several thousand more troops were needed.[20] Several months later, President Trump authorized up to 3,900 more troops, noting that future conditions may require additional military deployments.[21] In the fall of 2017, the Taliban unleashed a terrorism campaign in Afghanistan. Three attacks during September and October produced 98 deaths. On October 17, 2017, attackers in Ghazni boldly stormed a security compound and killed 25 police officers and six civilians.

The Philippines continue to be plagued by **Abu Sayyaf** (Arabic, Bearer of the Sword) and a surprisingly growing presence of IS. Abu Sayyaf may be morphing from

Romeo Gacad/Staff/Getty Images

a terrorist group to becoming a bandit gang. In a 12-month period, they attacked at least 13 foreign ships and took over 50 hostages they held for ransom. During that 12-month period, they appear to have committed more acts of piracy/hostage-taking as compared to initiating attacks on the government, although the government has initiated clashes with Abu Sayyaf. On at least one occasion when the ransom was not paid, Abu Sayyaf beheaded the hostage, a Canadian, man dumping his head in a street. Abu Sayyaf also has a record of raiding resorts and taking Western hostages for ransom. Abu Sayyaf's goal is to establish an Islamic state in the Southern Philippines.[23]

By September 15, 2017, Great Britain had suffered five terrorist attacks.

In South America, both Hezbollah and IS maintain a presence as well as to an extent in the Caribbean. Venezuela maintains a "permissive environment" for terrorists, most notably Hezbollah. The tri-border region of Brazil, Argentina, and Paraguay is a stronghold for terrorist fundraising activities, discussed in Chapter 6, "Critical Processes of Terrorist Organizations."

In 2017, the Russian Ambassador to Turkey was shot dead as he spoke at the opening of an art exhibit, "Russia in the Eyes of the Turks," in Ankara.[24] After murdering the ambassador, the lone gunman, a twenty-two-year-old off-duty policeman, was ranting before he was killed in a gun battle with security forces. He shouted, "Allahu Akbar" (God is greatest), "Don't forget Aleppo," "Don't forget Syria," and also "We are the ones who pledged allegiance to Muhammad to wage jihad."[25]

Quick Facts
Who Are the Kurds?

The Kurdish people (or Kurds) are a large ethnic group of some 30 million people inhabiting the mountainous region straddling the borders of Turkey, Iraq, Syria, Iran, and Armenia. Although they represent the fourth-largest ethnic group in the Middle East (behind Arabs, Turks, and Persians), they have never had a permanent nation state. In recent years, they have greatly influenced various conflicts in the region, especially in Iraq, Syria, and Turkey. For instance, the Kurdish Workers Party, or PKK, is a designated terrorist organization that has killed more than 25,000 people in Turkey over the last two decades. And in Syria and Iraq, the Syrian Kurdish Democratic Unity Party (PYD) and the Popular Protection Units (YPG) have emerged as powerful offensive allies in the fight against the Islamic State. The Kurds make up a sizeable part of the population in several Middle East countries:

Syria: Along with other minorities, the Kurds comprised about 10 percent of Syria's pre-war population of 23 million people.

Iraq: Kurds make up about 20 percent of the country's 37 million people and are located primarily in the mountainous northeastern part of the country.

Iran: Approximately 10 percent of the country's 82 million people are Kurdish and are concentrated in the northwest part of the country near the Iraqi and Turkish borders.

Turkey: The largest concentration of Kurds in the Middle East, comprising over 20 percent of the nearly 80 million people in Turkey, is located in the southern and southeastern provinces of Turkey.

Sources: Dion Nissenbaum, Gordon Lubold, and Julian E. Barnes, "U.S. to Arm Kurds, Vexing Turkey," *Wall Street Journal,* May 10, 2017, p. A1, A8. BBC News, "Who are the Kurds?" March 14, 2016. See: www.bbc.com /news/world-middle-east-29702440

FIGURE 1–1
A Marine returns home from a deployment and is greeted by a newborn child.

(PJF Military Collection/Alamy Stock Photo)

The motive for the murder is unknown, but three theories have emerged: (1) First, the killer was opposed to the increased economic ties between Turkey and Russia and the Russians' actions in the destruction of Aleppo, Syria, and support for Syrian President Assad; (2) Senior Turkish officials blamed Fethullah Gulen and his Gulenist Terror Organization. The Turkish language letters for the group are FETO. In 2016, there was a failed coup attempt against Turkish President Erdogan, which was blamed on the Islamic Imam Gulen, who lives in Pennsylvania. Turkey identified FETO as a terrorist organization and also asked the United States to extradite Gulen, which it declined to do. Given that history, it seems natural that Turkey would identify Gulen as being behind the assassination; and (3) suspicion has also been cast on the Kurds who are fighting against IS, which is allied with President Assad. It is a messy situation with several tentacles stretching toward entirely different motives as the explanation.[26]

4. It is said that those who make their living reading crystal balls are doomed to eat broken glass. Nonetheless, we accept the risk and assert there will be no quick and easy resolution to terrorism. The continuous possibility of an attack is akin to learning to live with an incurable disease.

5. Families are stressed by the deployment of their members to combat zones, struggle to adjust if they return with injuries, and grieve over their deaths. Service members who are deployed face dangers, often over multiple deployments. Their collective sacrifices give us a measure of security and deserve our respect. To demonstrate that respect, many people are joining efforts to help returning veterans adjust to their homecoming.

6. Robb makes a compelling argument that terrorists could wage a different kind of war against the United States, a "New War" that has the potential to have a major impact on America's homeland without **weapons of mass destruction** (WMDs).[27] Such a New War would be driven by two components: (a) crippling our infrastructures by cyber attacks, which can be launched covertly from anyplace in the world and would make our lives more difficult and (b) as IS is already doing in Western Europe, sending or activating small teams to wreak havoc and death. Cyber attacks can be waged indefinitely and launched covertly from anyplace in the world.

Terrorists have not forsaken using improvised explosive devices (IEDs), suicide bombers, or attacks on specific targets, such as the U.S. Consulate in Benghazi, Libya, during 2012, which killed Ambassador Stevens and others. However, the larger New War goal of sophisticated terrorist movements opposed to the United States is to render it economically impotent and unable to "throw its weight around in the Middle East."[28] Fallows thinks that while we have seemingly blunted al Qaeda's huge, spectacular attacks, a shift to New

Weapons of mass destruction
There are at least 50 official definitions of WMDs in the United States and other national governments, as well as international organizations such as the United Nations. A common thread in these definitions approximates the following: WMDs are nuclear, biological, chemical, radiological, and high explosive weapons capable of producing major destruction, mass casualties, and/or significant infrastructure damage.

Information Link
For a global examination of terrorism, visit the U.S. Department of State, Country Reports on Terrorism. U.S. law requires the secretary of state to provide Congress, by April 30 of each year, a full and complete report on terrorism with regard to those countries and groups meeting criteria set forth in its legislation.

War attacks may prove to be more threatening.[29] Robb asserts any New War will feature **Black Swan events**, which are so different from what we know that they will be difficult to predict.[30]

How would a New War be potentially able to make America economically impotent? It relies on the new strategic weapon of "**system disruption**,"[31] attacking elements of the infrastructure, including oil pipelines and refineries, and communication, transportation, electrical, and water systems. The 9/11 attacks illustrate this type of warfare because the towers were filled with banking, finance, insurance, and other important infrastructure enterprises. Al Qaeda spent perhaps $250,000 on those attacks, and in response, America has expended $500 billion[32] in the decades that followed.[33] In 2001, anthrax-tainted mail killed five people in the United States, cases that remain unsolved. In response, the U.S. Postal Service developed countermeasures costing $5 billion or $1 billion per fatality.[34] Attacks on Iraq's infrastructure disrupted its economy: Electricity was only available 8–12 hours daily, corporations were leaving the country, new investment money was scarce, and unemployment was a staggering 50 percent.[35] A single attack on an Iraqi oil pipeline cost $2,000 and none of the attackers were caught, but it produced an income loss of $500 million, creating a return of 25,000 times the cost of the attack.[36] In mid-2014, intelligence sources indicated that the Kingdom of Saudi Arabia was being targeted by the terrorist movement the **Islamic State** (IS).[37] In Chapter 4, we focus on the Islamic State as it has evolved over the last four years. Targets identified include desalinization plants, petroleum facilities, and government buildings,[38] all fitting within the strategy of system disruption.

To the public, IS seemingly came out of nowhere in 2014, but intelligence services were previously aware of it. Unlike other terrorist organizations that want to brutally inflict violence until their grievances, terms, or demands are met, IS's endgame is the establishment of an Islamic world under very conservative and strict Islamic law by establishing a global caliphate. Refer to Chapter 4, "The Rise of Radical Islam," for a much more in-depth discussion of the Islamic State.

As an example, in 2016, near Damascus, Syria, IS fighters pushed two blindfolded gay men off a roof and watched them hit the concrete, where they were stoned by women and children.[39] In 2013, a conservative Islamic scholar spoke at a mosque 30 miles from Orlando, Florida. Included was the idea that gay people should be killed "out of compassion" because they offend the human race and God.[40] A twenty-nine-year-old American-born man of parents from Afghanistan entered the *Pulse* nightclub in Orlando, Florida, three years after the "out of compassion" comment. *Pulse* was frequented by the lesbian, bi-sexual, gay, transgender, queer (LGBTQ) community.[41] Spraying the nightclub with gunfire, he killed 49 and wounded 53 before being killed by police after a several-hour ideal. Speaking with police by telephone while in *Pulse*, the man pledged allegiance to IS. A key question is whether he knew about and acted upon the Islamic scholar's words.[42] Then-President Obama called it a simultaneous act of terrorism and a hate crime.

As could be predicted, the radical right-wing groups (such as the Neo-Nazis, Skinheads, and Christian Identity Churches) within the United States applauded the *Pulse* nightclub shooting. Racist hate groups like the **Skinheads** are among the most dangerous radical-right groups in the United States and in Europe. Violent, and holding Neo-Nazi values about blacks, Jews, LGBTQs, foreigners, and others, they are organized into compact "crews" or act individually. They travel frequently and without notice, making it difficult for police to track them. The movement began in England and is now in its fourth decade in America.

The Emanuel African Methodist Episcopal Church in Charleston, South Carolina, was founded in 1816 and has a distinguished history of more than 200 years. The Church's history spanned slavery, the reconstruction of the South following the American Civil War, the Ku Klux Klan, the Jim Crow laws, segregation, the Civil Rights Movement, and the continuing discrimination against African Americans. None of that prepared anyone for one of the most horrific white supremacist attacks. On the evening of June 17, 2015, a twenty-one-year-old man filled with hatred entered the Church where congregants were gathered and began shooting them. When it was over, nine people were dead, including Reverend Pinckney, the Pastor of the Church. The crimes were so

Black Swan events
Black Swan events are so unique, so far from the norm, and so different from all other events and patterns that analysts will be unable to forecast them.

System disruption
System disruption attacks are called the New War. Instead of concentrating on attacks that produce mass casualties, system disruption attacks focus on the systems that are essential to our daily lives, such as mass transit, electrical grids, and water.

Islamic State
A terrorist organization and movement that has evolved to become a major international threat in 2014. Previously known as the Islamic State in Syria (ISIS) and the Islamic State in the Levant (ISIL). IS is an evolution of radical Islamic thought beginning with al Qaeda in Iraq (AQI) and al-Qaeda in the Arabian Peninsula (AQAP); both groups are presently in conflict against coalition forces in Iraq as well as Syria.

Islamic: of, or pertaining to Islam
Practices or persons that adhere to the beliefs of Islam. See Islam.

Skinhead
A white supremacist group that originated in London, England, among working class youths in the 1960s. Eventually becoming associated with a much larger subculture named for their shaved or close-cropped heads, military-style clothing, including Nazi-type "jack" boots and hard rock, punk-style music. Often heavily tattooed.

Dominic Dibbs/Alamy Stock Photo

Quick Facts
Ex-Girlfriends Testify Against Skinhead

A skinhead was on trial in Pennsylvania for murdering a black man. His ex-girlfriends testified against him, recounting how he had described the murder in detail. His motive, according to the women, was that he wanted to earn the spider web tattoo that skinheads wear to show they have killed an African American. Other violent aspects of his violence detailed in the testimony were his raping one of the women and beating her dog to death with a baseball bat.

---

ugly many people could not fathom the enormity of them. Although the gunman, Dylann Roof, has been tried, convicted on federal charges, and sentenced to death, his execution is by no means certain. Appeals might go on for years and the federal government hasn't executed anyone since 2003.

America has many infrastructure vulnerabilities, including oil platforms in the Gulf of Mexico, concentrated oil pipeline systems, lengthy railroad routes, numerous unprotected bridges and tunnels, and other sites, including the yet-to-be built second pipeline called Keystone. The new Keystone would run 1,179 miles from Alberta, Canada, to Steele City, Nebraska, carrying 830,000 barrels of oil daily. In Steele City, the privately financed pipeline would join an existing one that goes to American refineries on the coast of the Gulf of Mexico.

If systematically attacked by New War tactics, life as we know it would be considerably altered. In a New War, protecting the infrastructure is at least as important as fighting terrorists "over there" and perhaps even more difficult.

Finally, terrorism compels local, state, tribal, and national governments to have significant policy and diplomatic discussions about how to combat it. The National Security Agency's (NSA) massive anti-terrorism data collection programs were much in the news the last several years, illustrating how dealing with terrorism has implications for all of us. A recent survey discovered that 54 percent of respondents disapproved of the U.S. government's collection of telephone and Internet data, while 42 percent approved. However, a substantial portion, 74 percent, said they were not willing to sacrifice civil liberties to be safe from terrorism.[43]

Data such as this provokes serious national conversations about the balance between national security and Constitutional rights. We need to be able to follow such conversations knowledgeably because they are at the very heart of the relationship between a government and its citizens. This issue is discussed in Chapter 10, "Intelligence, Terrorism, and the U.S. Constitution." Benjamin Franklin captured the essence of this discussion in 1759, when he observed, "They that give up essential liberty to obtain a little temporary safety deserve neither liberty nor safety." Although the U.S. government is charged with preventing new attacks, it must simultaneously preserve those Constitutional liberties and rights that define it. Every citizen is affected by how well that balance is struck.

The Concept of Terrorism

There was terrorism before there was a word for it. The Romans conquered portions of the Middle East in the first century B.C. In Palestine for decades afterward, the Jewish Sicarii (dagger men) concealed knives under their robes and used them to murder Romans and their supporters in crowds. For example, in the market and on festival days, the Sicarii would strike and then quickly disappear into the crowd. The Sicarii believed that Jews were the chosen people and being subordinated to the Roman Emperor was antithetical to their religious beliefs, making them staunchly anti-Roman.[44] In Iran during the eleventh–twelfth centuries, a branch of Islam, the Nizari Ismailis, killed opposing leaders in the Middle East and became known as the "assassins."[45] There were nine European Crusades to the Holy Land, lasting from roughly the end of the eleventh to the end of the thirteenth century. During their travel to Palestine, some Crusaders slaughtered entire Jewish communities because they were not Christians.[46]

"Terrorism" only emerged as a term during the late Eighteenth century in France. Early terrorism in the United States was typically racial, labor, or **anarchist** related. Examples

Anarchist
An anarchist believes in the political theory of anarchy. Pure anarchy is characterized by the absence of a central government and strong cooperation among members of a society. Anarchists seek to overthrow rulers and governments. Practical anarchists recognize the impossibility of actually achieving pure anarchy. Consequently, they are willing to settle for a weak government that is minimally intrusive in the lives of its citizens.

include the following: (1) In 1856, John Brown, a vicious opponent of slavery, and his five sons went to Pottawatomie County, Kansas, where they murdered and mutilated five pro-slavery settlers.[47] Three years later, he seized a federal armory, thinking he could provoke and arm an uprising against slavery (see Figure 1–2). (2) Founded in 1867, the Knights of the White Camellia were a secret racist Southern society akin to the Ku Klux Klan (KKK), which was established two years earlier.[48] In order to get their candidate elected in 1868, the Knights terrorized Louisiana voters for two weeks before the election with secret murders and raids that left 2,000 voters dead or injured.[49] The Knights' candidate handily won the election. (3) Throughout the 1880s, Asians, especially the Chinese, were targeted for murder, assaults, and forced evacuation across all parts of the State of Washington.[50] (4) In 1886, a person believed to be an anarchist threw a bomb in Chicago's Haymarket Square that killed seven policemen present at a demonstration by striking workers.[51] (5) In 1892, Alexander Berkman, a Russian-born anarchist, shot and stabbed industrialist Henry Clay Frick in his Pittsburgh, Pennsylvania, office, wounding him.[52] Frick was chairman of the Carnegie Steel Company, where nine steelworkers were killed during a labor dispute. (6) Radical union leaders planted a bomb in the offices of the *Los Angeles Times* in 1910 that killed 21 people.[53] The bombing was in retaliation for the paper's anti-union stance. (7) In 1915, Eric Muenter planted a bomb with a timing device that detonated in the Reception Room of the U.S. Senate to dissuade the United States from entering World War I on the side of Great Britain and France. When arrested, he committed suicide by beating his head against the wall of his jail cell.[54] (8) A man driving a horse-drawn cart stopped at Wall Street in New York City in 1920 and disappeared into a crowd. Minutes later, a bomb exploded, killing at least 30 people and injuring 300 others.[55] The attack was attributed to anarchists and never solved (see Figure 1–3). During the 1880s–1920s, anarchists were also active in Europe, the most important example of which is the assassination in 1914 of Austria's Archduke Ferdinand and his wife Duchess Sophie, which led to World War I.

Despite such terrorist events, America's level of concern regarding terrorism has historically been quite low. As recently as 60 years ago, it got little attention. It was something that happened oceans away, "over there," in Europe and in the Middle East as several cases illustrate. In Spain, the Euskadi Ta Askatasuna (ETA, Basque Homeland and Freedom) was formed in 1959 with a goal to create a separate homeland in Northern Spain for ethnic Basques.[56] ETA quickly adopted terror tactics, such as assassinations. The Baader-Meinhof Group (BMG) wanted to create more socialist states in Europe, and between 1968 and 1977

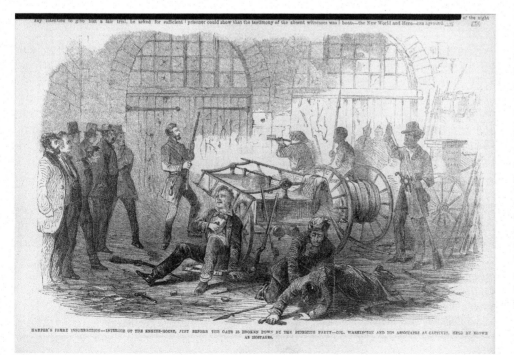

FIGURE 1–2
John Brown (1800–1859) stands alone in front of the left set of doors inside the federal armory at Harpers Ferry, Virginia. Brown and his followers seized the facility in the belief their action would provoke an uprising against slavery that they could arm. Robert E. Lee, then a colonel in the Union Army, led a force that killed some and captured others in this rebellious group. Brown was charged with treason and hung fewer than 90 days afterward. A song about the incident was popular among Union troops during the Civil War (1861–1865). Lee later commanded the Confederate Army.
(Library of Congress Prints and Photographs Division Washington, D.C. 20540 USA)

FIGURE 1-3
One of the early anarchist bombings in the United States occurred in New York's Union Square during 1900. The anarchist only succeeded in killing two people, himself and one other man. This photograph of their bodies is believed to have been taken 20 seconds after the bomb exploded.

(George G. Bain/Library of Congress Prints and Photographs Division Washington, D.C. 20540 USA)

Black September Organization

The Palestinian nationalist group that massacred members of the Israeli delegation at the 1972 Summer Olympics in Munich, Germany.

carried out deadly bombings.[57] Its successor was the Red Army Faction (RAF), which decided in 1998 that its goals could not be achieved and ceased operations. The Palestinian nationalist group **Black September Organization** massacred members of the Israeli delegation to the 1972 Summer Olympics in Munich, Germany.[58] The 1970s saw a handful of aircraft hijackings or "skyjackings." Despite these variations in attack modes, the country of Israel and its citizens have been the most consistent target of terrorists. Arguably, it has been under siege since its formation in 1948.

Despite these events, terrorism has until relatively recently been at the margin of U.S. policy. A variety of events account for this position. It was a distant event that was not directed at the United States. The National Aeronautics and Space Administration (NASA) had people focused on manned orbits of the earth and a landing on the moon. The American Civil Rights Movement was also prominent in news media reports. Finally, the Vietnam War consumed our resources and energy, particularly from 1965 through 1975.

From the 1960s to 9/11, several important radical movements, such as Students for a Democratic Society, existed in the United States, and some terrorist attacks were launched on Americans abroad. The Black Panther Party (see Figure 1–4), founded in 1966, was militant and violent from its beginnings, although it also provided some social assistance programs. It generally viewed governments as racist and repressive. Beginning in 1969, the Weather Underground, the "Weathermen," sought to overthrow the federal government, bombing the Capitol Building and the Pentagon in 1970 and 1971, respectively.

Quick Facts
The Assassination of Rabbi Meir Kahane

Rabbi Kahane formed the Jewish Defense League, a right-wing group, to protect elderly and poor Jews living in unstable neighborhoods in New York City.[59] El Sayyid Nosair, a naturalized U.S. citizen born in Egypt, was acquitted of murdering Kahane in 1990, but received a prison sentence for possessing a pistol.[60]

Nosair did so in the belief that Kahane declared war on Muslims, openly advocating genocide and ethnic cleansing.[61] Nosair later received a life sentence for being a co-plotter of the 1993 bombing attack on the World Trade Center.

In 1979, Iranian Muslim extremists seized the U.S. Embassy in Tehran and held Americans hostage for over a year. In 1988, two Libyan men planted a bomb on Pan Am Flight 103 that was flying from London to New York City. It exploded over Lockerbie, Scotland, killing all 259 passengers and 11 Scots on the ground.[62] From 31,000 feet, the explosion rained debris over 845 square miles,[63] creating what may be the largest crime scene ever processed. The motive for the bombing is believed to have been the reaction of Libya's leader, the late Muammar Gaddafi, to several sharp, but brief, military actions in which his country lost aircraft and a naval vessel to the United States. In 1983, truck bombs exploded in the U.S. Marine Corps compound in Beirut, Lebanon, killing 241 Marines and twenty-one members of other services.

In 1998, the U.S. Embassies in Kenya and Tanzania were simultaneously hit by truck-driving suicide bombers. Thousands of people were injured and 224 died from those attacks. President Clinton responded by authorizing cruise missile attacks on terrorist facilities in Afghanistan and the Sudan.[64] A U.S. missile strike was made on a pharmaceutical factory in the Sudan on the grounds it was making chemical weapons, but the accuracy of that assessment has been debated within the American government.

In 1993, radical Muslims made their first attack on the North Tower of the World Trade Center in New York City. A Ryder truck with 1,200 pounds of explosives was parked in the underground garage of one of the towers.[65] When the explosives detonated, a hole 100 feet wide and several stories deep was created. Six people were killed, more than 1,000 injured, and 50,000 people were evacuated.[66] Only one of the seven perpetrators has escaped capture and conviction. In custody, one of the perpetrators said the plan was to have the North Tower knock down the other tower.[67] Eight years later, the 9/11 attacks did cause both towers to collapse. In Yemen during 2000, two suicide terrorists detonated a boat filled with explosives alongside the USS Cole. This attack produced casualties and major damage, but more important, it also seized the attention of the American government. However, the event that would transform our national agenda was yet to occur.

The attacks on September 11, 2001, were devastating, frightening, and compelled a national response. The attacks focused the United States on preventing terrorism from reaching our shores. Terrorism is currently the most important word in our political vocabulary and America annually spends billions of dollars combat it.[68] Despite America's relatively short history of dealing with terrorism, knowledgeable observers have distinguished between the "old" and "new" terrorism. One of the early voices in calling attention to the new terrorism was Laqueur, who in 1999 foresaw that, "A new age of terrorism is dawning, but the **old terrorism** is far from dead."[69] Other historical accounts of terrorism appear in connection with other topics in subsequent chapters.

FIGURE 1–4
In 1970, the Black Panther Party called for a Constitutional Convention that would unite women, gays, blacks, and independence for Puerto Rico into a comprehensive revolutionary movement. They met on the steps of the Lincoln Memorial in Washington, D.C., to no great effect.
(O'Halloran Thomas J/Leffler, Warren K/ Library of Congress Prints and Photographs Division Washington, D.C. 20540 USA)

Old terrorism
Generally, it had specific political, social, and economic goals. Because the goals were limited, some could ultimately be resolved by negotiation.

Box 1-1
Black Swan Events

Black Swan events are so different from past experience that analysts will be unable to anticipate them. They are unpredictable. The following examples from 2015 illustrate Black Swan events: (1) the attack on the staff of *Charlie Hebdo*, a satirical magazine in France. During it, 12 people were murdered and 11 injured. In the three-day manhunt that followed, French citizens were fearful, not knowing what to expect next. The killers were from al Qaeda's Yemen affiliate, Ansar al-Sharia; and (2) at a San Bernardino County Department of Public Health training session and Christmas party, an American-born man of Pakistani descent and his wife, a Pakistani permanent resident of the United States, who are believed to have become self-radicalized, engaged in a mass shooting. When the two fled, they had killed 14 people and wounded 22 others. Later that day, the pair died in a shootout with police.

There is a growing body of literature on terrorism, but there is still much to learn. However, two case studies demonstrate that we have come a long way from our earliest understandings of terrorism:

Robespierre
A Frenchman and key architect of the reign of terror. He believed terror was the speedy, severe, and inflexible administration of justice from which virtue flowed. Seemingly, terror and virtue became synonymous to him.

Reign of Terror
Particularly violent period during the French Revolution (1793-1794) when the guillotine was used to behead over 16,000 people including Robespierre. See Robespierre.

1. The word "terror" gained currency in the modern era during the French Revolution (1789–1799), which was caused by political, economic, and social upheaval. **Robespierre** bears substantial responsibility for the period within the revolution called the **Reign of Terror** (September 1793–July 1794).[70] It would have been better for France if Maximilien Robespierre had remained an unimportant lawyer in Northern France.[71] Instead, he joined the revolutionary government in 1793. Robespierre quickly developed an appetite for using the guillotine to instill fear, and during the reign of terror, over 16,000 people lost their heads to the guillotine,[72] including the king and his wife.

   Robespierre lost the support of the people when he allowed a law to be passed that permitted the execution of those who were merely *suspected* of not supporting the revolution. Finally, the guillotine claimed Robespierre himself before the regime of terror ran its course. He attempted suicide to avoid public execution, but the gunshot merely shattered his jaw. In a 1794 speech, Robespierre claimed, "Terror is nothing but prompt, severe, and inflexible justice. It is thus the emanation of virtue."[73] Ultimately for him, it seems that terror and virtue became synonymous.

2. In 1877, Colonel Trepov was the Governor of St. Petersburg, Russia, and had a man flogged for not removing his hat as Trepov approached.[74] Outraged at this injustice, Vera Zasulich shot and severely wounded Trepov the next year. At trial, she was successfully defended by two claims by the defense. First, she was described as "a girl," although she was twenty-nine years old. Second, because she was acting to right a wrong as a terrorist, Vera could therefore not be a criminal.[75]

Terrorism (general/working definition)
The deliberate and unlawful use of threats or actual violence to inculcate fear, intended to intimidate or coerce individuals, groups, or governments to change their political, social, or religious basis.

A **general working definition of terrorism** is the deliberate, unlawful use of threats, force, or actual violence to inculcate fear, intended to intimidate or coerce individuals, groups, or governments to change their political, social, religious, or ideological basis. Although noted in Box 1–1, it bears repeating that presently the main victims of terrorist violence are usually unarmed civilians unable to defend themselves. Table 1–1 summarizes the United States' legal definitions for international and domestic terrorism.

Because the United States is just one political state and suffered significant terrorist attacks, it was easier to enact and amend terrorist legislation. In contrast, the United Nations has not been able to draft a definition of terrorism acceptable to all member nations because they reserve the political right to themselves to determine what acts constitute terrorism. In 2002, the **European Union** offered a framework for terrorism legislation that was adopted by all of its members. In 2008, that framework was amended by prohibiting certain activities associated with terrorism, for example, teaching others how to make bombs and use firearms for terroristic purposes.[76] Members of the European Union are free to add their own legislative concerns to the European Union's supplied framework.

European Union
The EU is a political and economic union founded in 1993 with 28 member nations that are primarily located in Europe.

Ethnic Arabs have suffered from acts of terrorism, often from neighboring nations. Arab states were early adopters of measures to combat terrorism. In 1997, the Arab League Ministerial Council resolved to fight terrorism in its 22-nation region with respect to its threats to security, economic, ideological, and social matters. This was followed

Quick Facts
The French Revolution, Royalty, and the Guillotine

In 1793, both King Louis XVI and his wife Marie Antoinette (1755–1793) were executed by the guillotine. It is alleged that when she heard peasants were complaining they had no bread to eat, she said, "Let them eat cake." While this "indictment" of her has been repeated often, there is no evidence that she actually uttered this phrase.

TABLE 1-1
United States' Definitions of International and Domestic Terrorism

International terrorism means activities that:

(A) Involve violent acts or acts dangerous to human life that are a violation of the criminal laws of the United States or of any State, or that would be a criminal violation if committed within the jurisdiction of the United States or of any State;

(B) Appear to be intended to:

   (i) intimidate or coerce a civilian population;

   (ii) influence the policy of a government by intimidation or coercion; or

   (iii) affect the conduct of a government by mass destruction, assassination, or kidnapping; and

(C) Occur primarily outside the territorial jurisdiction of the United States, or transcend national boundaries in terms of the means by which they are accomplished, the persons they appear intended to intimidate or coerce, or the locale in which their perpetrators operate or seek asylum.

Domestic terrorism means activities that:

(A) Involve acts dangerous to human life that are a violation of the criminal laws of the United States or of any State;

(B) Appear to be intended to:

   (i) intimidate or coerce a civilian population;

   (ii) influence the policy of a government by intimidation or coercion; or

   (iii) affect the conduct of a government by mass destruction, assassination, or kidnapping; and

(C) occur primarily within the territorial jurisdiction of the United States.

Source: 18 United States Code, Chapter 113B, January 1, 2012.

International terrorism

As provided for by federal law, international terrorism involves violent acts or acts dangerous to human life that violate federal or state laws if committed within the jurisdiction of the United States or any state, which appear to be intended to intimidate or coerce a civilian population, influence the policy of government by mass destruction, assassination, or kidnapping, and occur primarily outside of the territorial jurisdiction of the United States or transcend national boundaries by the means by which they are accomplished, the persons they appear to intimidate or coerce, or the locale in which the perpetrators operate or seek asylum. See the federal definition in Table 1–1.

Domestic terrorism

As provided by federal law, domestic terrorism involves violations of federal or state law that appear to intimidate or coerce a civilian population or affect the policy of a government by intimidation or coercion, or affect the conduct of a government by mass destruction, assassination, or kidnapping and occur primarily with the territorial jurisdiction of the United States. See the federal legal definition in Table 1–1.

in the next year by the Arab Convention for the Suppression of Terrorism. The Council of Arab Ministers of the Interior and the Council of Arab Ministers of Justice adopted a definition of terrorism: "Any act or threat of violence, whatever its motives or purposes, that occurs for the advancement of an individual or collective criminal agenda causing terror among people, causing fear by harming them, or placing their lives, liberty or security in danger, or aiming to cause damage to the environment or to public or private installations or property or to occupy or to seize them, or aiming to jeopardize a national resource."[77]

Mainline Muslims have been invested in seeing that their religion not be caught up in definitions of terrorism, which is both predictable and appropriate.

While the "new terrorism" targets non-combatants, this practice is in sharp contrast to **selective terrorism**. The Irish attempted to gain their country's independence from the British Commonwealth during the Anglo-Irish war of 1919–1921. Lacking a "real" military, their ragtag **Irish Republican Army** (IRA) fought a guerilla war. The IRA picked the places to attack and then quickly faded away. The IRA's commander, **Michael Collins** (see Figure 1–5), used selective terrorism, targeting supporters, key members, and the institutions of the British Commonwealth. This is sharp contrast to the practice associated with the new terrorism of using indiscriminate violence to cause mass casualties among defenseless civilians.

> **Information Link**
> Visit the United Nations at www.unodc.org/tldb/pdf/conv_arab_terrorism.en.pdf and read the "1998 Arab Convention on the Suppression of Terrorism."

Selective terrorism
Tactic advocated by Michael Collins, Commander of the Irish Republican Army (IRA). Instead of using unfocused, indiscriminate violence that killed many people, Collins used selective violence to focus on the people and institutions that supported continued British subjugation of Ireland. See Michael Collins and Irish Republican Army.

Irish Republican Army
Ireland's military arm during the Anglo-Irish War of 1919–1921.

Michael Collins
Commander of the Irish Republican Army (IRA) and advocate of selective terrorism.

Terrorism: Individual Perspective and Culture

Our views of terrorism are principally shaped by our individual perspectives and culture, a thread that runs throughout this book. A person's perspectives come from a process that incorporates multiple sources of data and at least some analysis of it. In contrast, culture is a pervasive collective experience that tends to produce people who share many values and ideas.

The EU's terrorism framework consists of:
1. An objective element, as it refers to a list of instances of serious criminal conduct (murder, bodily injuries, hostage-taking, extortion, fabrication of weapons, committing attacks, threatening to commit any of the above, etc.) and
2. A subjective element, as these acts are deemed to be terrorist offences when committed with the aim of

seriously intimidating a population, unduly compelling a government or international organisation to perform or abstain from performing any act, or seriously destabilising or destroying the fundamental political, constitutional, economic, or social structures of a country or an international organization.[78]

Individual perspective
A particular way of thinking about something, reduced to a simple image: On which side of the street do you stand?

Boston Tea Party
December 16, 1773, tax protest when colonists, disguised as Indians, threw tea from ships into Boston Harbor.

FIGURE 1–5
Michael Collins (1890–1922), often referred to as the "Big Fella," commanded the IRA and made effective use of selective terrorism. In 1922, he was the lone person killed in an ambush, suggesting he may have been the only target. Although a number of accounts have been written about the event, none has been widely accepted as authoritative.
(Library of Congress Prints and Photographs Division Washington, D.C. 20540 USA)

Individual Perspective

Individual perspective results from the process of evaluating issues, events, other people, groups, and nations and the underlying beliefs, intentions, and actions in order to assign meaning to them.[79] Individual perspective is produced out of a thoughtful and deliberate process that is to some degree analytical. In contrast, opinion is formed internally and may not rest on external observations or any degree of analysis. Opinion may be favorable, neutral, or malignant, such as racial hatred.

Reduced to a simple image, individual perspective is "what side of the street you stand on" for any given issue. Different people can see or know about the same event, but assign different meanings to it. The **Boston Tea Party** illustrates this point. In 1773, a group of 116 colonial men, some poorly disguised as Indians, boarded three ships at Boston's Griffin's Wharf, forced the crews below decks, and threw 90,000 pounds of the British East India Company's tea into the harbor (see Figure 1–6). Some colonists saw this is a bold act protesting English tax policy, whereas others were appalled by the act. Many colonists wanted no part of the subsequent revolution against England and moved to Canada, the Caribbean, and back to England. People in England saw the Boston Tea Party as defiance of the authority of Parliament and King George III. It is likely that everyone roughly had the same information. However, they formed radically different conclusions based on their perspectives. The Boston Tea Party happened before the idea of America becoming an independent nation took root in the colonies. However, it was an early event on the road to the American Revolution (1775–1783) and some theorists think it falls into the separatist/nationalism category of terrorism discussed in Chapter 8, "Typologies of Terrorism: The Right and Left Wings and Separatist or Nationalist Movements."

Another example of individual perspective comes from the terrorist attacks on September 11, 2001. The most common individual perspective is that al-Qaeda was responsible. However, conspiracy theorists have offered "competing" explanations, such as the government knew about the plot but didn't stop it because they wanted a reason to invade Iraq and Afghanistan. That reasoning is reminiscent of the allegation that President Roosevelt had prior knowledge of the Japanese plan to attack Pearl Harbor, but allowed it to happen to overcome Congress's sentiment to remain neutral in the war that was already being waged in Europe and Asia.

Al-Qaeda and the Islamic State view the United States and other Western powers through a radicalized, extremist Muslim prism. The late head of al-Qaeda, **Usama bin Laden** (1957–2011), helped plot the 9/11 attacks that turned four hijacked airliners into guided missiles. There were no survivors on any of the hijacked aircraft. American Airlines Flight 11 and United Airlines Flight 175 brought down the World Trade Center's Twin Towers in New York City, killing 3,000 civilians (see Figure 1–7). Trapped on burning floors, some people leapt to their death to avoid being burned alive.

THE DESTRUCTION OF TEA AT BOSTON HARBOR.

FIGURE 1–6
Thousands of jubilant colonists greet those involved in the Boston Tea Party. Two-thirds of the raiders were 20 years old or younger.

(Nathaniel Currier/Library of Congress Prints and Photographs Division Washington, D.C. 20540 USA)

Usama bin Laden
Saudi Arabian-born American ally who supported Afghanistan mujahedeen's resistance against the Soviets. When the Soviets left, he turned against the Americans and masterminded the 9/11 attacks. Head of al-Qaeda until his death in a 2011 raid on his compound in Pakistan by U.S. troops (Seal Team 6).

The attacks sent shock waves through city, state, and federal governments. Leaders debated whether more waves of attacks with deadlier weapons were coming. There was also a great deal of misinformation, such as the report that the U.S. Capitol had been bombed. The Federal Aviation Administration (FAA) ordered the immediate landing ("pancaking") of nearly 4,500 flights in America's airspace. Some 350,000 passengers found themselves grounded miles from their destinations.[80] All arriving international flights were immediately diverted to Canada. Both of these actions were taken because the United States was unsure of how many other planes might be used as weapons. Other measures implemented included the

Information Link
Visit the 9/11 Memorial & Museum at www.911memorial.org. Explore the website and listen to the oral histories of first responders, recovery workers, and survivors of the attack.

FIGURE 1–7
Two days after the 9/11 attacks, a rescue specialist searches for survivors in the smoldering wreckage of the World Trade Center.

(Andrea Booher/Federal Emergency Management Agency)

FIGURE 1–8
A portion of the damage caused at the Pentagon by the 9/11 attack that effectively used American Airlines Flight 77 as a guided missile.

(Courtesy Department of Defense)

Allah
Arabic, literally "The God"; the Islamic God.

Allah u Akbar
Arabic, Allah (God) is great or Allah is the greatest.

Culture
Culture is the shared beliefs, experiences, and behaviors, such as language, values, customs, history, law, and religion, that cause its members to substantially interpret things in a similar manner and distinguish them from other cultures.

FIGURE 1–8
A portion of the damage caused at the Pentagon by the 9/11 attack that effectively used American Airlines Flight 77 as a guided missile.

(Courtesy Department of Defense)

FIGURE 1–9
Anwar al-Awlaki in Falls Church, Virginia, about five weeks after 9/11, looking benign or perhaps smug. Several of the 9/11 hijackers attended the mosque where al-Awlaki was an imam. Because of his involvement in al Qaeda operations against the United States, he was killed in Yemen from a missile fired from an American drone. That action ignited a debate over whether the president can authorize the death of a U.S. citizen without a trial and based on secret intelligence findings. Despite his death in 2011, al-Awlaki's videos remain on the Internet and even in 2017, some Western recruits mention them as being important in making the decision to join a terrorist group.

(Site Intelligence Group/AP Images)

evacuation of some elements of the federal government from Washington, D.C., and closing the U.S.-Mexican border.

Cultural Perspective

President George W. Bush characterized the September 11, 2001, attacks as "evil, despicable acts,"[81] and Palestinian leader Yasser Arafat also condemned the attacks.[82] However, others in Middle Eastern countries crowded into the streets and celebrated joyously, praising **Allah** and chanting "**Allah u Akbar.**"

Culture is defined as the shared beliefs, experiences, and behaviors that cause its members to substantially view things in a similar manner. In contrast to individual perspective, culture is a collective, accumulated experience. This shared experience often distinguishes one culture from another, including language, values, customs, history, law, and religion. Of course, sharing a common culture is not a guarantee that all members will have the same perspectives.

Anwar al-Awlaki (1971–2011) represents someone who was born in one culture, but changed his cultural identity. He was born in New Mexico to Yemeni parents and earned degrees from Colorado State and San Diego State universities. After becoming a Muslim cleric, al-Awlaki was linked to over 19 terrorist operations.[83] He was adept at using social media to spread his propaganda messages of hatred and violence against the West and to attract and radicalize recruits. **Radicalization** describes the process of acquiring and holding extremist views. **Violent extremism** describes violent action taken on the basis of those extreme beliefs.[84]

The present radical Muslim culture views Western nations in general, and the United States in particular, very negatively. The people of Western nations are seen as the new or neo-crusaders making war on Islam, occupying its countries, misleading some of its

Box 1-2
The Old and New Terrorism

These descriptions of the "old" and "new" terrorism are broad. As a consequence, there are exceptions to the way they are profiled here. Moreover, the "old" never really disappeared. Instead, the amount of terrorism fitting its description simply declined. Simultaneously, the "new" had its roots in the old, yet produced its own identity. To some extent, the new terrorism arose as the motives changed from predominately secular, non-religious reasons to a high frequency of religion-based reasons. As a result, the news media, governments, and scholars substantially shifted their attention to the new forms of terrorism. The descriptions of "old" and "new" terrorism provide some understanding of where terrorism has been and how it has changed.

The "old terrorism" generally is described as having specific political, social, and economic goals.[85] Because many, if not most, old terrorism goals were subnational, they had some potential of being achieved by negotiation between the terrorists and the national government. As an illustration, ETA was ultimately able to obtain a Basque "homeland" with substantial autonomy within Spain. The old terrorism movements had a clearly defined organizational structure[86] and they targeted symbols of the government or social order being opposed.[87] Illustrations include embassies, national airlines, banks, and kidnappings and assassinations of business, military, and diplomatic personnel.[88] A communiqué in the name of the movement was issued after an attack that claimed responsibility for the attack and explained why it was carried out. In short, the old terrorism was comprehensible, albeit reprehensible.[89]

It is often difficult to specify with precision when a new trend begins. Some authorities point to 1979, when radicalized Muslims in Tehran, Iran, took U.S. Embassy staff hostage, as the onset of the "new terrorism." Others point to attacks in 1993 and 1995 as its starting period. In 1993, radicalized Muslims exploded a truck bomb in the parking garage under the North Tower of the World Trade Center.[90] In addition to the deaths and injuries,

some $500 million in damages were caused.[91] In 1995, sarin, a nerve agent, was released in the Tokyo subway system by Aum Shinrikyo. The sarin killed six and 6,000 others received medical treatment. Aum is a religious cult that teaches that the end of the world is near and only its believers will survive the apocalypse.[92]

The new terrorism deliberately targets unarmed civilians with the desire to inflict mass casualties. The number killed is of vital importance because mass casualties create greater fear in the general population. A radical religious interpretation undergirds many terrorist attacks around the globe. Believing they are carrying out the will of God, some terrorists willingly become suicide bombers because they believe immediate entry into Paradise will be their reward.

The new terrorist organizational structures are often difficult to discern because many of the new terrorism groups are autonomous or only loosely affiliated.[93] Unlike the prior generation of terrorism, the new terrorism is more international.[94] Such movements also inspire the "amateur" **lone wolf attacks**.[95] The new terror organizations are nimble, quick to learn, and increasingly technologically savvy and operationally competent.[96] Terrorist movements based on radical religious interpretations may not claim responsibility for their attacks. They are uninterested in negotiating settlements, and some groups seem eager to acquire weapons of mass destruction (WMDs).[97]

It is important to note that as terrorism continues to evolve, there are new "**new terrorisms**." Illustratively, system disruption attacks as well as cyber attacks represent a "New War," and IS's conquering lands in which to establish a new country is also a new iteration, as is its recently adopted practice of sending small teams to kill people in Western Europe, while continuing its large-scale combat operations in Iraq and Syria. Many of these new types of events are discussed throughout the book.

How are the old terrorism and the lone wolf attacks contrasted?

leaders, plundering its riches, and defiling its women and holy sites. These issues are discussed in more detail in Chapter 4, "The Rise of Radical Islam."

Issues in Conceptualizing, Defining, and Understanding Terrorism

A number of factors contribute to the difficulties we have in understanding terrorism, including (1) multiple and complex definitions have proliferated; (2) the evidence base for terrorism is insufficient; (3) terrorism is a contested concept; (4) terrorism is evocative—it appeals to emotion and not intellect; (5) political power often determines those who are labeled "terrorists"; and (6) past prosecutorial decisions within the United States have confused people.

Anwar al-Awlaki
Born in New Mexico to Yemeni parents. Became radicalized Islamic cleric linked to 19 terrorist operations. Killed in Yemen by drone in 2011.

Radicalization
The processing of acquiring and holding extremist beliefs. See violent extremism.

Violent extremism
Violent action taken on the basis of extremist beliefs.

Lone wolf attack
A violent attack by a single perpetrator, acting alone, without any direction or assistance from an organization or another person.

Quick Facts
Not all Muslims are Arabs

Intuitively it seems correct to think that all Muslims are Arabs. Statistically, there are about 1.6 billion Muslims in the world.[98] Most—66 percent—live in just 10 countries: Indonesia, India, Pakistan, Bangladesh, Nigeria, Egypt, Iran, Turkey, Algeria, and Morocco.[99] Worldwide, only 18 percent of the entire Muslim population is actually Arab.[100]

Box 1–3
Anwar al-Awlaki

Born in Las Cruces, New Mexico, Anwar al-Awlaki became a leading member of al-Qaeda's affiliate in Yemen. He was a senior recruiter as well as a spiritual motivator for al-Qaeda. He met with Umar Farouk Abdulmutallab (the Christmas Day bomber), who in late 2009 attempted to blow up a Northwest Airlines plane with a bomb concealed in his underwear. Major Nidal Malik Hasan, who killed 13 people and wounded many others at Fort Hood, Texas, exchanged emails in 2009 with al-Awlaki. Faisal Shahzad, who tried in 2010 to set off a car bomb in New York City's Times Square, called al-Awlaki an "inspiration."

Because al-Awlaki was involved in many operations, the federal government took the unprecedented action of placing him on a 2010 "capture or kill list" approved by President Barack Obama. After several attempts to capture him failed, al-Awlaki was killed in Yemen (September 30, 2011) by a Hellfire missile fired from a remotely flown drone.[101] Al-Awlaki's death caused significant controversy. The "targeted killing" of an American citizen was unprecedented in the United States. He was never charged nor convicted of a crime, yet was killed by a CIA-led drone attack. The same attack killed three other individuals linked to al-Qaeda.

Should the U.S. intelligence and military forces use drones to kill terrorist suspects, including American citizens, in foreign countries?

Box 1–4
al-Awlaki's Daughter Killed in Yemen Raid

In 2017, a U.S. Special Operations raid in Yemen to seize computers for intelligence purposes ended unsuccessfully with one American death.

An additional casualty of the raid was Nawar, the eight-year-old daughter of al-Awlaki, who was accidentally shot in the neck during what was described as a brutal gunfight. Her grandfather, a former government minister, said, "I don't think this was intentional."[102]

Should the U.S. intelligence and military forces use drones to kill terrorist suspects, including American citizens, in foreign countries?

New terrorism
Most commonly, a religious belief undergirds the violence. New terrorism is more transnational than the old and, unlike the old, it deliberately targets civilians/non-combatants to create fear. Many groups are autonomous or loosely affiliated with another group. Inspires lone wolf attacks. The new terrorism is nimble, quick to learn, technologically savvy, and operationally competent.

Bermuda Triangle of Terrorism
The hundreds of competing definitions of terrorism.

FIGURE 1–10
The Definition Triangle
(Drawn with modification from Alex Schmid, "The Definitional Problem,"[105] *Case Western Reserve Journal of International Law*, Vol. 36, No. 2/3, Spring 2004, Table 1–18, p. 400.)

Definitions Have Proliferated

The existence of many definitions of terrorism was mentioned earlier in this chapter and needs further comment. There is a natural, physical world that exists and can be scientifically analyzed, for example, the composition of soil. To make sense of other things, we intellectually construct meanings. The Fujita Scale (F-Scale) was created in 1971 to measure the intensity of tornadoes. The F-Scale and other constructs are artifacts or products of our intellect.

What we call reality largely consists of the world we create in our heads, which are filled with social constructs. They help us understand and organize our lives by virtue of the meaning we attach to them. Examples include marriage, loyalty, social status, happiness, and "bad neighborhoods." Some things such as gender have inherent qualities, but we create stereotypes about them, for example, "Women aren't good at science" and "Men are sloppy."

Terrorism is a non-natural world event and cannot be measured and characterized with scientific accuracy. Terrorism requires constructs to explain it. Figure 1–10 depicts how we construct our understanding of terrorism. It is a process that can be endlessly repeated, which accounts for numerous and complex definitions. Scholars and governmental agencies often develop definitions of terrorism that meet their needs. The combined efforts to define terrorism have created what Jenkins describes as the "**Bermuda Triangle of Terrorism**."[103] Definitions are intended to allow people to accurately distinguish one construct from another so that when we apply a label, such as terrorism, it is done with clear meaning. However, the surplus of terrorism definitions prevents us from doing so.

The Evidence Base for Terrorism Is Insufficient

The terrorism evidence base supporting planning, strategic thinking, and policymaking is weak. A 2008 review of 14,006 terrorism articles over a 32-year period revealed that 54 percent of them were written in 2001 and 2002,[104] immediately following 9/11. Articles in peer-reviewed

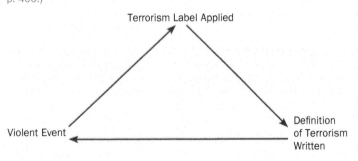

Terrorism Label Applied

Violent Event

Definition of Terrorism Written

journals numbered only 4,458.[106] Ninety-six percent of those were "think" pieces, only 3 percent were based on empirical analysis, and case studies accounted for just 1 percent.[107] Without a publically accessible empirical database, the question can be fairly raised: What do we really know about terrorism? Undoubtedly, such data exists within the control of intelligence and some other agencies and much of it should not be revealed because it may disclose methods and agents. Still, the lack of publically accessible empirical data may contribute to some misunderstandings about terrorism.

Terrorism Is a Contested Concept

Hezbollah (Arabic for the "Party of God") is a Muslim group that is simultaneously viewed as a political organization, terrorist group, and militia. It is primarily located in the Middle Eastern country of Lebanon and is headed by the radical cleric Sheik Hassan Nasrallah. Hezbollah was formed in response to the Israeli invasion of Lebanon in 1982. Hezbollah receives substantial arms, training, money, and intelligence from Syria and Iran.[108] This support is a **force multiplier**, which increases Hezbollah's operational capabilities and lethality. In late 2012, Hezbollah obtained a drone from Iran and assembled it. Hezbollah flew the unmanned aircraft into Israel, where it was shot down.[109] The addition of many strike-capable drones to Hezbollah's inventory would be a significant escalation of its operational capabilities. Syria describes Hezbollah as a militia resisting Israeli aggression.

Military clashes between Hezbollah and Israel Defense Forces (IDF) are not uncommon, and there was some escalation in late 2016 and early 2017. In the latter year, Hezbollah set off a roadside bomb that is believed to have killed two IDF members of an armored patrol and a Spanish UN Peace Observer. Amid other clashes, Israeli planes struck an arms shipment intended for Hezbollah, apparently from the Assad-led government.

Hezbollah has operatives worldwide—in Europe, South and North America, and Africa. It is not presently viewed as a security threat by Latin American nations. They see it as a legitimate political organization.[110] However, some host nations have concerns that Hezbollah's presence could complicate their relationship with the United States.

Latin America's view of Hezbollah as a legitimate political organization hampers America's counterterrorism efforts. Hezbollah's presence in Latin America gives it a closer geographic location to the United States than its Middle East home. From this forward position, Hezbollah could more easily launch attacks on the United States at the urging of its state sponsors of terrorism, Syria and Iran. Hezbollah is based on the minority Shi'a tradition of Islam and opposes the primary tradition of Sunni Islam, more commonly found throughout the Middle East and the world. Hence, on religion, Hezbollah is at odds with most Islamic nations. The principles of Shi'a and Sunni Islam are discussed in Chapter 3, "Understanding the Middle East and Islam"; the radical perspectives of Hezbollah are elaborated upon in Chapter 4, "The Rise of Radical Islam."

Hamas (The Palestinian Islamic Resistance Movement) is another radical fundamentalist Muslim Middle East organization designated as an FTO (**foreign terrorist organization**)

Hezbollah
Arabic, "Party of Allahu." Fundamentalist Islamic FTO, supported by Iran and Syria, originally Lebanon-based, now present in many other locations.

Force multiplier
A military term that means a capability that when added to, and employed by, a combat unit significantly enhances its combat potential and increases the likelihood of a successful mission.

Hamas
Arabic, "zeal," fundamentalist foreign terrorist organization (FTO) that provides extensive social services. It also has a well-armed militia/paramilitary arm. Opposed to the existence of Israel, Hamas has a strong presence in Palestine and Israel.

Foreign terrorist organization (FTO)
The U.S. Department of State lists an organization as a "foreign terrorist organization" if it engages in terrorist activity or has retained the capacity or intention to do so and it threatens U.S. nationals or America's national security.

Quick Facts
"Paper Terrorism"

Related to the proliferation of terrorism definitions is that "terrorism" is an elastic term that can be used in many contexts. "Paper terrorism" refers to bogus suits, baseless liens, and other measures that are filed to clog the courts, harm the credit of public officials, hold up the sale or refinancing of property, and consume public resources to deal with them. A "sovereign citizen," angered by getting a traffic citation, filed false liens totaling $800,000 against the chief of the police department employing the officer who issued the citation.[111]

To bolster their frivolous actions, "sovereigns" create fictitious or misuse genuine documents, their own license plates, and driver's licenses. Right-wing anarchists at heart, sovereigns believe all existing governments are illegitimate.[112] Sovereigns tend not to be violent, but the potential of dealing with sovereigns does pose a threat. During 2000–2012, sovereigns killed six police officers.[113]

Perhaps most paper terrorism is initiated by members of the Sovereign Citizen anti-government movement and sympathizers. There may be 300,000 sovereigns in a loose collection of groups.[114] The FBI considers sovereign-citizen extremists as a domestic terrorism movement.[115] At least 15 states have made it a crime to file "paper terrorism"–type actions. The Sovereign Citizen movement is further discussed in Chapter 8, "Typologies of Terrorism: The Right and Left Wings and Separatist or Nationalist Movements."

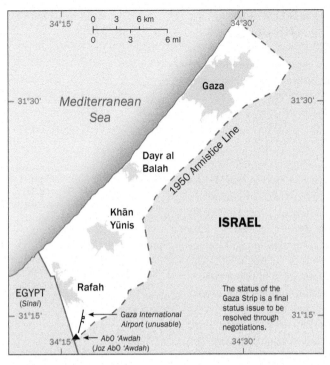

FIGURE 1–11

The Gaza Strip is 25 miles long and has a width of 3.5 to 7 miles with a population of 1.5 million Palestinians.

(Courtesy of the U.S. Department of State)

Gaza Strip

Administered by the Palestinian Authority, 25 miles long and from 3.5 to 7 miles wide. Situated on Eastern Mediterranean, bounded by Egypt to the south and Israel to its east and north.

by the U.S. government. Hamas is opposed to the existence of Israel and maintains a well-armed militia or paramilitary arm. It also provides substantial social services in Gaza, the West Bank, and Israel. Hamas funds have traditionally come from private donors in Saudi Arabia, oil-rich Persian Gulf nations, and charities operated for its benefit. Syria and Iran also provide support to Hamas.

Since the legislative elections of 2007, Hamas has been consolidating its control in the **Gaza Strip** (see Figure 1–11). Under the 1947 United Nations plan that partitioned Palestine, Israel was created. The Gaza Strip was to be an independent Arab country. However, Arab leaders rejected the plan because it created a Jewish homeland from territory formerly occupied by Arabs and religious sites sacred to Islam were located in Israel. The Gaza Strip is now claimed and governed by the Palestinian Authority under the 1993 Oslo Peace Accords between Israel and the Palestinian Liberation Organization (PLO). The Gaza Strip's long border with Israel has been problematic, and the historical development of this conflict is further explored in Chapter 2, "Political Ideology and the Historical Roots of Terrorism." Attacks by terrorists on Israel and retaliation raids can easily be launched because of their geographical proximity.

In 2012, Hamas was actively fighting against terrorist groups affiliated with al-Qaeda because their presence and activities threatened an unofficial cease-fire between Hamas and Israel.[116] Israel killed the Hamas military commander Ahmed al-Jabari in 2012. As a consequence, a wider exchange of rockets took place between the two countries. This violence threatened to spiral out of control, but fortunately did not, begging the hotly contested question of "who is the terrorist?" To make matters even more confusing, Hamas won a majority of seats in the Palestinian Parliament in the January 2006 election, making it the legitimate ruling power in the Gaza Strip and the West Bank and forcing the United States and Israel to now negotiate with "former terrorists." In 2014, Hamas fired hundreds of rockets into Israel, which responded with hundreds of air strikes on launch sites, munitions storage locations, and Hamas command and control centers. This threatened to engulf the region in a wider conflict until an uneasy peace was restored.

Terrorism Is Evocative—It Appeals to Emotion and Not Intellect

Something that is evocative has the power to stir people. It produces strong feelings and causes them to recall potent images and revisit powerful memories. The mention of terrorism on the news rivets our attention and we are compelled to pay attention until we know

---

Box 1-5
The United States' View of Hezbollah

The U.S. Department of State lists Hezbollah as a foreign terrorist organization (FTO). An organization is listed as such if it engages in terrorist activity or has retained the capacity or intention to do so and it threatens U.S. nationals or America's national security.

Hezbollah's portfolio includes (1) two suicide truck bombings in 1983 in Beirut, Lebanon—the first was at the U.S. Embassy and the second at a peacekeeping compound largely staffed by American Marines; (2) the suicide bombings in Argentina of the Israeli Embassy (1992) and a Jewish Center (1994); and (3) the 1996 suicide bombing of Khobar Towers in Saudi Arabia

that killed nineteen Americans, one Saudi, and 372 members of other nationalities.

There are several actual terrorist organizations that include "Islamic Jihad" in their full name. After Hezbollah's most notable attacks, a mysterious "Islamic Jihad" claimed credit for them. In some quarters, it is believed this particular Islamic Jihad is a fictional group whose purpose is to confuse enemies and draw attention away from Hezbollah.[117]

Why is it difficult to accurately link a specific act of terrorism to particular terrorist groups? Are there drawbacks to labeling a group an FTO?

the details. The public reaction to the 9/11 attacks was evocative and instructive. In the immediate wake of the attacks, a majority of Americans reported difficulty paying attention at school or work, felt depressed, and experienced sleep disruption or anger.[118] People with direct experience were six times more likely to experience post-traumatic stress disorder (PTSD) and they were nearly three times more prone to anxiety disorder.[119] They also had twice the probability of having some emotional difficulty.[120] Once a terrorist attack is experienced, the fear or anticipation of future attacks is intensified.[121] This intensification occurs because the attack becomes part of our frame of reference and lexicon. The attacks become embedded in our collective national conscious and some blame the government for failing to protect them. Some conspiracy-minded people believe the government committed the attacks or were complicit in them. A Pew Research Poll gathered data from persons who were at least eight years old on 9/11. Of them, 97 percent remembered where they were and what they were doing on that day.[122] By comparison, only 58 percent remembered where they were when the Berlin Wall fell.

Nations use the "terrorism" label to describe certain types of violent acts committed against them. However, they sometimes seem to lack the capability of critical introspection, which would require them to closely examine their own violent reprisals carried out in response to those acts.[123] Terrorism is a term that is so evocative and laden with meaning that many of us cannot entertain the thought that our allies or the United States would commit terroristic acts. Indeed, Americans generally believe that terrorism is "what the bad guys do."[124] What better way to distort the sovereign and legitimate interest of people than to associate them with illegitimate actions or sources? Such phrases as "guerrilla warfare," "revolutionary movement," and "radical extremist" only heighten ideological sentiment and play to emotion rather than intellect.[125]

The Ottoman Empire fought World War I as a German ally. At the end of the war, England and the allied powers occupied a large portion of the former Ottoman Empire. That area included what is now Syria, Palestine, Jordan, Lebanon, and Iraq. In 1923, one remnant of the Ottoman Empire became the Republic of Turkey. Britain ruled Palestine from 1923 to 1948.

Both before and after World War II, the Jewish people agitated for a homeland in Palestine and committed acts of terrorism. Illustratively, in 1944, Jewish operatives assassinated Lord Moyne (1880–1944), the British Minister of State, in Cairo to hasten the departure of the British from the Middle East. Two years later, they bombed the King David Hotel in Jerusalem, causing over 200 casualties. The hotel was headquarters for the British Army and the offices of the Civil Administration of Palestine. In 1948, Yitzak Shamir, who later served two terms as Israel's Prime Minister, was part of a team in Jerusalem that assassinated Swedish Count Folke Bernadotte (1895–1948), a U.N. negotiator sent to the Middle East to mediate the Arab-Jewish violence that followed the partitioning of Palestine.

Many of the acts called terrorism by the British were committed by the Irgun Zvai Leumi, an underground Jewish defense organization. Its leader, Menachem Begin (1913–1992), later served his nation in different leadership positions, including that of Prime Minister. Begin was known to have a body double or look-alike at public functions to confuse would-be assassins.

In the war against terrorism, the United States uses armed drones to inflict casualties and destroy targets. America considers it an effective military use of technology (see Figure 1–12). However, those on the receiving end are likely to view it as terrorism because it, albeit unintentionally, causes the deaths of unarmed non-combatants. Although no country wants to be accused of terrorism, the military value of the drones is such that the United States defends their use and suffers the allegations. The potential use of drones for surveillance domestically is controversial in the United States, an issue covered in Chapter 10, "Intelligence, Terrorism, and the U.S. Constitution."

Some people recall evocative events with great accuracy. In contrast, others disassociate with gruesome details to prevent being emotionally overwhelmed. They develop "cognitive blind spots" to preserve themselves. In one study, subjects were asked to put five key events about 9/11 in order. Surprisingly, 63 percent could not do so, even though they believed it was "the most unforgettable day" of their lives.[126] The greater the time lapse between an

FIGURE 1–12
An MQ-9 Reaper fires a Hellfire missile at a target in Afghanistan. The unmanned reaper is used for both operational and surveillance missions. Reapers have a 55' wing-span and a 27' length. They can be armed with several types (as this one is) or a variety of optics (cameras) and other sensing capabilities such as infrared and heat illumination and detection.

(HIGH-G Productions/Stocktrek Images/Getty Images)

evocative event and an attempt to recall the details, the more likely distortions will occur for one reason or another.[127] Distortions occur when the mind unconsciously "fills in" blank spots in its memory. Another source of distortion comes from people receiving information after an event and unconsciously incorporating it into their memories, accepting it as their own genuine experience. People who are highly cooperative are particularly susceptible to "filling in" their memories.[128]

Political Power Determines Who Are Terrorists

It is well understood that governments have the political authority to apply labels; examples include "mentally ill," "poverty level," "child molester," and "disabled." These labels carry significant consequences; for example, they may determine eligibility for various types of assistance or preclude people from certain rights.

The difference between a group being labeled "insurgent" or "terrorist" may turn less on what they actually do and more on what the ruling government calls it in pursuit of national policy agendas. Chechnya is a rural, lightly populated land rich in oil, natural gas, and other deposits.[129] Geographically, it is a combination of flatlands and the Caucasus Mountains. Chechens have been recognized as a distinctive people since the seventeenth century and

Box 1-6
Drone Use Attracts Sharp Criticism

Former President Jimmy Carter criticized the use of drones to kill terrorist leaders as an abuse of human rights. A Pakistan official says drone strikes made in his country bases are a violation of its sovereignty and he believes the attacks push people toward extremist groups. At the same time, he thinks, it pulls people away from democracy. Others have described the strikes as terroristic, arbitrary, and summary executions.

The exact number of civilian deaths from drones is unknown, or those reported are in dispute. Washington officials report a downward trend in civilian deaths. Some believe the reduction is caused by a "new method of scorekeeping." If a military-age male is killed during a drone strike, he is counted as an enemy unless his innocence is proved posthumously. The United States has "downsized" drone munitions to reduce casualties and employs longer periods of surveillance to ensure target identification. In Chapter 10, "Intelligence, Terrorism, and Homeland Security," we further discuss the use of drones domestically, as well as by the Islamic State against coalition forces in Syria and Iraq.

Do you think this use of drones constitutes an act of terrorism?

Quick Facts
Weaponized Drones

Weaponized drones are known to have been used in Iraq, Yemen, Afghanistan, Iraq, Somalia, Libya, Algeria, Pakistan, Nigeria, and Syria. The United States also flies drones out of a little-known base in Cameroon to fight Boko Haram[130] and has used them in the Philippines against terrorist leaders of Abu Sayyaf and Jemaah Islamiyah.[131]

---

are mostly Muslims. During 1818–1917, the Russians conquered and ruled Chechnya. Since that time, Russia has periodically been faced with Chechen independence movements. For instance, during World War II, the Chechens' hatred of Russia resulted in their cooperation with the Nazis. In retaliation, at the end of the war, Russian dictator Josef Stalin deported the Chechens to Siberia and Central Asia.[132]

During the late 1950s, surviving Chechens were allowed to return to their homeland. Since then, several insurgencies, some using terrorist tactics, have been waged against Russia. Following 9/11, Russian President Vladimir Putin "relabeled" the insurgents as "terrorists." Russia ostensibly seemed to join the global war on terror.[133] In 2004, Chechen terrorists seized control of a school in Beslan, Russia, and held 1,300 hostages, most of them schoolchildren and teachers. The Chechens threatened to kill their hostages if Chechen prisoners were not released. A three-day standoff ended when Russian security forces stormed the school. In the end, over 700 hostages were wounded and 186 children and 145 adults were killed![134]

Because Russia seemed to be "on board" with the fight against terrorism, the West substantially turned a blind eye to the "botched" Beslan siege. By relabeling Chechen insurgents as "terrorists," Russia's subsequent conduct averted a more immediate and higher level of international scrutiny and criticism.

Past Prosecutorial Decisions Confuse Us

The public does not have an expert knowledge of terrorism. We form our opinions on a basic and incomplete understanding of events and the laws that we think should be applied. It is not surprising that sometimes we agree and at other times disagree with how the government charges suspects. At the heart of our confusion is the expectation that certain perpetrators should be charged with terrorism, and instead authorities charge them with a conventional criminal act.

Analysis of two prominent cases is used to examine the points made above: (1) Abdulhakim Muhammad's murder and wounding of servicemen at a recruiting office and (2) Major Nidal Hasan's shooting rampage at Fort Hood.

Case Study 1

American-born Carlos Bledsoe converted to Islam in Memphis, Tennessee, as a teenager and later took the name Abdulhakim Muhammad.[135] He spent 16 months in Yemen and received training in a terrorist camp.[136] He was deported from Yemen on several charges, including overstaying his visa, carrying falsified Somali identification papers, and possessing other forged documents.[137]

The twenty-three-year-old Muhammad shot a soldier to death and wounded another outside a Little Rock, Arkansas, recruiting office. Prior to the shooting, he was of interest to the FBI, but they lacked sufficient cause for a full investigation and no further action was taken. After the recruiting office shooting, the federal government deferred prosecution to the State of Arkansas, which charged Muhammad with capital murder, attempted capital murder, and ten counts of unlawful discharge of a firearm.[138] Muhammad pled guilty to the charges to avoid the death penalty. He is currently serving life in prison without the possibility of parole.

Although there was a connection with a foreign terrorist organization and several claims by Muhammad that he was on jihad or "holy war," to protest American attacks on his Muslim brothers, terrorism was not charged, raising questions. Some wonder if we are trying to classify as many events as possible as anything but terrorism to artificially keep the number of such attacks low and the public feeling safe. Others ponder

FIGURE 1–13
A photograph of a friendly appearing Major Nidal Malik Hasan prior to his military trial. His smile may have concealed an inner rage.

(Polaris/Newscom)

Islamaphobic
An unfounded hostility toward Muslims resulting in a fear or dislike of all or most Muslims. Coined in 1991, the term was developed in the context of Muslims in the United Kingdom in particular and Europe in general.

Uniform Code of Military Justice (UCMJ)
The UCMJ was established by the Congress and is the basis for military law in the United States.

Accelerator sanctions
For certain types of crimes, such as hate-based and terrorism, the law provides more severe sentences for persons convicted of them. It is how society demonstrates its revulsion about such crimes.

whether Muhammad was charged with murder because a terrorism trial would have forced the disclosure of counter-intelligence assets and capabilities. Some people believe if Muslims are involved in terrorist violence, they are charged with something other than terrorism to avoid a backlash by **Islamaphobic** "loose cannons" against the vast majority of Muslims who are loyal citizens. In the final analysis, it may simply be that the evidence better suited a capital murder as opposed to a terrorism charge against Muhammad.

Case Study 2

Nidal Malik Hasan (see Figure 1–13) was born in Virginia to Palestinian parents and raised as a Muslim. As an adult, he became a physician and advanced to the rank of major in the Army. Hasan, a psychiatrist, was assigned to Fort Hood, Texas, while awaiting deployment to Afghanistan, which would have been his first assignment to a combat zone, an assignment he resented as a devout Muslim. He met and conversed with several well-known Muslim radicals, including Anwar al-Awlaki, with whom he had a long relationship over the Internet. In 2009, Nidal Malik Hasan shot 13 people to death in a medical processing unit at Fort Hood and wounded 32 others while shouting "Allahu Akbar" as he fired.[139] All but one of his victims were soldiers.

Just before the shootings, Hasan gave away all of his possessions,[140] something sometimes done in anticipation of one's own impending death. When moving, we might have a yard sale or give some things away, but it is unlikely that we would dispose of everything. Speculatively, Hasan was prepared to die or perhaps wanted to die during his attack. However, he was unsuccessful in his attempt to become a martyr and was, instead, wounded and paralyzed from the waist down while on his shooting spree. Hasan was convicted in a military court of charges that included 13 counts of premeditated murder, but not any terrorism charges.[141] Sentenced to death, Hasan is currently imprisoned at Fort Leavenworth, Kansas. The Army has not executed a soldier since 1961.

The U.S. Department of Defense (DoD) characterized the Fort Hood shootings as "workplace violence." The federal government asserts that because there was no co-conspirator and no foreign direction, the Fort Hood shooting was not terrorism. Officially, Hasan simply snapped, "went postal," and started shooting—there was no violent radical religious underpinning.

Characterizing the attack as workplace violence seemingly ignores what we know about Hasan's Islamic radicalization, his advocacy for extremism, his series of communications with al-Awlaki, and his shouts of "Allahu Akbar" as he murdered people. In contrast to the DoD's position, a 2011 Senate report sharply concluded the Ft. Hood attack was "the worst terrorist attack on U.S. soil since 9/11."[142]

The decision not to charge Hasan with terrorism raises important issues. In some circles, it is believed Hasan was charged with murder because federal agents and military officials mishandled identifying him as a terrorist threat and wanted to shift attention from themselves to Hasan. A murder charge is more immediately understood as compared to the more complicated terrorism charge. Others assert the military wanted to appear politically correct, and not anti-Muslim, and therefore used the murder rather than a capital terrorism charge.

These possibilities notwithstanding, it may simply be that the **Uniform Code of Military Justice (UCMJ)** does not, in and of itself, contain a capital terrorism charge. Under the UCMJ's Article 134, the federal Assimilative Crimes Act (ACA) can be used to "incorporate" state and certain federal laws into the UCMJ for the state in which the military installation is located. However, no capital crimes can be incorporated.[143] Thus, to charge Hasan with capital terrorism, the Army would have to waive jurisdiction to the federal courts, a choice that senior military commanders reasonably did not make when a workable murder charge was available.

Box 1-7
Could the Fort Hood Shootings Have Been Prevented?

A case can be argued that Hasan's signs of religious radicalization were glossed over, ignored, or given insufficient weight by his superiors and federal agents. Nine different points support this position.

1. Hasan's supervisors at the Walter Reed National Military Medical Center expressed serious concern about his questionable behavior and judgment. Among their concerns were his strident views on Islam and worries about his competence. Despite these concerns, they gave him positive performance evaluations that helped promote him.[144]

2. Hasan made three PowerPoint presentations titled "Why the War on Terror Is a War on Islam" when he was supposed to be presenting medical information.[145]

3. In a class presentation, Hasan argued that U.S. military operations were not based on legitimate national security needs. He claimed that they were actually a war against Islam. The class was halted when the audience of military officers erupted in opposition. Some class members labeled him a "ticking time bomb."[146]

4. A questionnaire to be distributed to Muslim soldiers was prepared by Hasan. It included a question asking whether they should help enemies who were Muslims.[147] The question could also be understood to be encouraging the soldiers to be disloyal. The questionnaire was not approved for distribution.

5. Hasan told several contemporaries that he thought Sharia law takes precedence over the U.S. Constitution. This position is contrary to Hasan's military oath to defend the Constitution against all enemies, foreign and domestic.[148]

6. Three 9/11 hijackers attended a Northern Virginian mosque at the same time Hasan did. His prayer leader was the radical cleric Anwar al-Awlaki, who also presided over the funeral of Hasan's mother.

7. In 2004, Anwar al-Awlaki went to Yemen. He was detained for allegedly plotting to kidnap a military attaché assigned to the U.S. Embassy.[149] Hasan ultimately exchanged some 20 emails with Anwar al-Awlaki, who federal agents knew was a radical extremist. Prior to Hasan's attack, federal agents were aware of only some of those emails. Federal agents concluded no threat or crime was involved and further investigation was not warranted because Hasan was thought to be conducting terrorism research using his actual name.[150]

8. The background check for a high-level security clearance for Hasan was seriously flawed. It did not include interviews with him, his coworkers, or supervisors.[151] Properly conducted, the issuance of the security clearance would have been at least problematic and Hasan would have been subject to a more thorough scrutiny.[152] Such an examination may have led to Hasan's separation from the military. A senior FBI official testified that, in retrospect, Major Hasan should have been interviewed after the emails with al-Awlaki were known.[153]

9. In the aftermath of the shooting, nine Army officers were disciplined for inaction, ranging from an oral reprimand to what is considered a career-ending letter of censure.[154] One officer explained some of the lapses: "People are afraid to come forward and challenge someone's ideology ... because they're afraid of getting an equal-opportunity complaint that will end their careers."[155]

Do you think the Fort Hood shooting involving Nidal Malik Hassan could have been prevented? At what point do you think there was enough information to closely investigate him?

Box 1-8
Title 18, United States Code, Section 249, The Matthew Shepard and James Byrd, Jr., Hate Crimes Prevention Act (HCPA, 2009)

State and federal hate crimes legislation has enhanced or "**accelerator sanctions**" for crimes rooted in hate or bias. Terrorism charges follow the same principle. It is the means by which society signals its revulsion about such offenses by specifying severe sentences for them. The HCPA was passed because of the realization that federal and state hate crimes legislation was inadequate. Two incidents provided the impetus for HCPA's passage.

In 1998, James Byrd, a forty-nine-year-old African American, was seized by three white men in Jasper, Texas.[156] He was chained by his ankles to the back of a pickup truck and dragged down a road. The next morning, police found 75 pieces of his body along a three-mile stretch of bloodstained road; his torso and an arm were located a mile from his head. Two of the three perpetrators were members of a white supremacist organization with racist tattoos. One man is serving a life sentence and the second is appealing his death sentence. The third perpetrator was executed in 2011 by lethal injection.

In 1998, two twenty-one-year-old men saw Matthew Shepard drunk in a lounge. They offered him a ride with the intent to rob him.[157] The two perpetrators were disappointed they only got $30. Believing Shepard to be gay, the men savagely beat him. They tied him to a post, where he was found 18 hours later. Shepard died after five days in the hospital. His assailants later pled guilty. Shepard's parents did a remarkable thing and asked the court to show mercy in sentencing their son's killers. Both men pleaded guilty to murder and were given life sentences.

The heart of HCPA makes it unlawful to willfully cause bodily injury—or attempting to do so with fire, firearm, or other dangerous weapon—when (1) the crime was committed because of the actual or perceived race, color, religion, national origin of any person; or (2) the crime was committed because of the actual or perceived religion, national origin, gender, sexual orientation, gender identity, or disability of any person and the crime affected interstate or foreign commerce or occurred within federal special maritime and territorial jurisdictions.

The law also provides funding and technical assistance to state, local, and tribal jurisdictions to help them to more effectively investigate, prosecute, and prevent hate crimes.

The law provides for a maximum 10-year prison term, unless death (or attempts to kill) results from the offense, or unless the offense includes kidnapping or attempted kidnapping, or aggravated sexual abuse or attempted aggravated sexual abuse. For offenses not resulting in death, there is a seven-year statute of limitations. For offenses resulting in death, there is no statute of limitations.

What do you think produces the kind and extent of hatred portrayed in the Byrd and Shepard cases? What, if any, potential connections do you see between the HCPA and terrorism?

These two case studies illustrate that the specific charges applied in terrifying and perhaps terroristic events are impacted not only by the fact situations, but also by a matrix of legal, operational, and political factors whose weight the public rarely learns. Moreover, we are not privy to the clash of views and needs among agencies in making such decisions. To some degree, our confusion about what is terrorism is grounded in the reality that charging decisions are a "witch's brew" of factors. One alternative is to conclude that the federal government invariably makes charging decisions solely on the legal merits of cases. The second and perhaps more likely alternative is that the United States is devolving itself from the "war on terrorism"—which means charging as many terrorists as possible in America with specific criminal acts instead of terrorism whenever possible.

Traditional and Irregular War and War Crimes

Traditional and Irregular War

War can result from the failure of political states to resolve their disputes by diplomatic agreement. The United States views war as sanctioned violence to achieve a political purpose. By doctrine, the U.S. Department of Defense recognizes two types of warfare: (1) traditional/conventional and (2) irregular.

Conventional warfare occurs between nations and relies on direct military confrontation to defeat an adversary's armed forces, destroy its war-making capacity, or seize or retain territory in order to force a change in the adversary's government or policies.[158] Conventional war seeks to force "decisive battles" that will end the war.

In irregular war (IW), a less powerful adversary seeks to disrupt or negate the military capabilities and advantages of a more powerful military force, which usually serves that nation's established government. IW usually involves a state and an opposing sub-state force, although sometimes it may include several sub-state forces.

IW encompasses "small wars," insurgencies, low-intensity warfare, and similar terms, and is a messy and ambiguous term that does not lend itself to concise definitions.[159] Khalil characterizes this lack of concise definitions as being so messy that it is "futile" to try and distinguish between terrorists and insurgents.[160]

Because states are typically better organized and armed than the sub-state forces opposing them, the sub-state forces cannot engage them in conventional military engagements. They therefore use guerilla and often terror tactics, resulting in a style of warfare called **asymmetrical**. To illustrate, enemies of the United States would be pressed to defeat America in a conventional war because of our military strength. They would seek to fight us by mixing modern technology and irregular warfare. They do not seek military victory on the field. Our enemies' goal is to exhaust our national will by undermining and outlasting our public support, as happened in Vietnam.

In Afghanistan, the United States and its allies are fighting the Taliban in a type of IW called an insurgency. An **insurgency** is an organized movement aimed at overthrowing a duly constituted government through the use of subversion and armed conflict.[161] It is a protracted political-military struggle designed to weaken the government's control and legitimacy and increase that of the insurgents.[162] In insurgencies, political power is the central issue.[163] As an aside, many countries, including the United States, did not regard the Taliban government in Afghanistan to be duly constituted.

What "muddies the waters" when thinking about the Taliban as insurgents is the fact that it uses terror tactics in addition to more conventional armed conflict methods and receives both material and operational support from al-Qaeda and other Islamic radical groups, which attacked the U.S. Embassy and NATO Headquarters in Kabul, Pakistan, in 2011. Originally an anti-Soviet movement, the Taliban network became a mafia-like criminal enterprise that morphed into a terrorist organization and became officially identified as such by the U.S. Department of State.

Asymmetrical Warfare
In warfare, it is the attempt to circumvent or undermine an opposing force's superior strengths while exploiting its weaknesses. Asymmetrical warfare often has a major psychological impact, such as shock or fear and often involves the use of non-traditional strategy, tactics, and weapons. Examples include the use of guerilla tactics against a powerful conventional army or flying hijacked planes into buildings.

Insurgency
A type of irregular warfare characterized by subversion, armed conflict, and occasional terrorism to overthrow the legally constituted government of a country.

War Crimes

Terrorism is not a type of irregular warfare; it is a tactic. International Humanitarian Law (IHL) prohibits, without exception, all acts during war that would constitute terrorism. Such acts are charged as war crimes; examples include executing civilians and prisoners of war (see Figure 1–14), taking hostages, bombing civilian population centers, reprisals against non-combatants, failing to provide medical care to captured prisoners, declaring that no quarter will be given, deliberately targeting religious and medical personnel, attacking non-defended locations, using prisoners for scientific experiments, and destroying property not required by military necessity.

The United Nations (UN) International Criminal Court (ICC) is located in The Hague, Netherlands, and is the body that adjudicates war crimes. A more contemporary case was the trial of former Yugoslavia President Slobodan Milosevic (1941–2006), the so-called "Beast of the Balkans," on 66 counts of crimes against humanity, including genocide during the Balkans War of the 1990s. Tens of thousands of Bosnian Muslims were massacred during ethnic cleansing. Milosevic died in custody before his trial was concluded.

The Syrian War

The Syrian War began as part of the Arab Spring in mid-2011 and, unfortunately, continues today. As of the fall of 2016, 250,000 people had been killed and 4.2 million people have left Syria to become refugees in other countries. Within Syria, 7.6 million people were forced to relocate to avoid living on a battlefield. Many of the buildings in the country have been destroyed from air strikes and artillery shells. Both sides have committed atrocities. Terrorist or other armed groups have used children as soldiers, kidnapped people, targeted civilians, and used summary executions freely.[164]

The flashpoint for the beginning of this insurgency was a minor event. In the surge of excitement of the pro-democracy Arab Spring, fifteen teenagers wrote anti-government graffiti on a wall. In the city of Deraa, people protested the arrests and called for their release and greater democracy and freedom for all people.[165] At some point, the arrested teenagers were reportedly tortured.[166] The protests continued, and on March 18, 2011, the Army opened fire on the protesters, killing four of them. The next day at the funerals for those who were killed, the Army fired on mourners, killing another person.

It appears that the killings by the Army tapped into the public's stored-up anger or rage because of decades of repression by President Assad, who had ruled since 1971. Within weeks, the next development unfolded, which included calls for Assad to resign and, across

FIGURE 1–14
Just before the end of World War II (1941–1945), a Japanese officer executes an Australian prisoner of war, which constituted a war crime.

(Bettmann/Getty Images)

Quick Facts
Nazi Reprisals Later Tried as War Crimes

In 1942, German General Reinhard Heydrich was assassinated in Prague by Czechoslovakian partisans. In reprisal, the Germans surrounded the villages of Lidice and Lezaky, which were believed to be the home of some partisans. All men and many boys were quickly executed. Women were sent to concentration camps. Some young children were adopted by German families, but others were gassed. Both villages were razed to the ground and their names removed from all German maps. After World War II ended, some Germans were charged with war crimes for their acts at Lidice and Lezaky. Lidice was rebuilt after the war, although Lezaky was not.

FIGURE 1–15
War brings death and destruction.
Syrians able to flee the war in their
country become refugees in other
Middle East countries. It is estimated that it will take decades to
rebuild the cities and infrastructure
that have been destroyed.

(Samet Dogan/Anadolu Agency/
Getty Images; OBJM/Shutterstock;
YOUSSEF KARWASHAN/Stringer/AFP/
Getty Images; Agencja Fotograficzna
Caro/Alamy Stock Photo)

Syria, hundreds of thousands of people taking to the streets in protests.[167] The government's reaction was like a reflex; they moved to crush all dissent, but that action had an opposite effect: It stiffened the resolve of the protestors.[168] Assad made some conciliatory gestures, such as freeing prisoners and lifting an emergency ban, but it was a case of too little, too late.

More people were killed at demonstrations, and the public began arming itself, first for protection, but later to drive the government's security forces away. Violence escalated and rebel brigades were formed to fight government forces for control of areas and cities. The Free Syrian Army (FSA) was formed in August 2011 to provide centralized leadership for the numerous independent insurgent factions. At the apex of the FSA was its Supreme Military Council. By 2012, the insurgents had reached the capital of Damascus and the second-largest city, Aleppo. Over a period of years, well over 100 different groups joined the FSA, including terrorists. Al Qaeda in Iraq sent fighters to overthrow Assad. They split into two warring camps that still fight government forces and each other: al-Nusra Front and the Islamic State in Iraq and the Levant (ISIL), now the Islamic State (IS). Roughly, the Levant consists of the countries that form an arc across Northern Africa.

In mid-2016, the al-Nusra Front rebadged itself as Jabhat Fateh al Sham. Other supporters of the insurgents include the U.S.-led coalition, Turkey, Kurds (Syrian Democratic Forces), France, Saudi Arabia, and the Gulf States. To help remove Assad from power, the United States has pursued an awkward policy of logistically helping the "moderate rebels," some of whom are almost certainly terrorists seeking to carve out a homeland for themselves or to capture the government's weapons depots. During the war, Assad used chemical warfare. The United Nations required him to surrender the chemical weapons to inspectors, but there's some question whether some of them may have been kept.

Examples of those aligned with Assad and the Syrian government and providing fighters and materials include Iran, its Revolutionary Guards (Quds Force), and its proxy, Hezbollah, Russia, and IS. Russia uses airstrikes against IS in support of Turkey and has some advisors on the ground, as does the United States.

Complicating the situation is that the population of Syria is religiously predominately Sunni Muslims and Assad, who is an Alawite, has ruled them since 1971. The Alawite religion is considered a part of the Shi'a tradition within Islam. Among the foreign fighters who have entered Syria and are Muslim, the Shi'a versus Sunni distinction reflects the major schism in that religion that has existed for close to 1,500 years. This split in religious traditions within Islam is further discussed in Chapter 3, "Understanding Islam and the Middle East," and Chapter 4, "The Rise of Radical Islam."

Chapter Summary

1. **State six reasons why it is important to understand terrorism.**

   (1) For most of its history, terrorism was subnational or regional. In recent decades, a few movements have shown the ability to launch attacks transnationally. This leaves people wary and changes how some people live. (2) Terrorism can be adapted with terrifying speed to the needs of many causes. It is the violent equivalent of a Swiss Army Knife. (3) Terrorism is not a uniquely American problem. (4) There will be no quick and easy resolution to terrorism. The continuous possibility of attacks is like learning to live with an incurable disease. (5) Families stress over their members being sent to a combat zone and dealing with some members who are injured or killed. These families deserve our respect. (6) Terrorism evolves and adapts, presenting a series of new challenges.

2. **Trace the history of key events in terrorism from the nineteenth century to 9/11/2001.**

   (1) John Brown's murder and mutilation of pro-slavery Kansas settlers in 1856. (2) Knights of the White Camellia terrorized voters in 1868 to get their candidate elected. (3) During the 1880s in the State of Washington, Asians, and particularly the Chinese, were targeted for murder, assaults, and forced evacuations of that state. (4) In 1886, a bomb killed seven police officers at a demonstration of striking workers in Chicago's Haymarket Square. (5) In 1892, Henry Clay Frick, a Pittsburgh industrialist, was shot and stabbed in his office, but survived. (6) The *Los Angeles Times* was bombed in 1910 for its anti-union stand. (7) The Reception Room of the U.S. Senate was bombed in 1915 to prevent America from entering World War I in Europe. (8) The 1920 unsolved Wall Street bombing. (9) In 1959, ETA began a campaign for a homeland for Basques in Northern Spain, quickly turning to the use of terrorist tactics. (10) Formed in 1966, the Black Panther Party was quickly militant and violent. (11) During 1968–1977, the Baader-Meinhof Group used terrorist tactics to try and create socialist governments in Europe. (12) Beginning in 1969, the Weather Underground ("Weathermen") tried to overthrow America's national government. (13) The Palestinian nationalist group Black September massacred members of the Israeli delegation to the 1972 Munich Olympics to call attention to their cause. (14) During the 1970s, terror groups hijacked a series of airplanes in an attempt to have authorities release imprisoned members of their group. (15) In Tehran, Iran, militant Muslims took members of the U.S. Embassy hostage. (16) In 1983, suicide truck bombers attacked the U.S. Marine Corps Compound in Beirut, Lebanon, killing 221 Marines and 21 other service members. (17) Two Libyan terrorists planted bombs on Pan Am Flight 103, which exploded over Scotland, killing the crew and all passengers as well as people on the ground in 1988. (18) In 1988, the U.S. Embassies in Kenya and Tanzania were simultaneously attacked by terrorist Muslims driving suicide bomb vehicles. (19) In 1993, militant Muslims made their first attack on the North Tower of the World Trade Center by exploding a truck bomb in the parking garage. (20) In 2000, while in a Yemeni port, the USS *Cole* was attacked by Muslim terrorists who drove a boat alongside the *Cole* and detonated the cargo of explosives, causing substantial damage to the American ship. (21) The 9/11 attacks.

3. **Contrast individual and cultural perspectives of terrorism.**

   Individual perspective results from the process of evaluating issues, events, other people, groups, and nations, and the underlying beliefs, intentions, and actions in order to assign meaning to them. Individual perspective is produced out of a thoughtful and deliberate process that is to some degree analytical.

   Cultural perspective is the shared beliefs, experiences, and behaviors that cause its members to substantially view things in a similar manner. In contrast to individual perspective, culture is a collective, accumulated experience. This shared experience often distinguishes one culture from another, including language, values, customs, history, law, and religion.

4. **Explain why there are so many definitions of terrorism.**

   There is a natural world filled with real, tangible things, such as weather and soil composition. Such things can be observed, measured, and analyzed. Our heads are also filled with what we call reality. In fact, these are social constructs that give us meanings about love, status, loyalty, and other non-natural world phenomenon. Terrorism is not a natural world phenomenon. It requires the development of social constructs to explain it. Individual observers and scholars of terrorism create social constructs to meet their needs, resulting in a staggering number of definitions of terrorism; additional definitions spring from other sources, such as the law and the definitions adopted by operating agencies. The result is a vast surplus of complex and varying definitions.

5. **Identify any six of the ten acts punishable as war crimes.**

   (1) Executing civilians and prisoners of war, (2) taking hostages, (3) bombing civilian population centers, (4) reprisals against non-combatants, (5) failing to provide medical care to captured prisoners, (6) declaring that no quarter will be given, (7) deliberately targeting religious and medical personnel, (8) attacking non-defended locations, (9) using prisoners for scientific experiments, and (10) destroying property not required by military necessity.

6. **Summarize the event that led to the Syrian War.**

   As word of the pro-democracy Arab Spring spread, 15 teenagers in Deraa, Tunisia, wrote anti-government messages on a wall. They were arrested. People protested the arrests and called for their release and more democracy. At some point, the teenagers were tortured. Demonstrations continued and security forces fired on one, killing four people. The funerals were also fired on, killing another person. Within weeks, demonstrations swept the country, calling for the resignation of the president, who did so several weeks later.

REVIEW QUESTIONS

1. Following 9/11, a national survey revealed some businesses and Americans made important changes to their lives. What are three of them?
2. What are homegrown terrorists?
3. Terrorism is not just an American problem. What data supports that assertion?
4. What four factors contributed to terrorism being at the margins of American policy going into the 1970s?
5. What does the "Bermuda Triangle of Terrorism" mean?
6. What is a "force multiplier"? What is an example of it?
7. What is a "foreign terrorist organization (FTO)"?
8. Under International Humanitarian Law (IHL), what are "war crimes"?
9. What is asymmetrical warfare?
10. What is meant by the term "Arab Spring" and how did it impact Syria?

CRITICAL THINKING EXERCISES

1. **Terrorism in History.** Think about some of the major historical events in history, from assassinations to revolutions to world wars. How many of these events could be perceived as acts of terrorism. For example, just considering World War II, think of all the incidents that occurred that could be "labeled" terrorist: the surprise attack on Pearl Harbor by Japan; the Bataan Death March; the treatment of Jews, gypsies, the mentally ill, homosexuals, and other political prisoners in the Nazi concentration/death camps; the Nazi bombing of civilian population centers, such as London, England; the Allied firebombing of Dresden; and America's dropping nuclear bombs on Hiroshima and Nagasaki. Some of these events caused heavy civilian casualties. Looking at them, how do they fit into the framework of acts of terrorism, acts of war, and war crimes?

2. **The Wounded Warrior Project.** Visit the Wounded Warrior Project at www.woundedwarriorporject.org. Why was the organization established and what is its mission? Review some of the programs that are offered through the project and consider how such activities assist others.

3. **The *Charlie Hebdo* Attack.** On January 7, 2015, a particularly grotesque terrorist attack occurred in Paris, France. Three gunmen attacked the headquarters of *Charlie Hebdo*, a satirical magazine that had published controversial cartoons of the Prophet Muhammad. A total of 12 people were killed and 11 wounded. The attackers spoke fluent Arabic and French and were heard shouting, "The Prophet is avenged." A massive manhunt for the attackers was conducted for three days across France.

What do we now know about this incident? Is it an example of ethnic Arabs who were French citizens radicalized in terrorist camps and who returned to carry out jihad? Why was the reaction to the cartoons so deadly? Is there an inherent conflict between freedom of expression and radicalized Muslims? In the three days following the attacks, what happened to the terrorists involved?

NOTES

1. Gallup Poll, "Terrorism in the United States," www.gallup.com/poll/4909/terrorism-united-states.aspx, accessed January 12, 2017. The first four pages are an historical record of polls of Americans concerning their concerns about terrorism, 2000–2015.

2. "Americans and 9/11: The Personal Toll," Washington, D.C.: Pew Research Center, September 5, www.people-press.org/2002/09/05/i-americans-and-9/11-the-personal-toll.

3. The contents of kits vary, but may include water, light sticks, orange vests, energy/protein bars, basic first aid/trauma items, whistles, toilet paper, dust masks, and 24″ pry bars. Some manufacturers provide kits for offices, homes, cars, and "bugging out." These kits may also be for one person, a family of four, a group of ten people, or other such configurations, including the type of emergency such as a pan epidemic or a biological/chemical agent attack.

4. Calvin Lawrence, Jr., "September 11th: 7 Ways 9/11 Has Changed Your Life," *ABC News*, pp. 4, 5, and 7, www.abcnews.go.com/us/september-11-ways-911-changed-life/story?id=14324226#7.

5. Adam Taylor, "Poll: 42% of Americans Say They Are Less Safe from Terrorism than Before 9/11, *Washington Post*, August 22, 2016, www.washingtonpost.com/news/worldviews/wp/2016/08/22/poll-42-percent-of-americans-say-they-are-less-safe-from-terrorism-than-before-911/?utm_term=.64e58bba4ae7, accessed January 22, 2017.

6. Fox News World, "Attacker Who Murdered Catholic Priest Under Police Supervision Wore Monitoring Bracelet," July 26, 2016, www.foxnews.com/world/2016/07/26/french-police-kill-2-attackers-who-took-several-hostages-at-church.html, accessed February 18, 2017.

7. Lindsay Issac and Ralph Ellis, "Man Killed After Knife Attack on Soldiers in Brussels," CNN, August 26, 2017, p. 1, http://www.cnn.com/2017/08/25/europe/man-attacks-soldiers-in-brussels/index.html.

8. Loc. Cit.

9. OP-ED Contributor, "The Growing Right-Win Terror Threat," *New York Times*, June 16, 2015, www.nytimes.com/2015/06/16/opinion/the-other-terror-threat.html?_r=0, accessed January 27, 2017.

10. Loc. cit.

11. This slogan was developed by DHS in cooperation with New York's Metropolitan Transportation Authority (MTA) and has been prominently displayed in transportation facilities.

12. Statista, "Global Terrorism Index 2016, Top 50 Countries," www.statista.com/statistics/271514/global-terrorism-index, accessed February 14, 2017.

13. Institute for Economics and Peace, Global Terrorism Index 2016, p. 14, http://economicsandpeace.org/wp-content/uploads/2016/11/Global-Terrorism-Index-2016.2.pdf, accessed February 15, 2017.

14. Brian Whitaker, "How a Man Setting Fire to Himself Sparked an Uprising in Tunisia," *The Guardian* (UK), December 28, 2010, accessed February 23, 2017.

15. Edwin Mora, "Taliban Surpasses Islamic State as World's Most Prolific Terrorist Group," Breitbart, June 6, 2016, www.cnn.com/2016/03/27/asia/pakistan-lahore-deadly-blast, accessed January 18, 2017.

16. Sophia Saifi, "I Pakistan, Taliban's Easter Bombing Targets, Kills, Scores of Christians," CNN News, March 28, 2016, www.cnn.com/2016/03/27/asia/pakistan-lahore-deadly-blast, accessed February 2, 2017.

17. Although "Osama" bin Laden is often used, his proper name is Usama bin Laden.

18. Ayaz Gul, "U.S. Military: Number of IS Members in Afghanistan Reduce to 700," VOA (Voice of America), March 1, 2017, p. 1, www.voanews.com/a/afghanistan-islamic-state/3745401.html.

19. Morgan Chalfant, "Afghanistan Lost 15% of Its Territory to the Taliban Last Year," The Washington Free Beacon via Business Insider, February 2, 2017, p. 1, http://www.businessinsider.com/afghanistan-lost-15-percent-territory-taliban-2017-2.

20. Michael R. Gordon, "U.S. General Seeks "A Few Thousand More Troops on Afghanistan, *New York Times*, February 7, 2017, www.nytimes.com/2017/02/09/us/politics/us-afghanistan-troops.html, accessed February 21, 2017.

21. Lolita C. Baldor and Matthew Pennington, "Trump's Plan Will Send 3,900 More Troops to Afghanistan, Officials Say," PBS NewsHour, August 22, 2017, p. 1, http://www.pbs.org/newshour/rundown/trumps-new-plan-will-send-3900-troops-afghanistan-officials-say/.

22. National Counterterrorism Center, "Abu Sayyaf (ASG), January 2014, p. 1, www.nctc.gov/site/groups/abu_sayyaf.html, accessed February 23, 2017.

23. Brandon Prins, Ursula Daxecker, and Ano Phayal, "What Do Pirates Want? To Steal Riches at Sea So They Can Pay for Wars on Land," *Washington Post*, January 25, 2017, www.washingtonpost.com/news/monkey-cage/wp/2017/01/25/what-do-pirates-want-to-steal-riches-at-sea-so-they-can-pay-for-wars-on-land/?utm_term=.ad87d5ae4682, accessed February 24, 2017.

24. Shaun Walker, et al., "Russian Ambassador to Turkey Shot Dead by Police Officer in Ankara Gallery," *Guardian* (UK), December 20, 2016, www.theguardian.com/world/2016/dec/19/russian-ambassador-to-turkey-wounded-in-ankara-shooting-attack, accessed February 19, 2017.

25. Loc. cit.

26. Katie Hunt, "Russian Ambassador Killed in Turkey: What Do We Know About Assassin?" CNN World News, www.cnn.com/2016/12/20/europe/ankara-russia-ambassador-shooter, accessed February 19, 2017.

27. See John Robb, *Brave New War: The Next Stage of Terrorism and the End of Globalization* (Hoboken, New Jersey: John Wiley & Sons, 2008) for the extension of this and related arguments.

28. Ibid., from Forward by James Fallows, p. 9. The authors read the Kindle copy of Robb's book, which does not display page numbers. Thus, page numbers are by our own count and may differ from those in a "hard copy."

29. Ibid., p. 8.

30. Robb, *Brave New War*, p. 17.

31. Ibid., p. 28.

32. Other estimates are higher, including one of $3 trillion.

33. Ibid., p. 77.

34. Ibid., p. 119.

35. Ibid., p. 46.

36. Ibid., p. 13.

37. "Saudi Braces for a Renewed Jihadist Threat," *StratFor*, July 18, 2014, www.stratFor.com.

38. Loc. cit.

39. Kelley Riddell, "The Ugly Truth About Sharia Law," *Washington Times*," June 13, 2016, www.washingtontimes.com/news/2016/jun/13/ugly-truth-about-sharia-law, accessed February 6, 2017.

40. Loc. cit.

41. Lesbian, bisexual, gay, transgender (LGBT). The *Q* was added to mean "queer," which includes a variety of sexual orientations or those questioning their sexual identity.

42. Ralph Ellis, et al., "Orlando Shooting: 49 Killed, Shooter Pledged ISIS Allegiance," CNN News, June 13, 2016, www.cnn.com/2016/06/12/us/orlando-nightclub-shooting, accessed September 30, 2016.

43. George Gao, "What Americans Think About NSA Surveillance, National Security, and Privacy," Pew Research Center, May 29, 2015, www.pewresearch.org/fact-tank/2015/05/29/what-americans-think-about-nsa-surveillance-national-security-and-privacy, accessed February 23, 2017.

44. There is literature that establishes the Sicarii as part of the Jewish Zealots, while other works identify them as separate, but allied, movements. See "Zealots and Sicarii," *Jewish Virtual Library*, 2008, www.jewishvirtuallibrary.org/jsource/judaica /ejud_0002_0021_0_21428.html.

45. "Time Trip," *Current Events*, Vol. 101, Issue 6, October 12, 2001, p. 2.

46. Shmuel Shepkaru, "'Death Twice Over' Dualism of Metaphor and Realia in 12th Century Hebrew Crusading Accounts," *Jewish Quarterly Review*, Vol. 93, Issue ½, July–October 2002, p. 217, and "The Crusades," *PBS*, 2014, p. 1, www.pbs.org/wgbh/pages/frontline /shows/apocalypse/explanation/crusades.html.

47. Wayne C. Lee, *Deadly Days in Kansas* (Caldwell, Idaho: Caldwell Well Press, 1997), p. 4

48. Paul Leland Haworth, *The United States in Our Own Time* (New York, New York: C. Scribner's Sons, 1920), pp. 55–56.

49. Loc. cit.

50. "Anti-Chinese Riots in Washington State," Dartmouth College, undated, p. 1, www.dartmouth.edu/~hist32/History/S01%20-%20Wash%20State%20riots.htm.

51. "Eight Anarchists," PBS, 2008, p. 1, www.pbs.org/wgbh/amex/chicago/sfeature/sf_haymarket.html.

52. "People and Events," PBS, 2004, p. 1, www.pbs.org/wgbh/amex/goldman/peopleevents/p_frick.html.

53. Richard Brookhiser, "Domestic Terrorism: The Killers Next Door," *American History*, Vol. 48, Issue 4, October 2013, pp. 7–18.

54. Norman Rozeff, "Fugitive in Early San Benito," *Sun Valley Times* (Harlingen, Texas), May 16, 2014.

55. "A Byte Out of History: Terror on Wall Street," Federal Bureau of Investigation, 2007, p. 1, www.fbi.gov/news/stories/2007/september/wallstreet_091307.

56. 1959 is the conventional date for the founding of ETA, but Shepard maintains it should be 1952. See William S. Shepard, "The ETA: Spain Fights Europe's Last Active Terrorist Group," *Mediterranean Quarterly*, Vol. 58, Issue 4, Winter 2002, p. 56.

57. For a detailed examination of the BMG, see Jillian Becker, *Hitler's Children: The History of the Baader-Meinhof Terrorist Gang* (New York, NY: Harper Collins, 1979).

58. See Simon Reeve, *One Day in September: The Full Story of the 1972 Munich Olympics Massacre and the Israeli Revenge Operation "Wrath of God"* (New York, NY: Arcade Publishing, 2000).

59. Michael B. Mukasey, "The War on Terror: Where We Are and How We Got There," *New York Law School Law Review*, Vol. 56, Issue 1, 2012, p. 10.

60. Loc. cit.

61. Richard A. Serrano, "Early Terrorist in U.S. Condemns Today's Jihad," *Los Angeles Times*, May 16, 2013.

62. "Byte Out of History: Solving a Complex Case of International Terrorism," Federal Bureau of Investigation, December 2003, p. 1, www.fbi.gov/news/stories/2003/december /panam121903.

63. Loc. cit.

64. "U.S. Missiles Pound Targets in Afghanistan, Sudan," *CNN News*, August 21, 1993, p. 1, /www.cnn.com/US/9808/20/us.strikes.02.

65. "1993 World Trade Center Bombing Fast Facts," updated to April 5, 2014, p. 1, www.cnn.com/2013/11/05/us/1993-world-trade-center-bombing-fast-facts/.

66. "1993 World Trade Center Bombing," 9/11 Memorial Organization, p. 1, www.911memorial.org/1993-world-trade-center-bombing.

67. "FBI 100: First Strike Global Terror in America," 2008, p. 1, www.fbi.gov/news /stories/2008/february/tradebom_022608.

68. Alex Schmid, "Terrorism—The Definitional Problem," *Case Western Reserve Journal of International Law*, Vol. 36, Issue 2/3, 2004, p. 376.

69. Walter Laqueur, *The New Terrorism* (New York: Oxford University Press, 1999), p. 32.

70. The information in this paragraph is drawn with restatement from Marisa Linton, "Robespierre and the Terror," *History Today*, Vol. 56, Issue 8, August 2006, pp. 23–29; and Marisa Linton, "Reign of Terror," *History Today*, Vol. 56, Issue 6, June 2006, p. 66.

71. Patrick L. Higonnet, "Robespierre's Rules for Radicals," *Foreign Affairs*, July/August 2012, p. 1, www.foreignaffairs.com/articles/137726/patrice-l-r-higonnet/robespierres-rules-for-radicals.

72. Tim McNeese, *The Age of Napoleon* (Boston, MA: Houghton, Mifflin, Harcourt, 2002), p. 11.

73. The speech, "The Republic of Virtue," appears in Richard C. Lyman and Lewis Spitz, editors, *Major Crises in Western Civilization*, Volume 2 (New York: Harcourt, Brace, and World, 1965), p. 27.

74. See Ana Sijak, *Angel of Vengeance: The Girl Assassin* (New York: St. Martin's Press, 2008).

75. The verdict was later annulled and she quickly went to Switzerland. Some years later, she was able to return to Russia, dying there in 1919.

76. Council of the European Union, "Council Framework Decision 2008/919/JHA of 28 November, amending Framework Decision 2002/475/JHA on Combating Terrorism," http://eur-lex.europa.eu/legal-content/EN/TXT/PDF/?uri=CELEX:32008F0919&from=EN.

77. The Arab Convention on the Suppression of Terrorism, signed in Cairo, Egypt, April 22, 1998, record deposited with General Secretariat of the League of Arab States, www.unodc.org/tldb/pdf/conv_arab_terrorism.en.pdf, accessed February 26, 2017.

78. "Europel TE-SAT 2013: EU Terrorism Situation and Trend Report," June 13, 2002, http://europa.eu/legislation_summaries/justice_freedom_security/fight_against_terrorism/l33168_en.htm.

79. Shali Wu and Boaz Keysar, "The Effective of Culture on Perspective on Perspective Taking," *Psychological Science*, Vol. 18. No. 7, July 2007, p. 600 with rephrasing and additions.

80. Undated video, USAToday.com/Graphics/News/gra/gclearskies/Flash.htm.

81. Staff and Wire Reports, "Bush Vows Retaliation for Evil Acts," *USA Today*, September 12, 2001.

82. Fox News, September 12, 2001.

83. Brian Ross, "How Anwar-al-Awlaki Inspired Terror From Across the Globe," September 30, 2011, www.ABCNews.go.com/Blotter/Anwar-al-Awlaki-Inspired-Terrorism/Story?Id=14643383#UDA1KLGNFI.

84. Jerome P. Bjelopera, *American Jihadist Terrorism: Combating a Complex Threat* (Washington, D.C.: Congressional Research Service, November 15, 2011), p. 2.

85. Ian O. Lesser et al., *The New Terrorism* (Santa Monica, CA: RAND Corporation, 1999), p. 8.

86. Loc. cit., with restatement.

87. Loc. cit., with restatement.

88. Loc. cit., with restatement.

89. The main points in this paragraph are drawn with restatement from Loc. cit.

90. Steven Simon and Daniel Benjamin, "America and the New Terrorism," *Survival: Global Politics and Strategy*, Vol. 42, Issue 1, p. 59 identifies 1993 as the "onset" of the new terrorism.

91. This account is drawn from Larry Neumeister, "WTC Bombing Ended Age of Innocence," *Washington Post*, February 17, 2008; "The World Trade Center Bombing" (Washington, D.C.: Department of Homeland Security, February 1993). It is doubtful that the February 1993 date is for publication. The attack occurred on February 26, 1993, leaving only two days to complete the report; "FBI 100: First Strike: Global Terror in America," undated, www.fbi.gov/news/stories/2008/february/tradebom_022608; Thomas Copeland, "Is the 'New' Terrorism Really New? An Analysis of the New Paradigm for Terrorism," *Journal of Conflict Studies*, Vol. 21, No. 2, Winter 2001, www.journals.hil.unb.ca/index.php/jcs/article/view/4265/4834; and "The World Trade Center Bombing," Anti-Defamation League, undated, www.archive.adl.org/learn/jttf/wtcb_jttf.asp.

92. See Dr. Yasuo Seto, "The Sarin Gas Attack in Japan and the Related Forensic Investigation," The Organisation for the Prohibition of Chemical Weapons, June 1, 2001, www.opcw.org.

93. "America and the New Terrorism," p. 8.

94. David Tucker, "What Is New About the New Terrorism and How Dangerous Is It?" *Terrorism and Political Violence*, Vol. 13, Issue 1, 2001, p. 1.

95. Loc. cit.

96. "America and the New Terrorism," p. 66.

97. Loc. cit.

98. "Not All Muslims Are Arab and Not All Arabs Are Muslims," Muslim Public Affairs Council, April 26, 2011, www.summits.mpac.org/blog/not-all-muslims-are-arab-and-not-all-arabs-are-muslims.

99. "Muslims," Pew Research, December 18, 2012, www.pewforum.org/2012/12/18/global-religious-landscape-muslims.

100. "Not All Muslims Are Arab and Not All Arabs Are Muslims," *Muslim Public Affairs Council*, April 26, 2011, www.summits.mpac.org/blog/not-all-muslims-are-arab-and-not-all-arabs-are-muslims.

101. "Anwar al-Awlaki," *New York Times*, July 18, 2012, www.NYTimes.com/Topics/Reference/Timetopics/people/A/Anwar_al_Awlaki/Index.html.

102. James Beal, "Yemen Raid Deaths, Terrorist's Eight-Year-Old Daughter Killed and U.S. Navy Seal Killed in First Special Forces Assault Under President Trump," *The Sun* (United Kingdom), February 1, 2017, www.thesun.co.uk/news/2753859/terrorists-eight-year-old-daughter-and-us-navy-seal-killed-in-first-special-forcesraid-under-president-trump," accessed February 20, 2017.

103. Brian Jenkins, Statement Before the Subcommittee on Emerging Threats and Capabilities, Committee on Armed Services, U.S. Senate, 107th Congress, First Session, November 15, 2001. Retrieved electronically.

104. The data in this paragraph is drawn from Cynthia Lum, Leslie W. Kennedy, and Alison Sherley, "Is Counter Terrorism Policy Evidence Based? What Works, What Harms, and What Is Unknown?" *Psicothema*, Vol. 20, No. 1, 2008, p. 36.

105. This point is made by Schmid, "Terrorism—The Definitional Problem," p. 395. The discussion of it is by the present authors.

106. Loc. cit.

107. Loc. cit.

108. Much of this information is restated from "Hezbollah," *New York Topics*, www.NYTimes.com/Top/Reference/Timestopics/Organizations/Hezbollah/Index.html, updated April 6, 2012.

109. Anne Barnard, "Hezbollah Says It Flew Iranian-Designed Drone into Israel," *New York Times*, November 11, 2012.

110. The "contested concept" phrase is from William Constanza, "Hezbollah and Its Mission in Latin America," *Studies in Conflict and Terrorism*, Vol. 35, Issue 3, March 2012, pp. 193–210.

111. "Georgia Bill Attacks 'Paper Terrorism' as FBI Takes Aim at 'Sovereigns,'" *Southern Poverty Law Center, Intelligence Report*, Issue 146, Summer 2012, p. 1.

112. "Sovereign Citizen Movement," Anti-Defamation League, 2005, p. 1.

113. "Georgia Bill Attacks 'Paper Terrorism' as FBI Takes Aim at 'Sovereigns,'" p. 1.

114. David Zucchino, "Police Teach Tactics for Handling 'Sovereign Citizens,'" *Los Angeles Times*, April 5, 2013.

115. Counterterrorism Analysis Section, "Sovereign Citizens: A Growing Domestic Threat to Law Enforcement," *FBI Law Enforcement Bulletin*, Vol. 80, No. 9, September 2011, p. 20.

116. Fares Akram and Isabel Kershner, "Hamas Finds Itself Aligned with Israel on Extremist Groups," *New York Times*, October 12, 2012.

117. Cyrus Miryekta, "Hezbollah in the Tri-Border Area of South America," U.S. Army, Combined Arms Center (CAC), Ft. Leavenworth, Kansas, Newsletter 11-15, February 2011, www.USACAC.Army.mil/CAC2/Call/Docs/11-15/Ch_11.asp.

118. Rachel Yehuda and Steven E. Hyman, "The Impact of Terrorism on Brain and Behavior: What We Know and What We Need to Know," *Neuropsychopharmacology*, Vol. 30, Issue 10, October 2005, p. 1774.

119. See Christine A. Henriksen, James M. Bolton, and Jitender Sareen, "The Psychological Impact of Terrorists Attacks: Examining a Dose-Response Relationship Between Exposures to 9/11 and Axis I Mental Disorders," *Depression and Anxiety*, Vol. 27, Issue 11, November 2010, pp. 993–1000.

120. Loc. cit.

121. Jackie Mardikian, "Mental Health Consequences of September 11: A Five-Year Review of the Behavioral Sciences Literature," *Behavior and Social Sciences Librarian*, Vol. 27, Issue 3/4, 2008, pp. 158–161.

122. "United in Remembrance, Divided in Policy," Pew Research Center, September 1, 2011, www.pewresearch.org/pubs/2095/911-september-11-attacks-terrorism-islamic-extremism-civil-liberties-iraq-afghanistan.

123. Kenneth J. Long, "Understanding and Teaching the Semantics of Terrorism: An Alternative Perspective," *Perspectives on Political Science*, Vol. 19, No. 4, Fall 1990, p. 203.

124. Brian Jenkins, *The Study of Terrorism: Definitional Problems* (Santa Monica, CA: The RAND Corporation, 1980), p. 1.

125. The concept that the word "terrorism" plays to emotion rather than intellect was first coined in 1982. See Robert W. Taylor and Harry E. Vanden, "Defining Terrorism in El Salvador: La Matanza," *The ANNALS of the American Academy of Political and Social Sciences*, 463, September 1982, pp. 106–118.

126. See Erik M. Altmann, "Reconstructing the Serial Order of Events: A Case Study of September 11, 2001," *Applied Cognitive Psychology*, Vol. 17, Issue 9, December 2003, pp. 1067–1080.

127. Elizabeth F. Loftus, "Intelligence Gathering Post-9/11," *American Psychologist*, Vol. 66, Issue 6, September 2011, p. 535.

128. Loc. cit.

129. Anup Shah, Crisis in Chechnya, Global Issues, accessed September 23, 2012, www.GlobalIssues.org/Article/100/Crisis-in-Chechnya#Background.

130. Warren Strobel, "Obama Sends U.S. Troops, Drones to Cameroon in Anti-Boko Haram Fight," Reuters, October 8, 2015, www.reuters.com/article/us-nigeria-bokoharam-usa-idUSKCN0S823F20151014, accessed February 20, 2017.

131. Akbar Ahmed and Frankie Martin, "Deadly Drone Strike on Muslims in Southern Philippines," The Brookings Institution, March 5, 2012, accessed February 20, 2017.

132. "Regions and Territories: Chechnya," November 22, 2011, www.News.BBC.Co.UK/2Hi/Europe/Country_Profiles/2565049.stm.

133. Dmitri V. Trenin, *The Forgotten War: Chechnya and Russia's Future* (Washington, D.C.: Carnegie Endowment for International Peace, November 2003), p. 1.

134. Nancy Ramsey, "The Horror of Beslan, Through the Eyes of the Youngest Survivors," *New York Times*, September 1, 2005, www.NYTimes/2005/09/01/arts/television/01best.html.

135. James Dao and David Johnston, "Report of Motive in Recruiter Attack," *New York Times*, June 6, 2009, www.NYTimes.com/2009/06/03/USRecruit.html.

136. Statement by Melvin Bledsoe, Father of Carlos Leon Bledsoe, AKA Abdulhakim Mujahid Muhammad, Committee on Homeland Security, U.S. House of Representatives, Washington, D.C., March 10, 2011, p. 3.

137. James Dao, "Man Claims Terror Ties in Little Rock Shooting," *New York Times*, January 21, 2010.

138. U.S. House of Representatives Tim Griffin, letter to President Barack Obama, June 1, 2012.

139. Steve Chapman, "Muslims and Mass Murder: Understanding the Fort Hood Attack," *Washington Report on Middle East Affairs*, Vol. 29, Issue 1, January/February, 2010, p. 30.

140. Maria Newman and Michael Brick, "Neighbor Says Hasan Gave Belongings Away Before Attack," *New York Times*, November 6, 2009.

141. James C. McKinley, "Suspect in Ft. Hood Case Is Said to Be Paralyzed," *New York Times*, November 14, 2009.

142. Joseph Lieberman, Chair, "A Ticking Time Bomb, a Special Report," U.S. Senate Committee on Homeland Security and Governmental Affairs," February 2011, p. 7.

143. ** For example, see *United States v. French* (1959).

144. "Army Reprimands 9 Officers in Fort Hood Shooting," *USA Today*, March 10, 2011, www.USAToday.com/News/Military/2011-03-10-Fort-Hood-Shooting_N.html.

145. Written Testimony of General Jack Keane, "A Ticking Time Bomb: Counterterrorism Lessons from the U.S. Government's Failure to Prevent the Fort Hood Attack," Hearing Before the Senate Committee on Homeland Security and Governmental Affairs, February 15, 2011, p. 2.

146. Loc. cit.

147. Ibid., p. 3.

148. Ibid., p. 2.

149. "Obituary: Anwar al-Awlaki," September 20, 2011, www.BBC.Co.UK/News /World-Middle-East-11658920.

150. Elisabeth Bumiller and Scott Shane, "Pentagon Report on Fort Hood Details Failures," *New York Times*, January 15, 2010.

151. Craig Whitlock, "Pentagon Inquiry: Supervisors Discounted Fort Hood Suspect's Worrisome Behavior," *New York Times*, January 16, 2010, www.WashingtonPost.com/WP-Dyn/Content/Article/2010/01/15/AR2010011502010.html.

152. Craig Whitlock, "Pentagon Inquiry: Supervisors Discounted Fort Hood Suspect's Worrisome Behavior," *The Washington Post*, January 16, 2010, www.WashingtonPost .Com/WP-Dyn/Article/2010/01/15/AR2010011502010.html.

153. "FBI Official Testifies on Hasan Report," *Military.com*, August 2, 2012, www.Military.Com /Daily-News/2012/08/02/FBI-Official-Testifies-on-Hasan-Report.html.

154. "Army Reprimands 9 Officers in Fort Hood Shooting."

155. Nancy Gibbs et al., "Terrified or Terrorist?" *Time*, Vol. 174, Issue 20, November 23, 2009.

156. The description of the Byrd murder is primarily drawn from Monica Rhor, "Texas Town Still Shadowed by Dragging Death," *USA Today*, June 6, 2008, www.USAToday.com /News/Nation/2008-06-06-2161250099_x.html; and Carter. T. Coker, "Hope-Fulfilling or Effectively Chilling? Reconciling the Hate Crimes Prevention Act with the First Amendment," Vol. 64, No. 1, *Vanderbilt Law Review*, January 2011, p. 272.

157. "New Details Emerge in Matthew Shepard Murder," *ABC 20/20*, November 26, 2004, www .ABCNews.go.com/2020/Story?Id=277685&page=1#.UEexzOJgPFJ.

158. Special Forces Unconventional Warfare (Ft. Bragg, N.C.: John F. Kennedy Special Warfare Center and School, September 2008), p. I–4.

159. Eric V. Larson et al., *Assessing Irregular Warfare* (Santa Monica: RAND Corporation, 2008), p. 8.

160. See James Khalil, "Know Your Enemy: On the Futility of Distinguishing Between Terrorists and Insurgents," *Studies in Conflict and Terrorism*, Vol. 36, Issue 5, May 2013, pp. 419–430.

161. Counterinsurgency Operations, FMI 3-07.22 (Ft. Leavenworth, Kansas: United States Army, October 2004), p. I–I.

162. Loc. cit.

163. Loc. cit.

164. No Author, "Syria," Human Rights Watch, October 2015, p. 1, www.hrw.org/middle-east/n-africa/syria, accessed February 24, 2017. The metrics in this paragraph came from this source and some ideas, which were rewritten.

165. No author, "What's Happening in Syria?" BBC, February 27, 2017, p. 2, www.bbc.co.uk /newsround/16979186, accessed February 28, 2017.

166. Loc. cit. Some sources claim two children died in police custody. In other accounts, the teenagers are described as "schoolchildren."

167. No author, "Syria: The Story of the Conflict," BBC, March 11, 2016 p. 2, www.bbc.com /news/world-middle-east-26116868, accessed February 22, 2017.

168. Loc. cit.

Political Ideology and the Historical Roots of Terrorism

CHAPTER

2

Learning Objectives

After completing this chapter, you should be able to:

1. Describe the concept of political terrorism.

2. Provide an overview of leftist terror cells, including Latin American and European groups.

3. Discuss how colonialism and the mandate system set the stage for future conflict in the Middle East.

4. Describe the secular "first wave" Palestinian terror groups.

5. Provide insight into how the United States and its policies have impacted terrorist ideology in the Middle East.

A member of the Black September Organization with a hood over his head on the balcony of a building holding Israeli athletes as hostages during the 1972 Summer Olympics in Munich, Germany. Probably no other picture in history is more symbolic of the beginning of terrorism in the modern age.

(Kurt Strumpf/AP Feature Photo Service/ Newscom)

Introduction

The subject of "politics" often provokes intense emotion, generates passionate discussion, and can frequently create extreme resistance to considering another person's point of view—this is obvious even during political discussions at the dinner table or seeing friends on Facebook tear into each other because of deeply held political convictions. Indeed, politics are sometimes so interwoven into people's psyches that it affects nearly every facet of their belief system.

And, as we learned in the previous chapter, the way that people think about or perceive their environment, government, and society—and the way they feel those entities should be structured—springs from a host of factors, including genetics,[1] family tradition, educational background, socioeconomic status, religious affiliation, and geographical location (individual perspective and culture). These factors are not mutually exclusive, they are not simple, and they have wide-ranging effects on a person's belief system. **Political ideology**, then, is (on an individual level) "the set of beliefs about the proper order of society and how it can be achieved."[2] On a group level, political ideology is the "shared framework of mental models that groups of individuals possess that provide both an interpretation of the environment and a prescription as to how that environment should be structured."[3]

Political ideology
The set of beliefs about the proper order of society and how that order can be achieved.

Identifying with a particular political theory or ideology has also been shown as calming, as strange as that may seem when discussing terrorism. It can help reduce uncertainty, make a person feel more secure, and increase feelings of solidarity with others.[4] Unfortunately, one's ideology is often somewhat intransient and intractable, and at its most extreme it doesn't allow for any deviation nor is it particularly tolerant of criticism. As such, it's easy to understand "how" terrorists can add to and indoctrinate their ranks, particularly during times of perceived societal upheaval. Early historical writers[5] on the subject of terrorism suggested that terrorism must be part of a revolutionary strategy and that it poses significant social consequences as well:

- Terrorism has a direct effect on the social structure of a society.
- Terrorism upsets the framework of precepts, images, and symbols on which society is based and on which society depends and trusts.
- Terrorism destroys the solidarity, cooperation, and interdependence on which social functioning is based and substitutes insecurity, distrust, and fear.
- Terrorism attacks the very bases of social order, culture, and government.[6]

In this chapter, the political and social theories that motivate certain groups will be examined—from their genesis and historical significance to their influence on modern terrorist groups.[7]

Revolutionary Ideology and Terror

As will be discussed in the coming chapters, much of the collective "modern" experience with terrorism from the Middle East is based in radical Islam. Terrorism today is not seen as purely a political phenomenon, but rather as something that is mostly motivated by religious zealots who misinterpret the peaceful constructs of various world religious, whether Islamic, Judaic, or Christian. In contrast, however, many other groups have their historical roots imbedded in political theory and ideological grievance. Even the definition of **political terrorism** (see Chapter 1, "Defining, Conceptualizing, and Understanding Terrorism"), according to most writers on the subject, relies on a definition from the early 1960s that defines it as "a symbolic act designed to influence political behavior based on extra-normal means, entailing the use or threat of violence."[8] Newer definitions of terrorism give religious ideology more emphasis or even equal footing with political motivations.

Political terrorism
A symbolic act designed to influence political behavior based on extranormal means, entailing the use or threat of violence.

Surprisingly, even those terrorist groups (like al-Qaeda) that spring primarily from religious ideology are deeply rooted in political and historical movements hailing from mid-nineteenth-century Europe. The ideologies that have had the greatest impact on modern terrorism are considered leftist, a term that has its roots in a French system of governmental continuum whereby more conservative politicians were physically seated on the right of an assembly and those considered more radical were seated on the left. This symbolism

FIGURE 2–1
Although often associated with Russia because of his perspectives on socialism and communism, Karl Marx (1818–1883) lived much of his life in Western Europe and is buried in London. At the funeral, his close friend and collaborator Friedrich Engels uttered only one sentence: "On the 14th of March, 1883, a quarter to three in the afternoon, the greatest living thinker ceased to think."
(INTERFOTO/Personalities/Alamy Stock Photo)

Left-wing
A political designation that encompasses ideologies more radical in nature, including anarchism and Marxism.

Marxism
The economic and sociological theories of Karl Marx and Friedrich Engels that encompassed a revolutionary view of social change.

Proletariat
A Marxist concept that describes the working class, peasants, or oppressed people.

Pierre-Joseph Proudhon
French philosopher who was the first person to declare himself an anarchist; instrumental in sparking French revolutionary activities in 1848.

Propaganda by the deed
An ideology that advocates acts of violence as a principal means of revolution.

has informed political designations globally (such as current American culture wars between the "right" and the "left"), and the "leftist" label has certainly been applied to describe both liberal and anarchist ideologies.

Left-wing extremism is heavily rooted in the works of Karl Marx (see Figure 2–1) and Friedrich Engels in Russia during the 1800s.[9] Their theory (now called "**Marxism**") seeks to change or eliminate a capitalist system that is perceived to be corrupt and oppressive in nature and restore power and autonomy to the working class. Although the goals are certainly laudable—to provide a better future for the working people (called the **proletariat** by Marx)—Marxism is heavily focused on the means to overthrowing government versus the maintenance of law and order. Left-wing theories are focused on revolution and anarchy, versus peaceful demonstration, to change governmental processes.

The ideology first gained traction after the political upheavals in 1848 Europe, known as the "Springtime of the People." The movement actually began in France, as a loose coalition of middle and working-class French people toppled the constitutional monarchy and advocated for self-rule. Within a few short years, similar movements were underway in Denmark—where their monarchy met a similar fate—as well as Poland, Germany, Austria, Hungary, and Italy.[10] Not all of the revolutionary uprisings were successful, but their violent nature left lasting impressions not only on the countries where they took place, but also on other revolutionaries around the world.

Anarchism

In Russia, some extremists identified with the most successful of the revolutionary theories expressed in France. As defined in Chapter 1, "Defining, Conceptualizing, and Understanding Terrorism," anarchism is a belief that there should be no centralized government and that society should be based upon voluntary cooperation and free association between individuals.[11] It was first expressed by a radical contributor to the ideology of the 1848 uprising in France, **Pierre-Joseph Proudhon**. He was the first person in history to declare himself an anarchist, and minted the phrase "property is theft," which spurred other anarchist groups in Russia and elsewhere (see Figure 2–2). Essentially, Proudhon posited that property ownership gives political power, and such power is all too often used to enslave those without it. The concept was convoluted and even Proudhon himself later refuted his catchphrase as being confusing.[12] However, his recantation was too late for Russia. Revolutionary actors like Peter Kropotkin, Mikhail Bakunin, and Sergei Nechayev took Proudhon's philosophies to heart, and began to violently advocate for the destruction of any centralized authority or government. The "people" of the middle and working class were to be the new "owners" of all property, and government would cease to exist.

For the most part, violent revolution and destruction were advocated via largely passive propaganda—accomplished by leaflets, parlor meetings full of intellectuals, and newspapers with pro-revolution language. Proudhon was much more the propagandist than the violent revolutionary that he often expressed in his writing. Violence in Russia began in 1869 when Nechayev and Bakunin published the groundwork for revolution and hence set the stage for the left-wing political theory:

> The revolutionary must have a single thought, a single goal: implacable destruction. Pursuing this goal coldly and relentlessly, he must be prepared to perish himself and to cause to perish, with his own hands, all those who would prevent him from achieving his goal.[13]

Nechayev and his contemporaries promoted "**propaganda by the deed**," wherein acts of violence were advocated as a principal means of revolution—and proponents of revolution were encouraged to infiltrate among the people and to win their support, and organize themselves into small, clandestine cells that could easily strike at the very heart of their enemy without detection[14]—a tactic observed in more modern terrorist organizations. Ultimately, Nechayev's and Bakunin's philosophical tactics would be used against the very people who were supposed to revolt. The general populace suffered decades of agony under the

THE STRUGGLE OF THE SLAV.

FIGURE 2-2
An anarchist wielding an axe fights the oppressive Russian government, symbolized as an octopus, trying to pull him down. The octopus wears a Tsar-like crown and royal robe. The powers the man fights are shown on the tentacles, such as graft, greed, oppression, and despotism.

(J. Ottmann Lith/Library of Congress Prints and Photographs Division Washington, D.C. 20540 USA)

Quick Facts
The Anarchist Cookbook

Anarchists believe that the world is in the epoch of capitalism and it is a historical necessity to advance socialism through violence and terrorism. As such, *The Anarchist Cookbook* by William Powell, first published in 1971, continues to be a popular manual for guerrilla and revolutionary tactics. It originally contained instructions for the manufacture of explosives, poisons, drugs, and rudimentary weapons. Later editions (available in PDF on the Internet) have added instructions on computer hacking and credit card fraud, basic electronic surveillance, sabotage, and GPS tracking. The familiar red Anarchist "Circle A" adorns newer editions of the book.

▲ The Anarchist "A" symbol.
(miloje/Fotolia)

totalitarian governments and dictatorships that would plague Russia and parts of Europe during the twentieth century. However, the seed had been planted among revolutionaries worldwide, inspiring the use of dynamite among French anarchists and, in particular, the man known as one of the first advocates of mass terrorism, Emile Henry. Henry famously attempted to bomb the offices of a mining company in Carmaux, France. He defended his use of explosives that harmed innocent women and children by stating that since the building was occupied by the **bourgeoisie** (or upper class), there could be no innocent victims.[15] A rash of political assassinations in the early twentieth century can also be traced to the anarchist tactics espoused by Nechayev and Bakunin.

Information Link
For more information on anarchism, visit the Spunk Library at www.spunk .org. Search the site and notice the number of other anarchist websites globally.

Bourgeoisie
The wealthy upper class, those who were property owners.

Marxism

The Marxist movement sprang from the belief that power and wealth were too concentrated in the hands of just a few—it championed the industrial working class as the creators of society's wealth, and sought to share that wealth equally, rather than putting it all in the hands of the very elite (the bourgeoisie). Marx and his associate, Friedrich Engels, were commissioned by

Quick Facts
The Invention of Dynamite

One technological advancement that changed the face of terror-ism was the invention of dynamite in 1867 by Alfred Nobel. Initially invented to aid in the digging of mines and to aid in the construc-tion of railroad tracks through difficult terrain, dynamite (made of the highly unstable nitroglycerin combined with the absorbent diatomaceous earth) was quickly adopted for more nefarious pur-poses by anarchist and populist movements in Russia and France and quickly spread to other movements around the globe.

▲ In 2014, an Arab fighter throws homemade dynamite toward forces loyal to Syrian President Bashar al-Assad. Dynamite has been an important weapon for revolutionar-ies and terrorists throughout time.
(Khalil Ashawi/Reuters)

Capitalism
Economies that focus on competition in a free market enterprise, valuing the ownership of private property to determine wealth.

Communism
The ideal utopian state as proposed by Karl Marx, characterized by the total elimination of privately held property and government.

Socialism
A Marxist perspective of a transitory and revolutionary period between capitalism and communism wherein the ruling class is "purged" from the land, all people are equal, and the government owns every-thing; the period is marked by violence and terrorism.

the Communist League (in 1847) to write down a complete theoretical and practical program for Russia. In their work, *The Communist Manifesto*,[16] Marx and Engel proscribe a political and social theory that directed the working class to violent revolution in an effort to overthrow the existing monarchies of Europe and Russia. Their target was **capitalism**, or governments with economies that focused on competition in a free market resulting in the ownership of pri-vate property. Capitalism was seen as exploitive, pitting one person against another for power; economic wealth was marked by the ownership of private property. Marx claimed that he had developed a scientific theory based on the laws of nature and the history of man.

According to Marx, man's history is that of a social class and class struggle (see Figure 2–3). Social class is based on wealth and the ownership of private property, and that all class struggle has been over attaining control of private property. Marx believed that man's history of exis-tence was based on materialism, or the ownership of private property. He strongly believed that there was no god or divine creator, and that all earthly functions are explained in terms of economic and social class based, again, upon the ownership of private property. According to Marx, capitalism breeds corruption and decay as the free competitive marketplace leads to overproduction, which in turn reduces the value of property. Wealth becomes concentrated in a few hands, while the masses suffer the fate of exploitation and alienation.

The entire history of man and society was a drive toward a new, utopian state of govern-ment: **communism**. Communism is characterized by the total elimination of private property as well as government (see Figure 2–4). Under the communist state, all goods and services are owned in common and are available as needed. The most relevant to our discussion of terrorism is the transitional stage or social state from capitalism to communism, known as socialism. It was during this transitional state that violent revolution through terrorism occurred, as individuals resisted surrendering their private property to the government (or state). **Socialism** is the elimination of private ownership of property and the means to production. The government or state owns everything, and all people are equal in the social order. Revolution, then, is inevitable as the ruling classes are "purged" during the transition to socialism.[17]

Marx's entire theory is based on his perspective of history as a constant struggle between classes of society. He contended that his theory was economic, political, and social, as society evolved through epochs of time by violent revolution and struggle (Marxism), ever seeking to equalize society by overthrowing the capitalist system and creating a more equal social order where government owns all private property and eventually withers away. Marx believed that revolution was sparked by the **vanguard**, described as advanced and tenacious representatives of the working class, who would organize revolution and overthrow the bourgeois ruling class.[18]

The Vanguard

The concept of the vanguard was further developed by Vladimir Lenin in the early twentieth century (see Figure 2–5). His Bolshevik Party was at the forefront of the Russian Revolution, and hence Lenin believed it was this party that would be the vanguard to arouse a level of political consciousness in all of society necessary for revolution. The vanguard exploits the differences in people existing in a heterogeneous population. They use differences among people to agitate and disrupt society, while at the same time attacking government through a variety of tactics. Terrorism is perceived as a legitimate military tactic designed to show the weaknesses and vulnerability of the existing government. As the government "cracks down" on individual civil liberties in an effort to stop terrorism, mass society further fractures with open antagonisms between groups of people and disruption of the existing way of life. Social order decays into rioting and eventual revolution.

FROM THE DEPTHS

FIGURE 2–3
Class struggle is depicted by this lavish social event in a large ballroom attended by the well-to-do. The party is disrupted as a fist erupts through the floor, where the exploited underclass masses work and provide the foundation on which the wealthy rest.
(Ker, William Balfour/Library of Congress Prints and Photographs Division Washington, D.C. 20540 USA)

Vanguard
A concept that advocates a method of arousing a level of political consciousness among proletariats in order to foster the belief among them that revolution and any changes it brings are far preferable to the status quo.

FIGURE 2–4
Historically, communists have tried to export their ideology. In Wisconsin, at a communist-sponsored summer camp in 1933, children are lectured on class struggle. Note the flag with hammer and sickle on it, the communist's symbol for the working people.
(Underwood & Underwood/Corbis/Getty Images)

Quick Facts
Guerrilla Warfare in Vietnam

North Vietnamese Army (NVA) troops were well-trained regular Army soldiers who were sent to South Vietnam to fight. Main Force Viet Cong military units were recruited from South Vietnam and were uniformed and received training. They typically had advisors from North Vietnam attached to them. Local Viet Cong (VC) lacked uniforms, had little or no training, and were used to snipe at opposing forces or conduct small operations and then fade quickly away.

FIGURE 2–5
Vladimir Lenin was born to a solidly middle-class family; his interest turned to revolution after his older brother was executed for plotting to assassinate the Tsar. Lenin was a founder of the Communist Party, a major force in the Russian Revolution of 1917, and later Chairman of the Soviet government.
(Soyuzfoto/Library of Congress Prints and Photographs Division Washington, D.C. 20540 USA)

Ernesto "Che" Guevara
An iconic, revolutionary figure in Latin America during the 1950s and 60s; he symbolized discontent with capitalism and colonization in the world, and believed that revolution was sparked by those most op-pressed in a country—poor farmers living in rural areas.

According to Lenin, the vanguard was inherently a righteous calling to arms; as a result of this action, his Bolshevik Party used widespread violence and terrorism as a successful tactic throughout the Russian Revolution. And while the Bolshevik Party ultimately became the Communist Party of Russia, the concept of the vanguard not only represented those that "start the revolution," but also as a concept described how a relatively small group of revolutionaries can be groomed and teased into a cohesive political movement…and eventually a ruling government.

"Che" Guevara and the Promotion of World Revolution

The concept of the vanguard has evolved over time and has been an instrumental force in revolutions throughout the world. **Ernesto "Che" Guevara** (1928–1967, see Figure 2–6) developed his ideas rooted in the establishment of a vanguard during the 1950s Cuban Revolution.[19] Guevara believed that there needed to be an immediate impact on the political consciousness of the ruling party, and that immediate impact involved an armed revolution sparked by those most oppressed—the rural, agrarian-based population of a country. A medical doctor by training, Guevara was a key figure in the Cuban Revolution, along with Fidel Castro. However, Guevara felt that only by taking Marxist principles outside Cuban borders to a global audience could he remedy the imperialism and capitalism that plagued the world. As such, he headed to Bolivia to rally a vanguard movement. Intellectual discourse was largely abandoned in favor of terrorism and guerrilla training; the tactic backfired when Guevara was unable to secure larger support from the local community. His "revolution in support of the people" of Bolivia was short-lived, and as a result, a small group, including Guevara, was killed by members of the Bolivian military advised by U.S. CIA operatives in 1967.

Guevara was a Marxist revolutionary who became an iconic cultural hero throughout the world during a time when the tenets of capitalism were questioned and the United States was engaged in the controversial Vietnam War (1956–1975). The Vietnam War was a long and unpopular armed conflict that pitted the communist regime of North Vietnam and its southern allies, known as the "Viet Cong," against South Vietnam and its principal ally, the United States.

The divisive war ended with the withdrawal of U.S. forces in 1973 and the unification of Vietnam under Communist control two years later. More than 3 million people, including 58,000 Americans, were killed in the conflict.[20] In the United States and the Western world, a large anti-Vietnam War movement developed. This movement was also part of a much larger counterculture movement of the 1960s. Much of Che Guevara's writing formed the basis for Communist rhetoric during the Vietnam War and his picture symbolized the anti-American sentiment prevalent during this time period.[21]

The concept of the vanguard did not die with Guevara. Today, elements of the process are seen in Islamic terror cells, and in many cases, terrorism remains the mark of the vanguard. Sayyid Qutb first wrote about that concept in his seminal work *Ma'alim fi al-Tariq* or *Milestones*—a book credited with informing much of Islamic jihad's ideology.[22] Qutb writes that the Islamic vanguard begins with preaching the movement, much like Marx and Lenin suggested, but then moves directly to violent means of terrorism as a means to spark wider revolution. Unlike Marx and Lenin, Qutb's movement had a strong religious overtone. He called it the duty of every Muslim to join in the "Holy Jihad" or "Holy War" against those who

FIGURE 2–6
A 2010 hand-painted mural of Che Guevara superimposed on Cuba's flag in Old Town Havana, Cuba. It demonstrates the immense popularity that Guevara continues to enjoy, although he was killed nearly 50 years ago.

(Robert Harding/Lee Frost/Alamy Stock Photo)

Quick Facts
Che Guevara's Death and Legacy

Guevara went to Bolivia and led an unsuccessful communist insurgency. On October 8, 1967, he and a few remaining followers were attacked by a special Bolivian Ranger Unit supported by U.S. Special Forces "Green Berets" and Central Intelligence Agency (CIA) operatives. Guevara was lightly wounded and captured. The Bolivian government did not want Guevara to have a public platform at what would be a highly publicized trial, so the

Bolivian Rangers were ordered to immediately execute Guevara and a cover story was issued that he was killed in combat.[23]

The emblematic and iconic photo of Che Guevara (see Figure 2–6) was very popular during the turbulent 1960s in the United States, especially after his death. It was often seen on posters, patches, hats, and T-shirts as both an expression of revolutionary Marxist thinking as well as contemporary style.

had "usurped the authority of God," Qutb knew that those in the ruling class would certainly not be inclined to surrender without a fight. This vanguard of violence and terrorism is the foundation for the modern concept of jihadism.[24] Refer to Chapter 4, "The Rise of Radical Islam," for a more detailed discussion of Sayyid Qutb and his radical Islamic philosophies.

Leftist groups, then, with their roots in mid-nineteenth-century Europe, have demonstrably influenced modern terrorism philosophically and tactically. Elements of Marxism and Leninism—particularly the concept of the vanguard—have made their way into different factions of terrorism, from leftist to Islamic terror, as have anarchist principles of "propaganda by the deed." Historically, terrorism (widespread killing, assassinations, and bombings) was a major part of the violent cultural and social changes in Russia, France, Cuba, and elsewhere, and has always been part of an accepted strategy among the revolutionary left.

Information Link
Visit bio.truestory at www.biography.com. Search the site for the biography of Che Guevara. Listen to his biography, and watch the popular 2004 film entitled *The Motorcycle Diaries*, chronicling the written memoir of a twenty-three-year-old Che Guevara as he rode his motorcycle throughout Latin America.

Latin American Leftist Groups

In Latin America, for example, several groups furthered Marxist ideology in action, engaging in guerrilla warfare just as "Che" Guevara advocated. Today, the most infamous of these is the *Revolutionary Armed Forces of Colombia (FARC)*, established in 1964 as the military wing of the Colombian Communist Party (see Figure 2–7). FARC purports to represent the rural, agrarian poor in Colombia by protecting their land interests against the wealthier classes of Colombia, the influence of the imperialist United States, the privatization of resources, and the influence of global corporations. FARC is a large operation with nearly 20,000 members. It operates in jungles and rural areas concentrated in southern

FIGURE 2–7
FARC—The Revolutionary Armed Forces of Colombia—was founded by the late Manuel Marulanda Velez in 1964. An estimated 50 percent of its nearly 20,000 members are under 19 years of age; more interesting, nearly 30 percent of the entire membership are female.

(Ricardo Mazalan/AP Images)

Egalitarian democracy
The political concept that all humans are equal in fundamental political, economic, and social worth; hence, social economic divisions or classes of people as well as centralized power should be diminished.

and eastern Colombia. Its presence is established in roughly one-third of the country.[25] FARC is heavily armed, and is primarily funded by the drug trade, though its involvement in illegal drugs can vary regionally. FARC also secures money from ransom deals related to kidnappings, extortion, and illegal "taxes" levied on those it claims to defend. FARC is responsible for the majority of kidnappings in Colombia targeting foreign tourists, government officials both foreign and domestic, and wealthy landowners. It has also been responsible for assassinations of hostages, Colombian political figures, and, in 1999, the murder of three U.S. missionaries. Since 2007, when several key FARC leaders were killed, the group has experienced declining membership but remains a major force in Colombian politics; currently, FARC is engaged in peace talks with the Colombian government. However, attacks on oil and energy infrastructure have continued during this timeframe, as have strikes, protests, and roadblocks related to oil pipelines in areas where FARC has a presence. More troubling is the merger of FARC with the second-largest guerrilla group in Colombia, ELN (the National Liberation Army). Leaders from both groups asserted in July 2013 that they were working in conjunction to "work for the unity of all political and social forces working to carry out profound changes in society" in Colombia.[26]

The *National Liberation Army (ELN)* is also a Marxist group that operates in the Colombian countryside. Though much smaller than FARC, it too has profited heavily from the drug trade as it looks to replace the Colombian government with an **egalitarian democracy** that represents the rural peasant class. The ELN is mostly concerned with Colombia's policies toward mining and energy investment and targets foreign businesses and oil pipelines for bombings, extortion, and kidnappings. ELN often targets multinational corporations that operate in the Colombian environment conducting lumber, mining, and drilling operations as well as the transportation of natural resources. Peace talks with ELN have not been fruitful—the Colombian government has asserted that it will not enter into any agreements or negotiations with the group until all hostages are released and reparations are made.

The *Tupac Amaru Revolutionary Movement (MRTA)* exists primarily in Peru and Argentina. However, the group, better known as the *Tupamaros*, was actually founded in neighboring Uruguay in the late 1960s. Named after the revolutionary Tupac Amaru, who led a major indigenous revolt against the ruling Spanish monarchy in Peru during the 1780s, the Tupamaros are steeped in Marxist ideology. Their goal was and is to reform the governments of Peru and Uruguay, removing all imperialist elements, and create a society in which power, property, and prosperity were/are shared equally.[27] The Tupamaros in Uruguay were one of the most successful Marxist groups of the 1970s, robbing banks, kidnapping executives, and extorting money from various businesses. Unlike many of its other Marxist predecessors, the Tupamaros were true to their word and often distributed money to poor people living in urban slums around Montevideo. One of their more infamous actions was the killing of FBI Agent Dan Mitrione, a police advisor who was killed while training police officers in Uruguay in 1970.[28] Today the Tupamaros have been virtually wiped out by the Uruguayan government, and remnants of the group are active only in Peru.

Like FARC and ELN, today's MRTA operates in rural areas in Peru and uses kidnappings to further its objectives; it's a relatively small operation though, with membership estimated to be fewer than a thousand people. Although MRTA distinguished itself from other groups in the region by refraining from attacking innocent and unarmed resident populations, it has been responsible for several high-profile events. For example, in 1997, the group was responsible for various assassinations of Peruvian government leaders and for an infamous attack on the Japanese ambassador's residence in Lima. The kidnapping played out over four months and resulted in the death of one hostage and the injury of nearly 30 others. The resulting international publicity since the event has relegated the group to working in the remotest of areas in the country.

However, Peru's most notorious leftist group is *Sendero Luminoso* or *Shining Path,* which adopted core Marxist principles and added the teachings of their leader Abimael Guzman, resulting in a mishmash of mysticism, Marxism, teachings of Mao, and even racial bigotry. Shining Path claimed to be the "vanguard of the world communist movement" and was brutal in its methods—massacring peasants, government bureaucrats, police officers, and other local authorities, frequently hacking them with machetes and publicly displaying their body parts. Nearly 70,000 people—11,000 of them civilians—have been killed in skirmishes between Shining Path and the Peruvian government. Shining Path leader Abimael Guzman was eventually captured in 1992 and called for his group to submit to a treaty with the government. The result of the capture caused Shining Path to splinter into factions, which today remain small and limited to the rural mountains of Peru. However, there is evidence of a resurgence of activity among the remaining factions, which have turned to narcotics trafficking to fund military-style attacks. The last five years have witnessed several small but deadly uprisings against police and military forces of Peru.[29]

In Argentina, complex political upheaval spawned several leftist groups. The *Montoneros* and the *People's Revolutionary Army* rose to infamy after a 1966 military coup in the country established an authoritarian-bureaucratic state. The Montoneros sprang from the Marxist left, viewing themselves as a vanguard for revolution, but also incorporating radical Catholic principles into their calls for justice and unity for all Argentinians. They formed urban guerilla cells and carried out political kidnappings and assassinations to achieve their means. The People's Revolutionary Army, meanwhile, retreated to the country to build a revolutionary base that would root out the Argentine government in favor of proletarian rule. They, too, formed urban guerilla groups that orchestrated political kidnappings with large ransoms, and frequently attacked military and police interests in the country.

The concept of the urban guerrilla was proposed in contrast to Guevara's rural guerrilla. A Brazilian revolutionary, **Carlos Marighella**, led a series of successful guerrilla groups in Brazil from 1964 to 1973. His ideas of "liberating" Latin American countries from oppressive regimes through urban warfare were chronicled in his book, *The Minimanual of the Urban Guerrilla*, which was a primer for the Tupamaros and the Montoneros.[30] Unlike their Peruvian, Uruguayan, and Colombian counterparts, however, today little is left of either the Montoneros or the People's Revolutionary Army, or of any of the more "urban" guerrilla groups. A military takeover in 1976 resulted in a brutal backlash against these leftist groups and any other dissenting political cells were destroyed. Much of the activities aimed at destroying such movements were centered around the cities, or large urban areas, crushing the "urban guerrilla" concept.

Carlos Marighella
A Brazilian revolutionary who expressed the concept of guerrilla movements stemming from urban areas. His book, *The Minimanual of the Urban Guerrilla*, was very influential in Latin American leftist movements.

European Leftist Groups

While leftist groups in Latin America were fighting ostensibly a "guerrilla" war on behalf of the peasant and agrarian classes, European leftist terror groups of the same period identified more as "revolutionary thinkers." The "new left," which came about in the 1960s and lasted only a short time—until about 1974—was born of a period of Western prosperity, quite counter to the ideas proposed by Marx. However, student groups and human rights movements took advantage of this period of unprecedented freedom to embrace extreme left ideologies. Such movements looked at the Middle East and underdeveloped countries as being exploited by imperialist powers (Western powers such as the United States and European countries). According to the "new left," the citizens of those places became in essence the "working class," the groups that supported insurgency were looked at as the vanguard, and the leaders of European leftist groups embraced their roles as advocates for a global class struggle between capitalist nations and their victims. European philosopher Leszek Kołakowski succinctly identified the "new left" philosophy:

> The existing world order deserves destruction in all its aspects without exception. The revolution must be worldwide, total, absolute, unlimited, all-embracing [and] universal, and all partial reforms [are] a conspiracy of the establishment .... Capitalist society [is] an indivisible whole and [can] only be transformed or defeated as such.[31]

FIGURE 2–8

Aldo Moro was twice Italy's Prime Minister. In 1968, he was within sight of his home when the Red Brigades killed his bodyguards and took him prisoner. Moro was forced to pose for this picture under their banner. After 45 days he was put in the trunk of a car, covered with a blanket, and murdered by multiple gunshots.

(EPA/Newscom)

Information Link

Visit the website www.baader-meinhof .com and learn about one of the most notorious terrorist gangs in history. Review the book by Richard Huffman cited on the website, *The Gun Speaks: The Baader-Meinhof Gang and the Invention of Modern Terror.*

One of the most active of these new left groups was the *Red Brigades*, based in Italy. The group formed in 1969 and became one of the largest leftist groups in Europe, with thousands of members at its peak. Their blend of Marxist and Leninist ideology sought to overthrow the government in three phases, all involving campaigns of urban terror: first, a period of "armed propaganda," followed by an attack on the "heart of the state," and finalized by a state of "generalized civil war" that would be the death blow to the existing government. Initially, the group sought only to destroy property, targeting symbolic political sites, especially those related to the center-right Christian Democratic governments of Italy, Germany, and France. Police and factories were also targeted with bombings and arson.[32] However, kidnappings and assassinations soon followed, with the 1974 kidnapping of Genoa's Assistant Attorney General Mario Sossi, whose five bodyguards were murdered by the group, and the 1978 kidnapping and killing of Christian Democratic leader and former Italian Prime Minister Aldo Moro (see Figure 2–8). In 1981, American Brigadier General James Dozier was kidnapped by the group, though he was rescued. In its nearly 20 years of existence, the Red Brigades were extremely prolific; they were responsible for nearly 14,000 terrorist attacks.[33]

In Germany, the notorious *Red Army Faction (RAF)*—also known as the *Baader-Meinhof Gang*—was the most prominent leftist group of its era. Spurred by the killing of an activist in Berlin who was demonstrating against the Shah of Iran, a young radical named Andreas Baader mobilized a young group of German aristocrats against the government. Though many have suggested that the RAF had no real political goals, the group positioned itself as the vanguard of the oppressed third world and asserted that terrorism was the only reasonable strategy of their movement. In 1968, Baader detonated homemade bombs in two Frankfurt department stores, both of which caused fires but did not injure anyone. Baader was arrested and imprisoned in 1970, but later escaped with the help from a left-wing journalist named Ulrike Meinhof. The pair fled with several associates to Jordan, where they trained with members of the Popular Front for the Liberation of Palestine (PFLP) in guerilla warfare tactics, then returned to Germany where they robbed banks to subsidize their underground lifestyle. Baader was captured in 1972, followed by girlfriend and active member Gudrun Ensslin a week later, and then Meinhof a few weeks later.

The trial for the members of the RAF started in 1975; in the meantime, a second generation of RAF had formed, composed of young German sympathizers. Soon the violence began anew. This new wave of violence diverged from any real political ideology, except to secure the release of the prisoners. The entire group disintegrated when Ulrike Meinhof committed suicide during a highly public trial (hanging herself in her cell). The remainder of the group, including Andreas Baader, was found guilty of murder and other crimes and sentenced to life in prison.

The RAF is one of the most notorious leftist groups in history. Three major incidents were carried out by its members, forever casting it in the lore of terrorist history. First, a public prosecutor in Berlin was killed by a hit squad in April 1977. Second, in July 1977, a banking executive was murdered in his home. Third, in September 1977, Hanns Martin Schleyer—a powerful industrialist linked to the old German Nazi party—was forced out of his car and kidnapped. These actions by the RAF heralded a bleak period in terrorist lore commonly referred to as the "German Autumn."[34] During a five-week period, Schleyer's release was offered in exchange for the discharge of Baader, Ensslin, and several others from prison. As that was being negotiated, former friends and comrades from the Popular Front for the Liberation of Palestine (PFLP) hijacked a Lufthansa flight bound for Frankfurt on October 13, demanding the release of the

RAF prisoners, two Palestinians held in Turkey, and $15 million in ransom. One pilot was executed as the plane hopped around the world for refueling. Finally, at a stop in Mogadishu, Somalia, on October 18, 1977, elite German federal police stormed the plane, killing all but one of the hijackers. Baader, Ensslin, and other members of the RAF committed suicide in their cells immediately following the failed attempt to garner their release from a German prison. Sadly, on October 19, 1977, at-large RAF kidnappers announced that they had also killed Hanns Martin Schleyer the day before.

The death of Baader and Meinhof signaled the beginning of the end for the RAF in Europe. Although splinter members perpetrated several assassinations and bombings well into the 1980s, it had weakened significantly. In 1998, members of the remnant group quietly dissolved into obscurity with a final statement: "The revolution says: I was, I am, I will be again."[35]

The *Revolutionary Cells*, and its feminist-leaning auxiliary group the *Red Zora*, were the least prominent of the three major European leftist groups. The group was Marxist in nature but eschewed the "underground" terrorist tactics of the RAF, preferring to integrate themselves into everyday life—holding jobs, raising families ... and waging bombing campaigns on the side. The anti-imperialist group (who viewed Israeli independence as an imperialist affront to Palestinians) was responsible for bombings at airports, military installations, and other symbolic government sites throughout the early to mid-1970s, and is probably best known for its role in the hijacking of Air France Flight 139 en route from Tel Aviv to Paris in 1976. Members of the Revolutionary Cell, in concert with members of the Popular Front for the Liberation of Palestine (PFLP), hijacked the Air France plane with 248 passengers. During the hijacking, Israeli and non-Israeli passengers were separated—the non-Israelis were allowed to depart the plane while Israeli passengers were held and eventually flown to Entebbe, Uganda.[36]

Acting on intelligence from various sources, the famous Operation Thunderbolt was planned for the raid on Entebbe. The operation was conducted at night on July 4, 1976. An Israeli Defense Force (IDF) special team of 100 commandos flew over 2,500 miles and landed on foreign soil in Uganda in an effort to rescue the Israeli passengers. The raid took only 90 minutes, during which 102 hostages were rescued, 5 Israeli commandos were wounded, and 1, the unit commander, Lt. Col. Yonatan Netanyahu, was killed, as were all the hijackers. The "Raid on Entebbe" became a significant world event and marked the beginning of elite commando forces of countries around the world in an effort to counter terrorism with opposing tactical and military means. See Chapter 14, "Combatting Terrorism," for more information on the development of counterterrorism units.

Historical Roots of Terrorism in the Middle East

As observed during the early 1900s, one particular political ideology—Marxism—formed the theoretical base of terrorism as part of a strategic or military tactic within a revolutionary movement. It is interesting to note that Marxism is considered an economic, social, and political theory, and that some groups used Marxist tenets to justify revolution in an attempt to end the plight of the working class and peasant people of a country (the proletariat), whereas others use a Marxist ideology as justification for participation in the illegal drug trade or as rationalization for the use of often indiscriminate force (bombings, assassinations, and kidnappings) against innocent individuals.

Marxist theory has also acted as the ideological foundation for groups interacting throughout the world—witness the collaboration between German leftist cells of the RAF and members of the Popular Front for the Liberation of Palestine (PFLP) during the 1970s. Groups like the Red Brigades and the Baader-Meinhof Gang viewed the Palestinian people as displaced working-class individuals without power being oppressed by the imperialist forces of the United States and Israel. This same ideological theme proved to be relatively dominant in the era of World War I and modern colonialism, an era that stretched through most of the twentieth century and greatly impacted the Middle East. Marxism was often the ideological justification for groups that fought newly established colonial rule by European countries in the Middle East after World War I.

On the ideological spectrum, leftist groups like the ones discussed here are at the very extreme—located far from moderate or centrist ideologies and even more distantly from fringe right-wing counterparts. What really sets leftist terror groups apart—and, in fact, distinguishes all ideological groups from each other—is the types of groups that they "advocate," their techniques, and their endgame. For example, most moderate or centrist groups tend to advocate for society in general, not focusing on one group, but rather seeing a society as a "whole." Their process for advancing causes is via a group consensus—generally as part of a partisan democratic event such as voting—and the outcome is generally a balance between a gradual change with a nod to tradition or status quo. This is a good characterization of traditional American political groups.

However, on the far-right fringe of the spectrum, groups advocate for a specific race or ethnicity, religion, or nationality. Their endgame is a change based on a reaction to a perceived threat—that is, a changing values system or a new and pervasive culture that is upending a long-standing social order. Their methodology for achieving their endgame involves a retreat or return to the "good old days"—a social movement that seeks to restore a cherished social order. These are characterized by the neo-fascist, neo-Nazi, and skinhead hate groups, such as the Ku Klux Klan, Aryan Nations, and the Christian Identity Church.

Far-left groups, by contrast, are more future-oriented; they look to radical change, hoping to topple the social order of the past on behalf of certain societal classes (e.g., the working class or proletariats). Their movements are often based in a complex theoretical groundwork that describes those that have wealth and those that are oppressed (e.g., anticolonialism, anticapitalism, Marxism). The ultimate goal is liberation from a real or perceived oppressive government. This designation contains groups that often self-identify as communist, socialist, or anarchist, such as the Black Blocs, Earth Liberation Front, Weather Underground, and Popular Front for the Liberation of Palestine (PFLP).

Far-right and far-left groups tend to hold sharply contrasting views on racial equality, law and order, patriotism, labor, economic issues, and religion; however, they do share some common ground. Both camps tend to be very alienated from mainstream society, mostly due to their zealousness and inflexible belief systems. They are also equally likely to embrace conspiracy theories and stereotypical views of social and political affairs.

Extremist groups on both sides of the spectrum are also similar in their pursuit of their goals: both sides will censor opponents and deal harshly with adversaries. Furthermore, both sides view civil liberties through an extremely partisan lens—calling for unyielding support of civil liberties when doing so supports their agenda, or completely eschewing them when they aid rival points of view.

What other similarities and differences can you think of between left and right extremist groups?

Colonialism and the Mandate System

Colonialism
A practice of domination, involving political and economic control of a territory.

The term **colonialism** refers to a practice of inhabiting a specific area outside the native country. Unfortunately, it often includes the social, political, and economic domination of the indigenous people of an area. Further, when a colonial power takes over a new territory, the natural resources and/or wealth of that territory are often transferred to the colonizing country.[37] For much of the early twentieth century, most of the known world lived under the sovereignty of European colonial powers: British, French, German, Dutch, and the Ottoman empires ruled much of the Middle East, the Caribbean, India, and Africa. At the end of World War I, the fate of the colonies in the Middle East of the defeated "belligerents" (Germany and the Ottoman Empire) was divided between the triumphant countries of Great Britain and France. Though some of the Allied forces tried to remain neutral (including the United States) and lobbied for the right to self-determination for many of these countries in the Middle East, it was clear that the Middle East would be subject to colonial annexation by the European victors of World War I.[38]

During World War I, both the British and the French realized the significant strategic importance of the Middle East, especially the potential wealth from oil that lies under its desert sands. Much of the Arabian Peninsula was open frontier ruled by individual tribes and no unifying government. At the end of the war, the Ottoman Empire was shattered and the British and French were eager to seize control of the area, particularly those areas that bordered the Mediterranean Sea (e.g., Egypt, Syria, Palestine), which could be used as easy shipping points to Western Europe. As a result, the **Sykes-Picot Agreement of 1916** was developed. The Sykes-Picot Agreement essentially carved up the Middle East into British and French "spheres of influence" upon the defeat of the Ottoman Empire. France would rule and colonize what is now the southeastern part of Turkey, plus territory in northern Iraq, Syria, and Lebanon; Great Britain would take possession of Transjordan, southern Iraq, and a few strategic ports in Palestine, allowing shipping access across the Mediterranean. Russia, the other victor of World War I, lay claim to the northern Ottoman territories, now known as the Ukraine, Azerbaijan, Armenia, and Georgia.

Sykes-Picot Agreement of 1916
An agreement between Great Britain and France as to the development of colonies resulting from the impending collapse of the Ottoman Empire after World War I.

To add insult to injury to the Arab Middle East, the **Balfour Declaration** emerged from Great Britain in 1917. It was essentially a diplomatic letter from British Foreign Secretary Alfred Balfour to a historically prominent Jewish family in Great Britain that formally signaled British support for the development of a new, sovereign Jewish state in the Middle East. The declaration was designed to win British Zionist support in England as well as provide a supportive ally in the Middle East. The Balfour Declaration was the first formal document from a European power to legitimize a "Jewish national homeland" in Arab-dominated Palestine.[39]

The end of World War I set forth the tenets of colonization in the Middle East and the potential for a Jewish state in the area. Arab interests were incensed—they had been promised by Allied forces during the war that the defeat of the Ottomans would begin the process of Arab sovereignty after the war. The Sykes-Picot Agreement and the Balfour Declaration sadly laid the early foundation of mistrust against Western countries that persists to this day.[40] The Paris Peace Conference in 1919 formally presided over by the "Big 4"—the United States, Great Britain, France, and Italy—formally created the League of Nations, a forerunner to the United Nations. Under Article 22 of the "Covenant of the League of Nations," the **mandate system** of dividing the Middle East into European colonies was established.[41] Syria, Lebanon, Tunisia, and Algeria were placed under French control, while Palestine, Transjordan (the area composed now of Israel and Jordan), and Egypt fell under Great Britain. The British also took, as part of their mandate, the three Ottoman provinces of Mesopotamia, Mosul, and Baghdad and Basra, defining what is now modern-day Iraq. The mandate system essentially charged Great Britain and France with administrative oversight of these territories, with responsibility for leading them toward eventual self-rule, but in reality, the two superpowers had no intention of ceding their newly acquired, wealthy territories (see Figure 2–9). Immediately following the implementation of the mandate, Arab nationalism rose throughout the Middle East and resistance against the new colonialism began.[42]

The fight against colonialism throughout the Middle East was informed by the same philosophical ideology: Marxism. Marx and Guevara identified colonialism as an outgrowth of a fully developed capitalist power. Colonialism was a natural extension of capitalism, according to Marx, because expansion of capitalism was necessary to obtain more resources and create new marketplaces. It was simply another mode of production in the capitalist machine.[43]

Arab uprisings began immediately as a result of the mandate system. They first began in 1920, as a revolt against British control in Egypt, followed by another in Iraq the same year. A rural guerrilla war in Iraq was organized against the British with much success; however, British control of the air proved fateful to revolting forces, killing thousands of Iraqis.

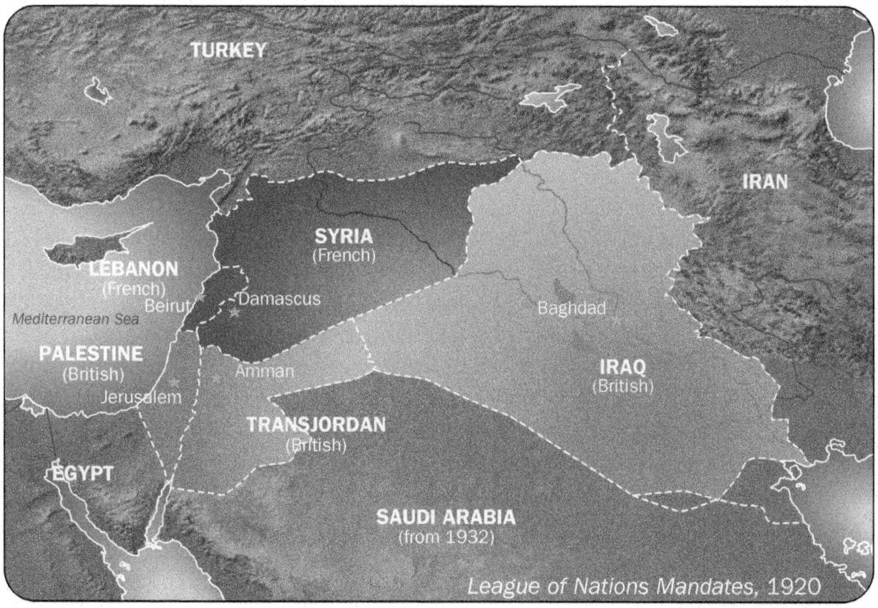

Balfour Declaration
A formal letter from British Foreign Secretary Alfred Balfour in 1917 signaling British support for the development of a new, sovereign Jewish state in the Middle East.

Mandate system
the system of colonization after World War I dividing areas in the Middle East, primarily between Great Britain, France, and Italy.

FIGURE 2–9
A map of the mandates or colonies established in the Middle East by the League of Nations after World War I.

Map: Geoffrey Gaudreault, NPR

Source: *A History of the Arab Peoples from The Middle East and the West: WWI and beyond by Mike Shuster. Copyright © 2004. Used by permission of NPR (National Public Radio).*

Box 2-2
Frantz Fanon

A more specific—and forceful—ideology stemming from the mandate system in the Middle East was espoused by Frantz Fanon. Fanon was born in the French colony of Martinique, served in the French army, and was eventually assigned to Algeria, a part of the French mandate. He was a black man trained as a psychiatrist, and practiced in the French government, leading him to have direct contact with Arabs dominated by French colonization. He was horrified by stories of torture by the French, and eventually resigned his position in order to advocate for the native Algerian cause. Fanon's two masterpieces were *The Wretched of the Earth*, published in 1961, and *Black Skins, White Masks*, published in 1952.

Fanon was influenced by the writings of Jean-Paul Sartre as well as Karl Marx, and is credited with characterizing the action of colonization itself as a form of violence, stripping the indigenous population of power, history, culture, and identity, particularly when the colonizing power was predominately white over lands inhabited by people of color. Hence,

CSU Archives/Everett Collection/Alamy Stock Photo

Fanon insisted that decolonization would always be a violent act as well, "... *revolutionary violence is a cleansing force. It rids the colonized of their inferiority complex, of their passive and despairing attitude. It emboldens them and restores their self-confidence.*"[44] Fanon's writings inspired not only a series of national liberation movements that signaled the end of the mandate system in the Middle East, but also sparked future revolutionary leaders globally, including Ali Shariati in Iran, Steve Biko in South Africa, Malcolm X in the United States, and Ernesto "Che" Guevara in Bolivia. He had a unique ability to write to the common man, indicating that each individual must be willing to sacrifice himself to strengthen the overall force of the revolution.[45] This is a concept that will be seen again and again in the evolution of terrorist ideology, from post-colonial Palestinian conflict to modern Islamic fundamentalism.

Can you think of other philosophers who influenced revolutionary writers in the future?

In 1925, a similar situation emerged against the French in Syria, and again the ruling country was able to use air power to reduce the revolt. Some scholars argue that these initial uprisings against the colonial powers of Europe via the post–World War I mandate marked the beginning of a sustained Arab resistance against the West.[46]

Nominal independence was granted to Egypt in 1922 and to Iraq a decade later in 1932; however, Great Britain maintained sizable military forces in the region. It was not until after World War II that Egypt and Iraq completely escaped British control. Syria, Lebanon, Algeria, and Tunisia also remained under French rule until after World War II.

Arab resistance also increased in the British mandate area of Transjordan, containing what is now the Palestinian Territory, Israel, and Jordan. Since the Balfour declaration, Jewish emigration to the Zionist homeland of current-day Israel had numbered in the hundreds of thousands. In 1922, the Jewish population rose to about 11 percent of the populace—and another 300,000 arrived within the next decade.[47] This huge influx of foreign Jews further antagonized the Arab population of the area (known as **Palestinians**), and continued to fuel outbursts of violence aimed not only at the new Jewish settlers but also against British forces in the area. Tensions and violence culminated in 1935 to 1936, when the "Black Hand" organization, a militant Palestinian group organized by Sheikh Izz ad-Din al-Qassam, attacked, murdered, and publically maimed Jewish settlers in the Palestinian Territory. Al-Qassam was killed by British forces, sparking further outrage among the greater Arab population. Combined with another major spike in Jewish immigration that brought the Jewish population to more than 25 percent of the total Palestine territory, conditions were like a powder keg.[48] The result was a year-long Arab revolt marked by massacres on all sides; Jewish settlers were killed, British troops were killed, and Palestinians were killed. After an attempt to relocate Palestinians, British military forces continued to resort to military tactics to thwart revolting Arab Palestinians. By the end of 1937, nearly 10 percent of the adult male Palestinian population had been killed, exiled, or maimed.[49] However, the events of World War II soon loomed large in the Palestinian Territory as well as throughout the Middle East, changing the course of Palestinian history and signaling the end of the mandate system of traditional colonialism in the Middle East.

Palestinians
People of Arab descent tracing their cultural heritage to an area known as Palestine, now occupied by the country of Israel.

The Impact of World War II and the Establishment of Israel

After World War II ended, areas subject to the mandate system in Syria, Lebanon, Iraq, and Egypt gained full independence from British and French rule. In the Palestinian territory (referred to as just Palestine), however, control of the land was handed over to the newly formed United Nations (1947). Again, there was increasing unrest between Arabs and Jews in the area due to a continued and massive influx of Jewish immigrants during and immediately after World War II (see Figure 2–10). Hundreds of thousands had fled Nazi persecution and settled in their religious and cultural homeland.[50] **Zionists**, or those sympathetic to the creation of a Jewish state in Palestine, began to demand that Britain establish such a state by immediately issuing 100,000 immigration certificates to Jewish survivors of the Holocaust. Previously, Jewish immigration had been strictly curtailed by the mandate. Regardless, 70,000 immigrants flooded into Palestine illegally. The Zionists intensified diplomatic efforts directed at the United States, and President Harry S. Truman unsuccessfully asked Britain to reconsider their immigration policy.

Nearly 400 people were killed by Jewish and Arab militant groups in 1946 during violent uprisings of both Jews and Arabs against the British and each other. Anti-Semitic graffiti perpetrated by Arabs became a common sight in Jewish settlements throughout Palestine. As an interesting note, since the 2016 presidential election, hundreds of new incidents of anti-Jewish graffiti, and a significant number of bomb threats against Jewish buildings have been reported to the police in the United States. Unfortunately, these new incidents reflect a growing pattern of anti-Semitism worldwide. In

Zionists
People sympathetic to the creation of a Jewish state in the Middle Eastern area of Palestine.

FIGURE 2–10
Following World War II, Jews, many of them recently rescued from German concentration camps, flocked to Palestine. Jewish migration to Palestine was strictly limited so hundreds of thousands came illegally. The passengers swarmed off of the ships as quickly as possible, before the British could collect and return them to their place of origin.
(AKG-Images/Newscom)

FIGURE 2–11
Vandalism on Jewish Synagogues and Cemeteries as well as over 100 bomb threats in dozens of states has prompted new concerns of anti-Semitism in the United States. Here, a swastika is painted over a directional sign at the Kollel Center for Jewish Studies in Providence, Rhode Island.
(Mike Derer/AP Images)

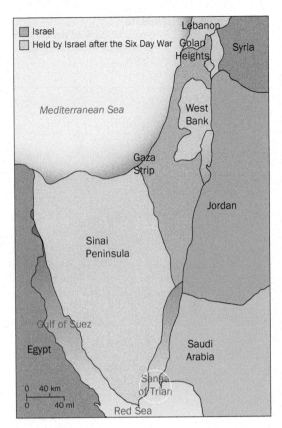

FIGURE 2–12

Israel was declared as a separate and independent country on May 14, 1948. It is a very small country, composed of only 8,500 square miles, located on the southeastern edge of the Mediterranean Sea, with a population of slightly over 8 million people (75% Jewish, 20% Arab, and 5% other). Its land mass and borders have significantly changed over the years as a result of wars and agreements with Palestinians and neighboring Arab states.

Information Link

Visit the Central Intelligence Agency Factbook on the Internet and learn about the histories of Israel, the Gaza Strip, and the West Bank at www.cia .gov/library/publications/the-world-factbook/docs/history.html.

the past two years alone, Jewish buildings and cemeteries have been vandalized in Poland, France, India, England, and Israel. (See Figure 2-11.) In March 2017, a news reporter, Juan Thompson, was arrested in St. Louis, Missouri, on charges of making bomb threat against Jewish sites in Manhattan. While Thompson was certainly not the sole actor in these recent incidents, his arrest points to an increased awareness of age-old problems of hate. Quite interestingly, the new graffiti has symbols often associated with radical Islamic groups, as well as traditional hate groups, like the neo-Nazis, Skinheads, and KKK.[51]

Political tension in the Palestinian area was at an all-time high just after World War II, leading British officials to surrender the entire problem to the newly formed United Nations. The UN developed a Special Committee on Palestine, which set forth two proposals calling for the creation of separate Arab and Jewish states. The Arab nationalists rejected both suggestions, and reiterated their position that Palestine was a crucial part of the Arab-Muslim world and that the UN had no right to separate Palestine into a "National Jewish Homeland" and an "Arab Palestinian State."[52]

Nonetheless, the United Nations adopted the partition plan on November 29, 1947. It gave just over 56 percent of Palestine to the Jewish state and about 43 percent to the Arab state, with the holy sites in Jerusalem remaining an international enclave. The approval prompted the withdrawal of British forces and immediately pitted Arabs against Jews living in the area. Zionist forces seized the moment to capitalize on British withdrawal and on May 14, 1948, declared an independent State of Israel to the United Nations, supported by only one vote, that of the United States. The action led to a full-scale war between the newly announced country of Israel and its neighboring Arab states of Jordan, Egypt, Lebanon, Syria, and Iraq. Arab military forces invaded Israel; most were unsuccessful, and hostilities ended in early 1949 with an armistice agreement that set the recognized boundaries of a new Israeli state and divided Jerusalem in half between the Jewish and Arab settlers. Israel retained a majority of the former Palestine, leaving only small areas along the Gaza Strip and the West Bank under Arab Palestinian control. These areas represented 25 percent of the former Palestinian territory.[53] (See Figure 2–12.)

Palestinians began to leave their homesteads "en masse" with the creation of the new state of Israel (1948–1949). The UN estimated that by 1949, almost a million Palestinian refugees fled to the smaller Arab-controlled areas of Palestine or to neighboring Arab countries like Jordan, Lebanon, and Syria. Destruction of the property of the fleeing Palestinians ensued, with many villages being leveled and subsequently rebuilt as new Jewish settlements.

The Arab position against Israel has not changed: The establishment of a Jewish state within Palestine was and is against all international law. The Zionist entity, according to the Palestinian Arabs, was never interested in sharing the lands as drawn in the original partition plan, but rather the development of a singular Zionist state (Israel) at the expense of the indigenous people of the land—the Arab Palestinians. Even today Israel is not formally recognized as a separate country by Palestinians and most Arab countries. On the other hand, Israel strongly argues that it has a right to exist as a separate nation, as a homeland for all Jews worldwide, and that the land is historically a Jewish homeland as well as an Arab location.

In addition to the dispute about whether Israel should even exist, other contentious factors are at work. Many of the sites located in Israel generally and in Jerusalem particularly have great meaning to all three of the monotheistic religions of Islam, Judaism, and Christianity, and often they are within just a few feet of each other.

The City of David, as Jerusalem is known, was the center of the first two Jewish commonwealths in Palestine. It was also the site of the first temple built to worship God. The Wailing Wall, part of this first Temple, still exists in Jerusalem and is the holiest of Jewish sites.[54] However, Jerusalem is also the third-holiest city in Islam. According to the Qur'an, Muhammad traveled to Jerusalem from Mecca and back in one night on a miraculous creature,

FIGURE 2-13
The Temple Mount as seen from the Mount of Olives, where Christians believe that Judas betrayed Jesus. The Middle East and Jerusalem have for centuries been the location of fierce fighting, often between religions. The Crusades, which lasted nearly 200 years, are just one example.

(Duby Tal/Albatross/Alamy Stock Photo)

accompanied by the angel Gabriel. While in Jerusalem, Mohammed visited the former site of the Hebrew temple, ascending to heaven while standing on a rock in the Temple Mount. This rock was enshrouded and is now known as the Mosque of Omar. Another sacred mosque, known as al-Aqsa, was built for public prayer nearby. Jerusalem is also an important city claimed by Christians as the area where Jesus died and was resurrected (see Figure 2–13).

Today, much of the dialogue around the Israeli-Palestinian conflict revolves around the proposed "two-state solution." This concept suggests a division of territories establishing an independent Palestinian state alongside the existing country of Israel. According to supporters of the concept, this action would effect a compromise between age-old enemies. Israel would achieve security and a demographic Jewish majority within its land—and Palestinians would have their own, separate and recognized state. While not official, in effect, this has been a diplomatic policy for the last 20 years and has formed the basis for the majority of international peace talks concerning this conflict.

However, there is no indication that the "two-state solution" will ever be officially implemented: the border issue is very complex, due in a large part to the development of new Israeli settlements in the West Bank that, if relegated to the Israelis, would result in a non-contiguous Palestinian state. Further, Jerusalem has overlapping holy sites that cannot be physically divided—both sides (Jewish Israelis and Palestinian Muslims) lay historical and religious claims to the city. There are also major concerns relating to security of Israel, as tactical geographic positions in a new Palestinian State (Gaza Strip and the West Bank) could cause imminent harm to Tel Aviv and other major cities in Israel should peace erode. Pointing to the final major issue, that both sides are deeply skeptical of the other, and trust is almost nonexistent. Palestinians argue that Israel continues to build settlements in disputed border areas against international and United Nation's objections, while Israelis complain about recent influxes in Arab refugees to the Palestinian territory (ostensibly escaping conflicts in Iraq and Syria) and who are members of radical Islamic groups like the Islamic State, that openly espouse the "annihilation of the Jewish State."[55]

The Palestinian Resistance Movement

The problem of Palestine quickly became the "lightning rod" for all Arab Muslims against Western influence in the region. In fact, Palestinians themselves became somewhat disenfranchised from the politics surrounding the issue. They were discouraged from using their

Box 2–3:
A New Era in U.S.-Israeli Relations Impacting the Palestinian Conflict

After nearly a decade of significant tension between the leadership of Israel and the United States, the Trump presidency has largely been viewed as a political win for the country of Israel. President Trump's daughter, Ivanka, is married to Jared Kushner, a Jewish developer in New York whose family has strongly supported West Bank settlements. More important, he is part of the Trump leadership team, and has been charged with diplomatic responsibilities toward Israel. During his campaign, President Trump expressed support for a move of the U.S. Embassy in Israel, from Tel Aviv to Jerusalem—a hugely controversial pledge that would effectively signal that the United States recognizes the holy city of Jerusalem as the capital of Israel. This action would certainly bring worldwide condemnation as the United Nations has declared Israel's annexation of that city a violation of international law. The fallout from such a move would likely be explosive—inciting Arab anger, and perhaps eliciting conflict among UN member nations.

However, President Trump's approach to the Israeli/Palestinian situation does not appear to be so clear-cut. After the last three presidential administrations have pushed for a "two-state solution," President Trump has backed off of that strategy during his first official meeting (February 2017) with Israeli Prime Minister Benjamin Netanyahu. President Trump stated that the two-state solution would be the easiest route to peace in the region; however, he urged Israelis and Palestinians to work together to determine their mutually beneficial solution. Further, he asked the Israelis to "hold back on settlements for a little bit" in disputed border areas, and expressed general support for the embassy move, stating that he was looking at that prospect "very strongly" and with "great care." These are important signals that reflect a much different tone than that of past President Barack Obama; his leadership corps continually voiced unequivocal support of the two-state solution, and whose tone—especially toward Netanyahu—was not as light and friendly as the one President Trump exhibited in their first meeting. President Trump also spoke to a wider, more regional approach relating to the Palestinian-Israeli issue than the Obama administration; advancing the concept of diplomacy between Israel and the primary Islamic countries of the area, including Saudi Arabia, Egypt, Jordan, and the United Arab Emirates, in an effort to influence Palestinian flexibility. First and foremost would be the recognition of the State of Israel by these important Arab countries in the Middle East.

How do you think President Trump's change in diplomatic policy, as well as his relationship with Prime Minister Netanyahu, will impact Israeli-Palestinian issues in the future?
Sources: *The White House, Office of the Press Secretary, "Joint Readout of Meeting Between President Donald J. Trump and Israeli Prime Minister Benjamin Netanyahu (February 15, 2017); and Peter Baker and Mark Landler, "Trump, Meeting with Netanyahu, Backs Away from Palestinian State," New York Times, (February 15, 2017). See: www.nytimes.com/2017/02/15/world /middleeast/benjamin-netanyahu-israel-trump.html?_r=0.*

own initiatives, and Egypt proclaimed that until the Arab states had a military superior to that of Israel and its allies, there should be no war. Syria claimed Egypt was ignoring the Palestinian problem in favor of unifying the larger Arab-Muslim world.[56] Arab perspectives on a Palestinian homeland were seriously divided.

In early 1964, Egyptian President Gamal Abdel Nasser convened the first Arab Summit Conference in Cairo regarding the plight of Palestine. As a result of this conference, a new entity was developed to represent the sole interests of Palestinian Arabs within the larger conflict with Israel. The conference, held in 1964, gave birth to a new organization known as the *Palestinian Liberation Organization (PLO)*, with a Palestinian Congress headed by **Ahmad Shukeiri**. The Palestinian Congress adopted a charter that affirmed a dedication to the liberation of Palestine and to the destruction of Israel. The Summit also established the Palestinian Liberation Army (PLA). However, neither entity (the PLO or the PLA) was independent of the greater Arab League, composed of Egypt, Saudi Arabia, Syria, Iraq, and other powerful Middle Eastern countries. Egypt retained effective control over the Palestinian Congress, emphasizing that broad military action was the most effective way to defeat the Israelis.[57] As a result, the PLA and the PLO were figureheads for the first three years of their existence. In fact, the creation of the PLO was more about restraining a growing Palestinian resistance movement and less about giving Palestinians a voice in a struggle that was co-opted by other Arab-Muslim nations. Consequently, those resistance groups began to criticize the passivity of the PLO and factions began to arise.[58]

Ahmad Shukeiri
The first head of the Palestinian Congress in 1964.

Quick Facts
Jewish and Arab Palestinians in Palestine

The population of Israel stands at 8,630,000: Of those, 6.45 million are Jews and 1.80 million are Arabs. The birthrate in Israel is the highest in the developed world, with birthrates among Jewish and Arab Israeli women almost identical in 2015.
Source: Central Bureau of Statistics, Israel. See: www.cbs.gov.il/.

Predictably, the PLO fractured into over a hundred different groups, each linked to the concept of a free and independent Palestinian state, but with a different ideology or methodology for achieving such a status. Many wealthy business entities within the PLO had links to more radical Palestinian organizations, some of them guerilla resistance groups, and began pushing for a more action-oriented position. Some of these groups had existed well before the PLO was even chartered. One such group was *al-Fatah*, which translates as "to open" from Arabic. The origin of this group was in the Union of Palestinian Students at Cairo University as early as 1952, under the leadership of an eloquent student named **Yasser Arafat**. The student group rallied Palestinians in support of direct assault against Israel, including clandestine commando raids against the general population of new Israeli settlers (terrorism as a tool of revolution). Al-Fatah was the largest of the PLO factions and was very successful in gaining support from other countries. Syria was an immediate ally; the Syrians had been waiting for a chance to challenge Egyptian president Gamal Abdel Nasser for control over the broader PLO. Syria provided funds, training, and equipment to the new al-Fatah group that began conducting raids against Israel.[59]

Yasser Arafat
The leader of the al-Fatah Palestinian group and later head of the Palestinian Liberation Organization (PLO).

Al-Fatah grew in strength and activity as Jordan and Saudi Arabia became strong supporters, both financially and militarily. By the end of 1965, al-Fatah had become an accomplished guerrilla force, carrying out a variety of bombings and attacks against Israeli military and citizen targets. As a result, the Israeli government became increasingly concerned that the stage was being set for a major invasion by combined forces of al-Fatah, Egypt, Syria, and Jordan. Israel retaliated by attacking al-Fatah strongholds in the West Bank, setting off back-and-forth violence that culminated in what is known as the Six-Day War (June 1967). (See Figure 2–14.) Israel further carried out a preemptive strike against Egypt and other Arab states, attacking airfields and destroying Egyptian as well as other Arab air forces. The Israeli military seized Gaza, the Sinai, and several other Arab-held strongholds throughout the region, nearly doubling the size of Israel and displacing an additional half-million Palestinians.

This defeat in 1967 led to the long-standing and dangerous belief by many Arabs that conventional warfare tactics would not work against the Israelis. With significant U.S. support, Israel maintained, and still boasts, one of the strongest and most modern military forces in the world. As a result, more radical and vocal leaders within al-Fatah began to gain legitimacy within the ranks of the PLO. Palestinians began to call for the resignation of Ahmad Shukeiri in favor of leaders willing to use guerrilla and terroristic tactics against the Israelis, expressed by the revolutionary ideologies of Karl Marx, Che Guevara, and Frantz Fanon. By 1969, Yasser Arafat became chairman of the PLO, now an umbrella group of over a hundred loosely connected organizations focused on the establishment of an independent

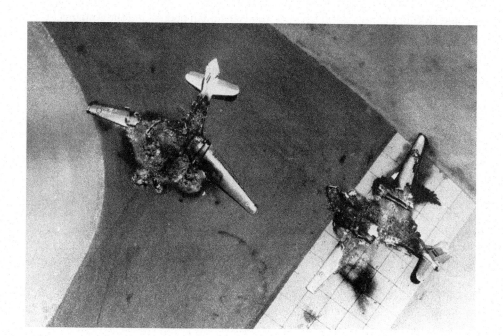

FIGURE 2–14
Egyptian warplanes lie destroyed on an airport tarmac after a preemptive Israeli airstrike during the Six-Day War in 1967.
(Hulton Archive/Getty Images)

Box 2-4
Yasser Arafat

Born in Cairo in 1929, Yasser Arafat became active in the struggle for a separate Palestinian state at an early age, rising to the leadership of al-Fatah, and then as head of the Palestinian Liberation Organization (PLO). In 1974, he became the first representative of a nongovernmental organization to address the

CNP/Contributor/Hulton Archive/Getty Images

United Nations. With a gun strapped to his hip, he compared himself to George Washington and Abraham Lincoln, and bluntly warned, "Today, I have come bearing an olive branch and a freedom fighter's gun. Do not let the olive branch fall from my hand."

In 1993, he was part of the U.S.-led Oslo Accords, meeting with Israeli Prime Ministers Shimon Peres and Yitzhak Rabin. Based on an agreement from these meetings, the implementation of Palestinian self-rule was granted in the West Bank and the Gaza Strip. A year later, Arafat shared the Nobel Peace Prize with his Israeli counterparts. On October 12, 2004, Yasser Arafat died after a relatively quick illness in Paris at the age of 75. Speculation abounded that he was poisoned with polonium, a radioactive metal, which led to the 2012 exhumation of his body. A Swiss team conducting the forensic investigation determined that he had 18 times the normal level of polonium in his bones and ribcage and stated they were 83 percent confident that polonium poisoning was the cause of his death. While controversy continues around his death, his life is remembered by fellow Palestinians as a constant struggle for his people, even amid accusations of widespread corruption and his continued support of terrorism and suicide bombing.

Do you think Arafat was a "thug" or a legitimate representative of his people?

Palestine.[60] A change in approach was immediate and obvious in the adoption of the following amendments to the Palestinian National Charter, some of which echo Fanon's ideological writings:

- *Article IX:* Armed struggle is the only way to liberate Palestine and is therefore a strategy, not a tactic.

- *Article X:* Guerrilla, commando, and revolutionary actions form the nucleus of the popular Palestinian war of liberation. This requires its escalation, comprehensiveness, and the mobilization of all the Palestinian popular and educational efforts and their organization and involvement in the armed Palestinian revolution. It also requires the achieving of unity for the national struggle among the different groupings of the Palestinian people (within the PLO), and between the Palestinian people and the Arab masses, so as to secure the continuation of the revolution, its escalation, and victory.[61]

Al-Fatah recognized that differences between PLO factions could quickly detract from their primary mission. The sole aim of the group became the elimination of Israel and the establishment of an independent Palestinian state. Although al-Fatah continued to be the largest faction under the PLO umbrella, other, more radical groups also formed.[62]

The *Popular Front for the Liberation of Palestine (PFLP)* was the second-largest group. The PFLP was a Christian-led Marxist organization founded by the late **George Habash** as a direct response to the Six-Day War of 1967. George Habash, code named "al-Hakim," or the doctor, was a Christian Palestinian doctor. He witnessed the mass expulsion of his people in 1948 and had previously led the Arab Nationalist Movement (ANM) as a medical student in Beirut. The PFLP established small cells throughout the West Bank and Gaza with support from Egypt and Syria. Habash's new group adopted a strong Christian Marxist ideology. It not only addressed the need to fight the Israelis, but also any imperialist nation (e.g., European nations or the United States) that was an active supporter of Israel or any Arab state that acted as a puppet government for perceived Western capitalist interests (e.g., Saudi Arabia and Jordan).[63] More interesting, Habash and the PFLP were Christian, strongly asserting that it was their Christian religious duty to assist the oppressed Palestinian people. Again, echoing the ideology of Che Guevara, the Palestinian struggle was seen by members of the PFLP as an integral part of a larger world revolution that

George Habash
A Christian Marxist physician who led the Popular Front for the Liberation of Palestine (PFLP).

included the Cubans, Vietnamese, North Koreans, and Chinese; the Palestinian struggle was but an extension of the world struggle against colonialism and capitalism sponsored by Western European countries and the United States.[64]

Leadership of the PFLP rested in the hands of two Christian Marxist physicians; George Habash became the political figurehead while his longtime friend, **Wadi Haddad**, directed military and guerrilla actions. In July 1968, the PFLP began a terrorist strategy aimed at bringing the Palestinian agenda to the attention of the entire world. The first modern hijacking of a commercial airline (skyjacking) was conducted by Haddad and other members of the PFLP against an Israeli El-Al airliner. Known as "the Master," Haddad meticulously planned and orchestrated the entire skyjacking. The airliner was diverted from its original flight from Tel Aviv to Rome and taken to Algeria. The PFLP gained world media attention from the event, and demanded that Palestinian prisoners be set free and that Israel retreat from all Palestinian lands. After nearly 40 days of negotiations, all passengers and skyjackers walked free, as well as many demanded prisoners; however, no Palestinian territory was ever surrendered. The event marked one of the most successful terrorist events in history and set the stage for a flurry of skyjackings to come.[65]

The PFLP came to the forefront of Palestinian organizations as a result of successful skyjackings that hit the world stage, forcing one terrorism expert of the time (Brian M. Jenkins from the RAND Corporation) to coin the phrase that "terrorism was grand theater."[66]

Events were soon to change, and in September 1970, the grandest of all skyjackings performed by the PFLP backfired in the Jordanian desert. A great deal of tension had arisen between Jordanians and Palestinians as a result of mass immigration of Palestinians into Jordan.[67] King Hussein of Jordan further fanned the flames of tension by openly supporting a new Israeli-Arab peace proposal sponsored by the United States. The proposal called for an end to Israeli occupation of the lands taken during the Six-Day War in 1967, but did not satisfy the Palestinian demands for a complete withdrawal of the Israelis from all Palestinian lands. As a result, the PFLP began to launch small-scale attacks against Jordan throughout the summer of 1970. King Hussein was viewed as an American puppet and at least two different unsuccessful assassination attempts were made against him by the PFLP.[68]

On September 6, 1970, Wadi Haddad again planned and set into motion a series of skyjackings specifically designed to attract world attention and embarrass Jordan. Two airplanes (an American TWA airliner and a Swiss Air airliner) were simultaneously skyjacked and diverted to an abandoned airstrip in the Jordanian desert. Passengers and crew were forced to deplane their aircraft and were held hostage for four days. Another plane, an American Pan-Am jet, was flown to Cairo and blown up as soon as the passengers and crew exited. A fourth hijacking aboard an El-Al flight was thwarted that same day, but the PFLP

Wadi Haddad
A Christian Marxist physician who directed the military and guerrilla actions of the Popular Front for the Liberation of Palestine (PFLP); credited for developing the modern-day hijacking of airliners as a methodology and tactic of terrorism.

Box 2-5
The Siege at OPEC: A Collaboration of Terror

In late December 1975, a collaborative exercise in terror brought members of the European Red Army Faction, June 2nd Movement, and Red Cells together with a group of Palestinian terrorists as part of the largest hostage-taking event in history. The combined group attacked the Vienna headquarters of the Organization of Petroleum Exporting Countries (OPEC). OPEC is composed of oil-producing countries primarily in the Middle East. Organized by "Carlos the Jackal" (whose real name was Ilich Ramirez Sanchez), a Marxist-Leninist radical and now member of the Popular Front for the Liberation of Palestine (PFLP), the group stormed the embassy, killing three and taking nearly 100 hostages. The terror group demanded that a statement be made on Austrian radio and television every two hours or else a hostage would be killed every 15 minutes; Austrian officials complied with that demand—as well as a request for an airplane bound for Algeria.

Upon confirmation that the airplane had been procured, the terrorists released 50 Austrian nationals and boarded a bus for

the airport. The plane flew to Algiers, where the remainder of the hostages (hailing from Saudi Arabia, Iran, Algeria, and the United Arab Emirates) were released and a $5 million ransom was obtained from Iran and Saudi Arabia. The PFLP retained $2 million of that sum; the rest funded various other Palestinian causes.

This siege was notable for several reasons. First, the level of partnership between the Palestinian PFLP and European leftist groups gave the Palestinians insight into Viennese and Austrian weaknesses, allowing them to exploit the hostage situation and leave the country successfully. Second, the sum paid in ransom was relatively huge, which likely set the stage for future ransom requests in a spate of hijackings throughout the late 1970s and into the early 1980s.

How do you think this incident impacted American policy? Do you think we should have a "no negotiation with terrorists" perspective, or have things changed with more sophisticated terrorist groups?

managed to later hijack a fifth plane, a British Air jet, and land it next to the previously two skyjacked aircraft in Jordan.[69] As a result of these hijackings, the PFLP demanded and obtained the release of Palestinian prisoners in Britain, Switzerland, and West Germany in exchange for the skyjacked hostages. However, the three empty jet airliners parked in the Jordanian desert were simultaneously blown up in front of onlooking TV cameras and a helpless Jordanian Army.[70] Skyjacking had again become "grand theater," and the PFLP was heralded as one of the most successful Marxist revolutionary groups of all time, spawning collaborations with similar groups throughout Europe (e.g., Red Army Faction, Baader-Meinhof Gang, Red Brigades).

Embarrassed on a global scale and in the midst of a civil war, Jordan reacted violently, sending troops to evacuate large settlements of Palestinians living along the Jordan River. Over the course of several days, up to 15,000 Palestinian men, women, and children were slaughtered and between 50,000 and 100,000 were left homeless.[71] The horrific event became known as Black September,[72] and pushed the PFLP to the edges of the Palestinian cause. Although the PFLP never regained its notoriety after September 1970, it continued to strike directly at Israel, often targeting innocent civilians. For the next several years, the PFLP conducted relatively small-scale car and bus bombings, assassinations, and killings of Jewish settlers primarily in the West Bank. The most spectacular of these attacks occurred in May 1972, in collaboration with members of the Red Army Faction and the Baader-Meinhof Gang that killed 24 people during an attack at Lod Airport in Israel.

The *Black September Organization (BSO)* is perhaps the most notorious, though short-lived, of the early Marxist Palestinian terrorist organizations. The BSO was primarily composed of former PFLP members and other smaller radical Palestinian factions expelled from Jordan during the events of Black September, 1970. The Black September Organization carried out a significant number of very violent attacks in Israel and left a lasting mark on the Israeli-Palestinian conflict of the time, as well as one of the most visible attacks associated with the concept of political terrorism as a whole. In November 1971, members of the BSO gunned down the Prime Minister of Jordan, Wasfi Tal, in broad daylight. One gunman knelt down and, in a gruesome display, appeared to lap up the blood of the slain Prime Minister.[73] A month later, the group tried to assassinate the Jordanian ambassador to England, Zeid al-Rifai, who had supported Jordan's crackdown on the Palestinians. Although severely wounded, al-Rifai survived the attack. In the same month, the group blew up a gasoline manufacturing plant in the Netherlands and oil tankers in Germany. In May 1972, the group hijacked a Belgian airliner, forcing it to land in Israeli territory. In July of that year, an Italian oil refinery was attacked and a bomb at a Tel Aviv bus terminal wounded eleven Israeli citizens.[74] Clearly, the BSO was actively at war using terrorism as its primary strategy.

No attack during this period was more shocking than the events at the Summer Olympic Games in Munich, Germany, in September 1972. Hooded and heavily armed Black September guerrillas jumped a fence and entered the Olympic Village in Munich. Two Israeli athletes were killed outright during the raid and another 11 were taken hostage. During an ensuing shootout with German police at the Munich Airport, nine of the eleven remaining hostages were killed, as were several of the BSO terrorists. Three of the gunmen were eventually captured but later released as part of the negotiations related to the hijacking of a Lufthansa aircraft just one month later. Their individual demise, as well as that of the mastermind of the attack, Abu Daoud, by members of the **Israeli Mossad** was chronicled in the 2005 movie *Munich*. Black September's actions at the 1972 Olympics in Munich were a direct affront to the entire world, as the Olympic Games have always been a symbol of global community and peace. The killings of the Israeli athletes alienated many who previously supported the Palestinian cause.

Outrage against the Palestinians was at an all-time high, and Yasser Arafat and his PLO were held responsible for the attacks, even though most Middle East experts seriously doubt that Arafat had prior knowledge of the earlier terrorist operations, much less power to actually control such activity within the highly radicalized BSO.[75] In an event, Arafat denounced all international terrorist attacks and mandated that further guerrilla actions be limited to the Israeli territories. As a result, BSO operations halted and the group faded into anonymity.[76]

Israeli Mossad
The intelligence and secret service unit of the country of Israel; responsible for carrying out extensive covert operations throughout the Middle East and the rest of the world.

Quick Facts
Revolutionary Physicians

Some of the most famous revolutionary thinkers and leaders were physicians. This association raises questions, such as, is it merely a coincidence, something in the makeup of people who are attracted to practicing medicine, or does the phenomenon arise out of the educational process for physicians?

Ernesto "Che" Guevara	- Medical Doctor – Infectious Diseases – Father of Marxist Revolutionary Ideals
Frantz Fanon	- Medical Doctor – Psychiatry – Revolutionary Writer in French Algeria
George Habash	- Medical Doctor – Pediatrics – Leader of Popular Front for Liberation of Palestine (PFLP)
Wadi Haddad	- Medical Doctor – Ophthalmology – Founder of Popular Front for Liberation of Palestine
Fathi Shikaki	- Medical Doctor – Pediatric – Founder of Palestinian Islamic Jihad
Ayman al-Zawahiri	- Doctor of Medicine – General Surgery – Current head of al-Qaeda

The *Abu Nidal Organization (ANO)* was the last of the first-wave, primarily Marxist-oriented Palestinian groups to gain major international notoriety. Headed by a former PFLP member named **Sabri al-Banna**, the group was highly entrepreneurial, meaning that the group worked for a variety of countries, conducting "missions" that included paid assassinations and bombings throughout the Middle East. Code-named Abu-Nidal (or "Father of the Holy Struggle"), al-Banna's group was highly radicalized and eschewed the moderate stance by senior PLO leadership like Yasser Arafat. Al-Banna believed that Israel must be destroyed at any cost, branding Arafat, the PLO, and the rest of the al-Fatah as traitors. The ANO launched international terrorist operations against the Israeli government as well as PLO interests, assassinating ambassadors and leaders within each group. The Abu Nidal Organization has been financially backed by Syria, Libya, Iraq, and even Iran,[77] and claimed responsibility for more attacks on foreign and Arab interests than any other Palestinian terrorist organization to date. At one point, the ANO was considered the most dangerous terrorist group in the world, seemingly conducting terrorist attacks for the highest bidder. Political ideology and cause gave way to financial benefit and mercenary action as Abu Nidal orchestrated attacks in the Middle East and Europe.

The Abu Nidal Organization was a very well-organized and technologically savvy operation that spanned the globe and reportedly had cells throughout the Middle East as well as in South America, Asia, and even the United States. From 1972 to 1994, the group conducted 90 attacks in 20 different countries, claiming the lives of over 900 people.[78] More interesting, Sabri al-Banna was never arrested and lived to the age of 65 in Iraq, under the protection of Saddam Hussein. In 2002, he was found dead in his flat as a result of three bullet wounds, two of which were in the back of his head. The official report reached the startling conclusion that he had committed suicide.[79]

Sabri al-Banna
A highly entrepreneurial revolutionary and mercenary who headed the Abu Nidal Organization (ANO).

Politics, Oil, and Terrorism in the Modern Era

The Palestinian groups discussed so far were the forerunners of modern Middle East terrorist organizations, but notably they were secular—meaning that their ideology was not based in religion, but more in the political theories of Karl Marx. These prominent Palestinian terrorist groups [al-Fatah, Popular Front for the Liberation of Palestine (PFLP), Black September Organization (BSO), and Abu-Nidal Organization (ANO)] clearly paved the way for more contemporary terrorist groups that eschewed political theory in favor of more radical Islamic (religious) ideology, as we discuss in Chapter 4, "The Rise of Radical Islam."

Since 1948, the Israeli-Palestinian conflict has been a central point of outrage by Arab radical groups in the Middle East. Bolstered by Marxist ideology and further inflamed by the perspectives of Fanon and other philosophers, these groups have also pointed to colonialism by European powers as the means of exploitation of the natural resources (particularly oil) in the Middle East. The United States has not been immune to this criticism, especially

Quick Facts
The Discovery of Oil in the Middle East

A British oil company (Burmah Oil) first discovered oil in Persia (now Iran) on March 26, 1908. However, large oil reserves were not fully developed until years later on the Arabian Peninsula (now Saudi Arabia) in 1938 by Standard Oil of California (SoCal) and the Texas Oil Company (Texaco); that same year, large oil finds were also discovered in the Kingdom of Kuwait by Gulf Oil Company. SoCal and Texaco were early partners in the development of Saudi Aramco, now boasting the largest proven crude oil reserves in the world, at more than 260 billion barrels.

▲ A 1932 view of an Iraq Petroleum Company oil well and camp near Kirkuk.
(American Colony (Jerusalem), Photo Dept., photographer/ Library of Congress Prints and Photographs Division Washington, D.C. 20540 USA)

concerning relatively recent foreign policies and military interventions. Arab groups have long resented perceived "imperialist" actions by the United States in its quest for oil in the Middle East. Relying heavily on Marxist principles to inform their perceptions of and reactions to the unwelcome advances of a capitalist nation, bent on corralling resources and establishing new marketplaces full of Western commerce at the expense of Arab sovereignty, radical Middle East groups have pushed their cause and justified their use of terrorism.

The chief natural resource of the Middle East is, in fact, oil. This was brought to light in the late 1930s, as American and British oil companies made major discoveries in the area. As a result, the United States—which had largely tried to remain neutral when the League of Nations was first formed in 1919—was suddenly involved more and more in the foreign policy of the Middle East. American politicians proclaimed that the Middle East was "a stupendous source of strategic power, and one of the greatest material prizes in world history."[80] Middle East scholars have long argued that the dominant and driving force behind every U.S. action in the region has been the security of its access to oil.[81] Aid has been given to U.S.-friendly governments in the region, often at the expense of democratic rule. "Regional stability" has been much more about the ease of getting U.S. interests to an oil pipeline than about ensuring that the Arab population is entitled to live under governments that do not oppress their citizens. Former U.S. Senator John Foster Dulles said it best during a crisis involving Lebanon in 1958:

> [We] must regard Arab nationalism as a flood which is running strongly. We cannot successfully oppose it, but we could put sandbags around positions we must protect: the first group being Israel and Lebanon, and the second group being the oil positions around the Persian Gulf.[82]

Many argue that this sentiment seemingly guided U.S. policies throughout much of the twentieth century: from Israeli partition, to the support of the Shah in Iran in the

1950s—which landed the United States ownership of 40 percent of the oil fields in that country as a reward[83]—to involvement in the Iran-Iraq war in the 1980s, and to more recent military entanglements in Iraq and Afghanistan.[84]

Fundamentalist Arab groups argue that the presence of the U.S. military in the Middle East was used to "fan the flames" of neocolonialism. Al-Qaeda, as well as other Arab groups, has always been violently opposed to the presence of American interests on Middle East soil, especially those on the Arabian Peninsula. Saudi Arabia is home to two of Islam's holiest sites (Mecca and Medina). The presence of half a million coalition soldiers near Mecca during the 1990s was seen as a defiling and defamation of Muslim holy land, and further represented America's desire for oil, backed up by a compelling military force in the region.[85] Radical Islamic groups led by Usama bin Laden rallied around his call to "purge" the United States from the Middle East (note the Marxian rhetoric), and sparked several international terrorist events against U.S. forces in the Middle East. Most notable was the attack on the USS *Cole* in 2000 while the ship refueled in the Yemen port of Aden. Bin Laden would justify his actions on 9/11 as an attack on the "Adulterous Nation" (United States) because of its support of Israel and the presence of military forces near the Islamic holy cities of Mecca and Medina in Saudi Arabia.[86]

On March 20, 2003, the United States launched ground attacks in Iraq to "disarm Iraq of weapons of mass destruction, to end Saddam Hussein's support for terrorism, and to free the Iraqi people."[87] The United States emphasized the links between Hussein and terrorism in a post-9/11 world, which was enough to sustain a presence in the country for more than a decade in what was deemed by some as a "creeping militarization of American foreign policy."[88] The invasion and the long-standing occupation of Iraq, which culminated in the capture of Saddam Hussein in 2003 and his execution in 2006, has resulted in a violent and unstable country. More important, most of the country's population is susceptible to the influence of a radicalized Iran. From March 2003 to February 20, 2014, 5,314 American soldiers died in Iraq military operations and another 51,895 were wounded.[89] Estimates for Iraqi deaths range from 120,000 to 200,000 people, and economic loss is in the billions of dollars.[90] American soldiers went to Iraq believing that they would secure their country from future terrorist attacks, and indeed, the financial and military strength of al-Qaeda has been significantly reduced because of U.S. military actions in Iraq, Afghanistan, and Pakistan (see Figure 2–15). However, Iraq has become the symbol of anti-American sentiment among terrorist groups, and again, a breeding ground for radical Islamic ideology; all aimed at further reinforcing Arab sentiments that the United States is not only an imperialist force, but also an enemy to all of Islam.

FIGURE 2–15
A Bradley Fighting Vehicle is engulfed in flames from an improvised explosive device (IED) during the Iraq War. A medic is profiled on top of the vehicle as he tries to enter the vehicle and rescue soldiers. He later received America's second-highest award, the Distinguished Service Cross, for extraordinary heroism.
(U.S. Army)

The discussion of terrorism in this chapter has traced its evolution from Marxism and left-wing terror groups full circle to Islamic fundamentalism. The historical roots of terrorism in the Middle East lay in nineteenth century France, and weave their way through Eastern Europe to World War I's colonial legacy of the mandate system. The establishment of Israel after World War II, the frequent intervention of military forces in the Holy Lands of Islam, and the quest for oil by Western nations only helped to coalesce bitter Arab groups against one enemy.[91] The vestiges of those actions remain a threat to the stability of the entire Middle East, and to the safety and security of Western nations—especially the United States.

Chapter Summary

1. **Describe the concept of political terrorism.**

   Political terrorism can be defined as "a symbolic act designed to influence political behavior based on extra-normal means, entailing the use or threat of violence." Recall that political terror is based on a set of ingrained beliefs that stem from the way people think about their environment, government, and society—and that those beliefs are often inflexible.

2. **Provide an overview of leftist terror cells, including Latin American and European groups.**

   Groups that espouse Marxist ideologies include the Revolutionary Armed Forces of Columbia, or FARC, which purports to represent the rural, agrarian poor in Columbia by protecting their land interests against the wealthier classes of Columbia, the influence of the imperialist United States, the privatization of resources, and the influence of global corporations. The National Liberation Army, or ELN, also a pro-Marxist group that operates in the Colombian countryside, seeks to replace the Colombian government with an egalitarian democracy that represents the rural peasant class. Tupac Amaru Revolutionary Movement (or MRTA) exists in Peru, and was founded in Marxist ideology to reform the Peruvian government, removing all imperialist elements, and create a society in which power, property, and prosperity were shared equally. Shining Path, or the Communist Party of Peru, claimed to be the vanguard of the world communist movement, and was brutal in its methods. Argentina's Montoneros sprang from the Marxist left, viewing itself as a vanguard for revolution and forming urban guerilla cells to carry out political kidnappings and assassinations to achieve their means. The People's Revolutionary Army, meanwhile, retreated to the country to build a revolutionary base that would root out the Argentine government in favor of proletarian rule.

   In Europe, Italy's Red Brigades formed in 1969, and became one of the largest leftist groups in Europe with thousands of members at its peak. Their blend of Marxist and Leninist ideology sought to overthrow the government in three phases, all involving campaigns of urban terror. The Red Army Faction—also known as the Baader-Meinhof Gang—was the most prominent leftist group of the era. The leaders of the group trained in Jordan with the Popular Front for the Liberation of Palestine in guerilla warfare tactics, then returned to Germany where they robbed banks to subsidize their underground lifestyle. They are notorious for the German Autumn, a series of kidnappings and hijackings that culminated in the fall of 1977. Finally, the anti-imperialist Revolutionary Cells was responsible for bombings at airports, military installations, and other symbolic government sites throughout the early to mid-1970s, and is probably best known for their role in the hijacking of an Air France airliner in 1976 with the Popular Front for the Liberation of Palestine (PFLP).

3. **Discuss how colonialism and the mandate system set the stage for future conflict in the Middle East.**

   At the end of World War I, a series of treaties divided the former Ottoman Empire into a series of British and French "spheres of influence." This encroachment into Arab lands engendered a series of uprisings throughout the Middle East, further inflamed by the mandate system—which gave Great Britain rule over Palestine, which had previously been legitimized as a Jewish homeland by the Balfour Declaration.

4. **Describe the secular "first wave" Palestinian terror groups.**

   The Palestinian Liberation Organization, or PLO, is dedicated to the liberation of Palestine and to the destruction of Israel. The PLO, which has been linked to the more radical guerilla group al-Fatah, adopted principles of armed resistance in the late 1960s under the leadership of Yasser Arafat. The Popular Front for the Liberation of Palestine (PFLP) is a Christian-led Marxist-Leninist group founded in 1967 by the late George Habash. The group rose to infamy in the late 1960s and early 1970s with a series of terrorist attacks, including airline hijackings, assassination attempts, and guerilla tactics aimed first at Jordan, then directly at Israeli targets. The Black September Organization is perhaps the most notorious of these first-wave Palestinian terror organizations, likely formed from radical members of both al-Fatah and the PFLP. Black September is best known for a series of brutal and high-profile terror attacks in the 1970s, including the 1972 attacks against Israeli athletes during the Munich Olympics. Finally, the Abu Nidal Organization (ANO) split from the PLO in the early 1970s. The Abu Nidal organization has been financially backed by Syria, Libya, Iraq, and Iran. It's responsible for more attacks on foreign and Arab interests than any other Palestinian terrorist organization to date, and moved its headquarters to Iraq in the mid-1980s. Its organizational prowess has inspired many modern terror organizations.

5. **Provide insight into how the United States and its policies have inflamed terrorist ideology in the Middle East.**

   United States oil interests—plus its long-standing support of the Israeli state—have long been a source of anger among Arab nationalists, who decry the imperialist actions of the United States and other Western countries. Nationalists and Islamic fundamentalists use Marxist-Leninist principles to inform their perceptions of and reactions to the unwelcome advances of the United States. Such sentiment has been further exacerbated due to U.S. actions in and around Iraq, most notably due to the U.S. presence in Arab holy lands as part of an offensive around Iraq and the long-standing occupation and destabilization of Iraq.

REVIEW QUESTIONS

1. What are the basic tenets of Marxism, and how do you see its effects in modern Middle Eastern terror?
2. How do you think Latin American and European terror organizations inspired present-day Arab terror organizations?
3. What was the mandate system and how do we see its lasting effects in Middle Eastern conflict?
4. Although the *Palestinian Liberation Organization (PLO)* fractured into over a hundred separate groups, identify the three primary groups and their respective leaders that gained worldwide notoriety for conducting terrorist attacks in the international arena.
5. How is the United States perceived by the Arab world, and why? How does this influence terrorist ideology?

CRITICAL THINKING EXERCISES

1. **The Impact of Oil in the Middle East.** Visit the homepage for Saudi Aramco at www .saudiaramco.com/en/home.html and *Life-Time Magazine* at http://life.time.com. Search these sites for stories on the discovery of oil in the Middle East. Learn about the history and culture of the Middle East in 1945 when the oil industry just began in that region. Notice the photos of the region and compare them to more modern times. How much has the landscaped really changed in half a century? Visit the homepages of some of the wealthiest Middle East countries like Saudi Arabia, Bahrain, Qatar, Kuwait, and the United Arab Emirates. Notice the significant improvements in health, education, and welfare of the individuals in those countries. Notice also that each of these countries is a royal monarchy. How do you think the form of government and the pervasive religion of Islam in the region have impacted the economic development of the Middle East—both negatively and positively?

2. **Terrorism as the Nexus of Politics and Violence.** In 1997, Bruce Hoffman, an international expert on terrorism and political violence at the RAND Corporation in Santa Monica, California, wrote a compelling article entitled "The Modern Terrorist Mindset: Tactics, Targets and Techniques" (New York: Columbia International Affairs Online Working Paper, October 1997). In that article, Hoffman explores the mindset of terrorists and the tactics they use in seeking political change. He contends that terrorism is where politics and violence intersect in the hopes of producing power ... power to dominate and coerce, to intimidate and control, and ultimately to effect fundamental political change. Discuss this concept in history. Has any terrorist movement ever been successful in achieving not just political change through revolution, but also long-term international recognition as a ruling party or existing government? Can you give any examples? Interestingly, Hoffman indicates that in modern times, most terrorist groups do not reach the final steps of authority and governance of their homeland or country ... but that was in 1997. Have things changed, particularly in the Middle East?

NOTES

1. Peter K. Hatemi and Rose McDermott, "The Genetics of Politics: Discovery, Challenges, and Progress," *Trends in Genetics*, Vol. 28, Issue 10, pp. 525–533.

2. R. S. Erikson and K. L. Tedin, *American Public Opinion* (New York: Longman, 2003).

3. A. D. Denzau and D. C. North, "Shared Mental Models: Ideologies and Institutions," *Elements of Reason: Cognition, Choice and the Bounds of Rationality*, Arthur Lupia, Mathew D. McCubbins, and Samuel L. Popkin (New York: Cambridge University Press, 1994).

4. J. T. Jost, C. M. Federico, and J. L. Napier, "Political Ideology: Its Structure, Functions, And Elective Affinities," *Annual Review of Psychology,* Vol. 60, pp. 307–337.

5. See the works of Ernesto Guevara, *Guerrilla Warfare* (New York: Vintage Books, 1961); Frantz Fanon, *The Wretched of the Earth* (Paris: Maspero Press, 1961); Carlos Marighella, *Minimanual of the Urban Guerrilla* (Baltimore, MD: Pelican Books, 1971); and Martha Crenshaw Hutchinson, "The Concept of Revolutionary Terrorism," *Journal of Conflict Resolution*, Vol. 16, No. 3, September 1972.

6. As an officer assigned to the Intelligence Division of the Portland Police Bureau in 1975–76, Dr. Robert W. Taylor was part of an interagency task force assigned to train officers on domestic terrorism. Their manual, from which these "social consequences" of terrorism were developed, was never published; however, it was used as a basis for training throughout California, Oregon, and Washington. See also Jennifer L. Merolla and Elizabeth J. Zechmeister, *Democracy at Risk: How Terrorist Threats Affect the Public,* Chicago Scholarship Online, DOI:10.7208/chicago/9780226520568.001.0001, March 2013.

7. See the works of Karl Marx and Friedrich Engels, including *The Communist Manifesto* (New York: Penguin Books, 1998) and *Das Kapital* (New York: Knopf Doubleday, 1977).

8. T. P. Thornton, "Terror as a Weapon of Political Agitation," *Internal War: Problems and Approaches*, Harry Eckstein (Westport, CT: Praeger Press, 1980) (New York: Free Press, 1964).

9. See the works of Karl Marx and Friedrich Engels, including *The Communist Manifesto* (New York: Penguin Books, 1998) and *Das Kapital* (New York: Knopf Doubleday, 1977).

10. R. J. W. Evans and Hartmut Pogge von Strandmann, eds., *The Revolutions in Europe 1848–1849* (New York: Oxford University Press, 2000), p. 4.

11. See *Anarchism and Anarcho-Syndicalism: Selected Writings by Marx, Engels and Lenin* (New York: International Publishers, 1972).

12. Pierre-Joseph Proudhon, *No Gods, No Masters: An Anthology of Anarchism* (Oakland, CA: AK Press, 2005).

13. A. Haynal, M. Molnar, and G. de Ruymege, *Fanaticism: A Historical and Psychoanalytical Study* (New York: Schocken Books, 1983).

14. Yves Ternon, "Russian Terrorism, 1878–1908," *The History of Terrorism: From Antiquity to Al Qaeda*, Gerard Chaliand and Arnaud Blin (Los Angeles, University of California Press, 2007).

15. Ibid.

16. Karl Marx and Friedrich Engels, *The Communist Manifesto* (New York: Penguin Books, 1998).

17. Ibid.

18. Laura Desfor Edles, *Sociological Theory in the Classical Era: Text and Readings* (Thousand Oaks, CA: Pine Forge Press, 2005).

19. Jon Lee Anderson. *Che Guevara: A Revolutionary Life* (New York: Grove Press, 1997).

20. See www.history.com/topics/vietnam-war.

21. See N. Van Hieu, *"Special War"—An Outgrowth of Neo-Colonialism* (Forest Grove, OR: Normount Armament Co., 1966).

22. Peter Kornbluh, *The Death of Che Guevara: Declassified* (Washington, D.C.: George Washington University, The National Security Archive, undated), p. 1. The most recent citation in this source is 1997, so it was published then or more recently.

23. Marc Sageman, *Understanding Terror Networks* (Philadelphia: University of Pennsylvania Press, 2004).

24. Sayyid Qutb, *Social Justice in Islam* (North Haledon, NJ: Islamic Publications International, 2000.)

25. Stephanie Hanson, "FARC, ELN: Colombia's Left-Wing Guerillas," Council on Foreign Relations, August 19, 2009, www.cfr.org/colombia/farc-eln-colombias-left-wing-guerillas/p9272.

26. colombiapeace.org., "Colombia Peace Process Update," www.colombiapeace .org/2013/07/16/colombia-peace-process-update-july-15-2013/.

27. Carlos Nunez, *The Tupamaros: Urban Guerrillas of Uruguay* (New York: Times Change Press, 1970).

28. David Ronfeldt, *The Mitrione Kidnapping in Uruguay* (Santa Monica, CA: RAND Corporation, 1987).

29. Kathryn Gregory, "Shining Path, Tupac Amaru (Peru, Leftists)," Council on Foreign Relations, August 27, 2009, www.cfr.org/peru/shining-path-tupac-amaru-peru-leftists /p9276.

30. Carlos Marighella, *The Minimanual of the Urban Guerrilla*, available at www.marxists .org/archive/marighella-carlos/1969/06/minimanual-urban-guerrilla/.

31. Leszek Kolakowski, Main *Currents of Marxism, Vol. 3: The Breakdown* (Oxford: Oxford University Press, 1981).

32. Mervyn F. Bendle, "Terrorism and the New Left in the Sixties," *National Observer*, No. 71, Summer 2006–2007, pp. 8–28.

33. Clarence Martin, "Understanding Terrorism: Challenges, Perspectives and Issues" (Thousand Oaks, CA: Sage Publications, 2013).

34. Clare Murphy, "Who Were the Baader-Meinhof Gang?" BBC News, February 12, 2007, http://news.bbc.co.uk/2/hi/6314559.stm.

35. Statement presented by the Red Army Faction, on its dissolution in Germany, March 1998.

36. Stanford University, "Mapping Militant Organizations: Revolutionary Cells," www.stanford .edu/group/mappingmilitants/cgi-bin/groups/view/353.

37. Stanford Encyclopedia of Philosophy, http://plato.stanford.edu/entries/colonialism/.

38. Nele Matz, "Civilization and the Mandate System under the League of Nations as Origin of Trusteeship," *Max Planck Yearbook of United Nations Law*, Vol. 9, 2005, pp. 47–95.

39. Gerard Chaliand and Arnaud Blin, "Terrorism in Time of War," *The History of Terrorism: From Antiquity to Al Qaeda* (Berkeley, CA: University of California Press 2007).

40. David Fromkin, *A Peace to End All Peace, The Fall of the Ottoman Empire and the Creation of the Modern Middle East* (New York: Holt 1989).

41. Rene Albrecht-Carrie, *Diplomatic History of Europe Since the Congress of Vienna* (New York: HarperCollins College Publishers, 1958).

42. Much of this discussion is taken from a discussion entitled "The Middle East and the West: World War I and Beyond" featured on National Public Radio's "All Things Considered" on August 20, 2004, available at www.npr.org/templates/transcript/transcript .php?storyId=3860950.

43. Karl Marx, *Capital: A Critique of Political Economy, Vol. 1 (1867)*, translated by Ben Fowkes (New York: Random House, Vintage Books, 1977).

44. See Frantz Fanon, *The Wretched of the Earth* (Grove Press, New York: 2004).

45. Erin McCoy, "Franz Fanon's Call to Anti-Colonial Violence," ProQuest Discovery Guides, www.csa.com/discoveryguides/fanon/review.pdf.

46. See Bernard Lewis, *The Middle East: A Short History of the Last 2000 Years* (New York: Touchstone, 1995).

47. BBC News, "A History of Conflict: Arab Discontent," http://news.bbc.co.uk/2/shared/spl/hi /middle_east/03/v3_ip_timeline/html/1929_36.stm.

48. Weldon Matthews, *Confronting an Empire, Constructing a Nation: Arab Nationalists and Popular Politics in Mandate Palestine* (London: I.B. Tauris and Co, 2006).

49. Rashid Khalidi, *The Iron Cage: The Story of the Palestinian Struggle for Statehood* (Boston: Beacon Press, 2006).

50. Mark Tessler, *A History of the Israeli-Palestinian Conflict* (Indianapolis, IN: Indiana University Press, 1994).

51. See Benjamin Weiser, "Former Reporter Charged in Bomb Threats Against Jewish Sites." *New York Times* (March 2, 2017).

52. Ibid.

53. British Broadcasting Company (BBC) News Online, "History of Conflict: Establishment of Israel," http://news.bbc.co.uk/2/shared/spl/hi/middle_east/03/v3_ip_timeline/html/1948.stm.

54. See Tessler, *A History of the Israeli-Palestinian Conflict.*

55. The leader of the Islamic State, Abu Bakr al-Baghdadi has openly called for the annihilation of the Jewish State of Israel in numerous communications, sermons, and public speeches. See Doug Bolton, "ISIS Leader Abu Bakr al-Baghdadi Remains Defiant and Threatens Israel in Rare Statement," *The Independent* (December 26, 2015). See: www.independent.co.uk/news/world/middle-east/abu-bakr-al-baghdadi-statement-released-a6786941.html

56. Aryeh Yodfat and Yuval Arnon-Ohanna, *PLO: Strategy and Tactics* (New York: St Martin's Press, 1981).

57. Shaul Mishal, *The PLO Under Arafat: Between Gun and Olive Branch* (London: Yale University Press, 1986).

58. John W. Amos II, *Palestinian Resistance: Organization of a Nationalist Movement* (New York: Elsevier Books, 1981).

59. See Tessler, *A History of the Israeli-Palestinian Conflict.*

60. See Mishal, *The PLO Under Arafat.*

61. Abridgement from the Palestinian National Charter: Resolutions of the Palestine National Council, 1967, affirmed in July 1–17, 1968, available at http://avalon.law.yale.edu/20th_century/plocov.asp.

62. See Amos II, *Palestinian Resistance*; and Helena Cobban, *The Palestinian Liberation Organisation: People, Power and Politics* (Cambridge: Cambridge University Press, 1984).

63. See Yodfat and Arnon-Ohanna, *PLO: Strategy and Tactics.*

64. See N. Van Hieu, *"Special War"—An Outgrowth of Neo-Colonialism* (Forest Grove, OR: Normount Armament Co., 1966).

65. International Policy Institute for Counter-Terrorism, "Terrorist Organizations: The Popular Front for the Liberation of Palestine," www.ict.org.il/.

66. Brian M. Jenkins, *International Terrorism: A New Kind of Warfare, 1974,* available at www.rand.org/pubs/papers/2008/P5261.pdf.

67. Ely Karmon, "Fatah and the Popular Front for the Liberation of Palestine: International Terror Strategies (1968–1990)," International Policy Institute for Counter-Terrorism, www.ict.org.il/.

68. See Tessler, *A History of the Israeli-Palestinian Conflict.*

69. Ibid.

70. See Karmon, "Fatah and the Popular Front for the Liberation of Palestine."

71. See "What Was the 1970 Jordanian-Palestinian Conflict Known as Black September?" *Israeli-Palestinian Conflict*, available at http://israelipalestinian.procon.org/view.answers.php?questionID=000435.

72. See ICT, "Terrorist Organizations: The Popular Front for the Liberation of Palestine."

73. See Tessler, *A History of the Israeli-Palestinian Conflict.*

74. See Yodfat and Arnon-Ohanna, *PLO: Strategy and Tactics.*

75. See Amos II, *Palestinian Resistance*; and Thomas L. Friedman, *From Beirut to Jerusalem* (New York: Farrar Straus Giroux, 1989).

76. See Yodfat and Arnon-Ohanna, *PLO: Strategy and Tactics.*

77. International Policy Institute for Counter-Terrorism, "Terrorist Organizations: The Abu Nidal Organization," www.ict.org.il/.

78. Ibid.

79. Ewen MacAskill and Richard Nelsson, "Mystery Death of Abu Nidal, Once the World's Most Wanted Terrorist," *The Guardian*, August 19, 2002.

80. Foreign Relations of the United States, Vol. 8 (Washington: Government Printing Office, 1945).

81. See Noam Chomsky and Gilbert Achcar, *Perilous Power: The Middle East and U.S. Foreign Policy: Dialogues on Terror, Democracy, War and Justice* (New York: Penguin Books, 2007); Bernard Lewis, *What Went Wrong? The Clash Between Islam and Modernity in the Middle East* (New York: Harper Perennial, 2003); and Daniel Yergin, *The Prize: The Epic Quest for Oil, Money and Power* (New York: Free Press, 1991).

82. Michael Bishku, "The 1958 American Intervention in Lebanon: A Historical Assessment," *American-Arab Affairs,* Vol. 31 (Winter 1989–1990).

83. See discussion entitled "Early US-Iran Relations" at www.strausscenter.org/hormuz/u-s-iran-relations.html.

84. Sheldon Richman, "Ancient History: US Conduct in the Middle East Since World War II and the Folly of Intervention," *Cato Institute Policy Analysis No. 59,* 1991.

85. Philippe Migaux, "Al Qaeda," *The History of Terrorism: From Antiquity to Al Qaeda* (Berkeley, CA: University of California Press 2007).

86. The motives of Usama bin Laden relating to his actions on September 11, 2001, have been well documented in his fatwas (or messages) delivered in August 1996 and February 1998, as well as his "Letter to America" (November 24, 2002) and his taped broadcast on the attacks in 2004.

87. "Operation Iraqi Freedom: President Discusses Beginning of Operation Iraqi Freedom," http://georgewbush-whitehouse.archives.gov/news/releases/2003/03/20030322.html.

88. David Drezner, "Diplomacy is Dangerous Business, a Fact Washington Needs to Remember," Foreignpolicy.com, November 19, 2012, www.foreignpolicy.com/posts/2012/11/19/diplomacy_is_dangerous_business_a_fact_washington_needs_to_remember.

89. See U.S. Department of Defense, available at www.defense.gov/news/casualty.pdf.

90. Exact numbers are unavailable; however, estimates are provided by Iraq Body Count. See www.iraqbodycount.org/

91. See Bernard Lewis, *The Crisis of Islam: Holy War and Unholy Terror* (New York: Random House, 2004).

Understanding the Middle East and Islam

CHAPTER

3

Learning Objectives

After completing this chapter, you should be able to:

1. Describe the geographical, historical, and cultural aspects of the Middle East.

2. Explain the misconceptions of Westerners over Muslims and vice versa.

3. Give a brief history of the development of Islam in the Middle East.

4. Describe the differences between the Sunni and Shi'a traditions within Islam.

5. Describe the concept of "jihad" from both an Islamic and Western perspective.

6. Name the five pillars of Islamic faith and briefly discuss them.

Mecca, Saudi Arabia, is Islam's holiest city and the birthplace of the Prophet Muhammad. Nearly 1 million Muslims, many of them on a pilgrimage, gather for Laylat al-Qadr (Arabic for "The Night of Destiny"). It is the anniversary of Allah's Messenger revealing the first portion of the Qur'an to the Prophet Muhammad. Laylat al-Qadr falls on the 27th day of Ramadan, the month of fasting.

(Zurijeta/Shutterstock)

Introduction

The world of the Middle East and Islam is very different in comparison to the United States. It is characterized by a unique history, culture, religion, and perspective not observed in the West. Most Westerners have a limited understanding of the Middle East and Islam, often diluted by stereotypes, misinformation, and inaccurate characterizations by the popular media. Movies such as *Lawrence of Arabia, the Sheik of Baghdad*, and *Raiders of the Lost Ark* all contribute to this dilution. In balance, people in the Middle East and other Islamic countries often have a corresponding misunderstanding of Westerners. Their understanding is often formed by information from religious zealots, old American television shows, MTV, and a local media that is simultaneously pro-Muslim and often anti-Western. People from the West and the Middle East have a great deal of room in which to increase their mutual understandings.

The Middle East: Strife, Misunderstandings, and Turmoil

Based both on real differences and misconceptions, terrorism often puts people and cultures against each other. Some Westerners leap to the conclusion that the radical Muslims they hear about on the news from faraway places like Afghanistan, Iraq, Lebanon, or Chechnya are representative of all Muslims from those countries. Conversely, drone strikes and news reports of crimes by Western troops confirm the worst notions that Muslims have about Westerners.

To genuinely understand terrorism requires something more than knowing a few definitions and laws. Comprehending terrorism in a deeper way requires a careful examination of the social, political, and/or religious positions taken by the parties involved in a conflict. After analysis, it may be possible to reach a conclusion about different ideologies. Illustratively, Usama bin Laden (UBL) urged Muslims to kill Americans wherever they found them because there were no "innocent" Americans. However, much of the world, including most Muslims, was repelled by the notion that even a radicalized view of a religion would urge the slaughter of non-combatant children and women.

Comprehending the "realities" involved in insurgencies, civil wars, insurrections, revolutions, or other labels of irregular warfare can also be difficult. Terrorism is a tactic commonly used in the irregular wars that seem so common in the Middle East. Is it the government or insurgents, both of which use terrorism, that really represent the best interests of the people? Could both or neither have those best interests in mind? Are these irregular wars really just over the form of government to be instituted or maintained and who is in power? Is it morally wrong for the majority to rise up against control by a minority that imposes their will, views, and practices upon them? When a democratically elected official suddenly institutes measures and practices that began to alter the form of government and there is no recall or impeachment provision, what should be done? These issues occupy center stage in the Middle East where the governments more than occasionally come face-to-face with groups in their population who violently pursue their visions of the future. The rise and fall of Egyptian President Mohamed Morsi illustrates some of these issues.

President Mohamed Morsi was democratically elected in 2012. He rapidly lost popular support because he seemed unable to govern, used excessive force to quell civic uprisings, and economic problems continued to increase. Even more troubling to a majority of citizens was that Morsi, a former leader and heavily supported by the **Muslim Brotherhood (MB)**, was moving Egypt toward an Islamic state, which the military also opposed. Seventy percent of Egyptians were dissatisfied with Morsi and 74 percent lacked confidence in the MB to actually govern.[1]

In 2013, after just one year in office, the military removed Morsi from power and established an interim government. However, the minority Muslim Brotherhood strongly supported Morsi and demanded his release and reinstatement. The MB and other pro-Morsi factions held massive demonstrations in Cairo and other Egyptian cities that produced over

Muslim Brotherhood (MB)
An Islamic fundamental movement stemming from the writings of the radical Islamic scholars Hassan al-Banna and Sayyid Qutb in twentieth-century Egypt. See Chapter 4.

Quick Facts
Soldier Sentenced to Life in Prison with No Possibility of Parole

An American Army Staff Sergeant with a total of four combat tours in Iraq and Afghanistan went on a rampage one night in an Iraqi family compound.[2] He murdered sixteen civilians, most of them women and children. Some Iraqi family members came to the military trial in 2013 to see how American justice worked and were disappointed that the Staff Sergeant was not executed. He did receive a life imprisonment sentence without the possibility of parole. Clearly, the concept of "justice" based on a Western Christian perspective was different from one based on a Middle Eastern, Islamic culture.

1,000 deaths among military, police, and pro- and anti-Morsi factions. At the same time, the MB and/or its supporters attacked, vandalized, and/or burned at least 60 Egyptian Christian churches and an unknown number of Christian businesses.[3] There were also pro-Morsi demonstrations in a number of other countries, although they were far less violent.

Initially, the Egyptian Armed Forces arrested some thirty-five Muslim Brotherhood members who died while in custody. There are two narratives for their deaths. The first is that while in a truck convoy the MB members suffocated from tear gas fired at them to prevent their escape. The second is that they were summarily executed (shot) while in the trucks.[4] No follow-up investigation was ever conducted to confirm the actual cause of death.

After the Muslim Brotherhood prisoners in the convoy were suffocated or executed, the MB canceled public demonstrations and rallies. The reason for the cancellations may be twofold. First, the convoy deaths, and second, the interim government continued arresting MB members on sight throughout the country, including most of its declared leaders. From among those arrested in the crackdown, 1,000 or more were killed in mass shootings.[5] Additionally, a court issued an injunction dissolving the Muslim Brotherhood and seized its assets.[6] However, the MB did not buckle under to the forces arrayed against it. The MB announced it had been an important historical and cultural element of Egyptian and Islamic society for nearly a century and that an illegal judicial decision couldn't change that fact.[7]

In addition, in 2015, Mohamed Morsi was arrested and sentenced to death along with over 100 other members of the Muslim Brotherhood, in connection to a series of violent jailbreaks during the 2011 Arab Spring, and the deaths resulting from pro-Morsi demonstrations in 2013. Ultimately, his trial was vacated as a political charade and his death sentence was commuted to life in prison.[8] See Figure 3-1. Thus is the story of Egypt's first democratically elected President, Mohamed Morsi, from leader of the Muslim Brotherhood to

Information Link
For more information on the Muslim Brotherhood, visit the official English homepage at www.ikhwanweb.com/.

FIGURE 3–1
A former leader of the Muslim Brotherhood and the first democratically elected President of Egypt, Mohamed Morsi now resides in prison.

(Xinhua/Alamy Stock Photo)

Quick Facts
The Decline of al-Qaeda?

Though al-Qaeda has largely been eclipsed in the international news arena by the shocking tactics and rise of the Islamic State, it is still a force to be reckoned with in the Middle East as well as the rest of the world. The group has developed a long-term strategy of building alliances with existing Middle East governments, and shifting their mission to align with social priorities in worn-torn areas of Syria and Yemen. Under the leadership of Aymen al-Zawahiri, the group has taken on a much more supportive role, such as

supplying food, shelter, and clothing to civilian populations, delivering gas, and supporting medical and humanitarian services in war regions. As such, it has gained the support of local populations—and terrorism experts warn that the emphasis on the Islamic State has allowed al-Qaeda to reform, restrategize, and reenergize.

Source: BBC News, "What Has Happened to al-Qaeda?" April 6, 2016. See: www.bbc.com/news/world-middle-east-35967409

beloved president of the country to condemned murderer and now prisoner. The United States finally called the removal of President Mohamed Morsi by the Egyptian military a **"coup d'état"** and cut off much of its foreign assistance to one of its few friends in the region. Today, however, Egypt is ruled by Field Marshal Abdel Fattah el-Sisi, the former chief-of-staff of the Egyptian Armed Forces; a president who was trained in the United States and thinks of the United States favorably. Many of his leaders have been trained in America as well, and annually, Egypt and the United States now conduct joint military exercises.

Coup d'état
The sudden and quick illegal seizure of a government by a small group of existing governmental people, usually a group from within the existing military.

The Middle East: Geography, History, and Culture

The Middle East extends from the western Saharan plains of Africa (Morocco, Algeria, and Tunisia) across the vastness of Libya and Egypt and the deserts of Saudi Arabia to the eastern mountains of ancient Persia—Iran, Afghanistan, and Pakistan (see Figure 3–2). The area is bordered to the north by the remnants of the great Ottoman Empire—Turkey, Kazakhstan, and Kyrgyzstan—and to the south by the beginnings of the jungles of the Dark Continent in southern Chad, the Sudan, and Somalia. The Middle East consists of over a billion people representing almost every religion and a variety of cultures. It also has significant historical sites, some of which are referred to as "the cradles of civilization," in the Nile River Valley in Egypt and Mesopotamia on the plains between the Tigris and Euphrates Rivers in Iraq. The geographical vastness of the Middle East produces such diverse cultures that none of them can singlehandedly represent the region.

The Middle East is also a region of the world dotted with thriving modern metropolitan cities such as Istanbul, Cairo, Tehran, Dubai, and Riyadh, where billions of dollars in commerce are exchanged each day; yet, in other areas people still live as they did centuries ago, herding a few sheep and making a marginal living out of the land. This contrast between the coexisting new and ancient ways is among the contradictions found in the Middle East. Another key contradiction is that the region hosts historical and implacable enemies of the West as well as friends and nations who stand shoulder-to-shoulder with it.

Americans Ask: "Why Attack Us?"

After 9/11, a question many Americans asked was "Why attack us?" Contained within that question is the notion that we see ourselves as "good people" living in a progressive, human-rights-oriented nation. There is data to support that view. A Pew Research Center survey concluded that 81 percent of Americans have a positive opinion about this country.[9] Moreover, the United States has a long history of helping others. Illustratively, following World War II (1941–1945), the United States gave its former foes Germany and Japan $29.3 and $15.2 billion, respectively, in foreign aid to help rebuild their economies.[10] Annually, America gives $4 billion for humanitarian and disaster relief in countries around the globe and advocates for human rights.[11] Other humanitarian aid is provided by private American organizations. In combination, these efforts deliver food to those suffering from malnutrition; produce safe drinking water; give refugee relief to those fleeing wars or droughts; provide training, seeds, implements, and farm animals to help people become self-sufficient; reduce deaths from common diseases by giving inoculations; build schools that reduce

FIGURE 3–2
The modern Middle
East is an enormous
area extending from
North Africa to Western
Asia. The area is
composed of multiple
cultures, races, eth-
nicities, tribes, and
nationalities.

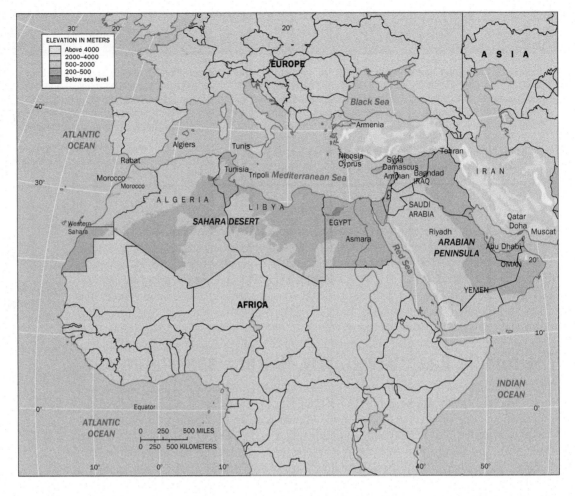

illiteracy; and lower infant mortality rates by 10 percent.[12] America leads the charge to end poverty and hunger throughout the world. Given such data, why was the United States attacked on 9/11? The answer to that question has nothing to do with what Americans think about their country and everything to do with what others think and how they experience the United States.

Surprisingly, a survey of countries whose population is predominately Muslim revealed substantially negative perceptions of the personal traits of Western people, particularly Americans. However, when the same survey queried non-Muslims in the United States, Russia, and Western Europe ("Westerners"), both negative and positive traits were associated with Muslims (see Table 3–1). Viewed as a country, America's reputation in countries with substantial Muslim populations is varied. There is no mono-lithic, global "Muslim view" of the United States (see Table 3–2). What is striking about the data is that Americans as individuals are seen nega-tively, but opinions of the United States as a country are more favorable.

Countries with populations that hold sharply negative opinions about Westerners and America may also have areas that terrorists can use as safe havens and a population from which they can recruit. However, those advantages are not suffi-cient to form a critical mass,[13] to move it from agi-tation to action.

There is an assumption that if the root causes of terrorism can be identified, then they can be eradicated.[14] There is, however, as we learned in

TABLE 3–1
How Muslims and Westerners See Each Other:
The Top Five Traits*

Muslims See Westerners as	Westerners See Muslims as
1. Selfish (68%)	1. Fanatical (58%)
2. Violent (66%)	2. Honest (51%)
3. Greedy (64%)	3. Violent (50%)
4. Immoral (61%)	4. Generous (41%)
5. Arrogant (57%)	5. Arrogant (39%)

*All "Westerners" were non-Muslims.

Source: "Muslim-Western Tensions Persist: Common Concerns about Islamic Extremism," Pew Research Center (Washington, D.C.), July 21, 2011. See: www.pewglobal.org/2011/07/21/muslim-western-tensions-persist/

Box 3–1
Who Was Usama Bin Laden?

The son of a wealthy construction magnate, Usama bin Laden (UBL) was born in 1957 in Saudi Arabia. He was raised as strict Sunni Muslim and rose to power within the fundamental Islamic movement as a student of Ayman al-Zawahiri in Egypt, who is the contemporary head of al-Qaeda. In 1979, he used his father's money and machinery to help the "mujahedeen" ("holy warrior") of Afghanistan to rid their country of the Soviets. It was during this time that UBL's notoriety and fame began to rise in the Arab world. For nearly 10 years (1979–1989), the United States provided financial aid to the mujahedeen through the Pakistani Army. Bin Laden became frustrated with Western influence in the Middle East, and particularly with U.S. support of then-King Fahd in Saudi Arabia. He became closely associated with Islamic radicals in Egypt who became the core members of his new group, al-Qaeda (the Base), and in 1996 declared war against the "Great Satan" (the United States). He was obsessed with destroying what he believed was a foreign government aimed at "adulterating" his sacred homeland of Saudi Arabia.

FBI MOST WANTED FUGITIVE

MURDER OF U.S. NATIONALS INSIDE AND OUTSIDE THE UNITED STATES; CONSPIRACY TO MURDER U.S. NATIONALS OUTSIDE THE UNITED STATES; ATTACK ON A FEDERAL FACILITY RESULTING IN DEATH

USAMA BIN LADEN

(JJM Stock Photography/Alamy Stock Photo)

The activities of al-Qaeda and bin Laden against the United States are significant:

1998: Suicide bombings of the U.S. embassies in Kenya and Tanzania killing 224 people

2000: Suicide bombing of the USS *Cole* in Yemen killing 17 American sailors

2001: Attacks on the World Trade Center and the Pentagon killing more than 3,000 people

As the mastermind and leader behind the September 11, 2001, attacks, Usama bin Laden became a major target of the War on Terror and was placed on the FBI's Ten Most Wanted Fugitives List with a $25 million bounty. On May 2, 2011, bin Laden was shot and killed inside a compound in Abbottabad, Pakistan, by members of the U.S. military (Navy Seal Team 6) in a covert operation authorized by President Barack Obama. The 2012 feature film, *Zero Dark Thirty*, chronicles the U.S. intelligence manhunt and neutralization of the "the world's most dangerous terrorist."

Did 9/11 impact you or your family? What impact did 9/11 have on the United States? Are there lingering effects? If so, what are they?

Chapters 1 and 2, no unified general theory that does so. As a behavior, terrorism is too complex and varied to be captured with the stroke of a single theory, although there are some gross similarities across different types of terrorism, for example, there must be a guiding purpose or doctrine that is compelling enough that it attracts recruits, financial supporters, and eventually, the willingness of some to die for the cause.

As pointed out in Chapter 1, terrorism is evocative—"it plays to emotion not intellect."[15] It strikes at the very heart of who we are as Americans. On September 11, 2001, for the first time in our modern history, the United States was rocked by an attack on its own land. People were afraid as

TABLE 3–2
Opinions of America by Countries with Predominately Muslim Populations*

Countries with Highest Disapproval Ratings	Countries with Most Favorable Opinions
Jordan: 83 percent	Senegal: 80 percent
Palestine: 70 percent	Nigeria: 76 percent
Pakistan: 62 percent	Malaysia: 54 percent
Lebanon: 60 percent	
Turkey: 58 percent	

*Surveys could not be conducted in some Muslim countries.

Source: Richard Wike, Bruce Stokes, and Jacob Poushter, "America's Global Image," Pew Research Center (Washington, D.C.), June 23, 2015. See: www.pewglobal.org/2015/06/23/1-americas-global-image/

their daily lives were impacted and changed forever; the privileges and lifestyle that we so enjoyed in this country appeared to be jeopardized. The ability to move about and travel freely was restricted. It was a contemporary day "of infamy" and one that not only changed the lives of many Americans, but also left them asking "why?"

Part of the answer to "why us?" lies with Usama bin Laden (UBL) and al-Qaeda. UBL announced to the world that one of the primary reasons for the attack was our lack of knowledge about the true political and economic conditions of the Middle East. UBL justified the 9/11 attacks as a response to America and its allies, which "disrespected" Islam by stationing their troops near holy sites (see Figure 3–3), exploiting the riches of the region, and supporting puppet right-wing dictators, for example, Egypt under former President Hosni Mubarak, who helped to further subjugate Muslims. UBL made it very clear that he believed Western goals in the Middle East were much more motivated by its self-interest and quest for oil than in safeguarding the human rights of the people in that land.

FIGURE 3–3
Marines near the border Saudi
Arabia shares with Iraq. Two of
Islam's holiest places, Mecca
and Medina, are located in Saudi
Arabia.

*(Sgt. Nathan K. LaForte/United
States Marine Corps)*

Secular
Separation of church (religion) and state
or government.

Muhammad
Born in 570 A.D. in Mecca, the Prophet
Muhammad was believed to be the final
messenger of God and the founder of the
Islam religion.

Muslim
From the Arabic root word for Islam, literally one who submits to the will of God;
westernized to "Moslem" or "Muslim."

Kingsley identifies four common "Whys" that explain terrorism: (1) Western scholars tend to blame it on radical Islamic
interpretations of the Qur'an; (2) liberal explanations rest on
the belief that social and political conditions foster authoritarianism, to which terrorism is a reaction; (3) others suggest that
social and political conditions are burning embers, often silently
opposed by people. Those embers are fanned into flames by
radical Islamic ideology, which gives rise and legitimacy to terrorism; and (4) globalization and modernity threaten religions,
such as Islam, disregard human rights, fracture traditional values and cultures, and blur national identity and sovereignty.[16]
Those opposed to what they regard as the adverse features of
globalization and modernity resort to terrorism in retaliation for
the things being forced upon them. Saighal takes a contrary view
of this explanation. He argues that Muslims push their communities back into medieval practices that perpetuate a clash of
civilizations between the Middle East and the West.[17]

Parenthetically, Muslims also ask "Why?" Illustratively, in
India and Myanmar, formerly Burma, there is a history of distrust and hatred between Buddhists and Muslims. Episodically,
one or the other goes on murderous rampages. In Myanmar during 2012, Buddhists killed 150 Muslims, causing 100,000 of them
to relocate to a less hostile place, including refugee camps.[18]

The Prophet Muhammad and the Beginning of Islam

To understand the Middle East, you must have a basic understanding of Islam. It is more than just a religion; it is a prescription for a total way of life, both individually and collectively.[19]
It visibly permeates life in the Middle East, including everyday
life, business, and government. This is in sharp contrast to nations like the United States (a
secular nation) where there is a separation of state and religion.

Like Judaism and Christianity, Islam traces its lineage to the "father of all people"
Ibrahim (Abraham). According to religious tradition, Abraham was the first of the significant prophets to make covenants (agreements) with God ("Allah" in Arabic). That covenant relationship became the foundation of the three faiths: Judaism, Christianity, and
Islam. In Islam, the Old and New Testaments are integral parts of their tradition and most
of the Hebrew prophets are revered as messengers from God. Muslims do not believe in the
divinity of Jesus, but honor him as an especially esteemed prophet. The ultimate and final
messenger within the Islamic tradition is the Prophet **Muhammad**. Muslims often say the
phrase "peace be upon him" after speaking or hearing the name of the Prophet Muhammad,
to show respect and humility in using the name of their most revered religious founder and
leader. "Muhammad" in Arabic means "highly praised."

Islam comes from the Arabic word "aslam," meaning total submission to Allah. A root
Arabic word for aslam is "salaam," which has several meanings, but is usually interpreted as
"peace."[20] The people of Islam are called **Muslim**. The word originates from the Arabic root
word for Islam—"s, l, and m." Arabic grammar rules allow different words to be combined
with root words and hence, a Muslim is literally one who submits himself/herself to the will
of God. This includes obeying Allah in his commandments, doing what is allowed, and avoiding that which is forbidden.

Muhammad was born around 570 A.D. in Mecca, on the western coast of the Arabian
Peninsula near the Red Sea. An orphan, Muhammad was raised by his grandfather. After
his grandfather died, his uncle, Abu Talib, assumed that duty, raising Muhammad alongside
his own son, Ali ibn Abi Talib, who after the Prophet's death became his fourth successor. Muhammad became a successful businessman who rejected the widespread worship of

Box 3-2
Women's Rights in Saudi Arabia and Iran

Both Saudi Arabia and Iran laud their societies as being progressive when it comes to women's right, with official changes and proclamations that value equality and education for women. For instance, Saudi Arabia allowed women to vote and run for office for the first time in 2015, and Iranian women make up the majority of university students in that country. However, there are still major limitations despite this progress. In both countries, women are limited in dress and must submit to restrictions related to marriage, divorce, and citizenship rights, and they face discrimination in sports, travel, work, and the subjects they are allowed to study at a university. Saudi women are still restricted from driving and the country bases much of its Constitution on Sharia law, making equality an almost impossible standard. And in the Islamic Republic of Iran, the Supreme Leader of the Revolutionary Council that governs the country is constitutionally headed by the leader of the Shi'a Islamic religion, currently Ayatollah Ali Khamenei. Women's rights are severely restricted in Iran, with disobedience carrying heavy penalties, including corporal punishment, such as flogging and stoning, to prison sentences and fines. According to Ayatollah Khamenei, "gender equality" is unacceptable to the Islamic Republic of Iran.[21]

As an example, in Iran, according to the *Islamic Penal Code of the Islamic Republic of Iran –Book Five:*

"Women, who appear in public places and roads without wearing an Islamic hijab [veil], shall be sentenced to ten days to two months' imprisonment or a fine of fifty thousand to five hundred Rials."

And in Saudi Arabia, *Fatwa from Sheikh Abdul Aziz bin Abdullah bin Baz, former chairman of the Senior Council of Ulama:*

"There is no doubt that such [driving] is not allowed. Women driving lead to many evils and negative consequences. Included among these is her mixing with men without her being on her guard. It also leads to the evil sins due to which such an action is forbidden."

Further, women must dress modestly in both countries, covering all part of the body except the hands and eyes. The custom of dressing modestly is call "**hijab**," which also refers specifically to a scarf that covers a woman's hair. Women in both countries, as well as for other Islamic women around the world who chose to do so, customarily wear a loose-fitting, long garment (abaya). If not wearing a hijab, a "niqab" that covers the head and face, except for a small opening for the eyes, may be worn. In the greater Islamic world today, hijab often reflects personal taste in color and personality.

Though women's rights in both countries have progressed, women are still quite restricted. Do you think that these limitations will continue to evolve? Further, many Muslim women feel that dressing hijab is quite progressive and "liberates" them from the pressures of Western style and influence, breaking stereotypic roles of "what" a women should look like and be. What do you think?

▲ Women (wearing niqab) vote in the Saudi election for the first time in 2015.

(Dina Fouad/Afp Photo/Stringer/Getty Images)

▲ Indonesian woman wearing hijab and abaya.

(Wf Sihardian/NurPhoto/Sipa USA/Newscom)

multiple deities and idols. Periodically, he would retreat to the mountains to a cave, "Hira." There, Muhammad meditated, reflected, and prayed alone, seeking truth about religion and life. Allah selected Muhammad to be "Rasul Allah," the final messenger of Allah. According to Muslim belief, Muhammad was 40 when *Jibra'il* (the Archangel Gabriel) visited him in Hira and revealed the first portions of what cumulatively became the **Holy or Noble Qur'an**. Gabriel's revelations continued over a period of 23 years, ending the year Muhammad died. As he received the revelations, Muhammad recited them to his daughter Fatima and an inner circle of friends and companions, which faithfully reduced them to writing.

The Qur'an consists of 114 "suras" (chapters) defining everything from the nature of God and Man to the everyday rituals of cleanliness and bathing. The Qur'an contains Islam's primary instructions and tenets. Muhammad shared the revelations with a growing number of believers. Similar to Jesus (and other religious founders), Muhammad was accepted in

Holy or Noble Qur'an
The central book of Islam consisting of 114 chapters developed through the visits of the Archangel Gabriel to the Prophet Muhammad. Simply, the Qur'an or Koran in Western nations.

Sunni
The "True Path of Allah" and the largest of the two primary Muslim traditions within Islam.

Shi'a or Shiite
One of the two primary Muslim traditions stemming from the "Shi'at Ali" or "The Party of Ali." Followers of the Shi'a tradition believe that Ali was given a divine right of successorship to lead the Muslim community after the death of the Prophet Muhammad.

Abu Bakr
The first Caliph or ruler of Arabia and the leader of the Muslim community after the death of the Prophet Muhammad.

Ummah
The worldwide community of the Islamic faithful.

Information Link
For more information on the Sunni and Shi'a traditions within Islam, visit the homepage for *The Muslim Observer*, an online periodical that provides news on Islamic issues both within the United States and internationally, at http://muslimmedianetwork.com/mmn/.

some places and denounced in others. A few times he was forced to flee for his life because of opposition to his message.

In early Christian tradition after the death of Jesus, his followers fell into two separate camps. One faction more closely followed the writings of the Apostle Paul and centered primarily in Constantinople (now Istanbul, Turkey) as the Eastern Church. The Apostle Peter was the first leader of the early Christian Church in Rome, which evolved into the Catholic Church, which is led by a "divinely inspired" leader, the Pope. The two camps were more than geographically separated; there were irreconcilable difference (e.g., the Eastern Church rejected the notion of the pope's infallibility in matters of church doctrine). Much later, during the sixteenth century, the Reformation in Europe resulted in the creation of Protestant churches, which separated from the Roman Catholic tradition.

In 632 A.D., Muhammad died, leaving the future of Islam to his followers. Like the early Christian Church, the response of the followers produced profound changes. One unintended consequence was a conflict that produced, again, two factions: **Sunni** and **Shi'a or Shi'ite**. These Islamic factions have existed continuously since the seventh century and their followers are, respectively, called Sunnis and Shiites. The Islamic scholar Husain Jafri explains the split within the Muslim world can be much better explained as a political difference rather than a spiritual separation.[22]

The Emergence of Two Muslim Traditions: Sunni and Shi'a

The death of the Prophet Muhammad led to a crucial question: Who is the rightful successor to the Prophet Muhammad? Those who came to be called Sunnis called attention to the fact the Prophet did not have a male heir, designate a successor, or establish a procedure for selecting his successor. Sunnis believed that the Prophet's successor should be selected by merit, not by inheritance, or birth or family.[23] Therefore, in their view it was proper for an assembly of distinguished clerics to elect a well-qualified pious person with wisdom who would follow the customs established by the Prophet Muhammad. An assembly of Muslim clerics elected **Abu Bakr** as the first Caliph of Arabia and the leader of the Muslim community, or **ummah**. Most of Muhammad's followers accepted Abu Bakr as the new leader. Abu Bakr (573–634 A.D.) was an early convert to Islam. He was a constant and close companion to Muhammad. Their relationship was strengthened by Muhammad's marriage to Abu Bakr's daughter, Aisha. During Muhammad's last illness he gave Abu Bakr the honor of leading prayer.[24] Aisha objected that her father was too frail for that leadership responsibility, but Muhammad insisted.[25] On his deathbed, Muhammad seemingly endorsed Abu Bakr as his successor by instructing his followers to close all doors to the mosque except for the door of Abu Bakr.[26] According to one Muslim tradition, Muhammad's last words were "God, have pity on those who succeed me."[27]

A small Hashemite group living in Mecca and the clan of the Prophet Muhammad advocated that Muhammad's cousin and son-in-law, Ali ibn Abi Talib, should be the Prophet's successor. According to early writings,[28] Ali alleged to have been given a divine right to successorship and had received a special mandate from the Prophet to become the next leader of the Islamic community. Ali was also married to Fatimah, the Prophet's daughter. Those calling for the election of Ali became known as the "*Shi'at Ali*" (or "party of Ali")— the Shi'a or Shiites. Although the Shi'a group actually arose several years after the death of

Quick Facts
Islam's Ummah and Caliphate

"Ummah" is used 60 times in the Qur'an.[29] It is also used frequently in the **Hadith**. The Hadith are reports of the words and deeds of the Prophet Muhammad, his closest companions, and the views of luminary Islamic scholars and religious figures.[30] Given its use in different contexts, there is some debate about its meaning. Ummah is the worldwide community of Islamic believers, which transcends race, geography, and national boundaries.[31] It roughly corresponds to those who believe in other transnational religions, such as Catholicism.

"*Caliphate*" means a single, worldwide Islamic nation. In modern time it is conceptualized by some as being ruled by both a religious head and an executive caliph. The last caliphate was dissolved in 1924 upon the founding of the Republic of Turkey. Iran is not a caliphate, but does have a Supreme Leader and a

President. The former is a religious figure with control over the military and judicial systems. The President has limited authority as the government's executive officer and is subordinate to the Supreme Leader. The President is elected by a popular vote, but the Supreme Leader is selected by the 86 clerics that form the Assembly of Experts.

Recently, the Islamic State has declared itself as the new Islamic Caliphate in the world and has claimed parts of Syria and Iraq as its country. While no other country or international organization such as the United Nations has recognized the Islamic State, it continues to dominate news through the use of horrific and barbaric tactics while fighting against coalition forces in that region. In Chapter 4, "The Rise of Radical Islam," we more fully analyze and describe the impact of the Islamic State on terrorism today.

---

the Prophet Muhammad,[32] they contended not only the divinely inspired right of Ali, but also the descendant leadership of the Muslim community through Fatimah, the daughter of the Prophet. Hence, the leadership of Islam should be transmitted exclusively through the Prophet's bloodline.[33]

The Party of Ali objected to Abu Bakr being selected by a vote. They believed that because Allah had selected Muhammad to be the final prophet, Allah intended that the male family member closest to Muhammad should follow. Therefore, the selection of Abu Bakr violated divine order. Ali was Muhammad's cousin and son-in-law by virtue of his marriage to the Prophet's daughter Fatima. Ali in his own right was a substantial candidate to become **caliph**. He was a great warrior and greatly respected as "The Leader of the Faithful" and "The Lion of God." Arguably, there was some ambiguity about the Prophet Muhammad's preference for a successor. Although he seemed to endorse Abu Bakr, he also publicly said of Ali: "Whoever has me as a master also has him as a master."[34]

Ali eventually became the fourth caliph, leading Islam from 656 A.D. to 661 A.D. He replaced numerous officials with trusted followers, ultimately provoking an Islamic civil war during his reign. Ali was assassinated in 661, as were his two sons, Hasan and Husayn, who also became caliphs. To avoid persecution, the Shi'a fled east into the mountains of Persia (now Iran). Although Persians are not Arabs, the effect of the Shiite on them has been profound, reflected in every aspect of life from literature and philosophy to politics and, of course, religion.

A key distinction between the Shi'a and the Sunni is that the latter elect separate spiritual and political leaders. For the Shias, leadership belongs to the successors of the Prophet Muhammad as ordained by Allah. Each successor occupies the office of Supreme Imam and selects the next Supreme Imam to maintain the direct lineage from the Prophet to the present time. The Supreme Imam leads not only the spiritual life of his Islamic community, but also the political and temporal aspects of everyday life—a modern caliph. Hence, Shia government is nonsecular, combining Islam with the political dimension of rule. On the other hand, the Sunni leader is elected by the leadership of Islam. Sunni government is secular, meaning that religion and government are separated. The Sunni or "True Path of Allah" remain as the majority group in the heart of the Middle East, electing their spiritual leaders after the death of Muhammad by the consensus of Muslim clerics and leaders (see Figure 3–4).

Today the Shi'a tradition remains a much smaller yet vocal minority in the Islamic world. Only 10 to 13 percent of the Islamic population is Shi'a, and those Muslims are primarily located in Iran, Lebanon, Pakistan, India, and Iraq.[35] The remainder of the Islamic community is Sunni and populates the entire Middle East and much of Southeast Asia. The largest Muslim country is no longer in the Middle East, but rather in Southeast Asia—Indonesia, with over 205 million people claiming Islam as their religion.[36] The center of Islamic faith

Hadith
A collection of the words and deeds of the Prophet Muhammad, his closest companions, and the views of luminary Islamic scholars and religious figures within the Islamic faith.

Caliphate
An Islamic state where the political and religious leader are the same.

Caliph
The political leader or head of a caliphate or Muslim state; a successor to the Prophet Muhammad.

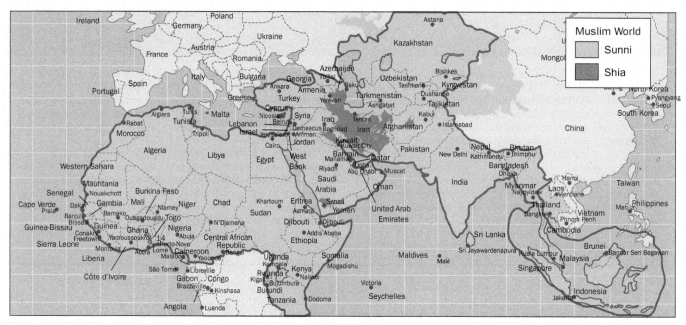

The Islamic Empire

FIGURE 3–4
The Shi'a population is primarily concentrated in modern-day Iran, Iraq, Lebanon, and Yemen, whereas the Sunni population is rapidly growing throughout the world, especially in Southeast Asia.

Mecca
The holiest city in the religion of Islam, located in southwest Saudi Arabia near the Red Sea. The birthplace of the Prophet Muhammad and the focus of the Hajj or Pilgrimage to Mecca.

Kaaba
According to Islam, the altar of Abraham (built by Abraham and his son Ishmael) and the focus of Hajj, or the pilgrimage to Mecca.

Jihad
Derived from the Holy Qur'an, the word *jihad* represents an internal struggle to overcome adversity and difficulty in submitting to the will of Allah (God). Perverted historically by Islamic fundamentalists to mean "holy war."

remains in the holy city of **Mecca**, the birthplace of the Prophet Muhammad and the site of the **Kaaba** (Arabic, cube), or altar of Abraham to which millions make pilgrimage each year.

The Concept of "Jihad"

Some 1.6 billion people embrace Islam in the modern world.[37] It is the fastest growing religion on Earth, with 80 percent of believers now outside the Middle East. Southeastern Asia generally, and Indonesia specifically, represent the concentrated new growth of Islam. For these people, Islam is an intimate personal connection with the same God worshiped by Jews and Christians—a source of strength, a way of life, and hope in a trouble world.[38]

The term *Islam* is Arabic, meaning "submission to the will of God," with roots firmly planted in the common Arabic word for peace: *salaam*. That may come as a surprise to most Americans, whose perceptions have been tainted by radical terrorists expressing the virtues of jihad against the United States, or the myriad of suicide bombers that have plagued Israel. In fact, the word "jihad" has a very special meaning to those following the Muslim tradition. Derived from the Qur'an, **jihad** means using all of one's strength to overcome adversity and difficulty in the struggle to submit to the will of God. It is a spiritual struggle, not a temporal (or worldly) struggle, to do good over evil. This strife occurs on two fronts: the internal and the external. The internal struggle can be described as the effort to attain one's own essence and perfection, whereas the external one is the process of enabling someone else to attain his or her own essence. In the words of the Prophet Mohammed, the first is the *greater jihad* and the second is the *lesser jihad*. As in Christianity, the body is considered weak, and is often tempted. The struggle for *greater jihad* characterizes a spiritual front over one's own ego and destructive emotions, desires, and thoughts (e.g., malice, hatred, envy, selfishness, pride, arrogance, and pomp), which prevent man from attaining perfection. It is not a struggle within the world itself. Aboulmagd-Foster observes that the inner struggle's work is within the soul.[39] It is a spiritual cleansing and, as such, an act of worship.[40] The purpose of the inner struggle is living a good life within the teachings of Islam.

The *lesser jihad* is much more materialistic in nature, consisting of physical acts to assist one's family, relatives, neighbors, and country; a call to strengthen the overall "ummah" or community of Muslim believers. Above all else, it is an idealized vision that reminds Muslims of what they should be: unified, connected, profoundly faithful, and practicing high moral standards.[41] Again, in parallel to Christianity, the *lesser jihad* can be acquainted more with acts of mercy and faith, or what are more commonly called "the beatitudes" that Jesus gave during his sermon on the mount. *Jihad* is the means of internal and external balance. It is a "holy war" that is fought within the spiritual context, and winning this war means reaching spiritual perfection and helping other so do the same.[42] In Chapter 4, we discuss the misinterpretation of the word *jihad* by radical Islamic scholars and clerics bent on rallying a war cry against the United States and the West.

In its truest sense, *jihad* was never meant to be associated with physical violence and most certainly not suicide bombing. Today, one of the most intense arguments within Muslim clerics is whether or not the suicide bombers observed worldwide will ever attain the spiritual bliss of Paradise since suicide within the Muslim tradition is strictly forbidden. The perversion of *jihad* began during the twelfth century (during the Crusades), with a tribal leader in Morocco rallying his people to repel the European Crusaders invading their land. It was a sacred duty to preserve their community, land, and culture from the invading "infidel" through physical war ... a "*holy war*" mandated by Allah to safeguard Islam (see Figure 3–5).

Similarly, other words were perverted and developed, such as the word "assassin" derived from the radical Shi'a Ismaili sect in Iran during this same period of time, the Ismailis. Literally translated, "assassin" means "hashish-eater"—in reference to

FIGURE 3–5
A page from a medieval book depicts Muslims and Crusaders fighting.
(Gianni Dagli Orti/REX/Shutterstock)

the ritual intoxication the assassins undertook before embarking on their mission of murder. Hoffman points out that violence for the assassins was a sacramental act: a divine duty, commanded by religious text and communicated by clerical authorities.[43] Similarly, the assassins were promised that, should they perish in the course of carrying out their attack, they would ascend immediately to Paradise. The same ethos of self-sacrifice and suicidal martyrdom can be seen in modern, radical Islamic terrorist organizations today (e.g., Islamic State, Hamas, Islamic Jihad, Jemaah Islamiya, al-Qaeda).[44]

Islam and Terrorism

The connectivity between religion and terrorism has not been without controversy. Several scholars have argued the role that religion plays in terrorism,[45] yet few accurately depict the immense complexity of a decision to commit oneself to violence and/or suicide. Religion may not be the reason or motivator for terrorism, but rather a means to understanding, and even accepting, political and social crisis. Without the crisis of living in dire poverty, in disease, in famine, and in suppression, Juergensmeyer argues there can be no suicide bombing, for such acts lose cosmic meaning without crisis.[46] Essentially, when people lose power in the present, they also lose hope for the future. It is in these conditions that the cosmic states of the afterlife (heaven, hell, paradise) take serious meaning in the justification of radical action, so often observed in terrorism and suicide bombing.

The words *jihad* and *assassin* have both been associated with Islamic terrorism today. Unfortunately, the spiritual and historical roots of these words are often forgotten and dismissed in our relatively weak understanding of the concept. This is particularly true in the West, as we struggle to understand such a different culture with such a vastly different historical and religious heritage. Unfortunately, it is often much easier to appeal to our emotional aspects by declaring the fanaticism of a religion that we do not understand or know, and that has been distorted by minority and radical perspectives for the last several centuries. Remember, religion—like terrorism—is evocative; it often appeals to emotion rather than intellect. Islam is a peaceful and beautiful religion that is *not* responsible for terrorism. The likes of Ayman al-Zawahiri and Usama bin Laden from al-Qaeda, Hassan Nasrallah

Eric Robert Rudolph was more commonly known as the Olympic Park Bomber. During the mid-1990s, he was responsible for a series of anti-abortion and anti-gay-motivated bombings across the southern United States, killing at least two people and injuring another 111. *David Koresh*, born Vernon Wayne Howell, was the leader of the Branch Davidian cult that was the subject of a 51-day siege near Waco, Texas, in 1993 that eventually led to the death of fifty-five adults and twenty-eight children after he set fire to his own compound. *James "Jim" Warren Jones* was the founder and the leader of the Peoples Temple. He is best known for instigating the mass suicide of over 909 individuals (over 300 children) in Guyana, South America, in 1978. All three of these individuals referred to scriptural passages in the Bible in order to justify their actions and strongly proclaimed their religion as Christian. Then, too, Adolph Hitler commonly referred to God, Jesus, and the Bible in many of his speeches and writings as well.

from Hezbollah, Sheik Ahmed Yassin from Hamas, and Sheik Abu Bakr Bashir from Jemaah Islamiya, as well as other leaders of radical Muslim groups in the Middle East that promote suicide bombing and the escalation of civilian casualties, no more represent Islam than Eric Rudolph, David Koresh, or Jim Jones represented Christianity.

The Five Pillars of Islam

Monotheistic
The belief in one God expressed by three major religions in the world: Judaism, Christianity, and Islam.

Islam is not a violent religion. It is a cousin to Judaism and Christianity in that all three have a **monotheistic** belief in one God. Islam emphasizes that all people are equal through the love of God (Allah) and it is based on five major principles or pillars of faith. These "pillars" represent the essential tenets of Islamic faith (see Figure 3–6). They are the primary obligations that Muslims must satisfy in order to live a good and responsible life according to Islam.[47]

Pillar 1: Testimony of Faith (Shahada)

Shahada means to testify or bear witness, and it is often cited as the most important of the pillars.[48] The Shahada is a testimony of faith in an eloquent yet simple prayer, similar to the Apostles Creed in Christian communities. It is the Muslim profession of faith, expressing its two most fundamental beliefs in a single statement.

> "La ilha illa Allah, Muhammadur rasoolu Allah."
> "There is no true god but Allah, and Muhammad is his Prophet."

A sincere recitation of this confession of faith before two Muslims is the sole requirement for those who wish to join the Muslim community. It must be correctly recited aloud with full understanding, sincerely, and without reservation. Although there is no requirement for the Shahada to be said publicly, there is some sentiment that it should be.[49] Others take the position that Allah is the best witness.[50]

FIGURE 3–6
The Five Pillars of Islam represent the essential tenets of the Islamic faith.

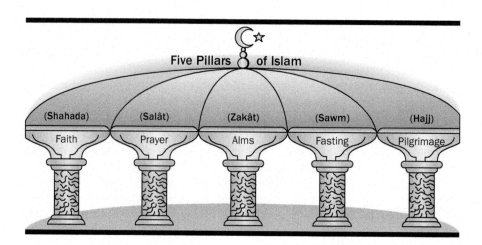

The Shahada declares that Allah is without equal and the only true God. He is all-knowing, all-powerful, and all-merciful. Allah is the creator of all things seen and unseen and everything is under his control and his command.[51] Only Allah deserves to be worshiped. Also acknowledged by the Shahada is that the Prophet Muhammad is Allah's servant and messenger. Muslims believe that understanding what Allah wants from us can be learned by adhering to the message sent to the Prophet by Allah through the Archangel Gabriel.[52]

The Shahada is recited in the Adhan (call for prayer) by the Muezzin (the person selected by each mosque to perform the Adhan) and is part of Salat (daily prayer).[53] It is whispered in the ear of the newborn and recited in anticipation of those immediately dying.[54]

Pillar 2: Prayer (Salat)

Muslims perform prayers five times each day. They do so at dawn, noon, mid-afternoon, sunset, and night wherever they happen to be (see Figure 3–7). Although each prayer takes only a few minutes, it is an acknowledgment by the supplicants of the importance of Allah in their lives. It is a quiet time, a time for reflection, a time of peace, and a time of prayer to Allah for guidance and mercy. When possible, Muslims go to a place of worship (a **mosque**) on Fridays for the noon prayer. Here, they listen to the local cleric (**imam**) discuss interpretations of the Qur'an or other topics which pertain to daily life and Islam. This sermon is known as the "khutba." The imams sing their praises to Allah over loudspeakers or raise their voices across windswept sands. Many Muslims carry prayer beads on which they murmur the phrase, "Allahu akbar!"—God is great!—as well as other phrases. In the Middle East, people actively engage with their religion five times a day. In contrast, in most western Christian nations (like the United States) worship is neither as public nor as visibly pervasive in daily life.

FIGURE 3–7
An Muslim man at prayer.
(Jasminko Ibrakovic/123RF.com)

Mosque
A holy place of worship in Islam.

Imam
Local spiritual leader of the Islamic faith, similar to a priest, rabbi, or pastor in other religions.

Although Islam is the dominant religion in the Middle East, it is by far not the only religion. By most standards, Islam is a very tolerant religion. As a reflection of the numerous and diverse ethnic populations residing throughout the Middle East, it is not uncommon to see Christian churches of almost every denomination, Catholic cathedrals, Jewish synagogues, and even the occasional Buddhist temple all existing within the same neighborhood in a Middle Eastern city. Potentially, radical Muslim extremists will impact negatively on this harmony.

Pillar 3: Giving Alms (Zakat)

"Zakat" denotes both purification and growth. Zakat is not a tax system that everyone pays in exchange for the delivery of some governmental service, such as the maintenance of roads. The compulsory annual payment of zakat by all adult Muslims and businesses that are able is both a reminder that what they have is a gift from Allah and of their obligation to help the needy and support Islam. Muslims owe zakat when they have or exceed more than a certain amount of money, called the **nisab**. The zakat is calculated as 2.5 percent or 1/40th of a percent of the amount that exceeds the nisaab. The collection of the zakat varies across Islamic nations. The state, zakat committees, charitable organizations, and mosques are all used to collect zakat.

Nisab
Arabic for "portion," the threshold after which a person is obliged to pay zakat; varies throughout the Middle East.

A list of people in need, such as orphans, the poor, and others, is detailed in the Qur'an. However, Muslims may also give other amounts on a daily basis to those in observable need, for example, the hungry, maimed, orphaned, or others who are reduced to begging (see Figure 3–8). This act is known as "sadaqah," which is voluntary charity that can be done in addition to the mandatory zakat per year. As one Muslim scholar noted, without beggars and paupers there could be no perfection for people striving to see Allah.[55] They provide the means by which the more fortunate can give, and hence grow in their own faith.

FIGURE 3–8
Afghan beggars pray outside of a mosque. Their appearance suggests a hard life and great need.

(Jalil Rezayee/EPA/Newscom)

Pillar 4: Fasting (Sawm)

Every year in the month of Ramadan, the ninth month of the Arab calendar, all Muslims fast from dawn until sundown, abstaining from food, drink, and sexual relations. Like many religions, fasting is regarded as a method of spiritual self-purification. By depriving one's self of worldly comforts, even for a short time, a fasting person gains true sympathy with those who go hungry, as well as achieves spiritual growth. Ramadan is similar to the Christian tradition of Lent or the Jewish tradition of Yom Kippur, wherein fasting and prayer often combine with spiritual reflection and purpose. The nights of Ramadan are often spent in congregational prayer at the mosque.

Pillar 5: Pilgrimage to Mecca (Hajj)

The final pillar of the Islamic faith is the pilgrimage to Mecca that takes place in the twelfth month of the Islamic calendar. This is a once-in-a-lifetime pilgrimage to the Holy Kaaba in Mecca. The Kaaba is a holy site built by Abraham and his son, Ishmael, according to Islamic tradition. It was the first mosque built by Abraham for worship. Again, the similarity to Judaism and Christianity in that Abraham is revered as the "father" of each religion is reinforced through the hajj.[56] Over 2 million people go to Mecca each year from every corner of the Muslim world. Most of the pilgrims wear simple clothes (usually two white pieces of cloth) that strip away distinctions of class and culture so that all stand equal before Allah. Symbolically, the hajj represents the spiritual journey that all Muslims are on, growing ever closer to Allah.

Quick Facts
The Hajj

The "Hajj" is Arabic for pilgrimage and represents the largest gathering of people in the world every year. Because there are so many people in one place, stampedes, trampling of people, fire, violence, and outbreaks of disease have occurred. For the first time in history, the Saudi government asked in 2013 that "elderly and chronically ill Muslims avoid the hajj." Additionally, the government has tried to restrict the number of people entering the country for hajj in order to avoid calamities.

Chapter Summary

SUMMARY BY LEARNING OBJECTIVE

1. **Describe the geographical, historical, and cultural aspects of the Middle East.**

   The geographical and cultural area of the Middle East extends from the western Saharan Plains of Africa to the eastern mountains of ancient Persia—current-day Iran, Afghanistan, and Pakistan. The area is bordered on the north by the Mediterranean Sea and to the south by the beginning of the jungles of Africa. It also has significant historical sites, some of which are referred to as "the cradles of civilization," in the Nile River Valley in Egypt and Mesopotamia on the plains between the Tigris and Euphrates Rivers in Iraq. The area historically represents some of the earliest and most advanced civilizations known to mankind and is the birthplace of the world's three major monotheistic religions—Christianity, Judaism, and Islam. Several countries compose the Middle East, including the recognized and major countries of Western Sahara, Morocco, Algeria, Libya, Tunisia, Egypt, Israel, the State of Palestine, Saudi Arabia, Lebanon, Syria, Jordan, Kuwait, Iraq, Iran, Oman, Bahrain, Yemen, Oman, Qatar, United Arab Emirates, Turkey, and Iran.

2. **Explain the misconceptions of Westerners over Muslims and vice versa.**

   Terrorism is evocative—"it plays to emotion not intellect." It strikes at the very heart of who we are as Americans and forces many people to have misconceptions about other people, cultures, and religions. For instance, Usama bin Laden (UBL) claimed that the attack on 9/11 was made in order to reveal America's lack of knowledge about the true political and economic conditions of the Middle East. He attempted to justify 9/11 as a response to America and its allies, which "disrespected" Islam by stationing troops near holy sites like Mecca and Medina in Saudi Arabia, exploiting the riches of the region, and supporting puppet right-wing dictators, for example, Egypt under former President Hosni Mubarak, who helped to further subjugate Muslims. UBL made it very clear that he believed Western goals in the Middle East were much more motivated by its self-interest and quest for oil than in safeguarding the human rights of the people in that land. Kingsley identifies four common misconceptions that explain terrorism, particularly involving Westerners and Muslims: (1) Western scholars tend to blame terrorism on radical Islamic interpretations of the Noble Qur'an; (2) liberal explanations rest on the belief that social and political conditions foster authoritarianism, to which terrorism is a reaction; (3) others suggest that social and political conditions are burning embers, often silently opposed by people. Those embers are fanned into flames by radical Islamic ideology, which gives rise and legitimacy to terrorism; and (4) globalization and modernity threaten religions, such as Islam, disregard human rights, fracture traditional values and cultures, and blur national identity and sovereignty. Those opposed to what they regard as the adverse features of globalization and modernity resort to terrorism in retaliation for the things being forced upon them. Others take a contrary view of this explanation, arguing that Muslims push their communities back into medieval practices that perpetuate a clash of civilizations between the Middle East (Islam) and the West.

3. **Give a brief history of the development of Islam in the Middle East.**

   Islam is one of the three great monotheistic religions of the world (along with Judaism and Christianity) believing in one God. The religion traces its roots directly to the Prophet Muhammad during the late 500s A.D. Muslims believe that Muhammad was visited by the Archangel Gabriel and presented with the word of God—that there is but one God—Allah. The communications between Muhammad and the angel Gabriel were compiled into the Qur'an, defining everything from the nature of God and man to the mundane rituals of cleanliness and bathing. In 632 A.D., Muhammad died and a struggle ensued between two primary traditions: Sunni and Shi'a. Both traditions maintain rightful successorship of the faith; however, the Sunni tradition has vastly outnumbered the Shi'a over the centuries.

4. **Describe the differences between the Sunni and Shi'a traditions within Islam.**

   The Shi'a stem from a group of followers of Ali, the son-in-law of the Prophet Muhammad who believed that Ali was divinely chosen to be the leader of the Islamic community after Muhammad's death in 632 A.D. They argue that the leader of Islam must provide political, governmental, and spiritual leadership to Islam as well as be directly descended from the Prophet. On the other hand, the Sunni or "True Path of Allah" tradition believes that the leadership of Islam should be elected and segregated from temporal and political life. Government should be secular, meaning that religion and government are separate. Sunnis represent about 85 to 90 percent of the Muslim population in the world; the Shi'a represent the minority and are primarily located in Iran, southeastern Iraq, and Lebanon.

5. **Describe the concept of "jihad" from both an Islamic and Western perspective.**

   From an Islamic perspective, the term "jihad" is derived from the Qur'an. The word represents an internal struggle to overcome adversity and difficulty in submitting to the will of God. The *greater jihad* characterizes a spiritual front over one's own ego and the destructive emotions often associated with malice, hate, envy, and pride that prevent man from attaining perfection; the *lesser jihad* is much more material and consists of acts of mercy and faith that are designed to help others. The Western perspective of "*jihad*" is based on a Middle Eastern perversion of the word meaning "holy war," and is often associated with violent actions and attacks by Islamic radicals and terrorists as exemplified by Usama bin Laden and al-Qaeda.

6. **Name the five essentials of Islamic faith.**

   The Five Pillars of Islam represent the five essentials of Islamic faith. They are: (1) Testimony of Faith (Shahada), (2) Prayer (Selah), (3) Giving Alms (Zakah), (4) Fasting (Sawm), and (5) Pilgrimage to Mecca (Hajj).

REVIEW QUESTIONS

1. Identify some of the major countries comprising the Middle East. Why is the Middle East such a unique geographic and cultural area?
2. How did Usama bin Laden view the United States (and other Western countries) and terrorism in the Middle East?
3. What does the word "Islam" mean?
4. Who was the Prophet Muhammad? And what role did he play in the development of Islam?
5. What is the "Qur'an"?
6. Describe the differences between the two Muslim traditions of Sunni and Shi'a.
7. What is the Kaaba?
8. Why is it important to understand the concept of terrorism from a Middle Eastern perspective?
9. What does the word "jihad" really mean to a Muslim, and how was it perverted to more contemporary Western perspectives?
10. What is meant by the term "monotheistic?" Name the three major monotheistic religions in the world.
11. What is Hajj?

CRITICAL THINKING QUESTIONS

1. **Monotheistic Religions.** As a class discussion, compare and contrast the three great monotheistic religions of Islam, Judaism, and Christianity. List the similarities of these three religions that all believe in one God. Then list the differences. Interestingly, they all tend to be exclusive in nature, meaning that they don't simply believe in and worship one God, but they also deny the existence of the gods of any other religious faiths. Do you think that this trait has made the monotheistic religions historically less tolerant than polytheistic religions?
2. **Compare and Contrast Islam with Judaism and Christianity.** Visit an Islamic mosque and talk with the local imam, visit a Jewish synagogue and talk to the rabbi, and visit a Christian or Catholic Church and talk to the local minister or priest. Ask them what they may know about the opposing monotheistic religions. Are they aware of each other's existence in the same community? Do they schedule meetings or events to share ideas and thoughts about the one God? Do the different faiths commonly mingle or worship with each other? Why not? How tolerant are they of each other?
3. **The Impact of the Crusades.** Explore the History website at www.history.com/topics/crusades. Watch the videos and read the articles relating to the Crusades. Were the Crusades sparked more by political and economic motivations or by religion? How do you think the Crusades of the eleventh through thirteenth centuries impact current events in the Middle East, and relations between Muslims and Christians?

NOTES

1. Omar Tewfik, "Poll: Egyptian Support for Morsi and the Muslim Brotherhood Plummets," *Arab American Institute*, June 17, 2013, www.aaiusa.org/index_ee.php/blog/entry/poll-egyptian-support-for-morsi-and-the-muslim-brotherhood-plummets.

2. This account is drawn with restatement from Jack Healy, "Soldier Sentenced to Life for Killing 16," *New York Times*, August 23, 2013; and Eric M. Johnson, "U.S. Soldier Who Killed Afghan Villagers Gets Life Without Parole," *Reuters*, August 23, 2013.

3. Abigail Hauslohner, "Ravaged Churches Reveal Sectarian Split Feeding Egypt's Violence," *Washington Post*, August 20, 2013.

4. Raja Abdulrahim, "In Egypt, More Than 35 Muslim Brotherhood Prisoners Reported Killed," *Los Angeles Times*, August 19, 2013.

5. David D. Kirkpatrick, "Egyptian Court Shuts Down Muslim Brotherhood and Seizes Its Assets," *New York Times*, September 24, 2013.

6. Loc. cit.

7. Loc. cit.

8. BBC News, "What's Become of Egypt's Mohammed Morsi?" (November 22, 2016).

9. "Opinion of the United States," Pew Research Center, Global Attitudes Project, 2013, www.pewglobal.org.

10. The dollar amounts are given in 2005 value. See Nina Serafino, "U.S. Occupation Assistance: Iraq, Germany, and Japan Compared" (Washington, D.C.: Congressional Research Service, March 23, 2006), p. CRS-1. The reason 2005 dollars are used is because the 2006 report was for Congress and the author wanted to use contemporary dollars for all three countries to make the comparison even.

11. Rhoda Margesson, "International Crisis and Disasters" (Washington, D.C.: Congressional Research Service, August 1, 2013), from the Executive Summary.

12. In part, the information is provided by "Fact Sheet: The U.S. Budget and Humanitarian Aid," www.care.org/getinvolved/advocay/budget_factsheet.asp.

13. On the notion of critical mass applied to social situations, see Gerald Marwell and Pamela J. Oliver, "Social Networks and Collective Action: A Theory of Critical Mass. III," *American Journal of Sociology*, Vol. 94, No. 4, January 1989.

14. An informative article on the causes of terrorism is Edward Newman, "Exploring the Root Causes of Terrorism," *Studies in Conflict and Terrorism*, Vol. 29, Issue 8, December 2006, pp. 749–772.

15. Robert W. Taylor and Harry E. Vanden, "Defining Terrorism in El Salvador: 'La Matanza,'" *The ANNALS of the American Academy of Political and Social Sciences*, Vol. 463, September 1982, pp. 106–117.

16. Okoro Kingsley, "Religion and Terrorism: A Socio-Historical Re-Consideration," *Journal of Alternative Perspectives in the Social Sciences*, Vol. 2, Issue 2, December 2010, pp. 550–576.

17. Vinod Saighal, *Dealing With Global Terrorism: The Way Forward* (Chicago: Independent Publishers Group, 2003), p. 20.

18. Thomas Fuller, "In Myanmar, Revival of Attacks on Muslims," *New York Times*, October 3, 2013.

19. T. R. Copinger-Symes, "Is Osama bin Laden's Fatwa Urging Jihad Against Americans Dated 23 February 1998 Justified by Islamic Law?" *Defence Studies*, Vol. 3, Issue 1, Spring 2003, p. 46.

20. Etim E. Okon, "Jihad: Warfare and Territorial Expansion in Islam," *Asian Social Sciences*, Vol. 9, Issue 5, May 2013, p. 171.

21. Human Rights Watch, "Women's Rights in Iran" (October 28, 2015). See: www.hrw.org/news/2015/10/28/womens-rights-iran.

22. Husain M. Jafri, *The Origins and Early Development of Shi'a Islam* (Cairo, Egypt: Qum, 1982).

23. "Islam-Sunni and Shia," London Inter Faith Center, www.londoninterfaith.org.uk/resources/islam-sunni-and-shia.

24. Wilferd Madelung, *The Succession of Muhammad: A Study of the Early Caliphate* (Cambridge, England: Cambridge University Press, 1997), p. 25.

25. Loc. cit.

26. Loc. cit.

27. Lesley Hazleton, "The Chosen Ones of Allah," *New Statesman*, Vol. 140, Issue 5058, June 20, 2011, p. 24.

28. According to the Shi'a tradition.

29. Robert A. Saunders, "The Ummah as Nation: A Reappraisal in the Wake of the Cartoons Affair," *Nations and Nationalism*, Vol. 14, Issue 2, pp. 303–304.

30. Ibid., p. 306.

31. Ishtiaq Hossain, "The Organization of the Islamic Conference (OIC): Nature, Role, and the Issues," *Journal of Third World Studies*, Vol. 29, Issue 1, Spring 2012, p. 291.

32. This group arose only after the death of the 3rd Caliph Uthman ibn Affan (656), at which point there was a great debate as to who would be the successor and leader of the community of Muslims.

33. Christopher M. Blanchard, *Islam: Sunnis and Shiites* (Washington, D.C.: Congressional Research Service, January 28, 2009), p. 1.

34. Lieutenant Colonel Adam Oler, "A Brief Introduction to the Sunni-Shi'ite Struggle: Six Key Points," *The Reporter*, Vol. 35, No. 2, June 2008, p. 3. Elsewhere this statement appears as "Whoever has me for a master, Ali is his master."

35. "Mapping the Global Muslim Population," Pew Research Center, October 7, 2009, p. 1, www.pewforum.org/2009/10/07/mapping-the-global-muslim-population.

36. "Muslim Population of Indonesia," Pew Research Center, November 4, 2010, www.pewforum.org/2010/11/04/muslim-population-of-indonesia.

37. "Muslims," Pew Research Center, December 18, 2012, p. 1, www.pewforum.org/2012/12/18/global-religious-landscap-muslim.

38. Don Belt, ed., *The World of Islam* (Washington, D.C.: National Geographic, 2001).

39. Brian Handwerk, "What Does Jihad Really Mean to Muslims," *National Geographic News*, October 24, 2003, p.1, www.news.nationalgeographic.com/news/2003/10/1023_0310023_jhad.html.

40. See Emad M. Al-Saidat and Mohammad Al-Khawalda, "Jihad: A Victim of Policy and Misinterpretations," *Asian Social Science*, Vol. 8, Issue 7, June 2012, pp. 202–207.

41. Garbi Schmidt, "The Transnational Umma: Myth or Reality? Examples of Western Diasporas," *Muslim World*, Vol. 95, Issue 4, October 2005, p. 575.

42. Fethullah Gulen, *Questions Put to Islam by the Ages* (Izmir, Turkey: TOV Yaymevi, 1997), pp. 186–219; and Ayatullah Kashif al Ghita, *The Ja'fari Sect and Its Essentials* (Istanbul, Turkey: Abdulbaki Golpinarli, 1979), pp. 70–79.

43. Bruce Hoffman, *Inside Terrorism* (New York: Columbia University Press, 1998), p. 89.

44. Ibid.

45. The role of religion as a motivator or causation of terrorism has been argued by several scholars. See David C. Rapoport, "Fear and Trembling: Terrorism in Three Religious Traditions," *American Political Science Review*, Vol. 78, No. 3 (September 1984); Walter Laqueur, *The Age of Terrorism* (Boston: Little, Brown, Inc., 1987); Mark Juergensmeyer, "Terror Mandated by God," *Terrorism and Political Violence*, Vol. 9, No. 2 (Summer 1997); Mark Juergensmeyer, *Terror in the Mind of God: The Global Rise of Religious Terrorism* (Berkeley, CA: University of California Press, 2000); and Jonathan White, *Terrorism: An Introduction* (Belmont, CA: West/Wadsworth Publishing, 2003).

46. Mark Juergensmeyer, *Terror in the Mind of God: The Global Rise of Religious Terrorism* (Berkeley, CA: University of California Press, 2000).

47. "Five Pillars of Faith," BBC, September 9, 2009, www.bbc.co.uk/religion/religions/islam/practices/fivepillars.shtml.

48. "What are the Five Pillars of Islam?" Islam Guide, p.1, www.islam-guide.com/ch3-16.htm.

49. "The Shahada Explained," August 28, 2014, p. 1, www.therevert.com/articles/the-shahada-explained.html.

50. Loc. cit.

51. Ibid., p. 2.

52. Loc. cit.

53. Loc. cit.

54. Loc. cit.

55. Ala al-Din 'Ali al-Muttaqi al-Hindi, *A Treasure of the Laborers for the Sake of the Prophet's Sayings and Deeds* (Beirut, Lebanon: Muassasat al-Risala, 1985).

56. See Bruce Feiler, *Abraham: A Journey to the Heart of Three Faiths* (New York: HarperCollins Publishers, 2005); and David M. Kay, *The Semitic Religions: Hebrew, Jewish, Christian and Moslem* (HarperCollins Publishers, Originally published in 1923 and reprinted in 2007).

The Rise of Radical Islam

Emin Sansar/Anadolu Agency/Getty Images

Learning Objectives

After completing this chapter, you should be able to:

1. Define fundamentalism, and provide a number of common assumptions observed in various fundamental groups, including Islamic fundamentalist groups.

2. Discuss the political and historical dimensions of Islamic fundamentalism.

3. Provide an historical overview of the Wahhabi movement in Saudi Arabia and the rest of the Middle East.

4. Describe the development and importance of the Muslim Brotherhood in Egypt, including the contributions of Hassan al-Banna and Sayyid Qutb.

5. Describe the differences between the Wahhabi, Salafi, Jihadist Salafi, and Islamic State movements.

6. Describe the roots of radical Islam from the Shi'a perspective (Khomeinism) and describe the group known as Hezbollah.

The Islamic State (IS) represents a movement of some 8 million people. With a philosophy rooted in radical Islam, they use barbaric tactics such as torture, maiming, beheading, and crucifixion to spread fear throughout the Middle East. Here, an IS fighter gestures with the raising of his index finger. The gesture goes well beyond the symbolic meaning of number 1, or victory, but signifies the *tawhid*, or belief in the oneness of Allah that implies the rejection of all other interpretations of Islam as idolatry. The raised sword gesture signifies death to all idolaters and disbelievers.

(Emin Sansar/Anadolu Agency/Getty Images)

Introduction

As discussed in the previous chapter, to understand the Middle East it is imperative to understand Islam as it permeates every aspect of life, both individually and collectively. Islam is not a violent religion, and is related to Christianity and Judaism in that all three have a common belief in one God. Islam is also the most rapidly growing religion in the world and radical Islam, as exhibited by certain terrorist groups operating throughout the world, represent dangerous threats to Western interests.

Fundamentalism

Fundamentalism
A strategy in which beleaguered believers attempt to preserve their distinctive identity as a people or group.

Marty and Appleby describe **fundamentalism** as a "strategy or set of strategies in which beleaguered believers attempt to preserve their distinctive identity as a people or group. Feeling this identity to be at risk, fundamentalists fortify this identity by a selective retrieval of doctrines, beliefs, and practices from a sacred past."[1] There are similarities between Islamic fundamentalists and other extremist ideologies that are seen in domestic terrorist groups found within the United States. These groups are discussed further in Chapter 8.

Selective Interpretation of Scripture and Doctrine

Both Islamic fundamentalist and many extremist or domestic terrorist groups rely on selective interpretation or misinterpretation of important documents. In the United States, the Bible and the U.S. Constitution with its amendments are selectively "twisted" to form the ideological basis seen in right-wing, neo-Nazi groups such as the Skinheads, Phineas Priesthood, and the Ku Klux Klan (see Box 4–1). An example of this selectivity is the interpretation of the Bible's account of human creation by churches belonging to the fundamental Christian Nation. These churches believe that when God created man, he made several "false starts." In this view, God used "mud" that became people of color. Although they had well-developed bodies, their intelligence was lower. Thus, these "false starts" were made by God to serve man. From clay, God created "true people" in his image and endowed them with superior intellect and gave them the Promised Land of the United States. Fundamentalist Christian churches also believe that Satan's temptation of man in the Garden of Eden resulted in the sexual union of Satan with Eve, which produced the Jewish race. This interpretation leads to the conclusion that the United States and the rest of the world are controlled by Jews, who are further demonized as the "killers of the Christ."[2]

Fundamentalist Christians believe they are locked in a vicious war (between good and evil) that will eventually culminate in an apocalyptic Armageddon pitting the Christian

---

Box 4–1
Memphis and the Three Parks

In 2013, the KKK Grand Dragon rallied members of the KKK, Aryan Nation, National Socialist Movement, and the Sadistic Souls Motorcycle Club in Memphis, Tennessee. The Memphis Rally protested renaming parks that formerly honored the Confederacy and two of its prominent figures: Confederate, Nathan Bedford Forrest, and Jefferson Davis parks became, respectively, Health Sciences, Mississippi River, and Memphis parks. Forrest was a controversial Confederate General and Jefferson Davis was the President of the Confederacy. In Memphis, African-Americans are a majority.

Organizations such as the Sons of Confederate Veterans and United Daughters of the Confederacy want to preserve and honor the history of their ancestors. These organizations are not hate groups. Is it right to simply erase their heritage? If you were defending the renaming of the parks, what would you say? What argument can you construct not to rename them? Is there any middle ground?

▲ *(Jim Weber/The Commercial Appeal/Zuma press/Alamy Stock Photo)*

white race against people of color and Jews. The U.S. Constitution and its amendments are similarly misinterpreted. Although fundamental and radical Christian groups strongly believe that the founding fathers of this country were divinely inspired, they only support the portions of the Constitution and its amendments that serve their purposes. The Second Amendment is interpreted as an inalienable right not only to own firearms, but automatic weapons as well. On the other hand, the Thirteenth Amendment, ending slavery, and the Fourteenth Amendment, requiring due process of law for all people, are dismissed by these groups as "fraudulent."

Misinterpretation of Symbolic Words

Fundamental and extremist Christian movements carefully select the words with which they identify themselves, such as "Christian Patriot," "free man," and "constitutionalist." These self-identifiers are intended to appeal to nationalistic and religious beliefs held by people for two purposes: (1) to soften the public image of fundamentalist and radical groups and (2) to attract new members who define themselves in similar terms.

Just as the fundamental and extremist Christians churches within the United States have misinterpreted certain passages within the Bible, fundamentalist and extremist Islamic clerics have done the same thing with portions of the Qur'an. Illustratively, the Arabic word "jihad" is a symbolic word focusing on an individual's inner struggle to submit to the will of God. In the Qur'an, jihad has little to do with physical war and nothing to do with a religious duty to kill Westerners. Fundamental and extremist Islamic scholars and clerics have misinterpreted jihad to fire the emotional response of people to fight for their personal identity, religion, culture, and the establishment of a worldwide caliphate. This chapter discusses the radical and fundamental Islamic movements that misinterpret the word "jihad" to serve their own violent purposes. And similar to their Christian counterparts, Islamic fundamentalists view their struggle as battle between the "pure" state of Islam that existed centuries ago with the "adulterated" world of today.

The Justification and Use of Violence Called by God

Demonstrations, counterdemonstrations, and violence are common denominators among fundamentalists and radicals on both sides of the religious equation (see Figure 4–1). They believe God is calling upon his faithful to challenge, refocus, and/or direct violence at the unworthy, nonbelievers, or other symbolic words they apply to justify their violence. Two benefits are derived from demonizing the group(s) at which they direct violence: (1) It

FIGURE 4–1
The clash of religions is readily seen as radical Muslims demonstrate in Turkey against a forthcoming visit of the Pope. About 25,000 radical Muslims of the Islamic Welfare Party participated in the demonstration. Paradoxically, the belief that Jesus is not the son of God is as offensive to Christians as the assertion that he is to Muslims.
(Alessandra Benedetti/Corbis Historical/Getty Images)

conforms their identities as a "good people" because they are doing God's work and (2) psychologically and emotionally within their movements they are absolved of any culpability or sin, for their actions are required by God and therefore not optional.

The misinterpretation of important documents by fundamentalist and extremist Islamic and Christian groups creates a problem. Uninformed people assume these characterizations are true and that they really represent Islam or Christianity. However, these extremist groups, movements, and their leaders represent an extremely small portion of the mainline religions they purport to be a part of: There are more than 2 billion Christians and 1.6 billion Muslims.

Eschatology
A part of religion that focuses on the last days, or ultimate destruction, of the world.

White's work on the **eschatology** of terrorism accurately depicts another commonality between fundamental and extremist movements, whether they are Islamic or Christian in origin.[3] Eschatology is derived from an ancient Greek word that essentially describes the end of the physical world. For many Christian extremists, the end of the world is shaped by their misinterpretation of the Battle of Armageddon as depicted in the Bible. These individuals often view themselves as the "last warriors" or "saviors of the White Christian race." In Islamic extremism, the oppressed Muslim views his or her culture, religion, and way of life as seriously jeopardized by Western ideology, and hence without future. There is only one choice before the end... the use of extreme violence and terrorism. White and others accurately point out that when violent eschatology is politicized on a cosmic battlefield in the mind of the religious extremist, all actions are justified in the eyes of their God.[4] The consequences are potentially devastating, with significant loss of innocent life and property. In the United States, we have seen two such events: the bombing of the Alfred P. Murrah Building in Oklahoma City (August 19, 1995) and the attacks on the World Trade Centers and Pentagon on September 11, 2001. Quite interestingly, both radical Christian as well as radical Islamic groups justify their use of violence because inexplicably, God (Allah) has given them the duty to purify their world. Hence, these groups are free to engage in ruthless bombings and the killing of innocent people to ensure their cause, such as radical Christians who bomb abortion centers. In a similar manner, some radical Islamic movements have misinterpreted the meaning of **tawhid**, or the indivisible concept of the oneness of Allah, to mean not only that there is but one God, but also that it is their mission to purify their world of nonbelievers by killing all others, including the destruction of Western nations, and anyone else who does not believe in their interpretation of Islam. Tolerance of other's beliefs is rarely a characteristic of terrorist groups.

Tawhid
The Islamic concept of the oneness of God (Allah). There is but one God (Allah)

Charismatic Leadership

Both Christian and Islamic fundamental movements have been heavily influenced by charismatic leaders. Within the Christian right, examples of charismatic fundamentalists include (1) David Koresh (1959–1993) and his Branch Davidian movement that ended after a 51-day standoff in Waco, Texas (see Figure 4–2); (2) Reverend Richard Butler (1918–2004) of Hayden Lake, Idaho, an early leader of the fundamental Christian ideology called the Aryan Nations; and (3) the flamboyant writings of William Pierce (1933–2002), for example, the *Turner Diaries*, that were found in Timothy McVeigh's (1968–2001) car when he was arrested within hours after bombing the Alfred P. Murrah Building in Oklahoma City in 1995.

Fundamental Islam has been led by the writings of various fundamentalist philosophers and ideologues. Several of these individuals wrote centuries ago about European colonization and the exploitation of their land, conditions that have long passed. Yet their philosophical ideology is given renewed credibility by charismatic religious leaders such as (1) Sheik Omar Abdel-Rahman (1938–), the "Blind Sheik," who was convicted and given a life sentence for his role in the 1993 bombing of the World Trade Center; (2) Sheik Ahmed Yassin (1937–2004), who as the former leader of Hamas (The Islamic Resistance Movement in the West Bank and Gaza) was responsible for hundreds of suicide bombings; and (3) Usama bin Laden and Ayman al-Zawahiri, both key leaders in al-Qaeda and the attacks on 9/11.

Information Link
Visit the Peabody Award–winning portrait of the standoff between FBI and ATF agents and David Koresh at the Branch Davidian compound in Waco, Texas, in 1995 at www.vimeo .com/13978271.

In each fundamentalist case, we see similar patterns. Selective interpretation of scriptures and misuse of symbolic words, combined with philosophical writings from years ago, are married to current political conditions by very charismatic writers and leaders.

FIGURE 4–2
In 1993, the Branch Davidian compound bursts into flames during the final assault by the FBI.
(Gregory Smith/Corbis Historical/ Getty Images)

Usama bin Laden not only had the ability to speak quite eloquently, but also had the financial means to support his ideological sentiments. Unfortunately as a government, we have grossly underestimated the power of such charismatic leaders and writers to influence other people and sustain such fundamental movements, whether they are Christian, Islamic, or any other religion.

The Political Dimension of Islamic Fundamentalism

Essentially, Islamic fundamentalist organizations attempt to "re-Islamize" societies that are already politically and economically ruled by powerful secular governments.[5] These governments are often allied with Western powers, including the United States, and often internally suppress their own people. In the past, some countries of the Middle East (e.g., Libya, Iraq, Egypt, Syria, and Saudi Arabia) represent suppressive governments or sheikdoms (kingdoms) where the tenets of democracy were nonexistent. There were no free elections, there were huge differences in socioeconomic classes within the population, and there was a concentration of wealth in the hands of only a few families, which often ruled the country and controlled all aspects of business and economic life. Many people in these countries lived in poverty, had no education, suffered from diseases and malnutrition, lacked access to medical care, and had no real political power. Most Arabs argue that this is the case in the West Bank and Gaza, where Palestinians live under the occupation of Israeli forces—freedom of movement is limited through imposed curfews, expression of divergent politics is often suppressed, and opportunities for a better lifestyle are severely limited. Faced with an unattractive future if nothing changes, some people are attracted to radical, fundamental, and extremist causes. Unfortunately, desperate situations spawn desperate actions, and the history of the Palestinian people as discussed in Chapter 2 highlights this type of desperation. Where there is no political power in the present, there is no hope in the future. For some, embracing fundamental Islam offers hope, if not in this world, in the next, for example, because of dying as a suicide bomber. The consequences of such desperation result in an opposing radicalization as well and the two sides are locked in a cycle of tit-for-tat marked by violence, terrorism, and military intervention.

The Arab Revolution

Beginning in spring 2010 in Tunisia, Egypt, Libya, and Yemen, events have yielded unprecedented changes in governments throughout the Middle East and North Africa. Many of these changes have come at the hands of violent uprisings, which frightened tourists away and deepened the poverty of the Middle East (see Figure 4–3). The **Arab Spring** is the term given

Arab Spring
Refers to a series of recent revolutions beginning in December 2010 in Tunisia aimed at increasing individual rights and freedoms for the people living in Middle Eastern countries.

FIGURE 4–3
Recent studies indicate that Islamic fundamentalism is most prevalent in poor, neglected, and impoverished rural cities in the Middle East. Here, a mother warms her two children near a bomb crater in Iraq.

(Mike Goldwater/Alamy Stock Photo)

Constitutional monarchies
A form of government commonly observed in the Middle East when a country has a ruling family or kingdom versus a democratically elected republic or dictatorship.

to these events (see Box 4–2). Civil protests, demonstrations, and in many cases violent uprisings from the masses have forced suppressive governments and dictatorships into exile or surrender. For instance, in 2011 one of the longest-serving rulers in the Middle East (41 years), Muammar Gaddafi in Libya, was killed and replaced by a Transitional National Council that installed a Constitution giving equal authority to various religious and ethnic groups in the country. And in 2011 in Egypt, the most populous nation in the Middle East, Hosni Mubarak resigned under siege and was replaced by a parliamentary government including newly elected members of the Muslim Brotherhood (a group designated as "terrorist" by the United States).

Stability in Egypt continues to be a problem as the newly elected leadership was ousted by the military in 2013. Similar changes have occurred throughout the Middle East; however, the oil-rich nations of Saudi Arabia, the United Arab Emirates, Qatar, Kuwait, and Oman have continued to maintain governments ruled by powerful families and/or sheiks in the form of **constitutional monarchies**.

The Historical Roots of Islamic Fundamentalism

Islamic fundamentalism is not a new phenomenon in the Middle East. Drawing on the early writings of Sayyid Qutb, Muhammad ibn Abd al-Wahhab, and Hassan al-Banna, radical fundamentalism can be traced to the early sixteenth century.

According to Murphy, the formation of Islamic fundamentalist movements can be historically attributed to a number of factors. These factors are the opposition to state authority; sociocultural and economic strife, which are associated with rapid urbanization and modernization; and the opposition to foreign occupation (colonization) in the Middle East.[6] Usually, more than one factor is needed for the formation of an Islamic fundamentalist movement.

Box 4–2
The Evolution of "Arab Spring": Chaos in Syria

—By Jamison Tolbert

The modern Arab revolution struggling for self-rule, autonomy, and freedom that began in Tunisia in December 2010 appears to have ended in a bloody civil war in Syria. What was denoted happily as the "Arab Spring," originated as a protest for human rights and freedom, has evolved into a bloody civil war, pitting old enemies against each other and forming new alliances that threaten the stability of the entire Middle East.

In early 2011, the Syria rebels demanded that President Bashar al-Assad step down from his leadership role. Rather than abdicate his power, he ordered open fire against demonstrators and stepped-up his military crackdown on the general public. What started as an internal group of protestors has now matured into a number of large rebel army encampments, collectively called the Free Syrian Army (FSA). Unfortunately, the Syrian Free Army is *not* primarily composed of Syrian rebels but rather of fleeing fighters from other countries like Iraq and Afghanistan. With new blood and strength in numbers, new alliances have also formed, ones with terrorist groups well-known to the United States. The largest of these unlikely alliances joined the Jabbat al-Nusra rebel army (part of the FSA) with the remnants of al-Qaeda (from Iraq). The new group has been successful, taking

credit for some of the most effective military victories against the al-Assad army and regaining control of northern Syria, including the city of Aleppo. In return, the al-Nusra have pledged their allegiance to al-Qaeda and their new leader, Egyptian jihadist Ayman al-Zawahiri.

The alliance has signaled the loss of international support for Syrian rebels and caused a significant and unforeseen backlash. Shi'a terrorist groups in the region have now linked with the al-Assad regime, pitting Sunni against Shi'a in a reflective war of historic proportions. Hezbollah, from Lebanon now sends armed troops to the al-Assad government, backed by the powerful government of Iran. With Hezbollah and Iran supporting the al-Assad regime, capitulation on the part of the Syrian government is doubtful. The United States is caught in the middle. Not wanting to support al-Assad, the United States has embraced funding for the FSA; unfortunately, this includes funding for members of al-Qaeda, the very fighters that were previously in conflict with U.S. forces in Iraq. Sadly for the people of Syria, the bloodshed and chaos continue in a stalemate.

Discuss how you think the United States can help in resolving the Syrian crisis. What do you think the U.S. policy toward Syria should be?

Quick Facts		
The Arab Spring (Timeline)		

Country	Date	Revolutionary Actions
Tunisia	December 2010–January 2011	Existing government dissolved; new Constitutional Assembly elected
Algeria	December 2010–January 2012	Military government ousted; change in government
Libya	February 2011–August 2012	Muammar Gaddafi killed; new rebel government
Morocco	February 2011–April 2012	Protests and peaceful changes in the existing government
Egypt	January 2011–	Hosni Mubarak replaced; Muslim Brotherhood elected to power; military junta oust (2013)
Lebanon	February 2011–	Civil war continues with protests and widespread violence
Syria	March 2011–	Violent civil war attempts to replace ruling Bashar al-Assad family; civil war persists and spreads to neighboring Lebanon and Iraq
Iraq	December 2006–	Saddam Hussein executed in Iraq; new Parliamentary government developed
	December 2011–	U.S. forces leave Iraq; open violence remains in many provinces
Jordan	January 2011–August 2013	King Abdullah Hussein monarchy continues with minor changes in governmental policies
Kuwait	February 2011–	Isolated protests; the constitutional monarchy continues
Bahrain	February 2011–	Isolated protests; al-Khalifa monarchy continues
Saudi Arabia	March 2011	Minor protests and no real government changes; al-Saud monarchy continues
Oman	January 2011–May 2011	Widespread protests yield government policy changes
Yemen	January 2011–February 2012	Violent protests succeed in change of government; still significant unrest in the country; al-Qaeda resurgent groups very active in country

Islamic fundamentalism is divided into two phases, which are represented throughout the history of the Middle East and the Muslim people.[7] Muslims and Islamic fundamentalists interpret the first phase as a positive period. During this positive period, the first Islamic state was created on the Arabian Peninsula and Islam was expanded outside of the Middle East (about 600 A.D. to the early 1900s). In addition, the Muslim culture and civilization were brought to their height with the spread of great Middle Eastern empires, such as the Hashemite and Ottoman Empires.[8] This positive period was soon followed by a second phase, which was the decline of Islam, marked by the Industrial Revolution of the West in the late 1800s and early 1900s. During this era, Muslims witnessed military defeat, loss of territory, and the insurgence of Western colonialism (especially after World War I), which continues to play a major role in the way Islamic fundamentalists interpret the world. According to radical Islamic leaders and writers, these conditions continue today, as witnessed by the **diaspora** of the Palestinian people and the establishment of Israel within the heart of the Middle East. Further, continued U.S. military involvement in Iraq, Afghanistan, and Qatar escalates radical beliefs that Western countries continue to destroy Islamic culture. These same radical clerics focus on the collusion of some governmental leaders with the West (primarily the United States) in an effort to exploit Middle East resources, especially oil. Again, these are not new concepts. Indeed, for Islamic fundamentalism, history holds the key to understanding not only the past but the future as well.[9]

Diaspora
The scattering or dispersion of people from their native homeland, often to a different, smaller, or less desirable geographic area.

Islamic Ideologies

Much like Christianity, Islam is a religion of "commandments," and most of them appear to be quite practical. As we learned in the previous chapter, these commandments shape all aspects of life. Islam not only deals with relations between God and man but also with everything that an individual believer or groups of believers encounter in everyday life, from politics to marital affairs to everyday eating and bathing.[10] The separation of religion and state (secular government) is primarily a Western perspective. However, in the Middle East and the world of Islam, it has been traditionally supported by the Sunni tradition. Conflict over secularism can be traced to the early split between Sunni and Shi'a traditions after the death of Muhammad. In the Shi'a tradition, as represented in Iran, strong emphasis is placed on the union of Islam and government, and enforcement of strict **Sharia** or Islamic

Sharia
Islamic law; the moral and religious code of Islam as prescribed by the Prophet Muhammad.

Quick Facts
Mustafa Kemal Ataturk

His father was a minor local official and his mother was religious and, unusual for women of that time, could read and write.[11] They named him "Mustafa" and he later graduated from a military academy (1905). While at the academy, one of his teachers gave him the name Kemal ("perfection") because of his academic record. After graduating he compiled an excellent combat record.

In 1923, Kemal Ataturk became the first president of the new country of Turkey and he became a comprehensive reformer. He abolished the office of the Muslim Caliphate, encouraged people to wear western-style clothes, discouraged Muslim women from wearing veils, abolished Islamic courts, and replaced Arabic script with a new alphabet based on Latin. The name "Ataturk" means father of the Turks; it was bestowed on him by the Grand National Assembly.

Secularism

The separation of church and state; the form of government where persons mandated to represent the state are not members of religious institutions nor are religious dignitaries.

Modernity

An epoch of time, usually referring to post-traditional and post-agrarian (feudal) states toward capitalism, industrialization, secularization, and technological innovation.

FIGURE 4–4
A 1923 photograph of Kemal Ataturk (1881–1938) with his well-educated wife, Latife Usakizade (1898–1975). They divorced in 1925 and she lived in seclusion, never discussing her marriage.

(Frank and Frances Carpenter Collection/Library of Congress Prints and Photographs Division Washington, D.C. 20540 USA)

law. Sunni radicalism is much more politically dynamic and focused on the development of puppet governments, the exploitation of people and natural resources (specifically oil), and other common conditions observed in colonialism. As discussed in Chapter 2, several non-Islamic philosophers such as Frantz Fanon[12] have also addressed these same issues as they relate to colonialism.

Muslim reactions to the term "secularism" have been influenced by Western history, politics and religion, and by the fear that **secularism** leads to the marginalization of their religion. Many Muslims interpreted European colonialism and attempts to introduce **modernity** as an attempt to impose Western customs, including secularism—separating religion from state and society—thus weakening the moral fabric and religious power of the Muslim community.[13] Other Muslims believed that secularism, and hence association with Western-developed countries, was necessary to build strong modern societies. Turkey, under the leadership of Kemal Ataturk during the 1920s and 1930s, illustrates this point (see Figure 4–4). Under his leadership, the country of Turkey was able to escape the strong secular beliefs of the time and has evolved into one of the only secular, democratic, stable Islamic countries in the world. Today, with a vibrant Islamic culture and a Western economic sentiment blending east and west, Turkey offers the Middle East a viable alternative to radical fundamentalism.

For others in the Middle East, Western ideologies and inventions such as democracy, capitalism, technology, and secularization are viewed as a direct challenge to Islamic existence. Secularism has been and continues to be equated (by most Islamic fundamentalists) with unbelief and thus is seen as a direct threat to the religious identity and values of a Muslim society.[14] Today, radical Sunni philosophers and traditional Shi'a beliefs merge to support the idea that government and religion should be one. This is a phenomenon that still rattles most scholars of the Middle East, as the Sunni and Shi'a traditions have been bitter enemies historically since their original split in the fourth century after the death of Muhammad.

The Ideologies of Islamic Fundamentalists

The inability of modern Islamic philosophers to resolve divisions within the Muslim world has created an opportunity for Islamic radicalism and fundamentalism. Islamic thinkers have borrowed various models of political, social, legal, and educational ideas from the West and adapted them to reflect and reaffirm Muslim goals.[15] Essentially, they have attempted to adopt Western organizational structure and mold it to fit Islamic values. Throughout the nineteenth century, often considered a period of Western colonial intrusion in the Middle East, the majority of people in the Muslim world watched as non-Muslim influences and ideologies eroded their religion, culture, values, and governments.[16] It was later, specifically during the early 1980s, that religious, economic, and cultural issues became the primary motivations of anti-Western Islamic fundamentalist movements.

According to Davidson,[17] Islamic radicalism and fundamentalism are rooted in the following assumptions:

1. The Muslim world has turned into a state of disorder because of centuries of political and moral decay. Islamic fundamentalists believe this decay began when the values within the Muslim religion were not respected or practiced diligently.

2. Islamic fundamentalists believe the Muslim world has been infected with immoral, secularist values and behaviors because of Western intrusion. These ways were an inherent part of the various Western-inspired governmental experiments of the nineteenth century, as well as the secularizing of legal, jurisprudence, and educational systems. Fundamental Islam viewed new trade and the potential for economic prosperity as a means to covet Western goods and adopt Western dress. They perceive these cultural changes as a direct threat to Islam and to the culture of the Middle East. New Western ideas of gender equality, sexual inhibition, and globalization are seen as further eroding Muslim society.

3. Fundamentalists believe that they need to fight this perceived decay by "re-Islamizing" the Muslim world. In order to re-Islamize the Muslim world, the Sharia (Muslim law) must be reintroduced (and strictly enforced) and most aspects of Western cultural and political influence must be purged, in most cases, violently.

4. The only way to re-Islamize society is to re-politicize Islam itself.

5. The West is seen as evil, as "adulterous nations" that pray to false gods, filled with men who abandon their families during divorce, are overly obsessed with sex, and adhere to corrupt practices that worship money above all else.

The radical movements active in most Muslim countries today work on these assumptions. Many of these movements began as fraternal orders, self-help groups, community action committees, or religious groups of clerics (such as the Muslim Brotherhood) that eventually evolved into political parties. Many of these fundamentalist groups have initiated some positive changes such as providing health care, education, and basic needs to the poor; for example, the Muslims Brotherhood operates hospitals in Egypt and Jordan. Others have been the spawning grounds for violent action and terrorism against many Middle Eastern governments as well as the West.

As previously discussed, jihad is a concept with multiple meanings that has been used and abused throughout Islamic history. Although jihad has always been an important part of the Islamic tradition, more recently, some Islamic fundamentalists and extremists have maintained that it is a universal religious obligation for all true Muslims.[18] Most Islamic fundamentalists believe that the restoration of Muslim power and prosperity requires a return to traditional Islam, and a political or social revolution to create a new caliphate, or Muslim-dominated state throughout the world. This revolution will undoubtedly be violent in nature.

Radical Islamic fundamentalists combine militancy with visions to inspire and mobilize an army of Allah, whose manifestation of a physical jihad they believe will liberate Muslims at home and abroad. Although the Qur'an states jihad is not to be used for justifying aggressive warfare, it has been and continues to be interpreted by some rulers, governments, and individuals as justifying extreme violence and terrorism. The scriptures of Islam have been misinterpreted to justify resistance and liberation struggles, extremism, suicide bombing, violent beheadings and executions, and unholy wars. Fundamentalist movements and groups, such as the Wahhabi and Salafi movements and the Muslim Brotherhood, go beyond classical Islamic interpretation of jihad and recognize no limits but their own.

The Wahhabi Movement

Among the more interesting movements in Islam is **Wahhabism**. It is the official form of Islam practiced in Saudi Arabia, other countries on the Arabian Peninsula, and elsewhere in the world. Wahhabi Islam was articulated by *Muhammad ibn Abd al-Wahhab* (1703–1792), who is recognized as the first modern Islamic fundamentalist.[19] In 1744, after receiving his religious education in Medina, he became the spiritual guide to the House of Saud (see Box 4–3).

Wahhabism
A fundamentalist interpretation of Islam stemming from the teachings of Ibn al-Wahhab in the late 1700s; widely adopted throughout the Arabian Peninsula expressing the radicalization of Islam and the alternative meaning of "jihad" as "holy war" against those that do not accept strict adherence to Sharia.

Box 4–3
The Founding of the House of Saud: The Holy Alliance of Abd al-Wahhab and Muhammad Ibn Saud

In the late 1700s, al-Wahhab joined forces with a young tribal chief, Muhammad ibn Saud, to lead a militant reform movement in Arabia. They united together to rebel against the Turkish Ottoman rule in Arabia. Muhammad ibn Saud hoped to harness al-Wahhab's religious passion and popular appeal to advance his own goal of political and territorial dominance in central Arabia.[20] In return, al-Wahhab sought ibn Saud's help for his own mission of reform, and an alliance of faith and power were born. They called themselves *muwahhidun*, "those who advocate openness" within the Islamic doctrine of the *Tawhid*, interpreted by al-Wahhab as "exclusiveness

Ibn al-Wahhab
(Courtesy of Extranewsfeed)

Ibn Saud
(INTERFOTO/Personalities/Alamy Stock Photo)

King Salman bin Abdul Aziz
(Xinhua/Alamy Stock Photo)

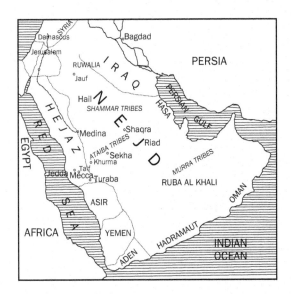

simply as ibn Saud) declared himself King of the Kingdom of Saudi Arabia. Ibn Saud fathered dozens of sons and daughters by his numerous wives. He divorced and married several times; however, in accordance with strict Wahabi law, he never had more than four wives at any one time. The Head of the House of Saud is the king of Saudi Arabia who serves as the head of state and monarch of the Kingdom of Saudi Arabia. In 1953, Ibn Saud died and leadership of Saudi Arabia was passed to his son. Today, the leader of Saudi Arabia is King Salman bin Abdul Aziz ascending to the throne in January 2015, the sixth son of Abdul Aziz and a direct descendant of Muhammad Ibn Saud.

of the One God."[21] Islam is one of the three monotheistic religions, and it is believed that all is possible through unity with the one God (Allah).

In 1788, with the help of al-Wahhab, the House of Saud ruled over the entire central plateau of the Arabian Peninsula, known as the *Najd*. There were literally hundreds of individual tribes of Arabs and Bedouins throughout the central Arabia plateau. Ibn Saud was the first to unite them under one ideology, and hence one leader. By the early nineteenth century, the entire Arabian Peninsula was under the rule of the House of Saud practicing the strict Wahhabi brand of Islam. Ibn Abd al-Wahhab did not live long enough to witness his vision as he died in 1792.

The House of Saud has ruled the Arabian Peninsula for nearly four centuries. All of the leaders have been direct descendants of Muhammad ibn Saud. In 1932, Abdul Aziz ibn Saud (known

(Stefanina Hill/123RF.com)

(Al-Tair/Shutterstock)

The Seal of the House of Saud

The Flag of Saudi Arabia with the Shahada emblazed upon it in Arabic, reflecting the *Muwahhidun*

"There is no god but Allah, and Muhammad is his Messenger."

What do you think are the "pros" and "cons" of long-lasting monarchies such as the House of Saud? Can you name any Western monarchies that continue today? How do monarchies differ from country to country?

Al-Wahhab labeled all who disagreed with him as heretics and apostates. He justified the use of force and violence in imposing both his beliefs and his political authority over neighboring tribes as the desire of God. These labels permitted him to declare a jihad, which he interpreted as a "holy war" on other Muslims perceived to not be practicing Islam as he interpreted it.

The central point of al-Wahhab's fundamentalism movement was that absolutely every tenet added to Islam after its establishment by the Prophet Muhammad was false and should be eliminated. Because of this, even today the people and government of Saudi Arabia, as well as some other Arab countries, wear traditional Arab clothing prevalent in the fourth century. These countries also maintain Islamic practices consistent with that time period, for example, having four wives simultaneously. Wahhabism rejects any attempt to interpret Islamic law from a historical, contextual perspective and treats the vast majority of history as a corruption of the true and authentic Islam.[22] Hence, Wahhabism is a very conservative, closed society tradition that is intolerant to non believers.

Al-Wahhab also emphasized the unity of God. He was upset at the widespread laxity in adhering to traditional Sharia (Islamic law) such as adultery, lack of attention to obligatory prayers, and the failure to allocate shares of inheritance fairly to women. According to al-Wahhab, only those who followed his teachings were true Muslims because they still followed the path laid out by Allah to Muhammad in the Noble Qur'an.[23] Many followers of Wahhabism prefer to be called "muwahhidun," or the unifiers of traditional Islamic practice.

The Wahhabis went on an unrelenting campaign against all others, for example, the Sufis, Shiites, and other tribes on the Arabian Peninsula deemed unfaithful to the Wahhabis' strict interpretation of the Prophet Muhammad. During the course of the late eighteenth and early nineteenth centuries, the House of Saud–led Wahhabis succeeded in conquering most of the Arabian Peninsula and much of what is present-day Israel, Jordan, and Syria. The Wahhabis occupied Mecca and Medina in 1802 and proceeded to destroy the shrines and tombs of the two holy cities. They continued their raids north and east into Syria and Iraq, destroying the Shi'ite shrines in the holy city of Karbala. These invasions and acts of violence still remain as points of hostility between Saudi (Sunni Wahabi) and Iranian (Shi'a) communities.[24]

Today, Wahhabism continues to be the dominant form of Islam practiced on the Arabian Peninsula, although its influence has been greatly diminished and its strict obedience vastly relaxed. Although Wahhabism is a minority position within the Middle East, it has nevertheless been influential in the formation of other extremist philosophies. The strict Wahhabi opposition to any reinterpretation of traditional Islamic law demonstrates a major influence throughout the Middle East. Radical and fundamental Islamists follow the Wahhabi example by opposing any attempt to reconcile traditional Islam with modern or Western culture, including issues such as gender and family, or the acceptance of modernity.[25] The Wahhabi movement has led not only to today's Saudi Arabia, but it has also encouraged Muslims to be concerned about society, politics, and the nature of the state (government). It was this growing concern among Muslims that set the stage for Salafism—another Islamic fundamental movement that has expressed violence as a methodology for reform and revolution.

The Muslim Brotherhood and the Beginning of the Salafi Movement

The **Muslim Brotherhood** movement was a political-religious movement beginning in Egypt in the twentieth century; its motivations and religious objectives were an ideological return to the nineteenth-century militant Wahhabism.[26] *Hassan al-Banna* (1906–1949) began the Muslim Brotherhood in 1928, specifically in reaction to British colonial presence in Egypt and its growing presence in the Islamic world (particularly in the Middle East)[27] (see Figure 4–5). In 1927, al-Banna took a position as a teacher in the Suez Canal Zone of eastern Egypt, which was then controlled under the British mandate. It was a critical time for the Middle East as European colonial powers took hold of much of the area through the mandate system described in Chapter 2. Al-Banna contended that the presence of the British and other European countries was eroding the Islamic values established by the Wahhabi movement in Egypt and elsewhere in the Middle East.

Muslim Brotherhood
An Islamic fundamental movement stemming from the writings of Hassan al-Banna and Sayyid Qutb in twentieth century Egypt.

FIGURE 4–5
Members of al-Gama'a al-Islamiya
(Islamic Group) demonstrating
against Egypt's then-President
Mubarak carry a picture of Hassan
al-Banna. It is believed Egyptian
security agents assassinated al-
Banna in 1949 because he was
getting too popular and was considered a threat to the oppressive
government. The United States
designated the Islamic Group as
a foreign terrorist organization in
1997.

(APAImages/REX/Shutterstock)

Through the Muslim Brotherhood, al-Banna had two basic goals: to liberate Egypt from all foreign powers and to develop a free state functioning under the rules of Islam. He believed that the Islamic faith was not just a religion, but an all-encompassing way of living and governing. By the late 1940s, the Muslim Brotherhood had become the most powerful Islamic movement in the world.[28] With over a half million members involved in a complex network of businesses, schools, universities, and clinics in Egypt, the Muslim Brotherhood began to engage populations throughout the Middle East (e.g., Syria, Lebanon, and Saudi Arabia).

The Muslim Brotherhood organized its followers into a close-knit, Islamic-oriented community designed to serve as the dynamic nucleus or vanguard in transforming the broader society from within.[29] All members comprised tight, socioreligious organizations with a network of branches and cells. Members were trained and reinforced in their faith and commitment to a stricter Islamic-oriented state and way of life. Religious instruction, youth work, schools, hospitals, religious publications, and social welfare projects were among the activities utilized to create a new generation of leaders within the new Islamic state to be created in Egypt. The Muslim Brotherhood grew rapidly as a mass movement, soon expanding from rural to urban areas throughout the Middle East, but particularly remaining very strong in Egypt, even to this day.

The Muslim Brotherhood regarded Islam as "the all-embracing ideology."[30] Again, Western secularization and modernity, with its separation of church and state, and the materialism often associated with capitalism, were seen, and still are seen, as evils that corrupt the very essence of man. The Muslim Brotherhood was not originally designed to be a political party, but its beliefs that the Islamic community was to exist in a state and society governed by Islamic law soon became drawn into the political arena. According to Munson,[31] the Muslim Brotherhood wanted to initiate several political, judicial, and administrative changes within Islamic countries including ending Arab rivalry, reforming the law so that it would conform to Islamic beliefs, strengthening the armed forces of many Middle Eastern countries, building mutual bonds and cooperation between all Islamic countries, and infusing the Islamic spirit throughout all governments.

In the years after 1936, the Brotherhood gained so much momentum that several leading politicians hoped to use it for their own political agendas.[32] In the pre–World War II era, the organization reached its height of power through violence, student demonstrations, political murders, riots, and the bombing of public places. Unable to use the Muslim Brotherhood for their purposes and confronted by its violence, Egyptian politicians became fearful and began listening seriously to its demands. By the time World War II broke out (1939), the Muslim Brotherhood was one of the most active and popular organizations in Egypt.[33] World War II provided a significant opportunity to extend the Muslim Brotherhood not only throughout Egypt, but the rest of the Middle East as well.

By the end of 1948, the Muslim Brotherhood became a hidden nation inside Egypt, with its own leadership, military, factories, weaponry, schools, and hospitals. Its members prepared themselves to take over Egyptian politics after the war. But Prime Minister Mahmud Fahmi al-Nugrashi Pash reacted to this threat by quickly jailing much of the Brotherhood's leadership, as well as other political adversaries.

The Muslim Brotherhood's dissatisfaction with the failure of Egypt's government to establish an Islamic state escalated into violence, armed conflict, civil war, and the assassination of its founder (al-Banna) in 1949.[34] Government repression drove the Brotherhood underground, but it could not escape the imprisonment and executions of its leaders and members in the mid-1960s. As in many movements, the suppressive tactics of the ruling government infuriated the Brotherhood, further radicalized its members, and to some degree increased its membership in the broader population. Although the Brotherhood was officially banned in Egypt and individual members were arrested and imprisoned, the Muslim Brotherhood continued to grow in many parts of the Muslim world. At the time of Hassan al-Banna's assassination, the group had over 70,000 members. Decades later, membership reached well into the hundreds of thousands and expanded into Sudan, Syria, Jordan, Palestine, and Kuwait.[35] The impact of the Brotherhood on Egyptian and Middle Eastern politics has been enormous as it maintains a majority of parliamentary seats in the government of Egypt and aligns itself with Hamas in the West Bank and Gaza against the country of Israel. Currently, the Brotherhood runs an extensive network of banks, investment companies, and schools focused in Egypt and the surrounding countries. It continues to serve as a catalyst for Islamic fundamentalism and radicalism, and has had a major impact on the interpretation and implementation of Islam in recent years. Almost every country in the Muslim world has an active chapter of the Muslim Brotherhood, fashioned on the model established by Hassan al-Banna in the 1930s.[36]

Today, the FBI reports that the philosophical father of all militant Islamic groups, the Muslim Brotherhood, has established cells in the American Islamic community as well, predominantly among students. For instance, the Muslim Brotherhood co-sponsored a convention in Phoenix, Arizona. The leaders of these groups urged their American supporters to "await an order to attack."[37] Nearly five years before 9/11, after the attacks on the American Embassies in East Africa, American intelligence sources discovered that other radical groups such as al-Qaeda may have merged with members of the Muslim Brotherhood.[38]

The Great Philosopher: Sayyid Qutb

Sayyid Qutb (1906–1966) has been called the "architect of radical Islam" and the "father of modern terrorism."[39] Qutb transformed the ideological beliefs of Hassan al-Banna and the Muslim Brotherhood into a revolutionary call to arms throughout the Middle East. He is remembered not only as a martyr of the Islamic revival, but also one of the greatest of all revolutionary philosophers.

Qutb was a devout Muslim and, like Hassan al-Banna, memorized the Qur'an as a child. Qutb was born in 1906 into a family of moderate means living in the village of Musha in Upper Egypt. He was sent to Cairo for an education that was largely of Western orientation.[40] Qutb served with Egypt's Ministry of Education until 1953 after his ministry had sent him as a representative to the United States. Visiting the United States was an experience that proved to be a turning point in his life. After his visit he became a harsh critic of the West, and shortly after his return to Egypt he joined the Muslim Brotherhood. During the 1930s and 1940s, Egypt was involved in the struggle to free itself from British imperial control. This struggle shaped Qutb's outlook much as it had that of his predecessor, Hassan al-Banna.[41]

> **Information Link**
> For more information on Muhammad Ibn Abd al-Wahhab, Hassan al-Banna, and Sayyid Qutb, visit the website at www.liveleak.com. Explore articles online about these influential and radical Islamic philosophers.

Quick Facts
Sayyid Qutb

Sayyid Qutb is often referred to as "the father of modern terrorism." He was an Egyptian author, writer, and revolutionary. He traveled extensively throughout the Middle East and Europe, and even lived in the United States from 1948 to 1952. He was a professor at Colorado State University of Education in Greeley, Colorado, as well as at Stanford University. He returned to Egypt after Gamal Abdel Nasser rose to power in 1952, and actively engaged in attempts to assassinate Nasser and overthrow the government. He spent more than a decade in Nasser's prisons and was eventually executed by hanging on August 29, 1966.

Qutb was disgusted by what he judged to be racial prejudice toward Arabs in the United States. The sexual permissiveness and promiscuity of American society, the free use of alcohol, and the free mingling of men and women in public violated his sense of Islamic law. He often referred to the United States as an "adulterous nation"; interestingly, Usama bin Laden was to later use the same terms in several of his video messages to the world shortly after 9/11. During the fifties, Qutb emerged as a major voice for the Muslim Brotherhood. His commitment, intelligence, and literary style made him especially effective within the group. His radicalization and confrontational views increased after being imprisoned and tortured in 1954 for his alleged involvement in an attempt to assassinate then-Egyptian President Gamal Nasser.[42] Qutb viewed society as being strictly divided into two camps, the party of God and the party of Satan.[43] There was no middle ground—only good and evil—a recurring theme in fundamental and radical religious doctrine. Qutb emphasized the development of a group of "true Muslims" within the broader corrupted society—the vanguard of Muslim revolution and militancy. He concluded that attempts to bring about changes from within the existing repressive Muslim political systems were futile and that a "jihad"—interpreted by Qutb as a physical "holy war"—was the only way to implement a new Islamic order.[44] In this manner, violence and terrorism were justified by Allah (God) as sanctified acts necessary for the reestablishment of Islamic order in Egypt and the rest of the Middle East.

Qutb's formulation became the starting point for many radical groups. In 1965, the Egyptian government massively and ruthlessly suppressed the Muslim Brotherhood after it was blamed for an attempt on Nasser's life.[45] Qutb and several other leaders were arrested and executed. Thousands of other Brothers were arrested and tortured as well. Some were able to escape this massive governmental crackdown by going underground or fleeing to other Middle East countries. Qutb became a martyr to the cause of Islamic reform. His writings and books, which number in the hundreds, continue to inspire fundamental and radical Islamic clerics and leaders who feel the need for confrontational action in the face of what they perceive as corrupt and un-Islamic regimes, backed and influenced by Western power and culture. Today, Qutb's writings are read throughout the Middle East, and his interesting commentary on life as a member of the Brotherhood, *Milestones*,[46] is one of the most influential works in Arabic today.

The Rise of Palestinian "Jihad"

In Chapter 2, we discussed the complex history and development of Palestinian resistance that gave way to several radical groups within the Palestinian Liberation Organization: al-Fatah, the Popular Front for the Liberation of Palestine, the Black September Organization, and the Abu Nidal Organization. Much of their rhetoric focused on the liberation of Palestine and the destruction of Israel through Arab unity. These previously identified Palestinian groups were described as politically motivated and revolutionary, not rooted in religious ideology. They were grounded in leftist ideologies expressed in the writings of Karl Marx, Che Guevara, and Carlos Marighella. Three important groups, however, emerged from the Palestinian cause that broke this mold, claiming that the liberation of Palestine is a religious mandate and the key to uniting all Arab countries into one great Islamic state. Israel and its supporters, such as the United States, were seen as major obstacles to not only the liberation of Palestine but also the establishment of an Islamic state throughout the Middle East. Violent actions taken in support of an independent and free Palestine are seen as a part of a much larger "holy war" or "holy jihad" within a worldwide Islamic revolution, beginning in the Middle East.

Al-Aqsa Martyrs Brigade
One of the first Palestinian terrorist groups to move from a secular to a radical Islamic ideology.

The **al-Aqsa Martyrs Brigade** grew out of the Palestinian-Israeli struggle, aligning itself with the original principles of al-Fatah—that armed struggle against Israel was the only way to achieve a Palestinian state (see Figure 4–6). The group considered terrorist attacks and the murder of Israeli citizens to be a legitimate means of accomplishing this goal, and believed that any Arab concession to Israel was treason to the Palestinian cause.[47]

The al-Aqsa Martyrs Brigade started as a radical nationalist movement within al-Fatah, but soon became ideologically aligned with the radical Islamic thoughts expressed by

FIGURE 4–6
Members of the al-Aqsa Martyrs
Brigade march in the streets of the
Gaza Strip, declaring allegiance to
Hamas.

*(Mohamed Atta/ABACAUSA.COM/
Newscom)*

Sayyid Qutb and others. Some of the earliest suicide bombings were reportedly conducted by this group against the Israeli military. Initially, their operations were targeted against Israeli military roadblocks and settlers in the West Bank. However, the religious radicalization of its members, combined with an overwhelming nationalist cause, gave way to increased suicide bombings and sniper attacks against Israeli civilians.[48] Since 2002, the group has been responsible for some of the bloodiest attacks in Israel, attacking innocent citizens as they sit in cafes, wait for public transportation, attend synagogue, shop in crowded malls, or ride buses.

The **Palestinian Islamic Jihad (PIJ)** is another of the primary Palestinian jihadist groups. Two men were particularly important to the development of the PIJ. Fathi Shaqaqi was expelled from Egypt with other Islamic radicals after the assassination of President Anwar Sadat in 1981. He relocated to the Gaza Strip, where he formed the PIJ. In 1988, Israeli authorities expelled Shaqaqi to Lebanon where he gained the support of Syria and Iran. Through the Iranian association, Shaqaqi enlisted the support of Hezbollah, the largest Shiite terrorist group in the world. Hezbollah perfected the use of suicide bombers to inflict mass casualties, for example, in 1973 at the Marine Barracks in Beirut, Lebanon. Shaqaqi was assassinated by Israeli forces in 1995 after the group began to dramatically increase its suicide bombing attacks against Israel. After Shaqaqi's death, Dr. Ramadan Abdullah Shalah stepped into the leadership role of the PIJ. Shalah was formally educated in England, earning a PhD in Banking and Economics. He is most known for his activities within the United States during the 1995–2008 investigation of a University of South Florida professor, Sami al-Arian.[49] Shalah and several others were indicted on 53 counts alleging involvement in a designated terrorist group (PIJ) and conducting a pattern of racketeering activities, such as bombings, murders, and money laundering, in support of that group. It was one of the first criminal indictments in the United States against a Middle Eastern terrorist using the federal Racketeer Influence and Corrupt Organizations Act (RICO).[50] Today, Shalah remains on the FBI's Most Wanted Terrorist list and is reportedly headquartered, along with other members of the Palestinian Islamic Jihad, in Syria as a long-standing ally of Hezbollah and the al-Assad regime.

The **Palestinian Islamic Resistance Movement (Hamas)** is clearly the largest and most successful of the Islamic fundamentalist groups identified within the Palestinian movement. Springing from the doctrine expressed by the Muslim Brotherhood, the Palestinian Islamic Resistance Movement was developed in the summer 1986. The ideology of Hamas was first observed in its charter, reflecting the common theme for the

Palestinian Islamic Jihad (PIJ)
One of the early terrorist groups to adopt a radical Islamic ideology that justified violence and suicide bombing as a means to liberate Palestine.

Palestinian Islamic Resistance Movement (Hamas)
The largest and most politically powerful group expressing radical Islamic ideologies to justify the liberation of Palestine and the destruction of Israel.

Oslo Accords
In 1993, the negotiation of a bilateral peace agreement between the Palestinian Liberation Organization (PLO) represented by Yassir Arafat and Israel represented by Prime Minister Yitzhak Rabin, moderated by President Bill Clinton.

Salafism
A broad intellectual movement spawned by the writings of Egyptian scholars such as Muhammad Abduh, Jamal al-Afghani, and Rashid Rida, focusing on the adoption of modernity and technology within Islam; soon became corrupted and blended with Wahhabism.

FIGURE 4–7
Sheikh Ahmed Hassan Yassin was an original founder of the Palestinian Islamic Resistance Movement, in Arabic *Harakat al-Muqawamah al Islamiyyah*—Hamas. He was a formally educated man and an inflammatory speaker; confined to a wheelchair as a quadriplegic stemming from an early childhood accident, he was quoted as saying that Israel "must disappear from the map." On March 22, 2004, while still on the steps of a mosque after an early morning prayer service in the Gaza Strip, Yassin was assassinated by an Israeli helicopter gunship that fired two Hellfire missiles at him and his bodyguards. The attack killed Yassin and his bodyguards as well as nine other bystanders and wounded another twelve people. The assassination escalated tensions in the West Bank and Gaza, sparking more suicide bombings against Israeli civilians and mass demonstrations in political support of Hamas.

(Hatem Moussa/AP Images)

liberation of Palestine and support of all Palestinian nationalist efforts. However, the document also expresses its belief that Palestine is an Islamic holy land and therefore no part of it may be inhabited by Israel. The charter is strongly anti-Jewish, peppered with stereotypes and bordering on paranoia in its description of Zionist conspiracies. Hamas rejects all peaceful solutions and accords, deeming them a retreat to its primary goal. Its charter reflects its closeness to Muslim Brotherhood doctrine and the writings of Sayyid Qutb, in that the only solution to the Palestinian problem is "jihad." It interprets this concept in a similar radical and fundamental way as meaning "a holy war" in which all Muslims are pitted against Israel and the West in a desperate fight for Islamic culture, land, heritage, and identity.[51] Specifically, the Hamas charter states "The day that enemies usurp part of Muslim lands, Jihad becomes the individual duty of every righteous Islamic person. In the face of Jews usurping Palestine, it is compulsory Islamic law that the banner of Jihad be raised."[52] Hamas calls for not only the liberation of Palestine, but also the destruction of Israel. Although Hamas recognized the Palestinian Liberation Organization (PLO), it rejected Arafat and any attempt at peace. During the **Oslo Accords**, a set of agreements between Israel and the PLO in 1993, Hamas rebelled against Arafat and conducted a flurry of bloody and destructive suicide bombings in Israel, effectively stopping negotiations during the Oslo process. As a result of the bombings and the ensuing Oslo Accords in 1993 and 1995, Arafat lost much ground to the Israelis, further destabilizing the political structure of the PLO. Hamas stepped in to fill the void left by Arafat's crumbling PLO, winning the loyalty and popularity of many Palestinians, especially young Palestinians facing a lifetime of perceived occupation by Israel.[53]

The primary modus operandi of Hamas has been suicide bombing against civilian targets in Israel. Hamas used this tactic frequently, especially during the late 1990s through 2005. This tactic was encouraged by Hamas founder *Sheikh Ahmed Yassin* (see Figure 4–7). In 2003, after the first U.S. invasion of Iraq, he urged Muslims to strike at Western interests anywhere in the world. His statements sparked concerns that suicide bombing might occur in the United States, because the FBI had long suspected linkages between Hamas and various sympathizers in the United States. Federal and local police began closely tracking thefts of explosives, such as those similarly used in Hamas backpack bombs, and unusual sales of fertilizer, chemicals, and fuel that could be used to make a truck or "personal" bomb.[54]

Israeli and American politicians were astounded and concerned when Hamas won a majority of the seats in the newly developed Palestinian Parliament in June 2007. Hamas had been formally designated as a "terrorist organization" by Israel, the United States, Canada, and the European Union. However, now they had to recognize Hamas as a freely elected representative of the Palestinian people—a group that has at the core of its charter the destruction of the country of Israel. Current leader Khaled Mashal refuses to change the Hamas charter; however, he has acquiesced in talks for peace with Israel. The election of *Mahmoud Abbas* as the President of the Palestinian Authority by the Palestinian Legislative Council has caused significant internal conflict between Hamas and the remnants of the PLO and al-Fatah organizations in which Abbas leads. Abbas is the only recognized leader within the Palestinian government by Israel and the United States, yet Meshai (and the rest of Hamas) remain a powerful internal force in Palestinian politics. Similar problems existed in Egypt in 2012 when the Muslim Brotherhood (the philosophical parent to Hamas) came to power in that country.

Salafism

Salafism is an Islamic philosophy founded in the late nineteenth century by Muslim reformers, such as Muhammad Abduh, Jamal al-Afghani, and Rashid Rida.[55] Salafism (al-Salafiyya in Arabic) comes from the word al-"Salaf," which refers to the companions of the Prophet Muhammad. Salaf means "the first" or the earliest, which in their movement is regarded as the first generation of believers who were the companions of the Prophet Muhammad. Jamal al-Din al-Afghani (1838–1897) was born and educated in Iran and British India. Afghani was a teacher and political activist who traveled throughout the Muslim world from Egypt to Pakistan, calling upon Muslims to "arise from their lethargy and reclaim their God-ordained purpose and identity."[56] While he lived and taught in Egypt, he served as an adviser to the Shah of Iran, and traveled Europe preaching a message that "challenged both Muslim and European authorities, the need for national unity to resist the danger of European intervention, the need for a broader unity of Islamic peoples, the need for a constitution to limit the ruler's power."[57] Themes of anti-imperialism, anti-colonialism, Arab unity, and Islamic solidarity were a major part of his legacy, as well as basic tenets of Salafism.

Afghani and his disciples were involved in the nationalist struggle against British and French influence in Egypt in 1882. Afghani was placed under house arrest in 1896, when Iran's Nasir al-Din Shah was assassinated by a reputed follower of Afghani's.[58] Afghani preached political ideas such as constitutionalism and political participation through elected assemblies. The revitalization of Islam and Muslim solidarity were the keys, according to Afghani, to attain the ultimate goal, independence from the West and the restoration of Muslim independence.

Afghani's protégé Muhammad Abduh (1849–1905) was the developer of the intellectual and social reformist dimensions of Islamic modern thought.[59] Abduh was responsible for beginning the Salafi movement, which sought legitimacy through identification of its Islamic modernist reformist with the elders of the early Muslim community, those who followed the example of the Prophet. Abduh was also an Egyptian trained scholar and taught at Azhar University, the oldest center of Islamic learning in the Middle East. Abduh was the most enthusiastic of Afghani's early students and worked closely with Afghani, publishing articles on sociopolitical reform, and was exiled to Paris with Afghani for his participation in early Egyptian insurgency. After his return from exile, Abduh turned away from political activism and focused on intellectual, religious, and educational reform. He was a critic of the Wahhabi movement and particularly polygamy and its negative effect on the Muslim family. Abduh argued that polygamy had been allowed as a concession to the prevailing social customs within Arabia at the time of the Prophet Muhammad. He also offered new interpretation of the Qur'an for application in a modern world, a concept that countered more radical and fundamentalist concepts of Wahhabism and the Muslim Brotherhood.[60]

Rashid Rida carried on the reformist tradition of Abduh, accepting the reality of modern states, technology, invention, and nationalism while maintaining the Islamic state and self-identity for all Muslims.[61] Afghani and Abduh influenced Rida's growing admiration for Saudi-Arabia's self-proclaimed Islamic state or caliphate. He emphasized the self-sufficiency and practical lifestyle of Islam, and in his later writings took a more critical attitude toward the threat of the West in the Middle East. He particularly focused on problems that he believed would stem from Saudi Arabia and the growing importance of oil to Western countries.[62]

Quick Facts
The Evolution of Terrorist Groups

Many of the same individuals who were involved in early Palestinian terrorist groups that expressed Marxist Revolutionary ideologies are now involved in leadership positions of radical Islamic fundamentalist groups. The evolutionary nature of group names has caused significant problems for police and intelligence personnel within the United States to monitor and identify specific individuals.

One group of individuals that has had an especially interesting evolution started out as young teenagers in the Arab Nationalist Movement, and then joined the al-Fatah Revolutionary Brigades that soon changed its name to the Arab Revolutionary Brigades (ARB). The Black September Organization (BSO) grew from members in the ARB and many joined the Abu Nidal Organization (ANO) after the 1972 Olympic Massacre. As the leader of ANO, Sabri al-Banna moved more toward mercenary actions without an ideology; these same individuals joined another group simply known as the Socialist Muslims. Today, these same individuals, now more experienced, are active in Hamas as spiritual and political leaders. The group names have changed but the actors and the terrorist methodology are the same.

Jihadist Salafism: The Ideology of al-Qaeda

Jihadist Salafism[63] is a label that has been given by many scholars to a second generation of Salafism. This group is a radical form of Salafism that emerged during the 1980s, rose in influence during the 1990s, and continues to dominate Middle Eastern and Islamic radical thought. Unlike traditional Salafis, Jihadists Salafis embrace violence as their *only* means to return to the original message of Islam. Jihadist Salafis are also distinct from the traditional Salafis because they have identified new enemies in the West and tend to see "jihad" as a global war that knows no boundaries. The Soviet-Afghanistan War (1980–1989) served as the catalyst for this explosive mixture of Salafi outlook and call to violence. The Soviet invasion of Afghanistan radicalized many Arab Salafis and had the effect of converting to the cause of "jihad" an entire segment of the transnational Salafi movement. Jihadist Salafis embrace a strict, literal interpretation of Islam, but combine it with an emphasis on "jihad," understood again as "holy war" against all those that threaten the historical, cultural, and religious existence of Islam in the Middle East. To them, violence becomes the prime instrument through which the Salafi desire to return to the original "purity" of Islam that controls all aspects of life.

The prime targets of Jihadist Salafi organizations vary according to the country and organization involved. Some concentrate their attacks on the "infidel regimes." These regimes, such as Saudi Arabia and Jordan, are denounced as Muslim in name only and for being subservient to the West. Jihadist Salafis also may engage in random violence against an entire society seen as having reverted to a state of pre-Islamic ignorance and for not siding with "true Muslims" in their struggle against the regime. For most Jihadist Salafi organizations (most prominently al-Qaeda) the main enemy is the United States. The United States is singled out because of its support for Israel and because of its support for Middle Eastern regimes and leaders that are perceived as betraying Islam and repressing Muslims. The charismatic and instrumental leader of the Jihadist Salafi movement was Usama bin Laden, emerging from the 1989 Soviet-Afghan War as a hero and religious icon strong enough to challenge the West. Bin Laden masterminded the 9/11 attacks, which surely excited all fundamentalist Islamic groups. All other Western nations learned a valuable and frightening lesson: If Jihadist Salafists can successfully attack America in its homeland, they are also vulnerable to such attacks.

Islamic fundamentalist movements such as Wahhabism, Salafism, Jihadist Salafism, and the Muslim Brotherhood all attempt to pursue change—many times through violence. These movements have created a cycle of violence and the insurgence of modern-day terrorism. Their goal is to re-Islamize the Muslim world. The fundamentalists view the Muslim world as being "infected" by the West's immoral, secularist values and behaviors. In addition, many Islamic fundamentalists embrace a strict, literal interpretation of Islam and combine it with an emphasis on "jihad," misinterpreted but understood by them as a "holy war." Although "jihad" as an inner struggle has always been an important part of Islam, many Islamic fundamentalists have restated it as a universal religious obligation for all "true" Muslims to join their war against the West in a worldwide Islamic revolution.

The Wahhabi movement has not only led to today's Saudi Arabia but has also encouraged Muslims to be concerned about politics and government. The Muslim Brotherhood, which emerged as a response to the Wahhabi movement, has grown in to be one of the largest and strongest fundamental Islamic organizations in the world. Sayyid Qutb's writings continue to inspire fundamental and radical Muslims who feel the need for confrontational action in the face of what they perceive as corrupt and non-Islamic regimes in the Middle East, backed and influenced by Western power and culture. Salafism has expressed itself in a multiplicity of movements that have given rise to historical self-reflection and hence created a foundation for Jihadist Salafis. Jihadist Salafis, acting through a variety of terrorist organizations such as al-Qaeda, al-Qaeda in the Arabian Peninsula (AQAP), the Islamic State in Iraq and Syria/Islamic State of Iraq and the Levant (ISIS/ISIL), and Jemaah Islamiah (based primarily in Indonesia and the Philippines) pose an enormous threat to Western nations and specifically the United States (see Table 4–1).

TABLE 4–1
Jihadist Salafist Groups Active Throughout the World

The Jihadist Salafist ideologies represent a significant threat to Israel, Europe, and other Western nations (including the United States). The philosophy represents the most virulent of radical Islamic fundamentalism and has been the foundation for several active terrorist groups throughout the world. These groups remain active and continue to pose a significant threat of attack in the United States and against American interests abroad.

Abu Sayyaf Group (ASG). ASG is a violent Islamic separatist group operating in the southern Philippine island of Mindinao. Split from the Moro National Liberation Front, the group has been active in narcotics, arms and human trafficking, as well as kidnapping as a means to fund its operations in Southeast Asia.

Al-Qaeda. Established in 1988 by Usama bin Laden in Afghanistan as a resistance movement against the invasion by the Soviet Union, al-Qaeda remains a viable terrorist group aimed at destroying Western influence (particularly the United States) and establishing a worldwide Islamic state. The group has been significantly reduced in number and resources due to military involvement in Iraq and Afghanistan. Al-Qaeda is currently headed by its long-time spiritual leader, Ayman al-Zawahiri, and remnants are still committed to their Jihadist Salafist cause.

Al-Qaeda in the Arabian Peninsula (AQAP). AQAP is a militant group following the ideological philosophies of the larger al-Qaeda. AQAP is based primarily in Yemen, and has been linked with other radical Islamic groups in that country, such as the Yemeni Islamic Jihad and the Aden-abyan Islamic Army. It has been strongly opposed to the House of Saud in Saudi Arabia and has been involved in several terrorist attacks in Saudi Arabia and Yemen. Interestingly, AQAP claimed responsibility for the Christmas Day attempted bombing of Northwest Airlines Flight 253 on December 25, 2009, by Umar Farouk Abdulmutallab. In that incident, Abdulmutallab attempted to set off plastic explosives sewn into his underwear. The explosives failed to detonate and Abdulmutallab was arrested.

Al-Qaeda in Iraq (AQI) or the Islamic State in Iraq and the Levant (ISIL), or the Islamic State in Iraq and Syria (ISIS), or simply the Islamic State. AQI is also known as the Islamic State in Iraq and more recently as the Islamic State in Iraq and the Levant (ASIL). It was established in 2004 by Abu Musab al-Zarqawi, a longtime and strong supporter of Usama bin Laden. AQI and ISIL/ISIS were primary forces against the U.S. military in Iraq, even after al-Zarqawi and other leaders were killed; a new revival of ISIL in Iraq and Syria under the leadership of Abu Bakr al Baghdadi continues to perform acts of terrorism against the established government of Iraq and threaten U.S. interests in the area. Attempting to identify all of the al-Qaeda cells and groups within Iraq is a difficult task as the names of groups often change and merge with new events. For instance, the Khorasan Group was relatively unknown until late 2014 when an American airstrike was directed against it within Syria. The group was headed by Muhsin al-Fadhli, a close associate of Ayman al-Zawahiri, and a strong supporter of al-Qaeda throughout the Middle East.

Al-Qaeda in Islamic Maghreb (AQIM). The Maghreb is a geographical region of northwest Africa, comprising the Atlas Mountains and the modern-day countries of Mauritania, Morocco, Algeria, Tunisia, Western Sahara, and Libya. AQIM has declared itself as an affiliate of the original al-Qaeda and carries out operations in an attempt to overthrow the Algerian government and institute an Islamic state throughout the Maghreb.

Harakat ul-Mujahidin (HUM). Formerly part of the larger radical Islamic movement in Pakistan and Afghanistan called Harakat al-Ansar, HUM operates primarily in Kashmir and can link direct associations with bin Laden and original al-Qaeda fighters in Afghanistan and Pakistan. The group maintains close ties to Jaish e-Mohammad (JEM) or the "Army of Muhammad" in Pakistan. These groups have maintained significant training camps in Pakistan and represent the primary groups that fight against U.S. forces in Afghanistan.

■ **TABLE 4–1**
Continued

Islamic State (IS). See Al-Qaeda in Iraq (AQI).

Jemaah Islamiya (JA). JA is an Indonesia-based terrorist group active throughout Southeast Asia. JI is headed by Abu Bakar Bashir, an Indonesian of Yemeni descent, and a highly charismatic cleric and leader. The group has active cells in Thailand, Singapore, Malaysia, and Indonesia, and has been linked to the Moro Islamic Liberation Front in the Philippines. The group has been responsible for several high-profile terrorist incidents in Southeast Asia, including the 2002 bombing of a nightclub in Bali killing 202 people and the 2003 car bombing of the JW Marriott Hotel in Jakarta, Indonesia, that killed twelve people.

Lashkar-i-Tayyiba (LT). The Lashkar-i-Tayyiba, or "Army of the Righteous," is one of the largest and best trained fighting groups in the Pakistan-Afghan region. It is headed by Hafiz Mohamed Saeed, and has conducted a number of terrorist attacks against India (Mumbai).

Source: The National Counterterrorism Center (NCTC) website, www.nctc.gov/site/index.html.

The Islamic State Today

The Islamic State (IS) represents the largest and most virulent strain of Jihadist Salafism in the Middle East today. It is a direct outgrowth of the Iraq War beginning in 2003 with the invasion of Iraq by the United States-led coalition forces that eventually toppled the government of Saddam Hussein. **Al-Qaeda in Iraq (AQI)** was the primary precursor entity that became the current Islamic State. It was established in 2004 by *Abu Musab al-Zarqawi*, a longtime and strong supporter of Usama bin Laden. Al-Zarqawi was a very militant Islamist, born in Jordan, and operating one of the first major paramilitary camps in Afghanistan. AQI and the emerging soldiers of the Islamic State were the primary forces against the U.S. military in Iraq. And, it was in Iraq that al-Zarqawi became much better known for his malicious tactics against military as well as civilian populations.

Al-Qaeda in Iraq (AQI)
The primary precursor entity that became the current Islamic State.

Al-Zarqawi was a strong and experienced leader of AQI, and had developed a relatively sophisticated organization to thwart the U.S. military and coalition forces in Iraq, particularly as the government and the country fell into turmoil. Al-Zarqawi was an ardent Sunni warrior and it was his bitter hatred toward the Shi'a majority in Iraq that set him apart as one of the most vicious terrorists of our time. It was his group and their radical ideology that turned the war in Iraq from one against Western interference to one of Shiite annihilation.[64] He specifically targeted Shiite mosques and civilians across Iraq, ostensibly because the Shi'a majority had cooperated with U.S. military and coalition forces. Indeed, all the Prime Ministers of Iraq and much of the government leadership since the provisional government led by Paul Bremer in 2003, have been or are now prominent Shiite leaders and/or dissidents under Saddam Hussein.

> **Information Link**
> For more information on the rise of the Islamic State, read Cole Bunzel's excellent analysis paper hosted by the Brookings Institute entitled, "From Paper State to Caliphate: The Ideology of the Islamic State" (March 2015). See: www.brookings.edu/wp-content/uploads/2016/06/The-ideology-of-the-Islamic-State.pdf.

It was al-Zarqawi who changed the focus of the Iraqi War from fighting U.S. and coalition forces, to a civil war between Sunnis and Shiites, in which al-Zarqawi and his new group *(Islamic State in Iraq and Syria - ISIS)*[65] were responsible for killing thousands of innocent Shiite civilians using barbaric tactics such as kidnappings, hostage beheadings, suicide and truck bombings, and mass killings.[66] Some of his most infamous atrocities included the killing of Laurence Foley, a U.S. diplomat in Jordan in 2002, the beheading of a U.S. engineer, Nicholas Berg, in 2004, and the car bomb attacks on Shia shrines in Karbala, Najaf, and Baghdad that killed over 250 people in Iraq, also in 2004. These violent and often videotaped killings earned him the nickname, "the butcher of Baghdad."[67] In September 2005, he declared an "all-out war" on Shiites in Iraq, and became one of the most wanted men in the world with a bounty of a $25 million reward for information that led to his capture and arrest, the same amount offered for Usama bin Laden in 2004. On June 7, 2006, fate caught up with Abu Musab al-Zarqawi as he was killed in a targeted bombing by U.S. forces in Iraq.[68] Five other people were also killed in the attack.

Interestingly, al-Zarqawi's nemesis was one of equal sentiment, only against the Sunni population in Iraq; an Iranian cleric named Muqtada al-Sadr who commanded the

Quick Facts
How Big Is the Islamic State?

In July 2016, the Islamic State occupied an area of some 60 to 90,000 square miles primarily in Iraq and Syria; an area roughly the size of the country of Jordan. Over 8 million people are influenced by this movement, which boasts between 25,000 and 32,000 hardened fighters. According to the U.S. Department of State and the CIA, the number of fighters in the Islamic State, surprisingly, did not decline between 2015 and 2016 despite significant conflict with Syrian, Kurdish, Russian, and American troops; their number of fighters is estimated at 30,000.[69]

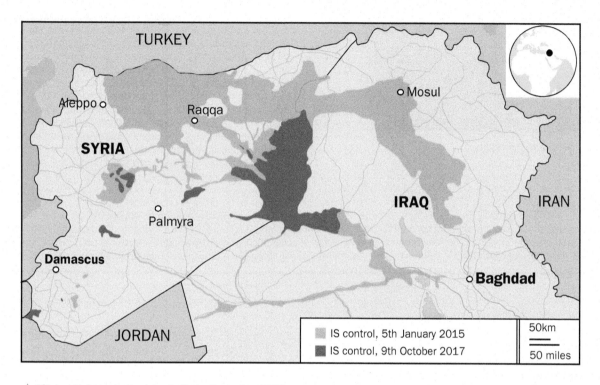

▲ "Claimed" Areas by the Islamic State, December 2016.

Mahdi Army. This group, also known as the Sadr Militia, fought directly against al-Zarqawi forces and was also responsible for significant battles against U.S. forces in Basra, Karbala, Kufa, and Baghdad (Al Kut, An Najaf, and Sadr City). While al-Zarqawi died relatively early in his life at the age of thirty-nine, Muqtada al-Sadr continues to be an important and powerful figure in the development of the Iraqi government under the strong influence of U.S. and coalition forces; a fact that continues to spawn new recruiting efforts and ideological sentiment in the Islamic State today.

Many of the radical Sunni fighters loyal to al-Qaeda suffered dramatic losses to U.S. forces during the Iraq War. Coupled with the loss of political power and the establishment of a majority Shiite-led government in Iraq, many fled to neighboring countries, and in particular Syria, where violent revolution already in progress was pitting Sunnis against a Shiite-backed al-Assad government. Under al-Zarqawi, the early name of this group became widely known as ISIS (or the Islamic State in Iraq and Syria). Syrian rebel groups quickly welcomed these hardened fighters; however, they soon realized that the Iraqi group had a much larger goal than toppling the al-Assad regime—their goal was to establish a new *"Islamic State in Iraq and the Levant - ISIL."* The Levant is a geographic and cultural area on the Eastern Mediterranean Sea, composed primarily of modern-day Syria, Lebanon, Jordan, and Israel.

A New Caliphate

The new Islamic State of Iraq and the Levant (ISIL) was successful in carving out a portion of land in the heart of the Middle East in which to build an Islamic State and recruit other like-minded Sunnis worldwide. The rise of ISIL was quick and historical, occurring along the

Box 4-4
The Leadership of Caliph Abu Bakr al-Baghdadi

(Pictures From History/Newscom)

Very little is known about the clandestine leader of the Islamic State, other than the numerous code names that refer to him, such as the "Invisible Sheikh, Abu Du'a Dr. Ibrahim, and of course, Caliph Abu Bakr al-Baghdadi. This is a "nom de guerre" or a code name that the Sheik has taken to conceal his real identity. Intelligence sources indicate that his real name may be Ibrahim Awad al-Badri, born July 28, 1971.[70] However, what is known about al-Baghdadi is often based on rumor, misinformation, exaggeration, and speculative intelligence information.[71] He is thought to be about forty-five years old, most likely born in the early 1970s near Baghdad, Iraq, and was radicalized during the harsh rule of Saddam Hussein. He certainly does not follow the profile of other, more recent radical Islamic leaders in al-Qaeda, like Usama bin Laden or Ayman al-Zawahiri, in that he does not come from a wealthy or elite family. His speech and manners suggest a strong middle-class background, which fits well with other rumors that he was a strong athlete and soccer player in his youth with a formal education in Baghdad. Al-Baghdadi emerged in 2014 as the leader of al-Qaeda in Iraq (AQI), taking the place of his predecessor Abu Musab al-Zarqawi. After a few initial public speeches and appearances, most notably in Mosul, Iraq (June 29, 2014), in which he declared himself the "Caliph" of the Islamic State and asked all Muslims everywhere in the world to pledge allegiance and support to him, he has been relatively quiet and most important, hidden from coalition forces. He most likely learned valuable lessons from al-Zarqawi (and bin Laden) in keeping a low profile while having a reward of $25 million on your head. Apparently escaping from a series of attacks by coalition forces, as well as an assassination attempt, according to the Pentagon, al-Baghdadi is still alive in early 2017 and still leading the Islamic State.[72] His whereabouts still unknown and his leadership team shrouded in secrecy.

Abu Bakr al-Baghdadi
The current leader of the Islamic State; while his true identity is unknown, his code name is Abu Bakr al-Baghdadi.

Islamic State
The primary radical Islamic movement active in Iraq, Syria and the rest of the Middle East; claims to be the new Islamic Caliphate in the world today. Previous names associated with this movement have been al-Qaeda in Iraq (AQI), Islamic State of Iraq and Syria (ISIS) and Islamic State of Iraq and the Levant (ISIL). Also known as its Arabic language acronym, Daesh.

Daesh
The Arabic acronym for the Islamic State comes from the root of the ISIS-ISIL inconsistency in the Arabic work "al-Sham," meaning "the Levant" or the "Greater Syria." Hence, the acronym is short for al-Dawla al Islamiya al Iraq al Sham.

banks of the Tigris and Euphrates Rivers, a region commonly known as the cradle of civilization and extending deep into Syria.

In July 2014, the leader of ISIL, **Abu Bakr al-Baghdadi**, declared himself "caliph" over the area he controlled and announced the establishment of the new "caliphate" (see Box 4–4). He then changed the name of the group to the **Islamic State**, and within a month (August 2014) he led attacks on Kurdish territories in northern Iraq, prompting an immediate response by the United States—retaliatory air strikes and bombing of IS-held areas. Quite interestingly, the Islamic State has had several name changes in its brief history. Moving from ISIS and ISIL to the Islamic State, as it is now referred to in most of the United States, particularly within academia and the general media; however, the U.S. government continues to refer to the movement as ISIS, as a subtle means to *not* recognize it as a legitimate state. However, in Europe as well as within the Middle East, the Islamic State is often referred to by its Arabic language acronym **Daesh**. As one BBC News report indicated, ISIS, ISIL, IS, or Daesh… all reflect the same radical Islamic "expansionist ambitions" or movement.[73]

Regardless of the name of his movement, Abu Bakr al-Baghdadi has called upon all Muslims around the world to pledge support and allegiance to him and his country. As we learned in the previous chapter, these are powerful words in the Muslim world, and ones that position al-Baghdadi and the Islamic State as a significant movement in the Middle East. The idea of a caliphate based upon radical Islam should not be thought of as an extension of al-Qaeda's philosophy, but rather an "evolution" of its ideology. Much of the leadership within the Islamic State has a strong disdain for al-Qaeda and its current leadership (Aymen al-Zawahiri). Usama bin Laden is revered as a great Islamic warrior; however, his view of terrorism as a prologue to the development of a new caliphate far in the future was wrong. The Islamic State believes it is the new Sunni Caliphate in the modern world today; and it is a mistake to think of the Islamic State as a group. Rather, it is a movement of some 8 million people who are well organized, well financed by captured oil wells and reserves, the development of a new legal and tax system based on the ideological premises set forth in radical Islamic thought, and supported by a continually growing, sophisticated, and powerful army.[74] In their mind, the Islamic State today is fundamentally fighting a "medieval war" against the West, in the modern age. It justifies the horrific use of violence (e.g., beheadings, assassinations, and rape) through isolated and perverted messages in the Qur'an, a phenomenon that we have witnessed before within radical Islamic ideology (see Box 4–5).

Box 4-5
Ruthless Violence and the Islamic State

—By Anne Speckhard and Ahmet S Yayla, PhD

The following material is adapted from actual interviews from thirteen Syrian Islamic State defectors. A fuller and more systematic account can be found in *ISIS Defectors: Inside Stories of the Terrorist Caliphate* (Washington, D.C.: Advances Press, July 2016) by Anne Speckhard and Ahmet S Yayla. Dr. Speckhard is Adjunct Associate Professor of Psychiatry at Georgetown University in the School of Medicine and Director of the International Center for the Study of Violent Extremism (ICSVE) Dr. Yayla is a 20-year veteran police officer and the former Chief of Counterterrorism and Operations Division for the Turkish National Police (TNP). He is currently working as the Deputy Director of the International Center for the Study of Violent Extremism (ICSVE) and as an adjunct professor at George Mason University in Washington, D.C. Ahmet was one of the first TNP officers to obtain a doctoral degree from a major university in the United States during a unique project started at the University of North Texas in 2002. He is a close friend and former student of Dr. Robert W. Taylor.

The Islamic State (IS) is the most powerful, ruthless, horrific, and well-funded terrorist group in recent history. Not only has IS managed to take and control a significant swathe of territory, it also has become a de-facto state. Since their 2014 claim of establishing a Caliphate, IS has also unleashed an unprecedented and prolific social media recruiting drive that has enabled them to attract up to 30,000 foreign fighters from more than one hundred countries. A steady stream of fighters continues to enter Syria and Iraq on a daily basis—with some estimates placing their number at over one thousand new recruits per month. As the Islamic State has arisen—seemingly out of nowhere—to become a powerful foe, the West has struggled to comprehend the ruthless violence observed within the movement and more important, to understand how to effectively counter it.

Takfiri Practices

The Islamic State claims to be following an authentic early version of Islam—following an extremist interpretation of Wahhabi and Salafi practices, observing what they claim were the original customs followed by the Prophet Muhammad and his companions in the 600 A.D. period. As such, the Islamic State engages in what is commonly referred to as *takfiri practices* (excommunication from Islam)—that is, they claim the right to label other Muslims, to whom they object, so-called "unbelievers." Most important, the IS believes that it is their duty to exterminate all those who do not adhere to IS ideology.

According to Islamic State informants, anyone who does not follow their extremist ideology is labeled *murtad* (a Muslim renegade), or *kafir* (unbeliever)—categories of people that, according to IS, can be killed with impunity. One informant recalled that when IS moved into Raqqa, Syria, the local population was told that they needed to follow the true Islam. "In November 2013, when IS took Raqqa," an informant named Abu Walid, recalled, "they told us, 'You are not Muslim, you are kafir (an unbeliever/rejecter of Islam). You are infidels.'" Other informants stated that those who had "sinned" according to IS dogma and agreed to live under IS rule are required to go through a process of *tawbah* (repentance), in which they openly had to declare sorrow over past sins and pledge never to repeat them. Tawbah takes place in front of a Shariah judge loyal to IS and then announced publicly one's allegiance to the Caliph (Abu Bakr al Baghdadi).

By this process, the label of "kafir" can be shed and the person then can live under the rule of IS as a "true Muslim" IS-style. Morality rules infractions with any hint of sexual impropriety are harshly punished under IS rule. One informant stated: "A man in a small village went to visit his neighbor. He knocked on the door of a woman whose husband was not there. He was caught waiting inside the front yard of the home [inside the outer gate of the yard] when the husband was absent, so he was arrested. He was brutally lashed forty times." The lashing was so harsh that, "he could not use the toilet and had to stay in bed for twenty days. Afterward he was forced to take the Shariah course for three weeks. The woman inside the house was lashed forty times as well because she opened the door to the yard for him"

Torture and Beheadings

Torture is also a central part of the Islamic State repertoire. One informant stated: "[They] took me by hand in iron cuffs, to torture me. They spread my arms wide and hung me by my forearms and wrists, held by the iron cuffs, from a steel bar [i.e., he was hung there with his full body weight pulling down on him]. They left me there for around two hours. I had so much pain, and started to cry many times from the pain in my hands and my body. I cried and shouted. They did this again the next day and I cried and shouted again throughout the day and night." This went on for thirteen days! Sadly, beheadings, crucifixions, torture, and executions are such a common occurrence that everyone "knows that life under IS is cheap and that not complying with their rules or wishes can bring a swift, harsh, and dire result." Interestingly, Anjem Choudary, an IS spokesman in London, voiced the opinion that killing or executing the enemy (such as Western infidels) by beheading and crucifixion is an IS obligation because it strikes fear in the enemy of Islam and hastens victory, thereby avoiding prolonged conflict.[75]

Rape and Female Slaves

The Islamic State also has the well-reported practice of taking female captives—particularly the Yazidi women—and then selling or granting them as sexual slaves to IS cadres. IS ideologues argue that Islam allows for taking and distributing female slaves as war booty. While the press has reported on the practice of taking Yazidi women captive, informants reveal that it is not only Yazidi women who are preyed upon but also the Sunni and Shia wives of

(News Pictures/Polaris/Newscom)

defeated enemy soldiers from the Iraqi army, the Free Syrian Army, and from the Syrian regime forces. According to one informant:

> There are special places in Raqqa, Syria, where they sell female slaves. It is in the center of the city. It is only for IS. It's in the building that was previously the government palace—the governor's compound. IS took it over. The female slaves, known as "sabiyya," are allowed only to the IS cadres. Only a fighter can buy a slave woman. He needs documents from the emir or the governor of IS in that region granting permission to him to buy a slave and only after getting this permission he can go to the slave market to buy slaves. They are sold by dollars. The minimum price is one thousand USD and the maximum is three thousand dollars. The slave girls can be sold between fighters [mujahideen], and there are rules, like you cannot take a mother and daughter slaves sexually at once, as you can only be with one of them [following Islamic incest rules].

Slaves are also given to the IS cadres as rewards—especially to the Westerners who do not have local wives. They reside with the fighter like a wife until he discards her, giving or selling her to another fighter. There are many rules governing the slave trade and how slaves ought to conduct themselves. Foreign fighters also receive additional rewards besides wives and sexual slaves ... sometimes they receive homes and cars. More recently, these practices have been in the national media as other Islamic State-pledged groups, such as *Boko Haram* in Nigeria, have adopted similar practices, particularly involving the kidnapping of innocent school girls to be sold as sex slaves as part of the "spoils of war."

To be sure, the Islamic State is fighting a barbaric and medieval war in the present day. Daily life inside IS as well as in their war against the West, is punctuated by brutal practices—including widespread floggings, rape, torture, and beheadings. Many of the comments in this abstract came from defectors

(Yavuz Sariyildiz/Alamy Stock Photo)

as a result of their exposure to extreme brutality, disgust over the slave trade, observations of deep hypocrisy, and a total mismatch between the words and deeds of the Islamic State. Charges of corruption and complaints about battlefield decisions that produced unnecessary deaths in their own ranks were also causes of disillusionment. The defectors and informants in this study all had come to hate the Islamic State and warn others not to join what they gradually came to see as a totally disappointing, ruthless, and un-Islamic organization.

What do you think has been the impact of the brutal tactics employed by the Islamic State on world opinion? Do you think these tactics have galvanized international opposition against the Islamic State, or have they attracted a huge wave of foreign recruits to the IS cause?

Khomeinism

Khomeinism
A Shi'a ideology that embraces Islamic worldwide revolution as well as Islamic unity and strict adherence to Sharia; based on the teachings of Ayatollah Ruhollah Khomeini.

As discussed in Chapter 3, the religion of Islam is divided into two primary traditions: Sunni and Shiite. The fundamentalists movements discussed to this point (e.g., Wahhabism, Salafism, and Jihadist Salafism) have been exclusively Sunni developments. There are also fundamentalist movements in the Shiite (or Shi'a) tradition; the most noted is **Khomeinism**. The most prominent of these radical movements stems from the teachings of *Ayatollah Ruhollah Khomeini* (known in the West as simply Ayatollah Khomeini), the conservative and radical cleric who led the 1979 Iranian Revolution against Shah Mohammad Reza Pahlavi. Khomeini strongly believed in Muslim unity and solidarity, and preached the union of all Muslim traditions. He also believed that secular states ultimately lead to the marginalization and ultimate destruction of Islam. Accordingly, he preached that government and religion must be united.[76] Khomeini viewed the development of the Islamic State on a worldwide basis as the revolutionary duty of all Muslims. Khomeini saw this revolution as starting in Iran and moving first throughout the Middle East, reclaiming the holy sites of the Islamic faith, and then on to the rest of the world.

Khomeini successfully led the downfall of the monarchy in Iran and subsequently rose to power in 1979 as the Supreme Leader of the new Islamic Republic of Iran. Under his rule, Sharia was strictly enforced by a new group of radical soldiers called the Islamic Revolutionary Guard. This military unit acted more as an internal police force that focused on the strict enforcement of Sharia law as interpreted by Ayatollah Khomeini, such as the establishment of new Islamic dress codes for men and women; the banishment of all alcoholic drinks; and the banishment of any music, television, or movies produced in the West. Communications and broadcasting within the country were strictly controlled by the government and the threat of surveillance and subsequent arrest by the secret police was always present. Life was harsh in Iran, marked by the execution of thousands of political prisoners and the persecution and torture of untold numbers in Khomeini's prisons. The oppressive government lasted for an entire decade while Ayatollah Khomeini remained as Supreme Leader. He died in 1989 at the age of eighty-six, giving rise to a more moderate, yet still very conservative, leadership under the current Supreme Leader of Iran, Ayatollah Ali Khamenei.

Hezbollah

Similar to other ideologues, Khomeini's radical philosophies of strict enforcement of Sharia law and the continuation of a world Islamic revolution did not die with him. Several of his edicts still permeate the Iranian government and way of life. However, the most visible of Khomeini's followers are observed in Lebanon—a small country adjacent to the north of Israel having a relatively large population of Shi'a Muslims (nearly one-third of the total population). As discussed in Chapter 1, **Hezbollah** (Arabic for "Party of Allah or God") is a paramilitary organization headed by Hassan Nasrallah, and originally developed by conservative Lebanese Shi'a clerics loyal to Ayatollah Khomeini. Trained by members of the Iranian Islamic Revolutionary Guard, Hezbollah members continue to wage the revolution of world Islamic order. The 1985 charter of Hezbollah focuses on Islamic unity, the destruction of Israel, and the expulsion of Western powers, including the United States, from the Middle East, "putting to an end any colonialist entity in our land."[77]

Hezbollah
"The Party of God (Allah)"; the largest Shi'a terrorist group in the world, led by Hassan Nasrallah and headquartered in Lebanon.

Backed by Iran, Hezbollah has been extensively involved in Lebanese and Syrian politics for years. Although it has not claimed responsibility for any attack, it has been widely suspected in a number of bloody and vicious suicide bombings, as well as open missile attacks and military raids against Israeli forces from their strong base in Lebanon. Acting in concert with other groups in Lebanon, Hezbollah was the group primarily responsible for the 1983 barracks bombing that killed 241 U.S. Marines, fifty-nine French paratroopers, and six civilians in Beirut.[78] More recently, Hezbollah has been an active ally (along with Iran) of Bashar al-Assad's regime, carrying out significant military actions against rebel forces in Syria.[79]

Similar to fundamentalist groups and ideologies from the Sunni tradition, the tenets of Khomeinism, as expressed by Hezbollah, pose a significant threat to not only Western countries, but also those Middle Eastern countries that are predominantly Sunni. The enmity between Sunni and Shi'a tradition is only exacerbated by Iranian rhetoric of a new Islamic world order that begins with Shi'a domination of the holy Islamic sites in Mecca and Medina, Saudi Arabia. To be sure, Khomeinism also poses a significant threat to Israel, the United States, and any other Western country with interests in the broader Middle East.

Chapter Summary

SUMMARY BY LEARNING OBJECTIVE

1. **Define fundamentalism, and provide a number of common assumptions observed in various fundamental groups, including Islamic fundamental groups.**

   Fundamentalism is a strategy in which believers attempt to preserve their distinctive identity as a people or group. Feeling this identity to be at risk, fundamentalists fortify this identity by a selective retrieval of doctrines, beliefs, and practices from a perceived sacred past. Common assumptions observed in various fundamental groups, including Islamic fundamentalism, include (1) the selective interpretation of scripture and doctrine, (2) the misinterpretation of symbolic words, (3) the justification and use of violence called by God, (4) an apocalyptic or "end of the world" mentality, and (5) charismatic leadership.

2. **Discuss the political and historical dimensions of Islamic fundamentalism.**

   Fundamental Islam has been led by the writings of various philosophers and ideologues, including Ibn al-Wahhab, Sayyid Qutb, Ahmed Yassin, and Hassan al-Banna. Some of these individuals wrote centuries ago about European colonization and the exploitation of the

Middle East, conditions that have long passed. Islamic fundamentalist organizations attempt to "re-Islamize" societies that are already politically and economically ruled by powerful secular governments. These governments are often allied with Western powers, including the United States, and internally they often suppress their own people. In the past, some countries of the Middle East (e.g., Libya, Iraq, Egypt, Syria, and Saudi Arabia) represent suppressive governments or sheikdoms (kingdoms) where the tenets of democracy were nonexistent. There were no free elections, there were huge differences in socioeconomic classes within the population, and there was a concentration of wealth in the hands of only a few families, which often ruled the country and controlled all aspects of business and economic life. Many people in these countries lived in poverty, had no education, suffered from diseases and malnutrition, lacked access to medical care, and had no real political power. Faced with an unattractive future, some people are attracted to radical, fundamental, and extremist causes. For some, embracing fundamental Islam offers hope, if not in this world, in the next, for example, because of dying as a suicide bomber. In part, the Arab Spring (beginning in 2010) was a result of a much wider Islamic fundamentalist movement. Civil protests, demonstrations, and in many cases violent uprisings from the masses forced suppressive governments and dictatorships into exile or surrender, such as those in Libya, Egypt, and Syria.

3. **Provide an historical overview of the Wahhabi movement in Saudi Arabia and the rest of the Middle East.**

The Wahhabi movement or Wahhabism is based on the writings of Muhammad ibn Abd al-Wahhab in the late 1700s. He believed that the only acceptable model for government in the Middle East was established by Muhammad in the fourth century, hence people should live like Muhammad and his followers during that time. Al-Wahhab teamed with a young and talented tribal chieftain in central Arabia named Muhammad ibn Saud. The two were able to unite the disparate tribes of the central plateau of the Arabian Peninsula called the Najd. Although al-Wahhab died in 1792, the House of Saud continues to govern the Arabian Peninsula. In 1932, a direct descendent of Muhammad ibn Saud, Abdul Aziz ibn Saud (simply known as ibn Saud), declared himself King of Saudi Arabia. Today, leadership of the kingdom and state of Saudi Arabia has passed to the sons of ibn Saud (now King Abdullah) and continues to follow the strict teachings of al-Wahhab.

4. **Describe the development and importance of the Muslim Brotherhood in Egypt, including the contributions of Hassan al-Banna and Sayyid Qutb.**

The Muslim Brotherhood represents a political-religious movement starting in Egypt in the 1920s with the writings of Hassan al-Banna. As prescribed by al-Banna, there were two primary objectives of the movement: the liberation of Egypt from all foreign powers and the development of a free state functioning under the rules of Islam. The Muslim Brotherhood grew to the largest and most powerful movement in the world and developed similar movements throughout the Middle East. Another of the influential writers from the Muslim Brotherhood and Egypt was Sayyid Qutb. He is often called the "architect of radical Islam" and the "father of modern terrorism." Qutb transformed the ideological beliefs of Hassan al-Banna into a revolutionary call for arms throughout the Middle East. He was particularly focused on revolutionary change in his home country of Egypt, and concluded that the only viable way to make such changes was through revolution, often led by groups of "true Muslims" that acted as a vanguard of Muslim militancy. Violence and terrorism were justified as sanctified acts under Qutb's new interpretation of "jihad" as a physical "holy war" designed to reestablish Islamic order in Egypt and the rest of the Middle East. Although Qutb spent much of his adult life in prison and was eventually executed in 1965, his writings were very influential in the development of future radical Islamic groups, including the Muslim Brotherhood, various Palestinian organizations, Shi'a revolutionary groups in Iran, and al-Qaeda under the leadership of Usama bin Laden.

5. **Describe the differences between the Wahhabi, Salafi, Jihadist Salafi, and Islamic State movements.**

Philosophically, Salafism is nearly identical to Wahhabism, except that Wahhabism is far less tolerant of diversity and differences of opinion. Whereas the liberal age of Salafism came to an end in the 1960s, Wahhabism was able to rid itself of its extreme intolerance and continues to be a major political and religious force throughout the Middle East, but most specifically on the Arabian Peninsula. Wahhabism has essentially co-opted Salafism until the two have become indistinguishable. Jihadist Salafism is a label that has been given to second-generation Salafists that express extreme radicalism. Jihadist Salfists embrace violence and revolution as their only means to an end. This is the ideology of al-Qaeda that has identified enemies not only in the Middle East but also in the West (particularly the United States). Jihadist Salafists believe that "jihad" is not just a physical "holy war" in the Middle East, but rather a global war that knows no boundaries. The Islamic State (IS) represents the largest and most virulent strain of Jihadist Salafism in the Middle East today. It is a direct outgrowth of the Iraq War beginning in 2003 with the invasion of Iraq by the United States-led coalition forces that eventually toppled the government of Saddam Hussein. In 2014, the leader of IS, Abu Bakr al-Baghdadi, declared himself "caliph" over the area he controlled and announced the establishment of the new "caliphate." These were powerful words in the world of the Middle East as set forth the Islamic State as the new Sunni Caliphate in the modern world today. It is a mistake to think of the Islamic State as a group. Rather, it is a movement of some 8 million people who are well organized, well financed by captured oil wells and reserves, the development of a new legal and tax system, and supported by a continually growing, sophisticated, and powerful army of hardened radical Islamic fighters who live in a brutally violent world.

6. Describe the roots of radical Islam from the Shi'a perspective and describe the group known as Hezbollah.

Radical Islam from the Shi'a perspective is embraced in the fundamentalist movement as expressed by Ayatollah Ruhollah Khomeini, known simply as Khomeinism. Khomeini was the conservative and radical cleric who led the 1979 Iranian Revolution against the monarchy of Shah Pahlavi. Khomeini strongly believed in Muslim unity and solidarity and preached against the secular state. He believed that government and religion must be united. Further, he believed in the development of a worldwide Islamic state that would begin in Iran, move to the Middle East, and extend to the rest of the world. Hence, the country of Iran is led by a Supreme Leader of the government as well as the Shi'a Islamic faith. Like so many other radical philosophers, his ideas did not die with him, but continue today in Iran as well as in various groups that practice the Shi'a tradition of Islam. The largest of these groups is in Lebanon and is called Hezbollah, meaning "the Party of Allah (God)." The group is headed by Hassan Nasrallah and is focused on the destruction of Israel and the expulsion of Western powers (including the United States) from the Middle East. Hezbollah is heavily funded and supported by Iran and has been suspected in a number of bloody and vicious suicide bombings, including the 1983 barracks bombing in Beirut, killing 241 Marines.

REVIEW QUESTIONS

1. What is fundamentalism and what are the similarities between Islamic fundamentalism and other extremist ideologies?
2. What is eschatology? How does it relate to religious fundamentalism?
3. What was the Arab Spring? Where did it begin and is it still continuing today? Give examples of countries where the Arab Spring was a prominent factor.
4. What are the common assumptions within Islamic fundamentalism and radicalism?
5. Who was Muhammad Ibn Abd al-Wahhab, and what are the basic tenets of Wahhabism?
6. Who was Hassan al-Banna and what was his contribution to fundamental Islam?
7. Who was Sayyid Qutb and why is he often referred to as "the father of modern terrorism"?
8. What are the differences between Salafism and Wahhabism?
9. Who was Ayatollah Ruhollah Khomeini and what was his significance to radical Islamic thought?
10. Who is Hassan Nasrallah, and what is Hezbollah?
11. How did the Islamic State burgeon to such international importance in such a relatively short time?
12. How does the Islamic State justify its brutal use of violence in war as well as daily life?

CRITICAL THINKING EXERCISES

1. **MEMRI and al-Jazeera America.** Visit the homepage for the Middle East Media Research Institute (MEMRI) at www.memri.org. MEMRI is a nonprofit research institute that provides timely translations of Arabic, Farsi, Urdu-Pashtu, and Dari media for an American and worldwide audience. Popular as well as scholarly media from the Middle East is translated into English, French, Polish, Japanese, and Hebrew. It is one of the most widely respected and utilized online media resources relating to the Middle East. Study the website and read newspaper articles from Cairo, Baghdad, and Istanbul as well as listen to news broadcasts

from Mecca, Beirut, and Damascus. Visit the "Jihad and Terrorism Threat Monitor" on the site as well. How do you think MEMRI serves an American audience in understanding the Middle East? How much meaning do you think is lost in the translation of an article from one language to another? Next visit the homepage for al-Jazeera America at www.america .aljazeera.com. Compare the two news media websites. How do they differ, or do they? How much of the media presented is formatted in an unbiased and fact-based style? What agenda does each site have, and how does this agenda impact fact-based reporting?

2. **Historical Problems in the Levant.** Research the Middle Eastern area known as the Levant—an area of land between Egypt, Anatolia, Mesopotamia, and the Arabian Desert. The Levant is an ancient land of great historical civilizations. From the center of the Ur civilization (2100 B.C.) to the kingdom of Babylonia (1700 B.C.), to the ancient Greek and Roman Empires (300 B.C. to 400 A.D.), to the great Ottoman Empire of the twentieth century, the Levant has been the crossroad for communication, trade, and commerce between the Middle East to the rest of the world (Europe). The Levant is a geographical area composed of the modern-day countries of Israel, the Palestinian territories of the Gaza and the West Bank, Syria, Jordan, and Lebanon. It is a fertile area located on the southeastern shores of the Mediterranean Sea. Great spiritual meaning has also been given to the area of the Levant as it represents the lands of Abraham, Moses, Jesus, and Muhammad. It is also an area that has witnessed significant historical conflict. Study the countries of the Levant and focus on the current conflict in Syria. Try to identify which groups discussed in this chapter are actively fighting or supporting a specific side in Syria. Next research the history of the al-Assad family in Syria. Who is Bashar al-Assad and do you think he will abdicate his monarchy in the near future? Why or why not?

NOTES

1. Martin E. Marty and R. Scott Appleby directed *The Fundamentalism Project* at the University of Chicago, funded by the American Academy of Arts and Sciences, from 1987 to 1996. Together, they published five volumes as a series on conservative fundamentalism between 1991 and 1995 distributed through the University of Chicago Press. See www.press.uchicago .edu/ucp/books/series/FP.html. This definition of fundamentalism is quoted from Volume 4; see Martin E. Marty and R. Scott Appleby (eds.), *Accounting for Fundamentalisms: The Dynamic Character of Movements* (Chicago, IL: University of Chicago Press, 1994), p. 1.

2. Much of the discussion on Christian Identity theology was informed by early writings of prominent leaders in the movement, such as William Pierce, author of the *Turner Diaries* and a leader in the National Alliance and American Nazi Party, and the Reverent Richard Butler, pastor of the Church of Christ's Christians of Hayden Lake, Idaho. Both Pierce and Butler are now deceased.

3. See Jonathan R. White, "Political Eschatology: A Theology of Antigovernment Extremism," *American Behavioral Scientist*, Vol. 44, pp. 937–956 and *Terrorism: An Introduction*, 3rd edition (Belmont, CA: Wadsworth Thomson Learning, 2002), pp. 46–61.

4. See White, *Terrorism: An Introduction*, pp. 53–54; and Bruce Hoffman, "Holy Terror: The Implications of Terrorism Motivated by a Religious Imperative," *Studies in Conflict and Terrorism*, Vol. 18, pp. 271–284.

5. Weitzman, *Religious Radicalism in the Greater Middle East.*

6. John Murphy, *The Sword of Islam* (Amherst, MA: Prometheus Books, 2002).

7. Lawrence Davidson, *Islamic Fundamentalism* (Westport, CT: Greenwood Press, 1998).

8. Ibid.

9. John Esposito, *Islam and the Straight Path* (New York: Oxford University Press, 1991).

10. Ibid.

11. This quick facts box is based on restated and reorganized information in Biography: Mustafa Kemal Ataturk, 2014, pp. 1–3, www.biography.com/people/mustafa-kemal-ataturk -20968109#synopsis, accessed August 19, 2014, and "Ataturk, Founder of the Turkish Republic and First President of the Republic," 2005, pp. 1–3, www.kultur.gov.tr/EN,31350/ biography-of-ataturk.html, accessed August 19, 2014.

12. See Frantz Fanon, *Black Skins, White Masks* (1961); *The Wretched of the Earth* (1963); and *A Dying Colonialism* (1965) (all translated from the French and published by New York: Grove Press, Inc.).

13. John Esposito, *The Islamic Threat: Myth or Reality?* (New York: Oxford University Press, 1965).

14. Ibid.

15. Esposito, *Islam and the Straight Path*.

16. Davidson, *Islamic Fundamentalism*.

17. Ibid.

18. Much of this section is derived from the works of John Esposito, *Islam and the Straight Path*, 1991.

19. Lansine Kaba, *The Wahhabiyya* (Evanston, IL: Northwestern University Press, 1974).

20. Davidson, *Islamic Fundamentalism*.

21. See Kaba, *The Wahhabiyya*.

22. Ibid.

23. Ibid.

24. David Benjamin, *The Age of Sacred Terror* (New York: Random House, 2002).

25. Ziyad Abu Amr, *Islamic Fundamentalism in the West Bank and Gaza* (Indianapolis, IN: Indiana University Press, 1994).

26. Henry Munson, *Islam and Revolution in the Middle East* (New Haven, CT: Yale University Press, 1989).

27. Fluehr-Lobban (ed.), *Against Islamic Extremism* (Gainesville, FL: University of Florida Press, 1998).

28. Ibid.

29. Murphy, *The Sword of Islam*.

30. Ibid., p. 103.

31. Munson, *Islam and Revolution in the Middle East*.

32. Benjamin, *The Age of Sacred Terror*.

33. Ibid.

34. Munson, *Islam and Revolution in the Middle East*.

35. Ibid.

36. Esposito, *Islam and the Straight Path*.

37. Benjamin, *The Age of Sacred Terror*, p. 124.

38. Ibid.

39. Ibid, p. 17.

40. Bruno Leone, *The Spread of Islam* (San Diego, CA: Greenhaven Press, 1999).

41. Ibid.

42. Davidson, *Islamic Fundamentalism*.

43. Benjamin, *The Age of Sacred Terror*.

44. Ibid.

45. Davidson, *Islamic Fundamentalism*.

46. Sayyid Qutb wrote over a hundred books mainly focusing on social justice and Islam. One of his central themes is the Islamic concept of *tawhid* (the singularity of God and, therefore, of the universe). See Sayyid Qutb, *Milestone*s (Beirut, Lebanon: The Holy Quran Publishing House, 1980).

47. International Policy Institute for Counter-Terrorism, "Terrorist Organizations: Martyrs of Al-Aqsa," www.ict.org.il/; and Council on Foreign Relations, "Al-Aqsa Martyrs Brigade: Palestinian Nationalists," www.terrorismanswers.om/groups/alaqa.html

48. Ibid.

49. The case against Sami al-Arian has been well publicized for the last decade. After his indictment on charges under the USA Patriot Act, a 13-day tumultuous trial was conducted in November 2005 under much media attention. The government's case was built on over 20,000 hours of surveillance and years of wiretaps on al-Arian. A jury acquitted al-Arian on the majority of the 17-count indictment and was deadlocked on the remaining charges. The case was viewed as a major defeat and embarrassment to the government and led to extensive review and commentary of the USA Patriot Act. The case has had international impact and has been the subject of books and movies. See *USA* v. *Al-Arian*, an award-winning 2007 documentary film by Norwegian director Line Halvorsen.

50. The Racketeer Influenced and Corrupt Organization Act (RICO) is a U.S. federal law (Chapter 96, 18 USC, Section 1961–1968) that allows civil as well as criminal charges

against individuals engaged in activities of an ongoing criminal organization. Enacted through the Organized Crime Control Act of 1970, the law was primary developed to assist in the prosecution of organized crime figures and cartels.

51. Don Peretz, *Intifada: The Palestinian Uprising* (Boulder, CO: Westview Press, 1990), pp. 104–106.

52. See *The Charter of the Islamic Resistance Movement,* August 18, 1988, Article 15. English interpretations can be located at http://avalon.law.yale.edu/20th_century/hamas.asp

53. See British Broadcasting Company (BBC) News, "Who Are Hamas?" http://news.bbc.co.uk/2/hi/in_depth/middle_east/2001/israel_and_the_palestinians/profiles/1654510.stm

54. UPI, "Report: Hamas Attacks Possible in the U.S." March 16, 2003.

55. Murphy, *The Sword of Islam.*

56. Ibid., p. 69.

57. Esposito, *Islam and the Straight Path*, p. 84.

58. For a more in-depth discussion of Salafism, refer to John Murphy, *The Sword of Islam.* Much of this section has been derived from his original work.

59. Munson, *Islam and Revolution in the Middle East.*

60. Ibid.

61. See John L. Esposito, *Islam and Politics*, 4th edition, www.docstoc.com/docs/68724700/esposito-islamic-threat

62. Ibid.

63. Ibid.

64. Anonymous, "The Mystery of ISIS," *The New York Review of Books*, August 13, 2016. See: www.nybooks.com/articles/2015/08/13/mystery-isis/

65. One of the first research pieces linking al-Zarqawi with the development of the Islamic State in Iraq and Syria, to modern-day Islamic State, can be found in the Pulitzer Prize-winning book by Joby Warrick, *Black Flags: The Rise of ISIS* (New York: DoubleDay Publishing, 2015).

66. Mary Ann Weaver, "The Short, Violent Life of Abu Musab al-Zarqawi," *The Atlantic*, July/August, 2006. See: www.theatlantic.com/magazine/archive/2006/07/the-short-violent-life-of-abu-musab-al-zarqawi/304983/

67. *Spiegel Online*, "The Butcher of Baghdad Is Dead," June 8, 2006. See: www.spiegel.de/international/iraq-confirms-death-of-al-qaida-s-zarqawi-the-butcher-of-baghdad-is-dead-a-420251.html

68. John F. Burns, "U.S. Strike Hits Insurgent at Safehouse," *New York Times*, June 8, 2006. See: www.nytimes.com/2006/06/08/world/middleeast/08cnd-iraq.html

69. Amre Sarhan, "CIA: 30,000 Foreign Fighters Have Traveled to Syria and Iraq to Join ISIS," Iraq News, September 29, 2016.

70. SITE Intelligence Group on the Jihadist Threat. See: https://news.siteintelgroup.com/

71. Alicia Kort, "How ISIS Leader Abu Bakr al-Baghdadi Came to Be." *Newsweek* (September 24, 2016). See: www.newsweek.com/abu-bar-al-baghdadi-isis-499594

72. Pentagon spokesman Peter Cook told ____CNN that U.S. security agencies "do think Baghdadi is alive and is still leading" the Islamic State, on December 30, 2016.

73. See Faisal Irshaid, "ISIS, ISIL, IS or Daesh? One Group, Many Names," BBC News, December 2, 2015. See: www.bbc.com/news/world-middle-east-27994277

74. Graeme Wood, "What ISIS Really Wants," *Atlantic*, March 2015, p. 2.

75. Andrew Anthony, "Anjem Choudary: The British Extremist Who Backs the Caliphate," *Guardian* (September, 2014). See: www.theguardian.com/world/2014/sep/07/anjem-choudary-islamic-state-isis

76. See Baqer Moin, *Khomeini: Life of the Ayatollah* (New York: Tauris Publishing, 2009); and Edward Willett, *Ayatollah Khomeini* (New York: Rosen Publishing, 2003).

77. See "The Hizballah (Hezbollah) Program," *The Jerusalem Quarterly,* No. 48, Fall 1988, ____www.ict.org.il/Articles/Hiz_letter.htm

78. Matthew Levitt, *Hezbollah: The Global Footprint of Lebanon's Party of God* (Washington, D.C.: Georgetown University Press, 2013).

79. Bassem Mroue, "Hezbollah Chief Vows to Continue Fighting in Syria," *USA Today*, November 14, 2013.

Terrorist Organizations and Structures

Learning Objectives

After completing this chapter, you should be able to:

1. Identify the five key dilemmas facing terrorist organizations.

2. Identify six organizational models of terrorist organizations and briefly describe each.

3. Explain how ideology helps terrorists identify targets and view victims.

4. State the ways Cronin sees terrorist organizations ending.

Security officials in Karachi, Pakistan, arrest alleged Taliban Commander Abdullah, who also uses the alias Abu Waqas. Abdullah was involved in recruiting female suicide bombers and planning terrorist activities.

(Xinhua Zuma/America/Newscom)

Introduction

Organizations have existed for centuries. Alexander the Great (356–323 B.C.) used one to conquer much of the known world, and the first bishops created the Catholic Church, and Catholicism became a worldwide religion.[1] These examples illustrate an important characteristic of organizations: They are oriented toward achieving goals. Organizations exist to do the things a single person or a few people are unwilling or can't do by themselves.[2] To illustrate, for a terrorist movement to launch a complex attack on a "hard" target, such as a military base, requires an organization that can effectively collect and evaluate intelligence; plan the attack; collect the equipment needed; train the attackers; get them to the point of the attack; make the assault; collect arms, intelligence, supplies (e.g., medical), and any prisoners; withdraw; and move to a safe position.

Even well-established organizations do not always run smoothly, and for new, "start-up" terrorist organizations "life" is very hazardous. Regardless of what organization model or structure is adopted, dilemmas invariably "pop up." This chapter examines a variety of topics, including the dilemmas facing "start-up" terrorist organizations, the types of organizational structures they might use, the selection of targets, suicide bombers and martyrdom, and how terrorist organizations end.

Dilemmas of Terrorist Organization

Terrorist movements have to develop some form of organizational structure. They need one to ensure their continued existence and to progress toward achieving their goals. Frisch notes that in choosing an organizational structure, terrorist movements face five key dilemmas.[3]

Action versus Secrecy

All terrorist movements are caught between two organizational imperatives: (1) taking action and (2) maintaining internal secrecy.[4] Action is necessary to advance the cause, publicize it, and gain recruits and supporters (see Figure 5–1 and Table 5–1). The dilemma is that as more attacks are made, it becomes more difficult to maintain internal secrecy because the success attracts more attention from security services. Internal secrecy means such things as protecting the location of operatives, the identity of future targets, and how the movement is financed. However, internal secrecy also complicates the task of communicating with and coordinating the various parts of the terrorist movement.[5]

In contrast to internal secrecy, a terrorist organization is not concerned about external security. A terrorist movement wants the public to know its name and cause and to fear it. Ironically, this publicity is provided for free by the news media. The Palestinian terrorist group Black September massacred Israeli athletes at the 1972 Olympics in Munich, Germany. Cronin recalls that Abu Daoud, one of the surviving gunmen, claimed that the murder of 11 Israelis forced "our cause" into the homes of 500 million viewers.[6]

Growth versus Control

Terrorist movements start off as a small collection of like-minded individuals. As a terrorist organization attracts new recruits, its numbers increase and there may also be a growth in the geographic area it can control or have an impact upon. To facilitate growth, the leader of a movement must relinquish a great deal of the operational control he or she had when the movement was smaller.[7] At some point, the leader has to delegate some tasks for running the organization to lower-ranking leaders.

One result of this is the leader has less actual contact or "face time" with fighters. This weakens the charismatic role and impact of the leader because he/she is increasingly busy with administrative tasks, such as securing financial supporters. As growth occurs, one of the key decisions is determining what organizational model the movement will adopt. This topic is discussed in a subsequent section of this chapter.

It would be difficult to overstate the importance of a vision and goals for a terrorist movement. In April 2013, al Baghdadi announced the formation of the Islamic State in Iraq and the Levant (ISIL, later shortened to the Islamic State). It was the first time in

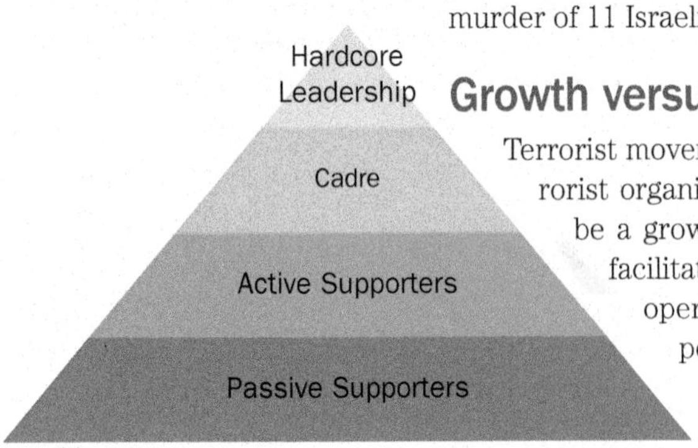

FIGURE 5–1

Levels of involvement in terrorist organizations

Source: "A Military Guide to Terrorism in the Twenty-First Century," United States Army, Fort Leavenworth, Kansas: TRADOC G2, August 15, 2007, p. 3–3, with minor changes.

TABLE 5–1
Levels of Involvement in a Terrorist Organization

Level of Involvement	Actions Taken
Hardcore Leadership	The hardcore leadership of a terrorist movement may have helped to establish the terrorist organization or been promoted multiple times. It has a vision of what the movement wants to achieve, articulates goals, establishes policies and rules, and approves operations. Finally, it ensures that the targeting and violence support the vision and goals.
Cadre	Overall, a cadre is a group of core members that form a dependable nucleus within a terrorist organization. They direct functions such as intelligence; counterintelligence; and targeting, finances, logistics, propaganda, communication functions and plans and conduct operations. Mid-level cadre tend to be trainers and specialists, such as surveillance experts; while lower-level cadre are often direct-action specialists such as snipers.
Active Supporters	Participate in fundraising and other activities, such as providing safe houses, medical care, and transportation. They are fully aware of their relationship with the terrorist organization. They may or may not be known to those outside of the terrorist organization.
Passive Supporters	Sympathetic to goals of the terrorist organization, but not committed enough to take an active role. May assist a front for the terrorist organization and not be fully aware of its true purpose.

Source: A Military Guide to Terrorism in the Twenty-First Century, United States Army, Fort Leavenworth, Kansas: TRADOC G2, August 15, 2007, pp. 3–4, with minor changes.

Hardcore leadership
The hardcore leadership of a terrorist movement may have helped to establish the terrorist organization or been promoted multiple times. It has a vision of what the movement wants to achieve, establishes policies, rules of administration and conduct, articulates goals, and approves operations. Finally, it ensures that the targeting and violence support the vision and goals.

Cadre
A cadre is a group of core members that form a dependable nucleus within a terrorist organization.

Active supporters
Participate in fundraising and other activities, such as providing safe houses, medical care, and transportation. They are fully aware of their relationship with the terrorist organization. They may or may not be known to those outside of the terrorist organization.

Passive supporters
These types of supporters are sympathetic to the goals of the terrorist organization, but not committed enough to take an active role. They may assist a front for the terrorist organization and not be fully aware of their relationship to the terrorist organization.

90 years that a movement had attempted to establish a sovereign Muslim state in the Middle East. (See discussions on the Islamic State and its attempts to establish a Muslim caliphate in Chapter 4.) Al Baghdadi urged Muslims to come to the Islamic State being forged out of land in Iraq and Syria and to bring their whole households. They would be given food and homes, children would be schooled, there would be electricity for heating and cooking, women for brides, and a pay of $1,100 for each fighter. Excitement was palpable and produced what has been called the Great Jihad Migration, swelling the ranks of IS.[8] It is thought that people from 100 countries may have joined IS in Syria.[9]

Omar Hammami
An American who went to Somalia and joined the clan-based Islamic terrorist movement al-Shabaab, which later killed him. Because Hammami was murdered by the movement he joined, Americans aspiring to be part of a foreign terrorist organization may have second thoughts about doing so.

Recruitment versus Retention

The terrorist movement Harakat Shabaab al-Mujahidin (al-Shabaab) organized a press conference in Somalia. Its purpose was to "show off" an American-born recruit (see Figure 5–2). The twenty-seven-year-old **Omar Hammami** (1984–2013) left Alabama in 2006 and joined the clan-based terrorist group al-Shabaab. Later, Hammami took the name of Abu Mansur al-Amriki (the American). Seven years later, after a series of public disagreements with al-Shabaab, the movement killed him in an ambush. A Department of Homeland Security report claims only 250 Americans have attempted to travel to, or actually reached and joined, a foreign terrorist organization.[10] The same report estimates 25,000 people have gone to the Syrian battlefield to join radical Islamic movements, 4,500 of whom are Westerners.[11]

The consequences of poor recruitment choices are severe for terrorist organizations. It may result in arrests, casualties, and having entire operations terminated or "rolled up" by governmental agents. Frisch argues that there are three main reasons why individuals choose to join a terrorist movement: (1) family members, friends, or individuals in the recruit's social network are going to join or have already done so; (2) the recruit, family members, or members of the recruit's social network have strong grievances against

FIGURE 5–2
A federal warrant was issued for Omar Hammami in 2007. It alleged several crimes related to supporting a terrorist organization. Fluent in Arabic, he rapped songs about the "glory of martyrdom." He was also known as Abu Mansoor Al-Amriki (the American).

(Farah Abdi Warsameh/AP Images)

Box 5-1
Retention in IS

Leaving the Islamic State (IS) is not a simple matter.[12] They make it hard to leave: On arrival, your passport and other identification are taken away. Your identity as a resident of another country is banished in lieu of an oath to the Islamic State. Your family is now second, again in lieu of IS that now becomes your sole obsession as a state, a family, and an identity. Some who joined do not like the idea of losing their nationality as a Jordanian, Iraqi, Syrian, or the like. They do not want to place their wife and family in the second priority of life, or they simply do not like the things they have to do. Some argue that the Islamic State may well break the tenets of Islam, and that female prisoners should not be physically and sexually abused, nor should they be forced into weddings with IS fighters. Others may dislike the way female recruits are treated, or for that fact, the way any Islamic fighter is treated. Many revolt at the idea of killing or executing fellow Muslims for very minor violations of the Islamic Law (Sharia), especially when proof of the violation is based on rumor or speculation. Sadly, the consequences of even expressing a desire to leave the Islamic State can be far-reaching and deadly; public humiliation, torture, and/or execution of the individual and their family are not uncommon. Gruesome beheadings, stonings, crucifixions, and shootings "remind" IS fighters to keep their ranks and not desert their duties.

Recently, members of the Islamic State executed 120 mostly foreign fighters who wanted to return home.[13] These executions were public, designed to intimidate followers and "encourage" blind obedience to the Islamic State and existing leadership. However, loyalty that is based on fear does not work, and today,

there are numerous accounts of individuals who have defected from IS. Many of these accounts are found in newspaper articles, books, movies, and scores of videos on the Internet. Yet, while some individual fighters may have been successful in physically escaping from IS in Iraq or Syria; many still live in fear for their family and their lives from a vengeful IS.

▲ IS fighters prepare to execute defectors from their ranks.
Handout/Alamy Stock Photo

Do you think that executing foreign fighters that want to return home within the Islamic State encourages discipline and order within the organization?

---

the government; and (3) deep religious and/or political beliefs inspire the recruit to fight for a cause.[14]

In addition to those three reasons, there are also much more pragmatic reasons: Often there are no other jobs, the recruit needs money to support himself and his family, and joining provides the family with services and assistance that the government does not. Occasionally, some terrorist groups coerce people to join, an unwise strategy because they are candidates to leave the movement and become informers. Some fighters switch from one movement to another because they will be paid better. If captured by another terrorist organization, even if fighting a common enemy, you may not be given the chance to change sides.

Although there may be a primary reason for joining terrorist organizations, there are others as well. Hezbollah has released a number of violent Internet games, such as "Special Force" and "Ash." **Jabhat Fateh al Sham (JFS)** in its former incarnation (al-Nusra) had a history of producing and distributing comic books, generating graphic novels, and releasing online videos such as *Mustafa Hamdi* that extoll the virtues of Islam and jihad in Syria. The purpose of these games, comics, graphic novels, and videos is to indoctrinate children and attract recruits.[15] However, the Islamic State (IS) excels at using social media to exploit teenagers. JFS and IS are the two most effective forces in Syria because of their financial resources. They attract fighters with the highest pay and the opportunity to use the best weapons.

Retention of current members is essential because: (1) they have already been trained; (2) current members may also be experienced and proven themselves to be reliable; and (3) some of them will be groomed for, or assigned, important, organizational roles, for example, making "pitches" to potential recruits, training them, or becoming couriers, reconnaissance specialists, and operational leaders. Recruiting is discussed in greater detail in Chapter 6.

Jabhat Fateh al Sham (JFS)
Al-Nusra was created by al Qaeda in Iraq (AQI) and sent to Syria in support of President Bashar al-Assad's government. With on-going fighting there AQI thought some advantage might be gained from doing so. In 2016, al Nusra, now renamed as Jabhat Fateh al-Sham (The Front for the Conquest of the Levant), separated from al-Qaeda and also remains separate from IS.

Success versus Longevity

Terrorist organizations must balance the risks associated with conducting operations with the need to ensure their own long-term survival.[16] The use of terror tactics against unarmed, defenseless civilian targets fulfills both of these needs. Terrorists feel assured their casualties will be light. If mass casualties can be inflicted in an attack, it will attract financial supporters and new recruits to the terrorist group. These supporters and new recruits are essential for the continued life of the movement. Still, only 5 percent of newly formed terrorist organizations exist after their first year.[17]

One way for an organization to ensure longevity is to reinvent itself. The classical example of this is the March of Dimes. In 1938, President Roosevelt created the Foundation for Infantile Paralysis (polio). It quickly became known as the March of Dimes because people were asked to contribute 10 cents by slipping a dime into a pouch on a card. When the Salk vaccine became available in 1955, polio cases dropped quickly. In 1958, the March of Dimes announced a new goal: the prevention of birth defects, which it continues to pursue.

Another potential way of acquiring longevity is to adopt long-term goals toward which the terrorist organization can work in perpetuity, but may not be able to ever achieve.[18] Al-Qaeda's stated goal is to establish a worldwide Muslim community. The neo-Nazi National Socialist Movement (NSM) wants to prevent all non-white immigration into the United States. The goal of ultra-violent skinheads is domination in America by "White Nationalists." Organizations that achieve their goals either go out of business or must reinvent themselves.

Gaibulloev and Sandler's statistical analysis of the longevity and demise of terrorist organizations over an eight-year period revealed some important patterns. Religious-based terrorist movements have longer longevity,[19] perhaps because it is easier to maintain ideological fervor. A homogenous society is hostile to the excessive actions of terrorist groups, whereas a heterogeneous one may to some degree be more tolerant about such "dissent."[20] Geography and terrain may also play a role in longevity: North Africa is conducive to durable movements,[21] although that finding may be a surrogate for the dense Islamic population from which some terrorist groups can recruit and the terrain in which bases can be hidden.[22] Conversely, landlocked nations are an adverse factor, because it is harder for terrorists to import weapons and fighters.[23]

Other features of durable terrorist organizations include an emphasis on diverse methods of domestic attacks, multiple bases from which to operate, and inflicting high casualties with their attacks.[24] A lack of one or more of these conditions could be fatal to a movement. Perhaps the most ominous sign for a terrorist group is experiencing high casualties in each attack it makes, causing fighters and supporters to fade away.

Resource Acquisition versus Constituencies

Olson described how ancient Chinese bandit gangs got their resources. He noted they used two strategies to obtain them: roving and stationary. Roving bandits go into a village, take everything they can, and leave. Stationary bandits settle down and receive something like steady tribute from the village. These bandits get small amounts over a longer period of time, creating a continuing flow of resources.[25] Modern terrorist organizations must also make decisions about how they obtain resources. Ones that select a stationary approach and use violence sparingly are able to attract more highly committed, ideologically motivated recruits while maintaining popular support.[26] The Islamic State (IS) contravenes this approach and

Quick Facts
The Islamic State and Recruiting

The Islamic State's recruiting effort is as much as a global brand marketing campaign as it is recruiting. That campaign resonates in the American heartland as periodically potential fighters leaving the country to join IS have their journey interrupted by being arrested. The IS media campaign is sophisticated beyond anything al-Qaeda has done. Key components of the IS campaign are effective use of social media and peer-to-peer communication.

Think of al-Qaeda's video with Usama bin Laden just talking as Version 1.0. Al-Shabaab's Anwar al-Awlaki's rapping in Arabic got us to 2.0, and IS's sophisticated manipulations propelled the state-of-the-art to 3.0.[27] In addition to global branding and recruiting fighters, IS wants to provide enough information and propaganda that some people will be self-radicalizing, becoming homegrown terrorists.

exploits people living in areas they control. In Syria, they "rent" equipment actually owned by farmers to the farmers. If a family in an IS-controlled area wants to travel to another IS city, there is a fee and a number of days set for the travel. If the family doesn't return on time, their home and all property are forfeited to IS. Several news media reports from Syria have noted that the terrorists live very well, but the rest of the people do not. Terrorist financing is further explored in Chapter 6, "Critical Processes of Terrorist Organizations."

Terrorist Organizational Models

Terrorist movements do not have total discretion about what organizational form they adopt. Many factors shape that decision, including (1) the number of active followers; (2) the geographical locations in which they will locate; (3) the operational pace[28] they intend to pursue; (4) the preferences of supporters; (5) their financial resources; and (6) the capabilities, intentions, and anticipated type of operations of their and opposing forces.[29]

The structure or "bones" of terrorist organizations may be selected by (1) a proactive and deliberate process, (2) using a limited amount of effort by selecting the first one that is "good enough," (3) intermittently reacting to the changing needs of the terrorist group and making incremental changes as needed from time to time, and (4) a reaction to drastic changes, such as significant combat losses or unceasing pressure from security forces or competing terrorist movements. Terrorist forms of organization covered in this section included the lone wolf, cells, networks, hierarchical, umbrella, and virtual models.

Lone Wolf Organizational Model

"Lone wolf" is like "terrorism" in that multiple definitions exist. Becker's definition is conceptually tight: A lone wolf is ideologically driven to violence or attempted violence and personally plans and executes the attack in the absence of collaboration with other individuals or groups perpetuates it.[30] This definition means the greatest number a lone wolf can be is one. However, other definitions of lone wolf allow the participation of two to four enablers or argue that when several lone wolves form a terrorist cell, they are a "wolf pack or wolf den." The discussion in this section substantially follows Becker's definition. Some researchers have shifted to using "lone actor terrorist" instead of lone wolf terrorist.[31]

Historically, American lone wolves are diverse, but tend to be single white males, often have created their own ideology, have a criminal record, spring from modest socioeconomic backgrounds, and have been unemployed or had part-time jobs. They are less well-educated and older than the average member of a terrorist group, are in their mid-thirties, and tend to suffer more from mental illness than members of the general population or members of terrorist movements.[32]

Quick Facts
The Lone Wolf Attack on Canada's Parliament

In 2003, al-Qaeda issued a video in 2006, *How to Fight Alone*, again calling for independent action. [33]

In June 2014, the Islamic State (IS) directed those who could not come to Syria to attack the "Westerners and unbelievers there."[34] Again that year, in its online, English language magazine, *DaBiq*, IS urged: "Every Muslim should get out of his house, find a crusader, and kill him. If you are not able to find an improvised explosive device (IED), smash his head with a rock, slaughter him with a knife, run him over with your car, throw him down from a high place, choke or poison him, but do not be contemptible.[35] If you cannot do these things, burn his home, car, or business." [36]

It seems clear that some of these appeals, whether made by al-Qaeda, IS, peers, family members, friends, or returning fighters can have an effect. Consider the case of Canadian Joseph Bibeau.

Born Joseph Paul Michael Bibeau in Canada, Joseph converted to Islam around 2005. Nine years later, as Michael Zehaf Bibeau, 32, he walked up behind an Honor Guard at the National War Memorial in Ottawa and shot him twice in the back, killing him. Bibeau then entered the National Parliament Building, but was shot to death by security forces before he could harm anyone else. Bibeau had a criminal record, a drug problem, was dismissed from studying at a Sunni Mosque in Canada, and wanted to go fight against Bashar al Assad in Syria. Yet, there were no apparent ties to Islamic terrorists, although some associates may have had extremist views. However, the Royal Canadian Mounted Police (RCMP) say they would have charged Bibeau with terrorism had he lived. [37]

Lone wolf terrorism shares some similarities with group-based terrorism, but there are also key differences. Nearly 50 percent of lone wolf terrorist attacks are abortion related versus only 17 percent for group-based movements. With respect to businesses, only 6 percent of lone wolves targeted them, while group-based terrorists did so 27 percent of the time.[38]

Using a definition consistent with Becker's, Hamm and Spaaj studied lone wolf attacks over two time periods;

1. From 1940 to 2000, there were 38 lone wolves who committed 171 attacks, killing 98 and injuring 305. Approximately 60 percent of the lone wolves made only one attack, while the rest made more, including the anti-technologist, Unabomber Theodore "Ted" Kaczynski, who made 16 bomb attacks over 17 years, and Joseph Franklin, who is believed to have murdered as many as 22 people, including mixed-race couples, in an attempt to start a race war.[39] The weapons primarily used were firearms and bombs.[40] Kaczynski is serving life in prison without the possibility of parole. Franklin was executed in 2013.

2. Post-9/11 to 2013, there was greater diversity in the weapons that were to be used or were actually used, including biological weapons, construction equipment, 20-ton vehicles, and knives. Post-9/11 has also produced a greater number of unfulfilled threats and hoaxes. Examples of these include anthrax threats against abortion clinics, downing an electrical grid, and use of a radioactive bomb in an assassination attempt against President Obama.[41] Using vehicles, particularly heavy trucks, as killing weapons increased after the 2014 attack in France (See Figure 5-3).

The smallest terrorist unit or "organization" is the lone wolf. The lone wolf's attack seemingly comes out of nowhere, with no warning. A lone wolf is one person acting alone and he or she can be every bit as dangerous or lethal as any major terrorist organization. Simon notes there are no constraints on their level of violence because lone wolves are not beholden to a financial or other type of supporter who might mediate their degree of lethality.[42] Lone wolves have no group decision-making process, peer pressure, or supervisor to stifle their inclinations. Simon notes that lone wolves were responsible for the first midair plane bombing, vehicle bombing, hijackings, product contamination, and anthrax attacks in the United States.[43] As Simon speculates, a lone wolf could deliver a crippling attack to our infrastructure by a cyber attack.[44] Box 5–2 illustrates violence done by people acting alone who were not charged with terrorism.

FIGURE 5–3
Lone Wolf Terror Attack in France
On the evening of July 14, 2016, a large crowd had gathered in Nice to celebrate Bastille Day (1789), which was a turning point in the long-running French Revolution. Mohamed Lahouaiej-Bouhlel, a thirty-one -year-old Tunisian man living in France, rented a 20-ton truck and drove it at high speeds through 1.2 miles of the crowd, where he was killed by gunfire from three police officers. Note the bullet holes in the windshield and driver's side door. The attack killed 86 people and estimates of the injured range from 202 to 434. The French government declared a three-day mourning period.
(Patrick Aventurier/Stringer/Getty Images)

FIGURE 5–4

A Model of Movement to Radicalization and Action.

Jeffrey Connor and Carol Rollie Flynn, Report: Lone Wolf Terrorism (Georgetown University: Security Studies Program, National Security Critical Issue Task Force, June 27, 2015, Figure 3, p. 1, http://georgetownsecuritystudiesreview.org/wp-content/uploads/2015/08/NCITF-Final-Paper.pdf, accessed March 3, 2017.

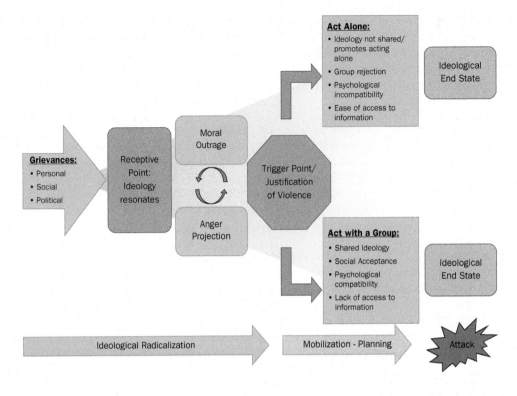

The extrapolation of Connor and Flynn's radicalization model in Figure 5–4 rests on the following five points:[45]

1. People who have a personal grudge/grievances and feel the need to call attention to something that is vitally important to them, for example, saving the rainforests, the need for different social institutions, including religion, and/or political processes.[46] They may also have some degree of affinity toward a particular domestic or foreign ideology, but the lone wolf is not controlled by, nor receives material assistance from, domestic or foreign terrorist movements, although their websites may be visited. A key dynamic for the lone wolf is that normal correction of the situation to which they are opposed is not possible and violence is required. Attacks committed by lone wolves conforming to Becker's are sometimes called "authentic" lone wolf attacks.

2. The receptive point or "cognitive opening" of a potential terrorist recruit occurs when external factors or events shake the lone wolf's reliance upon their traditional precepts and "opens them up"[47] to considering other ways of dealing with problems they perceive as being very important. To illustrate, consider two examples: (1) In San Antonio, a younger brother is framed for armed robbery and sentenced to confinement for eight years. The older brother knows his sibling couldn't have done it because the two of them were fishing when the robbery happened; and (2) In Syria, a younger brother who is arrested for writing anti-government graffiti on a wall, dies during interrogation the next day, and the body is not released to the family. In both cases, the psychological trauma of experiencing a great wrong creates a vulnerability to listening or attraction to extremist ideologies. In the first case, the older brother might resonate with the anti-government patriot movement and in the second one, a family may identify with radicalized Islam.

3. Few things promote in-group solidarity as quickly as having a target on which to vent your moral outrage and anger. That target is blamed for the unceasing injustices suffered, the moral decline of society, the pervasiveness of poverty, the absence of health care, the deaths of loved ones from drone attacks, or other reasons.

4. Bolstered by an adopted ideology and a focus for outrage and anger, individuals reach a trigger point, where they may just remain radicalized, which happens most

Wade Page served in the Army (1992–1998) but was never deployed to a combat zone. He was barred from reenlisting for showing up drunk at formations and field exercises.[48] Afterward, Page played in skinhead bands specializing in the lyrics of hate[49] and claimed membership in the white supremacist **Hammerskin Nation** (HN), which has a history of violence and hate crimes.[50]

Page entered a Sikh Temple in Wisconsin and shot six people to death, wounding three others. Page committed suicide after being wounded by the police. Page apparently dehumanized the ethnic Indians he killed. He called all non-whites, "dirt people" (Non-Whites). The FBI classified the crime as a lone wolf, domestic terrorist attack.

frequently, or they become actively involved because there is not only a justification for violence, there also is a need for it to rectify the wrong(s).[51] In love, we elevate the object of our affection. In contrast, the radicalized do just the opposite: They dehumanize those they will kill. It is an essential dynamic because it relieves the killers from moral responsibility from what they do.[52] Illustrations of this dynamic include on the American frontier, Native American women and children were killed because "Nits make lice" and in Vietnam, the enemy combatants were "slopes" and "zips."

5. The radicalized may act alone as a preference because of a lack of social skills, the inability to find others who have the same passion about their issue(s), fear of being rejected by a terrorist movement if they sought membership, the causes they championed crossed so many terrorist ideologies that no one movement of them could meet their all of their needs, or the movement didn't accept them.[53]

While it is commonly assumed people join terrorist organizations because they are primarily motivated by strong ideological or religious motives, Polko provides a different perspective: Wanting to improve their financial situation is an equally strong reason to join. In many countries from which terrorists are recruited, the economic situation of being a low-level terrorist is better than the average situation of a citizen in that country. "Joining a terrorist organization is treated as being the rough equivalent of having the worst job in a corporation: It is a pathway to higher, better-paying terrorist jobs in logistics or fundraising, where being the head of a unit or a mid-level leader pays ten times more than those who are actually involved in carrying out operations. The terrorist who volunteers to be a suicide bomber may be completely driven by religious fervor. The "career-minded" terrorist simply has a different balance between religious fervor and their own economic interest, albeit he or she surely is very secretive about it.[54]

Whether a citizen of the United States or a legal resident living here, the lone wolf is a "homegrown terrorist." An American lone wolf is self-radicalized and ordinarily shows little stomach for suicide attacks.[55] A homegrown terrorist who uses Islam as the ideological basis for his or her attacks may be called a "**homegrown jihadist**." When religion is the driving ideology for an attack, it is sometimes referred to as "deified terrorism."

A discrete lone wolf is hard to detect because he or she identifies the target; plans the attack; assembles the materials needed; doesn't have to communicate, coordinate, or get the approval of anyone; and executes the attack. Thus, the lone wolf is self-contained, which enhances **operational security** (OPSEC). Lone wolf attacks are more prevalent in the United States than elsewhere. Of all such attacks that occurred worldwide from 1968 to 2007, 42 percent happened in America.[56] Lone wolves are considered a very significant problem in the United States. This problem is heightened because of al-Qaeda's and IS's continuing emphasis on recruiting Americans.

The main advantage of the lone wolf is that he or she is totally independent and ordinarily has high OPSEC. The flip side of that advantage is the arrest of a lone wolf "rolls up" all pending operations. Historically, the lone wolf primarily has to rely on his or her own resources, which has limited attacks to the use of pistols, rifles, or rudimentary explosive devices. There are some trends in lone wolf terrorism in the United States that have occurred or are on the near horizon:

Wade Page
failed in the Army, where some believe he may have become a white supremacist neo-Nazi, and later played in a band that spouted lyrics of hatred. He may have attacked the Sikhs thinking they were Muslims or because they were simply what he called "dirt people."

Hammerskin Nation
The Hammerskin Nation is a leaderless Dallas-based movement that advocates a "White power skinhead" lifestyle and whose goal is "We must secure the existence of our people and a future for White children." At its earliest, leaderless resistance consisted of one or several people who formed cells to promote white supremacy and resist the oppressive government.

Information Link
West Point's Counter Terrorism Center has an excellent monthly journal, the *CTC Sentinel*, which has terrorism articles written by leading experts. Visit https://ctc.usma.edu for a research project or to stay abreast of things.

Homegrown jihadist
A homegrown terrorist is a self-directed citizen or legal resident who attacks his/her country using radicalized Islam as the ideological basis for doing so.

Operational security
A process to deny potential adversaries information about capabilities and/or intentions by identifying, controlling, and protecting unclassified information that gives evidence of the planning and execution of sensitive activities, such as future operations (OPSEC).

Box 5-2
The Carnage of "Loners"

Laqueur notes that all terrorism is violence, but not all violence is terrorism.[57] None of these examples of decades-spanning violent loners were charged with terrorism. However, their actions demonstrate how much carnage a single person can cause. These violent loners are distinguished from serial murderers in that the former's actions are committed publically, usually during one violent outburst or shooting rampage that ends with the capture or death of the loner.

From 1940 to 1957 in New York City, George Metesky (1903–1994) planted 33 pipe bombs in places such as theaters, restrooms, phone booths, music halls, and libraries. Although the so-called "Mad Bomber" didn't kill anyone, he wounded at least 15 people. A Marine during World War I, he "patriotically" halted his bombing campaign while the United States was involved in World War II. Metesky's personal grudge stemmed from a work-related injury at the Consolidated Edison electrical plant that caused him to lose his job. Metesky was only allowed 26 weeks of benefits. These events turned him bitter. Following his arrest, Metesky was declared incompetent to stand trial. He was confined in a mental hospital until his release in 1973.

On August 1, 1986, Charles Whitman, armed with several high-powered rifles and a shotgun, climbed to the top of a 307-foot tower on the campus of the University of Texas and barricaded himself. Earlier in the day he murdered his wife and mother-in-law. A former Marine, he killed 17 people and wounded another 32 before an Austin police officer went to the top of the tower and shot him dead.

A twelve -year-old girl was among seven people in the Chicago area who died from unknowingly taking an Extra Strength Tylenol laced with cyanide. Investigation revealed that the deadly drug had not been added in its production. Someone bought the Tylenol, added the cyanide, and returned it to the shelf of a store to be sold again. This 1982 incident resulted in many manufacturers adding tamperproof features, which previously had been nonexistent. Although these seven murders were never solved, investigators believe only one perpetrator was involved. This conclusion was based on the theory that if it was more than one, word would have slipped out and a suspect with knowledge of it arrested for an unrelated crime would have used it to bargain for leniency. Alternatively, the perpetrator may have murdered any co-conspirator to prevent being identified.

The phrase **"Going postal,"** becoming uncontrollably angry, originated in the Edmond, Oklahoma, Post Office. Patrick Sherrill, a disgruntled postal worker and former Marine, was a loner and socially inept.[58] Sherrill entered the Post Office on August 20,

1986, with three semi-automatic pistols. Apparently upset about a reprimand he had received, Sherrill walked through the facility, killing 14 people and wounding 6 before killing himself.[59]

A twenty-three -year-old South Korean senior majoring in English at Virginia Polytechnic Institute (VPI) bought guns and methodically killed people in several buildings on the VPI campus on April 16, 2007. Cho Seung-Hui murdered 32 people and also wounded a number of others before killing himself. Some people were injured jumping out of buildings to avoid contact with the shooter.

Joseph A. Stack loaded a light airplane with a 50-gallon drum filled with gasoline. He flew the plane into an IRS office in Austin, Texas. That February 18, 2010, attack killed Stack and an Internal Revenue Service (IRS) employee (see Figure 5–5). Several other people were injured. He left behind a rambling manifesto against the federal government, calling for "American zombies to wake up and revolt."[60] Stack is that rare exception to the general proposition that American lone wolves have no appetite for suicide attacks, that is, their death is contemporaneous with the detonation of explosives. However, it is not uncommon for mass shooters to kill themselves when the police have them cornered.

On January 8, 2011, U.S. House of Representatives member Gabrielle "Gabby" Giffords was meeting with constituents in the parking lot of a mall in the Tucson area when Jared Lee Loughner, 22, walked up to her and shot her in the head. Before he was done, Loughner shot another 17 people, six of whom died. However, Representative Giffords was not among them. Loughner had been displaying strange behavior in the months leading up to the shooting, posting videos in which he talked about mind control, the gold standard, and one in which he displayed a gun. He withdrew from a community college after five episodes of disruptive behavior on campus.[61] Loughner pleaded guilty to all charges and was sentenced to imprisonment for life, plus 140 years.

In Newtown, Connecticut, twenty-year-old Adam Lanza got dressed the morning of December 14, 2012, and killed his mother with a shot to the head as she was lying in bed. Armed with a semi-automatic rifle and two handguns, he went to the nearby Sandy Hook Elementary School. He shot up a security door to gain entrance to the school and quickly killed 20 children and 6 adults before shooting himself as the police closed in on him. All of the children killed were six or seven years old. The motive for Lanza's brutal massacre was not established by investigators.

The morning of September 16, 2013, Aaron Alexis, a Navy contractor, entered the Washington Naval Yard and killed 12 people

Going postal

The phrase "going postal," means becoming uncontrollably mad. It originated at the Edmond, Oklahoma, Post Office. In 1986, a disgruntled postal worker went on a murderous rampage and then committed suicide.

FIGURE 5–5
Joseph Stack set his home on fire and then flew his light plane into these offices, some of which were occupied by the U.S. Internal Revenue Service. The building was racked by 50-foot flames for three hours before the fire was brought under control.

(Ralph Barrera/PSG/Newscom)

with a shotgun. As is often the case in such crimes, a portion of the initial report was wrong: Alexis was not armed with a military-style assault rifle (AR-15), but a 12-gauge shotgun (Remington 870 pump), commonly used for hunting. The Navy Yard was sealed off and the hunt for Alexis began. Eventually, he was located and in the ensuing gunfight he was killed.

On April 2, 2014, Army Specialist Ivan Lopez opened fire on military and civilian personnel at Fort Hood, Texas. The eight-minute rampage ended with 3 people being killed and another 16 being wounded by Lopez, who was armed with a single Smith and Wesson 45-caliber pistol. He had a history of mental problems and had completed a tour in Iraq the previous year (2013). According to the ensuing investigation, Lopez was upset that he had only been given a 24-hour pass to attend his mother's funeral in November 2013.

Lopez subsequently committed suicide when confronted by a female military police officer. The event marked the second time in five years that a mass shooting had occurred on the grounds of Fort Hood Army Base in Killeen, Texas. The first was by an Army Psychiatrist and Medical Corps officer, Major Nidal Malik Hasan. Coincidentally, Lopez and Hasan purchased their weapons at the same gun store just days before their shooting rampages.

As Germanwings Flight 9525 flew from Spain toward Dusseldorf, Germany, on March 24, 2014, everything seemed normal. There were two pilots, four crew members, and 144 passengers. At some point during the trip, the co-pilot, twenty-seven-year-old Andreas Lubitz, locked the pilot out of the cockpit and deliberately put the plane into a premature descent, crashing in the French Alps. All aboard were killed on impact. Several motivations were advanced: (1) his girlfriend was pregnant, (2) Lubitz feared he would go blind and lose his job as a pilot, and (3) he was under treatment by a psychiatrist and had suicidal ideations/thoughts. Although his girlfriend was not pregnant, there is evidence Lubitz was treated for eyesight problems and he successfully hid his suicide ideations from his employer, Germanwings.[62] On the day of the crash, he had a medical excuse from his psychiatrist to be absent from work that was found torn up in Lubitz's home by investigators.

Located in Northern California, the Alturas Native American Tribe is perhaps the smallest, with only 35 members and 26 acres of land.[63] Cherie (aka Sheri) Lash, 44, went to Tribal Headquarters to discuss her eviction. She became enraged and murdered four people, wounded another, and when she ran out of bullets, she grabbed a butcher knife and stabbed the sixth victim. The jury approved the death sentence in this case.

Robert Dear, a fifty-seven-year-old man, moved from South Carolina to Colorado. On November 28, 2014, he entered a Planned Parenthood Clinic in Colorado Springs and killed three people, wounding nine others by gunfire. After a standoff with police he surrendered, murmuring "No more baby parts," revealing an anti-abortion motivation. In 2016, two psychiatrists testified he was under the delusion the government had persecuted him for two decades because of his anti-government and anti-abortion beliefs. He was found incompetent to stand trial and confined indefinitely in the state mental hospital.[64]

Umpqua Community College (UCC) sits on a small peninsula that juts out into the Umpqua River, some seven miles north of Roseburg, Oregon. The land is beautiful, but what happened on that campus October 1, 2015, was dark and evil. Christopher Harper Mercer was a twenty-six-year-old student at UCC. He entered a classroom and asked Christians to stand up. As they did, he said, "Good, because you're going to meet God in about one second" and shot them point blank. Ten people were killed, including a professor and students, while another nine were injured. Following a gunfight with responding Roseburg police officers, Mercer was wounded and committed suicide.[65]

On July 5, 2016, in Baton Rouge and July 6, 2016, in Minnesota there were highly publicized controversial fatal shootings of black men by police officers. These shootings were the catalyst for the July 7, 2016, peaceful demonstration in Dallas, Texas, which protested those incidents. Police officers monitoring the demonstration came under sniper fire from a lone black gunman, who "especially wanted to kill white police officers." As additional Dallas officers responded to the scene, they too came under fire. In the end, five Dallas police officers had been murdered and nine others wounded. After negotiations with the gunman broke down, police used a robot to deliver an explosive charge that killed the shooter. It was the deadliest day for American law enforcement since 9/11.[66]

On July 6, 2016, Esteban Santiago, 26, flew from Alaska to Fort Lauderdale, Florida, and picked up his luggage. He took it to a restroom, removed a handgun that had been legally checked in, loaded it, returned to the baggage claim area, and randomly shot and killed five people, wounding eight others. He surrendered to the police without any incident. An Iraq war veteran, Santiago's life was in disarray. After serving in the Puerto Rico National Guard, his unsatisfactory performance resulted in being discharged from the Alaska National Guard. He was arrested for roughing up his girlfriend and allegedly tried to strangle her. In November 2016, he entered the FBI office in Anchorage, Alaska, claiming the Central Intelligence Agency (CIA) was controlling his mind, and he was sent for a mental evaluation. He was indicted for 22 crimes associated with the airport shootings, none of them involving terrorism, and pled not guilty.[67]

On October 1, 2017, Stephen Paddock, a person that apparently had no ideological motive, opened fire at the annual Route 91 Harvest country music festival on the Las Vegas Strip killing 58 people and wounding another 550. When police searched his room in the Mandalay Hotel, they found 23 guns including several high powered assault rifles configured with "bump-stocks" mimicking fully automatic weapons, and re-fueling the gun control debate in the United States. The Las Vegas shooting represents the deadliest mass shooting in recent U.S. history.

On Sunday, November 5, 2017, Devin Kelly entered the Sutherland Springs (Texas) First Baptist Church and began firing, killing 28 and injuring perhaps another 20. Initial accounts from different news sources indicated an armed church member shot Kelly, an "armed resident" did so, the police killed him, one or more vehicles pursued Kelly as he fled and shot him. and he was found in his car, dead of a possibly self inflicted shot. This incident illustrates how terrifying or terrorist mass incidents produce conflict accounts which have to be sifted through to find the truth.

Do the actions of these "loners" represent a form of terrorism? What policies or actions may have prevented these mass shootings?

Quick Facts
How Alone Is a Lone Wolf?

While lone wolves act alone, they are not truly alone because of the Internet. Terrorists use Facebook, Twitter, and YouTube to lure people to their websites, where some will gradually become radicalized by audio and video recordings.[68] Arif Uka, a Muslim, shot and killed two American servicemen at the Frankfurt, Germany, airport. Uka said he was motivated to do so by a YouTube video that purported showing American soldiers raiding a home in Afghanistan and raping a daughter.[69]

Also on the Internet, lone wolves have access to terrorist training manuals on reconnaissance, bomb making, target selection, and related skills. They also find social support in digital chat rooms.

In one recent nine year span, there were 100 lone wolf attacks in the United States, the most of any Western country. These attacks resulted in 164 dead and 491 injured. Not all attackers were charged with terrorism.[70]

1. Law enforcement and military personnel are being increasingly targeted.
2. There is increasing radicalization via the Internet and in the civilian workplace.
3. Lone wolves offer their personal ideology for attacking versus expressing an affinity for a specific terrorist movement.[71]

Although the actual number of cases is small, there have been some terrorists using vehicles to injure and/or kill innocent people. With IS urging such attacks and some successful examples, we may well see more of them. In 2006, on the campus of the University of North Carolina, a Muslim man used his car to hit people, causing injuries, but no deaths. His motive was to avenge Muslim deaths. In 2014, two Canadian soldiers were deliberately hit by a terrorist, causing the death of one.[72] After leading the police on a high-speed chase, the driver was shot and died of his wounds. On July 14, 2016, there was the previously discussed Bastille Day truck attack and on December 19, 2016, a lone wolf drove a truck through a Berlin Christmas market, killing 12 and injuring 48. The driver, believed to be Anis Amri, 24, is still at large. Some of his associates were taken into custody, but their roles in the attack, if any, are not publically known. Previously, both Italy and France sought to deport Amri back to Tunisia, which declined to repatriate him because of paperwork difficulties.[73]

Cell Organizational Models

A **cell** is multiple terrorists working cooperatively toward achieving a particular goal, such as raising funds, gathering intelligence, or executing an attack. Alternatively, a cell may not be specialized and all of these functions may be performed within a single cell. Various sources assert that there are three to seven, four to twelve, or even more members in a cell. As a practical matter, the number of a people in a cell must be large enough to acquire all of the skills needed, but kept as small as possible to enhance OPSEC. A cell trying to manufacture explosive devices may consist of only one to three people. A cell assigned to executing a major attack will have more members and be supported by several different types of specialized cells, which are discussed later in this chapter.

Cell members do not necessarily have to be located in close physical proximity. However, this is frequently the case. Alternatively, they could be located in several localities or even different countries[74] and only meet face to face if necessary.

Al-Qaeda has adopted the concept of "**taqiyya**." This absolves cell members from religious condemnation for shaving off their required beards, not praying five times a day, and adopting a Western lifestyle as part of OPSEC.[75] Taqiyya allows Arabic terrorists to move with less scrutiny in Western societies.

A group of homegrown jihadists working collectively make up a "**homegrown jihadist cell**." Animal Liberation Front (ALF) and Earth Liberation Front (ELF) members may also act as cell members that have coalesced around a leader or be in a **leaderless resistance cell**. This type of cell is characterized by no leaders and equality of members who share the leadership functions.[76] Leaderless resistant cells are autonomous, self-enrolling, and self-organizing. Former Vietnam veteran Louis Beam popularized the leaderless resistance concept and although at one time he associated with right-wing, racist groups, he has since kept a low profile.[77]

Cell
A cell is multiple terrorists working cooperatively toward achieving a particular goal, such as raising funds, gathering intelligence, or executing an attack. Alternatively, a cell may not be specialized and all of these functions may be performed within a single cell.

Taqiyya
Taqiyya absolves Islamic fighters from religious condemnation for shaving off their required beards, not praying five times a day, and adopting a Western lifestyle as part of OPSEC.

Homegrown jihadist cell
A group of homegrown jihadists working collectively make up a homegrown jihadist cell.

Leaderless resistance cell
This type of cell is characterized by no leaders and equality of members who share the leadership functions.

> **Information Link**
> For more information on passport and visa fraud, visit the U.S. Department of State website at www.state.gov/m/ds/investigat/c10714.htm. Read the article, "Passport and Visa Fraud: A Quick Course."

Wolf pack
A group of lone wolves that form a cell are sometimes called a "wolf pack."

Quick Facts
A Homegrown Jihadist Cell's Activities

Six foreign-born Muslims from Jordan, Turkey, and the former Yugoslavia met in the United States. They eventually formed a cell in New Jersey because they all shared an interest in Internet images of jihad.[78] They acquired firearms and practiced shooting in the Pocono Mountains in northeastern Pennsylvania and played paintball to hone their military skills. Their intent was to murder as many soldiers as possible at Fort Dix, New Jersey. They had no leader and the cells' members just "fed off of each other." The "Fort Dix 6" had no apparent connection to any foreign terrorist organization. They were arrested and convicted of terrorism-related charges. This cell can be characterized three ways: "a homegrown terrorist cell," "homegrown jihadists," and using the "leaderless resistance" model.

Box 5–3
Terrorism and Passport Fraud

The greatest prize for transnational terrorists is a genuine passport issued in a false name.[79] South Africa and Venezuela have been two sources for them. A corrupt official in South Africa was arrested in conjunction with 4,000 stolen passports that were being sold on the black market.[80] Until South Africa recently instituted new security features in its passports, they were also forged with ease.

Venezuela has issued passports to terrorists,[81] a move that begun under its rabidly anti-American president, the late Hugo Chavez, and has continued after his death. It is known that 173 genuine Venezuelan passports with phony names were issued to members of the Lebanese terrorist movement Hezbollah.[82] A variety of false identification papers can be bought at many open-air markets around the world, although the quality varies considerably. Two of the largest of these markets are in Lima, Peru, and Manila's Recto District in the Philippines. Thailand also has a flourishing counterfeit identification business. A master forger previously known as only "The Doctor" was recently

arrested there. Although some documents were sold to people fleeing the Syrian War, The Doctor also did business with human traffickers, criminal gangs, and terrorist movements.[83] There are also reports of transnational criminal organizations (TCOs) providing identification papers to terrorists.

Examples of other ruses used by terrorists to obtain passports include getting them issued in the name of a dead person, but using the terrorists' photographs and descriptions in them. Passports are also stolen and the terrorists' pictures substituted for the actual bearer. A stolen passport may also be used if the fraudulent user sufficiently resembles the person to whom it was issued. The Department of Homeland Security (DHS) intercepted 30,799 passports in one recent year that were false in one or more aspects.[84]

Do you see any possibilities for reducing the number of stolen, forged, or otherwise fraudulent passports? What would you do about it?

Foreign terrorist organizations (FTOs) infiltrate individuals into the United States and other countries. Some may form as a cell after entry. Those infiltrated may enter a country illegally under assumed names or with forged identification papers. Terrorists entering under their legal names with student or tourist visas may have been issued "clean" passports by states sympathetic to their cause. Their "old" passports may have revealed travel to Yemen, Afghanistan, or Iran. Stamps on their old passports from those countries would have invited closer scrutiny by security services because terrorist camps are operated in them. Therefore, the terrorists are given a "clean" passport that doesn't reveal such travel.

There are different types of cells due to the fact that they are created under dissimilar circumstances and they can also have diverse responsibilities. Examples of cells with diverse missions include the following:

1. **Sleeper cells**: Members of FTO sleeper cells lead normal lives, engaging only in lawful employment and activities that call no attention to themselves. The jobs they select may facilitate future terrorist activities. Illustratively, a taxi driver will learn a great deal about a city's geography and can identify potential targets and move terrorists around. A sleeper cell may receive a signal that "awakens" it for a specific purpose, such as providing a safe house or sabotage. Iran has been inserting sleeper cells in Latin America with the goal of committing, fermenting, and fostering acts of international terrorism.[85]

2. **Command and Control Cells**: C2 cells make all of the final decisions about the execution of an attack and other matters pertaining to the activities of a cell.

3. **Tactical Operations Cells**: TAC-OPS cells actually execute attacks under the guidance of C2 cells.

4. **Intel Cells**: These cells collect data, make recommendations, may select targets, provide information about the best route to approach the target (ingress), and, if not a suicide attack, the best route to follow to when leaving (egressing) the area of the attack.

Sleeper cells
Members of sleeper cells lead normal lives and call no attention to themselves. The jobs they select may facilitate future terrorist activities. Illustratively, a taxi driver will learn a great deal about a city's geography and can identify potential targets and move terrorists around. A sleeper cell may receive a signal that "awakens" it for a specific purpose, such as sabotage or an assassination.

Command and control cells
C2 cells make all of the final decisions about the execution of an attack and other matters pertaining to the activities of a cell.

Tactical operations cells
TAC-OPS cells execute attacks under the guidance of C2 cells.

Intel cells
ICs collect data, make recommendations, may select targets, and provide information about the best routes for ingressing to and egressing from targets.

Quick Facts
A Hezbollah Fund-Raising Cell

An off-duty deputy sheriff noticed Arabic-speaking men buying 300 cartons of cigarettes each at a tobacco wholesaler and paying for them from wads of cash. A four-year investigation revealed that the men paid the North Carolina cigarette tax of $0.50 per

pack, sold to them by the truckloads in Michigan where the tax was $7.50 per carton, and pocketed the difference. The cell raised millions of dollars for Hezbollah.[86]

Logistics cells

LCs provide supplies and various types of support to other cells.

Fundraising cells

FRCs almost exclusively commit illegal acts to raise funds for their terrorist organization or to be used in support of a particular attack.

Network models

Network models include the chain, hub or star, spoke or wheel, and all channel structures.

Dead drop

A dead drop is a secret place where one courier hides documents, often encrypted, for the next courier to pick up.

Hubs

In terrorist network language, "hubs" are "chiefs," from local operational commanders to ideological leaders. The lines between nodes in a cell are called links or edges and represent a communication channel.

Nodes

In terrorist network language, "nodes" are more expendable members, such as fighters, whose loss is less critical to the terrorist movement.

Links or edges

In terrorist network language, the lines between nodes in a cell are called links or edges and represent a communication channel between nodes and/or hubs.

Compartmentalized information

Information to which access is restricted to those with a need to know.

5. **Logistics Cells**: LCs provide supplies and other support to other cells, especially TAC-OPS, including bomb-making materials and the names and locations of sympathetic doctors to use if there is a medical emergency.

6. **Fundraising Cells**: FRCs almost exclusively commit illegal acts to raise funds for the terrorist movement or to be used in support of a particular attack. Illustrations include kidnapping for ransom, arms and drug trafficking, operating bogus charities, extortion, credit card fraud, and pirating music and videos.

Network Organizational Models

The most important advantage of networks is that they are resilient against disruptions and attacks.[87] They are also effective in repairing damage to them and are highly effective in processing communications. Cells are the "building blocks" of **network models** that are illustrated by the (1) chain, (2) hub or star, (3) wheel, and (4) all channel structures.

The Chain Network

The simplest type of network model is the *chain network* (see Figure 5–6), which has no hierarchy. In its simplest form, each courier passes information, material, or encrypted documents to the next courier. In this form of the chain network, each courier knows the courier from whom they received the "package" and the courier to whom he or she gave it. OPSEC is improved when a dead drop is substituted for a face-to-face exchange by the couriers. A **dead drop** is a secret, innocuous place where the "package" the courier carries is left, to be later retrieved by the next courier. The dead drop can be as simple as a loose brick in a wall behind which a flash drive can be hidden.

Unless a courier runs surveillance on the dead drop, the identity of the retrieving courier is unknown to the courier who placed the material in it. It may be possible to take out a few couriers in a chain, but it is more difficult to "roll up" the entire network. However, the chain network is disrupted when some members go missing. Criminal groups and gangs also rely on the chain network when they smuggle goods and humans or launder money.[88]

The Hub or Star Network

In a terrorist hub or star network, the central "**hub**" may be a local operational commander, ideological leader, or other figure. In contrast, the outer "**nodes**" are more expendable members, such as fighters, whose loss is less critical to the terrorist movement. The lines between nodes in a cell are called **links or edges** and represent a communication channel between nodes and/or the hub.

Figure 5–7a depicts the hub or star network. The hub at the center (a) represents the leader who has substantial responsibilities. The leader is the only person communicating with higher levels of the terrorist movement and interacts directly with nodes B, C, D, E, and F, who have no contact with each other and may not be aware of how many other nodes there are or what their function is—this is an example of a high level of **compartmentalized information**.

In Figure 5–7a, the hub/leader can contact the members of his or her network, but they don't know how to contact their leader. Some hub networks allow two-way communication between the hub and its members, as is shown in Figure 5–7b. In both Figures 5–7a and 5–7b, the hub ensures that all outer nodes remain ideologically committed, are fully trained, maintain OPSEC, and makes sure the attack is a success.

A key advantage of a hub or star is that OPSEC is high when only the leader knows the identification of all of its members. This is also its disadvantage: If the leader is apprehended, the whole operation may be rolled up. Even if the leader discloses nothing during interrogation, cell members have no direction and may be isolated from each other until the higher-level command and control function establishes that the cell leader has "gone missing." There are several options for replacing a missing terrorist leader: train and infiltrate a new leader, which may take months; awaken

The Chain Network

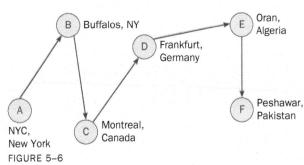

FIGURE 5–6
A chain network.

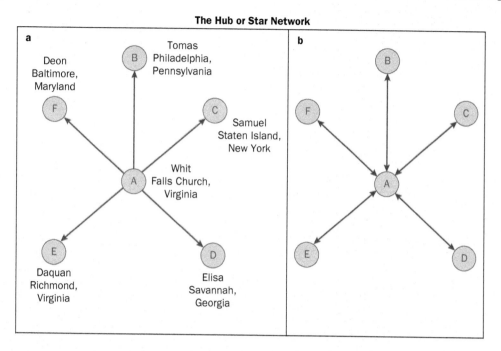

The Hub or Star Network

FIGURE 5–7
A hub or star network.
(A) The hub or star with one-way communication.
(B) The hub or star with two-way communication.

a qualified sleeper; or if there is a **redundant leader protocol**, one of the cell members will assume command of the cell.

Redundant leader protocol
If the leader of a cell is captured, killed, or otherwise not available, a designated member of the cell will assume the leadership role.

The Wheel Network

A variant of the hub or star is shown in Figure 5–8 and is called a wheel network. It primarily differs from Figure 5–7b in that nodes can communicate with the member to their "left" or "right" because of a link. This quickens the pace of sharing information, but increases OPSEC vulnerability.

The All-Channel Network

The all-channel model (see Figure 5–9) is highly decentralized and all nodes can communicate with each other and the hub. The advantage of this model is that it reduces the nodes' feelings of isolation and has great potential for collaboration in problem solving and other activities. The disadvantage is that it is the most difficult to create and maintain because so many horizontal communication channels are required, which also poses a greater threat to OPSEC.

Hierarchical Organizational Model

"Hierarchy" comes from the sixth century Greek words "hireros" (sacred) and "arkhia" (rule), meaning the governing of sacred things. By the early 1600s, it signified the differences in rank for the Catholic clergy, from the lowest parish priest to the pope.[89] The hierarchical model incorporates this idea of grades of rank and has the following characteristics:[90] (1) There is a **principle of hierarchy**—each lower organizational unit is under the direct control and supervision of a superior organizational unit. This produces a pyramid-shaped form with a single leader at the top of the pyramid (see Figure 5–10); (2) these organizational units are led by persons whose rank and authority ascend as we go from the lower to higher units, referred to as the **chain of command**; (3) organizational units are essentially stacked horizontal layers and the

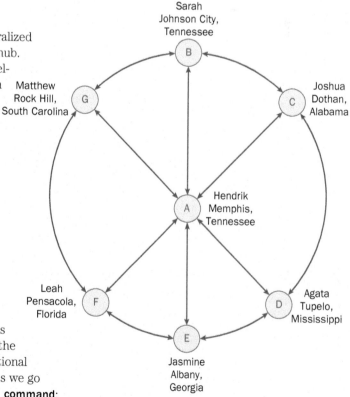

FIGURE 5–8
A wheel network.

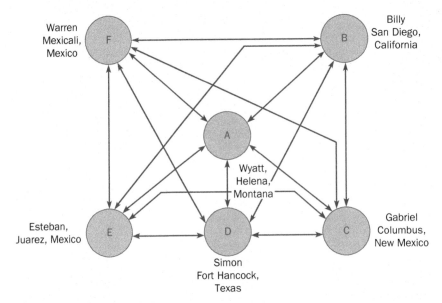

FIGURE 5–9
An all-channel network.

Warren
Mexicali,
Mexico

Billy
San Diego,
California

Wyatt,
Helena,
Montana

Esteban,
Juarez, Mexico

Gabriel
Columbus,
New Mexico

Simon
Fort Hancock,
Texas

Principle of hierarchy
This principle dictates that each lower organizational unit is under the direct control and supervision of a superior organizational unit. This produces a pyramid-shaped form.

Chain of command
The chain of command is a clear and unbroken line of authority and responsibility from the top to the bottom of the organization, which makes it possible to establish accountability.

more there are, the "taller" or more hierarchical the organization will be. "Tallness" may be produced by the organization growing in numbers and creating new units in which to place them, becoming geographically dispersed, or from the need to create specialized units, for example, snipers, hostage-takers, financial experts, and identification forgers. This creates the need for more hierarchy to coordinate the many parts of the organization; and (4) there is also an expectation that when lower-ranking members of the organization receive a "lawful" order from a superior authority in their chain of command that the orders will be followed. Members may be disciplined for not carrying out orders.

The chief advantages of the hierarchical model are that the chain of command is clearly understood, people know what their jobs are, specialization can be accommodated, and control is normally high. The disadvantages are that horizontal communication between units may be difficult or impossible; groups may compete for the leader's favor, causing goals to be distorted; there is low flexibility; if communication channels are clogged, decisions may not be received on a timely basis; and more geographically distant units may become more interested in their own interests versus the organization's goals.

Umbrella Organizational Model

The umbrella organizational model (UOM) has a core group that to some degree assists the groups that voluntarily associate with it. The UOM is a relatively recent hybrid organizational structure that is made up of two other organizational structures, the hierarchical and the networked. An internal (core) hierarchical group is at the top and provides some types of support to the organizations that are affiliated with it. The affiliated groups are networked or tied together by continuing vertical communication from the core and by horizontal communication between the affiliated movements (see Figure 5–11). The UOM is loose and decentralized in the sense that the affiliated organizations continue to have their own leaders and are to some degree autonomous.

In its beginning, al-Qaeda was a small, hierarchical organization with tight controls, but it has evolved into a UOM. Over a period of years, militant Islamic organizations joined forces with the "premier terrorist brand" and were "rebadged" as al-Qaeda. Illustrations include the former Tawhid wal Jihad, now al-Qaeda in Iraq (AQI), the Algerian group Global Salafist for Preaching and Combat, renamed as al-Qaeda in the Islamic Maghreb (AQIM, Maghreb is Arabic for northwest Africa, the area west of Egypt),[91] and Islamic Jihad in Yemen, one of the predecessors of al-Qaeda in the Arabian Peninsula (AQAP).[92]

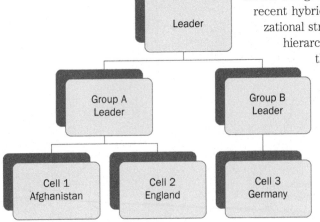

FIGURE 5–10
A simple hierarchical model with three "layers." More complex hierarchical organizations may have seven or more layers, making them much taller than this illustration.

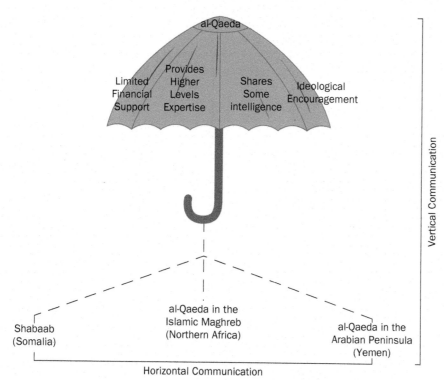

FIGURE 5–11
The umbrella model.

Services provided by al-Qaeda include ideological encouragement, articulating strategic goals, occasional operational funds, logistics support, advice from seasoned terrorist commanders, and radical Islamic propaganda from the Global Islamic Media Front (GIMF), founded by al-Qaeda around 2003. GIMF made a broadcasted video calling for the withdrawal of Austrian and German forces from Afghanistan and threatened terrorist attacks for the failure to do so.[93]

The shift to a UOM raises the question of whether al-Qaeda is still an operational terrorist organization or whether it has been reduced to just a support movement, roughly equivalent to a MacDonald's central office supporting its far-flung hamburger franchises.[94] The answer is that al-Qaeda retains some core operational capacity in its special operations unit, but it is substantially an umbrella organization, suggesting operations to affiliates. Because of this, Johnsen argues that al-Qaeda's core has ceased to be the most important part of the organization.[95] However, this argument may give insufficient weight to the fact the core is the cement that keeps the overall organization together and functioning.

The primary advantage of the UOM is its flexibility, allowing affiliates to conduct locally important operations and still participate in transnational terrorist attacks. The disadvantages are that affiliates have varying ideologies and they squabble with the core about strategic goals, the allocation of scarce resources, and because they are voluntarily associated with al-Qaeda they can leave whenever they choose. An ongoing al-Qaeda squabble was whether to attack "near enemies," rulers of Islamic countries who do not support the radicalized interpretation of the Koran or the "far enemies," Western nations in general and the United States in particular. The single most important disadvantage of the UOM is that the core does not have full authority over its affiliates. When AQI began beheading civilians and prisoners, al-Qaeda told it to stop using such harsh tactics because it was alienating people. AQI simply ignored the order.

Virtual Organizational Model

A **virtual terrorist organization** (VTO) exists in cyberspace (see Figure 5–12). It has no headquarters and needs no physical meeting space. Instead, the VTO exists in cyberspace by taking advantage of technology. There is no known large terrorist group that is completely virtual. VTOs are based on cell structures. They may be part of a large terrorist movement or be locally inspired and more independent.

Virtual terrorist organization
A virtual terrorist organization exists in cyberspace. It members can be dispersed geographically, but work together exploiting information technology to achieve their common goals by sharing their skills and knowledge collaboratively.

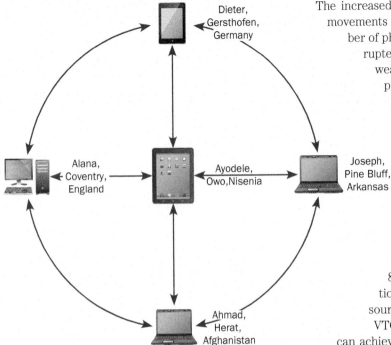

FIGURE 5–12
Virtual organization.

The increased reliance on information technologies by terrorist movements is to some degree caused by (1) the growing number of physical safe havens for terrorists that have been disrupted or eliminated.[96] Diplomacy, foreign aid, military weapons, training, raids, and drone attacks have all played a role in reducing the availability of physical safe havens, although they certainly have not been totally eliminated; and (2) simultaneously, terrorist organizations have been calling for the development of autonomous terrorist cells to attack whoever they consider their enemies to be.

A VTO may be temporary (gathering intelligence for a specific attack) or longer lasting, and requires a high degree of trust between its members. As an example, work by a VTO can be substantially substituted for a physical reconnaissance. A captured al-Qaeda manual asserts that 80 percent of the information needed for operations is available on the Internet in publicly accessible sources.[97]

VTO members may be dispersed geographically, but can achieve their goals by sharing their skills and knowledge collaboratively through information technology.[98] Judy's list of the technologies exploited by VTOs include computer networks, mobile phone systems, social media outlets, password protection, message encryption, messages embedded in photographs, online chat rooms, and electronic drop boxes.[99] Experts are wary that as terrorists gain greater cyberspace experience that it will lead to system disruption/netwar, for example, committing highly disruptive attacks on power, transportation, and other computer systems. The main advantages of the virtual organization are that it provides greater security and convenience than face-to-face (F2F) operations.[100] Illustratively, Israel reportedly has been unable to crack Hamas-encoded communications sent on the Internet.[101]

Target Selection and Attacks

Terrorist movements have a core set of beliefs and goals that define their ideology and focus their violence.[102] One way or another, ideology identifies "acceptable" targets and acts as a constraint against attacking other targets. Acceptable targets serve another important purpose. In the ideological framework of terrorist movements, victims are blamed for the violence inflicted on them. The essence of this argument is "They brought it on themselves." This construction both relieves terrorists of their moral responsibility for the deaths they have caused and glorifies them for doing so.

As a practical matter, some targets selected may have little to do with a group's ideology. For example, raids on police stations may be triggered by the need to avenge a popular terrorist leader who died while in police custody. Likewise, a target may be selected to meet several goals, for example, a terrorist attack inflicts mass casualties, which in turn provokes an unwise massive retaliation that causes the deaths of many Muslims, reinforcing the perception that Israel and Western powers nonchalantly kill them.[103] During 2014, Hamas fired at least 2,200 rockets from the Gaza Strip into Israel, breaking several truces of up to 72 hours to provoke a reaction. Hamas allegedly hid rocket launchers and rocket munitions in schools, hospitals, and government buildings, ensuring that to protect their citizens Israel would have to attack them, causing some civilian casualties. In some eyes, the retaliation caused the deaths of civilian Palestinians and provided Hamas with the opportunity to claim that the Israeli Defense Forces (IDF) was committing genocide. A devil's choice is a situation in which there are only unattractive alternatives to a decision. The devil's choice faced by the IDF was to protect its citizens or risk producing some civilian casualties.

Other variables impacting target choices include the symbolism of the target; the terrorist group's size, weapons, planning, and operational capabilities; ability to ingress and egress

Quick Facts
Center of Gravity, System Disruption, and Terrorist Selection of Targets

Center of gravity refers to the *primary* sources of strength, power, and resistance for a nation or organization and that of an adversary.[104] These sources are identified through an analytical process. Ideally, when the vulnerabilities of a center of gravity are identified and successfully attacked, decisive results are produced.[105] This concept is similar to Robb's system disruption.

During World War II, Americans sent badly needed war goods and troops across the Atlantic Ocean to England by convoys, which usually consisted of 45 or more ships. To prevent this, Germans deployed U-boats (submarines). In 1942, 1,664 ships were lost in the Atlantic to U-boats.[106] America was losing ships faster than they could be replaced.

Although warships and planes protected the convoys, losses remained high. The heart of the problem was that there was an area in the North Atlantic, the air-gap, which was beyond the range of the Allied Powers' aircraft.

The Germans' center of gravity in the Battle of the Atlantic was that area that could not be patrolled by the Allied Powers' aircraft. America's development of the very long-range B-24 bomber (The Liberator) contributed substantially to a decisive reduction of ships lost to the German submarines. The B-24s

provided a decisive victory that destroyed the Germans' center of gravity. By 1944, German submarines sank only 67 ships.[107] The result was that much-needed weapons, munitions, food, petroleum, and other essentials would reach England and be used in the war against the Axis Powers.

The major terrorist groups are sophisticated, and their recent announcements about attacking infrastructures reveal a well-developed targeting capability. These groups are developing and recruiting cyber experts, possibly to develop the tools needed for infrastructure attacks. The absence of infrastructure attacks against the United States (the "Great Satan") may reflect an absence of opportunity due to our vigilance. Alternatively, terrorists may not have a real intent to attack the infrastructure because just their announcements may cause us to spend perhaps billions to harden infrastructure targets. The lack of infrastructure attacks could also indicate that terrorists do not yet have the capability to do so. If such attacks do come, they are likely to cause Robb's system disruption or weaken our centers of gravity. If their future attacks do strike infrastructures, people might be illuminating their lives with candles for an unknown period of time. Note that netwar and system disruption essentially refer to the same actions.

---

from the target; and the need to make a demonstration for financial supporters who are impatient for results or from whom support is dwindling. Habash, founder of the terrorist Popular Front for the Liberation of Palestine (PFLP), asserts that when selecting a target the main point is to pick one that is 100 percent guaranteed to be successful.[108] Clarke and Newman use the acronym EVIL DONE to identify the characteristics that make a target attractive to terrorists. Attractive targets are:[109]

Center of gravity
The primary source of strength, power, and resistance for a nation or organization and that of an adversary.

1. *Exposed and publicly visible.* Damage done to hidden targets doesn't produce visually compelling images for the news media to broadcast;

2. *Vital to a society's day-to-day functioning or perhaps even survival.* Such targets are the elements of a country's infrastructure, such as electrical grids, pipelines, computer networks, water supply, and transportation systems;

3. *Iconic or symbolic.* When a picture of it is shown, many people can instantly identify it. Illustrations of icons in the United States include the Statue of Liberty, the White House, the Pentagon, and the Golden Gate Bridge. Global examples include the Eiffel Tower, the Colosseum, and the Taj Mahal;

4. *Legitimate, meaning that attacking them will not result in universal condemnation.* The 9/11 attacks were condemned, but they also were widely applauded. Children generally rank as the least legitimate target, but there is no ironclad protection for them. Tim McVeigh knew there was a nursery in the Oklahoma City federal building, but parked a truck eight feet from the building's door to ensure maximum destruction and lethality. The blast killed 19 children.

5. *Destructible.* Targets cannot merely be damaged; this is a failed attack and results in a lowered opinion of a movement's capabilities. Substantial damage to a target lessens, but does not eliminate, this response.

6. *Occupied, because mass casualties are essential to creating continuing fear.* What kind of people are occupying a potential target may also be important, for example, Buckingham Palace, the London residence and administrative space of Britain's sovereigns since 1837.

7. *Near,* as illustrated by the fact that the IRA in Northern Ireland struck many more targets there than on the British mainland; and

8. *Easy,* without significant and layered defense/security features.

Quick Facts
Why Do Terrorists Attack Tourists?

Terrorist groups attack tourists and resorts for foreigners for two main reasons: (1) For many countries, tourism is a multibillion-dollar industry. Depriving a country of some or a substantial portion of the revenue generated by tourists weakens a target country; and (2) tourists can be held hostage until a substantial ransom is paid. Secondary reasons are the terrorists can feel fairly certain they will get paid and operations need not be large or costly. "Flash kidnappings" are increasing. Only a handful of people are captured and quickly released because terrorists settle for a lower ransom. Kidnapping has signs of becoming a volume business.

Egypt's Red Sea tourism produces $10 billion annually. However, after a series of attacks, that sum was reduced to $4 billion. In Mali, three suitcases filled with five million euros were delivered to an obscure Islamic terrorist group to release 32 European hostages.[110] The funding source was from a German account labeled Humanitarian Aid.[111] Not all ransom paid comes from governments. Insurance companies offer "K and R" (kidnap and ransom) policies.[112] A businessperson in Iraq pays an annual premium of $3,000 to $6,000 for a K and R policy; shipping firms may pay as much as $7 million annually to cover large fleets in dangerous areas.

Few, if any, targets will satisfy all of the elements of EVIL DONE, but Clarke and Newman maintain that the final target selected will rank high on most of them.

Proximity to the target for a terrorist group may also play a role in selecting some targets. Although some notable terrorists have lived hundreds of miles from where they attacked, many others do not travel far. Examples of terrorists who traveled some distance to their targets include Tim McVeigh, the Oklahoma City bombing in 1995; Eric Rudolph, anti-abortion and anti-gay bombings and the 1995 Atlanta Olympic Park bombing; and the September 11, 2001 "9/11" hijackers.[113] An analysis of 60 cases determined that 44 percent of attackers lived with 30 miles of their target and 71 percent of attackers who were motivated by a single cause traveled only 12 miles.[114] These and other empirical studies of terrorism must be carefully considered: (1) they may be based on a small, nonrepresentative data set or (2) an available data set is analyzed that may be older and the researcher is "stuck" with whatever variables it examined.

Terrorist attacks come in all sizes and degrees of complexity. The 9/11 attacks required years of intelligence gathering, planning, and preparation. In 2001, less planning and preparation was used by Richard Reid, the "shoe bomber." He was caught trying to light a fuse that would explode his sneakers aboard American Airline Flight 63 from Paris to Miami. Passengers smelled smoke in the cabin and overpowered Reid, a British citizen who converted to Islam. On Christmas Day 2009, a Muslim from Nigeria, Umar Farouk Abdulmutallab, boarded Northwest Airlines Flight 253. The plane was flying from the Netherlands to Detroit, Michigan, when he attempted to light explosives sewn into his underwear and was subdued by passengers. Both Reid and Abdulmutallab had ties to al-Qaeda and received life sentences.

Suicide Bombing Attacks

For most Americans, trying to understand the motivation behind suicide bombing is very difficult. In our culture, such actions are often labeled unpredictable, irrational, and fanatical. However, a careful analysis of the phenomenon shows that suicide bombings are not spontaneous outbursts of emotion, but rather calculated, strategic moves by a particular group for a specific purpose. Deploying suicide bombers is not haphazard; they are carefully trained for their missions. They undergo a relatively long period of indoctrination filled with group pressure, pep talks, and organizational support, which fosters a personal commitment. Suicide is strictly forbidden in the Quran. However, some Islamic clerics have issued opinions that it is not forbidden when the act is committed in defense of Islam.

Between 2001 and 2004, Israel was the victim of rampant suicide bombers. Nearly half the attacks were attributed to Hamas. The radical Sheikh Ahmed Yassin* encouraged the bombings by publicly proclaiming that Muslims who engaged in suicide bombing against Israel became a "**shahid**," or martyr fulfilling a religious command.[115]

Shahid
A Muslim "martyr" who dies in defense of their faith; often inappropriately associated with those who conduct suicide bombings. Originates from the Qur'anic Arabic word for "witness."

---

* On March 22, 2004, Yassin was killed by the Israeli Mossad as he was returning from prayer services at a West Bank mosque.

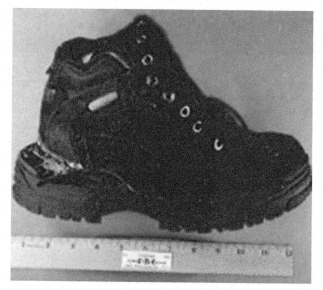

FIGURE 5-13
Richard Reid (1973–), the "Shoe Bomber." An Englishman, he became a Muslim while in prison. In 2001, he boarded American Airlines 63, scheduled to fly from Paris to Miami. During the flight he attempted to light the explosives in his shoe with matches, but was noticed and overcome by passengers.
(FBI Law Enforcement Bulletin)

Historically, suicide bombers striking Israel have overwhelmingly been male; predominately younger, although there was a range from 17 to 53 years of age; unmarried; had more than a high school education; and 81 percent came from households with eight or more members.[116] The motives for these suicide bombers were mixed. Some wanted to avenge some personal humiliation or wrong done to their family by Israeli officials, while others did it for nationalistic reasons, for example, to do something for their country, or for religious reasons, to be assured of a place in paradise.[117] However, as covered in the Quick Facts box below, the face of the suicide bomber is changing.

The effectiveness of suicide attacks is staggering. Between January 1, 2007, and October 16, 2016, worldwide there were 3,733 suicide bombers wearing a vest or using a car carrying explosives. These attacks resulted in 36,706 deaths and 83,149 wounded persons.[118]

The first recorded car bombing, which was not suicidal, was in New York's financial district during 1920 by Italian anarchists. In the modern age, terrorist attacks began with two attacks in Lebanon in 1983. The American Embassy was partially destroyed on April 18 when a suicide bomber in a truck killed 34 staff members. Later, on October 23, a suicide bomber driving a yellow Mercedes truck blew up a portion of a peacekeeping compound in Beirut, killing 241 service members, most of them American Marines. Hezbollah was responsible for both attacks. Suicide attacks communicate to supporters and the wider public that the members of a movement hold their cause more dearly than their lives.

Quick Facts
The Changing Face of Suicide Bombers

Although denied by insurgent/terrorist movements in Afghanistan, young boys are used as suicide bombers. The boys, as young as ten, are plucked off the streets and fed a diet of anti-Western and anti-government propaganda. When the handlers think they are ready, they are given an amulet with verses from the Qur'an on it and assured they will be protected and not die.[119]

In Nigeria, several women have carried babies to get past checkpoints and when they reach their targets, they detonate their hidden body explosives, apparently at the behest of Boko Haram. That terrorist movement is known to have used children and young women as suicide bombers in the past.[120]

Quick Facts
A Donkey and Dogs Used as Suicide Bombers

In 2014, Israel invaded the Gaza Strip after being shelled for days by Hamas. In response, Hamas announced that it would have "surprises" ready for the invading Israel Defense Force (IDF). In Rafah, near the Egyptian border, Hamas loaded a donkey with explosives and sent it toward IDF lines. The IDF fired on the approaching donkey to protect themselves, detonating the explosives. Similar incidents with dogs also occurred.[121]

A worldwide poll conducted by the Pew Research Center's Forum on Religion and Public Life of Muslims revealed that in Keep War: war-torn countries like Afghanistan, Iraq, and Palestine, 40 percent of the population supported the use of suicide bombing.[122] This high percentage was countered by less than 20 percent support in the vast majority of more moderate and economically stable Muslim countries.

Women are increasingly making their way into terrorist tactical roles, such as suicide bombings.[123] Nacos estimates that perhaps 20 to 30 percent of all terrorists are women, and they are well represented in regional movements.[124] The earliest record of a female suicide bomber is 1978.[125] In general, women are not viewed as threats or combatants, which may give them tactical advantages in avoiding detection and conducting a surprise attack.[126] In 1991, a woman approached former Indian Prime Minister Rajiv Gandhi, placed a garland on him, bowed at his feet, and killed both of them by detonating a bomb hidden in a basket of flowers.[127] The Liberation Tigers of Tamil Eelam (LTTE) of Sri Lanka was responsible for the assassination. Gandhi earned the wrath of LTTE when he sent Indian troops to help quell violence in Sri Lanka in 1987. Table 5–2 summarizes the work of Clarke and Newman, which examined suicide bombing from the key perspectives of both the bomber's handler and the bomber.

Although some research psychologists have described suicide bombers as loners, depressed, and suicidal, other researchers have rejected this position.[128] Radical Muslims reject the "suicide bomber" label as an attempt by Western journalists to limit the number of bombers. Studying bombers presents unique challenges. The bombers are dead and cannot be interviewed, although they may have made a martyr's video that provides some information.[129] Interviews with family and friends of suicide bombers must be carefully scrutinized: All of them may have a need to cast the deceased in the best light, but may not personally have knowledge of the bombers' true motivations.[130]

TABLE 5–2
Requirements of Handlers and Suicide Bombers

The Handler's Requirements	The Suicide Bomber's Requirements
• A safe house for operations	• Concealable explosives, preferably in the bomber's clothes
• Community support to maintain secrecy	• Means of detonating bomb
• A network to identify candidates	• Unless walking, means of getting to target
• Skilled personnel to: (1) train candidates (e.g., rehearse route and means to travel to target, dress to blend in with area, how to use detonator) and (2) indoctrinate candidates	• Cell phone or other means of communicating with handler
• Select suicide bombers	• Map or memorize route to target
• Reconnaissance tasks: acquire maps, gather intelligence (e.g., security vulnerabilities)	• Preferably a visit to target so can dress accordingly
• Skilled personnel to write, film, and edit suicide bomber's last statement	• Knowledge of alternative target if thwarted in attacking primary
	• Dedication to task

Data from Ronald V. Clarke and Graeme R. Newman, Outsmarting the Terrorists (Westport, CT: Praeger Security International, 2006), pp. 64–68 for an extended version of this chart.

Box 5-4
Suicide Bombing and the Shahid: Of Islamic Martyrdom

The Qur'an (2:195 and 4:29) forbids ordinary suicide (Arabic: *intihar*) and those who commit it will be driven into a fire (Qur'an 4:30). It is, therefore, unsurprising that Muslim countries traditionally have the world's lowest suicide rates.[131] Following the 9/11 attacks, some Muslim scholars issued religious rulings condemning suicide attacks, while others issued opinions supporting "martyrdom operations."[132]

Currently, radical segments of Islam see suicide bombers as heroic martyrs or *shahids*. Unlike those who will be driven into the fire, those who fight in the cause of Allah will receive a "great reward" in paradise (Qur'an 4:74).

Members of Hamas have accounted for over 90 percent of all suicide bombings in Israel and have certainly encouraged this type of radical Islamic tactic. The groups praise suicide bombers as dying in the most noble of causes...a misinterpreted perspective of "holy jihad."[133] Those who are martyred during jihad are told they will receive six bounties:[134]

1. Their sins are immediately forgiven;
2. they are immediately accepted into paradise and spared the judgment of the grave;
3. they avoid the great terror (a great frightening sound, all the dead will be made alive, and those alive will die except those who God wishes to spare, the sky will fragment, the mountains scattered, and all hearts will beat rapidly);
4. a great crown is placed on their head, one ruby in which is worth more than all there is in this life;
5. they are married to 72 maidens of paradise; and
6. they may intercede for 70 relatives.[135]

Do you think that suicide bombing is a viable tactic to win greater public support for a cause? Why or why not?

Quick Facts
Beyond the Six Bounties: Payments to the Family of Suicide Bombers

In addition, in the current era of radicalized Muslim suicide bombing, women who conduct such acts in the name of Allah receive one husband who will please them. Under Saddam Hussein, Iraq paid $25,000 to the families of suicide bombers.[136] Presently, both Syria and Iran make payments to the families of suicide bombers.

How Do Terrorist Organizations End?

In America, the failure rate for new small businesses is 50 to 70 percent in the first 18 months.[137] Similarly, Rapoport speculates that the vast majority of all terrorist groups don't survive their first year.[138] Intuitively, a high percentage of "start-up" terrorist groups failing in the first year makes sense. There are powerful forces and technological capabilities deployed against movements. To illustrate, start-up terrorist organizations are more at risk when recruiting because much of it must be done face-to-face. In contrast, more established movements recruit over the Internet. They can contact many candidates simultaneously while also reducing their risk exposure.[139]

Start-up small businesses and terrorist movements appear to be at significant risk of failure from four common factors. Stated in terrorist terms, those four factors are (1) inexperience, for example, leaders may not be able to sustain the zeal of followers because they neither know how to do so or don't recognize its importance; (2) bad operational decisions, such as attacking "hard" targets beyond the capabilities of the group; (3) a lack of capital, for example, either they cannot attract well-heeled financial supporters or such supporters are convinced by bad operational decisions the group does not have a future and stop contributing; and (4) an environment in which mistakes may lead to catastrophic failure, illustrated by failing to carefully vet followers, which results in penetration of the terrorist organization by informers or security agents.

Cronin envisions terrorist organizations ending in six different ways:[140]†

1. *The group's leader is captured or killed.* This is referred to as the "decapitation" strategy and its results are inconsistent. Capturing terrorist leaders is a better option than killing them because the leaders are cut off from the group; the group may be in turmoil while deciding what to do about their leadership; and the captured leaders

---

† We have used Cronin's endings and cited her work appropriately. In addition, we have added our own additional research and comments. Therefore, to avoid misrepresentation of her work, it will be useful to read it.

are humiliated as they are paraded in chains to court before the news media.[141] In balance, an imprisoned leader is a liability and there are some cases where hostages were taken to exchange for the release of the leader.[142] If a terrorist leader is killed, the group may go into decline or even split into factions, leaving no central figure with whom to negotiate, and if the group remains intact, a new leader may emerge who is much more effective than his predecessor.[143] In 1973, Israel killed Mohamed Boudia, who was a PFLP leader in Europe, apparently for his role in the Olympic Massacre the year before. On a temporary basis Ilich Sanchez (Carlos the Jackal) filled his shoes.[144] Two years later, the Jackal led a sensational attack on a summit meeting in Vienna, Austria, of the Organization of the Petroleum Exporting Countries (OPEC), killing 3 and taking 63 hostages, including 11 oil ministers.[145] OPEC didn't hold a summit for another 25 years.[146] There may be times when exercising tactical restraint and leaving a terrorist leader in place is the best course of action.[147]

2. *The group enters into negotiations.* All democracies publically maintain they do not negotiate with terrorists, but virtually all do so secretly.[148] Before agreeing to go to the table, governments must conclude what prospects there are for a reasonable outcome; groups with absolute goals are likely to demonstrate little flexibility, while those with political or narrower goals offer better prospects for negotiation.[149] Moreover, a determination must be made whether the organization is sufficiently centralized that the terrorist negotiators can actually get others to "toe the line" of any agreement.[150] State-sponsored terrorist groups offer a similar issue.[151] A precondition to all negotiations is a cessation of hostilities; if a group is not able to deliver on this issue, it suggests a lack of internal cohesion in it,[152] for example, a faction opposed to negotiating may use attacks to disrupt the process. Negotiations can be conducted indirectly through a third party.[153] A government will learn useful things about a terrorist group while negotiating, such as details about its structure, the identity of key figures, and something about the relative importance of those at the table.[154] Negotiations seldom end terrorism, but may be associated with producing a decline in terrorist operations.[155]

3. *The group's aims are achieved.* If a group claims success, saying it has "achieved its aims," the statement needs to be closely scrutinized. As the saying goes, "The devil is always in the details." For example, it may have accepted concessions granting it the achievement of some goals, but in exchange dropped other demands that may have been impossible to achieve. A Rand Corporation study found that only 10 percent of terrorist groups actually "achieve their goals."[156]

4. *There is an implosion or loss of the group's public support.* Cronin asserts that most terrorist movements end because the group eventually disintegrates.[157] A significant factor in this is the loss of support, for example, the ideology loses its relevancy, the group "loses the bubble" in understanding what its constituency wants or needs, and targeting errors provoke a backlash.[158]

5. *The group is defeated by force.* The application of military force accounts for 7 percent of the defeats of terrorist groups.[159] It is more effective with insurgency terrorism, whereas using the police is more effective with other groups. Policing produces 40 percent of terrorist endings.[160]

6. *There is a transition by the group from terrorism into other forms of violence.* Most commonly, terrorist groups shift to criminal acts, which implies a shift away from political or religious goals and toward acquiring goods and profits that are an end in themselves.[161] To illustrate, Rollins & Wyler note that the Philippines-based Abu Sayyaf Group (ASG) has sometimes prioritized criminal activities over ideological operations.[162] During its periods of high criminality, ASG focuses on maritime piracy, arms trafficking, and kidnappings for ransom.[163] Recruits seem less attracted by ideology and more motivated by promises of financial wealth.[164]

Information Link
Visit the National Consortium for the Study of Terrorism and Responses to Terrorism (START) at www.start.umd.edu. It has a broad range of terrorist information, including publications and annual updates on some datasets. The U.S. Department of State is responsible for submitting a terrorism report to Congress annually and START cooperates with USDOS in preparing that document.

7. Two important questions about how terrorist organizations end are: (1) What becomes of the military arms and supplies? If the terrorists "win," there is no issue, but if defeated by force or the group's aims are achieved, how much certainty can there be that all arms have been collected or otherwise accounted for? and (2) What becomes of the terrorist fighters? Do they join another cause? Start a new one elsewhere? Will they need to be treated for Post Trauma Stress Syndrome? Will they willingly "retire" to a life of peace?

Chapter Summary

SUMMARY BY LEARNING OBJECTIVE

1. **State the key dilemmas facing terrorist organizations.**

   These dilemmas are (1) action versus secrecy, (2) growth versus control, (3) recruitment versus retention, (4) success versus longevity, and (5) resource acquisition versus constituencies.

2. **Identify six organizational models of terrorist organizations, and briefly describe each.**

   There are six organizational models of terrorist organization. These include:

   - **Lone Wolf**: A lone wolf is ideologically driven to violence or attempted violence and personally plans and executes the attack in the absence of collaboration with other individuals or groups.

   - **Cell**: A **cell** is a group of multiple terrorists working cooperatively toward achieving a particular goal, such as raising funds, gathering intelligence, or executing an attack. Alternatively, a cell may not be specialized and all of these functions may be performed within a single cell. There is no set number of individuals that comprise a cell; hence, three or more individuals commonly make up a cell.

   - **Network**: Cells are the "building blocks" of network organizational models and are resilient against disruption and attacks; they are also highly effective in processing communication. There are four network models, including the chain, hub or star, wheel, and all channel structure.

   - **Hierarchical**: The hierarchical model incorporates the idea of grades of rank and is based on the principle of hierarchy; that is, each lower organizational unit is under the direct control and supervision of a superior organizational unit. This produces a common pyramid-shape form with a single leader at the top of the pyramid.

   - **Umbrella**: The umbrella organizational model (UOM) is characterized by a core group that assists (or gives leadership) to other groups that voluntarily associate with it. The UOM is a relatively recent hybrid organizational structure that is made up of two other organizational structures: the hierarchical and the network models.

   - **Virtual**: A virtual terrorist organization (VTO) exists in cyberspace. It has no headquarters and needs no physical meeting space. Its members can be dispersed geographically, but work together exploiting information technology to achieve their common goals by sharing their skills and knowledge collaboratively.

3. **Explain how ideology helps identify targets and view victims.**

   Terrorist movements have a core set of beliefs and goals that define their ideology and focus their violence. One way or another, ideology identifies "acceptable" targets and acts as a constraint against attacking other targets. Acceptable targets serve another important purpose. In the ideological framework of terrorist movements, victims are blamed for the violence inflicted on them. The essence of this argument is "They brought it on themselves." This construction both relieves terrorists of their moral responsibility for the deaths they have caused and glorifies them for doing so.

4. **State the ways that Cronin sees terrorist organizations ending.**

   Cronin's endings are (1) the group's leader is captured or killed, (2) the group enters into negotiations, (3) the group's aims are achieved; (4) there is an implosion or loss of the group's public support, (5) the group is defeated by force, and (6) there is a transition from terrorism to another form of violence.

REVIEW QUESTIONS

1. What are passive supporters of terrorist organizations?
2. Lone wolf terrorists are hard to detect. Why?
3. What is a cell?
4. How does a "leaderless resistance cell" function?

5. What are "sleeper cells?"
6. What is a "redundant leader protocol" in a cell?
7. The hierarchy organizational model has what major features?
8. What is the meaning of the acronym EVIL DONE?
9. As identified by Cronin, list the six different ways terrorist organizations commonly end.

CRITICAL THINKING EXERCISES

1. When IS conquers and occupies an area, it economically exploits the people living there and also executes people for even minor matters. In one instance, IS executed teenage boys who were watching a soccer game on television. Assuming IS remains in control of an area and maintains its strict policies, create three scenarios that could reasonably develop as a result and explain your rationale for each.

2. **Joining Terrorist Movements.** In the section "Recruitment versus Retention," Frisch asserts that people join terrorist organizations for three main reasons: (1) family members, friends, or people they know are going to, or have already done so; (2) family members and others have strong grievances against the government; and (3) out of deep religious or political convictions. Later in the chapter, Polko suggests that wanting to improve their financial situation is an equally strong motivation. Essentially, Polko argues that there are some "career-minded" terrorists who see their job as akin to having the worst job in a corporation. It is a pathway for upward mobility. Should that be added to Frisch's main reasons? Explain how you reached your decision about it.

Has Polko posited an interesting but unlikely possibility? People who join our armed forces expect to be promoted. Does that bolster the case for Polko's career-minded terrorist? Why or why not? Think of some possible other main reasons to add to Frisch's.

NOTES

1. Amitai Etzioni, *Modern Organizations* (Englewood Cliffs, New Jersey: Prentice Hall, 1964), p. 1 with restatement.
2. Charles R. Swanson, Leonard Territo, and Robert W. Taylor, *Police Administration: Structures, Processes, and Behaviors*, 8th edition (Upper Saddle River, New Jersey: Pearson, 2012), p. 174.
3. These five dilemmas are drawn with substantial restatement and some additions from Ethan Frisch, "Insurgencies Are Organizations Too: Organizational Structure and the Effectiveness of Insurgent Strategy," *The Peace and Conflict Review*, Vol. 6, Issue 1, 2010, pp. 19–24.
4. Ibid., p. 19.
5. Loc. cit.
6. Audrey Kurth Cronin, *How Terrorism Ends* (Princeton, New Jersey: Princeton University Press, 2009), p. 4.
7. Ibid., p. 20.
8. Michael McCaul, Chair, Final Report of the Task Force on Combatting Terrorism and Foreign Fighter Travel (Washington, D.C.: U.S. Department of Homeland Security), 2015, p. 10.
9. Ibid., p. 6.
10. Loc. cit.
11. Loc. cit.
12. Lori Hinnant and Paul Schem, "What It's Like Trying to Leave ISIS," Business Insider (via AP), February 3, 2015, www.businessinsider.com/what-its-like-trying-to-leave-isis-2015-2, accessed March 1, 2017. Several ideas from this source are included in this first paragraph.
13. Loc. cit.
14. Ibid., p. 22.
15. Bruce W. Don, *Networked Technologies for Networked Terrorists* (Santa Monica: RAND Corporation, 2007), pp. 12–13.

16. Ibid., p. 23.

17. Christopher Andrew, Richard J. Aldrich, and Wesley A. Wark, Secret Intelligence: A Reader (Florence, Kentucky: Routledge), 2009, p. 179.

18. Ibid., p. 24.

19. Khusrav Gaibulloev and Todd Sandler, "Determinates of the Demise of Terrorist Organizations," November 2012, www.utdallas.edu/~tms063000/website/Demise%20of%20 Terrorist%20Organizations.pdf, p. 3.

20. Ibid., p. 8.

21. Ibid., p. 15.

22. Loc. cit.

23. Ibid., p. 8.

24. Ibid., p. 7.

25. *Networked Technologies for Networked Terrorists*, p. 24.

26. Loc. cit.

27. Kevin Johnson, "ISIL's Sophisticated Recruiting Campaign Poses Persistent Threat in U.S.," USA Today, April 26, 2015, www.usatoday.com/story/news/nation/2015/04/26/ foreign-fighters-isil-fbi/26202741, accessed March 5, 2017.

28. Operational space is mentioned in Joshua Kilberg, "A Basic Model Explaining Terrorist Group Organizational Structure," *Studies in Conflict and Terrorism*, Vol. 35, Issue 11, 2012.

29. Resources and ideological preferences of supporters are identified in Luis De la Calle and Ignacio Sanchez-Cuenca, "The Production of Terrorist Violence: Analyzing Target Selection with the IRA and ETA," *Centro de Estudios Avanzados Ciencias Sociales, Instituto Juan March de Estudios e Investigaciones*, Madrid, Spain, 2006, p. 1.

30. Michael Becker, "Exploring Lone Wolf Target Selection in the United States," *Studies in Conflict and Terrorism*, Vol. 37, Issue 11, 2014, pp. 959–978.

31. Mark Hamm and Ramon Spaaij, "Lone Wolf Terrorism in America: Using Knowledge of Radicalization Pathways to Forge Prevention Strategies" (Washington, D.C.: U.S. Department of Justice, February 2015), p. 1.

32. Dalia Ghanem-Yazbeck, "Killing Alone: The Lone Wolf Phenomena," Carnegie Middle East Center, July 26, 2017, carnegie-mec.org/2016/07/26/killing-alone-lone-wolf-terrorist -phenomena-pub-64202, accessed March 13, 2017.

33. Dalia Ghanem-Yazbeck, "Killing Alone: The Lone Wolf Phenomenon," Carnegie Middle East Center, July 26, 2016, carnegie-mec.org/2016/07/26/killing-alone-lone-wolf-terrorist -phenomena-pub-64202, accessed March 11, 2016. With reorganization, restatement, and additional information for all four cites to this source.

34. Loc. cit.

35. Loc. cit.

36. Loc. cit.

37. Doug Mataconis, "The Attack on Canada's Parliament," *Christian Science Monitor*, October 23, 2014, www.csmonitor.com/USA/Politics/Politics-Voices/2014/1023/The -attack-on-Canada-s-Parliament-and-the-lone-wolf-terrorist, accessed March 14, 2017, and Benjamin Landy, "Canadian Parliament Attacked, Soldier Killed by Gunman," MSNBC, October 22, 2014, www.msnbc.com/msnbc/canadian-parliament-attacked-soldier-killed -gunman, accessed March 14, 2017.

38. Victor Asal, Kathleen Deloughery, and Ryan D. King, "Understanding Lone-Actor Terrorism: A Comparative Analysis with Violent Hate Crimes and Group Based Terrorism" (College Park, Maryland: National Consortium for the Study of Terrorism and Responses to Terrorism, September 2013), p. 1.

39. Hamm and Spaaj, "Lone Wolf Terrorism in America: Using Knowledge of Radicalization Pathways to Forge Prevention Strategies," p. 4.

40. Ibid., p. 6.

41. Loc. cit.

42. For an excellent analysis of this subject, see Jeffrey D. Simon, *Lone Wolf Terrorism: Understanding the Growing Threat* (Amherst, N.Y.: Prometheus Books, 2013). Also see Mark Thompson, "The Danger of the Lone-Wolf Terrorist," February 27, 2013, p. 1, www .nation.time.com/2013/02/27/the-danger-of-the-lone-wolf-terrorist.

43. Loc. cit.

44. Ibid., p. 4.

45. These five major headings were taken from Jeffrey Connor and Carol Rollie Flynn, Report: Lone Wolf Terrorism (Georgetown University: Security Studies Program), National Security Critical Issue Task Force, June 27, 2015, pp. 18–24, with considerable additions and restatement, georgetownsecuritystudiesreview.org/wp-content/uploads/2015/08/NCITF-Final-Paper.pdf, accessed March 3, 2017.

46. Ibid., p. 18, mentions personal, social, and political factors.

47. Ibid., p. 19 with restatement, the two examples are from the present authors.

48. Michael Laris, Carol D. Leonnig, and Sandhya Somashekhar, "Wade Michael Page: Excess Drinking Cost Sikh Temple Shooter His Military Career, Civilian Job," *Washington Post*, August 7, 2012.

49. Erica Goode and Serg P. Kovalesker, "Wisconsin Kill Fed and Was Fueled by Hate Driven Music, *New York Times*, August 6, 2012, www.nytimes.com/2012/08/07/us/army-veteran-identified-as-suspect-inwisconsin-shooting.html?pagewanted=all and Ryan Lenz, "White Supremacists React to Sikh Massacre," Southern Poverty Law Center, August 7, 2012. www.splcenter.org/get-informed/news/white-supremacists-react-to-sikh-massacre.

50. Anti-Defamation League, "Alleged Sikh Temple Shooter Was a Member of Hammerskins; A Hard Core Racist Skinhead Group with a Huge Presence in Florida," www.regions.adl.org/florida/news/sikh-temple-shooter.html, accessed September 4, 2012.

51. Ibid., with restatement.

52. Ibid., p. 22 with restatement.

53. Connor and Flynn, Report: Lone Wolf Terrorism, p. 22.

54. Paulina Polko, "Selected Problems Related to Managing Terrorist Organizations," Forum Scientiae Oeconomia, Vol. 2, No. 2, 2014, drawn from pp. 42–43, with reorganization and restatement.

55. Jerome P. Bjelopera, "American Jihadist Terrorism: Combating a Complex Threat" (Washington, D.C.: Congressional Research Service, January 23, 2013), p. 34. This statement was made with respect to Americans who are motivated by Islamic jihad, but by observation it also applies to American lone wolves.

56. Lone Wolf Terrorism (Rotterdam, Netherlands: Instituut Voor Veiligheids-en Crisis Management), June 6, 2007, p. 17.

57. Walter Laqueur, *The New Terrorism* (New York: Oxford University Press, 1999), p. 8.

58. "Edmond Post Office Massacre," Oklahoma State University Digital Library, undated, www.digital.library.okstate.edu/encyclopedia/entries/e/ed003.html.

59. Loc. cit.

60. Neil Katz, "Joe Stack Suicide Note Full Text: American Zombies Wake Up and Revolt," February 18, 2010, www.CBSNews.com/8301_504083_162_6220533_504083.html.

61. Marc Lacey and David M. Herszenhorn, "In Attack's Wake, Political Repercussions," New York Times, January 8, 2008, www.nytimes.com/2011/01/09/us/politics/09giffords.html, accessed March 7, 2017.

62. Patrick Sawyer, Montabaur and Raziye Akkoc, Telegraph, May 6, 2015, www.telegraph.co.uk/news/worldnews/europe/france/11496066/Andreas-Lubitz-Everything-we-know-about-Germanwings-plane-crash-co-pilot.html, accessed March 1, 2017.

63. No author, "Mass Shooting Kills Four Native Americans in Northern California," Reuters, February 21, 2014, www.rt.com/usa/four-killed-native-american-california-129, accessed March 3, 2017.

64. Trevor Hughes, "Planned Parenthood Shooting Suspect Found Incompetent to Stand Trial," USA Today, May 11, 2016, www.usatoday.com/story/news/nation/2016/05/11/planned-parenthood-shooting-suspect-found-not-competent-stand-trial/84243964, accessed March 6, 2017, and Isaiah J. Downing, "Planned Parenthood Says Colorado Shooter Opposed Abortion," Reuters, November 29, 2016, www.reuters.com/article/us-colorado-shooter-idUSKBN0TH05O20151130, accessed March 5, 2017.

65. This account was written with new content added by the authors and some details from CBS News, "New Details Emerge in Probe of Oregon College Shooter," May 23, 2014, www.cbsnews.com/news/

oregon-shooting-umpqua-community-college-chris-harper-mercer-investigation, accessed
March 1, 2017, and Dirk Vanderhart, Kirk Johnson,
and Julie Turkewitz, "Oregon Shooting at Umpqua College Kills 10, Sheriff Says," New
York Times, October 1, 2015, www.nytimes.com/2015/10/02/us/oregon-shooting-umpqua
-community-college.html, accessed March 1, 2017.

66. Manny Fernandez, Richard Perez-Pena, and Jonah Engel Bromwich, "Five Dallas Officers
Were Killed as Payback," New York Times, July 8, 2016, www.nytimes.com/2016/07/09/
us/dallas-police-shooting.html, accessed March 5, 2017, and Faith Karimi, Catherine E.
Shoichet, and Ralph Ennis, "Dallas Sniper Attack: 5 Officers Killed, Suspect Identified,"
CNN News, July 9, 2016, http://edition.cnn.com/2016/07/08/us/philando-castile-alton
-sterling-protests, accessed March 6, 2017.

67. Mark Berman, William Wan, and Sari Horwitz, "Five Killed in Fort Lauderdale Airport
Shooting, Suspect in Custody," Washington Post, January 6, 2017, www.washingtonpost
.com/news/post-nation/wp/2017/01/06/reports-shots-fired-at-fort-lauderdale-airport,
March 3, 2017, and Charles Rabin, "Airport Shooter's Life in Alaska Was Falling Apart,
Though Few Seemed to Notice," Miami Herald, January 11, 2017, www.miamiherald
.com/news/nation-world/article126025249.html, accessed March 3, 2017.

68. See Evan F. Kohlmann, "Home Grown Terrorists: Theory and Cases on Terror's Newest
Front," *The Annals of the American Academy of Political and Social Science*, Vol. 618,
No. 1, pp. 95–109.

69. Mark Hallam, "Frankfurt Shooter Described as Islamist-Influenced Solo Attacker,"
DW News, April 3, 2011, www.dw.de/frankfurt-shooter-described-as-islamist-influenced
-solo-attacker/a-14889904.

70. No author, Global Terrorism Index 2015 (Sydney, Australia: Institute for Economic and
Peace, 2015), p. 54.

71. Connor and Flynn, Report: Lone Wolf Terrorism, p. 10. Connor and Flynn had a fourth
point: "Overwhelmingly use firearms to conduct attacks, compared to LWTs in other western countries who rely on hijackings or bombs," which the present authors had essentially
made in the paragraph above it.

72. Ian Austen, "Hit-and-Run That Killed Canadian Soldier Is Called Terrorist Attack," *New
York Times*, October 21, 2014, www.nytimes.com/2014/10/22/world/americas/canadian
-soldier-run-down-in-what-officials-call-act-of-terror-dies.html, accessed March 15, 2017.

73. Catherine E. Shoichet, "Two Countries Tried to Deport Berlin Attack Suspect," CNN,
December 23, 2016, www.cnn.com/2016/12/22/europe/berlin-attack-suspect-deportation,
accessed March 14, 2017.

74. Loc. cit.

75. John Roach, "Estimation of Operations Security (OPSEC) in al Qaeda Operation,"
Newsletter of the OPSEC Professional Society, Vol. 3, Issue 2, July 2012, p. 12.

76. Chris Dishman, "The Leadership Nexus: When Crime and Terror Converge," *Studies
in Conflict and Terrorism*, Vol. 28, Issue 3, 2005, p. 243, www.cerium.ca/img/
dishman_2005_the_leadership_nexus.pdf.

77. "Louis Beam," Anti-Defamation League, www.archive.adl.org/learn/ext_us/beam.asp
?.xpicked=2&item=beam.

78. The account in this paragraph is taken with restatement from Dale Russakoff and Dan
Eggen, "Six Charged in Plot to Attack Fort Dix," *Washington Post*, May 9, 2007, www
.washingtonpost.com/wp-dyn/content/article/2007/05/08/ar2007050800465_2.html.

79. Richard Greenberg, Adam Ciralsky, and Stone Phillips, "Enemies at the Gate," NBC News
Today, December 28, 2007, www.today.com/id/22419963/ns/today/t/enemies-gate/
#.UjW30xavszY.

80. Emily Smith, "Terrorists Drawn to South African Passports," CNN, June 15, 2011, www
.security.blogs.cnn.com/2011/06/15/terrorists-drawn-to-south-african-passports.

81. Luis Fleischman, "Venezuela: Anatomy of a Dictator," *The Journal of International
Security Affairs*, No. 11, Fall 2006, www.securityaffairs.org/issues/2006/11/fleischman.
php.

82. Scott Zamost et al., "Venezuela May Have Given Passports to People with Ties to Terrorism," CNN News, February 14, 2017, http://edition.cnn.com/2017/02/08/world/venezuela-passports-investigation, accessed March 4, 2017.

83. Philip Sherwell, "Master Forger Arrested in Thailand over Fake Passports to Europe," *Telegraph* (United Kingdom), February 16, 2016, www.telegraph.co.uk/news/worldnews/asia/thailand/12149720/Master-forger-arrested-in-Thailand-over-fake-passports-for-migrants-to-Europe.html, accessed March 5, 2017.

84. Greenberg, Ciralsky, and Phillips, "Enemies at the Gate."

85. "Iran 'Sleeper Cells' Are Infiltrating South America, Argentine Prosecutor Says," Fox News Latino, May 30, 2013, www.latino.foxnews.com/latino/news/2013/05/30/iran-terror-sleeper-cells-are-infiltrating-south-america-argentine-prosecutor-says.

86. See David E. Kaplan and Monica M. Ekman, "Homegrown Terrorists," *U.S. News and World Report*, Vol. 134, Issue 7, March 3, 2003, pp. 30–34.

87. Markus Sabadello, "Comparing Terrorist and Internet Networks," Project Danube, Fall 2010, www.projectdanube.org/wp-content/upload/2012/02/comparing-terrorist-and-internet-networks.pdf.

88. A Military Guide to Terrorism in the Twenty-First Century (United States Army, Fort Leavenworth, Kansas: TRADOC G2, August 15, 2007), pp. 3–8.

89. Nicolas Verdier, "Hierarchy: A Short History of a Word in Western Thought," in Denise Pumain, ed., *Hierarchy in Natural and Social Sciences* (New York, N.Y., Springer, 2005), p. 13.

90. The hierarchical/ bureaucratic model is the centerpiece of organizational theory's traditional stem. It existed for centuries and was systematized by Max Weber. The bureaucratic model is compatible with administrative theory. For more information, see Charles Swanson, Leonard Territo, and Robert W. Taylor, *Police Administration: Structures, Processes, and Behavior*, 8th edition (Upper Saddle River, New Jersey: Pearson, 2012), pp. 174–208.

91. Rohan Gunaratna and Aviv Oreg, "Al Qaeda's Organizational Structure and Its Evolution," *Studies in Conflict and Terrorism*, Vol. 33, Issue 12, November 2010, p. 1052.

92. Jonathon Masters, "Al-Qaeda in the Arabian Peninsula," Council on Foreign Relations, May 24, 2012, www.cfr.org/yemen/al-qaeda-in-the-arabian-peninsular-aqap/p9369.

93. "The Global Islamic Media Front Issues Caliphate Voice Channel Video, Threatening Governments of Germany and Austria over Role in Afghanistan," Christian Action Network, March 12, 2007, www.christianactionnetwork.wordpress.com; and "Pair Sentenced for Terrorist Threat to Austria, Germany," DW (Deutsche Welle), March 13, 2008, www.dw.de/pair-sentenced-for-terrorist-threat-to-austria-germany/a-3189925-1.

94. See Peter Grier, "The New al Qaeda: Local Franchises," *Christian Science Monitor*, July 11, 2005, www.csmonitor.com/2005/0711/p01s01-woeu.html.

95. Siobhan Gorman, "Terror Links Spurred Alert," *Wall Street Journal*, August 6, 2013, quoting interview with Gregory Johnsen.

96. Major David M. Williams, "Nothing Virtual About It: An Emerging Safe Haven for an Adaptive Enemy" (Fort Leavenworth, Kansas: Monograph for the School of Advanced Military Studies, U.S. Army Command and General Staff College, 2010), p. 2.

97. Williams, "Nothing Virtual about It," p. 40.

98. Michael Judy, "Terrorism's Virtual Safe Havens and the Effects on Terror Organizations," *Global Security Studies*, Vol. 2, Issue 1, Winter 2011, www.globalsecuritystudies.com/judy%20virtual.pdf.

99. Loc. cit.

100. Loc. cit.

101. Loc. cit.

102. This paragraph, with restatement and new material, is drawn from Austin L. Wright, "Terrorism, Ideology, and Target Selection," March 5, 2013, www.princeton.edu/politics/about/file-repository/public/wright_on_terrorism.pdf. It does not appear to have been published other than on this Princeton University site.

103. Dallas Boyd and James Scouras, "The Dark Matter of Terrorism," *Studies in Conflict and Terrorism*, Vol. 33, No. 12, December 2010, p. 128.

104. Dale C. Eikmeier, "Center of Gravity Analysis," *Military Review*, Vol. LXXXIV, No. 6, August 2004, p. 2.

105. Loc. cit.

106. Joe Strange and Richard Iron, "Understanding Center of Gravity and Critical Vulnerabilities," Air War College, Maxwell Air Force Base, undated, p. 2.

107. Battle of the Atlantic Statistics, United States Merchant Marine, www.usmm.org/battleatlantic.html.

108. Terrorism in the Twenty-First Century (Ft. Leavenworth, Kansas: U.S. Army Training and Doctrine Command (TRADOC), G2, Handbook No. 1, December 10, 2010), p. A-1.

109. The discussion of EVIL DONE is drawn from Ronald G. Clarke and Graeme R. Newman, *Outsmarting the Terrorists* (Westport, CT: Praeger Security International, 2006), pp. 93–97.

110. Rukmini Callimachi, "Paying Ransoms, Europe Bankrolls Qaeda Terror," *New York Times*, July 29, 2014.

111. Loc. cit.

112. "I'm a Client … Get Me out of Here," *The Economist*, June 27, 2013, www.economist.com/blogs/schumpeter/2013/06/kidnap-and-ransom-insurance.

113. Brett Smith, "A Look at Terrorist Behavior: How They Prepare, Where They Strike" (Washington, D.C.: National Institute of Justice, July 2008), *NIJ Journal* 280, www.nij.gov/journals/260/pages/terrorist-behavior.aspx.

114. Loc. cit.

115. Ewen MacAskill, "Suicide Bomb Restarts Hamas Campaign," *Guardian* (England), July 9, 2001, www.theguardian.com/world/2001/jul/10/israel.

116. Sean Yom and Basel Saleh, "Palestinian Suicide Bombers: A Statistical Analysis," *Economists for Peace & Security*, 2004, www.epsusa.org/publications/newsletter/2004/nov2004/saleh.pdf.

117. Riaz Hassan, "What Motivates Suicide Bombers," *YaleGlobal Online*, September 3, 2009, p. 1, http://yaleglobal.yale.edu/content/what-motivates-suicide-bombers-0.

118. The data in these two sentences is drawn from the University of Chicago's Project on Security and Threats," Suicide Attack Database, current to October 16, 2016, http://cpostdata.uchicago.edu/search_new.php, accessed March 16, 2017.

119. Ben Farmer, "Afghan Boy Suicide Bombers Tell How They Are Brainwashed into Believing They Will Survive," Telegraph (UK), January 13, 2012, www.telegraph.co.uk/news/worldnews/asia/afghanistan/9014282/Afghan-boy-suicide-bombers-tell-how-they-are-brainwashed-into-believing-they-will-survive.html, accessed March 12, 2017.

120. No author, "Nigeria: Babies Used in Suicide Bombings, Officials Warn," BBC, January 23, 2017, www.bbc.com/news/world-africa-38725976, accessed March 9, 2017.

121. Robert Tait, "Donkey Suicide Bomb Stopped by Israeli Troops on Gaza," *Telegraph* (England), July 18, 2014.

122. The Pew Research Center Forum on Religion and Public Live, *The World's Muslims: Religion, Politics and Society* (Washington, D.C.: April 30, 2013).

123. Jessica Davis, "Evolution of the Global Jihad: Female Suicide Bombers in Iraq," *Studies in Conflict and Terrorism*, Vol. 36, Issue 4, 2013, pp. 279–291, online copy has no page numbers, www.tandfoline.com.proxy-remote.galib.uga.edu/dol/abs/10/1080/105763598#.uvgxhbavvur.

124. Brigitte L. Nacos, "The Portrayal of Female Terrorists in the Media," *Studies in Conflict and Terrorism*, Vol. 28, Issue 5, September 2005, p. 436.

125. Davis, "Evolution of the Global Jihad."

126. Loc. cit.

127. Nacos, "The Portrayal of Female Terrorists in the Media," p. 447.

128. See Robert J. Brym and Bader Araj, "Are Suicide Bombers Suicidal?" *Studies in Conflict and Terrorism*, Vol. 35, Issue 6, pp. 432–443.

129. Ibid., p. 438.

130. Loc. cit.

131. David Cook, "The Implications of Martyrdom Operations for Contemporary Islam," *Journal of Religious Ethics*, Vol. 32, Issue I, Spring 2004, p. 130.

132. Ibid., p. 131.

133. Ibn Warraq, "Virgins? What Virgins?" *Guardian*, January 11, 2002, www.theguardian.com/books/2002/jan/12/books.giardianreviews5.

134. Some of the current list of bounties do not comport to early descriptions. For example, the Prophet told a companion that those who are martyred will receive six bounties: (1) they shall be forgiven when the first drop of their blood is spilt; (2) they shall see paradise upon their death; (3) they will be spared the torment of the grave; (4) they will be kept safe from the great fright (a great frightening sound, all the dead will be made alive and those alive will die except those who God wishes to spare, the sky will fragment, the mountains scattered, and all hearts will beat rapidly), (5) they will be married to wives from among the wide-eyed houris in paradise (splendid, light skinned, dark-eyed women); and (6) they will be able to intercede for 70 members of their family (see the English Translation of Sunan Ibn Majah, Compiled by Imam Muhammad Bin Yazeed (Riyadh, Saudi Arabia: Darussalam Books, 2007), Volume 4, Hadith 2799, p. 67. When Gabriel took Muhammad on a visit to paradise, mention was made of 70 beds and on each of which was a (beautiful) woman, but there was no connection to martyrdom. Elsewhere, Muhammad was reported to have said that the least reward for a faithful Muslim in paradise would be 80,000 servants and 70 houris.

135. These bounties are commonly found in a variety of sources. There may be minor variations in their wording. See Shaykh Faraz A. Khan, "72 Virgins for Martyrs: Making Sense of One of the Rewards of Paradise," *Seeking Guidance*, July 29, 2011, www.seekersguidance.org/ans-blog/2011/07/29/72-virgins-for-martyrs-making-sense-of-one-of-the-rewards-of-paradise.

136. Suicide Bombing during the Current Israeli-Palestinian Confrontation, January 1, 2006, www.terrorism-info.org.il/data/pdf/PDF_19279_2.pdf.

137. Pamela Engel, "Small Business Owners Don't Fear the Devastatingly High Failure Rate," *Business Insider*, June 5, 2013, www.businessinsider.com/small-business-owners-are-optimistic-2013-6.

138. David C. Rapoport, "Terrorism," in Mary Hawkesworth and Maurice Kogan, editors, *Routledge Encyclopedia of Government and Politics* (London, England: Routledge, 1992), p. 1067.

139. Don, *Networked Technologies for Networked Terrorists*, p. 12.

140. These six ways of ending are drawn from Cronin's excellent book, *How Terrorism Ends*. We have added commentary and other research to these ways. Serious students of terrorism should carefully read Cronin's entire work.

141. Don, *Networked Technologies for Networked Terrorists*, pp. 14–15.

142. Ibid., p. 17.

143. Ibid., p. 26.

144. See John Follian, *Jackal: The Complete Story of the Legendary Terrorist, Carlos the Jackal* (London, Orion, 1999).

145. "Carlos the Jackal Attacks OPEC Headquarters," History, This Day in History (December 21, 1975), www.history.com/this-day-in-history/carlos-the-jackal-attacks-opec-headquarters.

146. Loc. cit.

147. Cronin, *How Terrorism Ends*, p. 34.

148. Ibid., p. 35.

149. Peter R. Neumann, "Negotiating with Terrorists," *Foreign Affairs*, January/February 2007, www.foreignaffairs.com/articles/62276/peter-r-neumann/negotiating-with-terrorists.

150. Loc. cit.

151. Loc. cit.

152. Loc. cit.

153. Cronin, *How Terrorism Ends*, p. 37.

154. Loc. cit.

155. Ibid., p. 34.

156. Seth G. Jones and Martin C. Libicki, "How Terrorist Organizations End, Lessons for Countering Al Qaeda" (Santa Monica, CA: RAND Corporation Summary, 2008), p. xiv, www.rand.org/content/dam/rand/pubs/monographs/2008/rand_mg741-1.sum.pdf.
157. Cronin, *How Terrorism Ends*, p. 34.
158. Ibid., pp. 105, 107, and 108.
159. Jones and Libicki, *How Terrorism Ends, Lessons for Countering Al Qaeda*," p. xiv.
160. Seth G. Jones and Martin C. Libicki, "How Terrorist Organizations End," RAND Research Brief (Santa Monica, CA: RAND Corporation, 2008), p. 1.
161. Cronin, *How Terrorism Ends*, p. 146.
162. John Rollins and Liana Sun Wyler, "Terrorism and Transnational Crime: Policy Issues for Congress" (Washington, D.C.: Congressional Research Service, June 11, 2013), p. 17.
163. Loc. cit.
164. Loc. cit.

Critical Processes of Terrorist Organizations

CHAPTER

6

An Afghan National Army soldier holds a poppy near the village of Karizonah, Afghanistan. Poppies are used to manufacture heroin. Like many other insurgent and terrorist groups, the drug trade is a major source of funding for the Taliban, as is illegal mining.

(Staff Sergeant/Joshua L.Demotts/U.S. Air Force)

Learning Objectives

After completing this chapter, you should be able to:

1. Explain what restrains a terrorist movement's capability to launch certain types of attacks.

2. State why it is important for terrorist groups to become learning organizations.

3. Identify and briefly describe a terrorist movement's four organization tools.

4. Identify and briefly explain a terrorist movement's six operational tools.

Introduction

Terrorist groups and movements represent complex organizations. And just like other organizations in society, they have a basic rationale and motivation for existence, specific goals and objectives, divisions of labor and function, and a hierarchy of authority and responsibility. This chapter addresses the wide range of processes and behaviors observed in terrorist groups and organizations aimed at successfully achieving political legitimacy; recruitment, training, and maintenance of new members; command and control for operational effectiveness; publicity, news, and social media attention; financial independence; and the development of new leadership.

Terrorist Motivations and Capabilities

Asal and Rethemeyer studied 395 terrorist organizations over an eight-year period.[1] During that time, 68 (17 percent) of them killed 10 or more people and only twenty-eight (7.1 percent) killed 100 or more in operations.[2] Clearly there is wide variance in how terrorist organizations behave. Ganor explains their actions by dividing them into groups based on their (1) motivations, meaning their intentions and (2) their capabilities to achieve specific objectives, for example, actually destroy a target.[3]

Table 6–1 profiles six terrorist behavioral groups on the basis of their motivations and capabilities. The six groups are not a progression through which terrorist movements inevitably progress. They may get stuck at any stage, advance, regress, or dissolve, or their motivations and capabilities may change. Describing a terrorist organization is much like a photograph; it portrays what exists in a particular point in time, but a second photograph, even one taken soon after the first, may show subtle to substantial differences as compared to the first photograph.

TABLE 6–1

Behavioral Groups for Terrorist Organizations

Group	Description
A	Group A maintains terrorist motivations (intentions), such as destabilizing its national government. However, its low operational capabilities cannot fully support them (e.g., cannot mount more than local small attacks on "soft" targets; possess a low level of tactical and technical competency; primarily have handheld firearms; cannot produce false identification papers that will pass close scrutiny; and lack the resources to deploy personnel to attack distant targets). May be in movement's early development stages. Lacks or has lost foreign government or other sponsorship. May have experienced significant losses that have degraded its capability. Possibly seeking a safe haven from which to operate.
	Perhaps the smallest and shortest-running terrorist movement in history was the Belgium-based Communist Combat Cells (CCC). The CCC espoused a violent communist ideology and carried out some two dozen bombings that resulted in two deaths between October and December 1985. The arrest of all four CCC members that same December put a permanent end to the group.
	In Northern Island, the Real Irish Republican Army (RIRA) has used terrorist tactics to support its ideology of a unified Ireland. RIRA is a successor to the original IRA. Formed around 1997, its intentions exceed its low capabilities.
B	This group possesses motivations and greater operational capabilities than Group A. However, Group B still lacks the full range of resources needed to conduct the kinds and scope of terrorist attacks it desires. Following 9/11, the United States and its allies have waged war against al Qaeda. They have killed many of al Qaeda's first-generation key leaders and cadre and reduced al Qaeda's safe havens in Iraq, Afghanistan, and parts of Pakistan. Drone strikes and special operations personnel have also been used to kill leaders, diminish command and control capabilities, and have disrupted training in a number of countries, including Yemen, Somalia, Burkina Faso (Burkina), Nigeria, and other African countries, as well as in the Philippines. These actions have degraded al Qaeda capabilities from Group C to Group B. Nigeria's Boko Haram also fits in Group B (see Figure 6–1).

TABLE 6–1
Continued

Group	Description
C	Motivation is high and so are capabilities (e.g., able to mount simultaneous and complex operations). Al Qaeda's four attacks on 9/11 illustrated this ability. Since then, as noted immediately above, al Qaeda's capabilities have been systematically degraded, but not eliminated.
	Since 2014, the rise of IS has been meteoric. With a bankroll of $2 billion[4] and seasoned commanders and fighters, IS motivations and capabilities are high. It maintains combat operations in Iraq and Syria against an international coalition, while sending or activating small teams or radicalizing individuals to make lone wolf attacks, for example, in France, Germany, Belgium, and England. Speculatively, the San Bernardino attack on December 2, 2015, and the car ramming of pedestrians and knife attack on the campus of Ohio State University (OSU) on November 28, 2016, may have been fueled by terrorist propaganda. IS refers to homegrown jihadists as terrorism by remote control.
	At OSU, Abdul Razak Ali Artan, a Somalian refugee by way of Pakistan, used a car to strike people, and then exited it, stabbing people with a knife. The toll: 1 dead and 11 injured. Artan was shot dead by a police officer. During the subsequent investigation, ample evidence was found suggesting Artan was influenced or radicalized by al Qaeda and IS propaganda. A sample of what he wrote: "I vow to kill a million infidels to save one Muslim." Artan also referred to the late jihadist rapper, Anwar al-Awlaki, as a "hero."[5]
D	Capabilities exceed motivation because terrorist organizations do not carry out a full range of attacks due to internal and external considerations. For example, due to *external considerations* a terrorist movement *might* refrain from using biochemical attacks out of fear of overwhelming reprisals, loss of public support, and/or potential loss of sponsors. An example of an *internal consideration* is when the late Usama bin Laden directed followers not to attack Western civilians because it was not having the desired effect on their governments.
E	Has the operational capabilities, but not the motivation to use them. Whereas Group D refrains from certain types of attacks, Group E has suspended all terrorist operations for some specific purpose (e.g., Hamas has been violently opposed to Israel in the Middle East for decades, but episodically agrees to a cease-fire while restraining its military arm, the Izz-al-Din al-Qassam Brigades).
F	Lacks both motivation and operational capabilities. It has abandoned using violence to achieve its goals in favor of the political process. Essentially, it has morphed into a political organization. In South Africa, Nelson Mandela, a member of the revolutionary, nationalist, and anti-apartheid African National Congress (ANC), was convicted of sabotage and conspiracy to overthrow the government. He was imprisoned during 1964–1990. Following the abandonment of the anti-apartheid policy, Mandela became the next South African president. In 2008, the ANC was removed from the U.S. Department of State's terrorism watch list. The ANC is now a major political party in that country. The Bodo Liberation Tigers (BLT) laid down its arms and left the path of terrorism when it signed a memorandum of settlement with India's government in 2003, which created an area to be administered by BLT's successor, the Bodoland Territorial Council (BTC). The Bodos are an ethnic people living in northeast India.

Source: Boaz Ganor, "Terrorist Organization Types and the Probability of a Boomerang Effect," *Studies in Conflict and Terrorism,*" Vol. 31, Issue 4, April 2008, pp. 279–280, with substantial restatement, and added narrative and examples, along with the addition of Group C.

Beyond motivation and capabilities, there are many other ways to look at terrorist organizations. Examples include the driving ideology, quality of leadership, demands made, stage of development, size, degree of specialization, sponsorship, and extent of public support. Other factors include tactics used, the selection of targets, whether they hit "soft" or "hard" targets (e.g., Hezbollah's bombing a bus in Bulgaria filled with Israeli tourists popular with Westerners versus attacking a closely guarded military facility), and ability to conduct a rapid series of attacks or complex multipronged attacks, degree of independence or subordination to another body, ability to control a territory as a safe haven, the numbers of casualties caused in individual attacks and cumulatively, and the organization's longevity.[6]

FIGURE 6-1
Overloaded cars help people flee attacks in 2016 by Boko Haram in Diffa, Niger, Nigeria, Boko Haram, crossed the international line from its native Nigeria into Niger to unleash a series of attacks on villages. Its goal is to establish a caliphate in Nigeria and to have nothing to do with anything Western. Boko Haram pledged allegiance to IS, but was disowned by it. Note the Diffa signpost on the right-hand side of the photograph.
(Issouf Sanogo/AFP/Getty Images)

Quick Facts
Two Different Terrorist Tactics: Occupy the Target versus a Raid

The Taj Mahal Palace Hotel and Benghazi Attacks. These two attacks represent very different tactics and targets. The Taj Mahal Palace Hotel was a soft target that terrorists held for several days, while Benghazi was a raid, following which the terrorists withdrew. Globally, the Taj Mahal Palace Hotel ranks twentieth among the most elite hotels. In 2008, terrorists attacked multiple targets in Mumbai, including the Taj Mahal Palace Hotel, which they held for three days. Despite the remarkable efforts of Taj Mahal Palace Hotel employees to protect guests, thirty-one people died and twenty-six were injured. In the end, all terrorists except one were killed, and the lone survivor was convicted and executed. The deadly 2012 attack on the American consulate in Benghazi, Libya, was carried out by a coalition that had connections to three radical Islamic movements. Ambassador Stevens and three other men were killed and ten injured. The failure to immediately send a quick reaction force (QRF) to the assistance of the beleaguered consulate was controversial. After several Congressional investigations, nothing noteworthy occurred. The Benghazi raid is an example of a Black Swan event.

Terrorist Organizations as Learning Organizations

To achieve some longevity, terrorist movements must become learning organizations. These are characterized by prizing the acquisition of new knowledge, being nimble when faced with new situations, and thinking "outside of the box." According to interrogated prisoners, by 2009 the success of drone attacks was being countered by the al Qaeda strategy of decentralizing training. Groups of roughly ten trainees were assigned to remote locations that consisted of a single shack that would not attract attention. Although effective, this strategy cost al Qaeda some trainees who objected to the primitive conditions under which they were forced to live.[7]

Becoming a learning organization is a survival mechanism for terrorist organizations. For terrorists and other organizations, being a learning organization is a survival mechanism. In the Port of Aden, Yemen, al Qaeda's January 2000 attack on the USS *The Sullivans* failed. The small boat that was to be used as a floating bomb was packed with too many pounds of explosives. As a result, it sank while accelerating toward *The Sullivans*. Although information about the failed attack was widely distributed by the Navy, it failed to foil a second attack. Nine months later, in the same harbor, al Qaeda successfully heavily damaged

FIGURE 6–2
The terrorist-damaged hull of the USS *Cole*. Both terrorists in the attacking boat were killed by the explosion. The USS *Cole* rode back to the United States "piggyback style" on the Norwegian *Blue Marlin*.
(Everett Collection Inc/Alamy Stock Photo)

USS *Cole*
Successfully attacked in 2000 by al Qaeda in the Port of Aden, Yemen, by a suicide "bomber" piloting a launch loaded with explosives.

the **USS *Cole*** by simply loading another launch with a manageable payload of explosives (see Figure 6–2).

The Two Essential Sets of Terrorist Organizational Tools

During the 1930s, the body of knowledge known as administrative theory emerged. Theorists and practitioners sought to identify "universal" methods of administration that could be applied in all organizational settings. In 1937, Luther Gulick coined the most enduring acronym of the functions of administration: POSDCORB: **P**lanning, **O**rganizing, **S**taffing, **D**irecting, **Co**ordinating, **R**eporting, and **B**udgeting.[6] Cragin and Daly, either directly or indirectly, accounted for all of these functions and reframed them in the particular needs of terrorist organizations. They determined that there are two essential sets of terrorist organization tools, four of which are organizational and six that are operational (see Table 6–2).

TABLE 6–2
Terrorist Organizational Tools

The Four Organizational Tools	The Six Operational Tools
• Ideology	• Command and Control System
• Leadership	• Weapons
• Recruiting	• Operational Space
• Publicity	• Training
	• Intelligence and Counterintelligence
	• Finance

Data from Kim Cragin and Sara A. Daly, The Dynamic Terrorist Threat (Santa Monica: RAND Corporation, 2004), p. xiv. We have combined some tools from this source.

The Four Organizational Tools

Broadly, "organizational tools" refers to the things an organization must accomplish to foster its viability. Cragin and Daly identified four organizational tools: (1) ideology, which represents the reason for existing; (2) leadership, which provides the oversight that steers the organization; (3) recruiting, which is acquiring followers; and (4) publicity, which calls attention to what the terrorist organization broadly intends to do and heralds its successes. In no particular order, a discussion of these factors follows.

The First Organizational Tool: Ideology

Adopting a guiding and motivating *ideology* is the key decision because it plays the central role in communicating what "We are about." It must also be powerful enough to motivate members to make sacrifices. Ultimately, it is at the heart of getting someone to "pick up the gun."[7] IS's ideology inspires its followers to believe that the violent acts they are committing fulfill the ordained will of Allah.[8] Skinheads believe they are preserving the "White way of life." The neo-Nazis admire the racial policies of Nazi Germany and hate Jews and LGBTQs. Terrorism occurs when opportunity, motivation, and ideology intersect.[9] Ideologies grow out of one or more conditions, such as human rights abuses, economic inequality, a sense of injustice, religion, and political repression.[10] Like radical Muslims, both the Ku Klux Klan and neo-Nazis focus their hatred, to some degree, out of a warped interpretation of religion that becomes part of their core ideologies.

Following 9/11, terrorism was widely commented on and occasionally studied. One of the early intuitive assertions was that poverty was one of the important root causes of terrorism. If this is true—and admittedly this is just one example—why of eight suspects arrested in Great Britain in 2007 for failed car bombings were six of them foreign-born physicians?[11] Arguably, this case may be a statistical abnormality, an outlier. The literature on this subject provides an answer.

Several empirical studies also assert that poverty causes terrorism. However, the accuracy of this assertion is questionable. Abadie concluded that terrorism is not significantly higher in poor countries and that the degree of political freedom was a better explanation for terrorism.[12] Countries with an intermediate level of political freedom or that are transitioning from an authoritarian to a more democratic model—for example, Iraq, Spain, and Russia—are more prone to terrorism than countries with a high level of political freedom or a highly authoritarian government.[13]

There may be a single factor that drives a terrorist ideology or there may be multiple factors. Regardless of the causes(s), all ideologies share three common characteristics: (1) a belief system that instructs people to do certain things (e.g., drive people of color or the "crusaders" out of "our" lands); (2) the belief cannot be questioned or violated; and (3) the things to be done must be directed toward achieving some objective or cause that resonates both with the general population, to ensure their support, and with potential recruits, so they can be brought into the organization.[14]

The Kurdistan Workers Party (Partiya Karkeren Kurdistan, **PKK**) has an ideology that resonates and is both separatist/nationalist and Marxist-oriented. Kurds are one of the world's largest ethnic populations without a homeland, numbering some 22 million people.[15] There is often an ethnic component to separatist/nationalist movements. The Bodo Liberation Tigers illustrate this point. Several other Kurdish groups actively involved in the Syrian War are also seeking homelands in Syria and Turkey and are discussed in several of the paragraphs that follow.

Formed in the 1970s, the PKK is composed of Turkish Kurds. Periodically, it has been in armed conflict with Turkey since 1984. Its goal is establishing a Kurdish homeland within Turkey and not a separate nation. The PKK has some bases in Northern Iraq. The Turkish PKK is one of several Kurdish movements in Turkey, Syria, and Iraq that are effectively contributing to combating Bashar al-Assad forces in the Syrian War.[16]

A substantial number of Syrian Kurds are fighting against President Bashar al-Assad's government. Among their grievances, they are denied citizenship and other basic rights. Moreover, the Syrian government has seized Kurdish lands and given them to Arabs to "Arabize" Kurdish regions.[17] Their Democratic Union Party's (PYD) military wing is the

Kurdistan Workers Party (PKK)

An ethnic Kurdish terrorist organization fighting to create a homeland for ethnic Kurds in Northern Iraq and Southeastern Turkey; responsible for significant deaths of Turkish civilians (over 20,000) during the past two decades.

FIGURE 6–3
PKK Returning from an Operation

The PKKs are carrying AK-47-type assault rifles A thick black stem to the right of the fighter wearing the blue and white shemagh around his neck is too thick to be a gun barrel and may be one end of a rocket-propelled grenade, possibly an RPG-7 or RPG-9.

(Eddie Gerald/Alamy Stock Photo)

People's Protection Unit (YPG). It has fought very effectively against ISIS.[18] In Northern Syria, the YPG has carved out a self-declared autonomous Kurdish region, Rojava. Although Both YPG and IS are fighting Bashar al-Assad's forces, the YPG also fights IS to gain as much territory as possible in Syria to add to Rojava. In turn, IS fights the YPG for dominance among insurgent forces. Turkey sees the YPG as a bigger threat than IS and periodically shells YPG. Turkey reasons that YPG's successes could stoke the fires of independence long sought by the PKK, Turkish Kurds.[19]

In Northern Syria, the YPG has carved out a self-declared autonomous Kurdish region, Rojava, where it is experimenting with direct democracy. In 2014, IS trapped some 400,000–500,000 members of the religious minority Yazidis on Mount Sinjar in Northeast Iraq. Is embarked on a policy of genocide of as many Yazidis as it could capture. Reports circulated that as many as 500 Yazidis were buried alive. Some women and girls were taken away to be sex slaves. American airpower and the YPG played key roles in opening a corridor along which many Yazidis escaped to Rojava, where they and other refugees from the war are welcomed. The Peshmerga, the military arm of the Kurdish Regional Government in Northern Iraq (KRG), is also fighting IS.

Over the decades there have been episodic peace talks between Turkey and the PKK, but no agreement about a homeland has been produced, nor does one seem close at hand. About 100 Westerners, including a handful of Americans, have joined Kurdish forces fighting IS, some of whom have been killed in combat operations.[20]

In Figure 6–3, PKK fighters are moving out of Turkey into their safe haven in Northern Iraq. Several women are in the group; they often serve as snipers in PKK units. These fighters are not expecting contact with their enemy or there would be greater distance between the fighters. Under military Western doctrine, if there was a possibility of contact with the enemy, they would be in several shorter columns so maximum firepower could be rushed to the front quickly. Several of the people in photographs are looking up and to their right and a woman is smiling, suggesting the column may be approaching a guide, meeting a PKK patrol, arriving at a place where trucks will pick them up, or are near or entering a base camp. In short, they are feeling safe.

In 2014, the military successes of the Islamic State, particularly in Northern Iraq, created thorny public policy problems for the United States. There was no interest in putting large numbers of troops back into Iraq, but the Islamic State was murdering people who did not share in and refused to join their faith. As previously noted, the Yazidis were given especially draconian treatment. The PKK fought the Islamic State on the ground, although they badly needed heavier weapons. However, because the PKK is designated as a foreign terrorist organization, the United States was reluctant to provide them. Moreover, doing so would be likely to anger Turkey, a strong American ally, who might later see the PKK use those weapons against it in a PKK drive for a Kurdish homeland. Nonetheless, as the Syrian War dragged on, the United States began arming the Kurds.

The Revolutionary Armed Forces of Colombia People's Army(FARC)

FARC has waged an insurgency against Colombia's national government for over 50 years. Growing out of the communist party, it has socialist ideas. In late 2016, FARC and the national government signed a treaty that presumably ended the hostilities.

Revolutionary Armed Forces of Colombia People's Army (FARC) The **FARC** in Columbia waged an insurgency against its national government, but that insurgency was not nationalistic. FARC grew out of the Colombian Communist Party of the 1960s.[21] It is, therefore, unsurprising that traditionally FARC's ideology has been based on seizing control of the government to institute socialist reforms. What is notable about FARC is that from its inception in 1964, until a peace agreement was reached, its ideology resonated with the people. In 2016, FARC and the national government reached a written agreement that ended the hostilities. FARC will now have get representation in Columbia's legislature. By the end of the Summer of 2017, demobilization of FARC continued, turning over their weapons to the government.

The Second Organizational Tool: Leadership

Providing *leadership* is a crucial enterprise. Terrorist organizations are often embedded in, operate in, or travel through countries that are opposed to them. Even in so-called safe havens, terrorist leaders and facilities are vulnerable to drone attacks, missiles, air strikes, and special operations. Moreover, because top leaders in terrorist organizations are subject to special efforts to capture or kill them, it is a hazardous occupation. In Afghanistan, the United States Joint Special Operations Command (JSOC) maintained a list of people it wanted to capture or kill.[22] The Joint Prioritized Effects List (JPEL) began with Taliban and al Qaeda leaders, but it eventually grew to some 2,000 names.[23] As a former member described it, JPEL had the best weapons, the best people, and plenty of money to burn, growing from a tight unit of 200 to several thousand people.[24]

The structure of a terrorist organization will dictate to some degree the importance of top and mid-level leadership. Charismatic leaders have personal qualities and express ideas that attract followers. An excellent public speaker, Hitler projected strength, national pride, and gave the people "enemies" to revile. People with charismatic qualities can draw people into terrorist movements and sustain their fervor.[25] If there are few levels of leadership in the organization, the chain of command is simple and the "supreme leader" becomes more important because the leader is often present and available to followers. In more complex bureaucratic organizations that are dispersed geographically and that have multiple layers of leadership, the "supreme leader" becomes more of a symbolic or spiritual figure and middle managers take on more substantial face-to-face leadership responsibilities, especially for operations. With reference to al Qaeda, Neumann, Evans, and Pantucci describe the role of middle managers as being the "connective tissue" that creates the organization's center of gravity.

The Third Organizational Tool: Recruiting

Recruiting identifies potential recruits and draws them into the organization, which fulfills four important needs for terrorist organizations: (1) import new energy; (2) acquire new sets of skills; (3) increase operational capabilities; and (4) replace losses caused by fighters being captured (see Figure 6–4), fighters "quitting the cause," defections to other terrorist movements or government forces, and casualties. Some recruitment efforts are aimed at recruiting people who don't fit the profile of a terrorist. For example, Boko Haram is recruiting women who are pliable enough to be suicide bombers with babies cuddled in their arms.

FIGURE 6–4
In Afghanistan, Taliban prisoners carry water back from a river to cook their evening meals. Note the AK-47-type rifle in the guard's hand.
(Itar Tass Photos/Newscom)

Quick Facts
A Sampling of the Categories of Islamic Unbelievers

Kufr ul-Nifaq: Openly believes, but conceals his/her disbelief

Kufr al-'Inkār: Disbelieves out of arrogance or pride

Kufrul-I'raadh: Knows the truth, but doesn't practice out of inconvenience[26]

A British woman, Aqsa Mahmood, living in IS-occupied territory in Syria, is a major recruiter for IS. On her blog she wrote, "if your parents have made friends with kuffar (plural of Kafir, a pejorative term for an "unbeliever") and they have abandoned jihad, it is your religious responsibility to leave the family and join jihad."[27]

A major challenge in recruiting new members is identifying those who can be indoctrinated to the degree that they are willing to risk death or die to help achieve the goals of the terrorist organization. Roughly 3 percent of terrorist movements fail because they cannot replenish their ranks.[28] Since 2002, women have carried out 50 percent of suicide bombings,[29] making them prized recruits. Olsson believes many jihadists get snared by terrorist organizations because they are vulnerable. More specifically, they are in transition or "betweeners." The transitions may be moving from high school to college, just jilted or divorced, lost a job and having difficulty finding another, just finished graduate school and don't know what to do next, or some other passage from one circumstance to another. Their vulnerability stems from being more open to listening to suggestions or more willing to try something different to relieve their anxiety.[30]

There is no single uniform recruiting process used to bring recruits into a terrorist organization; the process varies and is tailored to different geographic regions that have their own political, religious, and social histories, to the recruiting pool, and finally, the individual.[31] For example, a "pitch" to young men and women will differ according to the following circumstances: (1) if potential recruits are from a privileged class, the appeal might be framed in terms of patriotic or religious duty; (2) members from lower classes can be led to see joining as an advancement in social class; and (3) when parents are disapproving or opposed to their adult children involving themselves with a terrorist organization, recruiters tell their children that it is an opportunity to gain their independence through the "self-discovery" of who they really are.[32] MI5, the British intelligence agency, did a study of several hundred terrorists and extremists known to be involved as fund-raisers or planning bombings in Britain and concluded they were mainly males, "demographically unremarkable," radicalized in the early to mid-20s, and did not follow some "typical pathway to extremism." Most were British nationals, not recent immigrants, usually religious novices, and many lacked religious literacy.[33] Many were over 30 years of age, married, and had children. Those studied were neither gullible nor unaccomplished; most were employed in lower-level jobs and their educations ran from modest accomplishments to college degrees.[34] Over half of the sample were born in the United Kingdom and acquired radical views there. Both terrorists and extremists tend to be from the second generation of families, children of those who immigrated to Great Britain.[35]

Recruiting may take place at soccer games, on the Internet, and other places where people come together. Originally, Hamas recruited from refugee camps, but it now takes a longer view. It spends perhaps as much as 60 percent of its annual budget on orphanages, sports clubs, health clinics, and other social institutions, which has a double effect: It creates loyalty toward Hamas, as well as develops deep pools from which to recruit.[36] Recruiting may be conducted to acquire the people or skills needed for a specific mission or for some other purpose, such as simply increasing the number of "foot soldiers."[37] Hamas uses cartoons to indoctrinate the young. FarFour the Mouse bears a remarkable resemblance to Disney's Mickey Mouse, but is not amusing. He is used to teach children the importance of Islamic domination and hatred toward Israel (see Figure 6–5).

The recruiting process can be thought of as a funnel through which potential recruits pass (see Figure 6–6). According to Weimann, who identified some 5,000 terrorist websites, terrorist organizations are technologically sophisticated, using social media sites to recruit, including YouTube, Twitter, Facebook, MySpace, chat rooms, and other sites.[38] The Global

FIGURE 6–5
A child watches while in FarFour's last episode, he is beaten to death by an "Israeli official" for refusing to sell his land.[40] The teen host of the show, Sara, describes the death as being martyred for defending his land, killed by the killers of children.

(Mohammed Saber/EPA/Newscom)

Islamic Media Front (GIMF) released an encryption program on the Internet in seven languages to provide secure communication for popular messaging networks, including AOL Instant Messenger, Google Talk, and Yahoo Messenger.[39]

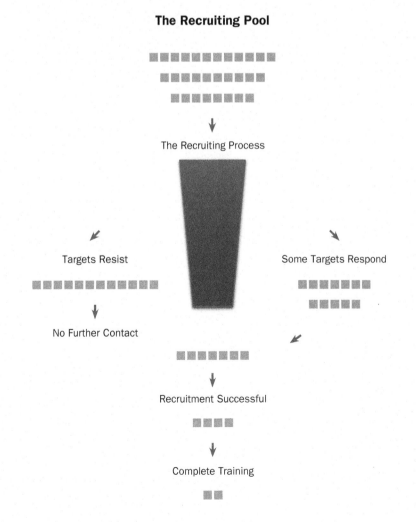

The Recruiting Pool

The Recruiting Process

Targets Resist   Some Targets Respond

No Further Contact

Recruitment Successful

Complete Training

FIGURE 6–6
The terrorist recruiting funnel.
Source: Scott Gerwehr and Sara Daly, *Al Qaida: Terrorist Selection and Recruitment* (Santa Monica: RAND Corporation, 2006), p. 77; and in D. Kamien, *Homeland Security Handbook* (New York: McGraw-Hill, 2007), p. 77. This figure represents a process and is not a precise mathematical representation.

Box 6-1
Recruiting Videos on the Internet

(Handout/Alamy Stock Photo)

Increased bandwidths and new software have allowed sophisticated terrorists users to develop and disseminate complex information via the Internet. The Islamic State has six different media institutions that focus on website development, propaganda, operational communication, and the development of professional quality training and recruiting videos, specifically for the Internet. Some of the videos posted instruct people on how to join the conflict in Syria or Iraq, while others display mechanisms of destruction like suicide bombs and vests. For instance, a recent 26-minute video teaches how to develop a suicide vest and how to use it on a bus.[41] Other videos present information on how to be a better marksman, how to make and set an improvised explosive device (IED), or simply how to conduct morning prayer. The videos are often shot in the field, on the "front lines" with Islamic State fighters and dubbed into several different languages (English, French, Dutch, German, Turkish, and of course, Arabic).

Many of the propaganda videos are directed at recruiting new and younger members to the cause. Hence, they often romanticize the bonding of brothers in combat, or fighting for one's belief, or living as in the days of old fighting the Crusaders that attacked the Middle East. Most of the videos have strong and forceful passages from the Holy Qur'an, with singing from other members in the background, or fiery speeches by Abu Bakr al-Baghdadi, the leader of IS.

During the initial stages of the IS movement, recruitment of individuals for the cause was an outcry to join the fight in the Middle East (in Iraq, Yemen, Jordan, and now Syria). Indeed, Abu Bakr al-Baghdadi often asked other radical Islamic groups to join the IS movement. However, one of the more dangerous trends in recruitment within the IS today, is a concerted focus to "take the attack to Western countries." Certainly since 2015, the numerous attacks in London, Paris, and Brussels support this new trend. Many of the new videos developed by IS focus on how to accomplish mass carnage in heavily populated European and American cities. Once on the Internet, these videos give the Islamic State a worldwide cyber footprint for training and recruiting. More important, they help to accomplish all four organizational tools of the movement: Ideology, Leadership, Recruiting, and Publicity; and the accomplishment of these tools suggests that the Islamic State will be a major threat to American and Western ideals for quite some time.

What mechanisms can Western nations employ to limit the impact of these types of training and propaganda videos? Compare and contrast the "romanticism" of films aimed at recruiting young people into our own armed services to those of the Islamic State. Do you see any similarities?

Islamic State training and propaganda videos often include speeches from Abu Bakr al-Baghdadi.

(World History Archive/Alamy Stock Photo)

The key advantage Internet recruiting provides is that it allows terrorist movements to recruit without any geographical boundaries. Recruiting foreigners is a priority because it reduces the effectiveness of profiles aimed at identifying ethnic terrorists. Therefore, Investigative agencies mine data from Internet sites for intelligence.

With some recruits, little or no recruitment is needed; they are already substantially self-radicalized. A Somali citizen legally living in Minnesota illustrates this point. Mahamud Said Omar made arrangements for 20 or more ethnic Somalian men to return to their native land and jihad against government troops with al-Shabaab, an al Qaeda affiliate. At least two of them are believed to have killed themselves in suicide bombings. Omar received a 20-year prison term plus probation for life following his release from confinement.[42]

Retention of existing members is somewhat akin to the ongoing recruitment of them. Despite such efforts, there is voluntary turnover in the ranks of experienced members, which Jacobson explains as (1) disillusionment with the strategies and tactics; (2) a lack of respect for the leadership; (3) resentment from taking orders from leaders who have never served on the battlefield, particularly when unnecessary casualties are seen to be caused by the leaders' inexperience; (4) a perceived inequity of compensation as compared to the members' contributions; (5) favoritism by leaders; (6) pleas to leave the movement from families and friends outside of it with whom the member has maintained contacts; and (7) switching from one group to another because they can be paid better, their families will be fed, or for other pragmatic reasons.[43]

The Fourth Organizational Tool: Publicity

In a half-dozen languages, terrorist movements achieve a substantial amount of publicity by using the Internet, the cheapest and fastest means available, for: (1) fostering public awareness of their existence and goals, (2) distributing propaganda, (3) shaping a favorable opinion of them by their relevant publics, (4) inciting violence, (5) influencing groups that have been marginalized or "left behind" to take up arms, (6) radicalizing visitors to the site, (7) raising funds, for example, by potential or actual supporters making donations or buying publications and discs with music or propaganda on them, (8) providing training material on homemade weapons, such as grenades and pressure cooker bombs, as well as information on other topics, for example, how to conduct countersurveillance, (9) tailoring messages to particular audiences, such as impressionable teenagers, (10) executing cyber attacks, (11) communicating with operatives, (12) a virtual dead drop (a message is posted on the Internet and only the person for whom it is intended has the password to access it), (13) spread misinformation about their intentions, and (14) demoralize opposing forces and public support for opposing regimes. The news media also meet some of these same publicity needs.[44]

On the Internet, al Qaeda distributed a 51-page, step-by-step manual, "The Art of Recruiting Mujahedeen." At each step, instructions are provided and points allowed for how successful the recruiter is in performing them. If in a particular chapter the recruiter doesn't get enough points, all steps need to be repeated until he/she does. Al Qaeda also publishes an online magazine to communicate its propaganda around the globe.

The Internet has no to little regulation and censorship, it provides global coverage, huge audiences can be reached, it's inexpensive to develop and maintain a website, there is anonymity for the communicator, and it provides a multimedia platform. Moreover, by providing information about their organization, terrorist movements can to some degree influence how the regular news media treats them.[45]

Typically, a site will provide a history of the organization and its activities; a detailed summary of its political and social background; accounts of notable exploits; biographies of its leaders, founders, heroes, and imprisoned comrades; information about its goals; fierce criticism of its enemies; identification of its allies and competitors; up-to-date news; and press releases.[46] Separatist and nationalist movements generally display a map of the contested geographical area: Hamas displays a map of Palestine. Most sites mention the "armed struggle" in which they are engaged. Even if they discuss the legitimacy of their use of violence, most sites refrain from mentioning their deadly actions and the fatalities caused by them. Two exceptions to this rule are Hamas and Hezbollah, whose sites feature updated statistical reports about their daily actions (daily operations) and tallies of "dead martyrs" and "collaborators" killed.[47]

On the Internet, there are also some known password-protected sites believed to be jihadist chat rooms. Al-Ekhlass is associated with al Qaeda, whose propaganda arm,

> **Information Link**
> Visit https://PublicIntelligence.net and search for "Inspire Magazine" to see a cross section of articles from that source.

Quick Facts
No Mercy

Hundreds of people had gathered near the post office where Leena worked. Ali Saqr al-Qasem walked with her to the center of the crowd. She had been reported as having urged her son to leave IS and the war. The son reported her to his commander and Leena received a death sentence. She was executed by being shot in the head by Ali Saqr al-Qasem, her son.[48]

The Islamic State continues to recruit young boys into their ranks at an alarming rate.

(ZUMA Press, Inc./Alamy Stock Photo)

al Sahab, releases approximately 80 "official" videos annually to keep al Qaeda in the public eye and to generate support for it.[49]

To counter the publicity terrorist groups seek, hackers, such as Ghost Security (GhostSec), work to make their sites inoperable. In one instance, a terrorist group lost use of one of its Internet sites for a day. By the time they could get it back online, the domain name had been reassigned and they were banned by the service provider. Credit for this action has not been claimed. It seems certain that governments also have their own hackers to do the same thing. It is claimed that about three dozen or more IS-related websites are using the services of a California company, CloudFlare, to be secure from hacking attacks.

IS, perhaps more so than any other terrorist movement, wants platinum grade publicity every day. They do so by their grotesque and wanton violence, which is intended to shock us. IS burned a captured Jordanian pilot alive in Syria.[50] In that same country it crucified nine Syrians who fought with pro-government forces.[51] IS is killing Coptic Christians in Egypt, simply because of their religion.[52] In France, IS operatives interrupted a Catholic Mass and cut the throat of an eighty-five-year-old priest.[53] In Northern Iraq, it buried hundreds of Yazidis alive.[54] It is reported that IS executed a seven-year-old child for cursing during a soccer game, and they tied ropes to two men and slowly lowered them into barrels of nitric acid, which slowly dissolved their body parts as they entered the acid.[55] A free press is a safeguard for all of us. There is, however, an irony that in the very act of being that safeguard, IS gets what it craves so much.

The Six Operational Tools

Terrorist movements need operational tools in order to generate attacks. We have modified Cragin and Daly's list of operational tools by combining several categories. The operational tools are:

The First Operational Tool: A Command and Control System

A command and control system is a necessary condition and the mechanism by which terrorist movements plan, staff, train, coordinate, and execute their attacks.[56] This mechanism is also referred to as C and C or C2. The stage of development and size of a terrorist organization influence how this function is executed. The **Provisional Irish Republican Army (PIRA)**, whose members were called "Provos," officially ended its terrorist campaign against Britain for a unified Ireland in 2005; two years later, an independent commission concluded PIRA had decommissioned its weapons and was committed to the political path.[57] However, when PIRA declared a ceasefire in 1997, a splinter group, the **Real Irish Republican Army (RIRA)**, broke away from PIRA to continue the fight for a unified Republic of Ireland. Today, both RIRA and the Continuity Irish Republican Army (CIRA) are considered terrorist organizations.[58]

Because RIRA is concentrated in a small geographical area, its C2 needs are limited and directions[59] can often be given face-to-face or by couriers who only have to travel a short distance. Still, British authorities have had great success in penetrating RIRA, imprisoning at least 46 of its members and disrupting operations.[60] In a similar fashion, in the early 1990s, Hamas was roughly in the same situation as RIRA, but now its C2 is more sophisticated and includes multiple C2 commands and "replacement teams" in the event that one or more members of a forthcoming operation are arrested or assassinated by Israeli security forces.[61] In terms of disrupting terrorist operations, having intelligence that allows targeting the C2 is a major asset.

The Second Operational Tool: Acquiring Weapons

Acquiring weapons and a reliable source of spare parts, replacements of combat losses, and resupply of ammunition are essential tools for terrorists (see Figure 6–7). The arms in the inventory of a terrorist movement are likely to consist of a mixture of those supplied by individual and state sponsors or by other terrorist organizations; purchased with drugs, money, or gemstones from the illicit weapons black market; or captured. In the first two decades of the last century, the Irish Republican Army helped Ireland achieve independence from

Provisional Irish Republican Army (PIRA)
The Provisional Irish Republican Army was the first and primary movement in Ireland to use terrorism as a means to justify its revolt against Great Britain and gain world status as a separate nation (Ireland). The group officially ended its campaign against Great Britain for a unified and separate Ireland in 2005, and now continues in political dialogue for the same goal.

Real Irish Republican Army (RIRA)
The Real Irish Republican Army in Northern Ireland uses terrorist tactics to support its ideology of a unified Ireland; RIRA is a successor to the original PIRA.

FIGURE 6-7
Pakistani security officials show vests and ball bearings to be used with them in suicide bomber attacks. In addition to the suicide vest materials, the raid resulted in the arrests of four men and the seizure of guns and ammunition.
(Rahat Dar/EPA/Newscom)

Great Britain by relying on captured weapons to a substantial degree. This tactic continues to work: In 2000, FARC raided a Colombian naval base and acquired substantial armaments, including mortars and claymore mines.

The arms inventory of terrorist movements is a crude indicator of their size, intentions, and capabilities. That inventory and the operational terrain also influence the tactics terrorists can use offensively and defensively. The opposing force also influences the weapons needed by terrorists. In 2013, antigovernment forces battling the Syrian government were desperate to be supplied with surface-to-air missiles to counter the government's aircraft attacks. The next year in Iraq, the Islamic State captured vast weapons from the Iraqi Army, including some armored personnel carriers and tanks, which enhanced IS's combat capabilities.

At the low end of the spectrum, small terrorist organizations are likely to have limited weapons, such as pistols, rifles, and light machine guns.* Explosives are also likely to appear in their inventory.

The Third Operational Tool: An Operational Space

Having an **operational space** means a physical sanctuary or safe haven where attacks can be safely planned, trained for, and rehearsed (see Figure 6–8).[62] During the Middle Ages in Europe (roughly 500 to 1450 A.D.), churches and monasteries could give "sanctuary" to persons fleeing justice or prosecution, a place where they would be safe. The laws regulating sanctuaries varied by period and kingdom, somewhat akin to the present conditions under which some nations tolerate the presence of terrorist movements within their borders.

Safe havens are a place or situation that allows illicit actors, including criminals, smugglers, and terrorists, to operate with relative impunity.[63] Other advantages include that the terrorists can organize, plan, raise funds, communicate, recruit, train, and operate with a reasonable or higher degree of security.[64]

In the modern terrorism period, Lebanon's **Bekaa Valley** has perhaps the longest continuous history as an operational space for terrorist groups.[65] Although some think a territory controlled by a terrorists is different from a safe haven,[66] we view it is being a special case of a safe haven, an area tightly patrolled and policed by a terrorist group.

One way of thinking about operational space is the types of settings that are used as safe havens. Lamb identifies four settings for safe havens:[67]

Operational space
This term means having a sanctuary or safe haven where attacks can be safely planned, trained for, and rehearsed.

Safe havens
Places or situations that allow illicit actors, including criminals, smugglers, and terrorists, to operate with relative impunity.

Bekaa Valley
Located in Lebanon, it has perhaps the longest continuous history as an operational space for terrorist groups.

---

*Light machine guns fire a round that is 7.62 mm or less.

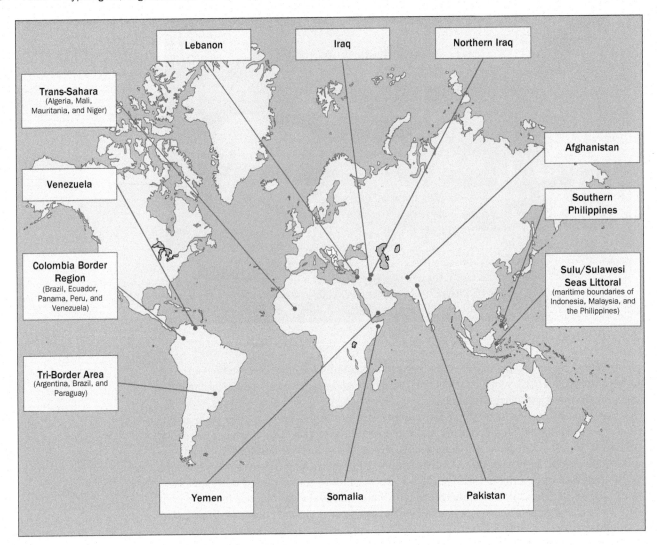

FIGURE 6–8
Remote Land Safe Havens.

Source: Jacquelyn L. Williams-Bridger, "Combating Terrorism." Statement before the House of Representatives Subcommittee on Oversight, Investigations, and Management of the Committee on Homeland Security, June 3, 2011, p. 5.

a) The classic *land safe haven* is a region that is remote, possesses rugged terrain, and has a low population density, little or no government presence, and a dense vegetation cover, although even some desert territory might provide adequate cover. A prime example of a remote land safe haven is Waziristan,[68] a mountainous region of 4,500 square miles in northwest Pakistan, bordering Afghanistan. In the 1950s, when Fidel Castro's communist July 26th Movement was waging an insurgency against Cuba's government, his forces used the Sierra Maestra mountains as a remote land safe haven. Those mountains are heavily forested, offering excellent concealment, with deep ravines and steep terrain, which provided the insurgents excellent defensive positions and broke up and isolated attacking forces. Safe havens are further discussed in the next chapter.

b) *Urban safe havens* include both traditional urbanized areas and nontraditional suburbs such as squatter villages and shantytowns. Carlos Marighella advocated attacking dictators from urban bases of operation, whereas Fanon argued for the opposite: rural-based fighters entering cities to inflict severe acts of terrorism to inspire fear. The sheer size of cities provides a degree of anonymity to terrorists because they can "hide in plain sight." Some European and Asian cities also have "no go" areas seldom visited by the police, such as the Islamic Sharia zones, which can provide safe houses for terrorists. The Provisional Irish Republican Army established no-go areas in the minority Catholic sections of some Northern Ireland cities, openly patrolling the streets and manning roadblocks while carrying weapons. If British soldiers entered the area, "Hen Patrols" would warn of their approach and movement by rattling the tops of garbage pails while children blew whistles.[69]

All of these same countries appear as safe havens in the U.S. Department of State's (USDOS's) 2015 annual report to Congress on terrorism. The report also added three additional safe haven countries in the USDOS's 2015 report: Libya, Mali, and a portion of Egypt's Sinai region.

In 2005, a series of bomb attacks by a homegrown jihadist cell in London, England, killed fifty-three people and wounded more than 700. The attacks demonstrate that an urban setting can be a safe haven. All four suicide bombers lived in cities near London.[70] Three men were second-generation British citizens of Pakistani parents. The fourth man was born in Jamaica and converted to Islam. In England, he met and married a British citizen who had also adopted Islam as her religion. The men apparently met in Muslim circles and bonded. On the day of the bombings, fixed video cameras recorded the men meeting and hugging, then going their separate ways. One of them entered a shop and bought a battery for his detonator. Soon bombs exploded on trains and a double-decker bus. Al Qaeda claimed credit for the attacks. One of bombers left behind a video in which he claimed the attacks were because democratically elected governments continuously perpetrated atrocities against Muslim people.

Some terrorist movements have no substantial alternative to using an urban sanctuary because the geography in which they are located has few or no remote land safe areas. The Real Irish Republican Army in Northern Ireland illustrates this point.

c) *Maritime safe havens* are situated on lands bordering littoral or shallow waters, such as the 7,100 islands in the Philippines,[71] as well as along rivers that flow to the ocean. Such safe havens allow terrorists to move equipment and personnel from one country to another rapidly on the vastness of oceans and to take advantage of poorly monitored coastlines.[72] Recognizing this threat and missions such as drug interdiction, the U.S. Navy began bringing littoral combat ships (LCSs) into its fleet in 2008. These smaller, high-speed ships can operate in waters of 20 or fewer feet.

Box 6–2
Sharia-Controlled Zones

Extremist Islamic Sharia-Controlled Zones (SCZs) are neighborhoods in Western nations where extremist Muslims have substantially or totally driven out non-Muslims to establish their own social, political, and legal control. The extremists' goal is to rule an area in which they can administer Sharia law, the Islamic moral and legal code. Where they are able to do so, the larger society's civil and criminal laws are ignored. For that reason, the indigenous population often refers to these areas as "No-Go" areas. Sixty-one percent of British Muslims surveyed want Sharia as opposed to English laws.[73] As such, SCZs are most often observed in England and other European countries like France, Denmark, Germany, Sweden, Belgium, and the Netherlands where there is a high percentage population of Muslims, particularly Muslim immigrants.

The Syrian War has created a humanitarian crisis of proportions not seen since World War II. Some European countries have accepted hundreds of thousands of refugees, many of them Muslims. It remains to see how this generosity will play out over the coming decades. Unfortunately, attacks in 2015–2017 by radicalized Muslims have stirred something of a backlash against Muslims in general in France, Belgium, Germany, and England. In England during 2017, a lone, British-born terrorist, Khalid Masood, 52, crossed over the Thames River on the Westminster Bridge, using his car to deliberately run people down. He exited his vehicle, used a knife to attack people, and entered the Parliament Building where he was shot and killed. Masood was previously investigated for having extremist views.

SCZs have immediate crime implications. To establish the zones, all non-Muslims living in the neighborhoods are displaced. This usually involves the use of harassment, threats, and some violence. Non-Muslim women passing through SCZs have been threatened with violence. They are told not to come back through the neighborhood unless their face is covered. Those suspected of being gay have also been threatened. These extremist Muslims reject integration into the larger society. In the end, they want to supplant the larger society. For instance, British authorities suspect that 117 Muslim women were murdered as "honor kills." Islamic practice permits fathers and brothers to kill wives, daughters, and sisters perceived to have brought dishonor to their families.[74] A lack of cooperation often thwarts investigation of these and other crimes. To make matters worse, police and emergency services vehicles are occasionally stoned if they enter SCZs. Radicalized Muslims are not tolerant of other lifestyles, cultures, and religions in designated SCZs. They represent an entirely different culture than their moderate European Muslim counterparts.

In France, there are some 717 Zone Urbaines Sensibles (ZUSs, Sensitive Urban Zones) that are deteriorated neighborhoods. An unknown number of them are controlled by extremist Muslims. Police may not patrol these SCZs aggressively because they are wary of a Muslim response if arrests are made. Although SCZs are not present in the United States, such areas seem to be increasing throughout European countries. In 2016, the Hungarian government released a report identifying nearly 1,000 SCZs in Europe, noting that the governments have lost control to the radical Islamic extremists and police officers are afraid to patrol them. Major cities with this problem include London, Berlin, Paris, and Stockholm.[75]

New SCZs have been observed in Belgium, Norway, and Sweden. These areas set up the prospect of continuous conflict with the host country and divert resources from other pressing issues. There is also the unsettling prospect of SCZs providing a comfortable urban safe haven for terrorists and imperiling a country's culture.

Why are Sharia-Controlled Zones (SCZs) somewhat common in Europe and not in the United States? What prospects are there to establish SCZs in the United States? If that happens, what governmental reaction do you expect?

Maritime safe havens also provide a base from which to attack sea targets (e.g., military and civilian vessels, ferries, and oil and natural gas platforms) and to attack resorts and port facilities from the sea.[76] As an illustration, in 2009, Egyptian authorities foiled an al Qaeda plot to bomb foreign ships in the Suez Canal and the pipelines adjacent to it; the terrorists included 24 Egyptian engineers and technicians led by a Palestinian man.[77] The plot was funded by contributions to Islamic charities and training was received via a jihad website.[78] The terrorists also robbed and murdered an Egyptian Christian jeweler to help fund their operation.[79]

d) *Virtual safe havens* exist in cyberspace and are used as a strategy to avoid being detected by security forces. As noted in the previous chapter, virtual terrorist safe havens are presently cell-sized and not complete organizations.

The Fourth Operational Tool: Training

For most recruits to terrorist groups, *training* begins with an initial emphasis on indoctrination, physical conditioning, small arms familiarization, marksmanship, and basic martial arts.[80] More advanced topics include planting bombs and tactics for assaulting military convoys and installations. Some terrorists will receive training for specialized functions, such as sniping, bomb building, car hijacking, hostage-taking, and eliminating sentries.

The war on safe havens seems to have spelled the end of large training camps, such as al Qaeda had in Afghanistan under the Taliban pre-9/11. The concurrent shift in al Qaeda's strategy to small independent cells and regional attacks has resulted in substantial terrorist "e-learning" courses becoming available on the Internet on a variety of courses, including

---

Box 6–3
Training and the Islamic State (IS) Fighters

Most Americans imagine fighters loyal to the Islamic State as a rather "ragtag" group of individuals, poorly trained and equipped to fight a modern war, or carry out a strategic military mission. Nothing could be further from the truth. The wars in Syria and Iraq are primarily fought in cities (with names like Tikrit, Kirkuk, Mosul, Qum, and Aleppo), in the midst of civilian populations. IS fighters are well aware of their vulnerability when "out in the open" to more technologically advanced forces, therefore, they use houses and buildings for cover, while deploying random explosive devices and deadly and accurate sniper fire. The battles are fought from street to street, neighborhood to neighborhood using ground forces, and limiting the effectiveness of more advanced warfare tactics using tanks, artillery, and airpower.

Islamic State fighters undergo extensive preparation, starting with basic training similar to a U.S. military boot camp. Physical exercise is emphasized as well as instruction in weaponry and tactics. More advanced instruction on reconnaissance, bomb-making, weaponry, and sniper shooting are available after basic training. Many of the instructors are battle experienced and some are former military personnel from the Syrian, Iraqi, and/or other Middle Eastern armies. Some have even been trained by U.S. troops in the past. Make no doubt about it, the IS fighters are a formidable foe and pose American and coalition forces a significant threat throughout the Middle East.

Islamic State recruits train similarly to a traditional army, with a heavy emphasis on physical fitness and small arms weaponry.

(Abed Rahim Khatib/Newzulu/ZUMA Press, Inc./Alamy Stock Photo, Ibrahim Khatib/Newzulu/Alamy Stock Photo, Stringer/Anadolu Agency/ Getty Images)

bomb-making manuals by one of al Qaeda's weapons masters, Abdullah Dhu al-Bajadin, an assumed identity. As part of the effort to monitor terrorist e-learning, the University of Arizona collects and analyzes data from 4,300 Islamic terrorist websites.[81]

The Fifth Operational Tool: Intelligence and Counterintelligence

From a terrorist organization's view, intelligence is the collection, processing, integration, analysis, evaluation, and interpretation of available information on a specific subject, for example, the current intentions of America against the Islamic State. Intelligence must be delivered with conclusions useful to the terrorist "client" in need of it. The mere collection of data without any processing does not constitute intelligence. In contrast, a terrorist's counterintelligence (CI) activities are a security tool consisting of activities dedicated to undermining the effectiveness of the intelligence activities of America and its allies.[82]

During the post-9/11 war in Afghanistan, the Taliban has been repeatedly characterized as having an impressive ability to collect and exploit intelligence.[83] It has advance knowledge of at least some impending Allied operations that transcends mere chance.[84] Illustratively, the United Kingdom's Prime Minister David Cameron was forced to cancel a visit to an Afghanistan military outpost because the Taliban was already aware of it.[85] Chapter 9 discusses intelligence and counterintelligence more fully.

> **Information Link**
> The Central Intelligence Agency has an excellent site for the study of intelligence. Visit www.cia.gov/library/center-for-the-study-of-intelligence.

The Sixth Operational Tool: Finance

With few exceptions, such as financially secure lone wolves, finance is of continuing concern to terrorist leaders, regardless of whether they are small cells or large transnational movements that are somewhat akin to international business conglomerates.

Following 9/11, substantial interest quickly developed in denying terrorists the use of normal banking channels. As a result, new banking regulations were put into place, new programs established, such as the U.S. Department of Treasury's Terrorist Finance Tracking Program (TFTP), interagency task forces were formed, and diplomatic pressure was placed on countries that were passive supporters of terrorism (e.g., generally not taking actions to create more control over their geographical space and/or financial transactions).[86]

Subsequently, the European Union arrested 80 people in a single year for financing separatist groups in Spain and France.[87] As financial intelligence was created, it became a formidable weapon. A sample of 500 FBI terrorist investigations revealed that 42 percent of them were aided by financial intelligence.[88] It also was important in preventing a terrorist attack on an English airport and in tracking down a senior terrorist leader, Hambali, the suspected mastermind of a bombing in Bali.[89]

The annual incomes of the nine wealthiest terrorists organizations range from IS's at the top with a robust $2.5 billion, to al Qaeda, in the middle of the pack with $150 million, to the Real IRA's dead last with $50 million (See Table 6-3). You might think that IS with $2.5 billion dollars is the deadliest terrorist organization in the world, but that dubious recognition goes to Boko Haram. However, in a single day that could change. IS has the funds to hire strongly qualified scientists to develop nuclear weapons, more deadly strands of chemical or biological agents, or weapons never seen or imagined before. Their wealth, ideology, and utter disregard for life make an ominous combination.

Hawalas

In response to growing pressure from formal banking systems, terrorists began making greater use of alternative remittance systems (ARSs), particularly the **hawala**. This is an informal and often unregulated remittance system that operates from many countries conducting domestic and international transactions.[90] It was developed in India before formal banking practices were introduced. In some cities of the world, Hawala services are openly advertised.[91] Hawalas are a faster and safer means than using a courier who could be arrested for currency violations or another offense while traveling. Illegal aliens also use the hawala or other alternative remittance system to send money home to their families in order to avoid all official contacts that might expose them to deportation.

Hawala
An Asian-based alternative remittance system that is based on trust and which allows users to remain unknown and escape contact with banking and other officials.

TABLE 6–3

The Nine Wealthiest Terrorists Organizations and Sources of Income

Organization	Sources
IS: $2.5 Billion	Exploit natural resources, including oil, gas, phosphate, agriculture, taxes, fees, extortion, and drugs
Hamas: $1 Billion	Strong financial aid from Qatar, taxes, fees
Hezbollah: $500 Million	Strong financial aid from Iran, drug production and trafficking, donations
Taliban: $400 Million	Drug production (opium/heroin) and drug trafficking
al Qaeda: $150 Million	Financial assistance, kidnap/ransom, drug trafficking
Lashkar-e-Taiba: $100 Million	Financial assistance and donations
Al-Shabaab: $70 Million	Kidnap/ransom, piracy, sponsorships
Boko Haram: $52 Million	Kidnap/ransom, fees, taxes, bank robberies, and lootings
Real IRA: $50 Million	Smuggling, illegal trade, donations

Data from Forbes International, "The 10 Richest Terrorist Organizations in the World," Forbes, Dec 12, 2014, https://www.forbes.com/pictures/ghki45efh/10-boko-haram-annual-turnover-52-million/#ee3191f3f51f, accessed March 23, 2017.

Hawalas are distinguished from traditional banks by (1) strong trust. They are illegal in some countries, yet they operate effectively and efficiently without regulatory oversight or any legal recourse; (2) hawala dealers are often bound together by family, business partners, or regional connections; (3) they make minimal use of formal negotiable instruments; (4) no money is actually transferred between hawalas; (5) the transactions take place based on communications between members of a network of hawaladars or hawala dealers; (6) hawalas operate with little paperwork and what exists is minimal and often in codes; (7) they provide better currency exchange rates than banks offer; (8) the person receiving the money gets it fast, within hours to a day or two at most; (9) some hawaladars are open and available 24 hours a day, such as local grocery stores; and (10) all taxes are avoided.[92]

Hawaladars typically charge a 2 to 5 percent transaction fee and operate out of a regular business, such as jewelry store, pawnshop, travel agency, or used car business. Being hawaladars is often not their principal work. Figure 6–9 depicts a hawala transaction. In Figure 6–9, Ibrahim in Karachi, Pakistan, wants to send $5,000 to his nephew Salim in Baltimore. Ibrahim goes to a Javeria, a Karachi hawaladar, and pays her $5,000, plus a transaction fee of 5 percent. Javeria sends the order by phone, fax, or Internet to Obaid, a hawaladar in Baltimore, but sends no money. In person, Obaid pays Salim in cash. Obaid now has a credit of $5,000 with Javeria for when he wants her to pay someone. For purposes of illustration, we will assume Salim will use the money to buy materials with which to make several bombs.

Among the other ways to disperse money secretly between entities is manipulating invoices with a colluding partner. Assume Company A is a foreign exporter who sends 50,000 scarves, actually valued at $2 each, to Company B, a domestic importer in another country. However, company A invoices the cost of the scarves at $1 each. Company B pays Company $50,000 and

FIGURE 6–9
A Hypothetical Hawala Transaction.

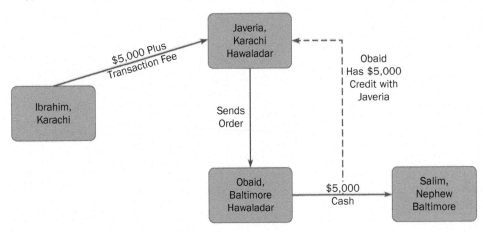

subsequently sells the scarves for $100,000, their actual value. Company B then disperses the excess $50,000 made according to the instructions of Company A.

BitCoin and PayPal

In mid-2014, **BitCoin** was being studied by several federal agencies to determine if terrorists could use it as an alternative remittance system or otherwise gain an advantage from using it. The system appeared online in 2009, apparently developed by an anonymous person identified as Satoshi Nakamoto. BitCoins can be bought, transferred to someone else, and sold online. If sold, a check is sent to your bank account, where all transactions are recorded. BitCoins are accepted by a few merchants online. Although it is an interesting system, BitCoin has struggled to find acceptance in the marketplace.

Bitcoin
is a new currency that was invented in 2009 by someone using the alias of Satoshi Nakamoto. It is a digital coin that doesn't rely on a central bank. You can buy and sell bitcoins at exchanges on the Internet.

Europol reports that terrorist movements are not using BitCoin and in this country experts have dismissed claims that they are, calling them overexaggerated. However, terrorist experts in Indonesia maintain terrorists are using bitcoin. This is a subject that bears some watching. Still, BitCoin has become the currency of choice for some transactions. In 2017, Los Angeles Valley College paid a ransomware "fee" of $28,000 in BitCoin to hackers who said if not paid in a week, they would destroy the college's data.[93] Conversely, terrorists are using PayPal as a means of accepting donations.

Narco-Terrorism

As the efforts to financially strangle terrorists continued, state and individual sponsorship of terrorists generally declined. An unintended consequence was that it pushed terrorist organizations toward the drug trade. The illegal global drug trade may amount to as much as $1.5 trillion annually and for some time terrorist movements have derived a portion of their income from it.[94] The United Nations estimates that $2.3 billion from the drug trade ends up in the coffers of terrorists, much of it with larger transnational organizations.[95] Interpol concluded that the main source of income for terrorist organizations comes from involvement in the drug trade.[96] The PKK, Taliban, al Qaeda, Kosovo Liberation Army, Hezbollah, ETA, Sendero Luminoso (Shining Path), and other terrorist groups all profit from drug production and/or trafficking.

Narco-terrorism originally referred to campaigns of extreme violence, including torture, beheadings, bombings, and assassinations by drug traffickers against competitors, the police, and others. Colombian Pablo Escobar (1949–1993) led the Medellin Cartel that controlled 80 percent of the cocaine shipped to the United States and was identified by *Fortune* and *Forbes* magazines as one of the ten wealthiest people in the world.[97] To build and maintain this empire, the Medellin Cartel killed three candidates for Colombia's presidency, over 200 judges, and in excess of 1,000 police officers.[98]

A common threat by the Medellin Cartel to public officials was "Plata o plomo" (Silver or lead), meaning accept the bribe or be killed. The mutilated bodies left on the streets of Mexican towns along America's southern border are a manifestation of narco-terrorism as drug traffickers fight each other for dominance. Among the major Mexican drug syndicates are Los Zetas, Caballeros Templarios, and the Sinaloa Cartel.

Quick Facts
Pablo Escobar

Escobar is described as being both from a poor family and from a lower middle-class family. Reportedly, as a child he was sent home from school because his family was so poor it could not afford the required shoes. He started life as a petty street criminal and later took over a drug trafficking ring. The head of it was reportedly killed on Escobar's orders.

As Escobar amassed wealth, he used some of it to curry favor with the people, for example, building soccer fields, hospitals, and schools, positioning himself as a modern-day Robin Hood. Escobar also built a private zoo that people could visit for free. Following his death, several hippos escaped. They reproduced, and now a small group of them runs wild in Columbia.[99]

After 15 months, Escobar escaped from his luxury prison and was soon on the run from Colombian authorities, who were reportedly aided by a constellation of U.S. law enforcement agencies and a highly skilled U.S. military counterterrorism unit. In 1993, he was killed in a gunfight with his pursuers.

Narco-terrorism also refers to some nexus or connection of terrorist organizations with the drug trade. To illustrate, terrorists may be (1) at the margin of the drug trade (e.g., for a fee they protect the coca plants from which cocaine is made or guard the clandestine laboratories that produce cocaine), or (2) engaged more fully in the drug trade to maximize their profit. In Columbia, FARC began its involvement with "taxing" coca plant producers for protecting them from government forces and right-wing paramilitary groups. FARC later gradually extended its participation to include production and trafficking in order to maximize its profits. Its earnings were estimated to be $400–$600 million annually. Al Qaeda and the Taliban control lands in Pakistan and Afghanistan that grow poppies, as well as the laboratories that turn them into heroin. With the help of drug lords, the heroin is moved to Europe and sold, creating an annual income of $20 billion.

To reduce the income of terrorists and criminal organizations, the police adopted the strategy of eradicating poppy fields and coca tree crops. In response, terrorist and criminal organizations began producing synthetic drugs to make up for their lost revenue. Millions of dollars now flow to the Middle East from the sale of synthetic drugs like K-2, Spice, and Blaze.[100] A nationwide raid on synthetic drug dealers in 29 states resulted in 150 arrests and the seizure of more than $150 million in cash and assets, along with approximately a ton of drugs.[101] At just one store selling synthetic drugs in Birmingham, federal agents discovered evidence of $38 million being sent to Yemen, where it is suspected that some portion of it ended up in terrorist hands.[102] Parenthetically, synthetic drugs are also called designer drugs, because new chemical formulations are created. Once a drug compound is banned, the manufacturers change the formula somewhat to make it legal and began selling it under a different name.

Traditional for-Profit Crimes

In Mali, a German official exited a military plane with three suitcases filled with 5 million euros.[103] Officially, the money was budgeted for humanitarian relief.[104] Instead, it was paid to obscure Islamic extremists for the release of 32 European hostages.[105] Although countries publically proclaim they do not pay ransom, some number of them do: In just 2013, al Qaeda and its affiliates were paid $66 million to free hostages they had taken.[106]

The U.S. Treasury calculates that in 2013, $165 million was paid in ransom to terrorists worldwide.[107] That figure almost certainly has increased. The U.S. Department of States maintains that 60–70 percent of kidnappings of American citizens go unreported.[108] One source estimates that it is now a multibillion business annually, which would be a very steep escalation in a few short years.[109] Table 6–4 shows a sample of kidnaping incidents by country, which suggest it is a brisk and profitable business. Each transaction reinforces the terrorists' belief that kidnapping is a good source of revenue. One al Qaeda leader described it as "an easy spoil."[110] Al Qaeda in the Islamic Maghreb, al Qaeda in the Arabian Peninsula, and al-Shabaab in Somalia are all abiding by a common protocol: The seizure of the hostages

TABLE 6–4
A Sample of Kidnaping Incidents, Captivity, and Ransom Costs

Country	Kidnapped Monthly	Days in Captivity	Average Ransom
Afghanistan	1	100	$500,000
Argentina	5	270	$350,000
Columbia	5	270	$350,000
Democratic Republic of Congo	5	60	$250,000
Iraq	3	110	$175,000
Philippines	1	90	$2 Million
Venezuela	1	90	$500,000

Data from data in Kidnap and Ransom Report, 1 August-1 September, 2016, Aegis Response by GardaWorld, 2016, https://www.thomasmillerspecialty.com/fileadmin/uploads/tms/Documents/Articles_of_Interest/SCR_Alert_24_Aegis_Kidnap_Ransom_Newsletter.pdf, accesse

On its face, cooperation between terrorist organizations and criminal groups does not seem likely. Terrorists seek publicity and organized criminal groups prefer to stay in the shadows, avoiding official attention. If terrorists groups are successful in establishing a homeland, or in the case of IS, a caliphate, the markets of transnational criminal organizations for drugs and other goods is likely to be destabilized. Terrorists are ideologically driven and criminal groups operate out of the profit motivation.[111] Terrorists desire to substantially alter the nature of government, replace it with their ideology, or destroy it altogether. Criminal groups want to neutralize government interference with their illegal activities and take money and things of value out of a society.

A salient advantage of cooperation between criminal organizations and terrorists is that in addition to, or in lieu of, money they can provide passports, intelligence, access to smuggling routes, and other things of value to the other party. This is a symbiotic relationship in that the exchanges between these dissimilar organizations are mutually beneficial. For example, terrorists can provide training in bomb making to drug traffickers seeking to eliminate rivals. This reduces competition in the marketplace and also helps to establish longevity.

When terrorist and criminal groups cooperate, they both ultimately end up with what they need or want. The terrorists need money to buy better weapons, attract seasoned fighters from other movements, finance attacks, expand their organizations, support their charitable activities, gather intelligence, and other uses. The criminal groups want their profits. While terrorism seeks to destroy ways of life, criminal organizations are a blight on them. They corrupt public officials, weaken the economy by not paying business or personal taxes, threaten the national security of weak nations, promote violence by arms trafficking, destroy families by trafficking in humans, reduce lawful earnings by pirating music and software, and cause countries massive expenditures to fight the importation and distribution of drugs.

is outsourced to criminal organizations, which get 10 percent of the ransom.[112] There are a small number of companies that specialize in arranging ransoms. Their daily fee is in the $3,000–$3,500 range.

Terrorists are not known to have counterfeited United States currency, although there is a report that a terrorist group counterfeited Indian rupees.[113] The best counterfeiter of the United States $100 bill is North Korea, which does so to bring in cash and to try and destabilize the American economy. Because it takes sophisticated examination to detect it, the bill is referred to as the "Super note." Terrorists do traffic in the global $500 billion counterfeit goods market, for example, Louis Vuitton purses and luggage.[114] In a single year, the black market counterfeit sales cost New York an estimated $1 billion in lost tax revenue.[115]

In Somalia, terrorists receive a portion of the money criminal organizations get from maritime piracy. Ever adaptable and quick to seize new opportunities, terrorists have a long-standing interest in using the Internet to raise money.[116] Illustratively, in the United Kingdom, twenty-two-year-old Younis Tsouli became the premier Internet jihadist, referring to himself as "Terrorist 007."[117] Using 1,400 stolen credit card numbers and their security numbers, the Moroccan-born man living in England raised and laundered the equivalent of $2.4 million, which was used to support 180 websites playing al Qaeda propaganda videos and to buy equipment for terrorists.[118] Tsouli was arrested and subsequently convicted.

Sponsorship, Donations, Charities, Zakat, and Sadaqah

Although it is accurate to state that state-sponsored funds and individual donations have generally declined, there are exceptions. Notably, the U.S. Department of State has called attention to the increase in Iran's support of Hezbollah, which has reached levels not seen since the 1990s.[119] As another means of growing their financial resources, some terrorist organizations have established shell corporations that claim they are for philanthropic and humanitarian purposes, but the funds collected are used to support terrorism.[120] Examples of overtly charitable organizations used for terrorism include the Global Relief Fund and the Holy Land Foundation for Relief and Development.[121] One of the duties of Muslims is **zakat**, annually giving money to be used for humanitarian purposes. Zakat is 2.5 percent of savings and earnings.[122] Some Muslims made zakat donations to charitable organizations, not realizing that instead of going for good works, the money was being funneled to terrorist organizations. In addition to zakat, the Qur'an and Islamic traditions also advocate additional charitable acts of giving, sadaqah, which in some instances has also ended up in terrorist coffers.[123]

Zakat
An annual humanitarian giving by Muslims.

Convergence

There is a significant danger to terrorist organizations becoming too involved in for-profit crimes: They may lose their ideological zeal because of the substantial profits to be made. When this happens, they convert from one type of an organization to another. The Philippines-based and ultra-violent Abu Sayyaf Group (ASG) illustrates this. Nominally, ASG wants to establish an Islamic state. However, it has become so involved in for-profit criminal activities that its ideological foundation appears to be temporally eradicated.[124] Stated simply, ASG is a movement that is at the slippery convergence of terrorism and for-profit crime, a position it shares with FARC.

Chapter Summary

SUMMARY BY LEARNING OBJECTIVE

1. **Explain what restrains a terrorist movement's capability to launch certain types of attacks.**

   Internal and external considerations restrain the launching of certain types of attacks. If, for example, terrorists contemplate using biochemical weapons, they might be *externally* restrained from doing so out of fear of overwhelming reprisals and loss of public support and/or potential loss of sponsors. *Internally*, terrorist leaders might restrain certain types of attacks. As an example, Usama bin Laden ordered followers not to attack Westerns civilians because it was not having the desired effect on their governments.

2. **State why it is important for terrorist groups to become learning organizations.**

   Learning organizations are characterized by prizing the acquisition of new knowledge, being nimble when faced with new situations, and thinking "outside of the box." It is important because it can be a survival mechanism for the terrorist organization: It allows them to analyze their failures and evolve.

3. **Identify and briefly describe a terrorist movement's four organization tools.**

   The four organizational tools are (1) ideology, which represents the reason for existing; (2) leadership, which provides the oversight that steers the organization; (3) recruiting, which is acquiring followers; and (4) publicity, which calls attention to what the terrorist organization broadly intends to do and heralds its successes.

4. **Identify and briefly explain a terrorist movement's six operational tools.**

   These tools are (1) establishing a command and control system, which is the mechanism by which terrorist movements plan, staff, train, coordinate, and execute their attacks; (2) acquiring weapons and a reliable source of spare parts to repair them, to replace combat losses, and to resupply ammunition; (3) securing an operational space, a sanctuary or safe haven where attacks can be safely planned, trained for, and rehearsed; (4) providing training, which begins with an initial emphasis on indoctrination, physical conditioning, small arms familiarization, marksmanship, and basic martial arts. More advanced topics include planting bombs and tactics for assaulting military convoys and installations. Beyond that for some members is specialist training, such as bomb making, car hijacking, sniping, eliminating sentries, and mission-specific training; (5) using intelligence and counterintelligence as key means by which terrorists reduce their risk exposure; and (6) obtaining funds from wealthy individual sponsors or states or acquiring funds from criminal activities such as maritime piracy, bank robberies, extortion, drug and arms trafficking, counterfeiting, kidnapping for ransom, and pirating movies, music, and software.

REVIEW QUESTIONS

1. Distinguish between terrorist motivations and capabilities.
2. Describe the difference between "soft" and "hard" targets.
3. What are the characteristics of a learning organization, and why is it so important for terrorist organizations to become one?
4. What ideology characteristics do all terrorist organizations share?

5. The Internet provides what key advantages to terrorist recruiting?
6. The arms inventory of a terrorist organization is a crude indicator of what?
7. How does a Hawala operate?

CRITICAL THINKING EXERCISES

1. European Sharia-Controlled Zones (or more commonly called "No-Go Zones") are predicated on Muslim preferences for Sharia Law over their current nation's law. Some No-Go Zones have their own police, courts, schools, and curriculum. To a substantial degree, they are self-contained. In some No-Go areas, street signs have been removed and replaced by new street names written in Arabic.

   Consider the Bill of Rights, the first ten amendments to the U.S. Constitution, written by our forefathers. In the First Amendment, there is no freedom of association mentioned. However, in *NAACP v. Alabama* (1958), the U.S. Supreme Court created one. The First Amendment also prohibits placing limitations on the practice of religion. Seemingly the rights just mentioned, and perhaps others, would prohibit some actions people may want to see taken if No-Go Zones come to America. Ordinarily, immigrants become acculturated and integrated into their new homeland.

   Do No-Go Zones create dangers? If so, what are they and how potentially serious are they to the fabric of our country? How do you think No-Go Zone issues should be handled in American communities?

2. Study the four organizational tools and the six operational tools in Table 6-2. Work alone to complete the following two tasks: First, identify any existing tasks from Table 6-2 you would move from one category to another and explain why. Second, assume you are going to start a terrorist movement. Develop your own list of tasks that you think you need to complete and list them in the order you think that you need to accomplish them. Then sort the tasks into whatever categories you think are useful. Form small groups and develop consensus lists. Assign one person to present your work to the rest of the class on a flip chart or whiteboard. After each group has completed this task, compare the various lists. Can a better list be made by combining items from the different lists? If so, what does that suggest about group decision-making, especially within initiating terrorist groups?

3. **The Evolution of Terrorist Tools and Tactics: Propaganda and Training Videos on the Internet.** Terrorist tools and tactics appear to be evolving over time. Terrorists may favor attack methods that exploit perceived vulnerabilities, such as adopting active shooter tactics and find new methods of concealing dangerous nuclear, biological, or chemical materials. Further, radical Islamic terrorists will likely pursue opportunities to inflict mass casualties, particularly considering recent upheaval in the Middle East (like the war in Syria and the advancement of the Islamic State). Recent attacks appear to be focused on causing mass casualties with contemporary weapons (e.g., shooting patrons in a theatre or restaurant). Scour the Internet for new propaganda and training videos that depict life as an Islamic State fighter. Can you imagine such videos that inform individuals on how to make a "dirty" bomb, or spread poison in a water supply, or use sophisticated software to cause train derailments? Discuss ways to combat these types of videos, and more important, discuss ways to reduce the desire for violence in the Middle East.

NOTES

1. See Victor Asal and R. Karl Rethemeyer, "The Nature of the Beast: Organizational Structures and the Lethality of Terrorist Attacks," *The Journal of Politics*, Vol. 70, Issue 2, April 2008, pp. 437–449.
2. Loc. cit.
3. Boaz Ganor, "Terrorist Organization Types and the Probability of a Boomerang Effect," *Studies in Conflict and Terrorism*," Vol. 31, Issue 4, April 2008, pp. 279–280.
4. Nic Roberson and Paul Cruickshank, "al Qaeda's Training Adapts to Drone Attacks," CNN. Com/Crime, July 31, 2009, www.cnn.com/crime/07/30/robertson.al.qaeda.training/index.html.
5. Almost all of these are mentioned in Ganor, "Terrorist Organization Types."

6. Charles R. Swanson, Leonard Territo, and Robert W. Taylor, *Police Administration: Structures, Processes, and Behavior* (Boston: Pearson, 2012), p. 188.

7. Kim Cragin, *Understanding Terrorist Ideology* (Santa Monica: RAND Corporation, 2004), p. 1.

8. See Christina Hellmich, "al Qaeda—Terrorists, Hypocrites, Fundamentalists? The View from within," *Third World Quarterly*, Vol. 26, Issue 1, February 2005, pp. 39–54.

9. Muhammad Hassan, "Key Considerations in Counter-ideological Work Against Terrorist Ideology," *Studies in Conflict and Terrorism*, Vol. 29, Issue 6, September 2006, p. 531.

10. The first four of these factors come from Edward Newman, "Exploring the 'Root Causes' of Terrorism," *Studies in Conflict and Terrorism*, Vol. 29, Issue 8, December 2006, p. 751. Newman rejects the notion that poverty is a root cause of terrorism.

11. "6 Doctors Among 8 Held in U.K. Bomb Plot," CBS/AP, February 11, 2009, www.cbsnews .com/2100-224_162-3004644.html.

12. Alberto Abadie, "Poverty, Political Freedom, and the Roots of Terrorism," Working Paper 1085 (Cambridge, Massachusetts: National Bureau of Economic Research, October 2004), pp. 1–2.

13. Loc. cit.

14. Randy Borum, *Psychology of Terrorism* (Tampa: University of South Florida, 2004), p. 40.

15. Amir Hassanpour, "The Kurdish Experience," *Middle East Report (MER)*, 189, Vol. 24, July/August 1994, p. 2.

16. No author, "Turkey v Syria's Kurds v Islamic State', BBC, August 23, 2016, www.bbc.com/ news/world-middle-east-33690060, accessed March 20, 2017, was helpful in understanding the major Kurd factions involved in the Syrian War.

17. No author, "Who Are the Kurds?' BBC News, March 14, 2016, www.bbc.com/news/world -middle-east-29702440, accessed March 16, 2017.

18. "Kurdish Groups, Turkey, and The Islamic State."

19. Ian Bremmer, "These 5 Stats Explain Turkey's War in ISIS-and the Kurds," Time.com, July 31, 2015, time.com/3980085/these-5-stats-explain-turkeys-war-on-isis-and-the-kurds, accessed March 20, 2017.

20. Roc Morin, "The Western Volunteers Fighting ISIS, Atlantic, January 29, 2016, www .theatlantic.com/international/archive/2016/01/peshmerga-isis-western-volunteers/433803, accessed March 18, 2017.

21. "Revolutionary Armed Forces of Colombia (FARC)," *National Consortium for the Study of Terrorism and Responses to Terrorism*, University of Maryland, p. 1. www.start.umd .edu/start/data_collections/tops/terrorist_organization_profile.asp?id=96.

22. Jeremy Scahill, *Dirty Wars* (New York: Nations Books, 2013), p. 167.

23. Loc. cit.

24. Loc. cit.

25. Cragin and Daly, *The Dynamics of Terrorist Threat*, pp. 32–34.

26. Abu Hamza al-Masri, "Islamic Scriptures Unveiled," undated, https://sites.google.com/site/ islamicscripturesunveiled/Home/dirtykuffar, accessed March 18, 2017.

27. Michael Petrou, "What's Driving Teen Girls to Jihad?," *MaClean's,* March 7, 2015, www. macleans.ca/society/teen-girl-jihadists, accessed March 16, 2017.

28. Leonard Weinberg and Arie Perliger, "How Terrorist Groups End," *CTC Sentinel*, Vol. 3, Issue 2, February 2010, from Table 1, p. 16.

29. Janine di Giovanni, "A Jihad of Their Own," *Time*, March 14, 2014, www.newsweek .com/2014/03/14/jihad-her-own-247935.html, accessed March 18, 2017.

30. Peter A. Olsson, "Homegrown Terrorists, Rebels in Search of a Cause," Middle East Quarterly, Summer 2013, Vol., 20, Issue 3, pp. 3–10.

31. Scott Gerwehr and Sara Daly, *Al Qaida: Terrorist Selection and Recruitment* (Santa Monica: RAND Corporation, 2006), p. 77 and in D. Kamien, *Homeland Security Handbook* (New York: McGraw-Hill, 2007), p. 75.

32. Ibid., pp. 74–75.

33. Alan Travis, "MI5 Report Challenges Views on Terrorism in Britain," *Guardian*, August 20, 2008, www.guardian.co.uk/uk/2008/aug/20/uksecurity.terrorism1.

34. Loc. cit.

35. Travis, "MI5 Report Challenges Views on Terrorism in Britain."

36. Cragin and Daly, *The Dynamics of Terrorist Threat*, p. 35.

37. Ibid., pp. 36–37.
38. See Gabriel Weimann, "The Psychology of Mass-Mediated Terrorism," *American Behavioral Scientist*, Vol. 52, No. 1, September 2008, pp. 69–86.
39. "GIMF Develops 'Islamic Encryption Plugin' for Chat Programs," Site Intelligence Group, February 13, 2012, www.news.siteintelgroup.com/component/content/article/6-jihadist-news/2733-gimf-develops-islamic-encryption-plugin-for-chat-programs.
40. "Mickey Mouse 'Twin' Killed on Hamas TV," *Washington Post*, June 30, 2007, www.washingtonpost.com/wp-dyn/content/article/2007/06/29/AR2007062902105.html.
41. Irving Lachow and Courtney Richardson, "Terrorist Use of the Internet," *National Defense University Press*, Issue 45, 2nd Quarter, 2007, p. 100.
42. This account is drawn from Amy Forliti, "Man Gets 10 Years in Somali Terror Investigation," MPR News (Minnesota Public Radio), May 13, 2013, minnesota.publicradio.org/display/web/2013/05/13/news/somali-terror-investigation.
43. Michael Jacobson, "Why Terrorists Quit: Gaining from al-Qa`ida's Losses," *CTC Sentinel*, Vol. 1, Issue 8, July 15, 2008, www.ctc.usma.edu/wp-content/uploads/2010/06/vol1iss8artl.pdf.
44. United Nations Office on Drugs and Crime, The Use of the Internet for Terrorism Purpose (New York: United Nations, 2012), pp. 3–11; and Gabriel Weimann, "How Modern Terrorism Uses the Internet," *Journal of International Security Affairs*, Number 8, Spring 2005, p. 5, www.securityaffairs.org/issues/2005/08/weimann.php, p. 4.
45. Weimann, "How Modern Terrorism Uses the Internet," pp. 5, 10–11.
46. Loc. cit., the content of this paragraph is drawn from this source with restatement.
47. Weimann, "How Modern Terrorism Uses the Internet," pp. 4–5.
48. Richard Spencer, "Islamic State Jihadist Executes His Own Mother in Public," Telegraph (England), January 8, 2016, www.telegraph.co.uk/news/worldnews/islamic-state/12088807/Islamic-State-jihadist-executes-own-mother-in-public.html, accessed March 22, 2017.
49. "Computer Image Shows Washington, D.C. Devastated by al Qaeda Nuclear Attack," *Telegraph* (United Kingdom), May 30, 2008, www.telegraph.co.uk/news/2052575/american-apocalypse-picture-shows-washington-dc-devastated-by-al-qaeda-nuclear-attack.html.
50. No author, "Jordan Pilot Hostage Moaz al-Kasasbeh Burned Alive," BBC News, February 3, 2015, www.bbc.com/news/world-middle-east-31121160, accessed March 20, 2017.
51. Harriet Alexander, "IS Crucifies Nine People in Syrian Villages, Telegraph (England), June 29, 2014, www.telegraph.co.uk/news/worldnews/middleeast/syria/10933851/Isis-crucifies-nine-people-in-Syrian-villages.html, accessed March 20, 2017.
52. Declan Walsh and Nour Youssef, "Targeted by ISIS, Christians Flee Violence," New York Times, February 24, 2017, www.nytimes.com/2017/02/24/world/middleeast/egypt-coptic-christians-sinai.html, accessed March 20, 2017.
53. Noemie Olive, "Islamics Attack French Church, Slit Priest's Throat," Reuters, July 27, 2017, www.reuters.com/article/us-france-hostages-idUSKCN1060VA, accessed March 20, 2017.
54. Corey Charlton, "They Started to Put People in Those Holes, Those People Were Alive: Yazidi Survivor's Horror Story Reveals How ISIS Threw Screaming Women and Children into Mass Graves," Daily Mail (England), August 20, 2014, www.dailymail.co.uk/news/article-2729130/They-started-people-holes-people-alive-Yazidi-survivors-horror-story-reveals-ISIS-threw-screaming-women-children-mass-graves.html, accessed March 20, 2014; and John Davison, "In Northern Iraq Yazidis Risk All to Flee Islamic State," Reuters, November 26, 2016, www.reuters.com/article/us-mideast-crisis-iraq-yazidis-idUSKBN13L07V, accessed March 20, 2017.
55. James Kirchick, "ISIS's Thirst for Blood Is Only Matched by Its Hunger for Publicity," *New York Post*, June 26, 2016, http://nypost.com/2016/06/26/isiss-thirst-for-blood-only-matched-by-its-hunger-for-publicity, accessed March 20, 2017.
56. Cragin and Daly, *The Dynamics of Terrorist Threat*, p. 40.
57. "Provisional Irish Republican Army (PIRA)," British Security Service, MI5, undated, but written sometime from 2007 forward, p. 5, www.mi5.gov.uk/home/the-theats/terrorism/northern-ireland/provisional-irish-republican-army-pira.html.
58. "Terrorist Designations and State Sponsors of Terrorism," U.S. Department of State, 2013, p. 1, www.state.gov/j/ct/list.
59. Cragin and Daly, *The Dynamics of Terrorist Threat*, p. 40.

60. Loc. cit.

61. Ibid., pp. 40–41.

62. Cragin and Daly, *The Dynamics of Terrorist Threat*, p. 45.

63. Robert D. Lamb, *Ungoverned Areas and Threats from Safe Havens* (Washington, D.C.: Final Report of the Ungoverned Areas Projects, U.S. Department of Defense, January 2008), p. 6.

64. Loc. cit.

65. "Terrorist Havens: Lebanon," Council on Foreign Relations, May 2007, www.cfr.org/lebanon/terrorism-havens-lebanon/p9516.

66. See Blake W. Mobley, *Terrorism and Counter-Intelligence: How Terrorist Groups Escape Detection* (New York: Columbia University Press, 2012), p. 14.

67. These settings, with additional commentary, are drawn from Robert D. Lamb, *Ungoverned Areas and Threats from Safe Havens* (Washington, D.C.: Department of Defense, January 2008),

68. Ibid., p. 25.

69. Mobley, *Terrorism and Counterintelligence*, p. 31.

70. This account is drawn from a preliminary report, Report of the Official Account of the Bombings on 7th July 2005, House of Commons (London: The Stationery Office, 2006).

71. *Terrorist Safe Havens* (Washington, D.C.: Department of State, May 30, 2013), Chapter 5, no page number, www.state.gov/j/ct/rls/crt/2012/2099987.htm.

72. Lamb, *Ungoverned Areas and Threats from Safe Havens*, p. 21.

73. Hearing Before the Subcommittee on the Middle East and Central Asia of the Committee on International Relations, U.S House of Representatives, 109th Congress, 2nd Session, September 14, 2006, p. 27.

74. James Brandon, "Britain Grapples with 'Honor Killing' Practice," *Christian Science Monitor*, October 19, 2005, www.csmonitor.com/2005/1019/p04s01-woeu.html.

75. No author, "Europe's No-Go Zones: List of 900 Areas Where Police Have Lost Control to Migrants," Express, April 2, 2016, www.express.co.uk/news/world/657520/Europe-no-go-900-EU-areas-police-lost-control, accessed March 21, 2017.

76. Some of these examples are drawn from Michael D. Greenberg et al., *Maritime Terrorism Risks and Liabilities* (Santa Monica: RAND Corporation, 2006), p. 9.

77. "Egyptian Authorities Foiled al Qaeda Terror Plot Against the Suez Canal," Maritime Terrorism Research Center, July 1, 2009, www.martimeterrorism.com/2009/07/01/egyptianauthorities-foiled-al-qaeda-terror-plot-against-suez-canal.

78. Loc. cit.

79. "Egypt Foils Terror Plot," CBN News, July 9, 2009, www.cbn.com/cbnnews/insideisrael/2009/july/egypt-foils-ssuez-terror-plot.

80. For more on this subject, see Joshua E. Keating, "What Do You Learn at Terrorist Training Camp?" *Foreign Policy*, May 10, 2010, www.foreignpolicy.com/articles/2010/05/what_do_you_learn_atterrorist_training_camp.

81. David M. Williams, "Nothing Virtual about It: An Emerging Safe Haven for an Adaptive Enemy," Monograph, School of Advanced Military Studies, U.S. Army Command and General Staff College, 2010, Fort Leavenworth, Kansas, p. 36.

82. Mark L. Reagan, *Introduction to U.S. Counter Terrorism* (Washington, D.C.: Department of Homeland Security, 2005), pp. 6–7.

83. Ben Brandt, "The Taliban's Conduct of Intelligence and Counterintelligence *CTC Sentinel*, Vol. 4, Issue 6, June 2011, p. 19.

84. Loc. cit.

85. Loc. cit.

86. Michael Jonsson, "Countering Terrorist Financing: Success and Setbacks in the Years since 9/11," *CTC Sentinel*, Vol. 3, Issue 7, July 2010, p. 198, www.ctc.usma.edu/v2/wpcontent/uploads/2010/08/CTCSentinel-Vol3Iss7-art71.pdf.

87. Loc. cit.

88. Loc. cit.

89. Loc. cit.

90. Patrick M. Jost and Harjit Singh Sandhu, "The Hawala Remittance System and Its Role in Money Laundering," *Financial Crimes Enforcement Network in Cooperation with INTERPOL/FOPAC*, 2013, p. 5.

91. Ibid., pp. 5–6.

92. Loc. cit.

93. John Haywood, "Indonesia: Authorities Say Jihadists Use Bitcoin, PayPal to Fund Terrorism," Breitbart, January 10, 2017, www.breitbart.com/national-security/2017/01/10/islamic-militants-fund-terrorism-indonesia-bitcoin-paypal, accessed March 22, 2017.

94. Emma Björnehed, "Narco-Terrorism: The Merger of the War on Drugs and the War on Terror," Global Crime, Vol. 6, No. 3–4, August–November, 2004, p. 310.

95. Loc. cit.

96. Nikesh Trecarten, "The Global Convergence of Terrorism and Narcotics Trafficking," Fraser Institute (Canada), Winter 2014, p. 31.

97. Bio: Pablo Escobar, undated, p. 1, www.biography.com/people/pablo-escobar-9542497#synopsis.

98. Loc. cit.

99. William Kremer, "Pablo Escobar's Hippos: A Growing Problem," BBC News Magazine, p. 1, June 26, 2014, www.bbc.com/news/magazine-27905743.

100. "DEA Takes Aim at Synthetic Drugs with Nationwide Raids," May 7, 2014, p. 1, www.pbs.org/newshour/rundown/dea-takes-aim-synthetic-drugs-nationwide-raids.

101. Loc. cit. and "Drug Busts Add to Suspicion that Profits Fund Terrorist Groups," CBS News, May 8, 2014, p. 1, www.cbsnews.com/news/synthetic-drug-busts-add-to-suspicion-that-profits-fund-terror-groups.

102. "Drug Busts Add to Suspicion that Profits Fund Terrorist Groups," p. 2.

103. This account is drawn with restatement from New York Times, July 29, 2014.

104. Loc. cit.

105. Loc. cit.

106. Loc. cit.

107. Loc. cit.

108. Dina Gusovsky, "The Multimillion Dollar Business of Ransom," CNBC, July 7, 2015, www.cnbc.com/2015/07/06/the-multi-million-dollar-business-of-ransom-.html, accessed March 23, 2017.

109. Loc. cit.

110. Rukmini Callimachi, "Paying Ransoms: Europe Bankrolls Qaeda Terror."

111. The points in this paragraph are taken with restatement from "Actual and Potential Links Between Terrorism and Criminality," Canadian Centre for Intelligence and Security Studies, Vol. 2006-5, pp. 2–3.

112. Loc. cit.

113. No author, "Fake Currency Seized," Times of India, July 25, 2014.

114. "Counterfeit Goods Are Linked to Terror Groups," New York Times, February 12, 2007.

115. Loc. cit.

116. The Use of the Internet for Terrorist Purposes (New York: United Nations, 2012), p. 7.

117. Loc. cit.

118. Loc. cit.

119. Guy Taylor, "Feds Say Iran's Support for Terrorism Growing," Washington Times, May 30, 2013.

120. Loc. cit.

121. Loc. cit.

122. Juan Miguel del Cid Gomez, "A Financial Profile of the Terrorism of al Qaeda and Its Affiliates," Perspectives on Terrorism, Vol. 4, No. 4, 2010, p. 3, www.terrorismanalysts.com/pt/index.php/pot/article/view/113.

123. Callimachi, "Paying Ransoms: Europe Bankrolls Qaeda Terror," pp. 1–2.

124. John Rollins and Liana Sun Wyler, Terrorism and Transnational Crime: Foreign Policy Issues for Congress (Washington, D.C.: Congressional Research Service, June 13, 2013), p. 17.

125. Forbes International, "The World's 10 Richest Terror Organizations," Forbes, November 28, 2014, www.forbes.com/sites/forbesinternational/2014/12/12/the-worlds-10-richest-terrorist-organizations/#2a2cacc4f8a9, accessed March 16, 2017.

126. Max Blau, Emanuella Grinberg, and Shimon Prokupecz, "Investigators Believe Ohio State Attacker Was Inspired by ISIS," CNN, November 29, 2016, www.cnn.com/2016/11/29/us/ohio-state-university-attack, accessed March 17, 2017.

Typologies of Terrorism: State-Involved and Single or Special Issue Movements

CHAPTER

7

Learning Objectives

After completing this chapter, you should be able to:

1. Identify and describe the four waves of terrorism.

2. Identify the three goals that differentiate religious and secular terrorism; provide an argument that supports the emergence of the Islamic State as religious terrorism.

3. Contrast state terrorism, state-enabled terrorism, state-sponsored terrorism, and state-perpetuated/international terrorism.

4. Explain why single-issue/special-issue movements are so important in the United States.

Ayatollah Khomeini (1900–1989) was exiled from Iran in 1962 because of his opposition to the existing government. He continued to foment and plan opposition to it. In 1979, the government finally collapsed and Khomeini returned in triumph. Later that year, he was elected Iran's political and religious leader for life. His radical views on Islam led to the capture of hostages in the American Embassy later that year.

(Keystone Pictures USA/Alamy stock Photo)

Introduction

Typologies and taxonomies are both methods of classification. Sometimes they are used synonymously. However, there is a crucial difference. **Typologies** rationally group related concepts and other things into categories. In contrast, **taxonomies** have categories that are formed by empirically studying observable and measurable characteristics.

Typologies bring clarity and patterns out of what otherwise would be a chaotic mass of information.[1] They allow us to quickly see the differences and similarities in concepts by using carefully reasoned categories. The use of typologies allows us to have shared understandings and a common language about the categories.[2] Despite such advantages, typologies have shortcomings. Their categories are artificial creations. They are ideal or pure descriptions that cannot fully account for the rich diversity of reality. Some concepts may fit equally well into more than one category. Cases that cannot be comfortably slipped into any category are forced into the best-fitting category despite the fact they have some features of other categories as well. Finally, typologies can lead to stereotyping.

There are many typologies of terrorism because unlike data-driven taxonomies, they are based on the reasoning of their originator. Johnson asserts that there are as many typologies of terrorism as there are analysts.[3] This chapter relies on the use of typologies because there is a dearth of well-developed taxonomies of terrorist organizations.

Typologies
Rationally group related concepts and other things into categories.

Taxonomies
Categories that are formed by empirically studying observable and measureable characteristics.

A Political-Orientation-Based Typology: The Four Waves of Terrorism

Rapoport analyzed the sweep of terrorism history beginning in the 1880s and identified points at which there were major shifts in terrorism. He called these the **four waves of terrorism**: the anarchist wave, the anti-colonial wave, the new left wave, and the religious wave.[4] Rapoport's four waves provide a good framework in which to summarize the various political, cultural, and religious ideologies historically developed to this point.[5] As useful as Rapoport's four waves may be, his work illustrates one of the shortcomings of typologies; his waves could also be categorized as political or historical with equal accuracy. Each of Rapoport's types of terrorism has a range of dates associated with it. However, each type doesn't neatly start and stop on those dates. The dates merely denote a predominate type of terrorism during any given period. For example, terrorism to establish a homeland or new nation for an ethnic minority or to establish a new form of government spans all four waves.

Four waves of terrorism
Typology developed by David Rapoport to better understand terrorism: anarchist, anti-colonial, new left, and religious.

The Anarchist Wave

Anarchy" comes from the Greek word "anarchos" and means "without a ruler."[6] According to Rapoport, the **anarchist wave** began in the 1880s and continued for some 40 years.[7] Practical anarchy recognizes the impossibility of actually achieving an idealized state of pure anarchy characterized by the absence of a central government. Consequentially, most anarchists are willing to settle for a weak government that is minimally intrusive in the lives of its citizens. Anarchy is inherently anti-authoritarian and revolutionary—it strives to overthrow an existing ruler and/or government. Anarchy is also used to describe chaotic social and economic conditions that are produced by the failure of the central government. A present-day example of this is Somalia. Gettleman described Somalia as "the most dangerous place in the world"[8] because it is a failed government, unable to control its own territory. This makes it an ideal safe haven for terrorists.

If idealized and practical anarchists knew the writings of American philosopher Henry David Thoreau (1817–1862), they would identify with his notion that the government that governs not at all or least is best. Anarchists have frequently used assassination to pursue their goals.[9] Victims of anarchists include Russian Tsar Alexander II's death at the hands of a bomb-throwing member of Narodnaya Volya (The People's Will) in 1881 and the stabbing murder of French President Carnot in 1894. Shooters killed Spanish Prime Minister Canovas in 1897, Italian King Umberto I in 1900, and American President McKinley in Buffalo in 1901. The assassinations of Archduke Ferdinand, heir to the Austrian throne, and his wife Sophie in 1914 triggered the onset of World War I a month later. Concern about anarchism

Anarchist wave
Roughly 1880-1920, anti-authoritarian and revolutionary concept that in pure form exists as a society without any government.

Box 7-1
Assassinations since the Anarchist Wave

Although the anarchist wave ended in 1920, the tactic of assassinating leaders has continued across waves. In the examples below, other states and/or terrorist movements may have been involved.

1963, President John F. Kennedy, Dallas, Texas. Lee Harvey Oswald was arrested for the murder and while in police custody was shot to death by nightclub owner Jack Ruby, who had terminal cancer and died before he was executed. Multiple and controversial theories surround President Kennedy's death. The Cuban government, Russian government, organized crime, and even the Central Intelligence Agency have all at one time or another been accused of complicity.

1968, Senator Robert Kennedy, presidential candidate and brother to the slain president, Los Angeles, California. He was shot to death by Palestinian Sirhan Sirhan, who is serving a life sentence. Sirhan's motivation was Senator Kennedy's support of Israel. In *The Forgotten Terrorist* (2008), Mel Ayton makes a case that "fanatical nationalism" drove Sirhan to assassinate Robert Kennedy.

1981, President Anwar Sadat, Cairo, Egypt. Sadat had recognized Israel as a legitimate state and had entered into a peace agreement with Israeli Prime Minister Menachem Begin regarding the Palestinian territory. Both men received a Nobel Peace Prize for this effort. However, many Arabs were outraged by it, particularly the Palestinians, who had not participated in the agreement. The radical Egyptian Islamic Jihad (EIJ), whose goal was to replace the national government with an Islamic state, assassinated President Sadat in 1981 as he reviewed a victory parade.

2004, Ezzedine Salim, President of the Governing Council of Iraq, Baghdad. If not a proponent of diversity, Salim was at least tolerant of it. In 2006, Salim was killed by a suicide car bomber because he was in a leadership position from which he might be able to create a more moderate climate. The bomber was from Abu Musab al Zarqawi's Jama'at al-Tawhid wal-Jihad, which went through several rebadging of names before becoming the Islamic State (IS).

2005, Rafik Hariri was a prominent business leader and prime minister of Lebanon when he and 21 other people were killed as nearly a ton of TNT explosives was detonated as his motorcade passed by the St. George Hotel in downtown Beirut. A lengthy investigation by Lebanese Internal Security Forces revealed evidence pointing to Hezbollah as the prime actor in the assassination, operationally and financially supported by Syria, a long-time, historical figure in the background of Lebanese politics.

---

resulted in the United States passing the Immigration Act of 1903. The Act made anarchists an excludable class of immigrants.[10]

The Anti-Colonial Wave

Anti-colonial wave
Prevalent during 1920s–1960s. Colonies sought independence from major powers controlling them.

Colonialism goes back to the early modern era, roughly 1500 to 1800. During that time, European nations used their military power to form colonies in other parts of the world that they could control.[11] Colonies were created in Asia, South America, the Caribbean, North America, Africa, and the Middle East. During the **anti-colonial wave** (1920s–1960s),[12] colonies sought their independence by negotiating; when that failed they often turned to terrorism.[13] Following the defeat of Germany and Ottoman Turkey in World War I, the League of Nations gave a mandate or authorization to a few member nations to rule the colonies of the defeated powers. Over time, many of these colonies were successful in freeing themselves from their largely European rulers. As the colonies struggled to gain their freedom, they invariably had the support of the people.[14] Some colonies gained independence by helping the Allies fight the Axis powers during World War II. As an example, the Philippines separated from the United States in 1946, and the country of Israel became a separate nation under a United Nations plan after the war (1948). India, formerly ruled by the British, was partitioned into India and Pakistan in 1947. Indonesia (1949) separated from the Netherlands. Algiers (1962) broke away from France, and the Republic of Kenya and Malaysia (1963) split from England as colonial territories.

The New Left Wave

New left wave
Concluded that terrorism was the way to reform governments.

Weather Underground
Originally called the Weathermen, this group broke away from the Students for a Democratic Society (SDS) in the late 1960s. It issued a "state of war" against the United States and was strongly opposed to the war in Vietnam, calling it an example of American imperialism in Southeast Asia. The group committed bombings of government buildings and banks; however, it was not responsible for anyone's death. The group disbanded in 1977.

The Vietnam War ultimately produced widespread opposition to it in the United States and abroad. America and its allies were viewed as engaging in a form of colonial imperialism, which the new left saw as the cause of inequality and oppression throughout the world.[15] Although the **new left wave** (1960s–1990s)[16] concluded that terrorism was a tactic to reform governments, it was notoriously unsuccessful in doing so.[17] For instance, in the United States, the violent leftist revolutionary **Weather Underground** (formerly the *Weathermen*) robbed banks to fund its operations. The group also bombed 12 federal buildings and facilities, including the Capitol Building and the State Department in Washington, D.C. Left-wing movements have often included socialists advocating programs to helping the "underclass," the weak and poor.

According to Rapoport, it is important *not* to overlook that during each wave other extremist movements did not stand still. For example, the American right-wing **National Socialist Movement (NSM)** was formed in 1974 and billed itself as "the premier white civil rights organization" of the time. Its root is the American Nazi Party founded by George Lincoln Rockwell in 1959. NSM membership is open to "heterosexual people of European descent" and its Viking Youth Corps (VYC) shapes the views of adolescents. Membership in NSM cannot be granted to Jews or homosexuals, and its platform calls for ending non-white emigration to the United States.[18] Clearly, right-wing as well as left-wing movements were active during same period of time.

National Socialist Movement (NSM)
Formed in 1974. Roots in the American Nazi Party. Self-billed as the "premier while civil rights organization."

The Religious Wave

There were major acts of secular terrorism prior to the beginning of the religious wave. For instance, the Black September Organization (BSO) was dedicated to creating a Palestinian homeland. In 1972, the BSO murdered Israeli athletes at the Munich Olympics. Israel quickly retaliated with military strikes against several Middle East countries, most notably Lebanon, Jordan, Egypt, and Syria. More important, the "Munich Massacre" was counterproductive because worldwide public opinion swung against the Palestinian cause.

According to Rapoport, the current **religious wave** began in 1979 with Iran's Islamic Revolution, which overthrew the ruling monarch, Shah (King of Kings) Pahlavi (1919–1980). Ayatollah Khomeini was installed in his place as Supreme Leader, creating the first modern national government based on Islamic beliefs. Two factors in 1979 helped birth the religious wave: (1) the taking of 53 American hostages[19] by radicalized Iranian Muslims at the American Embassy in Tehran,[20] which lasted 444 days (see Figure 7–1) and the subsequent aborted Operation Eagle Claw to rescue them, discussed in Chapter 14; and (2) the ill-fated Soviet military entry into Afghanistan.[21] Together, these two events communicated to the developing world that perhaps the superpowers were impotent and vulnerable "paper tigers."

Religious wave
Began in 1979 with Iran's Islamic Revolution and continues.

Weinberg and Eubank argue that the present wave of religious terrorism has killed more people, caused more injuries, and spanned the globe more widely in comparison to other waves.[22] Still, they reason that radical Islamic terrorism may be on the wane, although that view is not widely shared. In 2017, a United Nations (UN) report characterized IS as being a complex, diverse challenge with sustained military operations in Iraq and Syria and the

FIGURE 7–1
American hostages from the Embassy in Tehran, Iran, were occasionally let outside in small groups while armed guards watched them closely. The Iranians released them the same day President Reagan was sworn in as president.
(Mohsen Shandiz/Sygma/Getty Images)

ability to mount operations in other regions.[23] The U.S. Department of State sees IS as the greatest terrorist threat globally with a formidable military force in the same two countries the UN did.[24]

In explanation of their "terrorism waning" view, Weinberg and Eubank reason that after a thirty-eight-year-old effort to create a worldwide Islamic state, only one revolutionary Islamic state exists: Iran.[25] Mass movements tend to lose their momentum over long periods of time for two reasons. Governments develop better skills in dealing with them and over a succession of leaders the movement tends to become more moderate, allowing for less violent resolutions. There is also some difficulty in a cause being "translated" from one generation of terrorists to the next.[26] Using drones and raids, the United States and its allies have systematically killed radical Islamic leaders. This "decapitation of the core leadership" strategy has caused radical Muslims to take greater precautions about who knows where they are at any given time, but the strategy continues to have an effect.

Weinberg and Eubank's optimism may be correct, but it is not yet in sight. Still, by 2016, IS had lost 40 percent of the territory it controlled in Iraq and Syria, and the flow of foreign fighters had markedly slowed from where it was in 2014 and 2015.[27] While United Nations and other sanctions are in place, including travel bans, asset freezes and seizures, and arms embargo, their effectiveness is in question. The Islamic State is an extremely nimble, adaptable organization. The sanctions that worked against al Qaeda inadequately address IS's economic model, discussed later in this section. In 2013, IS appeared to be just another terrorist movement. Soon thereafter, it was also an insurgency and a government that sprawls over occupied territory in two countries.

Defining Religious Violence

As discussed in the first chapter, there are multiple definitions of terrorism. Here, we offer a distinction between secular violence, which has no genuine religious component, from religious violence. This is a slippery endeavor because some terrorism committed in the name of religion is secular; that is, the violence is politically based. The mere citing of scripture, displaying religious symbols, or including a religion's name in your movement or group's name is not sufficient to constitute religious terrorism.[28] The goal of the terrorist act or group must be considered.

For instance, some anti-abortion/pro-life terrorists have religious objections. The last words spoken by abortion clinic killer Paul Miller before lethal drugs were injected into his body were, "May God help you to protect the unborn as you would want to be protected."[29] However, the goal of the anti-abortion/pro-life movement is political: making abortions illegal. Similarly, just including the word "Christian" or some similar word may not be very illuminating.[30] The Christian Patriots are an anti-federal government organization and the Christian Identity Movement holds that white people are at the center of God's plan, while all others are lesser, "mud people." Both Christian Patriots and Christian Identity receive greater attention in the next chapter.

Gregg asserts there are three goals that differentiate between religious and secular terrorism:[31]

1. *To violently initiate an apocalyptical event that will save (destroy) the world, thereby ushering in the anticipated new world.*

   Illustratively, Shoko Asahara, the Japanese founder of Aum Shinrikyo (Supreme Truth), developed a group that was a strange combination of Hindu, Buddhist, and apocalyptic Christian beliefs. Asahara declared himself to be "both Christ and the first enlightened one since Buddha." In 1995, Aum Shinrikyo released deadly sarin gas in a Tokyo subway, killing thirteen people and injuring thousands more. One cult member participating in the attack evaded capture until 2012.

2. *To create a theocracy, a religious government based on the Word, Laws, and Commandments of God or Deity as interpreted by ecclesiastical authorities.*

   This tenet accurately describes the Islamic government of Iran since 1979. Muslims following the Shi'a tradition account for about 90–95 percent of Iran's population, Islamic Sunnis represent 5–10 percent, and combining Jews, Christians, and other denominations accounts for less than 1 percent of the population.[32] Iranian law dictates that the only acceptable religion is that of Islam within the Shi'a tradition, hence there are very few Christians and Jews, who can nominally practice their religion in secret. Although there are frequent reports of discrimination, imprisonment, and executions, small groups of other religions continue to evade oppression. In 2015, Iran executed at least twenty people on charges of "*moharebeh*," translated as "enmity toward God," as a violation against the religion and state of Iran. It was not an accident that many of those executed were Kurdish people, cultural and political enemies to Iran for throughout history, and members of the Sunni tradition within Islam.[33]

3. *To create a pure religious state where everyone practices the same religion.*

State law within Iran severely limits religious freedom to less than 1 percent of its population, and is at odds with actual practices experienced by those people. It is not a coincidence that many of those who practice religions other than the Shi'a tradition in Iran are also cultural or ethnic minorities. Interestingly, the greatest threat to Iran is the ultra-violent Islamic State (IS) that practices the Sunni tradition of Islam. The IS goal of a worldwide and transnational Islamic Caliphate is antithetical to Iran and meets this goal.

FIGURE 7–2
Shoko Asahara (1955–) and 12 followers were sentenced to death for their subway attack. None of them have been executed. Japan appears reluctant to execute those convicted of capital crimes.

(Chuck Nacke/Alamy Stock Photo)

The Islamic State: The Drive to Establish a Worldwide Caliphate

This section discusses the Islamic State's development, acquisition of military power, finances, and how, teetering on the brink of falling apart, has gained much more strength than it has lost.

The Islamic State (IS) is most fully understood in the context that American foreign policy, the Coalition's Invasion of Iraq in 2003 and its consequences, are among the catalysts that ultimately led to its formation. Other forces at work included a declining power and influence of al Qaeda in the Middle East, the continuing spread of radical Islamic theology, and the centuries-old Sunni-Shia conflict. In this section, IS receives the most coverage because presently it is the most capable global terrorist threat. Even if IS were to lose all the territory it occupies in Iraq, Syria, and even Southern Turkey, it would retain a demonstrated transnational jihadist capability to strike in Western countries.[34] Moreover, it appears to be preparing Southeast Asia as another operational arena.

During the Iranian War (1980–1988), President Saddam Hussein used chemical weapons against Iraqi Kurds and Iranian Forces. To prop up Iraq's economy after its long war with Iran, Hussein invaded Kuwait in 1990 and seized its revenue-producing oil fields. Iraq was forced to withdraw the following year by an international coalition led by the United States.

After Iraq was expelled from Kuwait in 1991, the United Nations (UN) Security Council passed more than a dozen resolutions, including requiring Iraq, under international supervision, to destroy its stockpile of chemical and biological agents and all supporting subsystems. Iraq was also required not to have or develop nuclear weapons, nuclear-weapons-usable material, or have ballistic missiles able to travel farther than 100 miles.

Saddam Hussein's lack of cooperation with arms inspectors became a major issue over a period of years as Iraq failed to account for stockpiles of weapons of mass destruction. Finally, in the absence of a clear United Nations resolution to take military action against Iraq, an international military coalition led by the United States invaded Iraq in 2003.

The invasion goals were reportedly to seize stores of weapons of mass destruction in Iraq, remove Hussein from power, and relieve the Iraqi people from the abuses of power,

Box 7–2
Views of the Iraqi War, 2003–2016

In 2016, England's government released its lessons learned from their participation in the Iraq War in the Chilcot Report. Notably, as some Americans had previously asserted, the report concluded that the war was based on (U.S.) intelligence that was flawed and unchallenged.[35] The existence of substantial stockpiles of weapons of mass destruction was overstated. Largely ignored before the 2003 invasion was the caution offered by Russian Foreign Minister Igor Ivanov, that such an action, if not sanctioned by the United Nations, "is only capable of worsening the already difficult situation *in the region*."[36]

There was a feeling among some U.S. government and military leaders that "Saddam may be a son-of-a-bitch, but at least he's our son-of-a-bitch," referring to Saddam Hussein's continuing war against Iran, which occupied Iran with a constant struggle for nearly eight years and away from sponsoring terrorism in the international arena. Nonetheless, 74 percent of Americans polled in 2003 supported the invasion, but by 2007, there was a reversal of public opinion: 67 percent concluded the war was not going well and 54 percent said invading Iraq was the wrong decision.[37]

De-Ba'athification
A term used to signify the elimination and subsequent banning of all members of the Ba'ath Party of Saddam Hussein from future Iraqi politics after the Second Gulf War (2003).

oppression, and corruption. Subsequently, Saddam Hussein was captured, tried by Iraqi authorities, and executed in 2006. Saddam Hussein's power came from the Ba'ath political party. Until an Iraqi interim government was formed in 2004, the country was governed by the Coalition Provisional Authority led by former U.S. Ambassador L. Paul Bremer. Under strong U.S. prodding, the coalition authority purged all mid- and senior-level Ba'athist party members from their military and civil positions, the so-called "**de-Ba'athification**" of Iraq. They were thought to be too corrupt and too loyal to their former leader, Saddam Hussein, to be a constructive part of a new government. Although some of the purging guidelines were relaxed the following year by the interim government, an estimated 80,000 to 150,000 people were eliminated from the Iraqi government.

Several months after the 2003 Iraqi Invasion, Abu Musab al Zarqawi and his Jama'at al-Tawhid group entered Iraq with significant military goods and training. Al Zarqawi's overall goal was to start a war in the Middle East that would crush Western influence and usher in a new Islamic-dominated world. Immediately, however, he needed to destabilize Iraq and create what Afghanistan had been under the Taliban, a glorified Islamic state practicing the Sunni tradition. He attracted many disgruntled Iraqi Sunnis who had been discharged from their duties by the Coalition Provisional Authority, as well as a variety of foreign fighters. As a radicalized Sunni, he attacked both coalition forces and Shiites, hoping to create open fighting between Iraq Sunnis and Shias to create even more chaotic conditions. In 2004, al Zarqawi pledged loyalty to al Qaeda and his new group became known as "al Qaeda in Iraq (AQI)." His tenure was short-lived, however; on June 7, 2006, he was killed by an American airstrike specifically targeting him. (Refer to Chapter 4.)

Following al Zarqawi's death, Abu Ayyub al Masri assumed leadership of AQI. A few months later, he announced the establishment of the next evolution of the group to the Islamic State in Iraq (ISI). The primary focus of this group was to begin a much larger movement across the Middle East that attempted to unify several resistant groups within Iraq as well as recruit new fighters to the entire area under the ISI title. During 2007 and 2008, the insurgent ISI was driven into the northern part of Iraq, and developed a stronghold in Mosul.[38] Its numbers were strongly diminished from 15,000 fighters to 3,800 due to deaths and captures by coalition forces.[39] The flow of foreign fighters also slowed from 120 per month to five or six.[40] Hence, two major factors contributed to the decline of the Islamic State in Iraq (ISI): (1) a surge in the number of U.S. troops in Iraq and (2) a growing discontent by Iraqi Sunnis against increasing numbers of foreign fighters in ISI. The Islamic State in Iraq had become too extreme in their version of Islam, conducting barbaric assassinations, beheadings, and crucifixions among mainstream Iraqi Sunnis who did not join their call for a new country, a new Islamic caliphate starting in the geographical location of Iraq. Thus, individual Iraqi Sunnis who had once been loyal to Saddam Hussein and continued to desire an independent country of Iraq rallied to U.S. forces. Today, many of these same individuals make up the ranks of the nearly 100,000 newly trained, Iraqi Army fighting against the Islamic State.[41]

In 2010, Abu Bakr al-Baghdadi became the new leader of ISI and called for the development of a new world Islamic caliphate … the Islamic State. (Refer to Chapter 4.)

The transformation of ISI from a declining terrorist movement to a new, vibrant, and growing embryonic Islamic State involved the following factors:

1. The emergence of al-Baghdadi as a leader who called for worldwide Islamic support was Iraqi, had jihadist experience with al Qaeda, military experience fighting the coalition forces, was religiously educated, charismatic, and articulate. Further, al-Baghdadi represented a new type of leadership that enjoined the ideas of other leaders within the radical Islamic revolution. He was successful in expressing the need for a worldwide Islamic state that would act as a theocracy, or religious government based on the Holy Qur'an and the word of Muhammad.

2. While confined in Camp Bucca (a large camp where some 24,000 fighters from various Iraq insurgencies were held in early 2000), al-Baghdadi was exposed to many different ideas, tactics that had worked and failed on the battlefield, and things that had worked well and poorly in other terrorist movements, such as failing to provide fighters with the support they needed to be successful. For al-Baghdadi and many other prisoners, Camp Bucca became advanced education in the theory and practice of insurgency.

3. The most important of al-Baghdadi's Bucca experiences was his exposure to military and civilian personnel who had been expelled in the "de-Ba'athification." This point cannot be over emphasized. Some number of them had attended American military schools, were battle hardened by eight years of fighting Iran, and had commanded everything from small to large infantry, artillery, armor, intelligence, counterintelligence, logistics, and other units in combat. Similarly, he had contact with civilians who had accounting, personnel management, engineering, city management, and information systems skills.

4. Following attacks on Sunni leaders in Iraqi by then-dominant Shi'a government officials, members of the Islamic State struck back at the government with a wave of bombings, including in the capital of Baghdad. The number of Sunni and foreign recruits slowly increased and al-Baghdadi began recruiting people he met in Camp Bucca.

5. In 2011, the coalition forces withdrew and the Iraqi government became totally responsible for fighting the insurgencies. Surprisingly, it was Ayman al-Zawahiri, Al Qaeda's leader, who apparently directed AQI to go to Syria and fight Bashir Assad's forces. In Syria, AQI quickly became known as Jabhat al-Nusra, or the al-Nusra Front, and members of ISI were ordered to focus on overcoming the Shiite government of Iraq. Al-Baghdadi disregarded the order and quickly began a strong ISI presence in Syria. His movement quickly became known as the Islamic State in Iraq and Syria (ISIS).

6. During 2012–2013, ISIS was credited with fighting their way into prisons in Mosul and Tikrit and freeing Sunni insurgents, which increased its visibility and growing favorable opinion within the Iraqi tribal population.[42] While many of these freed Islamic jihadists were common fighters, there were also skilled bomb makers, computer technicians, trained snipers, and other military specialists among them.

7. In Syria during 2013, al-Baghdadi rebadged ISIS more broadly, as the Islamic State in the Levant (ISIL). The historic and broader geographic area known as the Levant includes all or parts of Israel, Palestine, Lebanon, Jordan, Syria, Cyprus, Egypt, and Iraq.

8. In early 2014, members of al Qaeda diminished within the leadership ranks of ISIL and the distinction between the two groups became almost nonexistent. During 2014, ISIL forces dramatically seized large portions of Iraq, four large cities, oil fields, refinery facilities, military installations, and banks. These gains were made while they were virtually unopposed. Two Iraqi Army divisions, a fighting force of 30,000 men, retreated when approached by just 800 ISIL fighters.[43] ISIL stripped military bases of armored vehicles, artillery, small arms, munitions, and other goods. ISIL had become a regional power, pillaging banks of over $480 million, developing infrastructure with a strong economic base of oil trade and refinement, and, of course, building a strong and well-armed military.[44]

9. Simultaneously, al-Baghdadi announced the establishment of a worldwide Islamic caliphate, a new Islamic State, sprawling over Northern Iraq and parts of Syria. As noted in Chapter 4 and earlier in this chapter, he invited Muslims from all over the world to bring their households and rush to be part of the new caliphate. They would be given homes, and promises of a new life, children and women would be educated in the Sunni tradition, and men would have productive jobs … the dreams of a new Islamic renaissance had emerged.

10. Al-Baghdadi's statements precipitated a great Islamic migration from over 100 countries, with an estimated 30,0000 new fighters arriving in Iraq since 2016. Al-Baghdadi had set the Islamic State in motion and become the new "Caliph Ibrahim," presiding over the caliphate and Sunni Muslims everywhere. He has called for all Muslim to recognize the authority of the Islamic State as the new and pure religious state: an Islamic Caliphate where everyone practices the same Muslim faith. (Refer to Chapter 4.)

IS Sources of Revenue

IS is the richest and most powerful terrorist organization in history. Its financing strategy is based on controlling the territory it conquers to control and exploit the natural resources therein.[45] This makes IS financially self-sufficient and economically diverse. People living in conquered territory are also exploited by extortion, fees, confiscations, and criminal activity. The primary competing model is used by al Qaeda and most other terrorist movements: Without control of a territory, they are heavily dependent on donations from criminal activity, as well as individuals and institutions. The financial difference between IS and other terrorist movements can be reduced to self-sufficiency versus dependency.

IS places a very strong emphasis on finance, including income and careful accounting of expenditures. This emphasis is reflected in the position held by the Minister of General Finance (see Figure 7–4), who is on an equal footing with the other ministers who form the Cabinet. This figure reflects the upper reaches of a well-organized bureaucratic organizational structure. Although between January 2015 and March 2016, IS lost territory, it still controls vast natural resources and other streams of revenue. A French think tank asserts that the economic sanctions on IS are not working because they do not address its economic model.

The loss of territory, aging equipment, lack of technical expertise, inability to get replacement parts, airstrikes, and advancement on the ground by a coalition of forces led by the United States, and the flight of millions of people from Iraq and Syria caused IS's income to drop about $500 million between 2014 and 2015, to around $2.5 billion. A French terrorist think tank believes that economic sanctions have only a limited effect because they don't directly address the IS

FIGURE 7–3

Sources of IS Income in 2015
The total income was $2.4 billion. Extortion and sales of oil and natural gas on the black market accounted for 72 percent of total revenues. "K&R" stands for kidnapping and ransom.

(Jean-Charles Brisard and Damien Martinez, Coordinators, "ISID Financing, 2015 (Center for the Analysis of Terrorism, 2016), http:// cat-int.org/wp-content/uploads /2017/03/ISIS-Financing-2015 -Report.pdf, accessed April 3, 2017).

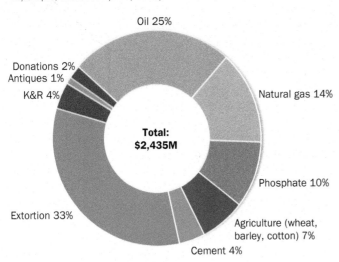

Oil 25%
Natural gas 14%
Donations 2%
Antiques 1%
K&R 4%
Total: $2,435M
Phosphate 10%
Extortion 33%
Agriculture (wheat, barley, cotton) 7%
Cement 4%

FIGURE 7–4

The upper portion of the organizational structure of IS showing the prominent position occupied by the Minister of General Finances. The eight ministers form the Cabinet, which reports directly to Abu Bakr al-Baghdadi.

(Jean-Charles Brisard and Damien Martinez, Coordinators, "ISID Financing, 2015 (Center for the Analysis of Terrorism, 2016), http:// cat-int.org/wp-content/uploads/ 2017/03/ISIS-Financing-2015 -Report.pdf, accessed April 3, 2017).

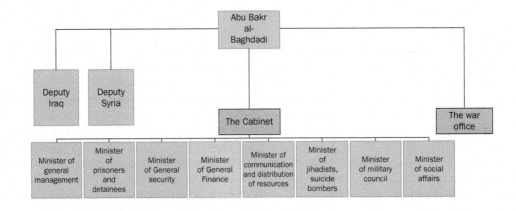

Abu Bakr al-Baghdadi
Deputy Iraq
Deputy Syria
The Cabinet
The war office
Minister of general management
Minister of prisoners and detainees
Minister of General security
Minister of General Finance
Minister of communication and distribution of resources
Minister of jihadists, suicide bombers
Minister of military council
Minister of social affairs

Quick Facts
U.S. Police Officer Arrested for Financially Aiding Islamic State

Terrorist organizations received money from some of the most unlikely sources. In August 2016, the first-ever arrest occurred of a U.S. police officer for financially supporting an undercover agent who posed as an individual who traveled abroad to join the Islamic State. The Washington Metropolitan Transit Authority (WMTA) officer, Nicholas Young, had been under investigation for over five years due to his association with individuals who supported IS

financially and had plotted to commit a terrorist act inside the U.S. Young had been a sworn police officer with WMTA since 2003.

Source: U.S. Department of Justice, "Fairfax Man Arrested Attempting to Support ISIL" (August 3, 2016). See: https://justice.gov/usao-edva/pr/fairfax-man-arrested-attempting-support-isil.

---

finance model, which is unprecedented for a terrorist organization: exploiting the natural and other resources in the territory it controls.

Motivation-Based Typologies

Motivation-based typologies are the most numerous of terrorism typologies. The types of terrorism identified in motivation-based typologies vary from one such typology to another. For the remainder of this chapter, the focus is on state-involved terrorism and single/special issue terrorism. In Chapter 8, the discussion of typologies of terrorism continues, focusing on those movements spawned by separatist or nationalist intentions, left- and right-wing sociopolitical changes, and radicalized religious causes.

State-Involved Terrorism

State-involved terrorism occurs when a national government supports, fosters, or commits acts of terrorism. Briefly, state-involved terrorism has four components: (1) State terrorism is the case in which an established government uses terrorism against its citizens and sometimes visitors within the confines of that country's national borders. (2) State-enabled terrorism occurs when a national government passively allows the presence of terrorists. The state neither provides material assistance nor conducts operations against the terrorists with the expectation that attacks will only be executed in other countries. (3) State-sponsored terrorism results when a government actively supports terrorism, typically as a tool of national foreign policy. (4) State-perpetrated/international terrorism ensues when a government uses its own security force operatives to commit terrorism in foreign countries, such as assassinating their expatriates who are former governmental officials or fermenting dissent or rebellion against the government of their home country.

Because terrorism is a tactic used both by governments and other entities, such as insurgents, the question fairly arises as to which, if either, really has the best interests of the people in mind. Long a champion of human rights, the United States has also turned a blind eye to terrorism on occasion as a matter of convenient foreign policy. Illustratively, the United States was well aware of Iraq's Saddam Hussein's use of terrorism against his own people to remain in power. However, it was ignored and we provided foreign aid to Iraq from 1980 to 1988 as it waged war against Iran, which was a nation hostile to the United States.

State Terrorism

State terrorism is terrorism committed by a national government, inside of its national borders and directed at its own people and sometimes visitors. This action contravenes a state's moral and legal duty to protect its citizens. The purpose of state terrorism is to repress and instill fear in citizens and sometimes visitors to consolidate the ruling regime's power and to maintain control over the country's civilian population. **Genocide**, the systematic killing of all or part of a racial, ethnic, religious, or national group within a specific country or area, is often linked to totalitarian regimes. These actions are often carried out by a state's security, police, intelligence, and/or military organizations, usually directed by one leader in an effort to "purge" or "clean" an indigenous population from the targeted group.

Some terrorism experts do not regard state terrorism as terrorism, preferring instead to label it as some form of political violence, or criminal acts such as genocide or murder.

State terrorism
Terrorism committed by a national government, inside of its national borders and directed at its own citizens and sometimes visitors.

Genocide
The systematic killing of all or part of a racial, ethnic, religious, or national group within a specific country or area; often linked to totalitarian regimes.

Box 7-3
Leaders of Totalitarian Governments that Conducted State Terrorism: Adolf Hitler, Josef Stalin, and Mao Tse-Tung

Adolf Hitler (1889–1945) became Chancellor of Germany in 1932 and ruled it as a dictator from the following year until his suicide near the end of World War II in the European Theater (1945). During the Holocaust, the Nazis killed millions of Jews from Germany and other European countries without even a pretense of a trial. Hitler imprisoned or executed his own citizens who were mentally ill, physically impaired, homosexuals, gypsies, political opponents, dissidents, Jehovah's Witnesses, and Jews. Post–World War II, many German officials were convicted of war crimes for atrocities committed in the concentration camps and elsewhere.

David Cole/Alamy Stock Photo

Pictorial Press Ltd/Alamy Stock Photo

Joseph Stalin (1878–1953) ruled Russia as a dictator (1928–1953). Without any trace of introspection, Hitler remarked of Stalin's murderous dictatorship: "He is probably sick in the brain...his bloody regime can otherwise not be explained."[46] Stalin moved national resources from agricultural to industry. He removed farmers from their lands and seized them as state property. The land was pooled to create large state-owned farming "collectives." Farmers working the land received just a small amount of what was grown. The rest was sold and the profit used to create industries. In doing so, perhaps seven million people were killed outright or deliberately starved to death in "troublesome" regions in the great famines of 1930–1933.[47] These victims were characterized as "socially harmful elements...enemies of the people."[48]

Stalin also instituted great "chistkas" (literally cleansing, but meaning purges) of political opponents and dissenters, particularly during 1935–1938, killing five million and sending millions into gulags (penal camps).[49] Russian historian Rogovin reports that during the purges a "court" would dispose of 500 cases in a single evening at a rate of several "trials" a minute.[50] The courts didn't have time to read the summons, let alone read the dossiers.[51] Some defendants were arbitrarily shot while others received various prison sentences.[52] Estimates of how many Russians Stalin killed vary considerably; a common uppermost estimate is 40 million,[53] which represents roughly one in every four Russians. In contrast, the Soviet Union experienced 8.6 million military combat deaths fighting the Germans in World War II.[54]

Mao Zedong (1893–1976), also translated as Mao Tse-Tung, received some formal education, but was largely self-taught.[55] In 1921, Mao helped formed the Chinese Communist Party (CCP). During the 1920s, the CCP was forced out of the larger Kuomintang (National People's Party, also known as the Nationalist Party), which

was oriented toward a democratic parliament and some socialist programs. The CCP and the Nationalist Party soon were fighting each other militarily. As a left-wing revolutionary devoted to overthrowing the established government, Mao resorted to terror tactics to control his small army; illustrative, on just one occasion he executed 3,000 officers and men who questioned his rule.[56]

The CCP and Nationalist Party called a truce in 1937 to independently fight the Japanese during World War II. Following the war in 1945, they again turned on each other. In 1949, the CCP militarily defeated the Kuomintang, forcing it to flee to Taiwan. Mao Tse-Tung announced the formation of the Communist People's Republic of China on the mainland. Once in power, Mao quickly launched a violent campaign to consolidate his power and executed perhaps 3,000,000 "class enemies."[57] As a totalitarian leader his policies resulted in some 30 million people starving.[58] However, unlike Stalin, Mao did not deliberately set out to starve "troublesome" regions; his policies were simply disastrous.

What compels some government leaders to be so harsh on their own people? Is it is just a coincidence that Hitler, Stalin, and Mao came to power at roughly the same period of time in history? Or is this period of time just unique in the annals of history? Why?

MARKA/Alamy Stock Photo

Others think that because the state has a legitimate monopoly on the use of force, it cannot be terrorism even if the violence is directed at its own citizens. We hold with other scholars, such as Baserne, who believe a state can turn terrorism inward, and be guilty of both state terrorism and genocide.[59] If a government terrorizes its own citizens as well as citizens of other countries, the character of those acts is the same. Is terrorism less repugnant when the state's victims are also its own citizens? We think not.

Terrorism by totalitarian states is the most extreme and often the most sustained form of state terrorism.[60] Unfortunately, it is the most common as well. The three most widely known names in state terrorism are Adolf Hitler, Josef Stalin, and Mao Tse-Tung (see Box 7–3).

There are numerous other examples of state terrorism, including the death squads in Brazil, El Salvador, Honduras, and Guatemala. In the sections that follow, state terrorism is further explored by examining lesser-known events in several countries.

The Dominican Republic—The Parsley Massacre: Ayuso regards the **Parsley Massacre** as "one of the ugliest and least known major events of the twentieth century."[61] Hispaniola, a major Caribbean island, hosts two nations, the Spanish-speaking Dominican Republic and Haiti, which has two official languages, French and Haitian Creole. In 1937, Dominican Republic dictator Rafael Trujillo alleged official outrage that Haitians were illegally crossing the border, taking up residence, using his country resources, and stealing from its citizens.[62] Trujillo directed his military to go the borderland, hold up a sprig of parsley to everyone they encountered, and ask them to say what it was. Those that answered "perejil" (parsley) in Spanish with the proper trill of the "r" were passed by because their answer suggested they were native Spanish speakers. Those who lacked the trill were instantly killed, often with a bayonet, on the presumption they were Haitians.[63] Perhaps as many as 30,000 people were murdered in what the Dominicans call "El Corte," the cutting.[64] Some historians note that Trujillo was an anti-Haitian and imply that he may have been a racist as well. They suggest his real intent was not protecting his citizens or maintaining territorial integrity, but racism: He wanted to "whiten" the Dominican Republic and rid it of the Afro-Haitians.[65]

Haiti—The Tonton Macoute: President Francois Duvalier ("Papa Doc," 1907–1971) ruled Haiti from 1957 to 1971.[66] He survived a military coup in 1959 and quickly took measures to ensure another would not occur, substantially dismantling the army and staffing its remnants with loyal allies. Papa Doc also created a volunteer private force answerable only to him, the **Tonton Macoute**,[67] which was also the name of a mythological Haitian bogeyman that kidnapped disobedient children in a sack and ate them for breakfast.[68] Carrying machetes and some firearms, the Tonton Macoute hacked to death or shot opposition leaders and reformists in extrajudicial executions, often at night, and put their victims' bodies on public display[69] to strike terror in the people. Soon, anyone suspected of harboring anti-Papa Doc sentiments, even in remote villages, was murdered. In 1971, Papa Doc's son, Jean Claude Duvalier ("Baby Doc," 1951–) came to power and ruled Haiti until he was deposed in 1986. By that time, the Tonton Macoute had killed an estimated 60,000 Haitians.[70] Aponte describes the Tonton Macoute as "the central nervous system of Haiti's reign of terror."[71] Its violence continued for years even after Baby Doc lost power. Notably, in 1988, the Tonton Macoute invaded a mass at St. Jean Bosco Catholic Church in Port-au-Prince, killing 12 parishioners and wounding another 77 using spears, machetes, and guns.[72] Eventually, Haitians turned on the Macoute, occasionally killing them.

Cambodia—The Khmer Rouge: The communist **Khmer Rouge** (Red Cambodians) ruled during 1975–1979, having come to power by overthrowing the existing government. Its leader, Pol Pot, wanted to turn the clock back to "**Zero Year**," empty the cities, and return to an agrarian society. He set in motion a massacre of Buddhists, Catholics, Muslims, intellectuals, businessmen, foreigners, and other classes, such as people who wore glasses (which suggested they were literate), spoke a foreign language (possibly tainted by outside ideas), or lacked any agricultural or mechanical skills (not useful in the future).[73] Approximately 1.7 million Cambodians died from executions, overwork, starvation, and disease before the Khmer Rouge were overthrown by the intervention of Vietnam.[74]

Parsley Massacre
1937, Dominican Republic dictator Trujillo ordered the military to kill all people immediately who could not pronounce the Spanish word for parsley with the proper Spanish trill on the "r," on the suspicion they were Haitians who had illegally entered the country.

Tonton Macoute
A long-standing private force answering only to the president of Haiti. Hacked and shot to death opposition leaders and reformists in extra-judicial executions.

Khmer Rouge
"Red Cambodians," communists who came to power by overthrowing the existing government. See Zero year.

Zero year
Pol Pot, leader of the Khmer Rouge, wanted to "turn the clock back" to "zero year." This "required" emptying the cities and returning to an agrarian society. In doing so 1.7 million Cambodians were killed, often beaten to death because they were Catholics or some other religion, businessmen, intellectuals, and others.

Information Link
This box belongs with the section below on Argentina. It is wildly out of place. Consequences continue from Argentina's period of the "disappeared." People continue to search for missing family members and when a child is found, that child has to decided what to do with new information about who they are versus the life they have been leading. Visit www.nytimes.com/2015/10/12/us/children-of-argentinas-disappeared-reclaim-past-with-help.html and see and hear from those who lost family members and those who were found.

FIGURE 7–5
Tuol Sleng Genocide Museum shows thousands of skulls from the "killing fields" in Cambodia under the Khmer Rouge (1975–1979).

(Photo courtesy of Robert W. Taylor)

Military junta
A government led by a group or committee of military leaders in a specific country; a military dictatorship.

Desaparecidos
From roughly the early 1970s to the early 1980s, a military junta (group) ruled Argentina. The junta labeled anyone who opposed them as communists or subversives. When the junta came to power, it had a "kill list" of perhaps 30,000 people who were abducted and placed in concentration camps. Most often they were killed. Their bodies were thrown from aircraft into the ocean or other large bodies of water and the deceased were never found. Therefore, they were called the disappeared. Children born to women in the camps were given to families the junta thought were "reliable." Children were also abducted for the same purpose.

Kurds
A Middle East ethnic minority that does not have a homeland. Kurds live in parts of Iraq, Turkey, Syria, and Iran.

Argentina—"The Disappeared": State domestic terrorism occurred during Argentina's "dirty war" against opposition leaders and leftists, as well as their families and friends. The dates assigned to the dirty war vary, but it was conducted roughly between the mid-1970s and early-mid-1980s when a **military junta** ruled the country. In the course of combating what the junta described as a subversive Marxist threat, government agents abducted perhaps as many as 30,000 unionists, intellects, reporters, Jews, and others, of which approximately 30 percent were women."[75] The abductees were confined without due process in one of 340 detention camps where they were interrogated, tortured, and sometimes executed.[76] Approximately 500 children were also abducted or taken from their mothers at birth in concentration camps and given to "reliable" parents in favor with junta.[77] Other children were also abducted for the same purpose. Some women arrived at camps pregnant and others became so after rapes by guards. After nursing their babies, the women were "transferred." They were drugged, placed on roughly weekly "death flights," and thrown from aircraft into the Atlantic or other large bodies of water.[78] Because their bodies and those of executed men were seldom found, they were collectively referred to as the **desaparecidos**, the disappeared.

Iraq—The Kurds: In 1987, the Iraq–Iran war was winding down. The President of Iraq, Saddam Hussein (1937–2006), ordered planes to drop poison gas on Kurdish civilians living in the Northern portion of his country. Hussein believed the ethnic minority Iraqi **Kurds** had been assisting his enemies, the Iranians, and in retaliation ordered his Air Force to deploy the gas. Estimates of deaths range from 3,200 to 5,000 with perhaps

Quick Facts
"An Act of Charity"

Jorge Rafael Videla (1925–2013) was Chief of Staff of Argentina's military forces. He led the 1975 coup that effectively let him function as President of Argentina. After being forced from office he was tried on several charges and sentenced to life in prison. Videla admitted that prior to the revolution, its leaders drew up a "first kill" list. Those on the list were labeled as "subversives,"

their children were taken from them, and the "subversive" parents were summarily tortured and executed.

Videla called his actions (taking or abducting the children from their parents prior to their execution and giving them to individuals that supported his regime) as an "act of charity."[79]

another 10,000 injured.[80] Hussein also pursued a general policy of ethnic cleansing of both the Kurds and Shiite Muslims and also murdered all who opposed his regime's policies. Numerous mass graves have been found attesting to the butchery authorized by the late Hussein. Although the actual number of those murdered will never be fully known, it was certainly hundreds of thousands.

Syria—April 4, 2017, a lone plane fired one rocket believed to be filled with poison gas in the insurgent-held town of Khan Sheikhoun. At least 58 deaths resulted and more than 500 people sought treatment at the hospital for respiratory problems. Entire families died right where they were standing. The Syrian government denied involvement and blamed it on a poison gas factory the rebels were building that exploded.[81] The Russians said they flew no missions near the area of the gas attack. On April 5: (1) the Russians claim they hit a rebel munitions site that had chemical weapons. (2) The United Kingdom's Foreign Minister, Boris Johnson declared, "I've seen absolutely nothing to lead us to think that it was anything other, but the regime."[82] (3) President Trump blamed President Assad and called on its patrons—Iran and Russia—to prevent another occurrence.[83] There are prior reports of IS flying drones, but not planes and it is generally thought the Syrian government had both the gas and the motive to use it. Moreover, it has previously used gas with impunity. On April 6, 2017, the Syrian Air Force under the direction of al-Assad dropped canisters of sarin gas (or a similar compound) on the defenseless city of Khan Sheikhoun in Northern Syria. Over 70 innocent people, including children, were killed, and another hundred wounded from the asphyxiation caused by the chemical weapon. As a result, President Trump ordered a strike of 59 Tomahawk missiles that hit the air base from which al-Assad's planes flew. The result was significant damage to warplanes and ammunition depots, including those that may have held other chemical weapons. The strike was a strong diplomatic statement to Syria, as well as the primary countries that support the al-Assad regime (Iran and Russia): The United States will no longer stand by and watch the horror of war in Syria that takes the lives of innocent people, and more important, that the use of chemical, biological, and nuclear weapons will simply not be tolerated.[84]

State-Enabled Terrorism

State-enabled terrorism occurs when a state doesn't provide direct support to a terrorist group so long as it conducts no operations against the state or its citizens. The state (1) passively allows its own nongovernmental entities and individual supporters to assist it; (2) implicitly condones the existence of the terrorist group by not conducting operations against it; and/or (3) fosters a safe haven for a terrorist group because *it cannot govern* its own territory, the case of the failed state.[85]

    Safe havens also include ungoverned, under-governed, or ill-governed geographic areas where terrorists are able to organize, plan, raise funds, communicate, recruit, train, transit, and operate in relative security because of the government's *lack of political will.* A 2015 U.S. Department of State report identified Somalia, Mali, Egypt, the Southern Philippines, Iraq, Lebanon, Libya, Afghanistan, Pakistan, and Venezuela.

    National governments are the primary building blocks of order. To a substantial degree, international security relies on states to prevent chaos at home so they do not become incubators for international anarchy and terrorism.[86] Failed states are in default of meeting this international political obligation. Afghanistan, Angola, Burundi, the Democratic Republic of the Congo, Liberia, Sierra Leone, Somalia, and Sudan are or have been have failed nations.[87]

State-enabled terrorism
A state that tolerates the presence of terrorists in the country so long as they only attack other states and citizens of other states.

Safe havens
A place or situation that allows terrorists and other types of criminals to operate with relative impunity because the state is unable or lacks the political will to expel them.

Quick Facts
Ungoverned Space

Few places in the world are literally "ungoverned"; the term also includes places that are under-governed, misgoverned, areas where governance is contested, and exploitable arenas, such as virtual safe havens on the Internet. Ungoverned areas are not necessarily terrorist safe havens; they are prospective or potential terrorist safe havens.[88]

FIGURE 7–6
In Buenos Aires during 2012, people continue to search for the babies and children stolen from them. About 100 adults have learned of their real families. Each year, there is a march to commemorate the disappeared and a wall of photographs erected in their remembrance.

(Imago Stock/People/Newscom)

Failed states
States that cannot govern their own territory. Their governments may be unstable, corrupt, cannot provide basic services, their citizens resent the government, and the government cannot guarantee the security of any weapons of mass destruction in its possession. See Collapsed state and Ungoverned space.

Ungoverned space
A government that cannot control its borders usually ends with space it cannot govern, "ungoverned space." The term also includes space that is misgoverned, under-governed, and where governance is contested. See Failed state and Collapsed state.

Collapsed state
The most extreme example of a failed state. See Ungoverned space and safe haven.

Characteristically, **failed states** (1) may be in conflict or recently emerged from one; (2) have governments that lack stability, are corrupt, and cannot provide basic services to its citizens; (3) are unable to control their borders or their territory, resulting in "**ungoverned space**" for terrorists to occupy;[89] (4) have civilian populations that resent the central government, which provides a pool of potential terrorist recruits;[90] and (5) lack the capacity to guarantee the security of any weapons of mass destruction or other advanced technologies in their possession.[91]

Other ills that result from failed states include increases in criminal and political violence; rising ethnic, religious, and culture hostilities that can spiral into open warfare; a collapsed health system in which infant mortality rates escalate and life expectancies decline; and increasingly severe food shortages that lead to starvation.[92]

Failed states become the equivalent of a corporation's international headquarters for terrorists.[93] They provide the opportunity to acquire territory on a scale much larger than a collection of scattered safe houses—enough to accommodate entire training complexes, arms depots, and communications facilities.[94] Generally, terrorist groups have no desire to assume complete control over an area they occupy; they just want to be unmolested.[95] The desire of radicalized Muslims, such as the Islamic State movement, to create an Islamic state is an exception to this general observation.

At one time Somalia was the most extreme example of a failed state, the **collapsed state**. It is an Eastern African nation that has enabled terrorism. Somalia has a long coastal nation that borders the Indian Ocean and the Gulf of Aden. Transit from Yemen on the Arabian Peninsula to Somalia is easily made by Islamic jihadists by a boat trip of roughly 100 miles. Somalia was without an effective central government since Soviet-supported President Siad Barre was overthrown in 1991 by warring clans. The clans then turned on each other and the country was plunged into chaos, famine, and disease. Somalian warlords regularly hijacked humanitarian shipments of food and medicine, using them to pay their troops and secure the loyalty of their local citizens. During 1992–1994, the United States Army put "boots on the ground" in a humanitarian effort authorized by the United Nations to help stabilize the situation.[96] The movie *Black Hawk Down* (2001) depicts the 1993 U.S. raid to arrest a warlord in Mogadishu, which resulted in Army Rangers being engaged by a numerically superior foe. The Ranger casualties in the battle played a key role in the United States subsequently withdrawing from Somalia without stabilizing the situation.

Somalia once more descended into chaotic conditions largely because of the insurgent radical Islamic al Shabaab movement that affiliated with al-Qaeda in 2012. Beyond politics and

FIGURE 7-7
Members of al-Shabaab parade in Mogadishu, Somalia. Al-Shabaab is a radical Islamic clan based in Somalia that been very active during the last two decades of insurgency in that country. The African Union is an organization of all 55 nations on the African continent. Through its multiyear African Mission in Somalia (AMISOM), al-Shabaab has been degraded by the some of the military forces deployed to assist Somalia. While problems still remain, there have been two presidential elections held, and although they were imperfect as clans jockeyed for control, Somalia is at long last on an upward trajectory.

(AFP/Stringer/Getty Images)

battlefield there has been a humanitarian crisis with perhaps a million or more people who are malnourished and undernourished; in just one four-month period 30,000 children died.[97] There has been some speculation and thinly documented press reports that the United States has been in an alliance with some of the warlords it fought during 1992–1994 to fight al-Shabaab, including use of drones armed with Hellfire missiles being flown in from neighboring countries.[98] If true, the effort would be subject to the criticism that the United States erred by using warlords instead of strengthening and working through the central government.

State-Sponsored Terrorism

State-sponsored terrorism is a relatively recent development. Historically, terrorism has been between a state and a group of people or an organization; however, in the second half of the twentieth century, state-sponsored terrorism grew as states used terrorist individuals and organizations as their proxies in international affairs. Before its breakup in 1991, Russia was particularly adept at working mischief with proxies for its adversaries. Russia has its eye on the Ukraine and is covertly supporting and arming breakaway nationalists rebels in that country.

The U.S. secretary of state issues a report annually and can designate a country as a state sponsor of terrorism if it has repeatedly provided support for acts of international terrorism; upon such a finding, four main categories of sanctions can be applied: (1) restricting the receipt of foreign assistance, (2) a ban on the sale and export of defense materials to it, (3) limiting the export of dual-use material (i.e., materials that can be used for commercial and military purposes, such as highly advanced computers, or that could be used to develop weapons and technologies of mass destruction), and (4) miscellaneous financial and other restrictions.[99]

As of 2015, the U.S. Department of State (USDOS) lists only three state sponsors of terrorism: Iran, Syria, and Sudan:[100]

1. The USDOS considers *Iran* as the "most active state sponsor of terrorism."[101] Iran has been on the USDOS terrorist list since 1984. It supports Hezbollah in Syria and in Iran, Palestinian terrorist groups, Shi'a terrorist groups in Iraq, such as Kata'ib Hezbollah (KH), and is violently opposed to the Sunni-dominated Islamic State movement throughout the Middle East. Iran has also sent its own troops to bolster Syrian President Assad's forces; as well provides arms, financing, and training to other Shi'a fighters supporting the Syrian regime.

State-sponsored terrorism
A relatively recent development. States use terrorist groups as proxies to further their agenda in international affairs.

In 2011, the United States accused Iran of plotting to assassinate the Saudi ambassador to the United States, and planning to attack the Israeli Embassy in Washington, D.C.[102]

2. Since 1979, *Syria* has been on the USDOS terrorist list. It also supports a cross-section of terrorist groups that affect the stability of the region. Politically, financially, and with arms, Syria supports Hezbollah, which is a Shia movement based primarily in Lebanon. Opposed to the existence of Israel, Hezbollah has accumulated significant combat experience during its support of Assad in the Syrian War and large stores of missiles to use against Israel. Consistent with Iran's desire to destabilize the region, Hezbollah, particularly if supported by large numbers of Iran's elite Revolutionary Guard, is Israel's major security concern.

The Syrian government and elite businessmen are complicit in terrorist financing, including money laundering. Unregulated hawalas are often used by terrorists for sending and receiving funds. Iran has also historically supported Hamas. However, Palestinian support for rebels fighting Assad created a chill between the two countries. In early 2017, hardliner Yahya Sinwar became prime minister within the Palestinian Territory, and remains a key figure in Hamas. He is regarded as uncompromising. Since then, there has been a public thawing of Syrian and Hamas relations. By supporting both Hezbollah and Hamas, Syria keeps the region tense and at time in flames.

More distantly, Iran also arms numerous insurgent movements battling coalition forces in Afghanistan and Iraq, as well as providing a transit point through which foreign fighters could enter Iraq to fight coalition forces. Ironically, Syria portrays itself as a victim of terrorism because its opponents are armed.

3. In the mid-1990s, Sudan was a safe haven and training hub for several international terrorist groups, including the Abu Nidal Organization (ANO), Palestine Islamic Jihad, Hamas, Hezbollah, and al Qaeda. It gave sanctuary to Usama bin Laden for five years, and in 1998, al-Qaeda operatives based in Sudan were reportedly involved in the bombing of the American Embassies in Kenya and Tanzania. Insurgencies in Uganda, Tunisia, Kenya, Ethiopia, and Eritrea have also received aid from Sudan. In 1999, Sudan signed the International Convention for the Suppression of Terrorist Bombing and expelled Usama bin Laden. Sudan considers Hamas as the legitimate representative of Palestine and in 2014, allowed Hamas to enter Sudan, travel freely, and raise funds. In 2015, there was some cooperation between the United States and Sudan in reducing that country being used as a transit route by terrorist movements, although al Qaeda and some Islamic State-linked groups still maintained some presence. However, the use of Sudan by Palestinian terrorist groups has declined. Sudan was placed on USDOS's terrorist list in 1993.

Refer to Chapter 4 for a list of other known terrorist groups associated with Iran, Syria, and Sudan.

Cuba was placed on the USDOS's list of state sponsors of terrorism in 1982 because of its efforts to spread communism in South America and Africa. For 33 years it remained there. However, in 2015, it was removed as part of President Obama's push to normalize relations between the two countries. Congress had a 45-day period to object, but did not do so. Figure 7–8 is a wanted poster for Joanne Deborah Chesimard, a convicted murderer of a New Jersey State Police Trooper. She escaped from prison in 1979 and is thought to have entered Cuba in 1984, where she is still believed to reside. In the last four days of President Obama's second term, he signed a law enforcement agreement with Cuba's President Raul Castro on wide-ranging law enforcement topics, including the harboring of law enforcement fugitives. The agreement stipulated that no fugitives residing in Cuba would be returned to the United States.

Some members of Congress believe North Korea should be included in the USDOS's next list of state sponsors of terrorism. It has attacked South Korea numerous times without provocation, provided arms to be used by Hezbollah against Israel, abducted an estimated 180,000 people from twelve countries,[103] committed genocide against its own people, and exported technology that could lead to the proliferation of nuclear weapons.[104] North Korea refers to its own nuclear capability as its "treasured sword."[105]

Information Link
Stanford University has one of the very best sites for information on terrorist organizations with current, informative profiles of them and useful maps. Think of some terrorist organizations you'd like to know more about and visit this site.

Act of Terrorism - Domestic Terrorism; Unlawful Flight to Avoid Confinement - Murder

JOANNE DEBORAH CHESIMARD

Multimedia: Images

Aliases:

Assata Shakur, Joanne Byron, Barbara Odoms, Joanne Chesterman, Joan Davis, Justine Henderson, Mary Davis, Pat Chesimard, Jo-Ann Chesimard, Joanne Debra Chesimard, Joanne D. Byron, Joanne D. Chesimard, Joanne Davis, Chesimard Joanne, Ches Chesimard, Sister-Love Chesimard, Joann Debra Byron Chesimard, Joanne Deborah Byron Chesimard, Joan Chesimard, Josephine Henderson, Carolyn Johnson, Carol Brown, "Ches"

DESCRIPTION

Date(s) of Birth Used	July 16, 1947; August 19, 1952	Hair:	Black/Gray
Place of Birth:	New York City, New York	Eyes:	Brown
Height:	5'7"	Sex:	Female
Weight:	135 to 150 pounds	Race:	Black
		Citizenship:	American

Scars and Marks: Chesimard has scars on her chest, abdomen, left shoulder, and left knee.

Remarks: She may wear her hair in a variety of styles and dress in African tribal clothing.

CAUTION

Joanne Chesimard is wanted for escaping from prison in Clinton, New Jersey, while serving a life sentence for murder. On May 2, 1973, Chesimard, who was part of a revolutionary extremist organization known as the Black Liberation Army, and two accomplices were stopped for a motor vehicle violation on the New Jersey Turnpike by two troopers with the New Jersey State Police. At the time, Chesimard was wanted for her involvement in several felonies, including bank robbery. Chesimard and her accomplices opened fire on the troopers. One trooper was wounded and the other was shot and killed execution-style at point-blank range. Chesimard fled the scene, but was subsequently apprehended. One of her accomplices was killed in the shoot-out and the other was also apprehended and remains in jail.

In 1977, Chesimard was found guilty of first degree murder, assault and battery of a police officer, assault with a dangerous weapon, assault with intent to kill, illegal possession of a weapon, and armed robbery. She was sentenced to life in prison. On November 2, 1979, Chesimard escaped from prison and lived underground before being located in Cuba in 1984. She is thought to currently still be living in Cuba.

REWARD

The FBI is offering a reward of up to $1,000,000 for information directly leading to the apprehension of Joanne Chesimard.

SHOULD BE CONSIDERED ARMED AND DANGEROUS

If you have any information concerning this person, please call the FBI Toll-Free tip line at 1-800-CALL-FBI (1-800-225-5324). You may also contact your local FBI office , or the nearest American Embassy or Consulate.

FIGURE 7–8

Wanted poster for Joanne Deborah Chesimard, the first woman to be placed on the FBI's Most Wanted Terrorists list.

(Federal Bureau of Investigation)

There are different ways of thinking about state-sponsored terrorism, such as (1) the amount of control a sponsor is actually able to exert over a proxy, (2) the amount and kinds of support (e.g., substantial amounts of arms and ammunition), (3) the frequency of such support (e.g., only infrequent sharing of low-level intelligence on anticipated movement

Box 7–4
The Assassination Attempt on Pope John Paul II

In 1981, Pope John Paul II, a native of Poland, was riding in an open car in St. Peter's Square in Vatican City when he was shot four times by Mehmet Ali Agca, a Turkish citizen and a member of the ultra-nationalist "Grey Wolves" in Turkey. Before attacking the Pope, Agca was imprisoned for murdering a newspaper editor. He mysteriously escaped from a maximum prison in Turkey, traveled to Italy, and attempted to assassinate Pope John Paul II on May 13, 1981.[106] For that attempt he served 19 years in an Italian prison, and then was deported back to Turkey and imprisoned for murder (of the newspaper editor) for another 10 years. When released, he shouted, "I am the Christ eternal. The Gospel is full of mistakes. I will write the Perfect Gospel. Everyone will die by the end of the century."[107]

Agca originally claimed that he shot the Pope at the behest of Russian and Bulgarian secret service agencies, which wanted to eliminate the Pope's influence in Eastern Europe. Agca later recanted those assertions. Perhaps he was afraid of retaliation against his family for the disclosures[108] or because they were untrue.

Based on Agca's statements, do you think that the assassination attempt on Pope John Paul II should have been classified as an act of "state-sponsored terrorism?"

▲ A Polish statue of Pope John Paul II in the standing position.
(Günter Lenz/imageBROKER/Newscom)

---

of vessels in the region), and (4) the degree of openness with which it assists terrorist organizations.

State sponsors of terrorism generally prefer to act covertly, without other nations being aware of their actions (see Box 7–4). Doing so offers a number of advantages: (1) the use of terror groups as proxies offers an attractive alternative to open, all-out warfare because the state's homeland and conventional forces are not placed at risk; (2) compared to conventional warfare it is a low-cost alternative that may have a high impact, such as destabilizing a rival regime or affecting voting outcomes; (3) if the connection to the sponsoring state is discovered, the terrorist attack(s) may not lead to open war (e.g., the attacked state may not be able to stand toe-to-toe with the conventional military forces of the sponsoring nation; it may seek sanctions supported by the international community; or it may simply wait for a more opportune time to seek its revenge, such as waiting until the terrorist sponsoring state is waging war with some other state and therefore weakened); and (4) by acting clandestinely, sponsoring states have plausible deniability.[109]

Periodically, the United States has been accused of being a state sponsor of terror. A common, yet relatively isolated example is our support of the Contras in Nicaragua, which is the largest and least populated country in Central America. In 1979, the left-wing revolutionary **Sandinistas**[110] overthrew President Anastasio Somoza (1925–1980) and began ruling the country; the following year Somoza was assassinated in Paraguay.[111] The Sandinistas were characterized by the United States as puppets of Russia and Cuba, which had established a "communist beachhead" in Central America.[112] The American government was soon supporting a counterrevolutionary force dubbed the "**Contras**," some of which had camps in neighboring Honduras (see Figure 7–9). Reports of atrocities, including murder, rape, torture, and mutilation, committed by the Contras resulted in U.S. military aid to them being officially cut off;[113] human rights groups subsequently reported continuing violations.

Sandinistas
Left-wing revolutionary group that overthrew the government of Nicaragua in 1979.

Contras
Nicaraguan counter-revolutionary group battling the Sandinistas for control of the country (see Sandinistas).

In the mid-1980s, the United States secretly and illegally arranged the sale of military arms to Iran in return for its help in freeing American hostages held in Lebanon by various factions of Iran's proxy, Hezbollah.[114] The profits from these sales were clandestinely used to support the Contras, in contravention of Congressional legislative actions that forbade such assistance.[115] Ultimately, America's clandestine practices were discovered and the resulting "**Iran-Contra Affair**" brought President Reagan's administration under blistering criticisms from the Congress.

Subsequently, Nicaragua sued the United States in the United Nations' International Court of Justice (ICJ). In 1986, the ICJ ruled that the United States had breached its international duty by intervening in Nicaragua's internal affairs by training, arming, equipping, financing, and supplying the Contra forces or otherwise encouraging, supporting, and aiding military and paramilitary actions against Nicaragua and also breached its duty under a friendship treaty.[116] The ICJ noted that although the United States produced a manual on guerrilla war that encouraged the commission of acts contrary to humanitarian law, no such acts were imputable to the United States.[117] The IJC also concluded that the United States had a duty to make reparations to Nicaragua for its breaches of duties and for damages caused, but Nicaragua has never sued to collect damages.

State-Perpetrated/International Terrorism

State-perpetrated/state international terrorism occurs when governments that lack the economic or military resources necessary to achieve their policy objectives use their own internal security forces to commit acts of terrorism on foreign soil to further their agenda or a country with resources chooses to do so using their own operatives. It is this reliance upon and use of the state's own internal resources that distinguishes this type of terrorism from state-sponsored terrorism's use of proxies.

State-perpetrated terrorism has been used to spy on, harass, and assassinate a state's vocal dissidents and opposition leaders living abroad. Several examples illustrate this point. Orlando Letelier (1932–1976) was Chilean President Allende's (1908–1973) Ambassador to the United States (1971–1973).[118] Allende was overthrown in a coup orchestrated by General Pinochet, who ordered Letelier arrested; he was later released, came to the United States,[119] and became a powerful voice against Pinochet. In 1976, Letelier was assassinated in Washington, D.C. by a bomb planted under his car; his American administrative assistant Ronni Moffitt was also killed in the incident.[120] Two men with ties to the Chilean secret service were later convicted for the bombing.[121]

Since Iran's Islamic Revolution in 1979, at least 83 Iranian exiles living in foreign countries have been murdered by Iranian officials.[122] Iran's former Prime Minister Bakhtiar (1914–1991) fled to Paris, where he led the Iranian government in exile. Although he had survived a previous attempt on his life, he was not so fortunate in 1991. Three Iranian men

Iran-Contra Affair
Reports of human rights violations/atrocities by the Contras caused Congress to prohibit further U.S. funding for them. To secure the release of hostages taken during Iran's 1979 Islamic Revolution, American illegally sold them arms. The profits were then secretly used to fund the Contras. This became known as the "Iran-Contra Affair" and brought significant Congressional criticism of President Reagan's administration.

State-perpetrated/state international terrorism
A state uses its own internal security forces to commit acts of terrorism in another country to promote its own international policy objectives.

FIGURE 7–9
Anti-Sandinista forces preparing a raid across the Honduras border into Nicaragua to fight the communist Sandinistas during the Iran-Contra Affair.
(Mike Goldwater/Alamy Stock Photo)

entered his home and executed Bakhtiar and his secretary.[123] Two killers were apprehended and convicted; French prosecutors alleged they were tied directly to the Islamic Republic of Iran's Ministry of Intelligence and National Security (VEVAK).[124] In 2012, there was a similar incident. Manssor Arbabsiar, who holds dual U.S. and Iranian citizenship, pled guilty to criminal charges involving a plot to assassinate the Saudi Arabia Ambassador to the United States in a Washington, D.C., restaurant. Arbabsiar admitted that he was acting at the direction of Iranian military officials.[125]

State-perpetrated terrorist acts are also illustrated by planting bombs on airplanes and at popular spots, such as foreign discotheques and hotels, frequented by exiles or civilians from enemy states. For instance, after the United States bombed Libya in 1986 for supporting terrorism, Muammar Gaddafi knew his country could not stand toe-to-toe with the United States militarily. He responded with state-perpetrated terrorism. In 1988, a Libyan intelligence officer, Abdelbaset al-Megrahi, planted a bomb on **Pan Am Flight 103**, flying from England to New York City. The bomb exploded in flight, causing the deaths of all 259 people on board and 11 more in the small village of Lockerbie, Scotland.[126] Al-Megrahi was subsequently found guilty in 2001 of 270 counts of murder and sentenced to life in prison, and in 2001, Libya offered $2.7 billion to settle claim by the families of those killed in what has been called the "Lockerbie Bombing."[127]

Pan Am Flight 103
Blown up in 1988 by a Libyan intelligence officer killing 259 people on board, as well as some people on the ground in Scotland, over which the plane exploded. Believed to have been ordered by Libya's dictator Muammar Gaddafi in retaliation for the United States bombing his country in 1986.

Homegrown violent extremist (HVE)
A person of any citizenship who mostly lives in the United States and who commits terrorist activity to advance an ideology when that person is influenced by a foreign terrorist organization (FTO), but acts alone.

Single-Issue or Special-Issue Threats and Extremism

A **homegrown violent extremist (HVE)** is a person who encourages, endorses, condones, justifies, or supports the commission of a violent criminal act to achieve political ideology, religious, social, or economic goals by a citizen or long-term resident of a Western country who has rejected Western cultural values, beliefs, and norms[128] and is influenced by a foreign terrorist organization (FTO). HVEs are not to be confused with single-issue/special-issue interest extremists who may be charged with violations of state or federal laws or as domestic terrorists. A key distinction between HVEs and all domestic terrorists is that the influence of an FTO is absent in the latter. At the national level the FBI has primary responsibility for terrorism investigations. Although not part of the domestic terrorism law, the FBI uses the phrase "Influenced by U.S.-based extremist ideologies" to identify cases as domestic terrorism.

There is some ambiguity about what "U.S.-based extremist ideologies" means.[129] Illustratively, some white supremacy groups in the United States reflect themes from Germany's Nazism and the skinhead movement evolved originally in several foreign countries,[130] but criminal acts by extremists from such ideologies will be charged with domestic terrorism or other violations of federal and state laws, but not as HVEs.

Presently, the federal government does not generate an official and public list of domestic terrorism individuals or groups;[131] there is no domestic terror organization counterpart to the secretary of state's list of foreign terrorist organizations (FTOs). Instead, federal agencies use a more cautious language, describing some causes as "threats" and those who commit criminal acts on their behalf as "extremists." Single-issue/special-issue terrorism is not ordinarily committed to effect widespread societal change. Its purpose is to change policies and practices with respect to a specific cause.

Groups with extreme views enjoy all the protections of the U.S. Constitution, including the free speech right to advocate for their cause.[132] Such groups may have a "front group" that performs their "public information" function and may be regarded as terrorist threats, but not as terrorists. They may also have a subgroup that carries out attacks to further their ideology.

Quick Facts
Who Could Be a Homegrown Violent Extremist (HVE)?

HVEs are a diverse group of individuals who can include U.S.-born citizens, naturalized citizens, green card holders (permanent residents) or other long-term residents, foreign students, or illegal residents.[133]

Box 7-5
Hacktivists Fighting IS

In 2015, a twenty-five-year-old Boston man watched radical Islamic Internet sites trumpet the success of a team that murdered staffers in the Paris, France, office of a satirical magazine, *Charlie Hebdo*. Incensed, he took the nom-de-guerre of XRSone and initiated #OpISIS. The man had begun writing code when he was seven years old and had the knowledge and experience to fight IS in cyberspace.[134]

XRSone called the loose-knit, leaderless hacktivist group, "Anonymous," to action. Soon splinter groups, such as GhostSec

and CtrlSec, were collaborating. Altogether, it was a swarm of neophyte and seasoned hackers who decided to take on the most powerful terrorist movement in the world, the Islamic State. Some hacktivists infiltrated jihadi forums, 149 websites were dismantled, 101,000 Twitter accounts and 5,900 propaganda videos were flagged, and one real-world terrorist attack was aborted. After some time, the hacktivists went on to other pursuits and others split their time targeting IS and other interests. However, in cyberspace, an unknown number of hacktivists still have IS in their sights.

Single-issue/special-issue extremists may (1) be members of groups or movements with extreme views; (2) be loosely affiliated with extreme causes; (3) never have contact with extreme causes, but have an affinity for their ideology; or (4) have their own unique ideology, such as "**hacktivists**" who use the Internet to attack hate sites, damage them, and release personal information about their members.

As a rule of thumb, single-issue/special issue extremists target property and not people (e.g., burn federal offices or ski resorts). Nonetheless, large-scale property attacks place emergency responders in dangerous situations. Other tactics include "spiking trees" to make them too dangerous to cut by hammering spikes into them, filing a barrage of frivolous suits, and destruction of research files. Attacks by single-issue/special-issue extremists may range from annoying vandalism to arson that destroys millions of dollars of property.

Single-issue/special-issue attacks are the most common form of violent political extremism in the United States and most of the industrialized nations of the world.[135] Examples of extremist single-issue/special-issue groups include the **Animal Liberation Front (ALF)** and the **Earth Liberation Front (ELF)**, anti-genetically modified organisms groups, anti-technologists, and anti-abortionists.

The Animal Liberation Front (ALF) and the Earth Liberation Front (ELF)

Both ALF and ELF share a common ideology. They take terrorist actions that call attention to and further their related causes; however, the methods they use are selected so that no human casualties will occur. Unfortunately for their causes, when fires are set, responding firefighters are put in harm's way and the use of pipe bombs cannot guarantee that people will not be injured or killed.

Although the number of perpetrators in attacks is unknown, ALF and ELF and/or sympathizers committed 2,000 attacks over a 29-year period, causing $110 million in damages (see Table 7–1).[136] Three people who later claimed to be ALF members broke into a facility at the University of Iowa and freed 300 rodents being used for research; broke equipment; and poured acid on computers, papers, and books, producing losses and added expenditures of $875,000. They also publicized the mail addresses and other personal information of the researchers and their spouses, resulting in numerous intimidating calls. Five faculty members also received over 400 unsolicited magazine subscriptions under the "bill me later" option. And in the State of Washington, ALF poured bleach and corrosive chemicals into two mobile meat slaughter trucks in 2014, resulting in the need for expensive repairs.[137]

ELF's term for economic sabotage is "**monkeywrenching**"; they also refer to it as **ecotage**, a corruption of eco—pertaining to the environment—and sabotage. Monkeywrenching may involve both destructive acts and acts of obstruction (e.g., tree sitting to avoid clear cutting of forests). An ELF arson attack on a U.S. Forest Station Research Station in Pennsylvania caused $700,000 in damages and destroyed 70 years of research.[138] During 2015, "Elves" raided Canada's RBR Fur Farms and released 6,800 minks[139] and destroyed seven cars at a Honda dealership in Mexico.[140]

Single-issue/special-issue extremists
As a rule of thumb, typically attack property as opposed to persons. Most common form of violent political extremism in the United States. May be members of, or loosely affiliated with, extreme group, may never have contacted group, but has an affinity for it, may have their own unique cause. Typically espouse a single issue or narrow range of issues.

Hacktivists
Single-issue/unique cause extremists who use the Internet to attack hate or other sites and disclose personal information about their members.

Animal Liberation Front (ALF)
ALF rejects the institutional position that animals are property and can be used as test subjects by corporations. ALF members or sympathizers may "liberate" animals and find "good homes" for them or return them to the wild and damage or destroy associated research facilities.

Earth Liberation Front (ELF)
ELF's mission is to cause as much economic loss to persons and other entities whose selfish greed and desire for profits result in the destruction of the natural environment and life. By doing so, ELF members and/or sympathizers hope to compel them to discontinue their destructive practices.

Monkeywrenching
Earth Liberation Front (ELF) term for economic sabotage. Involves acts of destruction and obstruction. See ecotage.

Ecotage
Earth Liberation Front's (ELF"s) corruption of eco (pertaining to the environment) and sabotage; used synonymously with monkey wrenching. See monkeywrenching.

TABLE 7–1
ALF and ELF Missions[141]

ALF	ELF
1. To liberate animals from places of abuse, that is, laboratories, factory farms, fur farms, etc., and place them in good homes where they may live out their natural lives free from suffering;	1. To cause as much economic damage as possible to a given entity that is profiting off the destruction of the natural environment and life for selfish greed and profit;
2. To inflict economic damage to those who profit from the misery and exploitation of animals;	2. To educate the public on the atrocities against the environment and life; and
3. To reveal the horror and atrocities committed against animals behind closed doors, by performing direct actions and liberations; and	3. To take all necessary precautions against harming life.
4. To take all necessary precautions against harming any animal, human, or non-humans; any group of people who are vegetarians or vegans and who carry out actions according to these guidelines have the right to call themselves part of the Animal Liberation Front.	

Box 7–6
Greenpeace: Peaceful Protest or Eco-Terrorism?

Greenpeace (GP) incorporated in 1971 with just a small nucleus of supporters. Today, it has 2.8 million supporters, five ships, twenty-seven national and regional offices, and a presence in forty-one countries. It rarely shows up on databases that list terrorist groups and extremist threats. It takes "direct action" to call attention to the situations it opposes, such as deforestation; nuclear testing; illegal whaling; releases of hazardous chemicals; deep ocean oil drilling; unsustainable fishing methods that needlessly kill baby tuna, sharks, and turtles; protecting seals; and opposing oil pipelines and toxic dumping in oceans.

The techniques used by GP include chaining themselves to equipment to prevent its use and climbing terrain and buildings to place their banners where many people will see them. In Australia, protesters perhaps affiliated with GP attacked a genetically modified wheat plot wearing hazmat suits and used weed string trimmers to destroy an entire experimental crop.[142] GP has also been accused of interfering with the navigation rights of whalers and conducting their direct actions in ways that are dangerous to the GP personnel and security personnel. In 2013, Greenpeace representatives attempted to board a Russian oil-drilling platform in the Arctic to display a banner calling for an end to drilling in that region. The Russians quickly responded and seized the ship and thirty people on it. By the end of 2013, all personnel had been allowed to leave the country. GP is working to secure the release of the ship.

GP differs from terrorist and extremist groups in important ways. It is incorporated, has legal responsibilities, and largely operates out of the tradition of protest, albeit sometimes over the top. Most often its "direct actions" are intended to change the

practices of businesses rather than the policies of governments. GP has a major interest in not harming people, and destruction of property is a relatively unusual act, even by sympathizers. It has also been the victim of violence; the French blew up one of its ships and killed a photographer because of GP's opposition to nuclear testing in the Pacific.[143]

However, Greenpeace is under close scrutiny by several governments around the globe. Some 200 miles south of Lima, Peru, is the Nasca Plain (also spelled Nazca), named after the ancient people who lived there. Between 200 B.C. and 300 A.D., 70 enormous biomorphs (animal and plant figures) and 900 geoglyphs (geometric shapes, with the longest line stretching a mile) were created. Portions of them can be faintly seen from orbiting spacecraft. In 2014, more than 20 Greenpeace activists damaged the Nasca figures and shapes, which is a United Nations World Heritage Site. Walking on the ancient site is strictly forbidden because it is very fragile and shoe prints can last hundreds or even a thousand years. Greenpeace activists walked out into the area, disregarding signs to do so, and unfurled giant letters spelling a message to a climate change conference then going on in Lima (see Figure 7–10).[144] It seems convoluted that a movement claiming dedication to protecting the earth would cause damage to the very ground that constitutes a World Heritage Site. In 2015, Greenpeace was banned from India. It had been at odds with that country's government over reliance on coal and deforestation. India accuses Greenpeace of committing fraud and falsifying data, which Greenpeace denies.[145]

Do you think Greenpeace should be labeled as a terrorist group? Why or why not?

FIGURE 7–10
On December 8, 2014, 20 Greenpeace activists significantly damage the Nasca Plain when placing the letters that form the message shown in this aerial photograph.

(*Rodrigo Abd/AP Images*)

Anti-Genetically Modified Organism (GMO) Groups

GMO extremist groups appeared in the 1980s in Germany in reaction to large-scale research on genetically altered agricultural plants, such as wheat and potatoes, which were resistant to diseases and provided a higher yield per acre. Extremists believed to be associated or have an affinity with lesser-known movements such as "Take the Flour Back" and the "Field Liberation Movement" invaded test plots and destroyed "**Frankenfood**" plants. In contrast, Greenpeace is an internationally recognized name of an environmental protection movement with broad interests. It has also been involved in protests against GMOs. "Concerned Oregon State University Students and Alumni" took credit for destroying 700 poplar trees, some of which were genetically engineered as part of research conducted by an OSU forestry professor; the research was being conducted to determine if the fast-growing poplar trees were suitable for use in the timber industry.[146]

Frankenfood
Term developed by anti-genetically modified organism (GMO) groups to describe genetically altered agricultural plants, such as wheat and potatoes.

Anti-Technologists

Theodore Kaczynski, a PhD mathematician (see Figure 7–11), became notorious as the **Unabomber** until his identity was established. An anti-technologist, he anonymously sent 16 bombs through the mail that exploded when opened during 1978–1995. Three people were killed and dozens injured.[147] Referred to as the *Unabomber* by the FBI, Kaczynski lived a Spartan, survivalist lifestyle in a remote Montana cabin. The bombs expressed his rage against technology; a key event radicalizing him was when a road was built though a pristine area he enjoyed visiting. His brother came to the conclusion "Ted" was the Unabomber and contacted the FBI. Kaczynski is serving multiple life sentences without the possibility of parole in a Colorado federal prison.

Theodore Kaczynski
Nicknamed the "Unabomber," Kaczynski was a mathematician and murderer who carried out a nationwide bombing campaign against people associated with industrialization and modern technology in the United States. Most of his bombs were crude, homemade bombs that were mailed to his victims.

Unabomber
See Theodore Kaczynski.

Quick Facts
The Unabomber's Manifesto

In 1995, writing as "KC" to confuse investigators, the Unabomber demanded that *The New York Times*, *The Washington Post*, and *Penthouse Magazine* publish a 35,000-word manifesto explaining his actions or he would strike again. Only *Penthouse* refrained from doing so. It part, the manifesto read "The industrial revolution and its consequences have been a disaster for the human race ... [It has] destabilized society, made life unfulfilling, and subjected human beings to indignities ... the continued development of technology will worsen the situation ... we therefore advocate the overthrow of the economic and technological basis of our society."[148]

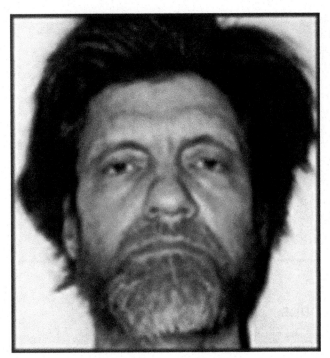

FIGURE 7–11
The April 4, 1996, jail booking pho-
tograph for Unabomber Theodore
Kaczynski.

(FBI Law Enforcement Bulletin)

Army of God
Anti-abortion group, underground
Christians, who produced manual on
how to attack clinics.

Anti-Abortionists

In *Roe v. Wade* (1973), the U.S. Supreme Court held that abortions were legal, which fueled the anti-abortion move-ment. The anti-abortion movement fully emerged in the early 1980s, peaked around 1984, and substantially disappeared until another spike in 1996. Since then, anti-abortion attacks have trended down, but have never disappeared.[149] Some right-wing movements and individuals may include an anti-abortion element within their multiple cause agendas, which is distinguishable from movements in this section that have it as their single issue.

Planned Parenthood Clinics have been a common target of anti-abortionists, who can be divided into two camps: (1) those who peacefully seek to end abortions through the passage of laws forbidding them, providing education to rally public sup-port, giving financial aid to pregnant women who might other-wise have an abortion, and peaceful demonstrations; and (2) violent extremists who engage in practices such as throwing acid on the property of abortion clinics, bombing them, committing arson of facilities, and assaults upon and murders of abortion providers. The **Army of God** is an underground Christian terrorist organization that produced a manual on how to attack clinics, including the use of bombs. Attacks attributed to the Army of God have virtually disappeared since 1998.[150] Most attacks since then have simply been attributed to "anti-abortion activists." The murder of a physician, George Tiller, provides insight into the minds of violent anti-abortion extremists.

In Wichita, Kansas, Dr. George Tiller performed late-term abortions. While Tiller was passing out bulletins for the Sunday services at his Lutheran Church, Scott Roeder shot him point blank, killing him.[151] The fifty-two-year-old Roeder was subsequently convicted of first degree murder with no possibility of parole for fifty years.[152] Roeder was unrepen-tant about the murder, claiming he stopped Tiller so he "could not dismember another innocent baby."

Chapter Summary

SUMMARY BY LEARNING OBJECTIVE

1. **Identify and describe the four waves of terrorism.**

   These four waves are: (1) anarchist, which predominated during 1880s–1920s. Pure anarchy requires an absence of a central government and people who respect and help each other; (2) colonialism began in the early modern period (1500–1800) when powers used their mili-tary might to impose their will on other parts of the world; (3) the new left wave (1960s–1990s) saw America and its allies engaging in a form of imperialism and were opposed to it. They saw revolution as the way to reform governments, but were very unsuccessful; and (4) the religious wave began in 1979 during Iran's Islamic Revolution and continues. It is fundamentally, but not exclusively, Islamic in nature. Its ultimate goal is a worldwide Islamic religion entwined with Islamic government.

2. **Identify the three goals that differentiate religious and secular terrorism; provide an argument that supports the emergence of the Islamic State as religious terrorism.**

   There are three goals that differentiate between religious and secular terrorism:

   1) *To violently initiate an apocalyptical event that will save (destroy) the world, thereby ushering in the anticipated new world.*

Clearly, it was the goal of early leaders like Abu Musab al Zarqawi and Abu Ayyub al Masri to begin a war in the Middle East that would crush Western influence and usher in a new Islamic-dominated world. However, al Zarqawi's first task was to destroy past governments in Iraq and begin a worldwide revolution that would spawn a new caliphate ... the Islamic State.

2) *To create a theocracy, a religious government based on the Word, Laws, and Commandments, of God or Deity as interpreted by ecclesiastical authorities.*

The emergence of Abu Bakr al-Baghdadi as the leader of the Islamic State in Iraq (ISI) was a pivotal move in establishing a new world order. ISI soon evolved into the Islamic State and would act as a theocracy, a religious government based on the Holy Qur'an and the word of Muhammad.

3) *To create a pure religious state where everyone practices the same religion.*

The ultra-violent Islamic State (IS), with its goal of a worldwide/transnational caliphate, fits neatly in this category. Abu Bakr al-Baghdadi announced the establishment of a caliphate, the Islamic State, sprawling over Northern Iraq and parts of Syria. He invited Muslims from all over the world to bring their households and rush to be part of this new ideal caliphate wherein they would be given homes, children and women would be educated, and men would have jobs. This announcement by al-Baghdadi precipitated the Great Islamic Migration from over 100 countries. Al-Baghdadi is now referred to as Caliph Ibrahim. He has called for all Muslim insurgents to recognize the authority of the Islamic State as a new and pure religious state, an Islamic caliphate where everyone practices the same Muslim faith.

3. **Contrast state terrorism, state-enabled terrorism, state-sponsored terrorism, and state-perpetuated/international terrorism.**

   State terrorism is terrorism committed by a national government, inside of its national borders and directed at its own people. This action contravenes a state's moral and legal duty to protect its citizens. The purpose of state terrorism is to repress and instill fear in citizens to consolidate the ruling regime's power and to maintain control over the country's general population. Many of the totalitarian governments of recent history conducted state terrorism in efforts to control their population, including Nazi Germany under Adolf Hitler (1932–1945), Russia under Joseph Stalin (1928–1953), China under Mao Tse-Tung (1949–1976), Haiti under Francois "Papa Doc" Duvalier (1957–1971), Cambodia under the Khmer Rouge (1975–1979), Argentina under the its military junta (early 1970s to early 1980s), Iraq under Saddam Hussein (1979–2003), and Syria under Bashar Assad (2000 to present). ***State-enabled terrorism*** occurs when a state does not provide direct support to a terrorist group so long as it conducts no operations against the state or its citizens. Thus, the actual state is not the terrorist, but rather a group inside the state that is allowed to flourish. In these cases, the state (1) passively allows its own nongovernmental entities and individual supporters to assist it; (2) implicitly condones the existence of the terrorist group by not conducting operations against it; and/or (3) fosters a "safe haven" for a terrorist group because it cannot govern its own territory, as in the case of the failed states, such as Afghanistan, Angola, Burundi, the Democratic Republic of the Congo, Liberia, Sierra Leone, Somalia, and Sudan. ***State-sponsored terrorism*** is a relatively recent development. Historically, terrorism has been between a state and a group of people or organization; however, in the second half of the twentieth century, state-sponsored terrorism grew as states used terrorist individuals and organizations as their proxies in international affairs. Good examples of countries that are designated by the U.S. Department of State as "state sponsors of terrorism" are Afghanistan, Iran, Iraq, Sudan, and Lebanon. Finally, ***state-perpetuated/international terrorism*** occurs when governments that lack the economic or military resources necessary to achieve their policy objectives use their own internal security or intelligence forces to commit acts of terrorism on foreign soil to further their agenda, or a country with resources chooses to do so using their own operatives. It is this reliance upon and use of the state's own internal resources that distinguishes this type of terrorism from state-sponsored terrorism's use of proxies. A good example of state-perpetuated/international terrorism was the 1988 bombing of Pan Am Flight 103, flying from England to New York City, causing the deaths of all 259 people on board and 11 others in the small village of Lockerbie, Scotland. This heinous act was conducted by a Libyan intelligence officer ordered by Muammar Gaddafi, then-dictator of Libya.

4. **Explain why single-issue/special-issue movements are so important in the United States.**

   Single-issue/special-issue attacks are the most common form of violent political extremism in the United States.

REVIEW QUESTIONS

1. What is the root meaning of anarchy and what does it mean?
2. Who are the three most widely known persons in state terrorism?
3. What were the main factors in the Parsley Massacre?
4. In mythology, what did the Tonton Macoute do and what did the Tonton Macoute actually do for Papa Doc?
5. Which nation is the most active sponsor of state terrorism?
6. What are ALF and ELF?
7. What is "Frankenfood"?
8. What are the three goals that differentiate between religious and secular terrorism?

CRITICAL THINKING EXERCISES

1. **The Holocaust and Genocide.** Visit the homepage of the United States Holocaust Memorial Museum at www.ushmm.org/. Learn about the Holocaust under Adolf Hitler and listen to the survivors and victims of this horrific event. Search the latest news and discover that genocide sadly continues today in several countries throughout the world. How do you think that genocide impacts the development of a country? Can a government ever overcome the history of genocide? Research and discuss as a class some of the more contemporary genocides observed in countries like Sudan, Rwanda, and Bosnia. Has the World Court been successful in preventing such tragedies through the prosecution of war crimes? Why not? Now, compare these contemporary genocides with the loss of Aboriginal people in Australia and Native Americans in the United States during the eighteenth and nineteenth centuries. Do you think genocide only occurs in developing nations? What can be done to prevent these types of horrific events?

2. **Greenpeace and PETA.** Search the web for articles on Greenpeace. Notice how many depict the organization as a group of radical environmentalists that potentially use violence and dangerous interventions to stop whaling and pollution in the world's oceans. What motivates some entities to characterize Greenpeace in this manner? How does Greenpeace differ from the groups discussed in the chapter that are commonly referred to as "eco-terrorists," like the Animal Liberation Front (ALF) and the Earth Liberation Front (ELF)? Now, visit the People for Ethical Treatment of Animals (PETA) website at www.peta.org. What is PETA's position on the Animal Liberation Front? Are Greenpeace and PETA alike, or do they differ? How?

NOTES

1. Ruth Lupton, Rebecca Tunstall, Alex Fenton, and Rich Harris, *Using and Developing Place Typologies for Policy Purposes* (London: Department for Communities and Local Government, February, 2011), p. 11.
2. Loc. cit.
3. Chalmers Johnson, "Interpretations in Terrorism," in Walter Laqueur ed., *The Terrorism Reader* (New York: New American Library, 1978), p. 276.
4. David C. Rapoport, "Modern Terror: The Four Waves," in Audrey Cronin and J. Ludes, eds., *Attacking Terrorism: Elements of a Grand Strategy* (Washington, D.C.: Georgetown University Press, 2004), p. 47.
5. We have faithfully cited Rapoport's excellent work that should be read in its original entirety if there any questions about what he and the present authors contribute herein.
6. Jeff Shantz, "Beyond the State: The Return to Anarchy," *Disclosure: A Journal of Social Theory*, Issue 12, 2003, pp. 87–103, http://uknowledge.uky.edu/disclosure/vol12/iss1/7/.
7. David C. Rapoport, "The Four Waves of Rebel Terror and September 11th," *Anthropoetics*, No. 1, Spring Summer 2002, pp. 1–19, www.anthropoetics.ucla.edu/ar-chive/ap0801.pdf.
8. Jeffrey Gettleman, "The Most Dangerous Place in the World," *Foreign Policy*, Issue 171, March/April 2009, p. 60.

9. Rapoport, "The Four Waves of Rebel Terror and September 11th," p. 2.

10. Julia Rose Kraut, "Global Anti-Anarchism: The Origins of Ideological Deportation and the Suppression of Expression," *Indiana Journal of Global Legal Studies*, Vol. 19, Issue 1, Winter 2012, p. 182.

11. Robert Taylor, *History of Terrorism* (San Diego: Lucent Books, 2002), p. 38.

12. Rapoport, "The Four Waves of Rebel Terror and September 11th," p. 2.

13. Loc. cit.

14. Loc. cit.

15. Ibid., p. 59.

16. Rapoport, "The Four Waves of Rebel Terror and September 11th," p. 2.

17. Loc. cit.

18. Taken from the NSM website, www.NSM88.org/25pointsengl.html.

19. At the beginning, there were 66 hostages, but by January 1981 the Iranians had released 14 of them. See Christine Coker, "Planning in Hostage Rescue Missions, U.S. Operation Eagle Claw and U.K. Operation Barras," *Military Technology*, Vol. 30, Issue 9, September 1, 2006, p. 66.

20. Six American diplomats escaped being captured and in 1980 were whisked out of Iran by courageous members of the Canadian Embassy. The 2012 movie *Argo* was loosely based on that event.

21. Leonard Weinberg and William Eubank, "An End to the Fourth Wave of Terrorism?" *Studies in Conflict and Terrorism*," Vol. 33, Issue 7, 2010, p. 595.

22. Weinberg and Eubank, "An End to the Fourth Wave of Terrorism?" p. 598.

23. Security Council Committee, "Monitoring Team's Nineteenth Report to the United Nations Security Council," S/2017/35, January 13, 2017, www.un.org/sc/suborg/en/sanctions/1267/monitoring-team/reports, p. 3, accessed March 26, 2017.

24. Bureau of Counterterrorism and Countering Violent Extremism, "Country Reports, 2015, Chapter 1, Strategic Assessment" (Washington, D.C.: U.S. Department of State, 2016), p. 1, www.state.gov/j/ct/rls/crt/2015/257513.htm, accessed March 26, 2017.

25. Ibid., p. 598.

26. Defining Terrorism, WP 3, Deliverable 4, A Project Funded by the European Commission, October 1, 2008, p. 45.

27. "Country Reports, 2015, Chapter 1, Strategic Assessment," p. 1 and "Monitoring Team's Nineteenth Report to the United Nations Security Council," p. 3.

28. This section was inspired by Heather S. Gregg, "Defining and Distinguishing Secular and Religious Terrorism," *Perspectives on Terrorism*, Vol. 8, No. 2, 2014, pp. 1–8. We have used, with citation, some of her ideas and substituted our own or added to a sentence from her work. In this instance, the sentence footnoted here is from p. 1.

29. Michael E. Miller and Yanan Wang, "The Radical, Unrepentant Ideology of Abortion Clinic Killers," *Washington Post*, November 30, 2015, www.washingtonpost.com/news/morningmix/wp/2015/11/30/the-radical-unrepentant-ideology-of-abortion-clinic-killers/?utm_term=.968412d17176, accessed March 29, 2017.

30. This content that follows is our extension of Gregg's point at footnote 28.

31. Ibid., with restatement, p. 1.

32. Index Mundi, Iran Demographics Profile 2016, p. 1, www.indexmundi.com/iran/demographics_profile.html, accessed March 29, 2017.

33. Bureau of Democracy, 2015 Executive Summary, Bureau of Human Rights, and Labor, International Religious Freedom Report, 2015 (Washington, D.C.: U.S. Department of State, 2016), www.state.gov/j/drl/rls/irf/religiousfreedom/index.htm, accessed March 29, 2017.

34. Bruce Hoffman, "The Global Terror Threat and Counterterrorism Challenges for the Next Administration," *Sentinel*, November 30, 2016, p. 1, www.ctc.usma.edu/posts/the-global-terror-threat-and-counterterrorism-challenges-facing-the-next-administration, accessed April 1, 2017.

35. No author, "Analysis: Britain's Iraq War Inquiry," *New York Times*, July 6, 2016, www.nytimes.com/live/britain-inquiry-iraq-war/report-points-finger-at-americans-for-de-baathification-policy, accessed March 29, 2017.

36. Richard W. Stevenson and David E. Sanger, "Threats and Responses; U.S. Resisting Calls for 2nd U.N. Vote on a War with Iraq," *New York Times*, January 16, 2003, www.nytimes.com/2003/01/16/world/threats-responses-white-house-us-resisting-calls-for-2nd-un-vote-war-with-iraq.html, accessed March 29, 2017.

37. "Public Attitudes toward War in Iraq: 2003-2008," Pew Research Center, March 19 2008, www.nytimes.com/2003/01/16/world/threats-responses-white-house-us-resisting-calls-for-2nd-un-vote-war-with-iraq.html, accessed March 29, 2017.

38. Loc. cit.

39. Loc. cit.

40. Loc. cit.

41. No author, "Mapping Militant Organizations: The Islamic State," Stanford University, March 29, 2017, p. 2, http://web.stanford.edu/group/mappingmilitants/cgi-bin/groups/view/1, accessed March 3, 2017.

42. Aki Peritz, "The Great Iraqi Jail Break, Foreign Policy, June 26, 2014, p. 1, http://foreignpolicy.com/2014/06/26/the-great-iraqi-jail-break, accessed April 3, 2017.

43. Martin Chulov, Fazel Hawramy, and Spencer Ackerman, "Iraq Army Capitulates to ISIS Militants in Four Cities," *Guardian* (England), June 11, 2014, www.theguardian.com/world/2014/jun/11/mosul-isis-gunmen-middle-east-states, accessed March 3, 2017.

44. Loc. cit., p. 1.

45. No author, ISIS Financing, 2015, Center for the Analysis for Terrorism, May 2016, p. 1.

46. Hiroaki Kuromiya, "Stalin's Great Terror and International Espionage," *Journal of Slavic Military Studies*, Vol. 24, Issue 2, April–June 2011, p. 240.

47. See Arch Puddington, "Denying the Terror Famine," *National Review*, Vol. 44, Issue 10, May 25, 1992, pp. 33–36.

48. Cynthia Haven, "Stalin Killed Millions. A Stanford Historian Answers the Question 'Was it Genocide?'" Stanford (University) Report, September 23, 2010, www.news.stanford.edu/news/2010/september/naimark-stalin-genocide-092310.html.

49. See Robert Conquest, *The Great Terror: A Reassessment* (New York City: Oxford University Press, 2007), which addresses Russia during the 1930s.

50. See Vadim Z. Rogovin, *Stalin's Terror of 1937–1938: Genocide in the USSR* (Oak Park Michigan: Mehring Books, 2009). Rogovin is the author of a highly regarded five-volume history of Russia.

51. Loc. cit.

52. Loc. cit.

53. J. D. Lindy and B. Kolk, "Notes from Moscow (1990): Some Thoughts on the Politics of PTSD during Perestroika," *Journal of Traumatic Stress*," Vol. 4, No. 3, 1991, p. 439.

54. Ria Novosti, "Russia's Losses in WW II Estimated at Some 27 Million People," www.en.rian.ru/russia/20100506/158896419.html, accessed January 15, 2013. This figure varies by source from a low of 6 million to a high of 11 million. The higher figure also includes an unknown number of missing service members.

55. Fox Butterworth, "Obituary, Mao Tse-Tung: Father of the Chinese Revolution," *New York Times*, September 10, 1976, www.nytimes.com/learning/general/onthisday/bday/1226.html.

56. Loc. cit.

57. Loc. cit.

58. Vaclav Smil, "China's Great Famine: 40 Years Later," *BMJ*, 319, December 1999, p. 1619.

59. Sertac H. Baserne, "Terrorism with Its Differentiating Aspects," *Defence Against Terrorism Review*, Vol. 1, No. 1, Spring 2008, p. 5.

60. "The State as Terrorist," *Stanford Encyclopedia of Philosophy*, August 8, 2011, www.Plato.stanford.edu/entries/terrorism/#StaFer.

61. Monica G. Ayuso, "How Lucky for You That Your Tongue Can Taste the 'r' in Parsley: Trauma Theory and the Literature of Hispaniola," *Afro-Hispanic Review*, Vol. 30, No. 1, Spring 2001, p. 47.

62. Ezra Fieser, "Haiti, Dominicans Try to Move beyond the Parsley Massacre's Long Shadow," *Christian Science Monitor*, October 19, 2012.

63. The account of the "Parsley Test" is taken from Ayuso, "How Lucky for You That Your Tongue Can Taste the 'r' in Parsley," p. 47.

64. Ezra Fieser, "Haitians and Dominicans Remember the Parsley Massacre 75 Years Later," *Miami Herald*, October 9, 2012. One source places the publication data two days later, although that may have been when it was posted to the Internet.

65. Fieser, "Haiti, Dominicans Try to Move beyond the Parsley Massacre's Long Shadow," p. 1.

66. "Francois Duvalier," *New York Times Topics*, December 3, 2012, www.topicsnytimes.com/top/reference/timestopics/people/d/francois_duvalier/index.html.

67. See Graham G. Diederich, *Papa Doc & the Tontons Macoutes* (Princeton, N.J.: Markus Wiener Publishers). Originally published in 1970, re released in December 2005.

68. David Aponte, "The Tonton Macoutes: The Central Nervous System of Haiti's Reign of Terror," *Council on Hemispheric Affairs*, March 11, 2010, www.coha.org/tonton-macoutes/.

69. Stephen Kurczy, "5 Reasons Why Haiti's Jean Claude Duvalier Is Infamous," *Christian Science Monitor*, January 20, 2011, p. 1.

70. Aponte, "The Tonton Macoutes."

71. Loc. cit.

72. Don A. Schanche, "9 Top Haitian Officers Fired, But Action Fails to Halt Military Unrest," *Los Angeles Times*, September 22, 1988.

73. There are a number of sources describing the victims. For example, see Douglas B. Levene, "Reflections on Cambodia," *National Review*, November 12, 2012, p. 1, www.nationalreview.com/articles/293017/reflections-cambodia-douglas-b-levene?pg=2; "Cambodian Genocide," William Mitchell College of Law (an independent college of law), p. 1, www.worldwithoutgenocide.org/genocides-and-conflicts-/cambodian%20genocide; and Peter Walker, "Behind the Cambodian Killing Fields," *Guardian* (daily newspaper, England), September 19, 2007.

74. "Khmer Rouge," *New York Times Topics*, November 23, 2011, www.topics.nytimes.com/top/reference/timestopics/organizations/k/khmer_rouge/index.html.

75. Stephen G. Michaud, "Identifying Argentina's Disappeared," *New York Times Magazine*, December 27, 1987, www.NYTimes.com/1987/12/27/Magazine/Identify-Argentina-s-disappeared.html.

76. Ernesto Sabato, President, Argentina National Commission on the Disappearance of Persons, Section D, Detention Centers, unnumbered manuscript, 1984. The report was later translated into English as Nunca Mas (Never Again) and published in New York by Farrar, Straus, Giroux, 1986.

77. Alexei Barrionuevo, "Daughter of Dirty War Was Raised by Man Who Killed Her Parents," *New York Times*, October 8, 2011.

78. Francisco Goldman, "Children of the Dirty War: Argentina's Stolen Orphans," *New Yorker*, March 19, 2012, p. 54.

79. "Rafael Videla Admits His Government Killed and Disappeared Thousands," Fox News Latino, April 16, 2012, www.latino.foxnews.com/latino/news/2012/04/16/rafael-videla-admits-his-government-killed-and-disappeared-thousands.

80. "On This Day: 1988: Thousands Die in Halabja Gas Attack," BBC, undated, www.News.bbc.co.uk/onthisday/hi/dates/stories/march/16/newsid_4304000/4304853.stm.

81. Kareem Khadder et al., "Suspected Gas Attach in Syria Reportedly Kills Dozens," CNN, April 4, 2017, www.cnn.com/2017/04/04/middleeast/idlib-syria-attack, accessed April 4, 2017.

82. Based on Laura Smith-Spark and Juliet Perry, "Suspected Gas Attack in Syria Reportedly Kills Dozens," CNN, April 5, 2017, https://www.google.com/webhp?sourceid=chrome-instant&ion=1&espv=2&ie=UTF-8#q=news,+latest+news+syria+gas+attack&*, accessed March 5.

83. Anne Barnard and Michael R. Gordon, "Worst Chemical Attack in Years," *New York Times*, April 4, 2017, www.nytimes.com/2017/04/04/world/middleeast/syria-gas-attack.html?_r=0, accessed April 5, 2017.

84. Lauren Said Moorhouse and Sarah Tilotta, "From Airstrike to U.S. Intervention: How a Chemical Attack in Syria Unfolded," CNN, April 7, 2017, www.cnn.com/2017/04/05/middleeast/syria-airstrike-idlib-how-it-unfolded/index.html.

85. Daniel Byman, "Passive Sponsors of Terrorism," *Survival: Global Politics and Strategy*, Vol. 47, Winter 2005, No. 4, p. 118. These points come from Byman, but we have restated them.

86. Robert I. Rotberg, "Failed States in a World of Terror," Council on Foreign Relations, July/August 2002, www.foreignaffairs.com/articles/58046/robert-i-rothberg/failed-states-in-a-world-of-terror.

87. Ibid., p. 5.

88. Robert D. Lamb, *Ungoverned Areas and Threats from Safe Havens* (Washington, D.C.: Department of Defense, January 2008), p. 6.

89. Liana Sun Wyler, *Weak and Failing States: Evolving Security Threats and U.S. Policy* (Washington, D.C.: Congressional Research Service, August 28, 2008), pp. 4–5.

90. Most of these factors are discussed in James A. Piazza, "Incubators of Terror: Do Failed and Failing States Promote Transnational Terrorism?" *International Studies Quarterly*, Vol. 52, Issue 3, 2008, pp. 469–488.

91. Robert S. Litwak, "Assessing the Nexus of Proliferation and Terrorism," Ridgway Center on the Determinants of Security Policy in the 21st Century, 2007, p. 3.

92. Rotberg, "Failed States in a World of Terror," p. 5.

93. Ray Takeyh and Nikolas Gvosdev, "Do Terrorists Need a Home?" *Washington Quarterly*, Vol. 25, No. 3, Summer 2002, pp. 98–99.

94. Loc. cit.

95. Loc. cit.

96. In 1993, Americans went into Mogadishu to arrest warlords and it escalated into fierce fighting that is depicted in the movie *Black Hawk Down*.

97. Ted Dagne, Somalia: *Current Conditions and Prospects for a Lasting Peace* (Washington, D.C.: Congressional Research Service, August 31, 2011), p. 1.

98. One report in this genre is Mark Mazzetti, "Efforts by CIZ Fail in Somalia, Officials Charge," *New York Times*, June 9, 2006.

99. Bureau of Counterterrorism and Countering Violent Extremism, "Chapter 3: State Sponsors of Terrorism," U.S. Department of State, 2015, www.state.gov/j/ct/rls/crt/2015/257520.htm, accessed April 4, 2017.

100. Loc. cit.

101. Greg Bruno, "State Sponsors: Iran," Council on Foreign Relations, October 13, 2011, www.cfr.org/iran/state-sponsors-Iran/p9362.

102. Loc. cit.

103. Ibid., p. 3.

104. Sebnem Arsu, "Man Who Shot Pope in 1981 Is Freed," *New York Times*, January 18, 2010.

105. Justin Conrad, "Interstate Rivalry and Terrorism: An Unprobed Link" *Journal of Conflict Resolution*, Vol. 55, No. 4, February 21, 2011, http://jcr.sagepub.com/content/55/4/529.

106. The Sandinistas took their name from Augusto Sandino. He was a popular leader, executed by his government, who was opposed to a series of American military interventions in Nicaragua from 1912 to the 1930s. Among the reasons for these interventions was protecting the interests of the American-owned United Fruit Company that exported bananas to the United States and Europe. Parenthetically, from 1889 until the mid-1930s, America often intervened in the internal affairs of Caribbean and Central American nations to protect its commercial interests, a period referred to as the "Bananas Wars."

107. Guy Gugliotta, "Assassinating a Tyrant: How Somoza Died," *Chicago Tribune*, July 19, 1989.

108. See Michael J. Schroeder, "Bandits and Blanket Thieves, Communists and Terrorists: The Politics of Naming the Sandinistas in Nicaragua, 1927–36 and 1979–1990," *Third World Quarterly*, Vol. 26, Issue 1, February 2005, pp. 67–86.

109. Loc. cit.

110. The Tower Commission Report (1987) is the official inquiry to "Irangate"; it suggests that the purpose of the sales was for this assistance, but stops just short of plainly asserting it. See John Tower, Chairman, *The Tower Commission Report: The President's Special Review Board* (Washington, D.C.: Government Printing Office, 1987).

111. "The Iran-Contra Affair, www.pbs.org/wgbh,americanexperience/features/general-article/reagan-Iran, accessed April 8, 2013. The Tower Commission Report found considerable evidence, but no hard proof that the arms deal money had gone to the Contras.

112. The information in this paragraph is drawn from the 11-page decision "Case Concerning the Military and Paramilitary Activities in and Against Nicaragua" (*Nicaragua v. United States of America*) (Merits), Judgment of 27 June 1986, International Court of Justice, The Hague, Netherlands.

113. Loc. cit.

114. Robert Pear, "Chile Agrees to Pay Reparations to U.S. in Slaying of Envoy," *New York Times*, May 13, 1990.

115. Loc. cit.

116. Loc. cit.

117. "TNI and the Pinochet Precedent," August 12, 2009, www.tni.org/primer/tni-and -pinochet-precedent.

118. Ely Karmon, "Counterterrorism Policy: Why Tehran Starts and Stops Terrorism," *Middle East Quarterly*, Vol. 5, Issue 4, December 1998, pp. 35–44. Karmon records number of deaths by separate periods.

119. Dan Geist, "A Darker Horizon: The Assassination of Shapour Bakhtiar," PBS, p. 2, www .pbs.org/wgbh/pages/frontline/tehranbureau/2011/08/a-darker-horizon-the-assassination -of-shapour-bakhtiar.html.

120. Loc. cit.

121. Chad Bray and Evan Perez, "Guilty Plea in Plan to Kill Saudi Arabian Diplomat," *Wall Street Journal*, October 17, 2012.

122. Richard Obina Iroanya, "Implications of State and State Sponsored International Terrorism for Africa: The Case of Libya and Sudan," a thesis submitted in partial fulfillment for the Master of Security Studies, Department of Political Sciences, University of Pretoria, South Africa, November 2008, p. 22.

123. The Lockerbie Trial. See: http://webarchive.loc.gov/all/20020913003025/http%3A//www .thelockerbietrial.com/.

124. Awareness Brief: Homegrown Violent Extremism (Washington, D.C.: Community Oriented Policing Services, U.S. Department of Justice, 2014), p. 1. The content of the site is drawn from several sources of the International Association of Chiefs of Police. See www.theiacp. org/portal/0/homegrownviolentextremistawarenessbrief.pdf.

125. Ibid., p. 5.

126. Loc. cit.

127. Jerome P. Bjelopera, *The Domestic Terror Threat: Background and Issues for Congress* (Washington, D.C.: Congressional Research Service, January 17, 2013), p. 9.

128. Ibid., p. 10.

129. Loc. cit.

130. The facts in this box were drawn from the citation, but information around them was reorganized, and rewritten, with some paraphrasing. E.T. Brooking, "Anonymous vs. the Islamic State," *Foreign Policy*, November 13, 2015, http://foreignpolicy.com/2015/11/13/ anonymous-hackers-islamic-state-isis-chan-online-war, accessed April 5, 2017.

131. William Dyson, The Emergence of Special-Interest/Single-Issue Terrorism," State and Local Anti-Terrorism Training (SLATT) Program (Tallahassee, Florida, Institute for Intergovernmental Research, 2001), p. 1.

132. Federal Bureau of Investigation, "Putting Intel to Work Against ELF and ALF Terrorists," June 6, 2008, www.FBI.gov/News/Stories/2008/June/Ecoterror_200208110011.

133. Mateusz Perkowski, "Two More Slaughter Units Vandalized," *Desert News*, July 16, 2014, www.capitalpress.com/Livestock/20140716/two-more-mobile-slaughter-units-vandalized, accessed April 5, 2017.

134. University of Maryland, Global Terrorism Database, Incident Summary Number 200208110011, www.Start.Umd.edu/gtd/Search/Incidentsummary. Aspx?gtdid=200208110011, August 6, 2015, accessed April 5, 2017.

135. Kate Dubinski, "Mink Liberation or Economic Terrorism?" *National Post*, August 6, 2015, http://news.nationalpost.com/news/canada/mink-liberation-or-economic-terrorism -activists-free-mink-from-three-southern-ontario-fur-farms, accessed April 4, 2017.

136. No author, "Mexico: Attack Against a Honda Dealership in Mexico," Earth First! Newswire, October 6, 2015, http://earthfirstjournal.org/newswire/2015/10/06/mexico-attack-against-a -honda-dealership-by-earth-liberation-front/, accessed April 5, 2017.

137. This table is prepared from information contained in Jerome P. Bjelopera, *The Domestic Terrorism Threat: Background and Issues for Congress* (Washington, D.C.: Congressional Research Service, May 15, 2012), p. 47.

138. Jessica Narim, "GP Destroyed GM Wheat," ABC News, July 14, 2011, www.abc.ner.au/news/2011-07-14/20110714-greenpeace-gm-protest/2794272.

139. Scott Neuman, French Agent Apologizes for French Blowing Up Greenpeace Ship in 1985," NPR, September 6, 2015, www.npr.org/sections/thetwo-way/2015/09/06/438036449/french-agent-apologizes-for-blowing-up-greenpeace-ship-in-1985, accessed April 5, 2017.

140. Katia Hetter, "Peru Claims Greenpeace Damaged Ancient Nazca Lines," CNN, December 12, 2014, www.cnn.com/2014/12/12/travel/greenpeace-nazca-lines-damage, accessed April 5, 2017.

141. No author, "India Bans Greenpeace in Ongoing Row over Foreign Donations," DW News, June 11, 2015, www.dw.com/en/india-bans-greenpeace-in-ongoing-row-over-foreign-donations/a-18832539, accessed April 5, 2017.

142. "Vandals Attack Forestry Research Project," *OSU News and Research Communications*, March 23, 2001.

143. The Unabomber's manifesto appeared as an eight-page supplement to the *Washington Post*'s September 25, 1995 edition. See www.washingtonpost.com/wp-srv/national/longterm/-unabomber/manifesto.text.htm.

144. Gordon Witkin and Ian Greenberg, "End of the Line for the Unabomber," *U.S. News and World Report*, Vol. 124, Issue 4, February 2, 1998, p. 34. No author, "Attack Against a Honda Dealership in Mexico by Earth Liberation Front, Earth First! Newswire, October 6, 2015, earthfirstjournal.org/newswire/2015/10/06/mexico-attack-against-a-honda-dealership-by-earth-liberation-front, October 6, 2015, accessed August 31, 2017.

145. "Chart of Abortion Attacks," *National Consortium for the Study of Terrorism and Responses to Terrorism*" undated, www.start.umd.edu/gtd/search/results.aspx?Search=abortion&sa.x=0&sa.y=0&sa=search, p. 1.

146. "Terrorist Organization Profile: Army of God," *National Consortium for the Study of Terrorism and Responses to Terrorism*," undated, www.start.umd.edu/start/data_collections/tops/terrorist_organization_profiles.asp?id=28.

147. See Robin Abcarian, "Abortion Doc's Killer Convicted," *Chicago Tribune*, January 30, 2010; and "George R. Tiller," *New York Times*, January 29, 2010.

148. CNN Wire Staff, "Doctor's Killer Sentenced to Life in Prison," www.cnn.com/2010/crime/04/01/kansasabortion.roeder.sentence/index.html.

149. This information is drawn from Ray Moseley, "Pope 'Plot' Central to Trial of Century," *Chicago Tribune News*, May 14, 1981.

150. Loc. cit.

151. Robert Park, "North Korea's Legacy of Terrorism," *World Affairs*, June 6, 2013, www.worldaffairsjounal.org/article/north-korea's-legacy-terrorism, p. 2.

152. Ibid., p. 2.

Typologies of Terrorism: The Right and Left Wings and Separatist or Nationalist Movements

Learning Objectives

After completing this chapter, you will be able to:

1. State what is at the core of American right-wing ideology.

2. Identify three major right-wing ideologies in the United States.

3. Compare and contrast the traditional goals of left-wing terrorism with the current goals of today's left-wing groups.

4. Define NLO and identify groups that are involved in NLO movements across the world.

Norwegian terrorist Anders Breivik bombed a government building and went to a youth camp and shot people, killing a total of 77. Breivik cited the far-right English Defence League as an inspiration. The man standing in the foreground has blood on his hands and arms, perhaps from trying to help someone or from his own injuries. He is gazing upward, possibly stunned or asking "Why?" Although it is easy to think of terrorism as being committed by radicalized Muslims, it should not deflect us from noting others also commit acts of terrorism—in this case, by a person philosophically from the international far right.
(Kamerapress Sweden/Photoshot/Newscom)

Introduction

This chapter represents the remaining categories of terrorism identified by leading scholars. This includes the right and left wings, as well as those that are separatist or national movements. Although we have briefly mentioned some of these movements in earlier chapters, they are now addressed in more detail.

Examples of the far right include the Ku Klux Klan, neo-Nazis, and the Hammerskin Nation (Skinhead movement) and the Christian Patriot Movement. Many right-wing groups include "hate" focused against people of different races and/or ethnicities in their ideology. A new group, originally founded in Finland in 2015 called Solider of Odin is a sign of the times and represents a vigilante anti-refugee movement. Also in 2015, Germany accepted more than a million refugees, and the far right there quickly emerged using a new word: *Überfremdung* or "over foreignization." In contrast, terrorist left-wing organizations want to replace their governments with ones based on Marxist-Leninist principles. Examples include the Anarchist Left and Black Blocs in the United States, Sendero Luminoso in Peru, and Italy's Red Brigades.

As a rule of thumb, as a country's diversity increases, tensions rise between segments of the population. If a nation's subpopulation is substantial, they may wish to have their own self-governed area, but remain within their country. For instance, the Basques in Spain have long and successfully fought to have a measure of autonomy in that country. Nationalists movements in a country, like the historic Irish Republican Army (IRA), want to break away and form their own country.

The Right Wing in the United States

Right-wing movements and politics are by nature conservative; illustrations of this in the United States include the Tea Party and the American Family Association. However, as used here, "right wing" denotes individuals and groups whose views exceed being merely conservative. They are sometimes characterized as the "far right," "extremist right," "radical right," and sometimes collectively called hate or extremist groups. To shed such labels, the far right has adopted the new identity of the "alternative right or alt-right" to make it appear more acceptable. The right wing potentially poses a serious threat, both here and abroad. The most popular forum for the right wing is Stormfront, an Internet site.

Right-wing Nationalist Front (NF) organizations exist in a number of Western countries. America's NF was formed in 2016 as a loose coalition of Neo-Nazis, white supremacists, and kindred hate groups. By the fall of 2017, the NF was in disarray and barely functioning. Other "umbrella" hate organizations in the United States like the Aryan Nationalist Alliance (ANA) have also failed.

Movements within the American right wing have different ideas about the "enemies" and ideas they oppose. Illustrations of these include illegal immigrants, the "Zionist Occupied Government" (ZOG) in Washington, D.C., African-Americans, feminist views, lesbians, gay, bisexual, transgender, and queer (LGBTQ) people, and Muslims. Simultaneously, they often share beliefs such as politicians and political parties do not properly represent them, the Constitution is being subverted, the government cannot be trusted and is eating away individual freedoms, the federal government is part of a plot to impose a "one world government" on U.S. citizens, and even claim that the Federal Emergency Management Agency (FEMA) has 800 concentration camps for people who protest government policies and programs.[1]

Quick Facts
The Christian Patriot Movement

In the mid-1980s, the **Christian Patriot Movement (CPM)** appeared. It was anti-government and strongly anti-gun control. Members were also racist and hostile to Jews and non-whites.

---

[a] The SPLC's numbers for hate groups were questioned in 2017. A researcher noted that some of the groups listed were not known to be active, had only a post office box address and a website, or their existence could not be confirmed. See John Perazzo, "Left Wing Hate Groups" (Sherman Oaks, California: David Horowitz Freedom Center, 2017), pp. 7–8.

TABLE 8-1

Number of American Hate Groups by Representative Years, 1999-2016

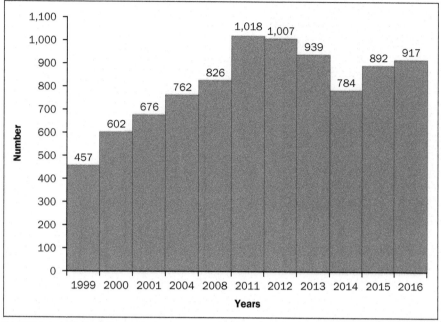

Heidi Beirich et al., "The Year in Hate and Extremism," Southern Poverty Law Center, Spring Issue, February 15, 2017, https://splcenter
.org/fighting-hate/intelligence-report/2017/year-hate-and-extremism. (3) There are no page numbers in cite. The data is from about 8
pp. or so.

The American right wing can collectively be referred to as hate groups. Table 8-1 summarizes the variation in such groups from 1999 to 2016.[a] From 1999 until 2011, the number of hate groups increased. The upward trajectory began before the al Qaeda attacks on September 11, 2001. The strong gun control measures taken by President Clinton's administration (1993–2001) moved some people to join right-wing groups, and the 9/11 attacks did likewise as conspiracy theories quickly sprang up, for example, Jewish people working in the Twin Towers didn't go to work on 9/11 because they knew about the attacks in advance, aluminum planes can't bring down massive steel structures, and what actually happened was the government planted bombs to ensure the Twin Towers came down to justify the wars in Iraq and Afghanistan.[2]

The election of Barack Obama as President in 2008 shook the far right. Even before President Obama took office in 2009, the Great Recession of 2007–2009 began. The housing market tanked, unemployment soared, banks failed, some cities cut the pensions of retirees, and the far right believed government failed them. The number and size of militias soared. Although the Great Recession was officially declared over in 2009, in some areas evidence of the recovery was not seen for several more years.

The far right was also alarmed by media disclosures about the breadth of data collection by the National Security Agency (NSA) and renewed efforts for gun control. Nonetheless, during 2013–2014, the number of American right-wing groups substantially declined, largely because of enforcement efforts directed at anti-government "Patriot" movements, an improving economy, and the failure of some nightmarish right-wing predictions to materialize[3] and followers fell away. To some degree, the reelection of President Obama may have also contributed to the decline because a portion of the far right may have become resigned to his presence.

In 2016, the Bureau of Alcohol, Tobacco, Firearms and Explosives (ATF) established an Internet Investigation Center (ICC) to regulate gun sales on the web. Under rules published by the Social Security Administration (SSA) in that same year, people could lose their right to possess a gun. If someone receiving checks from the SSA was adjudicated as being mentally impaired and unable to manage their own affairs, their right to own a firearm could be taken away.[4] In 2017, the Congress passed legislation overturning the SSA's gun rule.

Donald Trump was a Washington outsider and businessman whose campaign went from disjointed to populist. In some quarters of the Republican Party, the campaign was snidely referred to as the "populist insurgency." Some political observers and the news media linked his name to labels such as racist, xenophobic, and misogynist.[5]

The Southern Poverty Law Center (SPLC) asserted that some of the rhetoric of Trump's campaign may have energized the far right and contributed to a resurgence in the number of hate groups.[6] However, paralleling the campaign, there were a highly publicized series of IS terrorist attacks in France, Belgium, and Germany. In January 2015, 73 percent of Americans were already worried about an IS attack.[7] Between 2015 and 2016, anti-Muslim movements increased from 34 to 101.[8] Overall, hate groups saw a modest increase during the same period, from 892 to 917. Moreover, the Gallup Poll conducted 26 surveys during the campaign, revealing an overall average that two of every three respondents were dissatisfied with the way things were going "right now" in the United States.[9]

FIGURE 8–1
Followers of the neo-Nazi National Democratic Party participating in an anti-Muslim demonstration near a mosque in Duisburg, Germany.
(Roland Weihrauch/EPA/Newscom)

The International Right Wing

Terrorist attacks continued in Europe and elsewhere in 2017. Khalid Masood drove a car across the Westminster striking people. When he crashed his vehicle, he charged toward Parliament with two large knives, killing unarmed Constable Keith Palmer, and entered Parliament and was shot to death. Apart from attacks, there are also a number of important right-wing movements.

Europe has right-wing political parties with aggressive environmental and/or anti-immigration platforms. Examples of these parties include the National Front Party (France), Freedom Party (Austria), and the National Democratic Party (NDP, Germany). The neo-Nazi NDP believes "immigrants should go back to the Middle East on flying carpets"[10] (see Figure 8–1). Italy's Northern League takes positions across the political spectrum, but its strong stances against illegal immigration and Islam are popular with voters.[11]

The most recent iteration in Europe's right-wing movements is a product of the Syrian War. In some circles, there is focused opposition to receiving any more refugees, sentiment for getting rid of as many as have been admitted to the country, and a flat rejection of the multicultural society that began being touted in Europe in the mid-1980s. Terrorist attacks, like those in France, Germany, and Belgium, have poisoned the public opinion well for receiving more refugees. In Hungary, only ten people a day are accepted and they are detained in camps until their cases are decided. Only 10 percent will be allowed to stay in the country.[12] Greece is holding thousands of Syrian refugees on islands while decisions are made about them.[13] Frontex, the European Union's external border patrol agency, has stepped up boat patrols to cut off refugee flow from Turkey to Greece.[14]

In one way or another, organizations have sprung up in opposition to refugees, for example, UKIP, Front National, Alternative for Germany (NfG), and Soldiers of Odin (see Figure 8–2). The battle cry of the European right wing is "Take Back Our Country."

As in other European countries, the general unwillingness of immigrant and refugee Muslims in Italy to be assimilated is causing significant social strains. The fact that the Northern League and other right-wing parties have enjoyed moderate success at the polls reflects sentiments loose in the populations of their respective nations. Outside of the political arena, there are examples of right-wing violence. In Florence, Italy, a man with reported

Quick Facts
Soldiers of Odin USA

The Anti-Defamation League characterizes Soldiers of ODIN USA as a controversial, anti-refugee, vigilante group. Notably, the Soldiers of Odon are already changing the landscape of the far right since the first charter was received in early 2016: It is attracting members from both of America's largest extreme-right movements, the white supremacists and anti-government Patriot movement. The "Odins" held their first patrol in a Denver suburb during March 2016 and have been compared to the anti-immigrant Minutemen.[15]

FIGURE 8-2
Soldiers of Odin Canada rally in Toronto. In 2017, Parliament passed a bill that condemns Islamophobia the fear, dislike, or hatred of Muslims. While it passed, it was controversial. Odin is a warrior God in Norse mythology. The Odin movement started in Finland and members say they patrol the streets to protect people, especially from Muslims. The Soldiers of Odin movement has spread to a halfdozen European countries, Canada, and the United States.
(Roland Hoskins/ANL/REX/ Shutterstock)

Quick Facts
Right-Wing Violence in Sweden

Anders Breivik bombed a building in Oslo, Sweden—killing eight people—and drove to a youth camp, where he killed another 69 and wounded hundreds more. His personally created ideology combined the hate of the right wing with his own rage against Muslims. According to Breivik, Muslims are engaged in the "Islamic colonization of Europe.[16] He declared his victims were "traitors," guilty of embracing multiculturalism, and deserved to die.

ties to the right-wing anti-immigration group Casapound shot and killed two African street vendors and wounded another before killing himself.[17] In Germany, a three-member group described as neo-Nazis and calling themselves the National Socialist Underground are thought to have killed seven men of Turkish origin and one Greek.[18] In Japan, right-wing movements are substantially nationalistic, anti-Korean, and anti-Chinese. Right-wing movements in Africa include labor groups and white separatists. Right-wing groups from Hindu India and Islamic Pakistan often clash and the violence is fueled by a volatile combination of religious hatred and nationalism.

Although denying any aspiration to become a political party, the **English Defence League** (EDL) represents a growing phenomenon in Europe: groups that are not simply right wing, anti-Muslim, or overtly racist, but **xenophobic**, profoundly hostile toward immigration.[19] Between 2009 and 2012, the EDL organized over fifty street demonstrations, each with 1,000 to 3,000 supporters.[20] It has eighty local divisions in England and 80,000 Facebook followers.[21] Other defense leagues have been established in Belgium, Scotland, Australia, Denmark, and Norway. The public face of EDL is that it exists to peacefully demonstrate against the spread of Islam; however, without assigning any blame, it has been a counterforce at pro-Islamic demonstrations that turned violent. The larger right-wing anti jihad movement includes the defense leagues and other groups, such as the Citizen's Movement Pax Europa in Germany, Generation Identity in France, and the American Freedom Defense Initiative, that are united in their belief that Islam and Muslims are a fundamental threat to the resources, identities, and survival of Western nations.[22]

Issues in Defining the Right Wing

The difficulties in defining terrorism also apply to defining the "right wing." Terminological chaos and the absence of a clear conceptual framework also hinder our understanding of right-wing terrorism.[23] Consider the array of terms used: right

English Defence League
The EDL represents a growing phenomenon in Europe: right-wing groups that are not simply racist, but profoundly hostile toward Islam and their immigration into Western Europe. The EDL and other anti jihad movements are united in their belief that Islam and Muslims are a fundamental threat to the resources, identities, and survival of Western nations.

Xenophobic
A person who manifests xenophobia. See xenophobia.

Information Link
The English Defence League
The EDL has a well-developed website with instructive content about what it is and stands for. Illustratively, it is opposed to the Islamic distinction between Muslims and Kuffars, or non-Muslims. According to EDL, the idea that Kuffars are inferior to Muslims permeates the Koran, sharia law, and the Islamic worldview. The EDL website gives a good look at the public face of this controversial organization.

Quick Facts

The citizens Movement Pax Europa promotes itself as a Human Rights Organization for Freedom and Democracy Against Islamization.

TABLE 8–2
Murders by Extremists in the United States, 2007–2016[24]

Movement	Percent Killed	Number Killed
Right Wing	74	242
Domestic Radical Islamic	24	78
Left Wing	2	7

James Earl Ray
He assassinated civil rights champion Reverend Martin Luther King in Memphis, Tennessee, in 1968.

Nativism
The right wing rests on nativism, the ultra preference for the traditional culture of a homeland to the exclusion of immigrants and their alien ways, as well as opposition to foreign ideas and influences. Nativism also rejects those in the homeland who champion immigrants, "alien" ways, and nontraditional ways of looking at the world.

Xenophobia
An irrational fear, hatred, and hostility toward people who are "different," including not only immigrants but also those with different lifestyles or sexual preferences, and "strange" ideas.

Homophobic
Describes a range of negative attitudes and feelings toward people who are gay, lesbian, bisexual, transgender, or queer (GLBTQ).

wing, the far right, extreme right, radical right, alternative right/alt right, right-wing populist.[25] Geography and religion also affect what constitutes right-wing extremism. In Europe, there frequently isn't a religious component to right-wing extremism, but in Israel and the United States there is often one.[26] In Israel, extreme right-wing views are linked to justifications for using extreme measures to maintain control over the West Bank and the Gaza Strip; in the United States, religion is part of the ideology of white supremacy and other right-wing movements.[27]

Right-Wing Attacks and Ideology in America

Right-wing attacks in America have risen. Annual attacks by far-right individuals and groups averaged 70.1 during the 1990s, but during 2000–2011 that figure rose to 307.5, an increase of more than 400 percent.[28] Between 2007 and 2016, domestic extremists killed at least 327 people in America (see Table 8–2). Despite our fears of a radicalized Islamic attack, we should also be wary of movements closer at hand: America's right wing.

Figure 8–3 summarizes the affiliation of extremists who killed people in 2016 versus 2015. In most years, as it was in 2015, American right-wing extremists kill more people than any other type of domestic extremism. The following year was an anomaly. Omar Mateen committed what at the time was largest mass shooting in American history at the Pulse nightclub in Orlando, Florida, where many LGBTQ people found acceptance. Over 100 people were shot and forty-nine killed. During conversations with the police, Mateen pledged his support to IS and al Baghdadi, referred to the brothers involved in the Boston Marathon bombing, the Tsarnaev brothers, and complained about American air strikes in Afghanistan and Syria. Mateen was killed in a gun battle with police and his wife was later arrested on impeding an investigation and terrorism-related charges.

The murder of even a single person can have a terrible impact. Even if the person is not a public figure, a murder takes a spouse, parent, child, sibling, and friend. **James Earl Ray** (1928–1998), set off riots and demonstrations in 100 American cities when he used a rifle to assassinate the civil rights leader Reverend Martin Luther King Jr., who was standing outside of his room at the Lorraine Motel in Memphis, Tennessee.

At its core, American right-wing ideology envisions having a homeland population that is homogeneous with respect to ethnicity, language, culture, and beliefs, as well as a systematic rejection of all those who are different.[29] The right rests on the notion that "being American" equates to emanating from European Anglo-Saxon stock, being

FIGURE 8–3
Domestic Extremist-Related Killings in the United States 2015–2016.

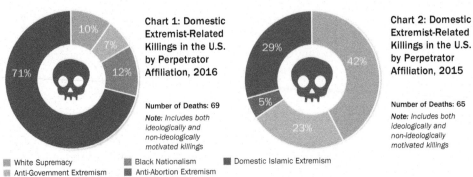

Chart 1: Domestic Extremist-Related Killings in the U.S. by Perpetrator Affiliation, 2016

Number of Deaths: 69
Note: Includes both ideologically and non-ideologically motivated killings

Chart 2: Domestic Extremist-Related Killings in the U.S. by Perpetrator Affiliation, 2015

Number of Deaths: 65
Note: Includes both ideologically and non-ideologically motivated killings

■ White Supremacy   ■ Black Nationalism   ■ Domestic Islamic Extremism
■ Anti-Government Extremism   ■ Anti-Abortion Extremism

Box 8–1
Anti-Immigration Attacks and Groups

In Brockton, Massachusetts, Keith Luke—who carved a swastika on his forehead while awaiting trial—murdered two immigrants from the Republic of Cape Verde and raped another as part of his plans to deal with African-Americans, Hispanics, and Jews. His motive was to fight for, and help preserve, "a dying race."

It is believed that Joseph Paul Franklin's crime spree in the United States started in 1977. In addition to bank robberies, this racist and anti-Semitic murdered Jews and visitors leaving a synagogue and mixed-race couples, killing twenty people. He also targeted persons who were friendly to minorities. Franklin believed that God wanted him to start a race war. He was convicted of murder in 1980 and committed suicide in prison in 2014.[30] Some sources report Luke was executed.

The most visible American anti-illegal immigration groups are often located in states along the Rio Grande River, the boundary with Mexico; they include the California Coalition for Immigration Reform, Border Guardians, Border Patrol Auxiliary, Texas Border Volunteers, American Freedom Riders, and Mountain Minutemen (see Figure 8–4).

Christian, nationalistic, and ruggedly independent.[31] To one degree or another, the right wing rests on **nativism**, the ultra-preference for the traditional culture of a homeland to the exclusion of immigrants and their alien ways, as well as opposition to foreign ideas and influences.[32] Nativism also rejects those in the homeland who support immigrants, "alien" ways, and nontraditional ways of looking at the world.[33] Nativism incorporates **xenophobia**, which involves an irrational fear, hatred, and hostility toward people who are "different," including not only immigrants but also those with different lifestyles, sexual preferences, and "strange" ideas; racism rests on the same dynamics, but is rooted in a narrower race-based hatred, driven by the belief that "we" are naturally superior to "them."[34]

The Three Major Ideological Right-Wing Movements in the United States

Perliger identifies three major ideological right-wing movements in the United States: (1) The Racist/White Supremacy Movement, including the development of the Ku Klux Klan, the rise of neo-Nazism in America, and the emergence of the Hammerskin Nation, (2) The Anti-Federalist Movement, and (3) The Christian Identity Movement. Their ideological orientations affect the targets they select, the tactics used, and the operations conducted.[35]

The Racist/White Supremacy Movement

To no small degree, the abominable practice of slavery has engendered the lingering *voluntary sickness* of racism in America. Racism essentially birthed the wider white supremacy movement with its volatile mixture of nativism, xenophobia, anti-immigration, **homophobic**, Christianity, and anti-Semitic components. As a society, the United States does not have "clean hands" when it comes to racism/white supremacy. Although not to the same degree as African-Americans, other ethnic groups have also suffered.

In the pre-revolution English colonies in America, free Irish immigrants usually arrived here impoverished, joining African-American slaves at the bottom of society's ladder. Ships' captains bringing servants to the colonies were paid a bonus for non-Irish males because Ireland had a long history of rebellion against England and were Catholics, a religion abandoned by England.[36] If the Irish indentured themselves, they were required to perform more years of service than indentured people from England.[37] Indentured Irishmen were often given more dangerous jobs than slaves because the latter were more valuable.[38] The Irish were so lowly regarded that even slaves could safely tell anti-Irish jokes.[39]

In 1845, as Americans pushed westward, newspaper editor John O'Sullivan coined the term "**manifest destiny**," meaning the United States had a divine obligation to push its boundaries ever-forward.[40] "At the heart of manifest destiny was the

FIGURE 8–4
Near Naco, Arizona, a Minutemen volunteer watches the Arizona/Mexico border for illegal aliens crossing into the United States. When observed, Minutemen call the Border Patrol to apprehend the "crossers."

(Andrew Holbrooke/Sipa Press/Newscom)

Manifest Destiny
In 1845, as Americans pushed westward, newspaper editor John O'Sullivan coined the term "manifest destiny," meaning the United States had a divine obligation to push its boundaries ever-forward. At the heart of manifest destiny was the pervasive belief in American cultural and racial superiority.

FIGURE 8–5
Racial hatred is often a precursor to racial terrorism. During the 1870s and 1880s there were 153 anti-Chinese riots in the American West. In 1880, anti-Chinese sentiment was loose in Denver, inflamed by a local newspaper that called the Chinese the "Pest of the Pacific" and prophesied that if more arrived, white men would starve and women would be forced into prostitution. During Denver's riot, one Chinese man was beaten to death, the Chinatown section was burned down, and their laundries were destroyed. Some citizens hid the Chinese in their homes, as did a brothel. No criminal charges were ever filed.[53]

(Library of Congress Prints and Photographs Division Washington, D.C. 20540 USA)

Japanese-American internment camps
At the outbreak of World War II, Japanese-Americans were placed in internment camps for "national security." Some volunteered to serve in the 442nd Regimental Combat Team to demonstrate their loyalty. In 1988, the Congress recognized the "grave injustice" done to those interred and awarded each surviving camp member $20,000; each reparation paid was accompanied by a letter of apology from President Reagan.

pervasive belief in American cultural and racial superiority."[41] The westward movement was particularly fueled by the discovery of gold at Sutter's Mill, California (1848), the availability of free land to settlers under the Homestead Act (1862), and the end of our Civil War (1865), which released large numbers of restless men who sought adventure and fortune in the West.[42] As manifest destiny made the shift from a slogan to unofficial government policy, the previous practice of going onto Indian lands, making genocidal war on Native Americans, then treaties, and then more wars when the treaties didn't suit the federal government became virulent. The refrain attributed to General Philip Sheridan that "The only good Indian is a dead Indian" was commonly voiced. Despite the refrain's endless repetition, there is considerable doubt that Sheridan ever said it.[43]

Hispanics were also subject to racism during the westward movement. There were 597 documented lynchings of Latinos, about one-fifth the number for African-Americans for the same period.[44] Although crimes were alleged in many cases, Latinos were also lynched for being "uppity," refusing to leave land coveted by Anglos, being "too Mexican" (speaking Spanish too loudly), and even a few Mexican women were lynched for resisting Anglo advances "too vigorously."[45]

Excitement about the discovery of gold at Sutter's Mill led to waves of Chinese coming to America to seek their fortune.[46] However, they were quickly pushed off any productive claims they found and forced into menial laborer jobs, most notably the construction of railroads. Still, within 30 years, the Chinese represented 10 percent of California's population.[47] Their "strange" language, Buddhist religion, manner of dress, physical appearance, and living in Chinese enclaves made assimilation in nineteenth-century America an impossibility. During the economic depression of 1873–1879, the Chinese were considered a threat to white employment[48] and racial violence quickened, including the burning of some "China Towns" (see Figure 8–5). Numerous racist laws regulating the Chinese were passed. For example, in California the Chinese couldn't testify in court or live within incorporated areas because they were considered a dangerous presence to the state.[49] The outcry against them grew so ferocious that in 1882 the Congress enacted the Chinese Exclusion Act, effectively barring Chinese immigration to America. In 1924, the National Origins Act restricted immigration from all Eastern Asian nations, which remained unchanged until the 1960s.

The surprise attack on Pearl Harbor, Hawaii, on December 7, 1941, led the American government to fear an imminent West Coast invasion by Japanese military forces. In 1942, the United States placed 120,000 mainland ethnic Japanese-Americans, two-thirds of whom were native United States citizens, behind barbed wire in ten guarded **Japanese-American internment camps** located in Western states and Arkansas as a "national security measure" (see Figure 8–6); this action was taken despite the fact that thousands of them had been investigated by federal agents and deemed not to be a threat.[50] The interred were forced to abandon their homes and businesses or sell them at distressed prices. However, it was impractical to enter the Japanese-Americans on Hawaii because they were the majority population and they were therefore left in place.

In 1942, the Army discharged all Japanese-American citizens from its Reserve Officer Training Corp (ROTC) program and changed their draft status to 4C, "enemy alien."[51] Remarkably, many of the interned Japanese-American men volunteered to serve in the army and formed the **442nd Regimental Combat Team**, along with volunteer Japanese-Americans from Hawaii. We have been unable to find a single case of espionage or sabotage by Japanese Americans during World War II. In 1988, the Congress recognized the "grave injustice" done and awarded each surviving camp member $20,000; each reparation paid was accompanied by a letter of apology from President Reagan. Longitudinal health studies showed that incidents of heart disease and premature death among internees were twice that of the general American population.[52]

FIGURE 8–6
In 1942, behind the barbed wire at the Manzanar Relocation Camp, California, Japanese-American citizens recognize Memorial Day, which honors the men and women who died while serving in the Armed Forces of the United States. As indicated by their American Legion hats, some of these men were veterans of World War I.

(U.S. War Relocation Authority/ Library of Congress Prints and Photographs Division Washington, D.C. 20540 USA)

Box 8–2
Dan Inouye

Dan Inouye (1924–2012) was deployed to the European Theater as an officer in the 442nd Regiment Combat Team. It became the most heavily decorated unit of its size in military history.[54] Inouye lost an arm from a combat wound, and received the Congressional Medal of Honor, America's highest award for valor. He served with great distinction in the United States Senate from 1963 until 2012.

The **German-American Bund** (GAB), a pro-Nazi organization, sprung up in this country in the 1930s to proclaim the virtues of Hitler and the Third Reich and to encourage America to remain neutral in the approaching European war (see Figure 8–7).[55] The anti-Semitic Bund's membership was made up of 25,000 German-American citizens, including 8,000 uniformed Storm Troopers, who occasionally clashed with American Jewish veterans of World War I.[56] Although the Bund was outlawed at the onset of World War II and a few leaders incarcerated, its Anglo-Saxon members, unlike the Japanese-Americans, were not rounded up and incarcerated.

During World War II, racist violence toward Chicanos erupted. **Zoot suit** fashion originated out of the African-American jazz movement and jumped to the Chicano culture. The zoot suit featured exaggerated shoulders, long coattails, a high waist, pleated pants with pegged legs, thick-soled leather shoes, and a long watch chain.[57] On the West Coast, American servicemen saw the style as not only a waste of materials needed for the war effort but subversive as well.[58] There were a number of violent clashes between servicemen and Chicano "zoot suiters" (see Figure 8–8), including one in 1943 in which the "suitors" were beaten, stripped naked, and their clothing burned in the street.[59]

In the wake of 9/11, anti-Islamic attacks in America skyrocketed from 28 in 2000 to 481 in 2001.[60] In 2015, there were 307 religious-based hate crimes committed against Islamics.[61]

Ten years after 9/11, the number of anti-Islamic attacks had fallen to 157, or 12.7 percent of all hate crime that is religion based; the anti-Jewish figure was 62.5 percent of the total.[62] Although "Islamophobic" attacks were down, gruesome violence against Muslims continues. Notably, in 2012, a thirty-one-year-old New York City woman was charged with second degree murder. She allegedly pushed a man, who she mistakenly identified as a Muslim, onto the subway tracks where he was killed by an oncoming train. The woman told investigators: I've hated Hindus and Muslims ever since 2001, when they put down

442nd Regimental Combat Team
A Japanese-American unit that served in the European Theater, consistently serving with valor. Members of the 442nd were Japanese-American volunteers from Hawaii and the internment camps. The 442nd became the most heavily decorated unit of its size in military history. See Japanese-American internment camps.

German-American Bund
In the 1930s, the GAB emerged in this country as a pro-Nazi movement that sang the praises of Hitler and the Third Reich, encouraged Americans to stay out of the war in Europe, and was anti-Semitic. Its members were largely drawn from German Americans. Unlike the wholesale internment of Japanese-Americans, only a small number of the GAB were incarcerated after it was outlawed.

Zoot suit
A men's fashion that moved from the African-American jazz movement into Chicano style. The exaggerated style was offensive to World War II American servicemen who saw the style as wasteful and subversive. The result were some violent clashes between the Chicano "zoot suiters" and servicemen.

FIGURE 8–7
In 1937, German-American Bund members marched in uniforms on Long Island, New York. A portion of a flag bearing the Nazi swastika appears to the right of the first American flag.

(World Telegram photo/Library of Congress Prints and Photographs Division Washington, D.C. 20540 USA)

Slave patrols
The first formal racist organization in America.

FIGURE 8–8
Chained together, "zoot suiters" are lined up outside of the Los Angeles jail waiting to board the bus that will take them to court after an evening feud with sailors. These encounters were sometimes brutal because servicemen beat the "suitors" with clubs.

(Acme Newspictures/Library of Congress Prints and Photographs Division Washington, D.C. 20540 USA)

the Twin Towers. I've been beating them up since then.[63] In the wake of the Boston Marathon bombing in 2013 by the two Tsarnaev brothers, both ethnic Chechens and Muslims, many feared a repeat of the widespread anti-Islamic attacks that followed 9/11, but this did not happen. African-Americans continue to suffer disproportionally from reported race-based hate crime, constituting some 71.1 percent of all of it, while Hispanics represent 56.2 percent of all reported ethnicity/national origin hate crimes.[64] Gay, lesbian, bisexual, and transgender (GLBT) persons accounted for 20.8 percent of all reported single-bias incidents.[65]

In early 2017, Kori Ali Muhammad, 39, was a suspect in shooting a motel security guard in Fresno, California. He decided that's not the way he wanted to be remembered. Instead, he wanted to be known as someone who killed a bunch of white people.[66] So, he shot three white people, while yelling in Arabic, "God is great."[67] Muhammad was captured and charged with four counts of murder.[68] Muhammad's actions contributed to a little-noticed statistic about single-bias hate crimes based on race: Whites are 19 percent of all victims.[69]

A fundamental truth of hate statistics is that African-Americans, Jews, Hispanics, and GLBTs continue to suffer disproportionately from right-wing extremism.

The Development of the Ku Klux Klan

Conventionally, the Ku Klux Klan (KKK) is "recognized" as the first formal racist organization in this country. However, that "distinction" actually belongs to the **slave patrols** that began in the colonial era and were highly regulated in some states. Beginning in 1704, South Carolina enacted laws controlling such slave patrol matters as district patrol boundaries, patrol authority, and relief from militia duty if serving on slave patrols.[70] These patrols were not informal, spontaneous, or episodic groups, but organizations created by law and are therefore the earliest formal racist organization in this country. Inasmuch as this section covers the racist/white

supremacy portion of the American right wing, the discussion here is focused on its most visible components, the Ku Klux Klan and the neo-Nazis.

Pulaski, Tennessee, was a sleepy town in 1865. The Civil War was over and several former Confederates played in a band to help raise money to buy artificial limbs for some of their maimed comrades. Bored Confederate veterans formed the Ku Klux Klan in 1866[71] to create a stir and excitement at parties. They made up nonsensical names like the Grand Cyclops and Imperial Wizard and rode off to parties wearing costumes and masks.[72] Very quickly the KKK began intimidating former slaves, referred to after the Civil War as "freedmen," and then jumped to committing violence against them. Many Southerners approved of KKK actions because it restored what they saw as the natural order of things. By 1868, the KKK was a full blown terrorist organization that its members called the "Invisible Empire of the South."[73] Beginning in 1870, Congress passed a series of laws that were aimed at defeating the KKK.

FIGURE 8–9
On August 8, 1925, 35,000 Klansmen marched in Washington, D.C., a substantial display of its power. The white-robed men paraded in orderly military formations as far as the eye could see. Barely visible in the distance is the dome of the United States Capitol building.
(National Photo Company/Library of Congress Prints and Photographs Division Washington, D.C. 20540 USA)

Originally a Southern phenomenon, the first KKK was substantially eroded and became a marginal movement not later than 1900. In 1915, a second, revitalized KKK appeared that was prominent into the 1930s; its membership extended into regions outside of the South and at its height it had 5,000,000 members.[74] The 1915 KKK was the most successful far–right-wing movement in U.S. history in terms of the power to elect political candidates, recruit dues-paying members, and turn out supporters at rallies.[75] To no small measure, the silent film "Birth of a Nation," released in 1915, aided recruitment by portraying African-Americans negatively and the Klan as a heroic force holding back this "threat" to America.

This "second" KKK pursued a national agenda that was virulently anti-immigration, anti-Catholicism, anti-Semitic, and anti-African-American, while at the same time being pro-family, pro-protestant, pro-prohibition, and pro-American white nation (see Figure 8–9). These themes resonated across class lines, causing the regular KKK membership rolls to bulge. The KKK also distributed a magazine to reinforce these messages and allowed for local agendas, such as targeting Mormons and labor radicals. Additionally, there were affiliate organizations, including the Women's Ku Klux Klan (WKKK), the Junior Order of the Ku Klux Klan for boys, and the Tri-K Klan for girls.[76] The Great Depression that began in 1929 and lasted until the late 1930s gutted the ability of many to pay KKK dues and membership declined. The entry of the United States into World War II diverted potential recruits to military service and the Klan substantially disappeared until after the Korean War (1950–1953).

The resurrection of the "third" Klan was inhibited by many states passing anti-Klan laws, the passage of the federal Civil Rights Act of 1964, the enforcement of its provisions by the FBI, arrests made on cold cases, including the bombing of African-American churches, and a series of civil suits that cost the Klan millions of dollars (e.g., the KKK was ordered to pay $38 million because it incited the hatred that resulted in an African-American Church being burned in Manning, South Carolina).[77]

Beginning in the 1970s and continuing into the 1980s, the Klan toned down its racial rhetoric and reframed its messages in a neo-conservatism shift. Jews were at the heart of a conspiracy to destroy America. They were blamed for an increasingly liberal national government that the Klan dubbed the "**Zionist Occupied Government**" (ZOG) and condemned as the "Jewish dominated news media" that espoused the acceptance of "deviant lifestyles," such as homosexuality, the mixing of races, and feminist views. To fight this menace, the Klan appropriated the warped notion of Christianity Identity, which established the Bible as the authority for what they did, while retaining their nativist and xenophobic views of what constituted being "American." In doing so, the Klan morphed from being a hate organization to a "theologically based, patriotic white supremacy movement." The Christian Identity movement is discussed later in this chapter and is sometimes referred to by mainstream theologians as "**Counterfeit Christians**."

Zionist Occupied Government
A right-wing term sometimes used to refer to the U.S. government.

Counterfeit Christians
Sometimes used to refer to Christian Identity adherents.

FIGURE 8–10
An Imperial Wizard of the KKK heads a klavern, while the Grand Wizard is the national head of the Invisible Empire of the Knights of the Ku Klux Klan. Note the KKK symbol over the heart, often called the MIOAK (an acronym for "Mystic Insignia of a Klansman," signifying the pure Aryan blood drop within the Christian cross, often worn as a tattoo by members.

(Jeremy Hogan/Polaris/Newscom)

Klaverns
Local chapters of the KKK.

George Lincoln Rockwell
Founder of the American Nazi Party who ran for president to change the U.S. Constitution and laws to align with the racist perspectives of the Nazi Party.

Dr. William Luther Pierce
As Andrew MacDonald authored *The Turner Diaries*, still considered one of the right wing's most influential publications. He also wrote *Hunter*, which did not receive nearly the acclaim that *The Turner Diaries* did.

The KKK has been fragmented for some time; there are at least 40 different Klan groups of various sizes with perhaps 100 local **Klaverns** or chapters between them. Each klavern is headed by an imperial wizard (see Figure 8–10). Until recently there was only an estimated total membership of 5,000.[78] As an indication of its impotence, at a 1999 protest in downtown New York, the Klan could muster only 16 members in the face of 8,000 New Yorkers who came out to counterdemonstrate.[79] Since 2006, the Klan has attempted to exploit fears about immigration, amnesty, gay marriages, crime, gun control, and other issues;[80] as a result, it is believed there has been a rapid expansion in size. Although some Klansmen still wear robes and burn crosses, some younger ones are virtually indistinguishable from racist skinheads and neo-Nazis, adopting their music, dress, tattoos, and imagery.[81]

The Rise of Neo-Nazism in America

"Neo-Nazi groups share a hatred for Jews and a love for Adolf Hitler and Nazi Germany. While they also hate other minorities, gays and lesbians and even sometimes Christians, they perceive 'the Jew' as their cardinal enemy, and trace social problems to a Jewish conspiracy that supposedly controls governments, financial institutions, and the media."[82] There is not one neo-Nazi organization; there are many. Estimates vary, but there may be as many as 200 neo-Nazi groups in the United States, many of which share agendas.

The goal of **George Lincoln Rockwell** (1918–1967) was to use his American Nazi Party (ANP) to become president of the United States in 1972 and then "exterminate all treasonous Jews, banish all American Negroes to Africa, and amend the Constitution to suit the Nazi party."[83] The FBI's official 1965 threat assessment of the ANP was "Though small in numbers and influence the ANP is a dangerous organization of misfits ... capable of perpetrating acts of violence."[84] In 1967, Rockwell was at a carwash when a sniper killed him; the perpetrator was a man Rockwell had dismissed from the ANP. Despite the hatred it spewed out and the extensive news media coverage it received, the ANP was never a major force. A more recent parallel to Rockwell's political ambitions is Billy Joe Roper, who in 2002 founded the neo-Nazi White Revolution as an Arkansas-based political party that seeks to promote cooperation among supremacy groups.[85] Roper, who was expelled from the neo-Nazi National Alliance (NA) in a leadership struggle, ran an unsuccessful write-in candidacy in the 2010 Arkansas governor's race.[86]

Shortly after Rockwell's death, the ANP was rebadged as the National Socialist White People's Party (NSWPP) and **Dr. William Luther Pierce** (1933–2002), a former physics professor at Oregon State University, became one of its principal leaders.[87] Beginning in 1974, Pierce headed the neo-Nazi National Alliance (NA)[88] and it was there that he became the leading figure of the racist/white supremacy movement for nearly 30 years. Pierce envisioned NA as being the vanguard of a white nationalist movement. The NA used right-wing magazines, bands, record companies, music (National Socialist Black Metal, NSBM), weekly radio talks, the Internet, and Internet games to spread its gospel.[89] NA's National Vanguard Press eventually had a list of 700 books to spread the NA's message.[90]

Writing under the name of **Andrew MacDonald**, Pierce wrote two influential racist/white supremacy novels, *The Turner Diaries* (1978) and *Hunter* (1984). The former depicts an Aryan revolution in America that spreads globally, includes nuclear attacks, and results in the elimination of all "impure races." The revolution begins with the truck bombing of the FBI Headquarters in Washington, D.C., a scenario that many think was a model for Tim McVeigh's 1995 attack on the Murrah Federal Building in Oklahoma City.[91] The fictional and McVeigh's attacks occurred at almost the same time of day, both featured truck bombs, and when arrested McVeigh had a portion of *The Turner Diaries* in his car. *Hunter* is considered the prequel to *The Turner Diaries*. In *Hunter*, The protagonist assassinates mixed-race couples and public figures advocating racial civil rights; battles other neo-Nazi enemies, including Jews; and becomes involved with a white nationalist movement.

Under Pierce, the NA became the largest and most active neo-Nazi organization in the United States; dozens of violent crimes were attributed to NA members or to those apparently influenced by its propaganda.[92] In 2005, many members defected to the newly formed National Vanguard, weakening the NA. By 2012, ten years after Pierce's death, the NA had been reduced to a tiny band of small-time propagandists.[93] Although small, the NA is dangerous; four recruits have been accused or convicted of carrying out at least a dozen murders.[94]

In 1974, two members of the ANP left it and formed the National Socialist American Workers Freedom Movement, which became the previously mentioned National Socialist Movement (NSM) 20 years later.[95] Ideologically, the NSM mirrors that of the original American Nazi Party; the NSM openly idolizes Hitler and describes him as "Our Fuhrer, the beloved Holy Father of our age."[96]

One of the NSM symbols is "88." The eighth letter of the alphabet is "H" and "88" means "Heil Hitler." The NSM rhetoric is anti-Jewish, homophobic, anti-immigration, racist, and white nationalist. The NSM demands territory for the creation of a union in which only whites of pure blood may be citizens; Jews and homosexuals are specifically excluded from citizenship.[97] All illegal immigrants must be returned to their homeland; non-whites can live in the white homeland only as guests under the law of aliens, meaning they have no legal right to remain in the country.[98] One of the NSM leaders asserts, "the Constitution was written by white men alone; therefore, it is intended for whites alone."[99] Unlike other neo-Nazi groups, the NSM allows members of other groups to join without abandoning their other memberships.[100]

Starting in 2004, the NSM began to overshadow all other American neo-Nazi groups,[101] primarily due to setbacks by other groups between 2002 and 2007.[102] It has members in every region of the United States, although the Northeast has the most local units.[103] NSM members tend to be young and they include some skinheads.[104] It is the most explicit "Nazi-like" movement,[105] specializing in provocative street demonstrations where its members show up in militant black battle fatigues. During the recent past, the NSM has emphasized immigration and amnesty issues (see Figure 8–11).

Organized in 1977, the Aryan Nations is a white supremacy group that, to some degree, operated as an umbrella organization, holding an annual World Congress for similar groups at its base of operations in Hayden Lake, Idaho. In 2000, it lost substantial assets due to a successful Southern Poverty Law Center civil suit. The death of Aryan Nations' founder in 2004 hastened some further disintegration of the group (see Figure 8–12).[106] Although there are a number of organizations that use "Aryan" in their title, it should be automatically assumed they are connected with the all-but-defunct Aryan Nations or the prison gang, Aryan Brotherhood. The original is badly splintered, lost members to better-organized movements, and is having difficulty reconstituting even a shadow of itself.

The Emergence of the Hammerskin Nation

The Hammerskin Nation (HN), founded in Dallas, Texas, in 1988, is the most violent, best organized neo-Nazi **skinhead** group in the United States.[107] Although primarily an American

Andrew MacDonald
See Dr. William L. Pierce.

The Turner Diaries
See Dr. William L. Pierce.

Hunter
See Dr. William L. Pierce.

Skinhead
A member of or affiliated with the white power or white nationalist movement commonly called the Hammerskin Nation.

FIGURE 8–11

An underground flyer from the American Nazi Party that rekindles hate and focuses on today's social and political issues. Note how the Nazi Germany flag is labeled as "the symbol of our race," while the American flag is "the symbol of our country." The "14 Words" is a reference to the most popular white supremacist slogan in the world (written in italics above the flags): "We must secure the existence of our people and a future for white children."

(Neo-Nazi Party)

Skinbyrd
A female skinhead.

Red Laces
Worn in the boots of skinheads, they denote the wearer has shed blood for the skinhead movement.

FIGURE 8–12
A small group of Aryan Nations adherents gather for a ritual.

(Jim Lo Scalzo/EPA/Newscom)

movement, HN has chapters in Canada, England, France, Germany, and several other countries[108] (See Figure 8–13). Although not large, American Front (AF) is the oldest continuously active skinhead group in the United States with members in several states.[109] Some local skinhead groups in the United States affiliate with HN or AF to have an umbrella organization to tie them together. Others affiliate with the England-based Blood and Honour organization. In 2011, four members of Tampa's Blood and Honour movement beat a homeless man to death and pled guilty or were convicted of the act.[110]

Skinhead organizations have a variety of names, including Blood and Honour, Aryan Strike Force, Aryan Terror Brigade, Crew 38, Old Glory Skinheads, and Confederate Hammerskins. Blood and Honour members believe white persons of Aryan descent are the superior race and consider the homeless to be an inferior class; "bum rolling" is the term given to targeting and committing acts of violence against homeless persons. Hammerskins and skinheads in general are disillusioned, unhappy young men who find the structure and exclusivity of the Hammerskins appealing; the probationary period for someone aspiring to join may last as long as two years.[111] Members may have shaved heads, be heavily tattooed, wear boots, jeans, and waist-length leather jackets. Like other movements, skinheads have their own language and symbols—for example, "**skinbyrd**" is a female skinhead and **red laces** in the boots means the wearer has shed his blood for the movement; some skinheads will randomly attack people to earn their laces.[112]

There are also right-wing groups that don't fit neatly into a violent racist/white supremacy mold. Neo-Confederates represent a revival of pro-Confederate sentiments and they advocate traditional gender roles, display hostility toward democracy, are opposed to homosexuality, favor segregation, and sometimes are openly secessionist from the United States.[113] The Institute for Historical Review (IHR) asserts its purpose is to promote truth and accuracy in history.[114] However reasonable that sounds, the real purpose of the IHR is to promote denials of the Jewish Holocaust and to defend Nazism.[115]

The Anti-Federalist Movement

The original anti-federalist movement opposed the ratification of the U.S. Constitution, but there are other early examples of people being opposed to, or fearing, America's federal government. When the new federal government passed a tax on homemade whiskey that was used as barter, farmers in Western Pennsylvania attacked agents attempting to collect taxes. The situation became serious enough that in 1794, President George Washington rode out at the head of a column of troops to restore order. The protester disbanded before his arrival. A handful of men were arrested, but with sympathetic local juries hearing the cases, there were no convictions.

The anti-federalist movement has many variations. Some individuals live the movement's tenets without formally joining any organization. The anti-federalist movement grew out of the **Posse Comitatus** and **Sovereign Citizen movements** that began during the 1970s and 1980s, which were anti-government and anti-tax.[116] Many were also racist and anti-Semitic as well.

From January 2, 2016, until February 11, 2016, a loose collection of armed anti-federalists, including some Sovereign Citizens, occupied the headquarters of the Malheur National Wildlife Refuge in Oregon (see Figure 8–14). The event was sometimes called the Sagebrush Rebellion or the Bundy Occupation, named after its leader. Its purpose was to espouse that under the Constitution, the federal government, specifically the Bureau of Land Management, was obligated to turn over the public land it owned in the various states to the respective states.

The anti-federalists' ideology is based on the idea that there is an urgent necessity to undermine the influence, legitimacy, and practical sovereignty of the federal government and its proxies.[117] In this view, America has been hijacked by external forces determined to make it part of a New World Order in which the United States would be embedded in the United Nations or a global government and policed by foreign peacekeeping forces.[118] An initial step toward that is taking up the guns presently in the hands of American citizens so they can't resist. Members see themselves as the successors to the nation's founding fathers, trying to restore America's true identity, values, and way of life.[119] In 1996, there was an 81-day standoff between Montana Freemen and federal agents.[120] Freemen adherents had

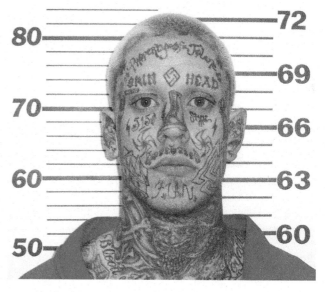

FIGURE 8–13
Skinheads are often adorned with multiple, racially-oriented tattoos, wear blue jeans, black "jack" boots, and, of course, a shaved head.
(Splash News/Newscom)

Box 8–3
The Posse Comitatus and Sovereign Citizen Movements

William Potter Gale founded the Posse Comitatus in 1970.[121] The Latin phrase translates to the "power of the county." It refers to a right-wing movement that opposes the federal government and holds that local authority trumps federal authority. However, the posse did not gain real momentum until Gale added Christian Identity "theology" to the anti-tax stance and spread it to the fiscally stressed farm belt.

In 1983, Posse adherent and tax protester Gordon Kahl killed two federal marshals in North Dakota; as a result, the entire movement became firmly fixed on law enforcement's radar. Kahl died in a gunfight with federal marshals, FBI agents, and local law enforcement officers in Smithville, Arkansas, in 1988. Although fledging remnants of the Posse Comitatus continue today, primarily in rural parts of the Midwest, the group and movement have withered away. Many of the former members left the Posse to join active groups in other right-wing movements.

The Sovereign Citizen movement is classified as a domestic terrorist movement by the FBI and has existed for decades.[122] The Sovereign Citizen movement was a natural evolution of the Posse Comitatus ideology. The sovereigns largely operate as individuals and come together in loose groups to provide mutual assistance, train, socialize, and talk about their ideology.[123] Sovereigns refer to themselves as "freemen" or "Constitutionalists" and believe they are free from all forms of government control because the federal, state, and local governments operate illegally.[124] Sovereigns assert that they have no obligation to pay taxes, get driver's licenses or vehicle tags, or otherwise comply with any governmental regulations or laws. If arrested or called into court, they try to clog it with frivolous claims and filings. Contacts with some sovereigns can be deadly. In 2010, a father-son sovereign team killed two West Memphis, Arkansas, police officers who had stopped their vehicle.[125] The Alabama-based Republic for the United States is the largest organized group of sovereigns currently in the United States. However, the Republic of Texas group is also relatively large and active with more than 100 members. In 2011, the Republic groups held a congress with voting members from forty-nine states to create a new "government in waiting"[126] for the entire United States. While the Republic for the United States and the Republic of Texas do not express a violent means to an end, they do openly advocate for political revolution.[127] Recently, they have received significant political support from more radical factions of the Tea Party, particularly in Texas.

Could there be a connection between periods of economic depression in the United States and growth in anti-government groups, hate groups, and other right-wing domestic followers?

Quick Facts
Republic of The United States

The Republic for the United States claims to be a functioning government working in parallel to our current United States of America national government, www.republicoftheunitedstates.org.

It claims that our current government subverts our rights and is controlled by foreign interests.

Posse Comitatus

The Latin phrase translates to the "power of the county." It refers to a right-wing movement that opposes the federal government and holds that local authority trumps federal authority. It was founded by William Potter Gale in 1970, but did not gain momentum until he incorporated Christian Identity (CI). The group was substantially defunct by 1990, several years after Gale's death.

Sovereign Citizen movement

Anti-government extremists who believe they are separate or sovereign from the federal government. Referring to themselves as freemen, or free patriots, the people associated with this movement do not pay taxes or recognize any federal or state authority, including the courts, motor vehicle departments, or law enforcement agencies.

Information Link

For more information on the Sovereign Citizen movement, visit the FBI story relating to such groups at www.fbi .gov/news/stories/2010/april/ sovereigncitizens_041310.

formed their own township, issued warrants, developed a court and banking system, and recognized no authority higher than their own. The Freemen's land was under foreclosure and a number of Freemen were wanted on various charges. Ultimately, the Freemen surrendered and a blood bath was averted.

The unregulated "volunteer" militias that spring up are solidly anti-federalist. Four Medicare-eligible men were arrested in plots to assassinate public officials, including the U.S. Attorney General, bomb federal buildings, and attack cities with deadly ricin made from plants.[128] The men may have been members of the Georgia Militia that is not fighting the "New World Order" but instead is grounded in racist, anti-Semitic, and neo-Nazi ideology.[129] Four Ft. Stewart, Georgia, soldiers formed a militia-style group called "Forever Enduring, Always Ready" (FEAR), which wanted to kill President Obama and start a revolution to give America back to the people. As they moved forward with their plans, they allegedly killed one of their members and his girlfriend, apparently fearing that they would reveal the plot to authorities. What both of these plots had in common was the killing of senior federal government officials.

The most deadly terrorist attack in this country until 9/11 was carried out by Timothy McVeigh and his accomplices at the Murrah Federal Building in Oklahoma City. McVeigh, a decorated army combat veteran, attended a few militia meetings and made a half-hearted attempt to start one in Arizona after being discharged from the army.[130] On April 19, 1995, McVeigh parked a rental Ryder truck filled

FIGURE 8–14
Early morning at the front gate guard post staffed by protestors at the Malheur National Wildlife Refuge. Eventually, protesters were arrested, some pled guilty, and at trial some were found not guilty.

(Jeffrey Schwilk/Alamy Stock Photo)

with a deadly mixture of agricultural fertilizers, diesel fuel, and other chemicals; he set a timer; and drove away.[131] The explosion killed 168 people, including nineteen children, and wounded more than 500 others (see Figure 8–15).[132] Ninety minutes after the explosion, McVeigh was stopped and arrested by an Oklahoma Highway Patrol Trooper on unrelated minor charges; among his possessions was a portion of *The Turner Diaries*.[133] While still in jail several days later, McVeigh was identified as a suspect in the Murrah Building bombing. McVeigh and his accomplices were convicted of the bombing, but only the unrepentant McVeigh was executed.

In 1992, federal agents tried to arrest Randy Weaver on federal weapons charges of selling illegally sawed-off shotguns at his home in **Ruby Ridge**, Idaho.[134] An 11-day standoff ensued and shots were exchanged. Federal agents killed Weaver's son and wife. McVeigh was angered by what he saw as an out-of-control government. Three years later, McVeigh was in Waco, Texas, where federal agents laid siege to the Branch Davidian Compound.[135] The Branch Davidians were a religious sect led by **David Koresh**. Federal agents had obtained a warrant to search the compound for weapons stockpiling. Resisted in their attempt to serve the warrant, federal agents besieged the compound for 51 days. Several federal agents were killed by Branch Davidians as they attempted to force entry into the compound. On April 19, 1995, federal agents again assaulted the compound and seventy-six Branch Davidians died by gunshot or by fire. McVeigh was at Waco and revenging it became his primary motivation. Two years to the day after the final assault at Waco, McVeigh detonated the bomb that gutted the Murrah Building.

FIGURE 8–15
Search and rescue teams work to save survivors trapped in the bombed Murrah Federal Building. (*Federal Emergency Management Agency*)

The Christian Identity Movement

British Zionism ideology achieved a degree of prominence in eighteenth century England; ethnic Western Europeans, especially the Anglo-Saxons of Great Britain, believed they were the progeny of the ten lost tribes of Israel[136] who had migrated to the British Isles. This meant the Bible was not written for the Jews, but for the white race.[137] This false form of Christianity placed the white race at the center of God's divine plan and all other ethnicities were lesser beings, soulless "mud people."[138] By the mid-late 1940s, the British Zionism ideology gained traction in America's West. In 1946, Wesley Swift, a Grand Dragon of the Ku Klux Klan, founded the Church of Jesus Christ Christian.[139] It is the root church for the U.S. **Christian Identity Movement**, which in its most extreme form postulates that the Jews were not God's chosen people, but instead are direct descendants of Satan,[140] the physical mating of Eve and the Serpent in the Garden of Eden.

Christian Identity churches are located throughout the United States. The first such church was originally located near Hayden Lake, Idaho, under the direction of Reverend Richard Butler, a former aerospace engineer for Lockheed. Butler combined the ideologies and symbols of neo-Nazism and fundamental Christianity with the racial hatred of the Ku Klux Klan to form the Aryan Nations. He constantly preached to his community the values of a white, Anglo-Saxon country devoid of foreign immigrants and people of color. He was indicted for seditious conspiracy to create a "race war" with 14 other right-wing leaders of the time (1987); however, federal prosecutors failed to prove the conspiracy among all members of the group. In 2000, Butler was successfully sued by Victoria and Jason Keenon, two Native Americans previously harassed and threatened by members of the Aryan Nations. The suit was filed by the Southern Poverty Law Center and a judgment of $6 million was issued against Butler and other members of his Christian Identity

Ruby Ridge (Idaho)
Federal agents went to Randy Weaver's rural home to arrest him on weapons charges. A standoff ensued and eventually gunfire was exchanged, killing Weaver's wife and son. The incident added fuel to the patriot, militia, and right-wing movements.

David Koresh
Leader of the Branch Davidians. Died at their compound in Waco, Texas.

Christian Identity Movement
The CI movement in its most extreme form postulates that the Jews were not God's chosen people, but instead are the spawn of the devil, the mating of Eve and the Serpent in the Garden. Different strands of CI believe it is wrong to mix with other races, interracial marriage is a sin, the Jews are the natural enemies of the Aryan race, racial treason is the greatest crime, and homosexuality should be punished by death. See Counterfeit Christians.

Quick Facts
The New American Right-Wing Alliance Today

Individual groups representing the right wing in America have banded together in 2016 to make a new alliance called *The Nationalist Front*. Born in a bar in Georgia, six different Ku Klux Klan chapters developed a formal national organization, originally called *The Aryan National Alliance,* to become more mainstream. *The Front* now represents such groups as the KKK, Neo-Confederates, Sovereign Citizens, Christian Identity Churches, Skinhead groups, a variety of Anti-Government Militias, and even several secessionist movements like the Texas Nationalist Movement and the "New State of Jefferson" Movement proposing a new state being formed from parts of Eastern Washington and Oregon with Northern Idaho

and Western Montana. The alliance has dropped the use of swastikas, calling minority groups by derogatory names, burning crosses, and even white robes and caps in an effort to broaden its appeal, build new membership, and become more politically powerful. The main goal of The Nationalist Front is to create an "ethnostate." As one imperial wizard of the KKK stated, "We want to see people stand up and make this country great again...we're tired of seeing white people lose everything."

Source: Jay Reeves, "White-Power Groups Banding Together," Associated Press, April 26, 2017.

movement. The judgment forced the Hayden Lake properties to be sold and Butler shrank into relative obscurity. He died in his sleep of a heart attack in 2004 and the Aryan Nations membership continues to decline.

The Christian Identity movement expresses a strong belief that is wrong to mix races and that interracial marriage is a sin. Further, they believe that Jews are the natural enemies of the white Christian and Aryan race, and that racial treason is the greatest of all sins or crime. The movement is also homophobic and openly advocates against gay rights and homosexuality, arguing that it is an "abomination before God" and should be punished by death.[141]

Benjamin Smith (1978–1999) was a disciple of the Christian Identity movement and member of the World Church of the Creator. He was an ardent follower of Matthew Hale, the son of an Illinois police officer who regularly preached racial hatred as justified through the Christian Identity movement. Smith went on a killing spree in Chicago and Northern Illinois in 1999, shooting people he identified as Jews by their dress. He also shot at African-Americans and Asians simply walking down the street, killing two and wounding nine others before finally committing suicide.[142] The Christian Identity movement, through Matthew Hale, did not take credit for the event. However, it did joyously exalt Smith as a good friend and hero to the Christian Patriot movement. In 2005, Matthew Hale was sentenced to 40 years in a maximum security prison for soliciting an undercover FBI informant to kill a federal judge in the Northern District of Illinois.

The tenets of the Christian Patriot movement have been openly expressed by neo-Nazis, Skinheads, and other far-right groups that have used violence to emphasis their hatred and bigotry. Examples of Christian Identity groups include the Anglo-Saxon Israel, Aryan Nations 88, Christian Patriot and Truth Ministries, Church of True Israel, the Aryan Nations, and the World Church of the Creator, which has been recast as the Creativity Movement.

The Left-Wing Movement

The traditional objective of left-wing terrorism is to overthrow the economic, political, and social structure of a society and replace it with one developed on Marxist-Leninist principles.[143] Groups historically in this category are located across the globe, including Sendero Luminoso (Shining Path) in Peru; the Red Army Faction (RAF) that operated mainly in Germany, but also in France, Switzerland, and the Netherlands; the Red Brigades in Italy; the Seung fein in China; and the Weather Underground in the United States.[144]

In the United States, the left wing originally sprang from labor/working class movements seeking to eliminate class distinctions,[145] setting the stage for later developments such as the Communist Party USA (CPUSA) that was formed in 1919. We have had a variety of communist/socialist political parties, but none have had lasting impact. The American left wing has essentially faded. To illustrate, there hasn't been a death in the United States attributed to it since an assassination attempt on President Truman in 1950.

Three factors may have contributed to the decline of left-wing movements in this country: (1) communism was seen by our government in past eras as a major threat and federal agencies, particularly the FBI, devoted a great deal of effort to eliminating the extremist right wing; (2) the demise of communism in European Eastern Bloc countries eliminated many ideological models from which left-wing movements could derive encouragement, learning, and perhaps some support; and (3) the lack of any success.

Using 1960 as a starting point, left-wing extremism and nationalism expressed itself through organizations such as the United Freedom Front, Weather Underground, Black Liberation Army, Black Panthers, May 19th Communist Organization (M19CO), and the Republic of New Africa (RNA), which sought a black majority homeland carved out of existing southern states and billions of dollars in reparations from the federal government for the enslavement of African-Americans and the discrimination they have suffered.

> **Information Link**
> For more information on the Patty Hearst Kidnapping, visit the FBI website: https://fbi.gov/history/famous-cases/patty-hearst.

Two of the most compelling events of the recent left wing involve the New Year's Gang (NYG) and Patty Hearst, a socialite heiress to a vast newspaper fortune established by her grandfather, William Randolph Hearst. The four-member NYG is often described as anti-war (Vietnam) activists; the FBI had tagged them as left-wing extremists. In 1970, the four men detonated a 2,000-pound bomb in a van at Sterling Hall on the campus of the University of Wisconsin, home to the Army's Mathematical Research Center. One researcher, the father of three children, was killed and others injured by the explosion that did $6 million in damages. It was the largest domestic terrorism attack until the bombing of the Murrah Federal Building led by McVeigh 25 years later. Three of the NYG were captured, convicted, and released after completing prison terms. Defying the odds, the fourth man, Leo Frederick Burt, has eluded capture since 1970.

Today, the left-wing groups in America have commonly gathered under a variety of anarchist movements that have rallied historically around ecology movements, some being violent in nature such as the "eco-terrorist" groups of Earth Liberation Front (ELF) and Animal Liberation Front (ALF) discussed earlier in Chapter 7. However, in

Quick Facts
The Black Panther Party

In 1966, Huey Newton and Bobby Seale founded the Black Panther Party for Self Defense in Oakland, California.[146] Its name was soon shortened to the Black Panther Party (BPP). The BPP saw Reverend King's nonviolent civil rights program as a failure and chartered a new and ultimately violent socialist course. Its original focus was to protect the black community from police brutality by using roving, armed patrols. The BPP also developed an impressive list of activities that included free health, dental, clothing, and children's breakfast programs, as well as legal aid, martial arts, and drama classes.

Because of their confrontational tactics, violent acts, and allegations of criminal acts, the BPP became a police target and many leaders and members were arrested and convicted. FBI Director Hoover called the BBP "the greatest threat to the internal security of this country." By the 1980s, the BPP had declined to fewer than twenty-five members and lost its national prominence. The BPP should not be confused with the New Black Panther Party (NBPP) discussed later in this chapter.

Quick Facts
Patty Hearst and the Symbionese Liberation Army (SLA)

In the 1970s, the Symbionese Liberation Army (SLA) wanted to use violent guerilla tactics to overthrow the government of the United States and replace it with a left-wing government. The SLA kidnapped Patty Hearst, a nineteen-year-old heiress and socialite, to create publicity. They successfully used crude brainwashing techniques to "convince" her to join their movement. She did so, and after being captured she was convicted of bank robbery and sentenced to seven years' imprisonment. After she served some 22 months, President Carter commuted her sentence to time served and she was released from prison. In 2001, President Clinton gave her a full pardon, wiping away her criminal record.

The beginning of the end for the SLA was a 1974 shootout with police that ended in the death of its founder Donald DeFreeze and several other members. Hearst was away from the house during the siege and escaped arrest for a short time thereafter. The last SLA member who had been "on the run" since the 1975 shootout was James Kilgore. He was finally arrested in 2002, nearly 27 years later, in South Africa by the FBI.[147] Kilgore was convicted of using a dead baby's birth certificate to get a passport under another identity and possessing a pipe bomb, which was found in his San Francisco area apartment in 1975. He served 54 months in a federal facility and was paroled in 2009.[148]

the late 1990s, much of the left-wing movement shifted focus to an anti-capitalist and anti-globalist position. Much of their unrest targeted the ultrarich, multinational corporations, and trade organizations. In 1999, the World Trade Organization held their annual meeting in Seattle, Washington, and was greeted with major demonstrations from the Anarchist Left, Black Army Faction, and Black Blocs movement. These groups had very little to do with race issues, and were much more about leftist ideology and the freedom presented by the "anarchist state." Most of the demonstrators were white, between 15 and 30 years of age, transient, and wore black masks and attire (hence the name "Black Blocs" or "Black Army Faction"). The groups were cell structure and conducted much of their violence, arson, and vandalism during the night. Most were heavily tattooed with anarchist slogans, and bore significant threat and hatred toward the police (see Figure 8–16). The demonstrations in Seattle completed the transition of the left wing from an ecology movement to an anti-wealth, antitechnology, and anticapitalist movement spewing rhetoric of class war and Marxist revolution.

FIGURE 8–16
The Anarchist Left poses a significant threat to the police as well as to industrialized nations. Their propaganda expresses revolution through class war as well as the use of violence directly against the police.
(David Ryder/Reuters; Michael Matthews/Alamy Stock Photo; Nicholas Kamm/Staff/AFP Photo/Getty Images)

Many of the causes to the left are centered around the perceived injustice toward individuals in America, such as Leonard Peltier, Mumia Abu Jamal, Pablo Escobar, "El Chapo" Guzman, and others who are serving life sentences in federal prisons, or have been shot by the police during their arrest. While the anarchist left, in general, has had significant problems formally organizing, remnants of these groups have appeared in recent demonstrations against some controversial police officer shootings, including St. Louis (MO), Chicago (IL), Detroit (MI), Los Angeles (CA), and Washington, D.C. The Black Blocs have conducted numerous acts of vandalism and arson, and their flyers continue to reflect an extreme violence against the police. The Anarchist Left continues to be very active in the United States, with primary groups on the West coast in Seattle (WN), Portland and Eugene (OR), San Francisco, Los Angeles, and San Diego (CA), as well as in various cities in Texas, Florida, and New York.

Quick Facts
Left Antifa vs. Alt-Right

On August 15, 2017, a crowd of alt-Right white supremacist and neo-Nazis marched in Charlottesville, Virginia. They were confronted by a large group of protestors from the left-wing, Marxist Antifa movement. As one report stated: On the one-side, a racist, identity-politics Left dedicated to the proposition that white people are innate beneficiaries of privilege and therefore must be excised from political power; on the other side, a reactionary, racist, identity-politics alt-Right dedicated to the proposition that white people are innate victims of the social-justice class and therefore must regain political power through race-group solidarity. As the two groups clashed, a young twenty-year old,

white nationalist, James Alex Fields Jr., plowed his car into the crowd, killing one and injuring another 19. Virginia Governor Terry McAuliffe declared a state of emergency as one of the worst assemblies of hate and racism erupted into violence, forcing one reporter to call the stand-off between right and left as a growing "cancer in body politic" of America."

Source: Ben Shapiro, "Antifa and the Alt-Right, Growing in Opposition to One Another." *The National Review* (August 15, 2017). See: http://nationalreview .com/article/450462/antifa-alt-right-twin-cancers-eating-america.

Separatist or Nationalist Movements

Ideally, a nation is a group that shares a common ideology, common institutions and customs, and a sense of homogeneity.[149] The people of a nation have a strong group sense of belonging together. In reality, many nations are not so homogenous; instead, they reflect some diversity in the characteristics of their population.

Episodically, some subnational groups express a desire for their own national identity. They may seek home rule, in which they can have their own customs, law, and institutions, but remain united with the larger nation in which they are located. Alternatively, they may want to establish their own state. A very early step in doing so is the formation of a national liberation organization (NLO), some of which resort to terrorism. NLOs do not possess legal authority over a specific territory; they are seeking to "liberate" it.

Examples of NLOs include (1) the Eritrean Liberation Front (ETA) in Spain, which obtained a strong measure of autonomy for the ethnic Basques in that country; (2) the Tamil Tigers, who have sought a nation for the Tamil people in northern Sri Lanka; (3) the Kurdistan Workers Party (PKK), which is committed to establishing a Kurdish country from parts of Turkey; and (4) the Liberation Front of Quebec, which desires an independent Quebec for its French-speaking constituencies.

Within the United States, there are also examples of groups desiring their own homeland: (1) the late secessionist Thomas Naylor founded The Second Vermont Republic in 2003; he believed that "America has truly lost its way and was no longer sustainable as a nation."[150] Naylor wanted Vermont to return to 1777, when it proclaimed itself an independent nation; (2) the League of the South (LOS) was founded in 1994 and is a nationalist movement whose ultimate goal is a free and independent South;[151] there are a number of affiliated LOSs in southern states. The LOS denies accusations that it is a neo-Confederate white supremacy movement; and (3) founded in 1989, the separatist/nationalist New Black Panther Party (NBPP) has a ten-point plan that has some similarities to the BPP's demands. The NBPP of demands include a homeland for Black Americans that can make its own laws, as well as reparations for slavery and the release of all black prisoners.[152] The Southern Law Poverty Center describes the NBPP as being "virulently racist and anti-Semitic."[153] Its leaders have encouraged violence against whites, Jews, and law enforcement officers.[154] The original BPP has rejected the NBPP as a "black racist hate group" and has contested its hijacking of the BPP's name and symbol.[155]

Nationalistic Puerto Ricans have made several attacks in Washington, D.C., to call attention to their ambition to have the Commonwealth of Puerto Rico become an independent nation. In 1950, two Puerto Rican men attempted to assassinate President Harry Truman (1884–1972).[156] After a shootout, a member of Truman's security detail and one of the attackers were dead (see Figure 8–17). In 1954, Puerto Ricans fired from the balcony of the House of Representatives, wounding several members but killing no one.[157] In 1978 and 1979, President Carter pardoned the men involved in both attacks. Puerto Rico has a long history of revolutionary nationalist organizations, including the Armed Forces for National Liberation, which carried out a series of bombings in Chicago and New York City during the 1970s, Armed Commandos for Revolution, Volunteers' Organization for Puerto Rican Revolution, the People's Boricua Army (also known as Los Macheteros or the Machete Wielders), and more recently, Nueva Lucha (New Struggle).

Quick Facts
Chinese Separatists/Terrorists Attack

During 2014, persons believed to be Muslim ethnic Uighurs reportedly massacred people at a kunming train station. The victims are thought to be majority Hun Chinese. Twenty-nine people were killed and 143 injured by people wielding large knives and machetes.[158] Uighurs resent increasing government controls on their religious life and believe the growing number of majority Hun Chinese in their province deprives them of jobs, land, and other opportunities.[159] The state-operated Xinhua News Agency blamed the attack on separatist, terrorist Uighurs.[160] During December 2016, a communist office in remote western China was allegedly attacked by Uighurs. China claimed an office worker and a security guard were killed and three attackers were also claimed to have been slain.

Case Study: Ireland

Ireland, roughly the size of Maine, looms large in the history of the United States. Although there were earlier Irish immigrants, the Potato Famine of 1845–1851 triggered horrific consequences. During it, one million Irish starved to death and another million immigrated to America. Together, these two events reduced the population of Ireland by some 25 percent.[161] The Irish were the first great wave of unskilled immigrants to the United States. They started life in America at the lowest imaginable rung, but over time became prominent in politics. Nine signers of the declaration of Independence were Irish-Americans[162] and 20 president's claim Irish ancestry.[163] During the American Civil War (1861–1865), Irishmen came to the United States and enlisted, primarily for the Union Army (see Figure 8–18). Some number of them did so to gain military experience to return to Ireland and continue fighting for Irish independence. Today 39.6 million Americans list their heritage as partially or primarily Irish.[164] Their nationalist drive mirrors our own in many regards (see Table 8–3).

In the early twentieth century, political party Sinn Fein (Gaelic for We Ourselves) and the Irish Republican Army (IRA) were also NLOs. The island of Ireland hosts the largely Catholic Republic of Ireland in the South, but is substantially protestant in Northern Ireland. How this came to be is a tumultuous history.

One of Ireland's minor kings promised loyalty and lands to England's King Henry II (1133–1189) if he would send a force to help defeat the minor king's foes. Henry II sent a force and some 850 years later the

TABLE 8-3

Comparison of the American Revolution (1775-1783) and the Anglo-Irish War (1919-1921)

Variable	American Colonies	Ireland
Language Spoken	Primarily English	Primarily English
Goal	Independence	Independence
Adversary	England	England
Scope of Military Capabilities	Limited	Limited
Scope of Adversary's Military Capabilities	World power	World power
Warfare Tactics	Guerilla, conventional	Guerilla, terrorism
Military Resources	Limited, improved with assistance from France. Spain, an informal ally, forced the British from Florida. This enabled Spain to send some supplies to the colonists through its port in New Orleans.	Limited, financial support from other Irish populations, especially in America and Australia, helped finance cause. Irish arms were largely captured by raids and ambushes.
Level of Domestic Support	Limited to moderate support initially. Clumsy and coercive reactions by British led to first Continental Congress (1774) and ultimately to the Declaration of Independence.	Low initially, grew swiftly due to numerous atrocities against civilians by the British. Irish patriots starved themselves to death, causing international opinion to swing against England.
Outcome	Independence	A period of substantial autonomy followed by full independence.

English have still not left. Those that Henry II sent mostly built strongholds in the large cities, sometimes fought the Irish, and at other times fought among themselves. The English occupiers gradually adopted Irish dress, laws, and language and intermarried with them, giving them control over even more lands.[165] Following another Irish rebellion in the northern province of Ulster, the rebels and their followers were granted pardons for leaving Ireland, referred to as the "Fight of the Wild Geese." Ulster was substantially repopulated with English protestants loyal to England, which set up the dynamics leading to what is now a protestant Northern Ireland, which is still part of the United Kingdom, and Catholics to the south in what is now the independent Republic of Ireland.

In addition to further forfeiture of lands to punish the Irish, laws were passed at different times that are collectively referred to as the Penal Code. Its purpose was to (1) ensure that the Catholic Irish could never achieve any measure of political or economic power and (2) separate the Catholic Irish from their church; among the provisions enacted was the Irish couldn't practice Catholicism, buy land, educate their children, hold public office, own arms, become lawyers, or live in important cities, or own arms.[166] Ultimately, these harsh measures were repealed, but not before culturally fixing in the minds of generations of Catholics and protestants that the other side was villainous.

Although the protestant majority in Northern Island was content to remain part of the United Kingdom, the "Southern" Irish had national aspirations. How these aspirations were achieved has some similarities to America's revolution, which it makes an important case study. Sinn Fein was formed in 1905 as a political party that originally advocated for Irish home rule within the British Commonwealth. It was not regarded as a serious threat, although England watched its fermentations. Ever opportunistic, the Irish operated on the principle that "England's difficulty was Ireland's opportunity."[167] So, while England was preoccupied with World War I in Europe (1914-1918), the Easter Uprising (April 24-30, 1916) occurred in Dublin, where the Proclamation of the Republic of Ireland was issued, a document analogous to America's Declaration of Independence.

The three major "military" components of the rising, the Irish Republican Brotherhood, the Irish Volunteers, and the Irish Citizen Army, were ragtag outfits that lacked proper weapons and were essentially untrained. In a week, the British Army defeated them. Some in the Dublin crowds lining the streets threw rotten vegetables and others emptied chamber pots (placed under beds and used for night urinals in the era before indoor plumbing) on the surrendered Irishmen as they were marched into captivity.[168] They may have done so because 254 civilians were killed in the fighting or because they had sons serving in the British Army during World War I.[169]

Fifteen of the rising's leaders were executed after perfunctory trials. Padraig Pearse (1879–1916) declared at his sentencing: "You cannot extinguish the Irish passion for freedom. If our deed has not been sufficient to win freedom, then our children will win it by a better deed."[170] James Connolly (1868–1916) was badly wounded in the fighting and could not stand. He was placed before the firing squad while tied to a chair in his hospital pajamas,[171] an ugly image to many leaders in the international community. Joseph Plunkett (1887–1916) was granted his request to marry his sweetheart Grace Gifford and shot hours later.[172] She never remarried. Two leaders of the uprising were initially sentenced to death, but their sentences were commuted to life imprisonment. Countess Markievicz[173] (1868–1927) strongly protested her commutation, claiming she had "done enough to be entitled to an execution,"[174] served a year, and was released; she later served as the Irish Minister of Labor.[175]

Eamon de Valera (1882–1975) was the sole signer of the 1916 Proclamation who was not executed, because his citizenship was in question and because of the politics of World War I. Although born in the New York City, de Valera had lived in Ireland for years.[176] Moreover, the United States, although officially neutral at that time in World War I, was supplying arms and other goods to England. The British were urging the Americans to help them and France by declaring war against the Germans. England had no desire to upset larger plans by executing de Valera, so he was spared. The English plans came to fruition and the United States fought alongside the allied powers from 1917 until the end of the war two years later.

De Valera was released from prison in 1917 and later became president of Ireland. Many of those who surrendered in the 1916 rising were interned in England and released the following year. The executions of the leaders of the Easter Uprising caused the Irish public to take another look at the rising. What they saw stirred them: a poorly armed force with courage taking on a mighty empire and holding it at bay for a week, trying to free the country from foreign domination.

One consequence of the Easter Uprising is that Sinn Fein became a focal point for the newly energized nationalist movement. In 1918, the Sinn Fein party won 73 of 105 seats to represent Ireland in the English Parliament.[177] However, they refused to take their seats and instead formed an Irish revolutionary legislative body, the Dail Eireann (Gaelic for Assembly of Ireland), which proclaimed Ireland an independent republic. The Anglo-Irish War (1919–1921) followed, fought by the newly created Irish Republican Army (1919, IRA). The Irish war in part was funded by solicitations and donations, particularly from the United States, New Zealand, and Australia.[178] The IRA was small and could not fight in a conventional manner. Many of its members came from the same groups involved in the Easter Uprising. The IRA used guerilla tactics, picking the time and places they would strike. The IRA also wisely used selective terrorism because they were fighting on the same ground occupied by their countrymen.

Quick Facts
Instructions to the Black and Tans

The Black and Tans[179] were mostly former mercenaries and out of work military veterans brought to Ireland by the British government in 1918 to assist the Royal Irish Constabulary in their work. The Irish soon viewed them as thugs opposed to the separatist movement in Ireland.

The attitude of the Black and Tans is best summed up by one of their divisional commanders, Lt. Colonel Smyth, on June 19, 1920, in Listowel, Ireland:

"If a police barracks is burned or if the barracks already occupied is not suitable, then the best house in the locality is to be commandeered, the occupants thrown in the gutter.

Let them die there—the more the merrier. Should the order (Hands Up) not be immediately obeyed, shoot and shoot with effect. If the persons approaching a patrol carry their hands in their pockets, or are in any way suspicious, shoot them down. You may make mistakes occasionally and innocent persons may be shot, but that cannot be helped, and you are bound to get the right parties some time. The more you shoot, the better I will like you. I assure you no policeman will get into trouble for shooting any man."[180]

Source: The Black and Tans from https://www.historylearningsite.co.uk. Used by permission of historylearningsite.

Because the Royal Irish Constabulary (RIC) was used by the British to gather intelligence, the IRA assassinated its members, raided their barracks for firearms, and burned over 400 RIC barracks to the ground, as well as many English tax offices. When disguised RIC members killed the Mayor of Cork in front of his family, the IRA found out who gave the order and the man was soon dead.

The British decided to supplement the RIC and formed the Royal Irish Constabulary Auxiliary Division, largely made up of out-of-work English veterans of World War I. The first of them reached Ireland in 1920 and because of the colors of their mismatched uniforms they were quickly dubbed the "black and tan." These auxiliaries soon gained a reputation for being undisciplined, drunkenness, and atrocities. They raped Irish women, looting and burning villages. If attacked, the Auxiliaries shot anyone they subsequently saw, such as uninvolved people working in a field or walking down a road, as a reprisal. These actions were encouraged by Auxiliary leaders. The IRA quickly killed Auxiliaries who committed crimes and Smyth was targeted by the IRA for issuing illegal orders and was killed within two weeks.

Late in 1920, the Lord High Mayor of Cork, Terence MacSwiney, rallied international opinion against the British Commonwealth, when after being arrested for sedition he starved himself to death in 74 days.

Wearing of fighting a guerilla war and withering under mounting international opposition to their Irish policies, Britain passed the Government of Ireland Act of 1920 that created the Irish Free State. Primarily protestant Northern Ireland and its six counties legally opted out of this arrangement to remain in the United Kingdom with home rule. The 26 overwhelmingly Catholic counties of "southern" Ireland rejected the Act so it could pursue full independence and the Anglo-Irish War continued. To some degree this effort was bolstered by Irishmen who had fought for England against Germany in World War I, returning home with combat experience in tactics and weapons.

Both sides in the Anglo-Irish War committed acts of terrorism. For example, when England used its 12-member "Cairo Gang"[181] to spy on the IRA, the IRA responded by sending teams to summarily kill each of them on November 21, 1921. Later that day, angry British troops, RIC, and Black and Tans fired at spectators at a hurling match in Dublin, killing 12 and injuring 65 others.[182] When the British announced that henceforth they would execute captured IRA members, the IRA responded they would randomly kill two Englishmen or their allies in return for every member they lost. The IRA also randomly executed members of their opposing forces for crimes committed against the Irish, such as burning parts of Cork.

The Anglo-Irish Treaty of 1921 ended the Anglo-Irish War and recognized "Southern" Ireland as the Irish Free State (IFS). The treaty provided greater independence than Northern Ireland enjoyed, for example, the IFS could maintain an army and have foreign embassies around the world, although it also remained tied to England under home rule. Michael Collins, the Big Fella, led the treaty negotiating team. The Republicans, Irish nationalists, felt he had "sold out" to the British and exceeded his bargaining authority by accepting the partition of Ireland and home rule, as opposed to the island becoming one sovereign nation. In the end, Sinn Fein split between pro- and anti-treaty factions.

The Irish Civil War (1922–1923) ensued between the Republicans and the "Free Staters" (see Figure 8–19) who supported the treaty. The original IRA split, some joining the Republicans but still using the name of the IRA, while others joined the new national army commanded by Collins.

Like most civil wars, the Irish one was ugly with former comrades killing each other, demonstrating the adage that "revolutions eat their own children."[183] The enormously popular "Big Fella" was among those killed in the Irish Civil War, dying in an ambush by split IRA members in 1922. The next year the Irish Civil War was over. The IRA was banned in the Irish Free State in 1936. The following year Ireland approved a new constitution, shed its identity as the Irish

FIGURE 8–19
Raw recruits of the Irish Free State (IFS) Army taking a break during their training in 1922.
(George Rinhart/Corbis/Getty Images)

Free State, and declared itself the independent Republic of Ireland, a measure made complete when it officially left the British Commonwealth in 1949.

There has been continued violence in Northern Ireland as Irish Catholics seek reunion with the Republic of Ireland and are countered by British military forces, the Ulster Defense League, and other groups. From Northern Ireland, the new IRA has made attacks on the English mainland. Illustratively, in 1974, it set a bomb off at the British Parliament. Although some Irish Catholics in Northern Ireland wish to reunite with the Republic of Ireland in the South, there is only tepid support for that in the Republic of Ireland. The major objection is that many people in Northern Ireland are on social welfare and there is little sentiment to take on that huge cost.

Chapter Summary

SUMMARY BY LEARNING OBJECTIVE

1. **State what is at the core of American right-wing ideology.**

   At its core, American right-wing ideology envisions having a homeland population that is homogeneous with respect to ethnicity, language, culture, and beliefs, as well as a systematic rejection of all those who are different. The right rests on the notion that "being American" equates to emanating from European Anglo-Saxon stock, being Christian, nationalistic, and ruggedly independent.

2. **Identify three major right-wing ideologies in the United States.**

   The three major ideological right-wing movements in the United States are (1) the Racist/White Supremacy Movement, including the development of the Ku Klux Klan, the rise of Neo-Nazism in America, and the emergence of the Hammerskin Nation, (2) the Anti-Federalist Movement, and (3) the Christian Identity Movement. Their ideological orientations affect the targets they select, the tactics used, and the operations conducted.

3. **Compare and contrast the traditional goals of left-wing terrorism with the current goals of today's left-wing groups.**

   The traditional goals of the left-wing terrorist movements were to overthrow the economic, political, and social structure of a society and replace it with one developed on a Marxist-Leninist perspective. Groups in this category include Sendero Luminoso (Shining Path) in Peru, the Red Army Faction (RAF) in Germany and across Western Europe, the Red Brigades in Italy, the Seung Fein in China, and the Symbionese Liberation Army and the Weather Underground in the United States. Many of these groups sprang from labor/working-class movements seeking to eliminate class distinction. Today however, the left-wing groups in America have commonly gathered under a variety of anarchist movements that have rallied historically around ecology movements, some being violent in nature such as the "eco-terrorist" groups of Earth Liberation Front (ELF) and Animal Liberation Front (ALF). Since the late 1990s, much of the left-wing movement has shifted focus to an anti-capitalist and anti-globalization position. Much of their unrest has targeted the ultrarich, multinational corporations, and trade organizations. Left-wing groups today in the Anarchist Left, Black Army Faction, and Black Blocs movement. These groups have very little to do with race issues, and are much more about leftist ideology and the freedom presented by the "anarchist state." The left wing has completed a transition from the ecology movements of the past to an anti-wealth, antitechnology, and anticapitalist movement spewing rhetoric of class war and Marxist revolution.

4. **Define NLO and identify groups that are involved in NLO movements across the world.**

   An NLO is defined as a **N**ational **L**iberation **O**rganization, and represents a subnational group that desires their own national identity. Examples of NLOs include (1) the Eritrean Liberation Front (ETA) for Basques in Spain; (2) the Tamil Tigers in northern Sri Lanka; (3) the Kurdistan Workers Party (PKK), which is committed to establishing a Kurdish country from parts of Turkey; and (4) the Liberation Front of Quebec, which desires an independent Quebec for its French-speaking constituency. Within the United States there are also examples of groups desiring their own homeland: (1) The Second Vermont Republic believes that

America has truly lost its way and is no longer sustainable as a nation and desires to make Vermont an independent nation as it was in 1777; (2) the League of the South (LOS) was founded in 1994 and is a nationalist movement whose ultimate goal is a free and independent South; and (3) the New Black Panther Party (NBPP) has a ten-point plan that includes a separate homeland for Black Americans.

REVIEW QUESTIONS

1. Why did racial violence against the Chinese increase during 1873–1879?
2. How were Japanese-Americans and members of the German-American Bund treated at the beginning of World War II?
3. Why were there violent clashes between Chicano zoot suiters and American serviceman during World War II?
4. What is the history of the 442nd Regimental Combat Team?
5. What American groups disproportionately suffer from right-wing extremism?
6. Is there a connection between *The Turner Diaries* and the bombing of the Murrah Building?
7. What does "88" mean?
8. What are three examples of the Penal Code the English applied to the Irish?
9. What happened following the assassination of the Reverend Martin Luther King?
10. What is the traditional objective of the left wing?

CRITICAL THINKING EXERCISES

1. **Hate on the World Wide Web.** Visit the website of the Southern Poverty Law Center (SPLC) and learn about hate in America at www.splcenter.org/.

   Study some of the available *Intelligence Reports* online and note the high number of active hate groups in the United States. Should you be a partner sharing the mission of the SPLC fighting hate and seeking justice? Think of your community: Are there any visible signs of hate or intolerance where you live?

2. Does the First Amendment to our Constitution confer unbridled free speech? It forbids Congress to pass laws that would abridge freedom of speech. Are there limits? If so, what are they and how are they applied? We not only give licenses for parades and meetings where people representing hatred advance vile arguments, we also assign our police to protect the very people whose ideas are repugnant to us. Free speech is a cherished freedom. To have it, must we also have to suffer things we abhor or that endanger us? This exercise requires you to execute two major tasks: (1) Do some basic research so you know any exceptions to freedom of speech. Also, make sure you understand the difference between the surface web and the deep web and its small portion called the dark web. Visit the Anti-Defamation League at https://adl.org/news/op-ed/google-must-do-more-to-pull-the-plug-on-online-hate. It is an article by Brittan Heller, "Google Must Do More to Pull the Plug on Online Hate" (2017).

   The issue for discussion is to what extent does our Constitutional right to freedom of speech also serve as an enabler for terrorists to recruit, solicit donations, control cells, and give commands to carry out terrorist acts? Does our freedom of speech give terrorists free rein to do whatever they like on any portions of the web? How do we curb what imperils us and be consistent with freedom of speech?

NOTES

1. Illustratively, see www.educate-yourself.org/cn/femaconcentrationcamplocations07sep05.shtml. A Google search locates further "information" on this subject.
2. Mark Potok, "The Patriot Movement Explodes," *Southern Poverty Law Center*, Intelligence Report Issue 145, Spring 2012, p. 1.
3. Mark Potok, "The Year in Hate and Extremism," Southern Poverty Law Center, Spring 2014, p. 1, www.splcenter.org/fighting-hate/intelligence-report/2014/year-hate-and-extremism, accessed April 10, 2017.

4. Fred Lucas, "Gun Rights Groups Hope Trump Nixes Social Security Role in Background Checks," Fox News, January 16, 2017, www.foxnews.com/politics/2017/01/16/gun-rights-groups-hope-trump-nixes-social-security-role-in-background-checks.html, accessed April 10, 2017.

5. Mark Potok, "The Year in Hate and Extremism," Southern Poverty Law Center, February 15, 2017, www.splcenter.org/fighting-hate/intelligence-report/2017/year-hate-and-extremism, accessed April 8, 2017.

6. Loc. cit.

7. No author, "Terrorism Worries Little Changed; Most Give Good Marks for Reducing Threat, "Pew Research Center, January 12, 2015, p. 1, https://ucr.fbi.gov/hate-crime/2015/topic-pages/victims_final, accessed April 10, 2017.

8. Southern Poverty Law Center, Anti-Muslim, p. 1. 2017, www.splcenter.org/fighting-hate/extremist-files/ideology/anti-muslim, accessed April 11, 2017.

9. No author, Historical Trends: Satisfaction with the United States," Gallup Poll, March 5, 2017, www.gallup.com/poll/1669/general-mood-country.aspx, accessed April 7, 2017.

10. Carla Bleiker, "Far-Right NPD Loses State Subsidies," *DW*, February 26, 2013.

11. "Not So Grim Up North," *The Economist*, October 14, 2010, p. 1.

12. Rick Lyman, "Already Hostile to Migrants, Hungary Starts Detaining Them," *New York Times*, April 19, 2017, p. 1.

13. Loc. cit.

14. Loc. cit.

15. No author, "Soldiers of Odin USA," Anti-Defamation League, 2016, p. 1, www.adl.org/sites/default/files/documents/assets/pdf/combating-hate/Soldiers-of-Odin-USA-Report-web.pdf, accessed April 10, 2017.

16. "Anders Behring Breivik," *New York Times*, August 24, 2012, www.Topics.NYTimes/Top/Reference/Timestopics/People/Anders_Behring_Breivik/index.html.

17. Nick Squires, "Florence Street Vendors Killed by Lone Gunman," *Telegraph* (England), December 13, 2013.

18. Marcel Furstenau, "Neo-Nazi Murder Spree Shocks Germany," *DW*, March 13, 2013.

19. Matthew Goodwin, "The Roots of Extremism: The English Defence League and the Counter Jihad Challenger," A Chatham House Briefing Paper, March 2013, p. 1.

20. Ibid., p. 5.

21. Ibid., p. 6.

22. Ibid., p. 3.

23. Arie Perliger, "Challenges from the Sidelines: Understanding America's Far-Right," (West Point, New York: Combating Terrorism Center, West Point, United States Army, November 2012), p. 13.

24. No author, "ADL Report: U.S. Deaths Linked to Domestic Extremists Second Only to Year of Oklahoma City Bombing," Anti-Defamation League, February 16, 2017, p. 2, http://sandiego.adl.org/news/adl-report-says-u-s-deaths-linked-to-domestic-extremists-second-only-to-year-of-oklahoma-city-bombing, accessed April 11, 2017.

25. Loc. cit.

26. Loc. cit.

27. Loc. cit.

28. Perliger, "Challenges from the Sidelines," p. 87.

29. Perliger, "Challenges from the Sidelines," p. 15.

30. This section as written with some information from Staff Reporter, "Brockton Rampage-of-Hate-Killer Keith Luke Commits Suicide in Prison," The Enterprise (Brockton, Massachusetts) May 12, 2014, http://enterprisenews.com/article/20140512/NEWS/140519379, accessed September 2, 2017 and Brian Ballou, "Self-Described neo-Nazi Guilty of 2009 Brockton Murders, Rapes," The Boston Globe, May 30, 2013, www.BostonGlobe,.com/metro/2013/05/30/self-described-white-supremacist-keith-luke-convicted-first-degree-murder-for-rampage/UOI1ACrfLJgGbny2QluitI/story.html, accessed September 1, 2017.

31. Some of these ideas are explored in Lindsay Perez Huber et al., "Getting beyond the 'Symptom' and Acknowledging the Disease: Theorizing Racist Nativism," *Contemporary Justice Review*, Vol. 11, Issue 1, March 2008, p. 42.

32. Perliger, "Challenges from the Sidelines," p. 16.
33. Loc. cit.
34. Ibid., pp. 16–17.
35. Ibid., pp. 1–2.
36. Bill Rolston, "Bringing It All Back Home," *Race & Class*, Vol. 45, Issue 2, October–December 2003, pp. 39–53. Copy accessed electronically on April 23, 2013, did not have page numbers.
37. Loc. cit.
38. Loc. cit.
39. Loc. cit. One joke was that the Irish didn't know how to walk upright until the wheelbarrow was invented. Shops seeking employees posted signs that read "Vacancy, inquire within. Irish need not apply."
40. U.S. History, "29. Manifest Destiny," undated, p. 1, www.ushistory.org/us/29.asp.
41. Loc. cit.
42. Charles R. Swanson, Leonard Territo, Robert W. Taylor, *Police Administration: Structures, Processes, and Behaviors* (Boston: Pearson, 2011), p. 6.
43. There is some question as to whether Sheridan actually made this statement. He denied it a number of times and there is no contemporary written record that he did.
44. Richard Delgado, "The Law of the Noose: The History of Latino Lynching," *Harvard Civil Rights-Civil Liberties Law Review*, Vol. 44, No. 2, Summer 2009, p. 299.
45. Loc. cit.
46. Walter Ko, "The Blood, Sweat, and Tears of Chinese in 19th-Century America," *Chinese American Forum*, Vol. 28, Issue 3, January 2013, p. 14.
47. Philip Chin, "The Chinese Exclusion Act of 1882," *Chinese American Forum*, Vol. XXVIIII, No. 3, January 2013, pp. 7–8.
48. Loc. cit.
49. Ko, "The Blood, Sweat, and Tears of Chinese in 19th-Century America," p. 9.
50. Cliff Akiyama, "When You Look Like the Enemy," *Brief Treatment and Crisis Intervention*, Vol. 8, Issue 2, May 2008, p. 210.
51. "442nd Regimental Combat Team," p. 1. www.goforbroke.org/history/history_historical_veterans_442nd.asp.
52. Michi Weglyn, "Children of the Camps," Public Broadcasting System, undated, www.pbs.org/childrenofcamp/history/.
53. David J. Wishart, "Denver's Anti-Chinese Riot," *Encyclopedia of the Plains*, undated, p. 1, http://plainshumanities.unl.edu/encyclopedia/doc/egp.asam.011.
54. Ibid., p. 2.
55. "German American Bund," *Holocaust Encyclopedia, United States Holocaust Memorial Museum*, p. 1. www.ushmm.org/wic/en/article.php?Moduleid=10005684.
56. Loc. cit.
57. Sarah Elizabeth Howard, "Zoot to Boot: The Zoot Suit as Both Costume and Symbol," *Studies in Latin America Culture*, Vol. 28, 2010, p. 113.
58. Ibid., p. 115.
59. Ibid., pp. 116–117.
60. Tanya Schevitz, "Hate Crimes Against Religious Groups, 2001," *San Francisco Chronicle*, November 26, 2002, www.sfgate.com/news/article/fbi-sees-leap-in-anti-muslim-hate-crimes-9-11-2750152.php.
61. FBI, 2015 Hate Crime, https://ucr.fbi.gov/hate-crime/2015/topic-pages/victims_final, accessed April 12, 2017.
62. FBI, "Hate Crime Statistics 2011," www.fbi.gov/about-us/cjis/ucr/hate-crime/2011/tables/table-1. Percentages computed from data in Table 1.
63. Marc Santora, "Woman Is Charged with Murder as a Hate Crime in a Fatal Subway Push," *New York Times*, December 29, 2013.
64. Loc. cit.
65. "Hate Crime Statistics 2011," Federal Bureau of Investigation (Washington, D.C.: Federal Bureau of Investigation), p. 1, www.fbi.gov/about-us/cjis/ucr/hate-crime/2011/narratives/incidents-and-offenses, accessed April 12, 2017.

66. No author, "The Latest: Brother of Fresno Shooter Shocked by Killings," *Mercury News*, April 18, 2017, accessed April 20, 2017.

67. Loc. cit.

68. Loc. cit.

69. "Hate Crime Statistics 2015," Federal Bureau of Investigation (Washington, D.C.: Federal Bureau of Investigation), p. 1 https://ucr.fbi.gov/hate-crime/2015/topic-pages/victims_final, accessed April 19, 2017.

70. K. B. Turner, David Giacopassi, and Margaret Vandiver, "Ignoring the Past: Coverage of Slavery and Slave Patrols in Criminal Justice Texts," *Journal of Criminal Justice Education*, Vol. 17, Issue 1, March 2006, p. 185.

71. Elaine Frantz Parsons, "Midnight Rangers: Costume and Performance in the Reconstruction Era Ku Klux Klan," *Journal of American History*, Vol. 92, Issue 3, December 2005, p. 811.

72. Ibid., p. 812.

73. No author, "General Article: Rise of the Ku Klux Klan," Public Broadcasting System, undated, www.pbs.org/wgbh/americanexperience/features/general-article/grant-kkk.

74. Kris Axtman, "How the South Outgrew the Klan," *Christian Science Monitor*, Vol. 93, Issue 112, May 4, 2001, p. 1.

75. Kathleen Blee and Amy McDowell, "The Duality of Spectacle and Secrecy: A Case Study of Fraternalism in the 1920s U.S. Ku Klux Klan," *Ethnic and Racial Studies*, Vol. 36, Issue 2, February 2013, p. 249.

76. Ibid., pp. 254–255.

77. "Klan Must Pay $37 Million for Inciting Church Fire," *New York Times*, July 25, 1998.

78. "About the Ku Klux Klan," Anti-Defamation League, 2013, http://archive.adl.org/learn/ext_us/kkk/default.html.

79. Alexandra Marks, "The Disruptive Face of a Dwindling KKK," *Christian Science Monitor*, Vol. 91, Issue 230, p. 2.

80. "About the Ku Klux Klan," p. 1.

81. "The Ku Klux Klan Rebounds," *Anti-Defamation League*, 2013, p. 1. http://archive.adl.org/learn_us/kkk/intro.asp?learn_cat=extremism&learn_subcat=extremism_in_america&xpicked=4&item=kkk.

82. "Neo-Nazi," *Southern Poverty Law Center*, 2013, www.splcenter.org/get-informed/intelligence-files/ideology/ne0-nazi#.uyux16vgofi.

83. "American Nazi Party," Confidential FBI Report, June 1965, p. 8. The document has typed and handwritten page numbers that do not coincide; we have used the handwritten page numbers.

84. Ibid., p. 98.

85. "White Revolution/Billy Roper," *Anti-Defamation League*, undated, © 2013, p. 1, http://archive.adl.org/learn/ext_us/w_revolution.asp.

86. Dianne Dentice, "The Nationalist Party of America," *Social Movement Studies*, Vol. 10, Issue 1, January 2011, p. 107.

87. "Extremism in America: William Pierce," *Anti-Defamation League*, 2005, http://archive.adl.org/learn/ext_us/pierce.asp.

88. Ibid., p. 2.

89. Ibid., pp. 4–5 with a few additions.

90. This information was taken from the National Vanguard Books website; see www.natvanbooks.com.

91. "Extremism in America: William Pierce," p. 3.

92. "Poisoning the Web: Hatred On-Line," *Anti-Defamation League*, 2001, p. 1, http://archive.adl.org/poisoning_web/national_alliance.asp.

93. Mark Potok, "Ten Years after Founder's Death, Key Neo-Nazi Movement a 'Joke,'" *Southern Poverty Law Center*, July 23, 2012, p. 1.

94. Loc. cit.

95. "National Socialist Movement," *Southern Poverty Law Center*, undated, © 2013, p. 2, www.splc.org/ger-informed/intelligence-files/groups/national-socialist-movement#.uyuzikvgofi.

96. Loc. cit.

97. Taken from the NSM website, "25 Point Party Thesis," undated, www.nsm88.org.

98. Loc. cit.

99. "National Socialist Movement," p. 2.

100. Loc. cit.

101. Loc. cit.

102. "The National Socialist Movement," Anti-Defamation League, 2013, p. 1, http://archive.adl.org/learn/ext_us/nsm/default.asp?learn_cat =extremism&learn_subcat=extremism_in_america&xpicked=3&items=nsm.

103. Loc. cit.

104. Ibid., p. 2.

105. Loc. cit.

106. "Aryan Nations," *Southern Poverty Law Center*, undated, p. 1, www.splcenter.org/ get-informed/intelligence-files/groups/aryan-nations.

107. "Hammerskin Nation," *National Consortium for the Study of Terrorism and Responses to Terrorism*, undated, © 2013, p. 1, www.start.umd.edu/start/data_collections/tops/ terrorists_organization_profile.asp?id=3483.

108. Loc. cit.

109. "American Front," *Anti-Defamation League*, undated, but © 2013, p. 1, www.adl.org.

110. See "Skinhead Convicted of Murder of Two Homeless Men in Tampa," *FBI Press Release*, October 18, 2011.

111. "Hammerskin Nation," p. 2.

112. "Racist Skinhead," *Southern Poverty Law Center*, undated, © 2013, p. 3, www.splcenter .org/get-informed/intelligence-files/ideology/racist-skinhead#.uyjliavgofi.

113. "Neo-Confederate," *Southern Poverty Law Center*, 2013, www.splcenter.org/ger -informed/inteligence-files/ideology/neo-confederate#.uygv_avgpfi.

114. "Institute for Historical Review," *Southern Poverty Law Center*, undated, © 2013, p. 1, www.splcenter.org/get-informed/intelligence-files/groups/instutute-for-historical -research#.uyfhw6vgpfi.

115. Loc. cit.

116. Michael Kimmel and Abby L. Ferber, "White Men Are This Nation: Right Wing Militias and the Restoration of American Masculinity," *Rural Sociology*, Vol. 65, Issue 4, December 2000, p. 586.

117. Perliger, "Challenges from the Sidelines," p. 28.

118. Loc. cit.

119. Ibid., pp. 30–31.

120. "Montana Freemen," *National Consortium for the Study of Terrorism and Responses to Terrorism*, University of Maryland, September 1995, p.1.

121. This content is drawn with restatement from "Hate Group Expert Daniel Levitas Discusses Posse Comitatus, Christian Identity Movement and More," *Southern Poverty Law Center*, Intelligence Report, Spring 1998, Issue 90, p. 1.

122. FBI Counterterrorism Section, "Sovereign Citizens: A Growing Threat to Law Enforcement," *FBI Law Enforcement Bulletin*, September 2011, p. 1

123. Ibid., pp. 1–2.

124. Ibid., p. 1.

125. Potok, "The Patriot Movement Explodes," p. 3.

126. Danny Lewis, "20 Years Ago Today, Montana Freemen Started Its 81-Day Standoff," Smithsonian.com, March 25, 2016, www.smithsonianmag.com/smart-news/twenty- years-ago-today-the-montana-freeman-started-its-81-day-standoff-180958568, accessed November 11, 2017..

127. Patrik Jonsson, "Right-Wing' Patriot' Groups Girding for Actual Class Warfare, Report Says," Christian Science Monitor, March 8, 2012,"/www.csmonitor.com/USA/2012/0308/ Right-wing-patriot-groups-girding-for-actual-class-warfare-report-says, accessed November 11, 2017.

128. Bill Morlin, "Georgia Militia Members to be Tried Later This Year in Movement's Latest Murder Plot," *Southern Poverty Law Center*, Intelligence Report, Issue 145, Spring 2012, p. 1.

129. Ibid., p. 2.

130. "Timothy McVeigh: The Oklahoma City Bomber," *Anti-Defamation League*, 2001, http://archive.adl.org/McVeigh/faq.asp.

131. "Terror Hits Home: The Oklahoma City Bombing," Federal Bureau of Investigation, undated, www.fbi.gov/about-us/famous-cases/oklahoma-city-bombing.

132. "From Decorated Veteran to Mass Murderer," CNN.Com Programs, hosted by Paul Zahn, 2001, p. 1, www.cnn.com.cnn/programs/people/shows/mcveigh/profile.html.

133. Jo Thomas, "Behind a Book That Inspired McVeigh," *New York Times*, June 9, 2001.

134. "From Decorated Veteran to Mass Murderer," p. 4.

135. Loc. cit.

136. Martin Durham, "Christian Identity and the Politics of Religion," *Totalitarian Movements and Political Religions*," Vol. 9, No. 1, March 2008, p. 79.

137. Loc. cit.

138. Loc. cit.

139. Rosemary Bradford Ruether, "Racist Extremists Use Bible Verse to Justify Killing," *National Catholic Reporter*, Vol. 35, July 27, 1999, p. 13.

140. Loc. cit.

141. To examine different CI websites, use the hyperlinks at www.thechristianidentotyforum.com/forum.net/index.php?/topic/94/-big-list-of-christian-identity.

142. Ruether, "Racist Extremists Use Bible Verse to Justify Killing," p. 13.

143. Concepts of Terrorism, Deliverable 5, Work Package 3, December 2008, p. 126, www.transnationalterrorism.eu.

144. Jeffrey M. Bale, "Definition of Terrorism, *Monterey Terrorism and Research Center Education Program*, undated, www.mils.edu/academics/researchcenters/terrorism/about/terrorism_definition.

145. Karl A. Seger, *Left Wing Extremism: The Current Threat* (Washington, D.C.: U.S. Department of Energy, April 2001), p. 1.

146. Much of this paragraph is drawn from information in D. J. Mulloy, "New Panthers, Old Panthers and the Politics of Black Nationalism in the United States," *Patterns of Prejudice*, Vol. 44, Issue 3, July 2010, pp. 217–238; Joe Street, "The Historiography of the Black Panther Party," *Journal of American Studies*, Vol. 44, Issue 2, May 2010, pp. 351–375; and Hugh Pearson, *Shadow of the Panther: Huey Newton and the Price of Black Power in America* (Cambridge, Massachusetts: De Capo Press, 1995).

147. Many of the facts herein are drawn from "The Patty Hearst Kidnapping," www.fbi.gov/about-us/history/famous-cases/patty-hearst-kidnapping.

148. Don Thompson, "Former SLA Member James Kilgore Paroled," *SFGate*, May 11, 2009, p. 1, www.sfgate.com/bayarea/article/Former-SLA-member-James-Kilgore-paroled-3162180.php.

149. The information in this paragraph is drawn from *Nationalist-Separatist Movements* (New York: United Nations, 2003), www.munfw.org/archive/47th/gal.htm.

150. "Thomas Naylor, Controversial Vermont Secessionist, Dies," *Southern Poverty Law Center*, © 2013, www.splcenter.org/home/2012/spring/thomas-naylor-controversial-vermont-secessionist-dies#uyryqqvgpf.

151. See the League of South website at www.dixienet.org/rights/whatisthels.shtml.

152. "New Black Panther Party," *Southern Poverty Law Center*, undated, © 2013, p. 2, www.splcenter.org/get-informed/intelligence-files/groups/new-black-panther-party#.uyv9vqvgpfi14.

153. Ibid., p. 1.

154. Loc. cit.

155. Loc. cit.

156. Allen Pusey, "November 1, 1950: Truman Escapes Assassination," *ABA Journal*, November 1, 2012, p. 1, www.abajournal.com/magazine/article/November_1_1950_truman_escapes_assassination.

157. Emma Brown, "Lolita Lebron, Jailed for Gun Attack at U.S. Capitol in 1954, Dies at 90," *Washington Post*, August 2, 2010.

158. "Death Toll Rises to 33 in Knife Attack on China Train Station," www.foxnews.com/2014/03/02/gang-knife-weilding-men-in-deadly-attacks-on-chaina-train-station.

159. Chris Buckley, "Attackers with Knives Kill 29 at Chinese Rail Station," *New York Times*, March 1, 2014.

160. Loc. cit. and "Dozens Stabbed to Death in Chinese Attack," CNN News, www.cnn .com/2014/03/01/world/asia/china-railway-attacks.

161. "The Famine of 1845," *The History Learning Site*, undated, www.historylearningsite .co.uk/ireland_great_famine_of_1845.htm.

162. Brendan Patrick Keane, "The Irish Who Signed the Declaration of Independence," *Irish Central*, July 4, 2014, www.irishcentral.com/opinion/others/the-irish-side-of-the-american -declaration-of-independence-97713259-238038151.html#.

163. Sean Murphy, "American Presidents with Irish Ancestry," *Directory of Irish Ancestry*, un- dated, http://homepage.eircom.net/~seanjmurphy/dir/pres.htm.

164. Irish Central Staff Writers, "U.S. Census Shows Seven Times More Irish Americans than Population of Ireland," *Irish Central*, August 5, 2013, www.irishcentral.com/ news/-census-shows-almost-seven-times-more-irish-americans-than-population-of -ireland-218344001-237779801.html.

165. Michael D. Greaney, "Last of the Norman Invasions," *Military History*, Vol. 15, Issue 5, December 1998, pp. 42–51.

166. *A Short History of Ireland: The Penal Laws* (London: BBC Home, undated), URL no longer available.

167. Richard F. Welch, "The IRA's guerrilla Wars," *Military History*, Vol. 20, Issue 1, April 2003, p. 58.

168. Peter De Rosa, *Rebels: The Irish Rising of 1916* (New York: Fawcett Columbine, 1990), p. 391.

169. Higher numbers are also cited; De Rosa claims 450 deaths and 2,614 wounded, which may include British casualties. See ibid., p. 1

170. De Rosa, *Rebels: The Irish Rising of 1916*, p. 417.

171. Ibid., p. 538.

172. Ibid., pp. 444, 452.

173. She was born in England as Constance Gore-Booth and became a countess by virtue of her marriage to a Polish count. They settled in Dublin in 1903. Countess Markievicz became an active Irish Nationalist around 1908.

174. Ibid., p. 464. For a closer examination of her life, see Suzanne Kennedy Flynn, "Countess Courageous," *World of Hibernia*, Vol. 4, Issue 3, Winter 1998.

175. De Rosa, *Rebels: The Irish Rising of 1916*, pp. 506–507.

176. See Phil Chapple, "'Dev': The Career of Eamon de Valera," *History Review*, Issue 53, pp. 28–33, December 2005.

177. "The Irish War," www.Theiririshwar.com/history/irish-war-of-independence/.

178. A fuller accounting of this point is found in Caoimhe Nic Dhaibheid, "The Irish National Aid Association and the Radicalization of Public Opinion in Ireland, 1916–1918," *Historical Journal*, Vol. 55, Issue 3, September 2012, pp. 705–729.

179. See "The Black and Tans" at www.historylearningsite.co.uk/black_and_tans.htm.

180. "The Black and Tans," *BBC Home*, www.bbc.co.uk/history/easterrising/aftermath/AF05/ shtml.

181. The reason for the unit being named the Cairo Gang is disputed. One version is that many of the people in the unit were military veterans who served in the Middle East. The sec- ond reason offered is that the group occasionally met at the Cairo Café in Dublin.

182. Loc. cit.

183. Welch, "The IRA's guerrilla Wars," p. 62.

Intelligence and Terrorism

Learning Objectives

After completing this chapter, you should be able to:

1. Define intelligence and counterintelligence.

2. Provide a brief overview of the U.S. Intelligence Community and discuss the role of the Office of the Director of National Intelligence.

3. Explain the differences between the CIA and the FBI relating to terrorism and intelligence.

4. Discuss the role of the National Security Agency as an intelligence agency.

5. List and describe the other agencies within the intelligence community.

6. Define and describe the four goals of a fusion center.

The U.S. Department of Homeland Security has spent nearly $1.5 billion since 2003 to build state and local fusion centers throughout the country. MOSAIC in the Dallas, Texas, Police Department represents state-of-the-art high-tech equipment and integrated information processing systems and is used tactically to fight everyday crime as well as more strategic activities designed to prevent terrorist attacks in the future.

(Alan Spearman/ZUMAPRESS/Newscom)

Introduction

The terrorist attacks on September 11, 2001, had a major impact on national homeland security policies and law enforcement strategies at the federal, state, and local levels. A recent report indicates that there are over 1,271 government organizations and 1,931 private organizations involved in homeland security, intelligence gathering, and counterterrorism issues.[1] The U.S. Department of Homeland Security (DHS) alone has contributed more than $500 million toward the development of new local and state agencies centered on the goal of improving the coordination of policing through intelligence sharing.[2] A deficiency that was quickly identified following the 9/11 attacks was that coordination and intelligence sharing between agencies and levels of government was nearly nonexistent.[3]

Several post-9/11 studies have been critical of the U.S. intelligence community's ability to collect and analyze important intelligence information on terrorist groups.[4] The most important of these inquiries was known as the **Gilmore Commission**, named after Virginia Governor Jim Gilmore, chair of the Congressionally sponsored commission to assess the domestic response of federal law enforcement and intelligence agencies against terrorism between 1999 and 2003. Five key issues were identified as problems: (1) failure to emphasize traditional human intelligence gathering and analysis in favor of an overreliance on technological tools such as satellites and computer programs; (2) failure to provide timely, accurate, and specific intelligence information to law enforcement agencies; (3) an overly bureaucratic and decentralized structure, particularly within the FBI, that hindered counterterrorism efforts; (4) outdated and obsolete computer systems that prevented the timely sharing of critical information with and between law enforcement agencies; and (5) overly restrictive guidelines and laws that hindered the effective use of informants and intelligence gathering on terrorists.[5]

Complicating these five potential problems is the structure of American government, which includes the cities and counties that form local government, state governments, and the federal government. Just what terrorism responsibilities should these different levels of government have and which of their agencies should have what responsibilities? To illustrate, should acts of terrorism be investigated only by the FBI and the appropriate state and/or local law enforcement agencies? Should ferreting out terrorist plots be the exclusive jurisdiction of the Central Intelligence Agency and the military? Within the military, which units should be involved? The answers to these questions are not simple. This chapter will define the role and scope of intelligence in combatting terrorism and describe the various agencies that make up the U.S. intelligence community.

Gilmore Commission
Congressionally sponsored inquiry after 9/11 to assess the domestic response of federal law enforcement and intelligence agencies against terrorism.

Defining Intelligence and Counterintelligence

The term "intelligence" often refers to information that is significant or relevant to an impending event and that will be a contribution to the positive outcome of that specific incident. It is paramount to understand the monumental differences between information and intelligence. Information is nothing more than data that has yet to be screened and interpreted through professional analysis. Once information has been analyzed, then it *may become* legitimate intelligence.

The analytical step toward processing gathered information into intelligence is often a misunderstood concept as well. Technology has offered analysts the comfort of reducing the number of people that can be responsible for categorizing and storing data. However, complete analysis of gathered information requires critical thinking that results in conclusions and recommendations stemming from the analyzed information. It is through effective analysis that government leaders and officials make informed decisions and base important responses to potential terrorist attacks (e.g., the deployment of police officers).[6]

Historically, the missing dimension in quality intelligence has been *analysis*. The transformation of raw data, whether acquired through human, technical, or open sources, must be collated, scrutinized, and processed accurately and timely. The ultimate goal of this analytic process is a finished product more intelligible, accurate, and usable than the data and information drawn upon to prepare it. **Intelligence**, then, is a product derived from systematic and thoughtful examination, placed in context, and provided to governmental executives and military leaders with facts and alternatives that can inform critical decisions.[7]

Intelligence
An information process and product derived from systematic and thoughtful examination (analysis).

Quick Facts
The Son Tay Raid: Well Executed, but an Intelligence Failure

In 1970, during the Vietnam War, intelligence was developed that American prisoners were being held under harsh conditions at the Son Tay POW Camp in North Vietnam. Army Colonel Arthur "Bull" Simons lead Operation Ivory Coast to free them. His ground force consisted of fifty-six Special Forces volunteers. Despite the operation being extremely well run, no prisoners were freed because they had been moved to another camp—an intelligence failure. Some military commanders believe that the 1976 Israeli raid to free civilian prisoners being held by terrorists in Entebbe, Uganda, was planned on precepts established by the Son Tay raid.

Counterintelligence (CI)
Activities intended to prevent adversaries from acquiring accurate information about another organization's capabilities.

FIGURE 9–1
The condition of this former POW underscores why freeing POWs is an urgent mission. This twenty-three year old man was a former communist in the Vietnam War. He defected to allied forces and then was captured by the Viet Cong, who were deliberately starving him to death.
(Corbis Historica/Getty Image)

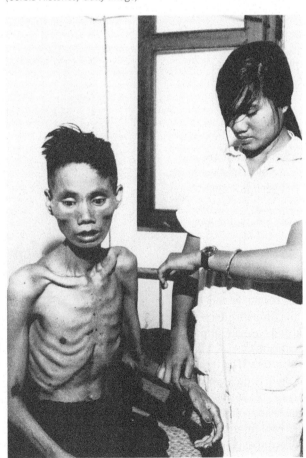

Intelligence is both a process and a product. Information is collected and analyzed and a finding is produced to meet the needs of a specific "customer."[8] Among the sources from which intelligence can be collected are humans (HUMINT), signals (SIGINT), geospatial (GEOINT), technical (TECHINT), imagery (IMINT), photographs (PHOINT), and open source (OSINT). Intelligence can be used for broad purposes, for example, shaping policy and doctrine. In those applications intelligence is not time sensitive, but in others it may be.

On rare occasions during the Vietnam War, a Viet Cong defector would reveal where prisoners of war (POWs) were being held (see Figure 9–1). Because those camps were often moved, raids had to be launched quickly. That situation describes tactical intelligence, which is perishable and therefore requires rapid action. On the other hand, **counterintelligence (CI)** is a constellation of activities, analyses, and decisions intended to prevent adversaries from acquiring accurate information about an organization's capabilities, intentions, personnel, and plans.[9] Counterintelligence is used by the U.S. intelligence services to disrupt the activities and operations of terrorist groups, and conversely, terrorist groups use counterintelligence to learn more about the methods used by the U.S. government to thwart their activities.

Pre-9/11, the Taliban ruled Afghanistan and had a substantial HUMINT collection capability: 20,000 spies and over 100,000 informants, at least one on every block, as well as in hospitals, military units, and aid agencies.[10] Following the 9/11 attacks, the Taliban refused to hand over Usama bin Laden and the United States and its allies waged war on both the Taliban and al-Qaeda, deposing the Taliban as the government of Afghanistan. It is widely believed that, subsequently, units of both terrorist groups evaded capture or destruction on a number of occasions based on their informants in Pakistan's Inter-Services Intelligence (ISI) unit.[11] The Taliban is also thought to have gathered intelligence from an Air Force officer's blog that discussed screening of passengers at airports, had photographs of his base, and pictures of his Afghanistan counterparts.[12] The Taliban continues to have a wide circle of informants and uses them to identify and eliminate suspected spies for Afghanistan security forces.[13]

As with intelligence, terrorists' counterintelligence practices are shaped by their numbers, the degree of popular support, and other resources. However, counterintelligence can be as simple as a thorough vetting of recruits to avoid being penetrated by government agents or potential informants.[14] The Provisional Irish Republican Army (PIRA) employed a variety of effective, but not necessarily costly, practices to thwart the British and the Royal Ulster Constabulary (RUC), Northern Ireland's police force. As an example, PIRA, which usually killed informants they discovered, undercut the effectiveness of British recruitment of informants by declaring an informer amnesty:[15] Come and tell us everything you gave up, what procedures were used to recruit you, what questions you asked, and no harm will come to you. This program revealed that the British were covertly operating a laundry so it could test the clothes of suspected PIRA members for explosive residues. [16] Also discovered was a bogus radio contest operated by the British Security Service MI5. It was rigged so targeted PIRA

The Provisional Irish Republican Army (PIRA) developed a "counter forensics" manual for its members that described the kinds of conclusions that could be reached by the forensic examination of different types of physical evidence.[17] One tip was not to wear wool clothes because wool picked up other materials and shed easily. The goal of the program was to limit the forensic evidence available to the British.

members "won" and when they left on their vacation, MI5 entered the homes and planted microphones.[18] In addition to reducing the number of informants, the PIRA program was able to assess the damage done and make adjustments to prevent further damage.[19]

Overview of the U.S. Intelligence Community

In order to address the problems identified by the Gilmore Commission, the Intelligence Reform and Terrorism Prevention Act of 2004 (IRTPA) established the **Office of the Director of National Intelligence (ODNI)**. The creation of the ODNI centralized all intelligence information from the myriad of agencies that had a mission to gather specific intelligence relating to their function. There are currently seventeen different agencies that report directly to the ODNI, including the Central Intelligence Agency and the FBI National Security Branch. These sixteen agencies represent the primary groups of federal government responsible for national security, including each branch of the military (i.e., Air Force, Army, Navy, Coast Guard, and the Marine Corps), the primary national intelligence agencies (e.g., National Security Agency and Central Intelligence Agency), and federal law enforcement (e.g., Federal Bureau of Investigation, Drug Enforcement Administration, and Department of Homeland Security). These agencies and the Office of the Director of National Intelligence are referred to as the **intelligence community (IC)** of the United States (see Figure 9–2).

The primary purpose of this new structure is to better coordinate, integrate, and manage the collection, analysis, and dissemination of intelligence information, including the intelligence that relates directly to international and domestic threats posed by terrorism. The ODNI administers the **National Intelligence Program (NIP)**, which funds the intelligence activities of the entire federal government. The estimated 2017 budget is nearly $54 billion per year and is critical in strengthening the nation's intelligence agencies.[20]

Office of the Director of National Intelligence (ODNI)
The national office created to centralize all intelligence information functions from all federal, state, and local agencies.

Intelligence community (IC)
Sixteen federal agencies representing various governmental groups reporting to the Office of the Director of National Intelligence.

Information Link
For more information on the Office of the Director of National Intelligence, visit the website at www.dni.gov/index.php.

National Intelligence Program (NIP)
The primary funding budget for the strengthening the nation's intelligence agencies.

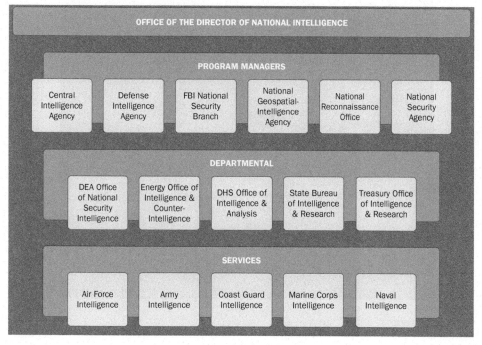

FIGURE 9–2
The Intelligence Community under the Office of the Director of National Intelligence (ODNI). United States Intelligence Community Seal and Organizational chart.
(National Intelligence Community)

The National Counterterrorism Center (NCTC)

The integration and analysis of terrorist threat information from various sources and the dissemination of that information to other members of the intelligence community, as well as other important state and local law enforcement partners, are accomplished through the National Counterterrorism Center (NCTC). The Center serves as the nation's "hub" for intelligence activity both domestically and internationally, coordinating intelligence information derived by individual members of the intelligence community. It also serves as a single point for the strategic and operational planning of counterterrorism activity. This is often accomplished through interagency meetings and secure teleconferences about terrorist groups, capabilities, plans and intentions, and emerging threats to U.S. interests.[21] The Center also operates a secure website (NCTC Online CURRENT) that serves as the primary dissemination mechanism for terrorist information to and from operational elements such as local FBI Joint Terrorist Task Forces (JTTFs) and military combatant commands. Located in Washington, D.C., the NCTC is part of the Office of the Director of National Intelligence and maintains the national repository of known and suspected terrorists and administers the Joint Counterterrorism Assessment Team (JCAT).* The JCAT is composed of public safety personnel from around the country. The goal of this coordination body is to inform public safety personnel in an effort to better identify, respond to, mitigate, and, most important, prevent the next terrorist attack against the homeland.[22] The National Counterterrorism Center also develops and distributes the *Counterterrorism Calendar* (see Figure 9–3) that commemorates particular events, traces the development of terrorist groups, has interactive timeline maps, and provides technical information on various topics

FIGURE 9–3
The NCTC maintains the Counterterrorism Calendar, which can be downloaded from the Internet and used by members of the general public. See https://www.nctc.gov/site/pdfs/ct_calendar.pdf.
(NCTC)

---

* JCAT was previously named as the Interagency Threat Assessment Coordination Group (ITACG).

such as biological and chemical threats.[23] The JCAT improves information sharing and public safety. It collaborates with other members of the intelligence community to research, produce, and disseminate products for federal, state, local, tribal, territorial, and private sector partners and advocates for the needs of those partners.[24]

The Central Intelligence Agency (CIA)

The framework for U.S. intelligence was created in a different time to deal with different problems other than terrorism. The National Security Act of 1947, which established the Central Intelligence Agency (CIA), envisioned the enemies of the United States to be nation-states such as Russia, North Korea, Iran, and China. The result was organizations and authority based on strict distinctions between domestic versus foreign threats, law enforcement versus national security concerns, and peacetime versus wartime operations.[25] The Federal Bureau of Investigation (FBI) was given responsibility for domestic intelligence inside the United States, and the CIA was charged with developing foreign intelligence outside the country. In contrast to the FBI and other law enforcement agencies (e.g., Drug Enforcement Administration, Secret Service), the CIA collects and analyzes information regarding national security in order to forewarn our government before an act occurs. The CIA, relegated to working outside the United States, has no arrest powers, and its activities are proactive in nature. Figure 9–4 compares the responsibilities of the CIA and FBI.

The Central Intelligence Agency is the principal foreign intelligence-gathering agency for the United States. For the most part, the focus of the CIA historically has not been on thwarting potentially violent groups in foreign lands (such as al-Qaeda) but rather on

FIGURE 9–4
Comparison chart between the CIA and FBI.

CIA
Central Intelligence Agency

FBI
Federal Bureau of Investigation,
U.S. Department of Justice

	CIA	FBI
Stands for:	Central Intelligence Agency	Federal Bureau of Investigation
Motto:	Ye shall know the truth and it shall set you free.	Fidelity, Bravery, Integrity
Formed:	September 18, 1947	July 26, 1908
Employees:	Classified. Estimated 20,000 agents and 35,000 staff in 2013	Classified. Estimated 13,785 agents and 22,117 staff in 2013
Headquarters:	George Bush Center for Intelligence Langley, Virginia	J. Edgar Hoover Building, Washington, D.C.
Agency Executives:	Michael R. Pompeo, Director	Christopher A. Wray, Director
	Mission executives (Chiefs of Station) are based in major embassies around the world and manage global operations on a regional or country basis.	Other directors (or Special Agents in Charge—SAC) are located in major large cities domestically and are responsible for regional geographic districts.
Website:	www.cia.gov	www.fbi.gov
Annual budget:	Classified	$8.1 billion (2013)

Source: CIA vs. FBI from Diffen.com. Used by permission of Diffen.com, and updated by R.W. Taylor (2017).

Box 9–1
Spies, Secret Messages, and Steganography

The earliest record of sending a secret message occurred in Greece in 5 B.C.[26] A man wanted to incite his son-in-law to revolt against the government. He shaved the head of one of his slaves, tattooed the message on his head, and when the hair grew back sent the slave to his son-in-law. During the American Revolution, invisible inks were used to send important messages. When treated chemically or with heat by the recipient, the hidden message would be revealed.[27]

Another method of sending secret messages during that war was based on books. If two people had the same edition of a book they could exchange secret messages. Upon receiving a message that began "43.21.6" the first word of the message could be found on page 43, line 21, word 6 of the agreed-upon book.[28] Obviously, the book selected had to contain a vocabulary that included the words that would commonly be used in messages.

In 1924, Thomas Dyer graduated from the U.S. Naval Academy and was assigned as an ensign to the battleship *New Mexico*.[29] Crossword puzzles had gained popularity during the 1920s. The Navy's Communications Research Desk (CRD) distributed crossword puzzles with "secret" messages hidden in them (steganography). Naval personnel were encouraged to work the crossword puzzles, find the hidden messages, and send their "solution" to CRD. Dyer routinely was able to find the hidden messages. As a consequence, he was transferred and trained in "making and breaking codes." The CRD crossword program was successful: It identified the few people with an aptitude for that kind of work.

In early 1942, Japan dominated the war in the Pacific Theater, enjoying an unbroken string of victories. That same year Japan planned to attack American forces on Midway Island. By then a lieutenant commander, Dyer was a member of Commander Rochefort's cryptanalysis ("code breaking") team. Dyer broke the Japanese naval code and Rochefort, fluent in Japanese, was able to read the subtle nuances in Dyer's translation and understood their foe's plans. The result was a stunning American naval victory at the Battle of Midway that reversed the tide of war in the Pacific Theater.

The steganography with which Dyer struggled in the 1920s was rudimentary and manually driven. However, the technological capabilities currently possessed by some terrorist groups have allowed them to exploit the new generation of digitally driven steganography to send secret messages that pose significant challenges.

Any picture, or other matter that can be reduced to a digital form, can be included in an altered file, creating a steganographic or hidden message. Consider the following:

1. There are 8 bits in a byte: 0-1-01-01-01;
2. The 8th or last bit always adds the smallest amount to the overall identity of a file;

3. Replacing the last bit can be done without causing an immediately detectable difference in a text, image, or auditory file; and
4. A PowerPoint file might easily contain 10 megabytes. This provides the opportunity for a hidden message of 1.25 megabytes (1/8 of 10 megabytes).[30]

In 2012, German police questioned Maqsood Lodin, who had just returned from Pakistan.[31] Digital storage devices were discovered in his underwear that included a pornographic video, *Kick Ass*. Contained within the video were al-Qaeda plans to hijack a cruise ship, dress passengers in orange jumpsuits like the ones worn by Islamic prisoners at the U.S. Naval Base at Guantanamo Bay, Cuba, and apparently videotape them being executed to pressure governments for concessions. Other plans included a series of attacks in London England.

Today, the battle over encryption remains something of an arms race—and those who prevail are more often not shadowy figures working for rogue elements or terrorist groups, but rather spies working for governments of world powers. In 2015, it was revealed that the United States was working closely with its "5-eyes" partners (including Great Britain, New Zealand, Canada, and Australia) to break the most widely used forms of Internet encryption.[32] And in 2016, the FBI was able to crack the encryption code that locks an Apple iPhone. This revelation came as Apple was preparing to defend itself from a legal challenge to hand over the encryption code to the government in a case involving files from the iPhone of Syed Rizwan Farook, who killed 14 people during a terrorist attack in San Bernardino, California. Instead of waiting for the court ruling, the FBI enlisted the help of an unknown professional hacker (within a corporate entity) to break the iPhone encryption and avoiding a legal confrontation. The 2016 case highlighted the chasm between intelligence needs and privacy concerns.[33]

Do you think the government still runs secret programs to identify people who have certain abilities?

What trade-off would you be willing to accept: Keeping intelligence safe versus sharing it more broadly with agencies that might be able to make use of it and potentially add to the intelligence you have, but increasing loss of security? Given the high-speed code-breaking capabilities of super computers, how safe is any encrypted data?

Information Links

For more information on the CIA, FBI, and NSA relating to the collection, analysis, and dissemination of terrorist intelligence information, refer to their websites at:

Central Intelligence Agency (CIA): www.cia.gov/index.html
Federal Bureau of Investigation (FBI): www.fbi.gov/
National Security Agency (NSA): www.nsa.gov/

individual nation-states that had the potential to conduct military attacks against the United States. The mission of the CIA is threefold: (1) Stop activities from terrorist organizations and nation-states that threaten the U.S. homeland or U.S. interests abroad by collecting intelligence information vital to U.S. decision makers; (2) conduct effective covert actions against enemies of the United States as directed by the president; and (3) safeguard national secrets that maintain the security of the United States (see Box 9–1). The **National Clandestine Service**, formerly known as the Directorate of Operations, is a major part of the structure of the CIA. It is the operation wing that carries out covert paramilitary operations against terrorist groups and cells outside the United States. It is also the part of the CIA that is most often romantically depicted in the popular media. The adventures of spies and secret agents have been depicted throughout literature as well as television and the movies. Recently however, the CIA has shifted focus from traditional counterterrorism activities to cyber intelligence and more offensive cyber operations.[34] Agencies that have intelligence responsibilities also have cryptanalysis (code breaking). The National Security Agency (NSA) globally monitors communications and collects, analyzes, and disseminates it as needed.

National Clandestine Service
The operational wing of the CIA that carries out covert paramilitary operations against terrorist groups and cells outside the United States.

The Federal Bureau of Investigation (FBI)

Headquartered in Washington, D.C., at the J. Edgar Hoover Building, the FBI is the largest investigative agency in the U.S. Department of Justice. It represents the nation's premier law enforcement agency. It has two distinct missions relating to terrorism: (1) The Federal Bureau of Investigation (FBI) is the primary criminal investigative body on any terrorist attack against the United States both domestically and internationally, and (2) the FBI collects, analyzes, and disseminates all domestic intelligence information relating to terrorist threats. The National Security Branch of the FBI houses the Directorate of Intelligence and is responsible for ensuring that accurate and timely intelligence is embedded into all counterterrorism activities. The FBI is an **intel-driven organization**; that is, it combines investigation and intelligence operations to be more predictive and preventative in nature—more aware of emerging threats and better able to prevent them from occurring.[35]

Intel-driven organization
An organization that combines investigation and intelligence operations to be more predictive and preventative in nature.

The primary vehicle for the collection of intelligence information relating to potential terrorist attacks and specific intelligence on individual terrorist groups is derived from the **Joint Terrorism Task Forces (JTTFs)** located throughout the United States (see Figure 9–5). The FBI is the lead agency in managing and directing these task forces. JTTFs represent a collage of highly trained federal, state, and local law enforcement officers and agents committed to gathering intelligence, investigating specific activities, making arrests, and responding to threats at a moment's notice. The task forces are based in 102 cities nationwide, including one in each of the fifty-six FBI field offices. As of 2014, a total of 71 of these JTTFs have been created since 9/11, composed of more than 4,200 members from over 600 state and local agencies and 50 federal agencies (e.g., U.S. Marshals Service, Secret Service, Immigration and Customs Enforcement, Drug Enforcement Administration, Transportation Security Administration, U.S. Military).[36]

Joint Terrorism Task Forces (JTTFs)
A group of highly trained federal, state, and local law enforcement officers and agents focusing on terrorism-related intelligence and investigations.

Blurred Lines and Conflicting Roles

The FBI and local and state police agencies within this country have a different role than the CIA, one that focuses on crime most often committed by citizens within the United States. With the passage of the USA PATRIOT Act in 2001,[37] the hard-and-fast distinctions between the FBI and the CIA, and hence the role of the police in combating terrorism, have become somewhat blurred. Law enforcement's primary focus has been to collect evidence *after* a crime was committed in order to support prosecution in a court trial. This process, called investigation, is reactive in nature (see Figure 9–6). Traditionally, police intelligence activity has been severely limited by law. A long and controversial history of abuse, particularly on the part of the FBI during the 1960s and 70s, led to the issuance of various Attorney General guidelines limiting the ability of the police to collect intelligence information.[38] The Church Senate Investigative Committee, named after Idaho Senator Frank Church in 1975, revealed a host of constitutional and human rights violations on the part of the FBI Counterintelligence Program (commonly referred to as COINTELPRO) designed specifically to disrupt and intimidate legitimate civil rights groups, including the National Organization for Women (NOW), the American Indian Movement (AIM), and the National Association for the

FIGURE 9–5
A member of a JTTF enters a home in North Bergen, New Jersey. Along with others, he conducted a search of the home. It is believed the home was connected to terrorist suspect, Mohammed Hamoud Alessa, who was arrested before he could be arrested in New York City.
(James Robinson/PennLive.com/ AP Images)

- **Investigation:**

  Reactive; occurs after the event, incident, or crime
  Reports are generally open
  Sources are generally known and open
  Arrests are made based on probable cause: evidence and facts

- **Intelligence:**

  Proactive; information gathered before the event or incident
  Reports are almost always closed
  Sources are confidential and closed
  Arrests are rarely made

FIGURE 9–6

The Differences between Investigation and Intelligence

Source: Robert W. Taylor, Eric J. Fritsch, John Liederbach, Michael R. Saylor, and William L. Tafoya, *Digital Crime and Digital Terrorism,* 4th edition (Upper Saddle River, NJ: Pearson, 2018), p. 267.

Advancement of Colored People (NAACP). These illegal activities (ranging from personal intimidation and threats, illegal eavesdropping, and even burglary) were detailed in the FBI's own internal documents.[39] As a result, the FBI and police were allowed to use intelligence information *only* to develop probable cause that would justify arrest and prosecution. In most incidents, a suspect had to actually break the law or threaten to break it before the police or the FBI could act on intelligence information. This was a frustrating predicament—police agencies could not act without probable cause, but at the same time they were prevented from engaging in the very activities that could establish probable cause![40]

The USA PATRIOT Act now allows the FBI and state or local police to engage in covert intelligence operations, greatly expanding the use of police surveillance through roving wiretaps, "sneak and peek" warrants, "trap and trace" pen registers on telephones, and the like. The police can now monitor surreptitiously your use of the Internet and receive a list of all sites visited by your IP address—all without a warrant or other judicial oversight mechanism. Arguably, the FBI and other police organizations indicate that they must have these tools to ferret out would-be terrorists living inside the United States, essentially to protect us from another terrorist attack.

On the other hand, many argue that our laws mandate civil liberties and constitutional rights for each individual citizen. These laws were developed to protect the individual and to balance the power of the police during an investigation…the police have never been given the right to collect intelligence information on individuals without judicial oversight. The right to be free from unwarranted searches and seizures as developed under the Fourth Amendment of the Constitution and to check illegal intrusions into our privacy without probable cause are two of the most basic and enduring rights enjoyed by all citizens of the United States. See Chapter 10 for a more thorough discussion of the issues presented by the collection of intelligence in a free society.

In 2017, Donald Trump became the President of the United States and was immediately embroiled in a political controversy with specific agencies within the intelligence community. Most prominent was his dismissal of James Comey as Director of the FBI, and the appointment of Mike Pompeo, a former Representative from Kansas having very little experience in national security issues, as the Director of the CIA. Both appointments further confused the role, scope, and perception of each agency. See Box 9–2.

Box 9–2
President Donald Trump and the Intelligence Community: An Uneasy Alliance

In the history of the United States, intelligence agencies have always evoked an uneasy and wary feeling in citizens: On the one hand, those agencies work hard to ensure defense of the country and to protect U.S. citizens against terrorist attacks or aggressions from hostile countries. On the other hand, though, the agencies have had a checkered past concerning human rights violations and, more recently, have been embroiled in various scandals related to surveillance and encryption-cracking-privacy-release incidents. Thus, many Americans struggle with how they perceive the national security apparatus—and the election of President Donald Trump has served to further confuse the perception of such agencies.

During his first 100 days, President Trump's relationships with intelligence agencies appeared tenuous at best. He has backed away from daily intelligence briefings that other presidents held sacrosanct; he has made appointments to the National Security Council—specifically that of his strategist Steve Bannon—that have caused major controversy; his NSA director (Michael Flynn) was fired due to dishonesty about meetings he held with Russian officials, and President Trump himself

has clashed with the FBI, CIA, and the NSA over leaks, purported surveillance, and investigations into ties between his 2016 campaign and Russia. Certainly, political maneuvering is not new to the intelligence process, and there have been other presidents in the past who have had significant friction with various intelligence agencies.

However, moving to an abridged *Presidential Daily Brief*, which is a collection of intelligence, threats, policy opportunities, and related concerns compiled by analysts and presented to the president six days a week, is something very different. President Trump reportedly prefers highlights from the briefings rather than intense analytic conclusions and predictions. Some analysts argue that the briefings must be kept short, with only terse factual statements and minus the analysis and viewpoints that past administrations often relied upon to make strategic and tactical decisions. Some intelligence officials characterize their agency's relationship with Trump as acrimonious, with many media outlets branding the tension as a "war." Tweets from the President in February of 2017 referred to intelligence officers who leaked information about investigations into ties between Russia and

(Bastiaan Slabbers/Alamy Stock Photo)

(REX/Shutterstock)

the Trump campaign as "low life leakers"; and in a speech to Congress the same day as the tweets, President Trump indicated that the former and current intelligence officers involved would "pay a price." Some intelligence experts have suggested that President Trump's "war of words" against the intelligence community will change the dynamic of the relationship to one that is highly guarded and political versus one that is trusted, informative, and open. Intelligence analysts fear that having to filter information to find pieces that please an agenda rather than inform is a potentially dangerous scenario. The dialogue has also caused personnel issues within the intelligence world, lowering morale and driving experienced intelligence analysts and officers out the doors. The departure of talented intelligence experts and analysts will certainly drain the knowledge base of the security apparatus.

The result of these incidents provides a different shape in intelligence administration for the future: one that may impact the overall effectiveness of the intelligence apparatus of this country to collect information, analyze threats associated with this data, and most important, prevent potential attacks in the future. Finally, this type of public display of distrust between intelligence agencies and the president further muddies the waters of perception for the public relating to the intelligence community. Ultimately, Americans continue to be split on their current perception of the national intelligence apparatus: some are suspicious

of their motives related to President Trump; others believe that they are being hamstrung and besmirched by the chief executive; and still others never trusted the intelligence community in the first place. Regardless, this turmoil will likely usher in significant changes to the administration, traditions, and structure of the United States intelligence community.

Sources: Frank Archibald, "Intelligence and the Trump Administration," The Cipher Brief, February 23, 2017, retrieved from www.thecipherbrief.com/column/network-take/intelligence-and-trump-administration-1091.
Andy Greenberg, "Trump ignoring US Intelligence creates risks beyond Russian hacking," *Wired,* December 12, 2016, retrieved from https://www.wired.com/2016/12/trump-cia-national-intelligence-briefings/.
Ashley DeJean, "Classified memo tells intelligence analysts to keep Trump's daily brief short," *Mother Jones,* February 16, 2017, retrieved from http://www.motherjones.com/politics/2017/02/classified-memo-tells-intelligence-analysts-keep-trumps-daily-brief-short.
Natasha Betrand, "The war between Trump and the intelligence community is heating up," *Business Insider,* February 16, 2017, retrieved from www.businessinsider.com/trump-intelligence-community-russia-cia-fbi-flynn-2017-2.

The National Security Agency (NSA)

The National Security Agency (NSA) bills itself as the nation's preeminent "cryptologic organization." In more familiar language, the NSA is primarily responsible for designing and maintaining computerized coding systems designed to protect the integrity of U.S. information systems.[41] (See Figure 9–7.) It has also become the lead agency responsible for monitoring and protecting all of the federal government's computer networks from acts of cyberterrorism.[42] In direct relation to these responsibilities, NSA agents are also responsible for detecting and exploiting weaknesses in an adversarial country's computerized secret coding systems. Headquartered in Fort Meade, Maryland, the NSA has been providing the nation with "code-breaking" capabilities since these operations began against the Japanese in the Pacific Theater of World War II. The NSA's role in providing information system security and information assurance has expanded with the parallel growth in computerized communications technology during the Cold War and the ensuing decades.[43]

The NSA's role in protecting classified computer data demands an eclectic mix of agents who specialize in a wide range of professional fields, including researchers, computer scientists, mathematicians, and engineers. Though much of the work of NSA agents

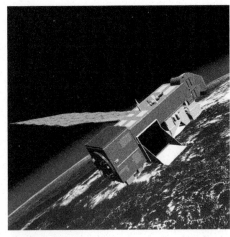

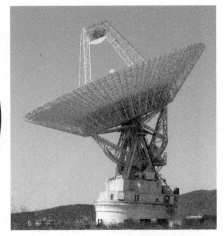

NASA   National Security Agency   NASA

FIGURE 9–7
The National Security Agency uses satellites, as well as other information system technologies, to collect data, information, and intelligence about potential terrorist groups and attacks. Recently, the agency has come under attack for eavesdropping on foreign telephone communication.

remains secretive in nature, the agency's expertise in the area of information systems has led to a number of collaborative initiatives intended to improve information security research, knowledge, and expertise through the federal law enforcement system. For example, the NSA has recently created the INFOSEC Service Center designed to increase research initiatives concerning computer security by the federal government. The NSA has also helped to form the National Computer Security Center (NCSC), which is designed as an avenue to create partnerships among the federal law enforcement and intelligence communities.[44]

The NSA has also assumed an active role in providing information security training to both government and private entities through the National INFOSEC Education and Training Program. This program provides training for security specialists, including risk assessment, security design, and information security evaluation. Through these initiatives, the NSA aims to provide government agencies and the private sector information system security expertise.[45] Additionally, the NSA works to provide information security through security tools, security products, threat warnings, analysis of potential attacks by terrorists, and security bulletins.[46] In 2013, the NSA came under considerable attack for spying on several U.S. citizens and foreign leaders (see Figure 9–8). In addition, the security of the agency appears to have been compromised by the effort of Edward Snowden, a former CIA employee and NSA contractor who disclosed classified NSA documents to several media outlets and revealed the agency's global surveillance activities.[47] These activities are further discussed in Chapter 10.

FIGURE 9–8
An aerial view of the NSA's Data Center in Bluffdale, Utah. Under a secret court order, the NSA has been collecting the telephone records of millions of U.S. citizens. Defenders of the program cite national security requirements and critics point to the lack of need to simply collect the records of citizens who are not under any suspicion.

(AP Photo/Rick Bowmer/AP Images)

Today, the fallout from Snowden's revelations continues in political, legal, and political talking points, but the NSA is embroiled in other controversies as well—including a statement from NSA director Admiral Michael S. Rogers in late 2016 that this year's election outcome had been influenced by a "nation-state." Further, an NSA contractor named Howard Thomas Martin was arrested in 2016 for theft of highly sensitive and classified computer codes that were developed for the purpose of hacking into the networks of foreign governments. Martin was indicted in 2017 and is awaiting trial.[48]

Intelligence and Cyberterrorism

Teams from the FBI, the CIA, and the NSA work together in a secure location known as the Remote Operation Center, the "ROC" ("rock"). With overlapping missions and legal authorities, combined with the best high technology equipment available, these teams have a dual mission:

- *Cyber Defense:* Protect current U.S. military and intelligence systems, as well as other critical infrastructure and information systems within the United States from foreign or terrorist attack; and

- *Cyber Offense:* Covertly exploit and infiltrate, via virtual methodologies, foreign systems and create a presence inside these targeted systems for advancing the interests of the United States.

These two missions provide a strong base in which to combat **cyberterrorism or digital terrorism**. These terms are often used interchangeably and can be defined as the premeditated, politically or ideologically motivated attack against information networks, computer systems, computer programs, and/or data that can result in violence against civilian targets.[49] According to Barry Collin of the Institute for Security and Intelligence, cyberterrorism is "hacking with a body count."[50] An early assessment by RAND's National Research Defense Institute concluded that cyberterrorism may also include attacks motivated by political or ideological objectives that can cause serious harm, such as a prolonged loss of infrastructure, like electricity or water (see Chapter 11 for a discussion of the vulnerabilities of critical infrastructure).[51] Yet another definition includes severe economic loss as a qualifier for cyberterrorism: If economic loss is harsh enough, a destabilization may occur that can result in serious harm to a society.[52] To muddy the waters even more, a less significant activity designed to protest, "spread the truth," or otherwise emphasize a particular belief or political bent without intentional harm to human life is referred to as "hacktivism."[53] In these cases, mostly involving website defacement, the actor is involved much more in vandalism and chaos versus economic gain and/or destruction—terrorism *without* the body count.

Terrorist organizations, including domestic left and right-wing groups as well as foreign, radical Islamic groups like al-Qaeda and the Islamic State have attacked information systems throughout the United States over the past decade. More recently, however, their attempts to strike at critical infrastructure within the United States has dramatically increased. See Box 9–3 for more information regarding this serious issue.

Cyberterrorism (or digital terrorism)
The premeditated, politically, or ideologically motivated attack against information networks, computer systems, computer programs, and/or data that can result in violence against civilian targets.

Box 9–3
The Islamic State (IS) and the Potential for Cyberterrorism

Much of the current interest in cyberterrorism sprung from the use of information technology by al-Qaeda in planning the events of September 11, 2001. Under the direction of Egyptian cleric Ayman al-Zawahiri, al-Qaeda apparently mounted a sophisticated system of communication, surveillance, and coordination via computer networks and other information tools. The group made no secret of its plans to commit what Sheikh Omar "Bakri" Muhammad, an Islamic cleric who was linked to Osama bin Laden, called a "cyber jihad" against the United States and its allies. Bakri identified the stock market as a major target and described how the fundamentalist Islamic groups are assembling cadres of computer science students sympathetic to al-Qaeda's cause in places like Pakistan and Malaysia.[54]

Upon the death of Usama bin Laden, much of the terror group's network was disrupted or destroyed, and no major cyberterror attack by the group has yet materialized—but today, experts emphasize that the Islamic State, or ISIS, may be planning such an event.

In 2016, Admiral Michael S. Rogers, Director of the U.S. Cyber Command, warned that the Islamic State had harnessed the power of cyberspace to recruit, spread propaganda, and incite attacks—and may be moving toward the disruption of critical infrastructure as part of their arsenal. Rogers emphasized that he has no indication that the fundamentalist terror group currently had the capability to carry out such an attack, but made it clear that an organization that has had great success in attracting collaborators sympathetic to their cause would have little difficulty attracting and recruiting highly technical associates

capable of such an attack.[55] Rogers pointed to a cyber event in the Ukraine in 2015, which is largely attributed to Russian state players. A sophisticated group of hackers were able to shut down the entire city of Kiev, Ukraine (with a population of over 3 million people), by disrupting its power grid. The rogue group gained access to networks from six different power companies, knocking out internal systems to restore power, and even taking down call centers where outages (and emergencies) could be reported. Though this event was not affiliated in any way with IS, Rogers believes that the attack demonstrated the potential disruption such an event could cause in a Western nation—as well as its relative ease and anonymity for the cyberterrorist, not to mention the difficulty in proving such an attack against a specific movement, group, or individual.

Until now, most IS-related cyberattacks (at least those that have been discussed publicly) have been focused on targets in Great Britain. For instance, in early 2017, National Health Service (in London) sites were exploited to show gruesome scenes from the Syrian civil war. An IS-linked group called the Tunisian Fallaga Team claimed responsibility for the cyber intrusion. Two other IS-related groups, the Global Islamic Caliphate and Team System DZ, have also been active throughout 2015 and 2016, coordinating operations against airlines, media companies, and the U.S. Central Command's Twitter and YouTube accounts.[56]

Many terrorism experts predict that the next major attack on the United States will be an attack on the digital and electronic resources of the country. Do you think that terrorist movements like the Islamic State have the capability to conduct acts of cyberterrorism?

Information Links
For more information on these agencies, visit their home pages at:
The Defense Intelligence Agency (DIA): www.dia.mil
The National GeoSpatial Intelligence Agency (NGIA): www.nga.mil/
The National Reconnaissance Office (NRO): www.nro.gov
Department of State Bureau of Intelligence and Research (INR): www.state.gov/s/inr/
Department of Homeland Security, Office of Intelligence and Analysis (ONI): https://www.dhs.gov/office-intelligence-and-analysis

Other Agencies within the Intelligence Community

As previously mentioned, there are 16 separate agencies reporting to the Office of the Director of National Intelligence (ODNI). Although the CIA, FBI, and NSA remain the largest and most well known of these agencies, there are a still a number of smaller, lesser-known agencies that collect, analyze, and disseminate intelligence related to potential terrorist activities, including the following.

The Defense Intelligence Agency (DIA)

The Defense Intelligence Agency provides intelligence in support of U.S. military planning and operations. It is the primary intelligence agency for the U.S. Department of Defense and focuses on preventing strategic surprise from a nation-state (similar to Pearl Harbor in December 1941) or an attack on U.S. military forces overseas (similar to the terrorist attack of the U.S. Marine barracks in Beirut, Lebanon, in 1983). The DIA houses the Office of the Inspector General that conducts audits, inspections, investigation, and intelligence oversight focused on preventing and detecting fraud, waste, and abuse within the defense industry.[57] The DIA also conducts security background investigations on all military or defense personnel relating to security clearances.

National Geospatial-Intelligence Agency (NGA)

Geospatial intelligence (GEOINT)
Intelligence information derived from maps, imagery, charts, and/or satellite data.

Using **geospatial intelligence (GEOINT)** derived from maps, imagery, charts, and satellite data, the NGA provides a foundation for the intelligence discipline (see Figure 9–9). Using high level geographic information systems (GIS)[58] and remote sensing techniques provides NGA analysts with critical information relating to terrain, elevation, and gravity.[59] Such information provides immediate intelligence relating to any physical or geographical point in the world, allowing strategic and tactical advantage to warfighters during combat as well as support for various types of counterterrorism operations.

National Reconnaissance Office (NRO)

The NRO is the government agency responsible for designing, building, launching, maintaining, and monitoring America's intelligence satellite system.[60] The NRO works closely with other members of the intelligence community and particularly those associated with the U.S. Department of Defense and the military.

State Bureau of Intelligence and Research

The primary intelligence division within the U.S. Department of State is the Bureau of Intelligence and Research (INR). Its mission is to provide intelligence information in support of U.S. diplomacy and is often the focal point for actions involving counterintelligence and law enforcement activities outside the United States.[61] The State Bureau of Intelligence and Research also provides intelligence support for the safety and security of embassies located throughout the world.

U.S. Department of Homeland Security, Office of Intelligence and Analysis

The Office of Intelligence and Analysis (I&A) is an agency that manages the collection, analysis, and dissemination of intelligence through the entire U.S. Department of Homeland Security. The Office tracks individual terrorists and groups as well as monitors threats against critical American infrastructure. One of the primary missions of the Office is to integrate the intelligence elements within DHS

FIGURE 9–9
Geospatial data has both military and civilian applications. A U.S. Air Force geospatial intelligence analyst studies images of the damage done by a large hurricane on the Gulf Coast. Information from such analyses allows for the rapid examination of damages and where resources need to be directed and prioritized.
(Kevin Wolf/AP Images)

and to share this information with state and local governments as well as the private sector.[62] To this end, the I&A has been instrumental in establishing and funding intelligence fusion centers throughout the United States. Fusion centers are discussed later in this chapter.

Other members of the intelligence community include smaller units within various governmental departments and agencies such as the Drug Enforcement Administration Office of National Security Intelligence, the U.S. Department of Energy Office of Intelligence and Counterintelligence, and the U.S. Department of Treasury Office of Intelligence and Research. The final members of the intelligence community represent the intelligence services within each branch of the military: Air Force, Army, Coast Guard, Marine Corps, and Navy.

Intelligence at the State and Local Level

In addition to federal effort, state and local police departments are implementing their own brand of intelligence gathering and analysis through the planned networking of large databases that seek to contribute to the national process of intelligence gathering and sharing. This new strategy, the **National Criminal Intelligence Sharing Plan (NCISP)**, combines the public partnership concepts of community policing with problem-solving tactics that aim to enhance police efficiency and draw attention to the primary concern of preventing terrorist attacks through effective communication and coordination. The strategic integration of intelligence, with an emphasis on predictive analysis–derived real data, defines a new style of policing called **intelligence-led policing (ILP)**. An important hallmark of ILP is the reliance on sophisticated computers and software programs to assist police decision makers in their daily duties. Ultimately, the goal of intelligence-led policing is to provide an expansive intelligence system involving local police that not only helps coordinate agency responses, but again, also informs objective decision making on how to prevent and combat both crime and terrorism.[63]

The Intelligence Process and Cycle

The National Criminal Intelligence Sharing Plan (NCISP) contained 28 specific recommendations for major changes in local policing. However, the key concept from the document emphasized the strategic integration of intelligence into the overall mission of the police organization. Rather than react and respond to past calls for service, the plan placed much more emphasis on predictive analysis derived from the discovery of hard facts, information, patterns, intelligence, and good crime analysis. Accurate and timely intelligence information, then, becomes a critically important element of the plan. In order to protect the civil liberties of all individuals, the intelligence process (from collection through analysis to dissemination) is developed with key evaluation points aimed at verifying source reliability and validity at the beginning of the collection cycle. The goal was to develop a universal process that would integrate both law enforcement and national security intelligence agendas, while at the same time provide mechanisms for securing individual freedoms, yet allow law enforcement agencies to be proactive in preventing and deterring crime and terrorism. The end result was the development of the "intelligence cycle", presented in an effort to bring varied pieces of information together in an effort to draw logical conclusions from a thorough and systematic process (see Figure 9–10). The intelligence cycle also provides the crucial means to communicate and share intelligence information between individuals and agencies through the dissemination process.

The intelligence cycle consists of six steps. The graphic in Figure 9–10 shows the circular nature of this process, although movement between the steps is fluid. Intelligence uncovered at one step may require going back to an earlier step before moving forward. The six steps of the intelligence cycle are:

Requirements are identified information needs—what we must know to safeguard the nation. Intelligence requirements are established by the Director of National Intelligence according to guidance received from the president and the national and Homeland Security advisors. Requirements are developed based on critical information

National Criminal Intelligence Sharing Plan (NCISP)
A national effort that combines public partnerships with problem-solving tactics aimed at enhancing police efficiency in preventing terrorist attacks through effective communication and coordination.

Intelligence-led policing (ILP)
A new style of policing that integrates intelligence, with an emphasis on predictive analysis derived from the discovery of hard facts, information, patterns, and traditional crime analysis.

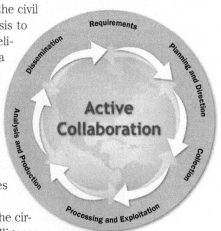

FIGURE 9–10
The Intelligence Cycle
The intelligence cycle is the process of developing unrefined data into polished intelligence for the use of policymakers.

(From Intelligence Branch. Published by Federal Bureau of Investigation.)

required to protect the United States from national security and criminal threats. The attorney general and the director of the FBI participate in the formulation of national intelligence requirements.

Planning and Direction is management of the entire effort, from identifying the need for information to delivering an intelligence product to a consumer. It involves implementation plans to satisfy requirements levied on the FBI, as well as identifying specific collection requirements based on FBI needs. Planning and direction also are responsive to the end of the cycle, because current and finished intelligence, which supports decision making, generates new requirements. The executive assistant director for the National Security Branch leads intelligence planning and direction for the FBI.

Collection is the gathering of raw information based on requirements. Activities such as interviews, technical and physical surveillances, human source operation, searches, and liaison relationships result in the collection of intelligence.

Processing and Exploitation involves converting the vast amount of information collected into a form usable by analysts. This is done through a variety of methods, including decryption, language translations, and data reduction. Processing includes the entering of raw data into databases where it can be exploited for use in the analysis process.

Analysis and Production is the conversion of raw information into intelligence. It includes integrating, evaluating, and analyzing available data and preparing intelligence products. The information's reliability, validity, and relevance are evaluated and weighed. The information is logically integrated, put in context, and used to produce intelligence. This includes both "raw" and finished intelligence. Raw intelligence is often referred to as "the dots"—individual pieces of information disseminated individually. Finished intelligence reports "connect the dots" by putting information in context and drawing conclusions about its implications.

Dissemination—the last step—is the distribution of raw or finished intelligence to the consumers whose needs initiated the intelligence requirements. The FBI disseminates information in three standard formats: Intelligence Information Reports (IIRs), FBI Intelligence Bulletins, and FBI Intelligence Assessments. FBI intelligence products are

Data fusion
The exchange of information from different sources, with analysis, that results in meaningful and actionable intelligence.

Quick Facts
Data Fusion

According to the U.S. Department of Homeland Security, *data fusion* is defined as the exchange of information from different sources—including law enforcement, public safety, and the private sector—and, with analysis, can result in meaningful and actionable intelligence and information that can inform both policy and the tactical deployment of resources.

(Toria/Shutterstock)

provided daily to the attorney general, the president, and to customers throughout the FBI and in other agencies. These FBI intelligence customers make decisions—operational, strategic, and policy—based on the information. These decisions may lead to the levying of more requirements, thus continuing the FBI intelligence cycle.[64]

Fusion Centers

The transformation of state and local police agencies into intelligence-led organizations involves several key objectives: (1) the creation of a task and coordination process, (2) the development of core intelligence products to lead the operation, (3) the establishment of standardized training practices, and (4) the development of protocols to facilitate intelligence capabilities.

This approach is intended to improve the capability of local law enforcement to respond to terrorist threats and the imperative to "fight crime." Intelligence-led policing blends community partnerships with crime fighting and police accountability in an effort to maximize police efficiency and effectiveness toward terrorism prevention and crime reduction. There is evidence to suggest that this initiative has started to alter the face of traditional policing in the United States. A national study found that a majority of local and state police agencies have conducted terrorism threat assessments since 9/11, and about one-third of these agencies have collaborated with the FBI's joint terrorism task force to assist in local crime investigations.[65] The movement toward intelligence-led policing has also been pushed by the creation of fusion centers inside local and state police agencies that serve as "clearinghouses" for all potentially relevant homeland security information that can be used to assess local terror threats and aid in the apprehension of more traditional criminal suspects.

Originally launched in New York City under the direction of Raymond Kelly in 2002, the concept of a **fusion center** blended the power of information technology with terrorism prevention and crime fighting. With a price tag exceeding $11 million, the Real Time Crime Center (RTCC) in New York City combs through tens of millions of criminal complaints, arrest and parole records, and 911 call records dating back a decade in an effort to provide NYPD officers with the information tools necessary to stop a terrorist event.[66] Fusion centers serve the function of distributing relevant, actionable, and timely information and intelligence incorporating a simultaneous vertical (i.e., federal, state, and local) and horizontal (i.e., within the agency, with other local agencies, and across disciplines such as fire, EMS, public works, private partners) approach in a timely and efficient manner within a given jurisdiction.

Fusion centers are composed of talented and trained individuals using sophisticated application software in crime analysis and mapping to manage and manipulate information and intelligence into a usable product. The resulting analysis acts as a basis for the deployment of police resources and directed operations in a real-time format—that is, almost immediately. The fusion center not only acts as a centralized host for intelligence information and analysis, but also serves as a conduit for passing critical information out to other regional, state, and national authorities. This is a particularly important point that fulfills the National Criminal Intelligence Sharing Plan in protecting the homeland.

Almost every state and several large metropolitan cities have undertaken the development of fusion centers with significant funding assistance from the Department of Homeland Security, Office of Intelligence and Analysis. For instance, the Chicago Police Department Deployment Operations Center (DOC) was one of the first centers to combine real-time intelligence analysis with the deployment of officers and other resources. In Los Angeles, both the city and county have well-developed fusion centers, and in Dallas, Texas, the Metropolitan Operations and Analytical Intelligence Center (MOSAIC) provides real time, tactical information to officers on the street 24/7.

The goals of a fusion center are fourfold:

1) Fusion centers support the broad range of activities undertaken by a police department relating to the detection, examination, and investigation of a potential terrorist attack and/or criminal activity. Similar to the NCTC, local and state fusion centers serve as a hubs of antiterrorist and anticrime operations in a specific region focusing on the recognition of patterns, indications and warnings, source development, interdiction, and coordination of critical criminal justice resources. These are critical

Fusion center
A "clearinghouse" or information "hub" that blends the power of information technology with terrorism prevention and crime fighting.

activities for any police agency attempting to be proactive and intelligence-led to be successful in deterring, detecting, disrupting, investigating, and apprehending suspects involved in terrorist activity.

2) Fusion centers provide support for operations that protect critical infrastructure and key resources (CI/KRs) in a given region, support major incident operations, support specialized units charged with interdiction and investigative operations, and assist in emergency operations and planning. See Chapter 11 for discussion on protecting America's infrastructure.

3) Fusion centers often maintain public "tip lines" or the capability to promote more public involvement/awareness to terrorist threats. The goal is to identify and recognize warning signs and potential threats in a timely manner in order to preempt potential terrorist attacks. Fusion centers accomplish this task on a daily basis, focusing on the analysis of crimes that are often linked to terrorist cells and activity for funding, such as narcotics trafficking, credit card abuse, armament and gun theft, prostitution, and human trafficking by distributing information relating to these linkages to all agencies within a given region. The timeliness of gathering, analyzing, and disseminating information is vital to successfully preventing acts of violence and threats to Homeland Security.

4) Fusion centers assist police executives in making better-informed decisions, especially during emergencies or critical incidents. Fusion centers serve as an ongoing deployment operations center with the real-time ability to monitor critical resources. This includes real-time status monitoring of major events, communicating with area medical facilities and trauma units, coordinating the allocation and deployment of multi-agency personnel resources (including military reserve units), monitoring changing weather conditions, and directing all support services through a centralized operations center.[67]

U.S. Department of Homeland Security and Fusion Centers

The U.S. Department of Homeland Security (DHS) has played an integral role in the development and implementation of fusion centers as part of the intelligence-led policing paradigm. The primary goal of DHS in this area has been to promote a strong relationship between state/local and federal law enforcement agencies through financial grants. Many states and larger cities have created fusion centers to share information and intelligence within their jurisdictions as well as with the federal government funded through DHS grants. The Office of Intelligence and Analysis within DHS provides support personnel with operational and intelligence skills to fusion centers when requested. This support is tailored to the unique needs of the locality and serves to help the classified and unclassified information flow, provide analysis expertise, coordinate with local law enforcement and other agencies, and provide local awareness and access to sensitive data (Department of Homeland Security, 2008).

As of 2017, there were 78 primary and recognized state and major urban fusion centers within the United States.[68] A "primary fusion" center typically provides information collection, collation, analysis, and sharing for an entire state, while a "recognized" fusion center typically provides services for a major urban area.[69] Almost every state has a statewide fusion center, as do most major urban areas (see Figure 9–11). The **National Fusion Center Association (NFCA)** is a formal group that represents the interests of state and major urban area fusion centers nationally. In addition, the NFCA promotes the development and sustainment of fusion centers to enhance public safety and the ethical and lawful collection of intelligence gathering, analysis, and dissemination.[70] Like many federal agencies and individual fusion centers, the goal of the NFCA is to prevent the next terrorist attack on the homeland. The **Homeland Security Data Network (HSDN)**, which allows the federal government to move information and intelligence to the states at the "secret" level, is deployed at most fusion centers. Through HSDN, fusion center staff can access the National Counterterrorism Center (NCTC) via a secure and classified portal to the most current terrorism-related information. Certainly, we have witnessed an unprecedented movement on the part of the federal government to employ local and state police agencies into the antiterrorism mission.

National Fusion Center Association (NFCA)
A formal group that represents the interests of state and major urban area fusion centers nationally.

Homeland Security Data Network (HSDN)
A classified information network that allows the federal government to move information and intelligence to state and local jurisdictions at the "secret" level.

The National Fusion Center Network

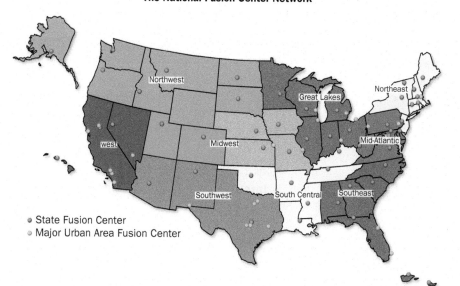

- State Fusion Center
- Major Urban Area Fusion Center

FIGURE 9–11
Locations of the 77 recognized U.S.
Department of Homeland Security
(DHS) fusion centers.
*(From Fusion Center Locations and
Contact Information. Published by
Department of Homeland Security.)*

Primary Fusion Centers

- Alabama Fusion Center
- Alaska Information and Analysis Center
- Arizona Counter Terrorism Information Center
- Arkansas State Fusion Center
- California State Threat Assessment Center
- Colorado Information Analysis Center
- Connecticut Intelligence Center
- Delaware Information and Analysis Center
- Florida Fusion Center
- Georgia Information Sharing and Analysis Center
- Hawaii Fusion Center
- Idaho Criminal Intelligence Center
- Illinois Statewide Terrorism and Intelligence Center
- Indiana Intelligence Fusion Center
- Iowa Division of Intelligence and Fusion Center
- Kansas Intelligence Fusion Center
- Kentucky Intelligence Fusion Center
- Louisiana State Analytical & Fusion Exchange
- Maine Information and Analysis Center
- Mariana Regional Fusion Center (Guam)
- Maryland Coordination and Analysis Center
- Massachusetts Commonwealth Fusion Center
- Michigan Intelligence Operations Center
- Minnesota Fusion Center
- Mississippi Analysis and Information Center
- Missouri Information Analysis Center
- Montana All-Threat Intelligence Center
- Nebraska Information Analysis Center
- New Hampshire Information and Analysis Center
- New Jersey Regional Operations Intelligence Center
- New Mexico All Source Intelligence Center
- New York State Intelligence Center
- North Carolina Information Sharing and Analysis Center
- North Dakota State and Local Intelligence Center
- Ohio Strategic Analysis and Information Center
- Oklahoma Information Fusion Center
- Oregon Terrorism Information Threat Assessment Network
- Pennsylvania Criminal Intelligence Center
- Puerto Rico National Security State Information Center
- Rhode Island State Fusion Center
- South Carolina Information and Intelligence Center
- South Dakota Fusion Center
- Southern Nevada Counter-Terrorism Center (Las Vegas, Nevada)
- Tennessee Fusion Center
- Texas Joint Crime Information Center
- U.S. Virgin Islands Fusion Center
- Utah Statewide Information and Analysis Center
- Vermont Intelligence Center
- Virginia Fusion Center
- Washington Regional Threat and Analysis Center (Washington, D.C.)
- Washington State Fusion Center
- West Virginia Intelligence Fusion Center
- Wisconsin Statewide Information Center

Recognized Fusion Centers

- Austin Regional Intelligence Center; Austin, TX
- Boston Regional Intelligence Center; Boston, MA
- Central California Intelligence Center; Sacramento, CA
- Central Florida Intelligence Exchange; Orlando, FL
- Chicago Crime Prevention and Information Center; Chicago, IL
- Dallas Fusion Center; Dallas, TX
- Delaware Valley Intelligence Center; Philadelphia, PA
- Detroit and Southeast Michigan Information and Intelligence Center; Detroit, MI
- El Paso Multi-Agency Tactical Response Information eXchange (MATRIX); El Paso, TX
- Greater Cincinnati Fusion Center; Cincinnati, OH
- Houston Regional Intelligence Service Center; Houston, TX
- Kansas City Regional Terrorism Early Warning Interagency Analysis Center; Kansas City, MO
- Los Angeles Joint Regional Intelligence Center; Los Angeles, CA
- Nevada Threat Analysis Center; Carson City, NV
- North Texas Fusion Center; McKinney, TX
- Northeast Ohio Regional Fusion Center; Cleveland, OH
- Northern California Regional Intelligence Center; San Francisco, CA
- Northern Virginia Regional Intelligence Center; Fairfax, VA
- Orange County Intelligence Assessment Center; Orange County, CA
- San Diego Law Enforcement Coordination Center; San Diego, CA
- Southeast Florida Fusion Center; Miami, FL
- Southeastern Wisconsin Threat Analysis Center; Milwaukee, WI
- Southwest Texas Fusion Center; San Antonio, TX
- Southwestern PA Region 13 Fusion Center; Pittsburgh, PA
- St. Louis Fusion Center; St. Louis, MO

Source: DHS and NFCA 2017, www.dhs.gov
/fusion-center-locations-and-contact-information.

Chapter Summary

1. **Define intelligence and counterintelligence.**

   Intelligence is an information process and product derived from systematic and thoughtful examination (analysis), placed in context and provided to governmental executives and military leaders with facts and alternatives than can inform critical decisions, particularly those involving the deployment of critical resources. Counterintelligence, on the other hand, is a myriad of activities intended to prevent adversaries from acquiring accurate information about an organization's capabilities, actions, personnel, and/or plans.

2. **Provide a brief overview of the U.S. Intelligence Community and discuss the role of the Office of the Director of National Intelligence.**

   The current U.S. Intelligence Community (IC) was established in 2004 in response to the Gilmore Commission. Sixteen different government agencies (including the CIA, FBI, and NSA) answer to the Office of the Director of National Intelligence (ODNI). The primary role of the ODNI is to coordinate, integrate, and manage the collection, analysis, and dissemination of intelligence information, including the intelligence that relates directly to international and domestic threats posed by terrorist organizations. The ODNI also administers the National Intelligence Program (NIP) representing the estimated $60 billion annual budget designed to strengthen the nation's intelligence capabilities.

3. **Explain the differences between the CIA and the FBI relating to terrorism and intelligence.**

   The Central Intelligence Agency (CIA) collects and analyzes information regarding national security issues, including potential strikes against the U.S. homeland and interest abroad. Its role is intelligence related and is relegated to working primarily outside the United States. It has no arrest powers within the United States; however, it conducts clandestine operations to thwart terrorist groups and potential attacks. In contrast, the FBI is the primary criminal investigative body on any terrorist attack against the United States both domestically and internationally and is responsible for collecting, analyzing, and disseminating all domestic intelligence information relating to terrorist attacks or threats.

4. **Discuss the role of the National Security Agency as an intelligence agency.**

   The NSA is primarily responsible for designing and maintaining computerized coding systems designed to protect the integrity of U.S. information systems. It has also become the lead agency responsible for monitoring and protecting all of the federal government's computer networks from acts of cyberterrorism. In direct relation to these responsibilities, NSA agents are also responsible for detecting and exploiting weaknesses in an adversarial country's computerized secret coding systems. The NSA's role in providing information system security and information assurance has expanded with the parallel growth in computerized communications technology. The NSA also has an active role in providing information security training to both government and private entities. Additionally, the NSA works to provide information security through security tools, security products, threat warnings, analysis of potential attacks by terrorists, and security bulletins.

5. **List and describe the other agencies within the intelligence community.**

   There are 16 separate agencies reporting to the Office of the Director of National Intelligence (ODNI). Although the Central Intelligence Agency, the Federal Bureau of Investigation, and the National Security Agency remain the largest and most well-known of these agencies, there are a number of lesser-known agencies that collect, analyze, and disseminate intelligence related to potential terrorist activities. These include the Department of Defense Intelligence Agency, the National Geospatial Agency, the National Reconnaissance Office, the Department of State Bureau of Intelligence and Research, and the Department of Homeland Security Office of Intelligence and Analysis. Other members of the intelligence community include smaller units within various governmental departments and agencies such as the Drug Enforcement Administration Office of National Security Intelligence, the Department of Energy Office of Intelligence and Counterintelligence, the Department of Treasury Office of Intelligence and Research, and the intelligence services within each branch of the military: Air Force, Army, Coast Guard, Marine Corps, and Navy.

6. **Define and describe the four goals of a fusion center.**

A fusion center is a "clearinghouse" or information "hub" that blends the power of information technology with terrorism prevention and crime fighting. Fusion centers are located throughout the United States and have four goals: (1) Support the broad range of activities undertaken by a police department relating to the detection, examination, and investigation of a potential terrorist attack and/or criminal activity; (2) provide support for operations that protect critical infrastructure and key resources (CI/KRs) in a given region, support major incident operations, support specialized units charged with interdiction and investigative operations, and assist in emergency operations and planning; (3) maintain public "tip lines" or the capability to promote more public involvement/awareness in an effort to identify and recognize warnings signs and potential terrorist threats or attacks; and (4) assist police executives in making better-informed decisions, especially during emergencies or critical incidents like a terrorist attack, a major criminal activity, or a natural disaster.

REVIEW QUESTIONS

1. Discuss the Gilmore Commission. What were the Commission's major findings?
2. Define the terms "intelligence" and "counterintelligence."
3. Discuss the structure of the U.S. intelligence community (IC) and identify several of its key component agencies.
4. What is the National Counterterrorism Center (NCTC) and what is its primary role and mission?
5. Discuss the differences between the CIA and the FBI. Discuss the role of each agency and the ways they may accomplish their respective missions.
6. What is a JTTF? What are the primary missions of these entities?
7. Discuss the differences between investigation and intelligence.
8. Discuss the primary role of the NSA.
9. Discuss the concepts of "cyberterrorism" or "digital terrorism." How vulnerable is the United States to such attacks?
10. Discuss the purpose of the intelligence cycle. Why is it important?
11. What are fusion centers? Discuss their four primary goals.
12. What is the role of the Defense Intelligence Agency?

CRITICAL THINKING EXERCISES

1. **Research Intelligence on Terrorist Organizations and Groups Globally.** Visit and preview the Terrorism Research and Analysis Consortium (TRAC), created by the Beacham Group, LLC on the Internet at www.terrorismresearch.org. Watch the preview and explore the site. TRAC is one of the most comprehensive terrorism research sites on the Internet and provides an efficient series of filters in which to study various types of terrorist targets, tactics, and groups. Play with the filters, watch some of the posted videos, read some of the articles on ideology, and read the intelligence reports about the latest information on active groups in any area of your choosing. Consider subscribing or having your university or college subscribe to the site. TRAC was specifically designed to fulfill the research and intelligence needs of faculty, scholars, students, and government and defense professionals studying terrorism.

2. **The National Counterterrorism Center (NCTC).** The Office of the Director of National Intelligence houses the National Counterterrorism Center (NCTC). The two core missions of the NCTC are to serve as the primary organization in the United States for the analysis and integration of terrorism intelligence, and the second mission is to conduct strategic operational planning for counterterrorism activities. Visit the NCTC website at www.nctc.gov. Name the key partners associated with the NCTC and view the Counterterrorism Calendar. Now explore career possibilities within the intelligence field. What types of career opportunities exist within the intelligence community at the federal level? As important, what are the knowledge, skills, and abilities required to fulfill these types of positions and are you qualified? Develop an action plan for yourself to accomplish education and training goals that would qualify you for an intelligence analyst position within the National Counterterrorism Center.

NOTES

1. D. Priest and W. Arkin, "Top-Secret America," *Dallas Morning News*, July 25, 2010, p. 26A.

2. A. L. Jackson and M. Brown, "Ensuring Efficiency, Interagency Cooperation, and Protection of Civil Liberties: Shifting from a Traditional Model of Policing to an Intelligence-Led Policing (ILP) Paradigm," *Criminal Justice Studies,* Vol. 20, pp. 111–129.

3. *The 9/11 Commission Report* (Washington, D.C.: USGPO, July 22, 2004), see www.gpo .gov/fdsys/pkg/GPO-911REPORT/pdf/GPO-911REPORT.pdf.

4. See K. Riley, G. Teverton, J. Wilson, and L. Davis, *State and Local Intelligence in the War on Terrorism, Volumes 1–5* (Washington, D.C.: RAND Corporation, 2005). These volumes are commonly referred to as the Gilmore Commission Reports, named after Virginia Governor Jim Gilmore, chair of the Congressionally mandated commission to assess the domestic response capability against terrorism between 1999 and 2003.

5. Summary of Classified Report to the U.S. Congress, House of Representatives Intelligence Subcommittee, *Report on Intelligence Gathering and Analysis pre September 11, 2001*, July 16, 2002.

6. Ibid.

7. Marilyn Peterson, *Intelligence-Led Policing: The New Intelligence Architecture* (Washington, D.C.: The RAND Corporation, 2005).

8. Richard J. Hughbank and Don Githens, "Intelligence and Its Role in Protecting Against Terrorism," *Journal of Strategic Security*, Vol. 3, No. 1, March 2010, p. 31.

9. Blake W. Mobley, *Terrorism and Counter-Intelligence: How Terrorist Groups Escape Detection* (New York: Columbia University Press, 2012), p. 8.

10. Ben Brandt, "The Taliban's Conduct of Intelligence and Counterintelligence," *CTS Sentinel*, Vol. 4, Issue 6, June 2011, p. 20.

11. Loc. cit.

12. Ibid., p. 22

13. Loc. cit.

14. Mobley, *Terrorism and Counterintelligence*, p. 8.

15. Ibid., p.40.

16. Ibid., p. 38.

17. Ibid., p. 41.

18. Ibid., p. 40.

19. Ibid., p. 55.

20. See www.dni.gov/index.php/newsroom/press-releases/215-press-releases-2016/1315-dni-releases-budget-figure-for-fy2017-appropriations-requested-for-the-national-intelligence-program.

21. See a description of the National Counterterrorism Center at www.nctc.gov.

22. Ibid.

23. See www.nctc.gov/calendar.html.

24. *Joint Counterterrorism Assessment Team (JCAT)*, Vol. 1, Issue 4, 2013, p. 4.

25. J. Deutsch and J. H. Smith, "Smarter Intelligence," *Foreign Policy*, 128 (2002), pp. 64–69.

26. This account is drawn from S. D. Murphy, "Steganography—The New Intelligence Threat" (Quantico, Virginia: Marine Corps War College, Research paper, 2005), p. 2.

27. See Jennifer Wilcox, "Revolutionary Secrets: The Secret Communications of the American Revolution" (Washington, D.C.: National Security Agency, undated paper), www.nsa.gov /about/_files/cryptologic_heritage/publications/prewil/revolutionary_secrets.pdf.

28. Loc. cit.

29. This synopsis is taken from Paul Stillwell, "The Lead Code-Breaker of Midway" (Annapolis, Maryland: U.S. Naval Institute, Proceedings 0041798X), Vol. 138, Issue 6, June 2012, pp. 62–65.

30. Loc. cit.

31. Restated from Nic Robertson, Paul Cruickshank, and Tim Lister, "Documents Reveal Al Qaeda's Plans for Seizing Cruise Ships, Carnage in Europe," *CNN World*, May 1, 2012, www.cnn.com/2012/04/30/world/al-qaeda-documents-future.

32. Ben Grubb. "Spies do happy dance after encryption cracked," *Sydney Morning Herald*, January 5, 2015, retrieved from www.smh.com.au/it-pro/security-it/spies-do-happy-dance-after-encryption-cracked-20150105-12i5lx.html.

33. Pierre Thomas and Mike Levine, "How the FBI cracked the iPhone encryption and averted a legal showdown with Apple," ABC News, March 29, 2016, retrieved from abcnews.go.com/US/fbi-cracked-iphone-encryption-averted-legal-showdown-apple /story?id=38014184.

34. Barton Gellman and Ellen Nakashima, "U.S. Spy Agencies Mounted 231 Offensive Cyber Operations in 2011, Documents Show," *Washington Post*, August 30, 2013, www .washingtonpost.com/world/national-security/us-spy-agencies-mounted-231-offensive-cyber-operations-in-2011-documents-show/2013/08/30/d090a6ae-119e-11e3-b4cb-fd7ce041d814_story_3.html.

35. See www.fbi.gov/about-us/intelligence/intel-driven.

36. See www.fbi.gov/about-us/investigate/terrorism/terrorism_jttfs.

37. The USA PATRIOT Act of 2001 was quickly rushed into law after the 9/11 attacks and signed by President George W. Bush on October 26, 2001. It was a rushed piece of legislation, without normal review and skirting traditional Congressional processes. The act changed 15 separate federal statutes, and has been attacked in court on various constitutional issues. Over the last decade, the appellate courts have struck down many parts of the act as challenges continue to be filed.

38. See Attorney General Edward Levi, *Guidelines for Domestic Security Investigations* (April 4, 1976), Attorney General William French Smith, *Guidelines on General Crimes, Racketeering Enterprise and Domestic Security/Terrorism Investigations* (1983), and Attorney General Dick Thornburgh, *Guidelines on General Crimes, Racketeering, Enterprise and Domestic Security/Terrorism Investigations* (March 21, 1989).

39. The constitutional and human rights violations of the turbulent 1960s were not just within the purview of the FBI. Several highlighted abuses by local police departments in Chicago, Los Angeles, and New York have also been detailed. See ACLU, *The Dangers of Domestic Spying by Federal Law Enforcement: A Case Study on FBI Surveillance of Dr. Martin Luther King* (January 2002); ACLU, *History Repeated: The Dangers of Domestic Spying by Federal Law Enforcement* (May 29, 2007); and W. Churchill and J. V. Wall, *The COINTELPRO Papers: Documents from the FBI's Secret Wars Against Dissent in the United States* (Cambridge, MA: South End Press, 1990).

40. J. B. Motley, *U.S. Strategy to Counter Domestic Political Terrorism* (Washington, D.C.: National Security Affairs) Monograph Series, 2 (1983), pp. 62–70.

41. www.nsa.gov.

42. Ellen Nakashima, "Bush Order Expands Network Monitoring: Intelligence Agencies to Track Institutions," *Washington Post*, January 1, 2008, www.washingtonpost.com/wp-dyn /content/article/2008/01/25/AR2008012503261_pf.html.

43. Ibid., p. 28.

44. Ibid.

45. Ibid.

46. www.nsa.gov/ia/ia_at_nsa/index.shtml.

47. Glenn Greenwald, Ewen MacAskill, and Laura Poitras, "Edward Snowden: The Whistleblower Behind the NSA Surveillance Revelations," *Guardian* (London), June 10, 2013.

48. Bill Chappell, "Ex-NSA Contractor Accused of Taking Classified Information is Indicted," NPR, February 9, 2017, retrieved from www.npr.org/sections/thetwo-way/2017/02/09/ 514275544/ex-nsa-contractor-indicted-for-taking-classifed-information.

49. Mark Pollitt, "Cyberterrorism—Fact or Fancy?" *Proceedings of the 20th National Information Systems Security Conference*, October 25, 1977, pp. 285–289.

50. M. Grossman, "Cyberterrorism," February 15, 1999, www.mgrossmanlaw.com/articles /1999.cyberterrorism.htm.

51. Ibid., p. 4.

52. Dorothy E. Denning, "Cyberterrorism," www.cs.georgetown.edu/~denning/infosec/ cyberterror-GD.doc.

53. For a more advanced discussion of cyberterrorism, refer to Robert W. Taylor, Eric J. Fritsch, and John Liederbach, *Digital Crime and Digital Terrorism,* 3rd ed. (Upper Saddle River, NJ: Pearson, 2015), Chapter 2.

54. "Al Qaeda Poses Threat to the Net," *Computerworld,* November 25, 2002.

55. Ryan Brown, "Top military official warns of ISIS attack," CNN, April 5 2016, retrieved from www.cnn.com/2016/04/05/politics/isis-cyberattacks-michael-rogers/.

56. Kim Sengupta, "ISIS-linked hackers attack NHS websites to show gruesome Syrian civil war images," *Independent,* February 7, 2017, retrieved from www.independent.co.uk /news/uk/crime/isis-islamist-hackers-nhs-websites-cyber-attack-syrian-civil-war-images-islamic-state-a7567236.html.

57. See www.dia.mil/Home.aspx.

58. Geographic information systems (GIS) are an integration of computer hardware, software, and data for capturing, managing, analyzing, and displaying all forms of geographic data from simple maps to complex remote sensing operations.

59. See www.nga.mil/.

60. See www.nro.gov/about/index.html.

61. See www.state.gov/s/inr/.

62. See www.dhs.gov/about-office-intelligence-and-analysis.

63. Jerry H. Ratcliffe and Ray Guidetti, "State Police Investigative Structure and the Adoption of Intelligence-Led Policing," *Policing: An International Journal of Police Strategies and Management,* Vol. 31, 2008, pp. 109–128.

64. This material on the intelligence cycle was taken from the FBI website at www.fbi.gov /about-us/intelligence/intelligence-cycle.

65. Kevin Riley, G. Teverton, J. Wilson, and L. Davis, *State and Local Intelligence in the War on Terrorism* (Washington, D.C.: RAND Corporation, 2005).

66. Joseph D'Amico, "Stopping Crime in Real Time," *Police Chief* (September 2006), pp. 20–24.

67. This section on fusion centers was adapted from Charles R. Swanson, Leonard Territo, and Robert W. Taylor, *Police Administration: Structures, Processes and Behavior,* 8th ed. (Upper Saddle River, NJ: Pearson, 2012), pp. 90–93; and Robert W. Taylor and Jennifer Elaine Davis, "Intelligence-Led Policing and Fusion Centers," in Roger G. Dunham and Geoffrey P Alpert, *Critical Issues in Policing,* 6th ed. (Long Grove, IL: Waveland Press, 2010), pp. 224–245.

68. U.S. Department of Homeland Security, "Fusion Center Locations and Contact Information," www.dhs.gov/fusion-center-locations-and-contact-information.

69. Ibid, Expanded States.

70. See https://nfcausa.org/.

Intelligence, Terrorism, and the U.S. Constitution

The Naval Station Guantanamo Bay, Cuba, is the United States' frontline facility for security in the Caribbean region. Enemy combatants from the Middle East, suspected of terrorism are also housed there. Two guards escort a detainee to the recreation area. Methods used to obtain information from detainees have been described by the government as "enhanced interrogation techniques"; other sources describe the methods as torture.

(PJF Military Collection/Alamy Stock Photo)

Learning Objectives

After completing this chapter, you should be able to:

1. Summarize the USA PATRIOT Act and its subsequent reauthorizations.

2. Discuss the conflicts between the PATRIOT Act and the First, Fourth, Fifth, and Sixth Amendments of the U.S. Constitution.

3. Articulate how the New York Police Department has instituted its own domestic intelligence program and discuss the implications of that on law enforcement agencies nationwide.

4. Explain the concept of *posse comitatus* and how our military might be called to supplement civilian policing functions.

5. Describe how drones are used both domestically and abroad for intelligence purposes and state the Constitutional issues that arise with each type of use.

6. Discuss the use of torture in intelligence functions in the United States and describe the Constitutional issues involved.

7. Outline the events surrounding the Chelsea Manning case, the WikiLeaks scandal, and the Edward Snowden intelligence leaks.

Introduction

After September 11, 2001, the intelligence shortcomings that allowed al-Qaeda operatives to carry out the terrorist attacks were highlighted, debated, discussed, and promoted as an example of a post–Cold War mentality that cost nearly 3,000 American lives. Government agencies responsible for intelligence gathering were denounced for failing to think beyond threats from nations-states (such as Iran, Libya, or even China), for failing to link together key pieces of intelligence information about terrorist groups, and furthermore, for failing to share those pieces of information with other agencies. This created an environment obviously ripe for communications and intelligence reform, and in the decade that has followed the attacks of 9/11, a number of such reforms have been enacted.

Some civil libertarians have raised alarms that new and sweeping intelligence powers and swift changes to the culture of American law enforcement and intelligence agencies—particularly as detailed in the USA PATRIOT Act—were pushed through opportunistically, at a time when the public was reeling from the horror of the attacks and unlikely to fight anything that potentially could prevent future occurrences of terror on American soil. There was controversy associated with the passage of many of these reforms; however, Americans would wrestle with the balancing of civil rights and individual freedoms with national security and safety. Increased and more coordinated intelligence efforts on the part of the military, the police, and the national intelligence agencies raise a host of questions related to the balance between liberty and public safety; for example, can there be Fourth Amendment guarantees related to the expectation of privacy when the government has a host of tools at its disposal for large-scale data exploration? What governmental body does an individual hold accountable if there are breaches in personal security in the name of national security? Where is the bright line between intelligence agencies and police departments ... and should this line ever be crossed? In this chapter, these questions will be explored, as will other issues related to the intersection of terrorism and the Constitutional rights guaranteed to all American citizens. Most dear of these rights are held in the Fourth Amendment guarantee against unreasonable searches and seizures; however, the First Amendment right to free speech and freedom of religion, Fifth Amendment protections related to due process, and the Eighth Amendment guarantees against cruel and unusual punishment all relate to the new "war on terrorism." This may be particularly true when the methods used by the United States to gather intelligence about terrorism are scrutinized.

The USA PATRIOT Act

USA PATRIOT Act
Act of Congress that was signed into law by President George W. Bush on October 26, 2001. The title stands for Uniting and Strengthening America by Providing Appropriate Tools Required to Intercept and Obstruct Terrorism Act.

In an effort to improve the collection of intelligence information by federal agencies after 9/11 and provide sweeping new powers to both domestic law enforcement and traditional intelligence agencies, President George W. Bush signed into law the **USA PATRIOT Act** on October 26, 2001. The USA PATRIOT Act (**P**rovide **A**ppropriate **T**ools **R**equired to **I**ntercept and **O**bstruct **T**errorism) changed over fifteen different statutes with little or no external review—in fact, many members of Congress themselves reported that they themselves had not read the entire act all the way through.[1] The law addressed not only terrorism and intelligence issues but also focused on more traditional money laundering, computer abuse and crime, immigration processes, and fraud. However, the most substantial part of the act is that it expanded traditional tools of surveillance used by law enforcement and intelligence agencies with significantly reduced checks and balances.

- *Records Searches:* Records kept on an individual's activity being held by third parties—including doctors, libraries, and Internet Service Providers (ISPs).
- *Wiretaps:* The surreptitious eavesdropping on a third-party conversation by wire, oral, or electronic communication. Usually conducted with a microphone receiver ("bug") on a telephone device; requires both a search warrant and a court order.

Search Warrant
Legal document that authorizes police to search a specific area for a specific person or item of interest. Must be based on probable cause and signed by a judge.

- *Search warrants:* A **search warrant** is a legal document signed by a judge directing police officers to search a specific area for a specific person or item of evidence/contraband. The document must be based on probable cause, but the PATRIOT Act allowed search warrants to occur without the "knock and announce" requirement outlined in the Fourth Amendment.

- *Pen/trap and trace orders:* Telephone call setup information only is intercepted without individual communications. A "**pen register**" provides the law enforcement agency access to the numbers dialed from a subject's phone, whereas a **trap and trace** provides the incoming numbers to the subject's phone (like caller ID).

- *Court orders and subpoenas:* A court document signed by a judge that instructs the police to perform a specific task. A subpoena is a court order that commands a person to appear in court at a specified date and time to testify.

Law enforcement and intelligence agencies can now easily and more surreptitiously monitor Web surfing and communication of individuals using the Internet, conduct nationwide roving wiretaps on cell and line telephones, and build profiles on the reading habits of people visiting public libraries. Under the act, police or government officials can force **Internet Service Providers (ISPs)** to "voluntarily" hand over information on customer profiles and Web-surfing habits *without* a warrant or court order.

Pen register
Provides law enforcement agency access to the numbers dialed from a subject's phone.

Trap and trace
Provides law enforcement agency access to incoming numbers on a subject's phone.

Internet Service Providers (ISPs)
An organization or private corporation that provides services for accessing, using, or participating on the Internet (e.g., AOL, NetZero, Comcast, Microsoft Network, EarthLink, Verizon, Google Prodigy, Sprint, and local telephone companies).

The Reauthorized PATRIOT Act—2006

In 2005, provisions of the USA PATRIOT Act were to sunset, and Congress acted to review, reauthorize, and pass this bill. The revisions were passed into law by President George W. Bush in March 2006. The roving wiretap provisions were maintained, though greater oversight was added to ensure that these powers would not be abused. The changes include judicial review and approval by the Director of the Federal Bureau of Investigation (FBI) or the National Security Administration (NSA), along with a more detailed application process to specify targets and actions. The provision that allowed library records to be subpoenaed was also removed to protect citizens from unwarranted search, with the exception of monitoring electronic communications through a library. The original USA PATRIOT Act also allowed law enforcement agencies to conduct covert, or "sneak and peek," searches in the homes of potential suspects without their knowledge or authorization. Since this was considered by some to be too extreme, the reauthorization act changed this portion of the law to limit the time when such a search could be conducted so as not to give unreasonable power to law enforcement. However, the ability to conduct surveillance against what are defined as "lone wolf terrorists" or individuals who seemingly act alone and without direction was increased to provide greater time to monitor a specific target. (Refer to Chapter 5 for more information on lone wolf terrorists.) The definition of terrorism was also expanded with several provisions: (1) to include receiving military-type training from a foreign terrorist organization; (2) engaging in narco-terrorism; and (3) criminalizing the act of planning a terror attack specifically against a mass transit entity or system (e.g., bus stations, airliners, GPS, and other navigation or communication systems).

Information Link
For more information regarding the USA PATRIOT Act, visit the website hosted by the U.S. Department of Justice at www.justice.gov/archive/ll/highlights.htm.

The Reauthorized PATRIOT Act—2011

Provisions of the USA PATRIOT Act were once again set to sunset in 2011 and Congress acted to review, amend, and reauthorize it. First, roving wiretaps in relation to foreign intelligence collection were reauthorized and allowed electronic surveillance of a person, without specifying the phone or computer, if that person demonstrates an intent to evade surveillance by, for example, switching cell phones on a regular basis. In short, the government may obtain an order to conduct surveillance that specifies a target but not a specific device (e.g., cell phone, home phone, Internet connection, specific website) to tap. Second, the reauthorization extended access to business records and other tangible evidence. The USA PATRIOT Act allowed the government to seek court-ordered production of "any tangible thing," including business records, in intelligence investigations. The new provision to the USA PATRIOT Act both expanded the scope of materials that may be sought and lowered the standard for a court to issue an order compelling their production. Third, the "lone wolf" provision was extended, which permits surveillance against a non-U.S. person engaged in international terrorism for which the government does not have evidence of ties to a specific foreign terrorist group.

The Freedom Act, 2015

On June 2, 2015, President Barack Obama signed the USA Freedom Act into law, in order to address three expiring provisions of the USA PATRIOT Act: Section 215 (which has been amended regarding bulk phone and Internet metadata), roving wiretaps, and lone wolf surveillance authority. Notably, the Freedom Act dissolved the provisions of Section 215 that allowed the NSA to collect bulk data on individual American telephone records and Internet metadata. The law limits the government's ability to collect data on American citizens to "the greatest extent reasonably practical,"[2] which prohibits mass collection based on variables like geographic area or area code. Other notable additions via the Freedom Act include:[3]

Foreign Intelligence Surveillance Act of 1978 (FISA)
Passed by Congress in 1978, the law was intended to increase counterintelligence capabilities and established procedures for the judicial authorization of foreign intelligence surveillance and established the Foreign Intelligence Surveillance Court.

- New reporting requirements to the **Foreign Intelligence Surveillance Act of 1978 (FISA)** courts and authorities. FISA focuses on issues surrounding the Fourth Amendment as discussed later in this chapter.
- Expands the ability of private companies to disclose the number of FISA requests they receive.
- Declassification of FISA Court opinions of significant legal significance—or in cases where full declassification isn't viable, it requires a summary.
- A requirement that the FISA Court appoint "amicus curiae," or advocates, to represent the public's interest in cases that involve significant legal issues.
- An increase in the maximum penalty for material support for terrorism from 15 years to 20 years.

American Civil Liberties Union (ACLU)
A national organization (primarily composed of attorneys and legal scholars) focused on defending and preserving the rights and liberties guaranteed to individuals within the United States Constitution.

- An authorization for the government to collect up to "two hops" of call records related to suspects, given reasonable suspicion that that person is linked to a terrorist organization.

Constitutional Rights and the USA PATRIOT Act

The expanded scope and breadth of the act have raised concerns from a variety of sources.[4] Most agree that intelligence gathering and analysis had to improve (especially since 2001) in order to prevent future domestic and international terrorist attacks. However, some argue that the USA PATRIOT Act may have gone too far. One group that has done so is the **American Civil Liberties Union (ACLU)**, a national organization composed primarily of attorneys that defends and preserves the individual rights and liberties that are secured within the U.S. Constitution. The first ten Amendments to the U.S. Constitution are commonly called the **Bill of Rights** (see Figure 10–2). The ACLU works to extend these freedoms to segments of the population that have traditionally been denied their rights. Historically, this includes people of color, women, lesbians, gay men, bisexuals and transgender people, prisoners, and people with disabilities.[5] Subsequently, the ACLU is often pitted against agencies of the federal government over Constitutional issues surrounding arrest, search and seizure, and the imprisonment of individuals. Relating to intelligence collection and gathering on potential terrorists as well as the investigation of individual terrorist groups, the First, Fourth, and Fifth Amendments to the U.S. Constitution are most often tested.

Bill of Rights
The collective name for the first ten amendments of the U.S. Constitution, explicitly enumerating such freedoms of religion, speech, a free press, freedom to assemble, the right to bear arms, freedom from unreasonable searches and seizures, security and privacy of personal effects, freedom from warrantless searches not based on probable cause, guarantee of a speedy trial and judgment by an impartial jury, prohibition of cruel and unusual punishments including torture, prohibition of double jeopardy, and the guarantee to live without unnecessary governmental intrusion.

The First Amendment

The First Amendment of the United States Constitution:

Congress shall make no law respecting an establishment of religion, or prohibiting the free exercise thereof; or abridging the freedom of speech, or of the press; or the right of the people peaceably to assemble, and to petition the Government for a redress of grievances.

Informational Link
To see the latest updates to the USA PATRIOT Act via the USA Freedom Act of 2015, visit www.congress.gov/bill/114th-congress/house-bill/2048/text.

Civil libertarians argue that the USA PATRIOT Act has a "chilling effect on free speech," and, in fact, some of its provisions have stirred controversy in this area. See Figure 10–1. The most high-profile of these First Amendment challenges can be observed in a 2010 Supreme Court decision, *Holder v. Humanitarian Law Project (HLP)*.[6] In this case, the government asserted that members of a charity group, The Humanitarian Law Project, were in violation of the "**material support**" clause of the USA PATRIOT Act, and formal charges were brought to bear. The clause prohibits supporting any designated terrorist group via "any property, tangible or intangible, or service, including currency or monetary instruments…expert advice or assistance…weapons, lethal substances, explosives, personnel…except medicine or religious materials."[7] In this case, the HLP—a group of human rights and peace activists—worked to "advise" the Workers' Party of Kurdistan (PKK)—a designated terrorist group by the United States—on how to file human rights violations with the United

FIGURE 10–1
President George W. Bush signed the USA PATRIOT Act on October 26, 2001.
(Shawn Thew/EPA/REX/Shutterstock)

Nations. Further, the HLP was actively advising the PKK on the peace negotiation process with the country of Turkey. The group challenged the "material support" on the grounds that peace negotiations were not a terrorist endeavor, and that the clause infringed on their ability to associate with a group for these purposes, thereby impinging on their First Amendment rights. The Supreme Court did not agree, stating that the HLP's services did indeed qualify as material aid under the "service," "expert advice or assistance," and "personnel" clause of the act. The government argued successfully that the PKK benefited from the assistance rendered by the HLP. The services and expert assistance could potentially benefit the terror group by legitimizing its interests, thereby potentially helping the terror group conserve resources.[8] The decision was quickly followed by a series of FBI raids on other peace activists' homes in Minneapolis and St. Paul, further bolstering the government's assertion that material support would be investigated and prosecuted.[9]

Material support
Defined by the PATRIOT Act as "training," "expert advice or assistance," "service," and "personnel" given to terrorist organizations.

In yet another case, Tarek Mehanna, an American pharmacist, was convicted of providing material support, conspiring to kill American soldiers in a foreign country, and lying to authorities in a terrorism investigation in Boston in late 2011. Mehanna travelled to Yemen in 2004 and joined a terrorist training camp. His plan was to attack American soldiers in Iraq; however, his plan failed. When he returned to the United States, he began translating Arabic material into English and posting it online in promotion and support of al-Qaeda and radical Islamic fundamentalism. He inspired others to engage in violent jihad against the West and the United States by posting Jihadist Salafist material online. He was successfully prosecuted under the "material support" clause of the USA PATRIOT Act and is currently serving a 17-year sentence in federal prison.[10] Unconvincingly, the ACLU argued that anyone researching and/or translating controversial material could be prosecuted, seriously compromising the freedoms established under the First Amendment.[11] Again, appellate courts disagreed, indicating that Mehanna went well beyond the scope of just translating documents; he did indeed "go down a treacherous path" that not only provided material support to al-Qaeda, but also jeopardized the safety and security of American soldiers in Iraq.[12] While appeals continue in the Mehanna case, it is clear that the current Supreme Court views terrorist activities and groups significantly different than international criminal organizations or enterprises. Like so many other areas of criminal law, cases involving the USA PATRIOT Act are often reviewed on a case-by-case basis—trying to balance individual freedoms with national security.

Interestingly, the freedom of religion clause within the First Amendment has also been tested under the USA PATRIOT Act. The American Civil Liberties Union asserts that the government's use of religious profiling to target Muslims for investigation infringes on their Constitutional right to practice religion. For example, in the months leading up to the November 2004 elections, the FBI engaged in large-scale surveillance or "fishing

FIGURE 10–2

In 1789, at the First Continental Congress, James Madison introduced a series of amendments to the newly ratified U.S. Constitution. The House of Representatives sent 17 of them to the Senate, which consolidated the amendments into 12. The 12 proposed amendments were sent to the respective states for ratification, and they ratified proposed Amendments 3–12. These became the Bill of Rights. The image is the Senate's changes to the first page of the House of Representatives' amendments.

(National Archives and Records Administration)

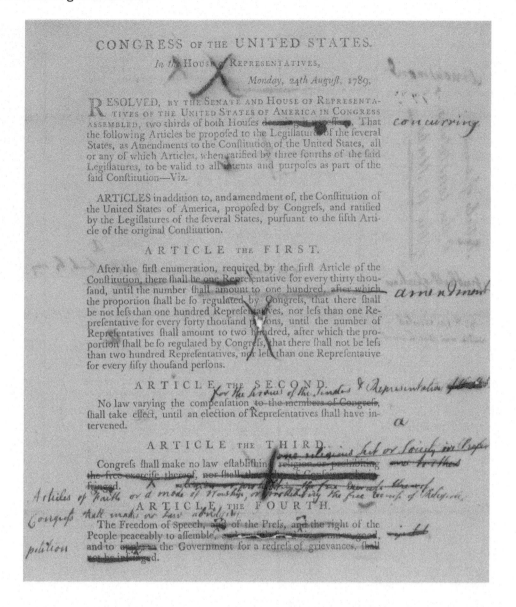

expeditions" on American Muslims in large cities. FBI agents visited mosques and questioned attendees in an attempt to identify suspected terrorist (al-Qaeda) sympathizers. Known as the "October Plan," the coordinated effort between the FBI and Immigrations and Customs Enforcement (ICE) outraged the Muslim-American community. Legal challenges against the huge intelligence gathering and investigative practices were defeated and subsequently allowed under the auspices of the amended USA PATRIOT Act.[13] Clearly, the Court sees nonspecific intelligence gathering of a wide audience in an attempt to uncover an act of terrorism significantly different than a targeted investigation of a specific individual leading to an arrest.

The Fourth Amendment

The Fourth Amendment of the United States Constitution:

> *The right of the people to be secure in their persons, houses, papers and effects, against unreasonable searches and seizures, shall not be violated, and no Warrants shall issue, but upon probable cause, supported by Oath or affirmation, and particularly describing the place to be searched and the persons or things to be seized.*

On cursory examination, this passage of the U.S. Constitution is particularly relevant to the USA PATRIOT Act and its subsequent reauthorizations. There certainly appears to be

Quick Facts
The Foreign Intelligence Surveillance Court (FISC)

The Foreign Intelligence Surveillance Court (FISC) meets in a high-security area of the E. Barrett Prettyman United States Courthouse in Washington, D.C. All proceedings are secret, and there are two separate parts of the court: One is a full lower court panel and the other is a "Court of Review." The lower court has a rotating panel of eleven Federal District Court judges, three of whom must reside within 20 miles of Washington, D.C. The Court of Review consists of three judges. All judges on the FISC are appointed by the Chief Justice of the United States.

contraction. For example, under the original PATRIOT Act, the government did not have to show probable cause, or even reasonable suspicion, to obtain third-party records, or conduct searches or wiretaps, as long as the government asserts a request for such records is related to an ongoing terrorism or foreign intelligence operation—or has a significant foreign intelligence purpose.[14] Note that the USA Freedom Act attempted to limit some of these issues, particularly related to the mass collection of telephone and Internet data. Collection of mass data was banned, and other call record collection was limited to cases where the government can prove it has "reasonable suspicion" that a target is linked to a terror organization. But despite that update, the USA PATRIOT Act still largely amends the Foreign Intelligence Surveillance Act of 1978 (FISA), which is widely used in foreign espionage and spying cases.

The Foreign Intelligence Surveillance Act of 1979

FISA was initially developed and passed in Congress in 1978 to address a difficult history of abuse by federal agencies using **wiretaps** and other forms of electronic eavesdropping during the 1960s and 70s. Law enforcement agencies were not required to gain a warrant in a criminal case until the passage of the Wiretap Act in 1968. However, the legality of warrantless searches and seizures, and the use of wiretaps and other electronic eavesdropping methods during intelligence and/or national security operations, was not settled until 1972. The Supreme Court unanimously held, in their landmark case *United State v. U.S. District* (known as the "Keith case"), that the federal government did not have unlimited power to conduct wiretaps and electronic surveillance without the approval of a neutral magistrate just by claiming that the act was for national security—warrantless wiretapping of U.S. citizens was found unconstitutional.[15] Indeed, the court recognized that a history of abuse (unauthorized governmental spying on U.S. citizens "suspected" of unnamed national security violations) had occurred during the turbulent 1960s and 70s Civil Rights/Vietnam War era. The Foreign Intelligence Surveillance Act of 1978 created a procedure, similar to the procedure for any governmental or law enforcement agency pursuing a criminal case, to present evidence to a judge (or court) and procure a warrant. Essentially, FISA severely limited unauthorized spying and provided a procedure for judicial oversight in cases involving foreign intelligence surveillance and investigation.

FISA is significantly different from law enforcement processes enacted to gain a warrant. First, it authorized the FBI to conduct surveillance on identified foreign intelligence agents operating in the United States because these actions are inherently different from a criminal investigation conducted by a law enforcement agency. FISA was justified at its inception because it was asserted that its authority could *not* be used for the purpose of investigating a crime against an American citizen. Hence, a FISA warrant could be obtained only if the primary purpose of the investigation was directly related to the collection of foreign intelligence by either surveilling a place or a specific person. However, the USA PATRIOT Act, as reauthorized in 2011, eliminated that primary purpose clause within FISA, allowing warrants to proceed without probable cause if the government intrusion had a "significant purpose" for collecting foreign intelligence.[16] Second, because of the secretive nature of the Foreign Intelligence Surveillance Act (FISA), individual and specific cases are presented to a special court, known as the **Foreign Intelligence Surveillance Court (FISC)**. This court serves to hear evidence and justification presented by government agencies relating to the securing of a warrant to eavesdrop or wiretap. Indeed, the FISC initially served to approve wiretapping orders. However, under updates to the PATRIOT Act, the secret FISA court functions only as the main arbiter of surveillance issues.

Wiretaps
Surreptitious eavesdropping on a third-party conversation by wire, oral, or electronic communication.

Information Link
For more information on FISA and FSIC, visit the website hosted by the Federal Judicial Center at www.fisc.uscourts.gov/.

Foreign Intelligence Surveillance Court (FISC)
Secret federal court created by the Foreign Intelligence Surveillance Act in 1978. The court authorizes wiretaps and other forms of electronic surveillance and authorizes searches involving suspected terrorists and spies by U.S. intelligence agencies.

The Fourth Amendment also guarantees an ancient common-law principle called "knock and announce" under its protections against unreasonable searches and seizures. This principle requires that law enforcement give notice of their authority and purpose to those occupants of a place or home about to be searched. The rule serves three important purposes: First, it reduces the risk of violence during a police entry by informing the person whose property is to be searched that it is indeed the police, as opposed to a criminal breaking and entering. Secondly, it allows the inhabitant to ensure that their privacy is indeed maintained, particularly when it involves activities not subject to the warrant. Finally, it protects a citizen's individual property interests.[17]

The PATRIOT Act expands the ability of the government to search places and homes *without* providing notice at the time of the search. In other words, a governmental intelligence agency (like the FBI) can enter a person's home, search through their belongings and gather evidence, and not inform the individual that a governmental agency was there for a "reasonable period thereafter." Before the passage of the PATRIOT Act, this activity could only occur under extreme circumstances, such as when a life was in danger or when evidence was likely to be destroyed. However, under the current PATRIOT Act, it occurs any time such notice would "seriously jeopardize" an investigation. More important, notifications to the searched individual are routinely *not* made fewer than 30 to 90 days after the intrusion, and extensions to this timeframe are possible (and often probable).[18]

This provision of the USA PATRIOT Act was tested in the case of Brandon Mayfield, a Portland, Oregon, attorney who had converted to Islam in the late 1980s after meeting his future wife, who was a practicing Muslim. Mayfield was linked, erroneously and through a litany of spectacular coincidences, to the 2004 train bombings in Madrid carried out by terrorists thought to be inspired by al-Qaeda. The FBI asserted that fingerprints on detonating devices found at the scene were identified as belonging to Brandon Mayfield. The FBI continued its investigation, offering completely false and ambiguous statements to a judge in order to procure a warrant for Mayfield's home. A warrant was issued, and Mayfield's home was searched and electronically surveilled ("bugged"), including a wiretap on his telephone. In reality, Brandon Mayfield had absolutely no involvement in the attacks and the FBI subsequently recanted that the fingerprints found on the scene were not Mayfield's (see Figure 10–3). Mayfield sued the FBI in 2005, asserting that the search and seizure under the USA PATRIOT Act were unlawful. The federal government settled the case with Mayfield for a reported $2 million; however, he continued to challenge the constitutionality of the USA PATRIOT Act. In an initial ruling, a U.S. District Court judge asserted that the provisions

FIGURE 10–3
Brandon Mayfield at a press conference moments after being released in 2005. He was erroneously charged with being a terrorist because of a mistake in analyzing a fingerprint left at the scene of a bombing of a train in Madrid, Spain, in 2004. The case rocked the forensics world as the veracity of fingerprints as unique human identifiers was initially challenged. The FBI eventually apologized, blaming the mistake on faulty supercomputer software compounded by human error during the initial fingerprint analysis.
(Greg Wahl-Stephens/Stringer/Getty Images News/Getty Images)

of the Fourth Amendment, particularly those related to the probable cause requirement and the lack of "knock and announce," were unconstitutional.[19] However, the ruling was overturned in a 9th Circuit Court of Appeals decision in 2009, and the USA PATRIOT Act remains as amended.

The Fifth and Sixth Amendments

The Fifth Amendment of the U.S. Constitution:

> *"No person shall be held to answer for a capital, or otherwise infamous crime, unless on a presentment or indictment of a grand jury, except in cases arising in the land or naval forces, or in the militia, when in actual service in time of war or public danger; nor shall any person be subject for the same offense to be twice put in jeopardy of life or limb; nor shall be compelled in any criminal case to be a witness against himself, nor be deprived of life, liberty, or property, without due process of law; nor shall private property be taken for public use, without just compensation."*

The Sixth Amendment of the U.S. Constitution:

> *"In all criminal prosecutions, the accused shall enjoy the right to a speedy and public trial, by an impartial jury of the State and district wherein the crime shall have been committed, which district shall have been previously ascertained by law, and to be informed of the nature and cause of the accusation; to be confronted with the witnesses against him; to have compulsory process for obtaining witnesses in his favor; and to have the Assistance of Counsel for his defense."*

One of the most controversial challenges to the Bill of Rights by the USA PATRIOT Act is the power to arrest and hold any **alien** (or foreign national) "certified" by the Attorney General as a "suspected terrorist" *without* any initial charge for up to seven days. The Attorney General must either place the alien in removal proceedings from the United States, or charge the alien with a criminal offense. At first glance, this power appears to be a blatant violation of the due process clause of the Fifth Amendment, and the speedy and fair trial concepts of the Sixth Amendment. The government only has to show "reasonable grounds" to believe that a foreign national has committed any of a wide range of violations related specifically to terrorism, or is engaged in any other activity that endangers the national security of the United States. The practice is not widely used, and it is specifically aimed at highly suspected "foreign nationals" that pose an immediate threat to the national security of the United States. So far, the clause has not been tested at the Supreme Court level for foreign nationals residing inside the United States. However, similar activities relating to the detention of foreign nationals from foreign lands have been the subject of much controversy.

Alien
A foreign national living in the United States.

The practice known as **extraordinary rendition** was started after 9/11 by the Central Intelligence Agency. It involves the detention and interrogation of foreign suspects without bringing them to the United States. The program allows the CIA to essentially apprehend and interrogate individuals from one country and place them into a jail or prison in another country without ever charging them with a crime in the United States. The extrajudicial transfer of these terrorism suspects became infamous when it became widely known that they were often tortured in the host countries. Individuals under the extraordinary rendition program were not labeled as an "enemy combatant," which will be discussed later in this chapter. Although the practice of extraordinary rendition has not been heard at the Supreme Court, several lower appellate courts have ruled that former prisoners of the program could not sue over their alleged torture in overseas prisons because such a suit may expose the classified information related to the government's fight against terrorism. Torture of prisoners is addressed later in this chapter. The courts have been reluctant to challenge the presidential privilege of executive secrets, a judicially created doctrine that shields the government from judicial review related to national security protections and measures.[20] The privilege has been successfully used by both Presidents Bush and Obama; however, recent leaks by Edward Snowden (see Box 10–1) have presented new challenges to the states-secret doctrine.[21] [22]

Extraordinary rendition
The apprehension, detention, and extrajudicial transfer of a person from one country to another, outside the confinements and jurisdiction of the United States.

Box 10-1
The Snowden Leak

In 2013, a classified intelligence leak from former defense contractor Edward Snowden revealed that the FISA court had authorized the collection of *all* phone-tracing **metadata** from *all* Verizon digital telephone communications under the PATRIOT Act. The FISC required the company to produce:

> ...ongoing, daily basis all call detail or telephony metadata created by Verizon for communications (i) between the United States and abroad; or (ii) wholly within the United States, including local telephone calls. Telephony metadata includes comprehensive communications routing information, including but not limited to session identifying information (e.g., originating and terminating telephone number, International Mobile Subscriber Identity (IMSI) number, International Mobile station Equipment Identity (IMEI) number, etc.), trunk identifier, telephone calling card numbers, and time and duration of call. Telephony metadata does not include the substantive content of any communication, as defined by 18 U.S.C. § 2510(8), or the name, address, or financial information of a subscriber or custom.[23]

The revelation from Snowden's leak made it clear that at least some intelligence agencies were overstepping their power under FISA and the USA PATRIOT Act. What also became clear after significant internal investigation was that most of the actual content of the calls was not being gathered. In other words, the most important and salient parts of the conversations were never being analyzed. The primary intelligence agency involved in the case, the NSA, appeared to be not only overstepping its bounds, but also inept in actually collecting the very information that may be used to thwart a terrorist attack or identify a specific terrorist individual. The actions by NSA continue to be a subject of much debate. Phone records can reveal a number of important personal items about individuals on their own, including the people who they communicate and associate with on a regular basis.

The collection of phone numbers alone may also conflict with Fourth Amendment protections against unreasonable searches and seizures, as a search generally must be based on individualized suspicion of wrongdoing to be considered "reasonable." Obviously, such a broad search cannot be individualized or based on any suspicion, and a "special needs" exception to this rule is problematic. At least one jurist has expressed a strong opinion relating to this issue: *"To my knowledge, no court has ever recognized a special need sufficient to justify continuous, daily searches of virtually every American citizen without any particularized suspicion.* In November 2014, in the wake of the Snowden leaks and a new civil suit filed by *Twitter* requiring the NSA to publish a full transparency report on its surveillance activities, the Senate failed to block the agency from continuing to collect individual phone records and other metadata from social media and Internet companies. In response, *Apple* and *Google*, as well as other companies, began offering an encryption program to secure private data and text messages on cell phones. The encryption program renders a locked cell phone impervious to external intrusion without a key, held only by the owner of the phone. These actions continued to fuel the push back against governmental snooping"[24] and can be directly tied to the passage of the USA Freedom Act in 2015, which effectively ended the mass collection of phone and Internet metadata. The Snowden leaks left an important legacy on the legislative evolution of the PATRIOT Act, and impacted public perception of the role of intelligence agencies in the fight against terrorism.

Do you think that the actions of the NSA were reasonable in weighing the impact of safety and security with personal liberties and privacy? Do you think that the USA Freedom Act eliminates many of the privacy concerns that the Snowden leak highlighted? Why or why not?

Metadata
Data that describes other data; for example, telephone metadata records the number called, what time the call was made, and how long it lasted.

Balancing Acts: Issues for Modern Intelligence

The events of the last decade have pounded into the American psyche one important message: We are not safe from domestic nor foreign threats. Remembering some of the consequences of such attacks as discussed in previous chapters, the primary goal of terrorism is to replace trust and social cohesiveness with distrust and insecurity. Terrorism plays to emotion rather than intellect. Clearly, America wrestles with this complex and difficult perspective. Random yet relatively consistent acts of violence and terrorism over a short ten-year period of time reinforce the concept that the United States (and its people) is vulnerable. As a reaction, the U.S. government has instituted a variety of new law enforcement, military, and intelligence operations that are designed to prevent acts of terrorism. Many of these measures have proven crucial to the government's ability to combat terrorism. However, the effort to provide these tools often conflicts with the need to protect Constitutional rights to privacy and due process—in essence, to ensure and secure not only our physical homeland, but also our way of life. This is an important balance to keep in mind while addressing the following issues.

NYPD and Intelligence

Increasingly, after the events of 9/11, local law enforcement agencies have taken on greater roles in domestic anti-terrorism. As discussed in Chapter 9, fusion centers have become the norm in large cities, and joint task forces composed of local, state, and federal law enforcement officers regularly work to identify and arrest terror suspects. Nowhere, however, has local law enforcement been more active in preventing terrorism than in New York City. The city bore the brunt of the 9/11 attacks and remains a place of huge symbolic importance in the American psyche. As such, the city has confronted its vulnerability to terror attacks by preparing an unprecedented response in the form of proactive and intelligence-led policing that yields a specific police counterterrorism unit within the New York City Police Department. It is a sophisticated unit that can respond by land, sea, or air in New York City and was founded in 2002 by then-Mayor Michael Bloomberg and Police Commissioner Ray Kelly. It is considered by the city to be the first line of defensè against terrorism, asserting that the failures of federal agencies like the FBI and the CIA to protect against the 9/11 attacks mean that New York City will no longer rely on those federal agencies alone to identify and disrupt potential terror attacks in their city (see Figure 10–4).

FIGURE 10–4
Members of the NYPD's Counterterrorism Unit stand guard at a building near Times Square, alert for indicators of a potential terrorist incident. CT officers are considered the first line of defense against terrorist attacks in the city.
(Erik Pendzich/REX/Shutterstock)

The unit is a well-funded and highly organized endeavor; it is, however, not without its problems. For example, there is no external (federal or state) oversight of the bureau—it functions largely at the discretion of the Police Commissioner and the Mayor of New York City. In addition, the unit deploys local NYPD police personnel overseas, to foreign countries, without the formal sanctions of diplomatic recognition through the U.S. Department of State. NYPD officers are commonly observed at the scene of terrorist strikes throughout the United States and around the world, collecting information and providing relevant intelligence back to NYPD commanders. As such, NYPD's counterterrorism unit has been accused of violating the Constitution and overstepping its bounds on more than one occasion.

For example, it was revealed in 2011 that the unit had been secretly monitoring the Muslim community extensively over a decade—conducting surveillance in mosques, and even sending out officers to act as "rakers" or "crawlers" within the Muslim community, essentially serving as part of a "human mapping program" within not only New York City, but also the entire United States.[25] Clearly, NYPD officers are out of their jurisdiction when operating outside the confines of New York City. The NYPD used its diverse force of officers to infiltrate ethnic neighborhoods in a number of other East Coast cities, going undercover to monitor individuals at bookstores, markets, restaurants, and religious centers. There was no criminal predicate and the only variable for being the target of surveillance was being Muslim. The unit also developed a team of informants, known as "mosque crawlers," who reported to their NYPD handlers on routine religious activities—an undertaking that would blatantly violate Constitutional and other legal protections against collecting intelligence on purely First Amendment activities had a federal agency been involved.[26]

In fact, a federal agency (Central Intelligence Agency) *was* involved in the original development of the unit. NYPD Intelligence Division and Counterterrorism Bureau officers were sent to CIA training academies, essentially equipping them with the skills needed for foreign intelligence operations. Unfortunately, these skills were then used in a domestic setting against U.S. citizens. Active CIA operatives were also sent on special assignment to assist the unit in undercover operations, further drawing criticism from civil liberties groups and the local Islamic population, which was the target of the unit's activities.[27]

The "New York Model" of post-9/11 policing with the development of the Intelligence Division and Counterterrorism Bureau has influenced police departments around the nation; several of their deployment models have been adapted by other law enforcement agencies. See Box 10–2. However, few police departments have the resources to develop their own intelligence and counterterrorism unit: NYPD has a massive budget—the 2014 proposed budget was $4.678 billion dollars[28]—and deep ties to the CIA, both of which are unique to the organization. It is also unique in that its citizens are tolerant of the sometimes questionable activities that the unit undertakes where civil liberties are concerned. For instance, a move to develop a similar unit in Los Angeles was scrapped due to protests from

Box 10–2
NYPD Intelligence Unit Infiltrated Activist Group

Although many in New York are supportive of the NYPD's efforts to prevent a terror attack like the one that happened on September 11, 2001, a report that surfaced in 2012 brought up questions about the Intelligence and Counterterrorism Bureau's focus—and its seeming overreach that skirts First and Fourth Amendment protections. Case in point: Undercover officers with the unit attended meetings of liberal political groups, keeping intelligence files on activists engaged in legal protests throughout the country.

NYPD asserts that they have good reason to go undercover in such organizations. Protests have turned into riots in other cities, such as Seattle in 1999, and police like to be prepared for elements within an organization that may cause a disturbance

to the peace. In a lawsuit related to similar surveillance before the Republican National Convention in 2004, former Intelligence Division Director David Cohen stated, "There was no political surveillance; this was a program designed to determine in advance the likelihood of unlawful activity or acts of violence." However, the activists were catalogued in intelligence reports not for violent acts or unlawful activity—but merely for being present at a meeting and associating with other group members.[29]

Do you think asking local police agencies to infiltrate political and religious groups blurs the line between policing and intelligence gathering? Should the police be involved in such activities?

local immigrant communities. It is likely that NYPD's unit thrives because the citizenry still bears deep scars from 9/11, and as former CIA officer and NYPD advisor Larry Sanchez testified on Capitol Hill, "We've been given the public tolerance and luxury to be very aggressive on this topic."[30]

Interestingly, there is little data that indicates that NYPD's counterterrorism program is effective. Though New York City officials claim that the unit has thwarted at least 14 terror plots (from 2001 to 2012), only three can actually be confirmed. The rest were predicated on such heavy-handed enabling by informants that federal officials declined to bring charges or were never brought anywhere close to fruition. In addition, the three terror plots claimed by NYPD were not actually disrupted by the Intelligence Division and Counterterrorism Bureau; in one case, a bomb was discovered in Times Square by street vendors, and in the other two cases, the plots were disrupted by agencies other than the NYPD.[31] Balancing security and safety with individual freedoms and Constitutional rights is a difficult task. There are those that argue that such aggressive tactics as described by the NYPD's Intelligence Division and Counterterrorism Bureau are actually counterproductive by eroding trust and driving those who might potentially be a good source of information on terror plots into silence. Muslim-Americans who may have otherwise been forthcoming about signs of jihadist radicalization in their community may fear that approaching law enforcement would only further invite intrusive and unconstitutional policing tactics into their neighborhoods and mosques.[32]

The NYPD Intelligence Unit and Counterterrorism Bureau represents one local agency's unique methodology to gain advantage over those who employ terrorism against the United States. In Chapter 14, other agencies are presented that have recognized counterterrorism missions.

The Military and Policing Functions: Posse Comitatus

Local and state police departments are not the only entities that have found it difficult to balance their activities in the wake of 9/11. Similar to law enforcement, U.S. military forces have increasingly found themselves participating in *domestic* intelligence and security operations—a role that has been historically illegal.

The Posse Comitatus Act was passed by Congress in 1878, as a reaction to the events that took place during the post–Civil War, Reconstruction era. (Please note that the Posse Comitatus Act is *not* to be confused with early right-wing terrorist group "Posse Comitatus" discussed in Chapter 8.) In one of the most hotly contested elections in national history (1876) between Democrat Samuel Tilden and Republican Rutherford B. Hayes, southern Democrats claimed that military officers who had been assigned to monitor voting stations had prohibited newly freed black men from casting ballots, resulting in the loss of the election. After much debate, a Congressional commission awarded Hayes 20 electoral votes and he was inaugurated the following year in 1877 as the 19th President of the United States. The Great Compromise of 1877 provided the needed electoral votes for Hayes, but also ended all federal military (army) interventions in the Southern states. The Posse Comitatus Act became law and set forth the provision that federal troops could not be used in a policing action within a State, no branch of the military could be used "*as a posse comitatus or otherwise to execute the laws of a State, except in cases and under circumstances expressly authorized by the Constitution or Act of Congress.*"[33]

The term **posse comitatus** translates from Latin into "power of the county," and hails from common law. It refers to a practice dating from England in the 1400s where a posse composed of ordinary citizens could be assembled by a local sheriff in order to enforce certain laws or quell certain disturbances. Because the military was once composed of average citizens, as opposed to professional soldiers, the term has evolved in the United States to refer to the use of the federal military to enforce state or civilian laws. The USA PATRIOT Act expanded the ability of the military to *assist* with domestic intelligence and security after 9/11, and thereby challenged the validity of the Posse Comitatus Act in modern history. Further the USA PATRIOT Act created the new U.S. Department of Homeland Security (see Chapters 12 and 13) and the new U.S. Northern Command (NORTHCOM). NORTHCOM is a military command responsible for the entire Northern American continent, plus the Caribbean basin. It also is responsible for protecting all U.S. borders and U.S. coastal waters up to 500 nautical miles from land. NORTHCOM's purpose is to support local and state authorities in the case of a domestic terror attack or natural catastrophe; it also is tasked with prevention, deterrence, and response to external threats to the security of the United States. Although this doesn't sound terribly intrusive on its face, the problem—as with many of the issues discussed so far—is that the word "support" often becomes broadly defined and blurs the line between military and local police separation. For example, the presence of government troops at large sporting events like the Super Bowl or the Olympics is justified because of their "support" to federal, state, or local law enforcement entities. The military involvement in anti-narcotics and border control functions has also been authorized, and the military was also greatly involved in supportive operations after Hurricane Katrina. However, formally staffing local fusion centers with military personnel who have access to intelligence systems used to help establish criminal cases against individual citizens has been severely questioned and abandoned. Similarly, using military officers as "partners" with state and local officers to routinely patrol parts of a city or the southern border with Mexico have also been met with significant resistance, as these types of initiatives "push the envelope" in violating the Posse Comitatus Act.

So far, the use of the military in post-9/11 domestic operations has indeed been rather ad hoc, and limited to a supplemental and supportive status. Many legal scholars have advocated that the Posse Comitatus Act be revisited as a means to clarify the role of the military during a national crisis, such as during another major terrorist strike on the order of 9/11.[34] Certainly, defining the role of the military, and specifically NORTHCOM, before such an emergency would greatly enhance the government's ability to effectively respond to such a crisis.

Posse comitatus
Common law term meaning literally "power of the county"; refers to the military's role in enforcing state or civilian law.

Information Link
For more information on The Posse Comitatus Act, visit the website hosted by the U.S. Northern Command (NORTHCOM) at www.northcom.mil /Newsroom/Fact-Sheets/Article-View /Article/563993/the-posse-comitatus-act/.

The Use of Domestic Drones

The use of domestic drones as a means to collect intelligence information is a hot-button topic in the United States. This is especially true considering that the use of domestic drones by law enforcement is posed to dramatically increase. **Drones** are unmanned aerial vehicles that are widely used for the purposes of both commercial and governmental endeavors, including the monitoring and/or surveying of commercial property, the scientific and academic research of geography and space, the surveillance of private and public transportation systems, and a host of intelligence gathering operations from crowd monitoring

Drones
Unmanned aircraft that can navigate autonomously.

to border enforcement to routine law enforcement and security monitoring. For example, a drone was recently used in a 2013 hostage situation in Midland County, Alabama.[35] Police and FBI agents deployed a drone with a camera to monitor the health and well-being of a five-year-old autistic boy being held captive by a sixty-five-year-old Vietnam War-era veteran. The drone also provided critical intelligence information regarding potential access into the underground bunker that was being secured by the suspect. Police officers used this information to breach the location and rescue the boy.[36]

The technology used in drones is evolving rapidly; one manufacturer has produced a device equipped with a 1.8 gigapixel resolution camera that is capable of the high-resolution monitoring and recording of entire cities. Pictures of individuals can then be analyzed by computer systems using high-speed visual recognition software and databases of known terror suspects and wanted persons. Additionally, the listening capability of drones has also dramatically improved. It is now possible to listen to and record normal conversations between individuals within a house, building, or office simply by having a drone hover nearby.

Similar to the discussion regarding the use of the military in supporting law enforcement, drones have only been allowed on an ad hoc, case-by-case basis in the United States. However, the proposed opening of U.S. airspace in 2015 to wider drone activity has created a general uneasiness among the American public and civil liberties advocates who fear the potential for wide-scale surveillance and invasions of privacy. Truly, the potential for "big brother" to spy from the sky has now become a reality.

Drones are becoming more and more popular among domestic law enforcement agencies. See Box 10–3. Police use drones to assist in locating bombs, finding lost children, monitoring weather, traffic, and wildlife patterns, and rescuing people during natural disasters. Most agencies also use the drones to assist in deploying personnel during emergencies as well as assist in monitoring existing problems or critical incidents. For the most part, drones are not practical for large-scale surveillance operations.[37] In 2013, Congress attempted to set limits on the use of drones during such types of nonspecific endeavors by federal law enforcement agencies. Further, several states, including Virginia, Florida, and Idaho, enacted specific limits on the ways that drones might be used by police agencies.[38] A recent survey showed that one-third of Americans fear the potential of domestic drones to spy on their daily activities.[39] In response, the ACLU has recommended that drone usage be subject to the following safeguards:

- *USAGE LIMITS:* Drones should be deployed by law enforcement only with a warrant, in an emergency, or when there are specific and articulable grounds to believe that the drone will collect evidence relating to a specific criminal act.

Box 10–3
Domestic Drones and Crime Fighting

In August 2016, the Federal Aviation Administration opened uncontrolled U.S. airspace for drone flights; in the years leading up to that date, though, several dozen law enforcement agencies throughout the country had already begun utilizing drones for law enforcement efforts.

One such agency is the Mesa County Sheriff's Department in rural Colorado, which flew more than 40 missions with their approved device in a three-year period. Armed with a GPS-enabled Draganflyer X6, weighing just 3.5 pounds, the agency utilized the device extensively for 3-D reconstruction of accident and crime scenes—the drone photographs the areas involved and downloads the pictures into an imaging program which then creates a virtual re-creation of the site. Deputy Ben Miller, who wrote the protocols for the agency's drone use and training, says that the device can revolutionize accident reconstruction, eliminating the need to shut down highways and other roadways after incidents. He also estimates that the device costs about $25 an hour to operate; most drones of this size and capability run about $10,000 to $20,000.

Drone use is also employed for searches that aid first responders in finding missing persons: The Royal Canadian Mounted Police have utilized them extensively when equipped with infrared cameras. One successful mission located an injured person in snowy conditions when his car flipped over. They've also been used after catastrophic floods to survey conditions, and to assist fire departments in assessing structure blazes from above. Though much of the worry related to domestic drone use centers on surveillance and Fourth Amendment overreaches, law enforcement agencies see much of the value in the devices outside of such purposes. As of early 2014, many states were considering limiting drone use for law enforcement purposes to situations where warrants had been obtained; however, many of those had clauses for exceptions due to emergency situations or activities not related to crime-fighting. This may be a fair compromise for many agencies. Miller states that tactical missions are few and far between anyway, and that no surveillance missions had been flown during the years that the program was in place.[40]

Do you think that domestic police agencies should be able to routinely use drones, or should their use be restricted to specific conditions?

FIGURE 10–5
With the assistance of the Arizona National Guard, the Border Patrol assembles and distributes rescue beacons across the remote desert area between Mexico and the United States. Illegal "crossers" often get in physical danger and some die in the rugged country through which they walk. The beacons are solar powered with metal panels that reflect sunlight in day and emit a blinking blue light that can be seen from 10 miles at night. Instructions about the operation of the beacon are written in several languages and are supplemented with a drawing for those who may not be able to read in order to lower the number of deaths of those making the dangerous journey from Mexico to the United States.

(U.S. Customs and Border Protection)

- *DATA RETENTION:* Images should be retained only when there is reasonable suspicion that they contain evidence of a crime or are relevant to an ongoing investigation or trial.

- *POLICY:* Usage policy on domestic drones should be decided by the public's representatives, not by police departments, and the policies should be clear, written, and open to the public.

- *ABUSE PREVENTION & ACCOUNTABILITY:* Use of domestic drones should be subject to open audits and proper oversight to prevent misuse.

- *WEAPONS:* Domestic drones should not be equipped with lethal or non-lethal weapons.[41]

Finally, there has also been much controversy about the use of drones to carry out "military-type strikes" against combatants on foreign soil. Drones have been a key weapon in the fight against al-Qaeda and the Islamic State in Pakistan, Yemen, Iraq, Afghanistan, and Somalia. These drones differ greatly from the ones previously discussed relating to domestic law enforcement use. These are militarized or "weaponized" drones, capable of firing missiles at targets or crashing into their targets with bombs, and are discussed more thoroughly in Chapter 14 as a counterterrorism tactic. Not all use of technology is used for apprehension. In Figure 10–5, rescue units are being readied to deploy in the desert.

Intelligence and Torture

The 9/11 attacks produced a series of unforeseeable events. The desire to strike back at terrorists was predictable, but the authorization of a new set of "harsh" or "enhanced interrogation techniques" (EITs) was not. The new methods were at odds with American values, our Constitution and case law, and the Third Geneva Convention (1949) that, in part, requires prisoners of war to be humanely treated and protected, particularly against acts of violence, intimidation, and insults. Enhanced interrogation techniques were also contrary to a 1994 United Nations international agreement signed by the United States that prohibited, as a matter of human rights, torture, and other cruel, inhumane, or degrading treatment or punishment.[42] However, all of these authorities were brushed aside in the pursuit of terrorists. Illustratively, in 2002, our government concluded that captured terrorists were not entitled to the protection of being prisoners of war (POWs) because they were "enemy combatants."[43] Part of the underlying logic was that because there was no declared war, there could be no POWs.

Quick Facts
The Lingering Results of Enhanced Interrogation Techniques (EITs)

Beginning with the Lieber Code during the American Civil War, the U.S. Military championed the humane and responsible handling of combatants and civilians.[44] EITs, which seemed so necessary in 2002, are now regarded as a national mistake by human rights, the courts, think tanks, and studies. Many known and suspected terrorists were confined at the United States facility at Guantanamo Bay, Cuba, and subjected to EITs. Other detainees were held abroad in facilities in foreign countries. In December 2014, the U.S. Senate Select Committee on Intelligence released a declassified study on the Central Intelligence Agency's Detection and Interrogation Program.[45] Although highly controversial upon its release, the report concluded that CIA personnel, aided by two outside contractors, initiated a program of indefinite secret detention and the use of brutal interrogation techniques in violation of U.S. law, treaty obligations, and American values.[46]

Intelligence officials knew that the techniques were verifiably painful and shocking—but they maintained that such techniques would not cause long-term psychological harm. Today, it's clear that those who were exposed to such techniques in Gitmo, Afghanistan, or other secret CIA facilities around the world have persistent mental health problems, many of which mimic the symptoms of American prisoners of war cruelly tortured during the Vietnam and Korean conflicts. At least half of those who went through the CIA's EIT program have shown psychiatric problems, including post-traumatic stress disorder, paranoia, depression, and psychosis.[47]

Though experts warn that mental illness cannot always be traced back to a specific cause, it does seem clear that the practices caused harm to their recipients—many of whom were later found to have been detained under mistaken identities, shoddy evidence, and only tangential connections to the other terrorists. Even for those who were clearly involved in terror plots, such as the one that destroyed the USS *Cole* in 2000, their mental status as a result of EIT has affected the U.S. ability to prosecute them effectively.

Information Link
Visit the National Security Archives at www2.gwu.edu/~nsarchiv/NSAEBB /NSAEBB127 to view documents relating to the use of enhanced interrogation techniques and U.S. policy.

The use of EITs is not simply a case of a few agents "going rogue." EITs were used globally. The American governmental apparatus was substantially involved in approving these new methods and their use was not just for a handful of isolated cases. A small bipartisan group of Congressional members were briefed on EITs by the CIA, with no dissent about the methods.[48] The U.S. Attorney General's Office approved them, as did the Secretary of Defense. Moreover, it is also clear that the White House supported these new measures or they could not have been implemented.

In retrospectively looking at the record, it is arguably true that on the issue of intelligence and torture that for a time America lost its way. Some people, groups, and institutions may readily endorse this conclusion, while others may say that is naïve and doesn't give sufficient weight to the urgent necessity of gathering potentially life-saving intelligence. The latter view does give rise to larger questions, such as "Do the ends justify the means? "Even if an action is legal, must it also be moral?"[49] "How reliable is 'evidence' obtained by coercion?"[50] "Is there a natural and unavoidable clash between individual rights and protection of the homeland?"

It is essential to note that many of the activities now labeled as "torture" were EITs previously approved by our government as "counter resistance measures" and legally permissible under existing guidelines. A partial list of EITs approved in 2002 includes:

1. *Category I Techniques:* During the initial interrogation, the detainee should be provided a chair in a generally comfortable environment. If cooperative, give cookies or cigarettes. If uncooperative, authorized techniques include yelling at the detainee, use of deception, multiple interrogator techniques, and leading the detainee to believe the interrogator is from a country with a reputation for harsh treatment of detainees.

2. *Category II Techniques:* The use of stress positions, such as standing for four hours, the use of falsified documents or reports, isolation for up to 30 days, use of other than standard interrogation techniques, use of hoods over heads while being transported and interrogated, 20-hour interrogations, removal of all comfort items, including religious items, reducing rations to standard military Meals Ready-to-Eat (MREs), removal of clothing, forced grooming (shaving of facial hair), and using detainee phobias to induce stress, such as claustrophobia and fear of dogs and snakes. See Figure 10–6.

3. *Category III Techniques:* Within the military, prior approval by a General grade officer was required to use Category III Techniques. Such techniques include the use of scenarios to convince the detainee that death or severely painful consequences were imminent for the detainee or his family, exposure to cold weather or water

with appropriate medical monitoring, use of waterboarding (although not actually referred to as such) to induce the misperception of suffocation, use of mild, non injurious physical contact such as grabbing, poking in the chest with the finger, and light pushing.[51]

It is easy to conclude that criticisms of EITs emerged only after the emergency climate created by 9/11 faded. However, it is more likely that as the secrecy surrounding EITs was peeled away and repugnant actions reported, opposition to them emerged. In 2004, the United States Army released the "Taguba Report,"[52] an investigation of alleged abuses and accountability lapses at the Abu Ghraib Prison in Iraq. It found that "numerous incidents of sadistic, blatant, and wanton criminal abuses were inflicted on several detainees."[53] This conclusion was supported by witness statements and photographic evidence. Among the abuses were a male military policeman having sex with a female detainee and a detainee who was sodomized with a chemical light.

FIGURE 10-6
An enemy combatant detainee undergoes "enhanced interrogation" methods at an unknown location at the hands of CIA and U.S. military personnel.

(Washington Post/Getty Images)

The Constitution Project formed an independent, bipartisan, blue ribbon group to examine the capture, detention, and treatment of suspected terrorists during the presidential administrations of Clinton, Bush, and Obama, called the Task Force on Detainee Treatment (TFODT).[54] In 2013, the Task Force released its report, which found that the U.S. government had engaged in the widespread use of sanctioned torture of detainees and suspected terrorists after 9/11, including some American citizens. The report describes interrogations of prisoners at Guantanamo Bay and other detention facilities controlled by the CIA, which included extreme sleep deprivation, waterboarding, chaining of prisoners to walls in painful positions, slamming prisoners into walls and floors, beating prisoners, extending long periods of nudity and humiliation, and a variety of psychological torture techniques.

In 2014, a report by the U.S. Senate Intelligence Commission concluded that the CIA had intentionally misled Congress and the public about the success of the brutal interrogation program.[55] The CIA had described the program to both the U.S. Department of Justice as well as to Congress as retrieving unique and otherwise unobtainable intelligence that helped disrupt terrorist plots and saved thousands of American lives both domestically and in combat throughout the Middle East (Yemen, Somalia, Iraq, and Afghanistan).[56] This representation may not be accurate. There are consistent findings that the information gained from torture is often unreliable, despite such claims, popular belief, and media representations to the contrary.[57] The report also documented a sprawling network of secret detention sites where some detainees were tortured. These secret detention sites, and the use of EITs, were finally dismantled and banned by President Obama in late 2009. However, the future of EIT's has recently come under speculation with the new Trump administration. See Box 10–4.

The use of torture is abhorrent to most Americans and most of the international community. Although mention has been made of U.S. authorities using torture, a closer examination of how it violates key constitutional provisions is warranted. The Fifth Amendment guarantees the right to a grand jury, protects against self-incrimination, guarantees due process, and precludes double jeopardy for the same offense. The Eighth Amendment prohibits cruel and unusual punishment, including torture, as well as excessive fines and bail. The USA PATRIOT Act of 2001 and the **Military Commissions Act of 2006 (MCA)** combine to provide exceptions to granting detainees Constitutional protections.

The MCA allowed the president to determine who is an "**enemy combatant**." Being labeled as such dispenses with the U.S. government's obligation to provide the protections of the Fifth and Eighth Amendments. Therefore, an enemy combatant "detainee" can be held indefinitely without being charged. The MCA also allows enemy combatant to be subjected to extraordinary interrogation methods. The U.S. Department of Justice has ruled that the Fifth and Eighth Amendments do not apply to foreign enemy combatants held abroad[58] and that even U.S. citizens are subject to the designation of "enemy combatant" when captured abroad.

Military Commissions Act of 2006 (MCA)
An act of Congress signed by President George W. Bush in 2006 to authorize trial by military commission for violations of the law of war and for other purposes. It prohibited detainees who had been classified as enemy combatants or were awaiting hearings on their status from using "Habeas corpus" to petition federal courts in challenges to their detention.

Enemy combatant
A special designation of an individual who has engaged in hostilities against the United States or its coalition partners.

In the previous chapter, we discussed conflicts between the Trump administration and the intelligence community. These tensions and differences have also been observed relating to important strategic techniques in intelligence gathering. One such area surrounds the use of enhanced interrogation techniques, or EITs. During his campaign, President Trump promised that he would "bring back a hell of a lot worse than waterboarding" if elected.[59] And indeed, one of his first actions when taking over the office of president was to draft an executive order that would have resurrected the enhanced interrogation techniques banned by his predecessor, President Barack Obama. Further support of these types of techniques was seen in President Trump's appointment of Jefferson Sessions as attorney general. Sessions was part of a strong contingent of U.S. senators that voted in favor of enhanced interrogation techniques during the Bush era and was questioned extensively on his position regarding "torture" during his confirmation hearings in 2017.

However, President Trump's executive order never made it past the draft stage. Career officials within the Central Intelligence Agency and the U.S. Department of Defense openly balked at the idea, citing evidence that EIT and torture simply does not work: (1) EIT and torture undermines long-term U.S. military, intelligence, and diplomatic strategy;

(2) Information derived from human intelligence sources is simply ____not as important or crucial in this age of cyber intelligence and drones as it was in the past; (3) Much of the information derived from prisoners under EIT programs was false and/or of "low priority" value; and most important (4) The use of EIT and torture undermines the ethical and integrity standards of the U.S. government as presented by military and intelligence agencies. General James Mattis, President Trump's new secretary of defense and a strong advocate for dropping the use of EITs, asserted that "a pack of cigarettes and a couple of beers" yielded better intelligence than enhanced interrogation techniques or torture.[60]

A return to the use of enhanced interrogation techniques (EITs), or the use of other forms of torture, as intelligence gathering strategies will not be as simple as an executive order. Techniques such as waterboarding, physical beatings, starvation, and sexual humiliation are now expressly prohibited—as is anything else that is not clearly listed in the *2016 Army Field Manual* and codified within the 2016 National Defense Authorization Act. Any modifications to the *Army Field Manual* must now be made public and would have to be fully supported by the secretary of defense—who, at this time, has made it very clear that he opposes such techniques.

The case of Jose Padilla clearly illustrates the excesses that can be inflicted on a person labeled an "enemy combatant." Padilla was born in Brooklyn, New York, in 1970. He was arrested in Chicago in 2002, after returning from a trip to Egypt, Saudi Arabia, Afghanistan, Pakistan, and Iraq. Padilla was suspected of plotting to detonate a "dirty bomb" (radiological bomb) somewhere in the United States. Then-President George W. Bush ordered him held as an "enemy combatant" and authorized "enhanced interrogation techniques," including extended solitary confinement and sensory deprivation, administration of psychotropic substances, and sleep deprivation. Padilla was not charged with a crime for nearly five years. He was never charged for conspiring to detonate a bomb within the United States, but for a much less grievous charge of conspiring with and supporting terrorist overseas. He was found guilty in 2007 and sentenced to 17 years in prison.

In a subsequent civil suit that reached the Ninth Circuit Court of Appeals in 2012, Padilla claimed he was entitled to a settlement from the U.S. government in light of the torture that he experienced during his detainment. The court, however, disagreed, stating that at the time, the things that Padilla experienced (shackling, stress positions, extreme sleep deprivation) were not considered torture and so the government could not be held responsible.[61] Furthermore, in 2012, the Seventh Circuit Court of Appeals ruled in *Vance and Ertel vs. Rumsfeld* that U.S. citizens labeled "enemy combatants" could not recover damages from military personnel and their commanding government officials for torture, leaving U.S. citizens without remedy against government officials who authorized or participated in their torture.[62]

The Padilla case is an example of a government gone awry post-9/11 and brings into clear relief the difficulty of finding an equitable and Constitutional balancing of homeland security and individual rights.

"Outing" Intelligence: Leaks and Insecurity

Beginning in 2010, a series of intelligence leaks by U.S. military personnel and contractors rocked American perceptions of intelligence and privacy, and laid bare shocking details related to nearly every facet of American intelligence gathering. Intelligence leaks have occurred throughout history—but in the past several years, it has become obvious that technology now enables those inclined to gather and leak classified materials to do so in large quantities and to gain widespread exposure and attention to their materials. The use of flash drives/thumb drives allows would-be spies to quickly and surreptitiously copy massive amounts of information; in the past, such gathering of mass data would have been cumbersome and extremely obvious to others. However, in the cases of Chelsea Manning and Edward Snowden, nobody was even aware of their access to and copying of mass information related to national security until it was headline news around the world.

The case of Chelsea Manning was the first major exposure of United States intelligence secrets and wartime tactics since World War II. The Army private was deployed to Iraq in 2009, and by 2010 she had surreptitiously downloaded hundreds of thousands of classified military documents onto a CD while passing the media off as a Lady Gaga record. Those documents were passed on to **WikiLeaks**, a nonprofit international organization claiming to be dedicated to publishing classified documents in the name of transparency. The classified items that Manning stole and subsequently leaked include the following:

WikiLeaks
A nonprofit international organization dedicated to publishing classified documents in the name of transparency.

- *Video:* Manning procured video documentation of an air strike that showed Apache helicopter pilots firing on a group of people in Iraq that included civilians, two of whom were Reuter's photographers. Those coming to the aid of the photographers were also fired on. The video was edited by WikiLeaks personnel and showcased callous dialogue from the helicopter pilots as they killed innocent civilians on the ground.

- *"War Logs":* This included thousands of incident reports from the combat engagements in both Afghanistan and Iraq.

- *State Department Diplomatic Cables:* A large number of diplomatic communications that revealed—among other things—that the U.S. government was secretly cooperating with several oppressive Arab regimes in the Middle East. The cables revealed the collusion of military and intelligence activities with governments, in stark opposition to U.S. Department of State public and policy positions.

- *Guantanamo Documents:* These documents were less shocking in nature, primarily because the reports on the prisoners and their detention, abuse, and torture had already been made public by the U.S. government.[63]

The effects of Manning's leaks were wide-ranging from a number of different perspectives. First, U.S. officials blamed her for putting a number of diplomatic relationships on ice, particularly those involving the governments of Syria, Egypt, Saudi Arabia, and Yemen. Second, government officials who testified against her in 2013 blamed the leaks for harming military relationships with Afghan villagers and for straining operational relationships with the Pakistan and Afghan governments. Accordingly, these "strained operational relationships" endangered the lives of foreign citizens who worked with U.S. diplomats and for hampering efforts of the U.S. Department of State to work with human rights groups overseas.[64] The United States also claimed that the leaks put the lives of U.S. soldiers and citizens at risk as they inflamed terrorist rhetoric. However, there is little to no evidence to support this contention.[65] Regardless, Bradley Manning was charged with 22 offenses related to the leaked documents. She pled guilty to 10 of those 22 offenses and was found guilty in a military court of all but one of the remaining charges. She was sentenced to 35 years confinement in a maximum security federal prison in Leavenworth, Kansas. She was, however, acquitted of the charge of "aiding the enemy," which could have carried the death sentence.

Adding to the controversy of the case, after conviction, Manning, who was born a male named Bradley, began to transition to a female gender identity, receiving treatment including sex reassignment surgery, hormone therapy, and psychological counseling, while in prison. See Figure 10–7. The procedures were approved by the U.S. Department of Defense Secretary Chuck Hagel, and raised question as to whether Manning would be transferred to a female prison. The prison at Leavenworth, Kansas, is all male. Some have argued that being transgender in an all-male prison could constitute "cruel and unusual punishment."[66] Manning attempted suicide twice while in prison, and in what many feel was a stunning turn of events, then-President Barack Obama overruled Secretary of Defense Ash Carter in the

(Alex Wong/Staff/Getty Images News/
Getty Images)

(Gail Orenstein/Zuma Press/Newscom)

FIGURE 10-7
Chelsea Manning's transgender
status added to the controversial
issues surrounding her leaking of
classified documents to WikiLeaks
in 2010.

closing days of his administration, and commuted Manning's sentence. While her conviction will stand, Chelsea Manning was released from prison on May 17, 2017.

President Obama's rationale for the commutation was not made clear, though many speculated that her transgender status and suicide attempts played a role. Regardless, the intelligence and military communities were less than pleased with the surprise announcement right before Donald Trump's inauguration. Manning is still largely considered a traitor who endangered military lives in Iraq and Afghanistan and damaged U.S. foreign relations.[67] Critics also pointed out that the action may decrease accountability for those who compromise national security.

Manning's legacy remains mixed: Some see her as nothing more than a traitor to her nation, while others point to her gender identity as proof that U.S. servicemen and women who are gay or transsexual are not fit for military service. Others credit her with being a whistle-blower who uncovered a series of injustices by the U.S. government in the Middle East. She may have even been a catalyst for the Arab Spring, in which indigenous populations rose up against the corruption detailed in some of the diplomatic materials leaked by Manning. The Manning case also served to legitimize WikiLeaks as a news source, bringing it to the forefront of journalistic source material.[68]

However, the reputation of WikiLeaks has also come into question since the initial publication of the leaked data. Its founder, Julian Assange, was indicted by the Swedish Prosecution Authority for multiple counts of sexual molestation and one count of rape. While denying the allegations and contending that the charges were brought in retaliation to the Manning case, Assange fled to the Ecuadorian Embassy in London, England, and subsequently was given political asylum by Ecuador.[69] With Metropolitan Police stationed outside the embassy in London, Assange remains confined to the Ecuadorian Embassy building.

Further, the WikiLeaks hacks of the Democratic National Committee during the 2016 presidential election, which exposed clear bias against Democratic candidate Bernie Sanders, and improper relationships between the media and Hillary Clinton's campaign, raised concerns that Assange was meddling in the U.S. electoral process, particularly since the same level of scrutiny was apparently not being applied to the Republican candidates.[70] Further revelations that the Russian government was somehow involved in these hacks and subsequent investigations may not only damage Assange's image, but also put his asylum at risk. Assange's fate may well hang in the balance of the Ecuadorian election cycle.

The legacy of Edward Snowden will likely be similarly mixed. Beginning in June of 2013, a series of leaks to news organizations (including British newspaper the *Guardian* and the *Washington Post*) began to surface that detailed orders from the Foreign Intelligence Surveillance Court (FISC) discussed earlier in this chapter. The court order required Verizon to hand over telephone metadata to the National Security Agency (NSA). Under a secret program, entitled PRISM, the leaks revealed that a total of nine Internet service companies were being forced to give the NSA broad access to audio and video chats, photographs, emails, documents, and connection logs of "suspected foreign terror targets."[71] This information allowed the NSA to document, trace, and conduct further surveillance on these individuals. One day after the initial leaks, it was further revealed that the U.S. government had developed a specific program (Boundless Informant) that listed these individuals as well as other targets for offensive cyber attack. **Boundless Informant** is/was a real-time global surveillance tracker that details and maps, by country, the metadata it receives from computer and phone networks. The leaked information about Boundless Informant revealed a surprising statistic: The NSA had collected 3 billion pieces of information in just one 30-day period (March 2013) from U.S. citizens alone, and 97 billion records from individuals worldwide![72] This was a surprising development, particularly since the NSA had long maintained—to Congress and the American public—that it was technologically not feasible to track, record, or analyze such abstract intelligence data and that such programs did not exist within the agency. To cap off the series of leaks (June 2013), the identity of the "leaker" was self-revealed as a twenty-nine-year-old former NSA and CIA information technology security contractor, Edward Snowden. Comments about his leaks indicated that he was well-aware of the consequence of his actions: *"I understand that I will be made to suffer for my actions ... but ... I will be satisfied if the federation of secret law, unequal pardon and irresistible executive powers that rule the world that I love are revealed even for an instant."*[73] Snowden also asserted that his case was different than that of Chelsea Manning. According to him, he "carefully evaluated" every single document disclosed to ensure that each was legitimately in the public interest, and that there were many other documents that he could have leaked but chose not to do so. In his words, his intention was not to "harm people" but rather to provide "transparency" to the U.S. government.[74]

Boundless Informant

A real-time global surveillance software tracker used by the NSA that details and maps the metadata it received from computers, phone systems, and the Internet.

Quick Facts
PRISM

The NSA program revealed by Edward Snowden in June of 2013 known as PRISM allowed U.S. intelligence agencies to tap into the servers of nine Internet companies, including Microsoft, Google, Yahoo!, Facebook, PalTalk, YouTube, Skype, AOL, and Apple. Materials collected include email content, chats, videos, photographs, stored data, VOIP (Voice Over Internet Protocol, or Internet phone calls), file transfers, video conferencing, social networking details, and notifications of targeted activity (such as log-ins). The program had been operational since 2007.

Dates When PRISM Collection Began for Each Provider

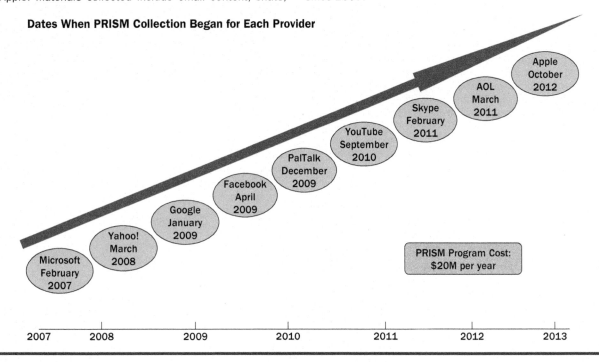

Microsoft February 2007 · Yahoo! March 2008 · Google January 2009 · Facebook April 2009 · PalTalk December 2009 · YouTube September 2010 · Skype February 2011 · AOL March 2011 · Apple October 2012

PRISM Program Cost: $20M per year

2007   2008   2009   2010   2011   2012   2013

The leaks didn't stop with the revelation that Snowden was the source. Information that the United States had spied on hundreds of Chinese and Hong Kong citizens and foreign diplomats, including the Chancellor of Germany, Angela Merkel, were also made public. Further, documents that illustrated a complete lack of judicial oversight on the part of the FISA court became accessible, as were NSA documents that detailed the technology used in gathering and analyzing domestic information used to track a billion cell phone calls a day. Snowden also released a list of over 500 servers used by the NSA to "capture nearly everything a user does on the Internet and store it in databases searchable by name, email, IP address, region and language," and it was revealed that the NSA has cracked the common encryptions used to secure email, commerce, and financial transactions domestically and worldwide.[75] Furthermore, the NSA's ability to peer into smartphones was revealed, as was its ability to trace social connections of Americans through phone and email metadata, social networking site information, and email contact lists or electronic address books. Snowden revealed how drone strikes in the Middle East had been informed by NSA data collection via cyber espionage, how the agency had intentionally propagated malicious surveillance software, how massive numbers of cell phone location records were archived in a NSA database, how U.S. intelligence agencies monitored online game playing such as World of Warcraft and Second Life, how the NSA cracked a common cellphone encryption methodology and captures every SMS text message, how the NSA can access data from any smartphone app, and most important, that the NSA maintains and stores this data for years on end without probable cause, warrant, or court oversight.[76]

Information Link

For more information on the NSA and PRISM controversy, refer to the NSA Prism Slides at: https://nsa.gov1.info /dni/prism.html. Explore the website for other information on "Boundless Informant," Snowden statements, and 2013 through 2017 Leaks.

Box 10–5
Reflections on Edward Snowden

For a time in June of 2013, every day brought a new and stunning revelation about the depth of U.S. intrusion into everyday communications. The world learned that the NSA could read its emails, intrude into its social networks, and learn intimate details based on phone records. It also learned that the man responsible for exposing the numerous spy programs was a twenty-nine-year-old intelligence contractor named Edward Snowden; a man who accepted that what he was doing would bring severe and immediate consequences from the government whose secrets were uncovered.

What differentiates Snowden's leaks from those of Chelsea Manning is that Snowden meticulously studied each document he released, making sure that he revealed nothing that could be used to identify specific targets, secret agents, or technical information, whereas Manning downloaded an unwieldy number of documents that contained information unknown to her, in many cases. While Manning's leaks alerted the world to serious abuses of U.S. power and authority throughout the world, the dump of data was, by definition, careless and arbitrary.

Snowden's leak, though, was far more deliberate. He chose documents that would highlight what he considered to be the government's deceptive practices: Just months before the information became public, the director of national intelligence told Congress that the NSA did not engage in widespread data mining that affected American people.

Similarly, General Keith Alexander, then-director of the NSA, denied that the agency had the technology to capture emails and other online communications. This testimony was cited by Snowden as a breaking point in the case:

"I would say the breaking point was seeing the Director of National Intelligence, James Clapper, directly lie under oath to Congress. There's no saving an intelligence community that believes it can lie to the public and the legislators who need to be able to trust it and regulate its actions. Seeing that

▲ During a demonstration in Washington, D.C., in 2014, a protestor holds up a placard supporting Edward Snowden. Many people believe he is a traitor, whereas others see him as a patriot.
(Miguel Juarez Lugo/Newscom)

really meant for me that there was no going back. Beyond that, it was the creeping realization that no one else was going to do this. The public had a right to know about these programs. The public had a right to know that which the government is doing in its name, and that which the government is doing against the public."[77]

Snowden obviously hopes that his actions will be seen as those of a whistle-blower as opposed to those of a traitor; the government clearly doesn't see it that way. In an extensive interview with the *New Yorker*, President Obama reiterated that Snowden had, in fact, harmed national security though he didn't offer any concrete examples—other than the fact that his relationship with German Chancellor Angela Merkel had chilled significantly since

Snowden's revelations that the United States had tapped into her cell phone. Obama also admitted, however, that he wasn't fully comfortable with the lack of oversight in the NSA's dealings, but then asserted that he was confident that the NSA's actions did not threaten the privacy and constitutional rights of Americans. This viewpoint could be bad news for Snowden, who has expressed hopes that he will be granted clemency by the government.

For now, as he resides in Russia on political asylum, Snowden's status as a hero is not solidified: In some circles, the pale computer geek is indeed a champion of civil liberties. In others, however, he is a man who betrayed the trust that his position

granted—and gave terrorists information that allowed them to burrow even further into communication rabbit holes—and even further out of our grasp.[78] Snowden has enjoyed a certain level of celebrity since his leaks: He's been the subject of a major Hollywood film, he's appeared via streaming video at panels about privacy and security, and he was the focus of an unsuccessful push to convince Barack Obama to exonerate him. He's also been accused of being a Russian spy—as of this writing, he will be eligible to apply for Russian citizenship in 2018.[79] See Box 10–5.

What do you think—is Edward Snowden a criminal or a patriot?

Immediately after the leaks, Edward Snowden was charged with three felony counts of espionage by the U.S. government. He initially fled to Hong Kong, and then, with the help of WikiLeaks, to Russia, where he has been granted asylum. The United States has agreed not to seek the death penalty in his case; however, requests to pardon Snowden as a whistle-blower have been strongly rejected by the U.S. government. Edward Snowden remains a wanted man. He remains something of a folk hero to U.S. civil rights advocates who assert that because of Snowden's actions, the American people are now aware of the "surveillance state" that undermines their guaranteed Constitutional right to privacy and freedom from unwarranted governmental intrusion. To others, he is a traitor to his government and a person who has made the country more vulnerable to foreign as well as terrorist attack. According to the then-Director of the NSA, General Keith Alexander, Snowden's leaks caused "irreversible and significant damage" to terrorist surveillance programs.[80] The government has also claimed that it caused unnecessary and difficult rifts between the United States and foreign allies (like Germany) who were spied on. It may take years to evaluate and assess the full effects of Snowden's actions: What is clear, however, is that his actions dramatically changed the perception of domestic intelligence in this country, laying bare a litany of constitutional breaches by the U.S. government, and drastically skewing the perceived balance between liberty and security.

Chapter Summary

SUMMARY BY LEARNING OBJECTIVE

1. **Summarize the USA PATRIOT Act and its subsequent reauthorizations.**

The USA PATRIOT Act was authorized after the 9/11 attacks and addressed not only terrorism and intelligence issues but also focused on more traditional money laundering, computer abuse and crime, immigration processes, and fraud. However, the most substantial part of the act is that it expanded traditional tools of surveillance used by law enforcement and intelligence agencies with significantly reduced checks and balances. It was reauthorized in 2006 and 2011 for the purposes of revision, clarification, and in some cases, expansion of powers set forth in the original document.

2. **Discuss the conflicts between the PATRIOT Act and the First, Fourth, Fifth, and Sixth Amendments to the U.S. Constitution.**

Provisions of the PATRIOT Act seemingly clash with First Amendment protections related to freedom of association because of the broadness of the "material support" clause in the Act. It also challenges freedom of religion as a result of religious profiling authorized under its authority, and freedom of speech by allowing the prosecution of those who advocate jihadist material. The PATRIOT Act conflicts with Fourth Amendment rights against unreasonable searches and seizures by skirting the probable cause requirement, allowing broad searches instead of ones based on individualized suspicion, and allowing intrusion into homes without a "knock and announce" warning.

3. **Articulate how the New York Police Department has instituted its own domestic intelligence program and discuss the implications of that on law enforcement agencies nationwide.**

   NYPD has developed a domestic intelligence program that sprang from the citizens' desire to not rely on the federal government to prevent and disrupt future terror attacks after the events of 9/11. It's a large unit within the NYPD, with a host of deployments at its disposal and the ability to take to land, air, or sea. Many law enforcement agencies across the country have emulated pieces of the NYPD unit; however, funding, the deep-rooted CIA involvement, and a permissible public sentiment that make the unit's activities possible are not available in any other American city.

4. **Explain the concept of *posse comitatus* and how our military might be called to supplement civilian policing functions.**

   Posse comitatus is a common law concept that asserts that military forces may not take on domestic law enforcement functions. However, the PATRIOT Act expanded the ability of our military to supplement civilian functions during major national security events, terror attacks, and natural catastrophes.

5. **Describe how drones are used both domestically and abroad for intelligence purposes and state the constitutional issues that arise with each type of use.**

   Domestically, drones are used for a variety of functions, from commercial land surveys to law enforcement surveillance and border patrol. The use of these types of drones is increasing with the approach of open air space provisions set in 2016, and Constitutional scholars are concerned about their impact on protections against unlawful searches and broad surveillance. Drones on foreign soil have been militarized and "weaponized," sometimes employed for the purposes of killing American terrorists. This is a direct conflict with protections found in the Fifth Amendment that guarantee due process of law.

6. **Discuss the use of torture in intelligence functions in the United States and describe the Constitutional issues involved.**

   Torture and intelligence have an uncomfortable association; recent reports prove that it was used extensively and authorized by the very highest levels of U.S. government to interrogate those suspected of involvement with al-Qaeda and other radical terror groups. Torture is specifically prohibited in the Eighth Amendment; however, courts have repeatedly denied relief to both foreign and domestic detainees under these protections.

7. **Outline the events surrounding the Chelsea Manning case, WikiLeaks scandal, and the Edward Snowden intelligence leaks.**

   Private Chelsea Manning downloaded hundreds of thousands of documents she had access to in her classified Army position and made them available to the WikiLeaks organization in 2010. As a result, videos of U.S. military strikes against civilians were made publicly available, as were incident reports from Iraq and Afghanistan, diplomatic cables that showed a disconnect between what the U.S. government reported publicly and how it conducted itself in communications with nations perceived to have oppressive regimes, and documents about the treatment of detainees in Guantanamo. The releases strained diplomatic relations and may, according to some, have further inflamed the hatred of America by extremist groups.

   The Edward Snowden leaks exposed the previously unknown techniques and tools that the NSA uses to spy on domestic cell phone, Internet, social network, and smartphone use, as well as those used to spy on foreign diplomats. The massive leak, enabled by Snowden's access to NSA files via his job as a contractor with the agency, made obvious that the intrusion of the intelligence community into everyday domestic communications is far broader than the average American ever thought.

REVIEW QUESTIONS

1. Discuss the PATRIOT Act. What reasons might the U.S. government have had to pass it so quickly after the events of 9/11?
2. How does the U.S. government determine what the balance should be between civil liberties and the protections against terrorist acts that the PATRIOT Act offers?
3. Which traditional tools of surveillance did the PATRIOT Act expand upon and why?
4. Has the PATRIOT Act had a chilling effect on First Amendment rights among certain populations? Why?

5. Describe the ways in which the PATRIOT Act defies the due process clause.
6. Give examples of searches under the PATRIOT Act that might otherwise be considered unreasonable.
7. Would the NYPD counterterrorism model work in other cities? Why or why not?
8. What should be the military's role in a domestic terror incident?
9. Why are civil liberties advocates concerned about drone use, both domestically and on foreign soil?
10. Is the torture of terrorist detainees ever justified? Why or why not?
11. What are the long-term implications on U.S. intelligence gathering as a result of the Manning and Snowden leaks?

CRITICAL THINKING EXERCISES

1. **Is the U.S. Constitution Out of Date?** The first ten amendments to the United States Constitution are more commonly known as the "Bill of Rights" and were ratified by Congress in 1791. The Bill of Rights and the U.S. Constitution have survived for nearly 225 years of history. However, the founding fathers never imagined a technological world marked by amazing global communication through computers and the Internet at the current scale, nor a lifestyle that often hinges on personal telephone usage, texting, gaming, and access to online and social media sites. Should the Constitution be updated and rewritten to address such changes in our society? Why or why not?
2. **Torture and the U.S. Government.** Search the Internet on the subject of "torture by the U.S. government" and read the accounts of such activity by members of the CIA and the military over the last decade. Now, search the Internet under *Human Rights Watch* and *Amnesty International* to gain a different perspective. Do you think that torture should be used to elicit information from suspects? How reliable is information obtained from torture? Are you willing to allow torture of some suspects in order to potentially prevent another terrorist attack on the homeland on the scale of 9/11 ... maybe nuclear or biological in nature?

NOTES

1. M. Moore, *Fahrenheit 9/11* (documentary), timestamp: 01:01:39-01:01:47.
2. HR2048: USA Freedom Act of 2015. 114th U.S. Congress, 2015–2016, retrieved from www .congress.gov/bill/114th-congress/house-bill/2048/text.
3. Ibid.
4. Electronic Frontier Foundation, "EFF Analysis of the Provisions of the USA PATRIOT Act," October 31, 2001, www.eff.org/Privacy/Surveillance/Terrorism_militias/20011031_ eff_usa_patriot_analysis.html.
5. See: "About the ACLU" at the American Civil Liberties Union website at www.aclu.org /about-aclu-0.
6. See *Holder v. Humanitarian Law Project*, 561 U.S. 1 (2010), 130 S.Ct. 2705.
7. 18 U.S. Code § 2339A - Providing material support to terrorists, www.law.cornell.edu /uscode/text/18/2339A.
8. "The Supreme Court goes too far in the name of fighting terrorism," Editorial, *Washington Post* (Washington, D.C.), June 22, 2010, www.washingtonpost.com/wp-dyn /content/article/2010/06/21/AR2010062104267.html.
9. Sheila Reagan, "FBI raids activist homes in Minneapolis, Chicago," *Twin Cities Daily Planet* (Minneapolis, MN), Sept. 24, 2010, www.tcdailyplanet.net/news/2010/09/24 /fbi-raids-activist-homes-minneapolis-chicago.
10. Travis Anderson, "Federal Appeals Court Upholds Tarek Mehanna Terror Convictions," *Boston Globe,* November 13, 2013.
11. American Civil Liberties Union, "Mehanna Verdict Compromises First Amendment, Undermines National Security," December 20, 2011, www.aclu.org/free-speech/ mehanna-verdict-compromises-first-amendment-undermines-national-security.
12. Ibid., see also *United States v. Mehanna* 735 F. 3rd 32, 2011.

13. American Civil Liberties Union, "FBI's New Surveillance Plan Chills Religious and Political Activity, Bay Area Civil Rights Groups Warn," October 5, 2004, www.aclu.org/national-security/fbis-new-surveillance-plan-chills-religious-and-political-activity-bay-area-civil-.

14. ACLU: Surveillance Under the USA Patriot Act, www.aclu.org/national-security/surveillance-under-usa-patriot-act.

15. See *United States v. U.S. District Court*, 407 U.S. 297 (1972) – The "Keith Case."

16. David Cole and James X. Dempsey, *Terrorism and the Constitution: Sacrificing Civil Liberties In the Name of National Security*, 3rd ed. (New York: The New Press, 2013).

17. M. Josephson, "Fourth Amendment: Must Police Knock and Announce Themselves Before Kicking in the Door of a House?" *Journal of Criminal Law and Criminology* Vol. 86, Issue 4, 1996.

18. David Cole and James X. Dempsey, *Terrorism and the Constitution*.

19. S. Herman, *Taking Liberties: The War on Terror and the Erosion of American Democracy* (New York: Oxford University Press, 2011).

20. See Adam Liptak, "Obama Administration Weighs in on State Secrets, Raising Concern on the Left," *New York Times*, August 4, 2009.

21. See Charlie Savage and David E. Sanger, "White House Tries to Prevent Judge from Ruling on Surveillance Efforts," *New York Times*, December 21, 2013.

22. "NYPD Counterterrorism Units," www.nyc.gov/html/nypd/html/administration/-counterterrorism_units.shtml.

23. Judge Roger Vinson, "In re Application of the Federal Bureau of Investigation for an Order Requiring the Production of Tangible Things from Verizon Business Network Services, Inc. on Behalf of the MCI Communication Services, Inc. d/b/a Verizon Business Services," *Top Secret order of the Foreign Intelligence Surveillance Court,* http://epic.org/privacy/nsa/Section-215-Order-to-Verizon.pdf.

24. Marjorie Cohn, "The Surveillance State: NSA Telephony Metadata Collection: Fourth Amendment Violation," January 16, 2014, http://jurist.org/forum/2014/01/marjorie-cohn-nsa-metadata.php.

25. Matt Apuzzo and Adam Goldman, "With CIA Help, NYPD Moves Covertly in Muslim Areas," Associated Press, August 23, 2011, www.ap.org/Content/AP-in-the-News/2011/With-CIA-help-NYPD-moves-covertly-in-Muslim-areas.

26. Diala Shamas and Nermeen Arastu, "Mapping Muslims: NYPD Spying and Its Impact on American Muslims," The Creating Law Enforcement Accountability & Responsibility (CLEAR) Project, City University of New York School of Law, 2012, www.law.cuny.edu/academics/clinics/immigration/clear/Mapping-Muslims.pdf.

27. Ibid.

28. "Hearing on the Fiscal Year 2014 Executive Budget for the Police Department," May 23, 2013, http://council.nyc.gov/downloads/pdf/budget/2014/execbudget/2police.pdf.

29. Sources for this box item are Matt Apuzzo and Adam Goldman, "NYPD Infiltrated Liberal Political Groups, According to New Documents," Associated Press, www.huffingtonpost.com/2012/03/23/nypd-infiltrated-liberal-political-groups_n_1374823.html; and the website of the NYPD Intelligence and Counterterrorism Bureau at www.nyc.gov/html/nypd/html/administration/counterterrorism_units.shtml.

30. Apuzzo and Goldman, "With CIA Help, NYPD Moves Covertly in Muslim Areas."

31. Justin Elliot, "Fact-Check: How the NYPD Overstated Its Counterterrorism Record," *ProPublica*, July 10, 2010, www.propublica.org/article/fact-check-how-the-nypd-overstated-its-counterterrorism-record.

32. Ben White, "NYPD Counterterror Investigations," *Harvard National Security Journal*, April 10, 2012, http://harvardnsj.org/2012/04/nypd-counterterror-investigations/.

33. J. Kayyem and S. Roberts, "War on Terrorism Will Compel Revisions to Posse Comitatus," *National Defense Magazine,* December 2002.

34. Ibid.

35. ABC News, *20/20*, "The Bunker Tapes: Alabama Hostage Standoff," May 31, 2013, http://abcnews.go.com/2020/video/bunker-tapes-alabama-hostage-standoff-19302211.

36. Ibid.

37. Somini Sengupta, "Rise of Drones in US Spurs Efforts to Limit Uses," *New York Times*, February 15, 2013, www.nytimes.com/2013/02/16/technology/rise-of-drones-in-us-spurs-efforts-to-limit-uses.html?_r=0.

38. Ben Wolfgang, "Congress Seeks to Regulate Drone Use, Looks for Bipartisan Ground," *Washington Times*, May 17, 2013, www.washingtontimes.com/news/2013/may/17/congress-seeks-regulate-drone-use/.

39. Joan Lowy, "AP-NCC Poll: A Third of the Public Fears Police Use of Drones for Surveillance Will Erode Their Privacy," Associated Press, September 27, 2013, http://ap-gfkpoll.com/uncategorized/our-latest-poll-findings-13.

40. For more information regarding this subject, see the sources used for this box item: Chris Francescani, "Domestic Drones Are Already Reshaping U.S. Crime-fighting," Reuters, March 3, 2013, www.reuters.com/article/2013/03/03/us-usa-drones-lawenforcement-idUSBRE92208W20130303 and Nidhi Subbaraman, "Swarms of Drones Could Be Next Frontier in Emergency Response," *NBC News*, January 25, 2014, www.nbcnews.com/technology/swarms-drones-could-be-next-frontier-emergency-response-2D11988741.

41. American Civil Liberties Union, "Domestic Drones," www.aclu.org/blog/tag/domestic-drones.

42. *International Convention Against Torture and Other Cruel, Inhumane and Degrading Treatment or Punishment* (1994). See United Nations, Treaty Series, Vol. 1465, p. 85.

43. Karen De Young, "Bush Approves New CIA Methods," *Washington Post*, July 21, 2007, www.washingtonpost.com/wp-dyn/content/article/2007/07/20/AR2007072001264.html. This article covers both the 2002 guidelines and the 2007 ones approved by "the second Bush."

44. The Honorable Patricia M. Wald, "Foreward" in Laurel E. Fletcher, et al., "Guantanamo and Its Aftermath" (Berkeley, CA: The Human Rights Center, International Human Rights Clinic in partnership with the Center for Human Rights, University of California, November 2008), pp. Vii–Viii, and p. 2, www.law.berkeley.edu/files/IHRLC/Guantanamo_and_Its_Aftermath.pdf.

45. Senate Select Committee on Intelligence, *Committee Study on the Central Intelligence Agency's Detention and Interrogation Program* (Washington, D.C: USGPO, declassified December 3, 2014).

46. Ibid., *Executive Summary*, p. 2.

47. Matt Apuzzo, Sheri Fink, and James Risen, "How US Torture Left a Legacy of Damaged Minds," *New York Times*, March 17, 2017, retrieved from www.nytimes.com/2016/10/09/world/cia-torture-guantanamo-bay.html.

48. Jody Warrick and Dan Eggen, "Hill Briefed on Waterboarding in 2002," *Washington Post*, December 9, 2007, www.washingtonpost.com/wp-dyn/content/article/2007/12/08/AR2007120801664.html.

49. Adolph Eichmann, one of the major architects of the Nazi Holocaust, defended himself at trial in Jerusalem by asserting he was "only following orders." In fact, Eichmann was acting on orders that were legal, but not moral. For more information on this issue, see Hannah Arendt, *Eichmann in Jerusalem: A Report on the Banality of Evil* (New York: Penguin Books, 1963).

50. John Clooman, Testimony Before the U.S. Senate of the Judiciary, Washington, D.C., "Coercive Interrogation Techniques: Do They Work, Are They Reliable, and What Did the FBI Know About Them?" June 10, 2008, www.loc.gov/rr/frd/Military_Law/pdf/Senate-Judiciary-Hearing-June-10-2008.pdf. Clooman, an FBI agent, took issue with the use of EITs.

51. These EITs are taken from a Memorandum from the Commander of Joint Task Force 170, Subject: Request for Approval of Counter-Resistance Strategies, 11 October 2002, which were approved by the Secretary of Defense on December 2, 2002. These documents can be located as described in the "Informational Link" in this chapter.

52. This common name for the report is derived from Major General Taguba, who directed the military investigation. It is formerly identified as "Article 15-5 Investigation of the 800th Military Police Brigade."

53. "Article 15-5 Investigation of the 800th Military Police Brigade," United States Army, 2004, p. 17.

54. "The Constitutional Project's Task Force on Detainee Treatment, 2013, p. 1, http://detaineetaskforce.org.

55. Greg Miller, Adam Goldman, and Ellen Nakashima, "Report Finds that the CIA Misled on Interrogation," *Washington Post*, April 1, 2014.

56. Ibid.

57. John W. Schiemann, "Interrogational Torture: Or How Good Guys Get Bad Information with Ugly Methods," *Political Research Quarterly*, Vol. 65, Issue 1, March 28, 2012, p. 3, DOI: 10.1177/1065912911430670.

58. U.S. Department of Justice, Office of Legal Council, "Memorandum for William J. Haynes II, re: Military Interrogation of Alien Unlawful Combatants Held Outside the United States," March 14, 2003, www.justice.gov/olc/docs/memo-combatantsoutsideunitedstates.pdf.

59. Sources:
    Jonathan Swan, "Trump calls for 'hell of a lot worse than waterboarding,'" *The Hill*, February 6, 2016.
    United States Army, "Cruel, Inhumane or Degrading Treatment Prohibited," United States Army Field Manuals: Human Intelligence Collector Operations, FM 2-22.3. 2006, retrieved from https://fas.org/irp/doddir/army/fm2-22-3.pdf#page=97.
    Philip Carter, "Thank the Deep State for quashing Trump's torture plans," *Slate*, February 10, 2017, retrieved from www.slate.com/articles/news_and_politics/jurisprudence/2017/02/meet_the_people_who_helped_quash_trump_s_plans_to_reinstitute_torture.html.
    Rebecca Shabad, "Jeff Sessions addresses race, Muslim Ban, and torture at confirmation hearing," *CBS News*, January 10, 2017, retrieved from www.cbsnews.com/news/jeff-sessions-senate-confirmation-hearing-attorney-general-live-blog/.

60. See www.businessinsider.com/james-mattis-trump-torture-2016-11.

61. Andrew Rosenthal, "Tortured Logic," *New York Times Taking Note Blog*, May 3, 2012, http://takingnote.blogs.nytimes.com/2012/05/03/tortured-logic/.

62. "Getting Away with Torture," *New York Times Editorial*, November 14, 2012, www.nytimes.com/2012/11/14/opinion/getting-away-with-torture.html.

63. Julian Barnes, "What Bradley Manning Leaked," *Wall Street Journal Washington Wire Blog*, August 21, 2013, http://blogs.wsj.com/washwire/2013/08/21/what-bradley-manning-leaked/.

64. Associated Press, "Bradley Manning Leak Has Had Chilling Effect on US Foreign Policy, Court Hears," *Guardian* (London), August 5, 2013, www.theguardian.com/world/2013/aug/05/bradley-manning-leak-foreign-policy-sentencing.

65. Abby Ohlheiser, "The U.S. Can't Connect a Single Death to Bradley Manning's Leaks," *The Wire*, July 31, 2013, www.thewire.com/national/2013/07/us-cant-connect-single-death-bradley-mannings-leaks/67851/.

66. See Philip Caulfield, "Chelsea Manning to Get Sex Change Treatments at Military Lockup, not Civilian Prison," *New York Daily News*, July 18, 2014, and Pauline Jelinek and Lollita C. Baldor, "Pentagon OKs Manning Treatment for Transgender," *AP Big Story*, May 14, 2014.

67. Ed Pilkington, David Smith, and Lauren Gambino, "Chelsea Manning's Prison Sentence Commuted by Barack Obama," *Guardian*, January 18, 2017; see: www.theguardian.com/us-news/2017/jan/17/chelsea-manning-sentence-commuted-barack-obama.

68. Joshua Keating, "According to WikiLeaks: The Journalistic Legacy of Bradley Manning," *Foreign Policy*, March 1, 2013, http://blog.foreignpolicy.com/posts/2013/03/01/according_to_wikileaks_the_journalistic_legacy_of_bradley_manning.

69. See Andrew Hough, "Julian Assange: WikiLeaks Founders Seeks Political Asylum from Ecuador," *Daily Telegraph*, June 19, 2012, and Nick Davies, "10 Days in Sweden: The Full Allegations against Julian Assange," *Guardian*, December 17, 2010.

70. Al Jazeera Staff, "WikiLeaks, Political Hacks and the US Election" October 23, 2016, Al Jazeera, retrieved from www.aljazeera.com/programmes/listeningpost/2016/10/wikileaks-political-hacks-election-161023102730794.html.

71. Barton Gellman and Laura Poitras, "US Intelligence Mining Data from Nine US Internet Companies in Broad Secret Program," *Washington Post*, June 6, 2013, www.washingtonpost.com/investigations/

us-intelligence-mining-data-from-nine-us-internet-companies-in-broad-secret-program/2013/06/06/3a0c0da8-cebf-11e2-8845-d970ccb04497_story.html.

72. Glenn Greenwald and Ewen MacAskill, "Boundless Informant: The NSA's Secret Tool to Track Global Surveillance Data," *Guardian* (London), June 8, 2013, www.theguardian.com/world/2013/jun/08/nsa-boundless-informant-global-datamining.

73. Barton Gellman and Jerry Markon, "Edward Snowden Says Motive Behind Leaks Was to Expose Surveillance State," *Washington Post*, June 9, 2013, www.washingtonpost.com/politics/edward-snowden-says-motive-behind-leaks-was-to-expose-surveillance-state/2013/06/09/aa3f0804-d13b-11e2-a73e-826d299ff459_story.html.

74. Ibid.

75. Ibid.

76. Much of the information in this paragraph was adapted from a timeline of Edward Snowden's revelations. See http://america.aljazeera.com/articles/multimedia/timeline-edward-snowden-revelations.html.

77. Excerpt from "Edward Snowden Says Motive Behind Leaks Was to Expose Surveillance State" from *Washington Post*, published by *Washington Post*, © 2013.

78. For more information about Edward Snowden, refer to John Cassidy, "Why Edward Snowden Is a Hero," *New Yorker,* June 10, 2013, www.newyorker.com/online/blogs/johncassidy/2013/06/why-edward-snowden-is-a-hero.html; Conor Friedersdorf, "What James Clapper Doesn't Understand About Edward Snowden," *Atlantic*, February 24, 2014, www.theatlantic.com/politics/archive/2014/02/what-james-clapper-doesnt-understand-about-edward-snowden/284032/; and David Remick, "Going the Distance: On and Off the Road with Barack Obama," *New Yorker*, January 27, 2014, www.newyorker.com/reporting/2014/01/27/140127fa_fact_remnick?currentPage=all.

79. Shaun Walker, "Edward Snowden's leave to remain in Russia extended three years," *Guardian*, January 18, 2017, retrieved from www.theguardian.com/us-news/2017/jan/18/edward-snowden-allowed-to-stay-in-russia-for-a-couple-of-years.

80. Tom Gjelten, "The Effects of the Snowden Leaks Aren't What He Intended," *National Public Radio*, September 20, 2013, www.npr.org/2013/09/20/224423159/the-effects-of-the-snowden-leaks-arent-what-he-intended.

Homeland Security

CHAPTER
11

Customs and Border Protection (CBP) is a component of the Department of Homeland Security (DHS). Border Patrol agents assigned to patrol remote areas of America's borders must be competent trackers. The CBP's elite tracking unit is referred to as the "Shadow Wolves." Membership in the unit is drawn from the Navajo, Lakota, and Blackfeet Native American tribes. The Shadow Wolves rely on traditional tracking techniques and are often used to track illegal migrants and smugglers moving through a wilderness area.
(Atomic/Alamy Stock Photo)

Learning Objectives

After completing this chapter, you should be able to:

1. Briefly state why and how the Department of Homeland Security (DHS) was created.

2. State the vision statement of DHS.

3. Explain the purpose of the Quadrennial Homeland Security Review.

4. Identify the five DHS core missions.

5. Name the steps in the DHS performance management framework.

6. State the broad purpose of Customs and Border Protection (CBP).

Introduction

This chapter focuses on the U.S. Department of Homeland Security (DHS) and its responsibilities, as well as key agencies within it. The reason to study DHS is its mission: To lead the unified national effort to protect America by deterring terrorist attacks and protecting against and responding to threats and hazards to the nation. DHS protects our national borders while welcoming lawful immigrants, visitors, and trade.[1] Understanding the organization and function of DHS is a civic responsibility. Those who protect us must be scrutinized so that in their zeal to accomplish their mission they do not also infringe upon on our rights as citizens.

The United States neither detected the oncoming 9/11 attacks nor was it prepared to deal effectively with their aftermath. To illustrate, President Bush's national security leadership met 100 times in the months before the attacks, yet terrorism was only a topic of discussion in two of those meetings.[2] Arguably, if some of the parcels of data relating to 9/11 which were "stove piped" or isolated in various agencies, had been shared and analyzed, the loss of life and destruction of property may have been mitigated to some degree or avoided altogether. As a matter of conjecture, a single key arrest may have caused the attacks to be delayed, providing further opportunity to derail them, or even aborted by the terrorists.

The 9/11 attacks inflicted terrible human losses and produced psychological wounds as well.[3] Nearly 3,000 people died, more deaths than were inflicted by the December 7, 1941, surprise attack on Pearl Harbor. Families lost loved ones in the attacks and rescuers died in desperate attempts to save trapped people. Families were left to cope with their bereavement and uncertain futures. Survivors who worked at or were visiting the Twin Towers, as well as firefighters, police officers, and utility workers, experienced high levels of continuing health problems, including alcoholism, acid reflux, sleep disturbance, and respiratory illnesses.[4] Similar results are reported for survivors and rescuers from the Pentagon on 9/11.[5]

Although mentioned in an earlier chapter, the valor of the passengers on the fourth hijacked flight is worthy of repeating as an important lesson both in courage and moral responsibility. Those passengers already knew how the other three hijacked flights had been used. They fought to give themselves a chance to live, but also to not let our enemies use their flight as another weapon against our nation. Flight 93 crashed in Shanksville, Pennsylvania, killing all aboard. It is speculated that the White House or the U.S. Capitol building, offices for members of Congress, was the terrorists' intended target. As did the people trapped in the Twin Towers, some passengers on the planes had brief conversations or left messages for loved ones as they lived out what little time they had left.[6]

Americans were anxious about their safety and security after 9/11, fearing more attacks. Many people experienced **post-traumatic stress disorder** (PTSD), while others struggled with panic attacks and other disorders. Stock markets closed for four days, and when they reopened there were significant declines. There was a precipitous drop in flights from overseas and fewer people took domestic flights.[7] Some people didn't pick up luggage that had been lost and then found, fearing it may have been booby-trapped.[8] Security screening intensified at sporting events, governmental building, and airports. Between 2001 and 2003, Trans World Airlines, U.S. Airways, United Airlines, and Air Canada all declared bankruptcy. For the first time in its history, America was fighting a non-state enemy on two fronts, Iraq and Afghanistan, which later resulted in a massive National Guard and Reserve Unit call up to active duty,[9] which further impacted American lives. What rights to extend to captured terrorists or "enemy combatants" and where they would be housed provoked important national conversations.[10] Human rights advocates unsuccessfully opposed America's use of extraordinary **rendition**—transferring captured terrorists to countries where harsh interrogation methods could be used. This may have involved over 130 prisoners sent to some 54 countries.[11]

Post-Traumatic Stress Disorder

Classically, some people involved in a terrifying, life-threatening event develop the anxiety disorder PTSD. They may relive the event frequently, have angry outbursts, dramatic bad dreams and frightening thoughts, be easily startled, or constantly seem "on edge."

Rendition

Rendition is the "handing over" or transfer of a person from one legal jurisdiction to another. Some apprehended terrorists have immediately been handed over to foreign countries to be able to use more harsh interrogation methods. Captured terrorists were placed on planes in the countries in which they were captured and taken to friendly countries where they could be interrogated using methods beyond those allowed by both U.S. military and Constitutional guidelines.

Box 11–1
President Bush Learns of the 9/11 Attacks

On September 11, 2001, as he was in route to Booker Elementary School in Sarasota, Florida, President Bush learned that a plane had hit one of the Twin Towers in New York City. Earlier he had been briefed of a nonspecific threat of a terrorist attack, but the connection of terrorism to this first plane was not immediately made. Later, while President Bush was reading to Booker students, Andrew Card whispered in his ear that a second plane struck the Twin Towers. At that point, a terrorist attack was abundantly clear. The president continued reading for perhaps another eight or nine minutes and left after commending the students for their reading ability. Although there was some discussion about President Bush not returning to the Capitol, he did so later in the day.[12]

That evening President Bush addressed the nation and vowed, "The search is underway for those who are behind these evil acts. I've directed the full resources of our intelligence and law enforcement communities to find those responsible and to bring them to justice. We will make no distinction between the terrorists who committed these acts and those who harbor them."[13]

▲ White House Chief of Staff Andrew Card interrupts President Bush to inform him of the terrorist attack on the Trade Center's Twin Towers.
(Doug Mills/AP Images)

The Department of Homeland Security: The Early Years

Eleven days after the 9/11 attacks, Pennsylvania Governor Tom Ridge was appointed as the first director of the Office of Homeland Security in the White House. His job was to develop, oversee, and coordinate a comprehensive national strategy to safeguard the country against terrorism and respond to any future attacks. Over a year later, on November 25, 2002, Public Law 107-296 created the new U.S. Department of Homeland Security (DHS) as a stand-alone agency, headed by a secretary who was to be a member of the president's cabinet.

The question has been raised because it was intelligence coordination failures that had some culpability for the 9/11 attacks, why wasn't there a major federal effort to reform America's intelligence agencies?[14] What happened instead was the creation of a sprawling new federal bureaucracy (DHS), created with some 178,000 employees and an appropriated budget of $29.28 billion.[15] Clark concluded that the real agenda was not solving a problem. Instead, politicians wanted to have the appearance of having taken swift and decisive action in light of the 9/11 catastrophes.[16]

TABLE 11–1

Movement of Agencies into the Department of Homeland Security (DHS)

Prior to 9/11, before DHS Existed	Now within DHS
The U.S. Customs Service (Treasury)	U.S. Customs and Border Protection—inspection, border, and ports of entry responsibilities
	U.S. Immigration and Customs Enforcement—customs law enforcement responsibilities
The Immigration and Naturalization Service (Justice)	U.S. Customs and Border Protection—inspection functions and the U.S. Border Patrol
	U.S. Immigration and Customs Enforcement—immigration law enforcement: detention and removal, intelligence, and investigations
	U.S. Citizenship and Immigration Services—adjudications and benefits programs
The Federal Protective Service	U.S. Immigration and Customs Enforcement (until 2009), currently resides within the National Protection and Programs Directorate
The Transportation Security Administration (Transportation)	Transportation Security Administration
Federal Law Enforcement Training Center (Treasury)	Federal Law Enforcement Training Center
Animal and Plant Health Inspection Service (part) (Agriculture)	U.S. Customs and Border Protection—agricultural imports and entry inspections
Office for Domestic Preparedness (Justice)	Responsibilities distributed within FEMA
The Federal Emergency Management Agency (FEMA)	Federal Emergency Management Agency
Strategic National Stockpile and the National Disaster Medical System (HHS)	Returned to Health and Human Services, July 2004
Nuclear Incident Response Team (Energy)	Responsibilities distributed within FEMA
Domestic Emergency Support Teams (Justice)	Responsibilities distributed within FEMA
National Domestic Preparedness Office (FBI)	Responsibilities distributed within FEMA
CBRN Countermeasures Programs (Energy)	Science & Technology Directorate
Environmental Measurements Laboratory (Energy)	Science & Technology Directorate
National BW Defense Analysis Center (Defense)	Science & Technology Directorate
Plum Island Animal Disease Center (Agriculture)	Science & Technology Directorate
Federal Computer Incident Response Center (GSA)	US-CERT, Office of Cyber Security and Communications in the National Protection and Programs Directorate
National Communications System (Defense)	Office of Cyber Security and Communications in the National Protection and Programs Directorate
National Infrastructure Protection Center (FBI)	Dispersed throughout the Department, including Office of Operations Coordination and Office of Infrastructure Protection
Energy Security and Assurance Program (Energy)	Integrated into the Office of Infrastructure Protection
U.S. Coast Guard	U.S. Coast Guard
U.S. Secret Service	U.S. Secret Service

Source: From DHS Organizational Chart. Published by U.S. Department of Homeland Security.

On March 1, 2003,* the U.S. Department of Homeland Security (DHS) became operational with parts or all of 22 different preexisting federal agencies (see Table 11–1). It was the largest reorganization of the federal bureaucracy since the **National Security Act of 1947**.[17] Some of the agencies assigned to DHS remained intact, such as the U.S. Coast Guard (USCG). Others, such as the Immigration and Naturalization Service (INS), had various units parceled out to three separate DHS organizations: U.S. Citizenship and Immigration Services (USCIS), Immigration and Customs Enforcement (ICE), and Customs and Border Protection (CBP).[18]

National Security Act of 1947

The Act reorganized the military and foreign policy elements of the federal government, including the creation of the Central Intelligence Agency (CIA). Illustratively, it also combined the War and Navy departments into the Department of Defense.

*Public Law 107-296, enacted November 25, 2002, created DHS, mandating it to take effect in 60 days (by January 24, 2003). However, March 1, 2003, is conventionally given as DHS's "inception date" and it is used here.

The creation of DHS created bureaucratic wrangling from individuals and agencies seeking to be prominently placed in it, as well as some Congressional political discontent, because of lost influence. For instance, one senator, furious about the changes, bluntly said, "Hell hath no fury like a committee chair whose jurisdiction has been taken away."[19] The numbers suggest, however, that Congressional committee chairs may have not lost any jurisdiction. More than 100 committees and subcommittees of the 112th Session of Congress (2011–2013) asserted some jurisdiction over DHS. There were 289 formal House and Senate hearings and another 28 before caucuses and commissions. Altogether, these events required 400 DHS witnesses. Congress made 4,300 inquiries or other engagements of DHS, the response to which involved 66 work years of effort at a cost of $10 million.

Grossman noted that Americans have proven supremely adept at war fighting, but not at creating long-term security bureaucracies.[20] This observation was accurate with respect to the early years at DHS, which were often politically, financially, and administratively bumpy and mostly uphill:

U.S. Government Accountability Office
The U.S. "Government" Accountability Office (GAO) is an independent, nonpartisan agency that works for Congress. Often called the "Congressional watchdog," the GAO investigates matters of concern to the Congress.

DHS Inspector General (IG)
The DHS OIG was created by Congress to ensure integrity and efficiency in the DHS. The office conducts or supervises studies and research to improve DHS administration and operations.

1. The enormity of the challenge to DHS for transforming its 22 constituent agencies and bureaus into a single agency was overwhelming. At the heart of this challenge was creating one dominant culture from 22 different cultures. In 2003, the **U.S. Government Accountability Office** (GAO) described this transformation as a "high-risk" proposition.[21] In GAO's view, this transformation and get it "up and running" quickly. Seemingly, efforts expended on one of these challenges detracted from accomplishing the other.

2. In 2002, 300 applications for aid relating to the 9/11 attacks were sent to the Federal Emergency Management Agency (FEMA), a new agency within DHS. They were sent back to the applicants stamped "Return to Sender." FEMA had forgotten to pay the rental fees for a Post Office box, adding to its reputation of failing to get things right.[22]

3. To make matters worse and add to the confusion, in 2005, a major hurricane devastated part of the Gulf Coast and particularly New Orleans—Hurricane Katrina (see Figure 11–1). The Department of Homeland Security and FEMA specifically had substantial responsibilities with respect to responding to the needs created by Hurricane Katrina. FEMA responded so slowly and performed so poorly that both DHS and FEMA came under scathing criticisms.

4. In 2006, the **DHS Inspector General (IG)** wrote a hefty 216-page report of FEMA's performance in the aftermath of Hurricane Katrina, confirming most of the criticisms, including that it took three days before FEMA understood the magnitude of the disaster, it was ill-equipped to conduct massive search and rescue operations, and FEMA workers had to order twice as many supplies as they needed because they had no confidence in their delivery system.[23] Another report concluded that state and local first responders were not adequately trained to handle large-scale disasters because FEMA had awarded 75 percent of its grant money for terrorist training.[24]

5. Senator Dayton (D-MN) claimed that the performance of FEMA before and after Katrina was "so dysfunctional or nonproductive it was frightening."[25] His observation underscored just how much of a high risk transforming DHS with new agencies like FEMA would be. Following the Katrina debacle, there was some Congressional sentiment to disband FEMA or remove it from DHS.[26] In the end, FEMA remained in DHS.

6. In 2012, as Hurricane Sandy plowed through the Atlantic Ocean toward the upper East Coast (see Figure 11–2), President Obama issued 25 emergency declarations for states. It was a chance for FEMA to redeem its image and demonstrate its nimbleness. Initially, FEMA received high marks for its efforts, but as time wore on, complaints became more common and familiar. Unfair

FIGURE 11–1
An aerial view of a portion of New Orleans. During Hurricane Katrina. In 2005, Hurricane Katrina caused levees, which had long protected New Orleans, to fail, producing catastrophic flooding. Some people waited too long to evacuate and retreated to their rooftops. There they waited to be rescued, attracting attention by making signs or waving to attract rescuers. As houses were cleared, their roofs were spray painted with US&R (Urban Search and Rescue) to avoid wasted effort in repeatedly visiting that home to check for survivors.
(Mary Bahamonde/Federal Emergency Management Agency)

comparisons were made to Hurricane Katrina in New Orleans. The reality is that FEMA has significantly improved since 2005. In mass catastrophes, inevitably there will be some mistakes because of the sheer volume of work that has to be done perfectly every time in an emotionally charged atmosphere.

7. Agencies were included in DHS whether or not it made sense—for example, the Secret Service, with a primary mission of protecting the president, became part of DHS, whereas more security-related agencies, such as the FBI and Central Intelligence Agency (CIA), "stayed outside."[27]

8. DHS grants to state and local governments were distributed without any analysis of whether the jurisdiction was rationally "at risk." One example of this is a small Vermont town of 18,000 that got a truck capable of boring through concrete to find survivors. Some grant funds were diverted by recipients to non-terrorism programs, such as a popular mayor's summer intern program and a computerized car-towing program to prevent fraud from private towing companies.[28] There is, however, no record of systematic fraud.

9. Many DHS agencies had never worked closely with their new "brothers and sisters" and numerous new routines had to be created, as well as clarifying the mission of each agency to eliminate competition and duplication of effort. They also had to agree upon how various terms would be defined so they could "speak the same language."

10. The 22 agencies DHS "inherited" had different operational and management systems that conflicted with or duplicated other capabilities. Across these agencies there were numerous areas that needed consolidation, which was time consuming. To illustrate, in the beginning there were 19 different financial centers, 22 human resource offices, and 27 different bankcard programs. In the absence of a single and mature procurement system, some misconduct occurred. One program official bought $500,000 in art and silk plants from a tool company that had never previously sold such merchandise.

11. DHS funding was not sufficient to perform all functions. For example, it could not take the lead in consolidating terrorist watch list information.[29] The imperative of making rapid progress meant, in retrospect, some decisions were made too quickly or initially overlooked entirely. Too often, the focus was overwhelmingly on protecting the homeland from terrorist attacks to the neglect of other responsibilities, such as the previously mentioned lack of training for state and local first responders for natural disasters.

12. The ability of DHS's human capital to lead the transformation was suspect. Only 93 of 175 program managers were certified (53 percent) to perform those duties. Although political appointees proliferate in bureaucracies, DHS accumulated "political hacks" far beyond what had been seen in any federal agency.[30]

13. In 2005, there was still no DHS unit tasked with the responsibility of establishing policies and procedures for program management.[31]

FIGURE 11–2
A portion of the damage done as Hurricane Sandy struck Union Beach, New Jersey, in 2012.
(Liz Roll/FEMA)

The Present Organization of DHS

DHS can no longer be described as a "high-risk proposition." It is a maturing organization that has overcome the initial hurdles facing it. An organization's vision statement is the most overarching statement that explains what it hopes to be or achieve. It may be written in such a way that it cannot ever be achieved and must be endlessly pursued. The DHS vision statement is: *A homeland that is safe, secure, and resilient against terrorism and other hazards, where American interests, aspirations, and way of life can thrive.*[32]

One impressionistic way of determining, in a preliminary way, if an organization's resources are aligned with its vision statement is to assess whether the structure facilitates

U.S. Department of Homeland Security

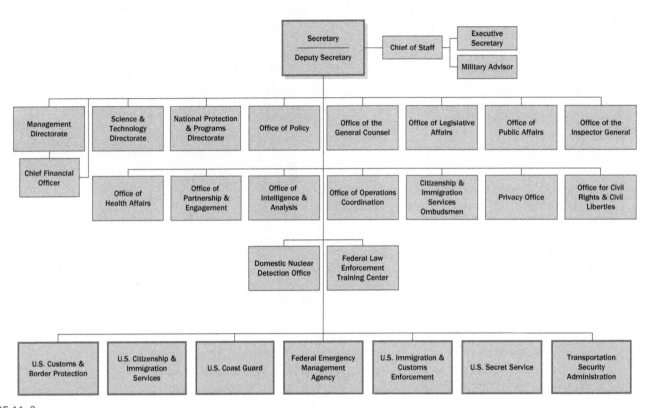

FIGURE 11–3
The DHS Organizational Chart

Source: (DHS Organizational Chart, February 1, 2017, www.dhs.gov/ sites/default/files/publications/ Department%20Org%20Chart_2.pdf.)

achieving the vision. A well-constructed organizational chart is visual depiction of an orga-nization, revealing such things as how work is organized, the function each unit performs, the distribution of authority, the relative hierarchical standing of the leaders of various units, and the lines of communication. Figure 11–3 is the organizational chart for DHS. Each "box" is a unit.

Note the number of specialized staff units in Figure 11–3 such as the Office of Policy, which will have fewer people staffing it as compared to the more heavily populated line units. Staff units, like finance, support line units, relieving them of many administrative duties. In turn, line units do the work for which the agency was created and are illustrated by the bottom tier on the organization chart with units such as Customs and Border Protection (CBP), the U.S. Coast Guard (USCG), and the Transportation Security Administration (TSA), which is commonly seen as we travel through airports. Each unit in Figure 11–3 will also have its own organizational chart, as will its subunits.

Organizational charts are relatively stable as agencies are "captured" by the roles assigned to them. This results in changes often being marginal or incremental. To illustrate, the Border Patrol may change its procedures, tactics, and use new technology, but their role is legislatively mandated and the budget enacted by the Congress for the Border Patrol also creates obligations for it to do even more specific things.

The Quadrennial Homeland Security Review (QHSR)

Beginning in 2010, the Department of Homeland Security produced a QHDR every four years. The most recent of these is the QHSR 2014–2018. It reflects a deep analysis of the evolving strategic environment and outlines the specific changes necessary to keep our nation secure. The QHSR assessed the threats and challenges DHS faces and is crucial to intelligence gathering, strategic planning, research, programs, performance goals, budget-ing, recruitment, training, and operations.

To illustrate, among the QHSR evolving risks identified later in this section is that terrorism is becoming decentralized. Some lone wolf attacks are based on personal,

Box 11-2
Decentralized Terrorist Attack in Garland, Arizona

In 2015, a cartoon drawing contest of the Prophet Muhammad was held in Garland, Arizona. Abdul Malik Abdul Kareem supplied guns to the two attackers, both of whom were killed by police officers in a gunfight outside of the convention building. The contest was provocative, even offensive, to some Muslims, but didn't warrant trying to murder numerous people attending the convention. The two officers are boxing up an AR15 used by one of the attackers. Note the yellow evidence cones. The gun supplier didn't accompany the attackers, but got 30 years in jail for facilitating terrorism.

(Brandon Wade/AP Images)

idiosyncratic beliefs rather than rooted in terrorist ideology. However, many are conducted as a result of the propaganda of some groups, such as the Islamic State, that encourage lone wolf attacks through their online videos and social media pages. Other attacks come from people who simply identify with terrorist dogma and act without direction or assistance from a terrorist movement.

Confronting decentralized terrorism gives rise to a series of questions. What are the motives, targets, and other characteristics of decentralized terrorism? Which of our partners in other agencies, academia, and elsewhere should we involve in this discussion? What programmatic options do we have? Scotland has a very low incidence of terrorism. What can we learn from them? What must we be able to do to counter this evolving risk? Do we now have the necessary skills? If not, what kind of skills do we need to develop or recruit? Does our organizational structure facilitate prompt action? Are our policies aligned with dealing with this threat? Do new delegations of authority need to be made? How do we balance resources between prevention and remediation? Two sections from the QHSR (2014–2018) follow: evolving risks in a changing world and strategic priorities for homeland security.

For DHS, key drivers of risks suggest several prevailing strategic challenges that will drive homeland security risk during 2014–2018. Many of these risk patterns are more thoroughly discussed in Chapter 15, relating to terrorism in the future:

1. The terrorist threat is evolving and remains significant as attack planning and operations become more decentralized. The United States and its interests, particularly in the transportation sector, remain persistent targets.

2. Growing cyber threats are significantly increasing risk to critical infrastructure and to the greater U.S. economy.

3. Biological concerns, including bioterrorism, pandemics, foreign animal diseases, and other agricultural concerns, endure as a top homeland security risk because of both potential likelihood and impacts.

4. Nuclear terrorism through the introduction and use of an improvised nuclear device, while unlikely, remains an enduring risk because of its potential consequences.

5. Transnational criminal organizations are increasing in strength and capability, driving risk in counterfeit goods, human trafficking, illicit drugs, and other illegal flows of people and goods.

6. Natural hazards are becoming more costly to address, with increasingly variable consequences driven by trends such as climate change and aging infrastructure.[33]

Box 11–3
U.S. Customs Seizes Counterfeit Goods

U.S. Customs seized 7,800 pairs of fake Ferragamo shoes in Long Beach, California. Had they been genuine, their market value would have been $4.3 million. If there is money to be made, counterfeit goods will be made. A small sample of items counterfeited include Glock magazines, condoms, tools, Louis Vuitton purses, prom and bridal dresses, electronics, baby carriages, children's toys, pharmaceuticals, and watches. The sale of counterfeit goods is one of the ways terrorist movements fund themselves.

(U.S. Customs Border Protection)

Strategic Priorities for Homeland Security

DHS and its partners will use the QHSR as a guide for the execution of its collective responsibilities and continued integration across its strategic priorities:

1. Address the evolving terrorist threat by focusing on enhancing Department of Homeland Security and partner capabilities abroad, and while at home, strengthening our understanding of possible indicators that someone is planning violence, and using that knowledge to help prevent mass-casualty attacks.

2. Strengthen cybersecurity by breaking down traditional barriers between cybersecurity and physical security, enhancing our investigative and incident response capabilities, and leveraging innovative technologies that work at the speed of cyberspace to support our partners across government and the private sector in securing their networks.

3. Manage the urgent and growing risk of biological threats and hazards through a homeland security strategy to prevent the occurrence of priority biological incidents where possible; but, when unable to prevent, to stop priority biological incidents from overwhelming the capacity of our state, local, tribal, and territorial partners to manage and respond.

4. Adopt a risk segmentation approach to securing and managing flows of people and goods that prioritizes facilitation of legal trade and travel while minimizing disruptions, targets illicit finance and increases organization's risk perception for market driven problems, and prevents entry of terrorists, diseases, and invasive species.

5. Improve mission execution through more agile, innovative, and effective public–private partnerships.

6. Continue our efforts to prevent a nuclear device from entering the United States.

7. Continue to evolve immigration policies and processes to respond to new trends in illegal migration and further align our enforcement policies with our goal of sound law enforcement practice that prioritizes public safety.

8. Continue to build resilient communities by implementing the National Preparedness System, consistent with the whole community approach to emergency management.[34]

The QHSR validated much of what DHS was already doing, but it also created an imperative to improve those things and modify or create new missions.

The Core Missions of DHS

DHS has five core missions, which are further articulated by their associated goals. These missions are:

Mission 1: Preventing Terrorism and Enhancing Security

Protecting the American people from terrorist threats is our founding principle and our highest priority. The Department of Homeland Security's counterterrorism responsibilities focus on three goals:

Goal 1-1: Prevent terrorist attacks
America's security forces have been successful interrupting terrorist attacks before they were implemented. We should be grateful for the sacrifices they and families make. National security and public safety personnel work long hours, often under harsh conditions. For reasons discussed in an earlier chapter, preventing apparent lone wolf attacks is very difficult unless the person does something to call attention to him/herself. Inevitably, some attacks by lone wolves and small cells will be successful. We cannot even be sure if the absence of attacks is due to excellent work security forces or an absence of intent by our enemies.

Denver Transit Officer Scott Von Lanken was murdered in early 2017 as he helped two women who were concerned they may have missed the last light rail trip to their destination. A recent convert to Islam walked up behind Officer Lanken and killed him with a gunshot to the head. Lanken had been a pastor for 30 years in several different states. The alleged killed was apprehended, described himself as a radical Muslim, and had been dismissed from a mosque in Texas. He was apprehended within 30 minutes without any incident. There is an apprehension that police officers are being targeted by radicals.

Goal 1-2: Prevent the unauthorized acquisition, importation, movement, or use of chemical, biological, radiological, and nuclear materials and capabilities within the United States.

Goal 1-3: Reduce the vulnerability of critical infrastructure and key resources, essential leadership, and major events to terrorist attacks and other hazards.

Mission 2: Secure and Manage Our Borders

The Department of Homeland Security secures the nation's air, land, and sea borders to prevent illegal activity while facilitating lawful travel and trade. The Department's border security and management efforts focus on three interrelated goals:

Goal 2-1: Effectively secure U.S. air, land, and sea points of entry;

Goal 2-2: Safeguard and streamline lawful trade and travel; and

Goal 2-3: Disrupt and dismantle transnational criminal and terrorist organizations.

Mission 3: Enforce and Administer Our Immigration Law

The Department is focused on smart and effective enforcement of U.S. immigration laws while streamlining and facilitating the legal immigration process.

The Department has fundamentally reformed immigration enforcement, prioritizing the identification and removal of criminal aliens who pose a threat to public safety and targeting employers who knowingly and repeatedly break the law. Four interrelated goals are:

Goal 3-1: Smart and effective enforcement;

Goal 3-2: Facilitate legal immigration;

Goal 3-3: Combat human smuggling and trafficking; and

Goal 3-4: Fulfill other department responsibilities

Mission 4: Safeguard and Secure Cyberspace

The Department has the lead for the federal government for securing civilian government computer systems, and works with industry and state, local, tribal, and territorial

1. Mexico may no longer be where most illegal immigrants originate.[35] In 2016, roughly 50 percent were Mexicans, but substantial numbers came from Central and South America, as well as Asia. In 2016, 2,867 people from India and 1,498 from China were apprehended while attempting an illegal border crossing. More non-Mexicans than Mexicans tried to entry this country illegally.

2. Of approximately 11 million illegal Mexicans living in the United States, 2.7 percent have been convicted of felonies. Most illegal Mexicans are long-term residents of this country.

3. In 2016, 1,222 persons entered Canada from the United States seeking asylum. That number is five times the 2015 figure.

4. The number of illegal Mexicans living in the United States has declined by 1 million since 2007.

5. A larger number of people attempting illegal crossings have ties to gangs or drug cartels. Although other illegal crossers have few skills, little education, and at best modest savings, they are like many of the colonists who came to what was later this country: Born elsewhere with few opportunities, seeking a better life, and willing to work hard.

governments to secure critical infrastructure and information systems. The Department focuses on three goals:

Goal 4-1: Analyze and reduce cyber threats and vulnerabilities;

Goal 4-2: Distribute threat warnings; and

Goal 4-3: Coordinate the response to cyber incidents to ensure that our computers, networks, and cyber systems remain safe.

Mission 5: Ensure Resilience to Disasters

The Department of Homeland Security provides the coordinated, comprehensive federal response in the event of a terrorist attack, natural disaster, or other large-scale emergency while working with federal, state, local, and private sector partners to ensure a swift and effective recovery effort. The Department builds a ready and resilient nation through efforts to:

Goal 5-1: Bolster information sharing and collaboration;

Goal 5-2: Provide grants, plans, and training to our homeland security and law enforcement partners; and

Goal 5-3: Facilitate rebuilding and recovery.[36]

DHS: Missions and Performance Management

Carefully written mission statements with corresponding goals mean nothing if the desired results are not achieved. The effectiveness of an agency rests on performance management, which involves the continuous monitoring and steering of a unit's performance toward achieving its missions and goals. Inadequate funding is an impediment to achieving those missions and goals.

DHS Performance Management

Like other organizations, the DHS was created to do the things people cannot do for themselves. This means its behavior must be purposeful and result in certain end states. To assess whether federal agencies are fulfilling their mandates, Congress passed the Government Performance and Results Act of 1993 (GPRA). Subsequently, it was modified by the GPRA Modernization Act of 2010. Among its most important features are:

1. Strategic plans must be for at least four years and aligned with presidential terms;

2. Annual performance goals must be linked to the strategic plan, which can be amended if changed circumstances warrant it;

3. Agencies must at least annually, or more frequently as needed, provide the Office of Management and Budget (OMB) with agency performance updates, formerly

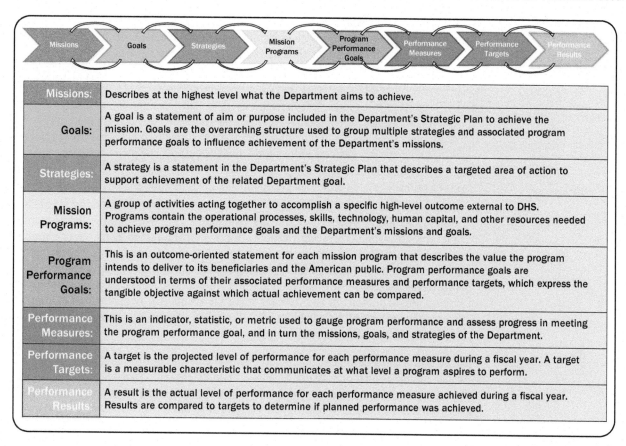

Missions:	Describes at the highest level what the Department aims to achieve.
Goals:	A goal is a statement of aim or purpose included in the Department's Strategic Plan to achieve the mission. Goals are the overarching structure used to group multiple strategies and associated program performance goals to influence achievement of the Department's missions.
Strategies:	A strategy is a statement in the Department's Strategic Plan that describes a targeted area of action to support achievement of the related Department goal.
Mission Programs:	A group of activities acting together to accomplish a specific high-level outcome external to DHS. Programs contain the operational processes, skills, technology, human capital, and other resources needed to achieve program performance goals and the Department's missions and goals.
Program Performance Goals:	This is an outcome-oriented statement for each mission program that describes the value the program intends to deliver to its beneficiaries and the American public. Program performance goals are understood in terms of their associated performance measures and performance targets, which express the tangible objective against which actual achievement can be compared.
Performance Measures:	This is an indicator, statistic, or metric used to gauge program performance and assess progress in meeting the program performance goal, and in turn the missions, goals, and strategies of the Department.
Performance Targets:	A target is the projected level of performance for each performance measure during a fiscal year. A target is a measurable characteristic that communicates at what level a program aspires to perform.
Performance Results:	A result is the actual level of performance for each performance measure achieved during a fiscal year. Results are compared to targets to determine if planned performance was achieved.

FIGURE 11–4
The DHS Performance Management Framework
This framework can be used in any number of settings. Understanding the basic concepts in this figure provides a good initial understanding of performance management.
(Courtesy Department of Homeland Security, DHS Annual Performance Report, Fiscal Years 2015–2017, p. 4, www.dhs.gov/sites/default/files/publications/15-17-APR.pdf, accessed April 30, 2017.)

called program performance reports. OMB is part of the Executive Office of the President; and

4. If an agency does not achieve its desired outcomes for a specific performance plan for three consecutive years, OMB can recommend defunding the activities involved. In years one, two, and three, OMB is authorized, in coordination with the agency, to take action that will foster improvement and avoid defunding.

The DHS Performance Management Framework is summarized in Figure 11–4. It is an integrated system that links the department's missions through a series of steps that begins with missions and goals, concluding with the determination of what level of performance results were achieved.

DHS Performance Evaluation

DHS will always have serious challenges because of its significant responsibilities, some of which are central to the survival of our nation. DHS will and must consistently receive scrutiny and there will be some criticisms. Senator Tom Coburn, who serves on the Committee on Homeland Security and Governmental Affairs, issued his individual assessment of DHS in 2015. Among his criticisms were:

1. DHS's primary counterterrorism programs are yielding little value for the nation's counterterrorism efforts. FEMA spent more than $39 billion on homeland security grants, originally intended to improve our ability to prevent terrorist attacks, and DHS has not effectively tracked how these dollars were spent.

2. The nation's borders remain unsecure. DHS has very few resources deployed to control thousands of miles of our border with Canada and vulnerable to illegal entry. In 2014, 700 miles of the Southern border were not secure because assets had not been deployed there, and DHS struggles to fulfill its mission to secure our ports.

3. DHS is not effectively administering or enforcing the nation's immigration laws and some immigration programs have significant vulnerabilities. DHS has not effectively tracked people who overstay their visas. Lax enforcement creates an expectation that people can violate our immigration law with no consequences. The department has also struggled with vetting, processing, and monitoring immigration benefits for noncitizens.

4. DHS struggles to execute its cybersecurity responsibilities and its strategies and programs are unlikely to protect us from adversaries that pose the greatest cybersecurity threat. DHS spends $700 million annually on a range of cybersecurity programs. Repeated Inspector General audits found that DHS offices and employees do not always comply with federal rules and policies for agency cybersecurity. DHS cybersecurity focuses primarily on mitigation, while our adversaries continuously develop new tools.

5. DHS is federalizing the response to manmade and natural disasters by subsidizing state, local, and private sector activity. Oversight of FEMA programs shows increasing levels of expenditures with little evidence that the nation is better prepared or more resilient to natural disasters. Some $37.6 billion of expenditures were related to Hurricane Katrina. Much of this spending is focused on subsidizing state, local, and private sector emergency management, including public safety, cleanup and rebuilding efforts, and after-the-fact disaster relief for events that occurred weeks, months, and years ago, as well as subsidizing flood insurance for people who continue to build and rebuild in flood-prone areas.[37]

Recall this is the assessment of an individual senator and not the findings of a committee, whose members may or may not have endorsed its content. That fact that the senator is one person should not persuade us he is wrong or right. One person advanced the theory of relativity, Albert Einstein. Senator Coburn's criticisms often rest on broad, general terms. In his first point, just exactly how much is "little value" and how much would the needle need to move to be in the "Some value range"? In point 2, DHS "struggles" to protect our ports. Does that mean they are protected, 86 percent, but not 100 percent? What we lack in evaluating Senator Coburn's criticisms is the point-by-point response, which DHS surely would have made. In balance, Senator Coburn notes that FEMA has improved its ability to quickly mobilize and render assistance after Hurricane Katrina.[38]

A 2016 Congressional Research Service Report concluded that DHS grants were being audited and evaluated, although that process is "evolving."[39] The report left unanswered the question of the effectiveness of the grants. It also raised the question whether after $33 billion in grants to state and local governments, should they now be prepared and able to take on responsibility for maintaining programs?[40] The American Civil Liberties Union (ACLU) praised DHS in 2014 for how it safeguards citizens' personal information, a cybersecurity issue.[41] The General Accountability Office in 2015 recognized "exemplary progress" in DHS making needed improvements. Two years later, the GAO praised federal efforts to safeguard the electrical grid in 2017, including contributions by DHS.[42] The Chairman of the Senate Committee on Homeland Security and Government Affairs "applauded" DHS's initiative in creating a Victims of Immigrant Crime Engagement Office (VOICE) in that same year.[43]

As is often the case in such matters, the performance of DHS is not bifurcated, either "poor" or "good." It's mixed. As an aside, evaluating the performance of an organization requires education, experience, open-mindedness, being even-handed, isolating strengths and performance deficits, determining how to sustain high performance, recognizing barriers to performance, and identifying pathways to improvement. Finally, while many barriers are organic, such as people being inadequately trained for their duties, other barriers are in the larger system, for example, legislation may need to be amended or enacted.

Information Link
For more information relating to the history and agencies within the U.S. Department of Homeland Security, visit the homepage at www.dhs.gov. There is also a continuing flow of current announcements and news.

DHS Funding

A budget is a plan stated in financial terms. It is also an agreement or contract between those who appropriate the funds and those who receive them. Appropriators have the reasonable expectation that if DHS requests funds to do certain things, such as hire and train 200 new Border Patrol Agents, it will in fact do so if the request is approved.

In Fiscal Year 2017 (FY'17, October 1, 2016–September 30, 2017), DHS's budget was just short of $50 billion dollars with 226,000 employees[44] deployed to every state and 75 foreign countries (see Figure 11–5 and Table 11–2).[45] A budget also reveals the priorities of an organization. In 2017, just five agencies—CBP, the Federal Emergency Management Agency/FEMA, the U.S. Coast Guard/USCG, the Transportation Security Administration/TSA, and Immigration and Customs Enforcement/ICE—accounted for approximately 78 percent of the requested budget (see Figure 11–5). Table 11–2 explains the acronyms used in Figure 11–5.

Historically, DHS has been a well-funded organization. Under the present administration, it is likely to retain that status, given that the president is concerned about securing our borders and extraditing illegal immigrants who have committed crimes. Early in his administration, the president issued an executive order to withhold funds from sanctuary jurisdictions and a federal district court issued a preliminary injunction (2017), blocking implementation of the executive order.

Major DHS Agencies

The major operational DHS components identified in Table 11–2 are discussed in this section; however, support and administrative units are not. The units discussed include the (1) U.S. Customs and Border Protection, (2) Federal Emergency Management Agency, (3) U.S. Coast Guard, (4) Transportation Security Administration, (5) U.S. Secret Service, (6) Immigration and Customs Enforcement, and (7) U.S. Citizenship and Immigration Services.

Customs and Border Protection (CBP)

Broadly, the purpose of CBP is to prevent harmful individuals and substances from entering the United States. This includes terrorists, criminals, illegal immigrants, and drugs, weapons, and other contraband, as well as harmful pests and diseases. A major CBP responsibility is regulating international trade, collecting import duties, enforcing trade laws, and protecting U.S. businesses from counterfeit goods and the theft of intellectual

TABLE 11–2
Understanding DHS Acronyms

Acronyms	Budget Units
A&O	Analysis and Operations
CBP	Customs and Border Protection
Depart. Ops	Departmental Operations
DNDO	Domestic Nuclear Detection Office
FEMA	Federal Emergency Management Agency
FLETC	Federal Law Enforcement Training Center
ICE	Immigration and Customs Enforcement
NPPD	National Protection and Programs Directorate
OHA	Office of Health Affairs
OIG	Office of Inspector General
S&T	Science and Technology Directorate
TSA	Transportation Security Administration
USCIS	U.S. Citizenship and Immigration Services
USCG	U.S. Coast Guard
USSS	U.S. Secret Service

Source: Department of Homeland Security, Budget-In-Brief 2017, www.dhs.gov/sites/default/files/publications/FY2017_BIB-MASTER.pdf.

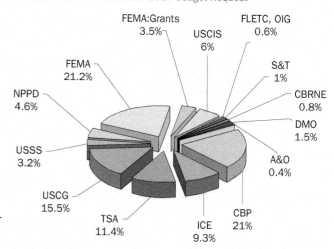

FIGURE 11–5
Pie Chart for DHS Fiscal Year 2017 Budget Request

FEMA:Grants 3.5%
FLETC, OIG 0.6%
USCIS 6%
FEMA 21.2%
S&T 1%
CBRNE 0.8%
NPPD 4.6%
DMO 1.5%
A&O 0.4%
USSS 3.2%
CBP 21%
USCG 15.5%
ICE 9.3%
TSA 11.4%

FIGURE 11-6
Motorists lined up at the border crossing in San Ysidro, California. It is the busiest land border crossing point in the world. Daily, 90,000 people pass through it.
(U.S. General Services Administration)

Agro-terrorism
Malicious acts directed at the agricultural or food supply system in the United States.

Texas Rangers
In 1823, when Texas was still part of Mexico, Stephen Austin gained permission to employ ten men to range over the territory and scout for Indian threats. These men were the first of the Texas Rangers.

Point of Entry (POE)
A specific location where one may lawfully enter the United States; typically where passports and visa are inspected (e.g., international airports, seaports).

Speakeasies
Unlicensed bars operating during the prohibition era gained the name of speakeasies because patrons desiring to enter were allegedly told to knock and softly say (speak easy) the password.

Blind pigs
In modern use, unlicensed bars that sell alcohol to patrons after legal bars have closed. Gambling and prostitution are activities in some blind pigs.

property,[46] such as software. CBP also works to prevent and intercept the illegal export of U.S. currency and other monetary instruments, stolen goods, and strategically sensitive technologies,[47] such as advanced radar. CBP began as a legal DHS entity on March 1, 2003, by transfers into it from:

1. The U.S. Border Patrol and the Inspections Program (IP), both of which were in the Immigration and Naturalization Service (INS), a unit in the Department of Justice. IP inspectors determined whether people seeking to enter the United States through a point-of-entry (POEs) are entitled to do so (see Figure 11–6).

2. The largest industry and employer in the United States is agriculture with more than $1 trillion in annual economic activity.[48] Nearly one in six jobs is linked to it.[49] Invasive species that slip into America cause an annual loss of $136 billion.[50] Agriculture is also a potential target for **agro-terrorism** because of its vulnerability: It is the least protected potential target.[51] Agro-terrorism is not new; the ancient Assyrians (1400–600 B.C.) poisoned enemy wells, and during World War I, German agents in the United States infected horses and cattle bound for the war effort in France.[52] About 2,300 plant protection inspectors were transferred from the Department of Agriculture to DHS (See Figure 3–7).

3. Approximately 2,500 people "came over" to DHS from the U.S. Customs Service in the Department of Treasury. Their role in CBP was to collect entry duties and tariffs and to prevent fraud. Investigators from the U.S. Customs Service became part of DHS's U.S. Immigration and Customs Enforcement (ICE) unit.

Customs and Border Protection: Legacy Agencies

Agencies that existed prior to the formation of DHS and "came over" to it, in part or whole, are called "legacy agencies." The two largest legacy agencies for CBP were U.S. Customs and the Border Patrol. Because of their sheer size, a brief, pre-DHS history of them is warranted. The U.S. Customs Service (USCS) was created in 1789 by the First Congress, making it the oldest federal agency.[53] The United States was in dire financial straits and on the brink of bankruptcy.[54] Six days after becoming operational, Customs collected its first duty, $774 on a cargo of miscellaneous goods from Italy; in its first year it collected approximately $2 million, a substantial boost for the cash-strapped government.[55] The customs service assesses and collects duties and taxes on imported goods, controls carriers of imports and exports, and combats smuggling and revenue fraud.[56] As early as 1904 "Mounted Guards," which were part of the U.S. Immigration Service, patrolled the border from Texas to California.[57] Never numbering more than 75 people, the patrolling was secondary to their immigration duties and therefore the border was only protected on an irregular basis.[58] The army and the **Texas Rangers** also patrolled the border episodically during this period.[59] The Immigration Act of 1907 required all immigrants entering the United States to pass through an official **port of entry (POE)**, submit themselves for inspection, and receive official authorization to legally enter the United States.[60]

The 18th Amendment to the U.S. Constitution, which went into effect in 1920, prohibited the importation, transportation, manufacture, or sale of alcoholic beverages. "Rum runners" brought "booze" in by sea while bootleggers smuggled it into the United States by land or transported it from illegal distilleries in America to "**speakeasies**" or "**blind pigs**," where it was illegally sold to drinkers. To no small degree, the 18th Amendment was an impetus to the creation of the U.S. Border Patrol in 1924[†] and expansion of its jurisdiction

---

[†]An excellent history of the Border Patrol is Kelly Lytle Hernandez, *Migra!* (Berkeley, California: University of California Press, 2010). The National Border Patrol Museum is in El Paso, Texas.

to the sea the following year. Ten years after its formation, the first Border Patrol Academy was held in Camp Chigas, El Paso, with an emphasis on horsemanship and marksmanship.[61] The role of the Border Patrol has been securing the border between POE inspection stations, particularly along America's southern border with Mexico.[62] Although Border Patrol Officers "patrolled the line"—the border with Mexico—they were also involved with liquor law violations, smuggling, and other violations of the law during prohibition. Away from the border during those early years, they used a "Mexican appearance" as a surrogate for an illegal border crosser,[63] a tactic referred to today as racial profiling.

Customs and Border Protection Activities

CBP has responsibility for approximately 5,000 miles of border with Canada, 1,900 miles with Mexico, and 95,000 miles of shoreline.[64] Watching for boats and land crossings is not sufficient because drug smugglers and human traffickers also use tunnels they have dug. In the air, drugs are being smuggled by ultralights (see Figure 11–8) and hang gliders. The ultralights may land or make a drop from the air to waiting confederates. Customs and Border Protection (CBP) officers, who number 22,910,[65] are law enforcement personnel who work at POEs (e.g., international airports, seaports, and land crossings), performing physical checks of travelers, luggage, cargo, containers, ships, and commercial and passenger vehicles.

Within CBP there are also 19,282 Border Patrol agents[66] with law enforcement authority. They retain their customary role of protecting the areas between POEs (see Figure 11–9). It has been estimated that presently there are 10.9 million undocumented migrants living in the United States.[67] Other resources of the CBP are 639 Air Interdiction Agents/Pilots, 334 Marine Interdiction Officers, and 2,416 agricultural specialists.[68] Daily, CBP deploys 1,462 canine teams and 400 horse patrols, and flies 217 hours of law enforcement air missions over the United States.[69]

The combined activity produced by CBP's 42,192 personnel with law enforcement powers is staggering. Annually, they process 390 million travelers a year at POEs, make 416,000 arrests, apprehend 8,030 wanted criminals, identify 320,150 persons with suspected national security concerns, refuse admission to 274,480 individuals, and seize 2.8 million pounds of drugs and $105 million in undeclared or illicit currency.[70]

FIGURE 11–7
A CBP agricultural inspection officer checks cut flowers for pests and drugs. Ninety percent of Valentine's Day gifts of flowers are imported, the majority from Columbia and Ecuador. England, Spain, and the United States are among the nations that have found drugs hidden in imported flowers. One technique is to cut a stem, insert drugs, and glue the stem back together.
(U.S. Customs and Border Protection)

FIGURE 11–8
An ultralight seized by U.S. Border Patrol Agents. The aircraft was loaded with 189 pounds of marijuana and 12 pounds of methamphetamine, together worth $557,650.
(U.S. Customs and Border Protection)

FIGURE 11–9

Border Patrol Officer has just jumped out of a patrol boat on the Rio Grande River separating Mexico and the United States. He is in hot pursuit of an illegal immigrant. The officer saw the man swim the last few strokes and then scramble ashore in the United States as the patrol boat approached.

(U.S. Customs and Border Protection)

Tunnel rats are members of the Border Patrol's Border Tunnel Entry Team (See Figure 11–10). Between 1990 and March 2016, authorities discovered 224 tunnels that originated in Mexico.[71] One incomplete tunnel was 70 feet below the surface, 2,700 feet long, equipped with rail, lighting, water pumping, and ventilation systems.[72] Tunnels are three to four feet wide, take six months to a year to complete, and cost between $1 and $2 million[73] if they are well developed. Most tunnels enter California or Arizona. Because the strong odor of marijuana is hard to conceal, the tunnels are mainly used to move tons of it. However, the tunnels are also used for human trafficking.

Tunnels start and end in homes or warehouses in industrial areas. People coming and going from warehouses in trucks is a common sight and helps cloak the operation. False walls and floors may be built to conceal a tunnel opening in a warehouse. As may be needed, some drug smugglers make any needed repairs to walls or floors and paint them after receiving each shipment to maintain a high level of concealment.

Being a tunnel rat is a dangerous job. The rat may encounter someone unexpectedly, cave-ins could trap them, and the ventilation system may be inadequate. Going into the tunnel, they wear special harnesses and carry meters to gauge the air. Specially trained tunnel rescue personnel are at the tunnel to extract rats by lines attached to their harnesses or take other needed action. Rats enter and map the tunnel, gather intelligence, and when they come back up, the tunnel will be filled with concrete after the investigation is complete.

Arizona's border region next to Mexico is largely a desert basin dotted with rugged mountains.[74] During much of the last century, the Border Patrol worked the area using their personal knowledge of it, trying to interpret tracks on the ground.[75] Were they made by a lost family who needed help or well-armed drug smugglers?[76] One veteran of that era likened working conditions to a doing surgery in a dark room.[77] One strategy to better secure the border was a substantial infusion of technology (see Figure 11–11). Radar was linked to cameras, night vision goggles were procured, unattended ground sensors (UGS) were deployed, color video surveillance cameras with long distance/thermal imaging were placed to cover miles of remote areas covered by fences, and where they were impractical to construct, radiation detection devices were distributed throughout the area, and manned aircraft and drones provide actionable intelligence.

FIGURE 11–10
A Tunnel Rat at Work

A Border Patrol Agent checks a rudimentary tunnel. Note that he wears a body camera on his helmet so rescue specialists monitoring his situation can see what he does. Elbow/knee pads and gloves offer some protection from sharp rocks. The camera hanging from his neck is used to take high-resolution photographs for analysis.

(U.S. Customs and Border Protection)

FIGURE 11–11
Technology at Work
Portable radar and video unit setup in a remote area. The Border Patrol Officer monitors the situation from a truck concealed nearby.

(U.S. Customs and Border Protection)

Federal Emergency Management Agency (FEMA)

The first piece of federal disaster legislation was in 1803, when Congress voted relief funds for a town in New Hampshire ravaged by a fire.[78] Over the next century, such federal **ad hoc** legislation was passed more than 100 times.[79] During the 1930s, some federal agencies were empowered to make loans to repair public buildings damaged by earthquakes, and they later expanded to include other types of disasters, and to repair roads and bridges damaged by natural disasters. Similar legislation was passed during the 1960s and 1970s.[80] For several years, governors claimed they had to go "hat in hand" to too many federal agencies when disasters struck. In 1979, by Executive Order 12127, President Jimmy Carter created the Federal Emergency Management Agency, which centralized several preexisting programs. To some degree, FEMA faced changes similar to DHS in terms of trying to build an effective organization quickly. FEMA has been periodically criticized for being too large, too bureaucratic, too ponderous, and too slow to react to large-scale disasters.

Ad hoc
A Latin phrase meaning "for this." Ad hoc generally means a process, decision, or solution that applies only to "this" particular situation and does not have a wider/general application.

Information Link
For additional information on Customs and Border Protection, visit the website at www.cbp.gov/.

Box 11–5
Cartels, Coyotes, Rape Trees, and Homeland Security

In the Pima County, Arizona, Medical Examiner's Office there are 774 sets of unidentified remains of illegal immigrants who died trying to cross the United States-Mexico border.[81] Since 2001, more than 2,100 migrants have ended up in the Pima County Medical Examiner's Office.[82] Migrant apprehensions are down in recent years, suggesting the CPDs strategies are working, but more immigrants are dying.

As security has become more stringent, border-crossers are trying more remote and dangerous routes.[83] Coyotes are paid guides who bring illegal immigrants into the United States from staging areas in Mexico. Immigrants who are unable to keep up with their coyote are left behind and many die in the desert. Some Americans trespass on ranch land and place water and food on coyote trails to prevent such deaths.[84] Many ranchers complain about crimes committed by coyotes and immigrants.

The Mexican cartels, known for their brutality, control most coyotes. Although some guides are strict about their behavior, others victimize immigrants. Girls as young as 12 are raped and their underclothes thrown onto "rape trees."[85] According to Amnesty International, 60 percent of these female immigrants are sexually assaulted.[86] Immigrants may also be robbed of any money they have, and some are taken to "stash houses" where they are held prisoner until a relative comes and pays an additional fee. Once "established," border crossers hope to send for family members.

Fees vary from a thousand to several thousand dollars. One immigrant reported that he paid $500 at the beginning of the trip and another $1,600 after crossing.[87] Immigrants save the fee or borrow money from friends and family with the hope of quickly paying it back from a well-earning job. The cartels charge substantially more to help people from Pakistan, Iran, and China, as much as $50,000–$100,000.[88]

Payan maintains that three wars are being waged along America's southern border: drugs, immigration, and homeland security.[89] Even a handful of enemies gaining illegal entry can potentially commit acts that produce mass casualties. Iran is an implacable enemy of the United States and there is substantial international concern about it developing a nuclear weapons capability, including small "backpack" devices. Radical Islamic groups want to have such a capability, and while waiting for them to be developed and acquired, they could use coyotes to move a handful of operatives into the United States to form sleeper cells or to conduct reconnaissance tasks. Border security and homeland security are closely linked.

Because some illegal immigrants commit crimes on remote U.S. border ranches, should ranchers and their "hands" be authorized to arrest and hold them for the Border Patrol when the illegals are on their ranch property? What are the dangers and advantages of such authorizations?

Category 4 hurricane
Hurricanes are characterized as being one of five categories. Category 1 is the least severe and has winds from 74 to 95 MPH and other descriptors also apply, such as damage to unanchored mobile homes. The most severe hurricane is Category 5, with winds of 156 MPH or greater and descriptors such as complete roof failures of many buildings and massive evacuations may be required.

With winds gusting to 137 miles per hour, Hugo plowed into South Carolina in 1989 as a **Category 4 hurricane**. It was on a course that had already done $9 billion of damage in Puerto Rico. Hugo was the strongest hurricane to strike the United States in 30 years. It made land-fall just north of Charleston, South Carolina. Despite advance knowledge of the ferocity of the storm, FEMA didn't open its first temporary disaster center in South Carolina until seven days later.[90] United States Senator Fritz Hollings (D-SC) related a conversation with a FEMA administrator who said before they could deliver any supplies they had to advertise in state newspapers for two weeks.[91] Senator Hollings concluded FEMA officials were "a bunch of bureaucratic jackasses." At the same time, he praised the U.S. Weather Service as a "superb outfit" and "constantly doing the government proud."

Quick Facts

The Two Versions are two versions to Senator Hollings's characterization of FEMA officials, the one above and "the *sorriest* bunch of bureaucratic jackasses."

FEMA's Role in DHS

FEMA was adsorbed by DHS on March 1, 2003. FEMA has a headquarters in Washington, D.C., ten regional officers, three area offices, and as many temporary disaster-related sites as are needed to accomplish its mission, as well as 14,844 employees.[92] FEMA's mission can be summarized as supporting our citizens and emergency first responders to ensure that the country can work together to build, sustain, and improve the capability to prepare for, protect against, respond to, recover from, and mitigate all hazards, including terrorist attacks.

FEMA's strategic plan for 2014–2018 established five priorities (see Figure 11–12). These priorities are each bolstered by a total of 16 key outcomes or indicators as to how well

FIGURE 11–12
FEMA's Five Priorities for 2014–2018
(Courtesy Federal Emergency Management Agency, 2014–2018 Strategic Plan, p. ii)

PRIORITY 1: Be Survivor-Centric in Mission and Program Delivery
- Disaster services are transparent, efficient, and effective in meeting the needs of survivors.
- Local leaders and tribal officials are better prepared and positioned for effective recovery and mitigation.
- Individuals and communities know the steps to take have the tools required, and take appropriate actions before, during, and after disasters.

PRIORITY 2: Become an Expeditionary Organization
- Unified and coordinated Federal response and recovery operations successfully support and complement state, local, tribal, and territorial incident operations.
- FEMA's incident workforce is appropriately staffed and managed to rapidly mobilize, efficiently deploy, and effectively engage in multiple sustained operations in the response, recovery, and mitigation mission areas.
- Incident operations are efficient, timely, and predictable.

PRIORITY 3: Posture and Build Capability for Catastrophic Disasters
- Capability gaps are identified and addressed in National Preparedness System planning, training, and exercises.
- Partnerships, tools, and resources are in place to support national-scale response and recovery operations for catastrophic disasters.
- Survivors, bystanders, and grassroots organizations are better prepared and positioned to take immediate independent response actions in catastrophic events.

PRIORITY 4: Enable Disaster Risk Reduction Nationally
- The whole community uses the best-available data and analytic tools to make better risk-informed decisions before, during, and after disasters.
- Whole community partners make resilient investments in development and rebuilding.
- Congressionally mandated reforms are implemented to advance flood insurance affordability. financial stability of the National Flood Insurance Program, and reduction of the risks and consequences of flooding nationwide.

PRIORITY 5: Strengthen FEMA's Organizational Foundation
- FEMA has a qualified, effective, and engaged workforce recognized for its excellence.
- Integrated analytics capabilities support effective and efficient operations and greater consistency and transparency in decision-making.
- FEMA's strategy, resources, and performance outcomes align to maximize mission impact.
- Business processes are transparent and produce consistent, high quality results.

the priorities were addressed. Although not revealed, each key outcome will be measured by one or more pre established metrics. For example, Priority 1's first indicator requires disaster services to be: (1) transparent, people will know what FEMA is doing and why, (2) efficient, which is the relationship of the resources required to achieve an outcome. The fewer resources (inputs) used to achieve an outcome (results), the higher the level of efficiency, and (3) effective, meaning the effort produced the intended results.

One of the most familiar artifacts of early homeland security efforts was the color-coded Homeland Security Advisory System (HSAS). Its replacement, the National Terrorism Advisory System (NTAS), is issued as a bulletin and distributed widely through the news media, DHS websites, Facebook, Twitter, and email by free subscription. NTAS has two levels of warning: (1) Imminent Threat Alert, meaning a credible, specific, and impending terrorist threat has been made against the United States and (2) Elevated Threat Alert, which denotes a credible terrorist threat has been made against the United States.

The Robert T. Stafford Disaster Relief and Emergency Assistance Act of 1988 amended the Disaster Relief Act of 1974. It is the statutory authority for most federal disaster response activities, especially as applied to FEMA and its activities. It has been amended by the Disaster Mitigation Act of 2000 and the Pet Evacuation and Transportation Act of 2006.

The president is authorized by the Stafford Act to issue emergency and fire management declarations, which enables federal agencies to provide assistance to state and local units of government overwhelmed by catastrophes.[93] The statute also authorizes the president to determine what types of assistance can be provided and the conditions under which aid is distributed.[94] A variety of assistance may be provided to qualified individuals with special needs (e.g., handicapped), including durable medical equipment, as well as to qualified persons or families needing such things as transportation, temporary housing, emergency food, consumables, unemployment assistance, crisis counseling, home repair grants, and financial assistance for uninsured expenses, including medical, dental, funeral, personal property, and other expenses. Nonprofit organizations, such as private museums, may also be eligible for assistance.

The definition of a *major disaster* is relatively restrictive and covers any natural catastrophe from storms, earth movements, and high water.[95] "Major disaster" declarations may be issued for a hurricane, tornado, storm, high water, tidal wave, tsunami, earthquake, volcanic eruption, landslide, mudslide, snowstorm, drought, or regardless of cause, after a fire, flood, or explosion.[96] In contrast, an *emergency* is a nonspecific word allowing the president to determine "any occasion or instance" in which assistance can be provided.[97] Between 2010 and 2016, there were 823 disaster declarations or an average of 118 annually. The data is skewed by 242 declarations in 2011.[98]

Requests for disaster declarations come from governors of the respective states to the president. A "state" also includes the District of Columbia, Puerto Rico, the Virgin Islands, Guam, American Samoa, and the Commonwealth of the Northern Mariana Islands. The Republic of Marshall Islands and the Federated States of Micronesia are also eligible to request a declaration and receive assistance through the Compacts of Free Association.[99]

From 2000 to 2013, president's annually denied an average of 11 declarations, referred to as "turndowns."[100] Presidential turndowns drop to 1.75 in election years.[101] During presidential election years, emergency declarations shift upward from an average of 2.6 to 5.6 per year,[102] suggesting a political motivation in some instances, although the data is not sufficient to make a definitive conclusion.

Presidential Policy Directive 8: National Preparedness (PPD-8) describes the nation's approach to preparing for threats and hazards that pose the greatest risk to the security of the United States. FEMA intends to achieve its National Preparedness Goal by the following activities:

1. Preventing, avoiding, or stopping a threatened or an actual act of terrorism.

2. Protecting our citizens, residents, visitors, and assets against the greatest threats and hazards in a manner that allows our interests, aspirations, and way of life to thrive.

3. Mitigating the loss of life and property by lessening the impact of future disasters.

Quick Facts
The Twin Fire Disasters of 1871

In legend, the Great Chicago Fire of 1871 was caused when a cow owned by Patrick and Catherine O'Leary kicked a lantern over. Skarbek notes The Great Chicago Fire resulted in 300 deaths, 300,000 people left homeless, and the loss of approximately 17,420 buildings.[103] The federal response was initially limited to sending troops to maintain order. Foreign governments, American cities, and wealthy Chicago citizens quickly donated approximately $4.8 million to help survivors. In 1872, Congress gave some relief to those caught up in the Chicago Fire. Individuals received tax relief and the duties on goods shipped to Chicago for the relief of sufferers was dismissed.

Ironically, at the same time as the Chicago Fire, another one was raging just a few hundred miles away in Wisconsin. The Peshtigo Fire caused 1.5 million acres of forestland to burn to the ground, 2,400 deaths, and the destruction of 17 towns. It remains America's most deadly and least-known fire. Because all telegram stations in the burned area were destroyed, the world did not learn of the disaster for several days. There does not appear to have been any federal relief for the Peshtigo Fire.

▲ A stereoscopic card depicting a horse-drawn carriage leaving a scene of ruins at the Great Chicago Fire of 1871.
(Stereograph Cards/Library of Congress Prints and Photographs Division Washington, D.C. 20540 USA)

4. Responding quickly to save lives, protect property and the environment, and meet basic human needs in the aftermath of a catastrophic incident.

5. Recovering through a focus on the timely restoration, strengthening, and revitalization of infrastructure, housing, and a sustainable economy, as well as the health, social, cultural, historic, and environmental fabric of communities affected by a catastrophic incident.

FEMA deals with potential catastrophes, including terrorist attacks, by a variety of activities (see Quick Facts: Examples of Extreme Mass Casualties). For example, a catastrophe or terrorist attack that produces mass casualties will overwhelm the capacity of morgues, funeral homes, and cemeteries to handle the dead. FEMA develops contingency plans to deal with that possibility, which includes Disaster Mortuary Response Teams (DARTs) consisting of citizens with, hopefully, some applicable background, such as a forensic anthropology. DMORTs become temporary federal employees.

FEMA also prepares states, tribes, and local communities by providing technical assistance, conducting residential and online training, as well as offering courses on-site supporting the continuous development of the emergency management profession, conducting exercises to identify areas that need corrective attention, and providing grants to acquire equipment and otherwise strengthen capabilities. Preparedness is not a destination; it's a continuous process. Mitigation is FEMA's strategy to reduce or eliminate long-term risks, such as flooding, by building dams and levees, which are man-made structures that restrain floodwaters or the direction in which they move. The Disaster Mitigation Act of 2000 allows additional funding to states, tribes, and local governments that take a comprehensive approach to mitigating the risks posed by natural hazards. FEMA is also discussed in Chapter 13, Emergency Management.

U.S. Coast Guard (USCG)

The United States Coast Guard is the descendent of the Department of Treasury's Revenue Cutter Service established in 1790 with ten ships to collect tariffs and enforce import laws.[104] This role was important to a new nation strapped for cash. In its long and distinguished history, the USCG also fought pirates, smugglers, and the British during the War of 1812. Today's USCG was created in 1915. At the same time, the U.S. Lifesaving Service was "folded" into it. Subsequent additions to the Coast Guard were the U.S. Lighthouse Service (1939) and the Bureau of Marine Inspections and Navigation (1942).[105]

In both the European and Pacific Theaters during World War II, the USCG was involved in combat operations. In 1940, Japan signed the Tripartite Pact, aligning itself with Germany and Italy. Spurred on by promises of being given new territory or coerced by Germany, some smaller European countries joined the Axis Powers coalition against America and its allies. The Magnuson Act (1950) solidified the USCG's responsibility for the security of America's harbors and ports.[106] The Coast Guard returned to combat duties during the Vietnam War (1965–1975),[107] conducting "blue water" (open seas) and "brown water" (inland waterways) patrol and surveillance duties. Similar duties were performed in the Arabian Gulf in support of Operation Iraqi Freedom (2003).[108] The U.S. Coast Guard is one of five U.S. armed services and the only one not "housed" in the Department of Defense.[109] Following its placement in the Department of Transportation (1967), the USCG was transferred to DHS by the Homeland Security Act of 2002. That act divides USCG missions into "homeland security" or "non-homeland security" missions (see Table 11–3).

The role of the USCG is to protect the public, the environment, and U.S. economic interests—in the nation's ports and waterways, along the coast, on international waters, or in any maritime region as required to support national security (see Figure 11–13). More specifically, the USCG retained traditional missions and assumed additional homeland security missions. It is responsible for executing both types of missions along 95,000 miles of coastline[110] and 4.5 million square miles of the sea, including the maritime Exclusive Economic Zone (EEZ), which typically extends 200 miles from a country's shoreline.[111] In the EEZ, the Coast Guard protects our fisheries from exploitation by foreign vessels. Forty-eight percent of the Coast Guard's annual budget goes for its traditional, non-homeland security missions, including protecting marine natural resources; preventing marine-related injuries, deaths, and property losses; protecting the environment from oil and hazardous substances; maintaining navigational aids; and icebreaking internationally and on the Great Lakes. The remaining 52 percent is allocated to homeland security missions.

Coast Guard programs to carry out the missions identified in Table 11–3. A homeland security mission, drug interdiction, is depicted in Figure 11–13 during a patrol in the Gulf of Mexico. One of the favored drug smuggling departure points is the Isthmus of Central America, which separates the Gulf of Mexico from the Pacific Ocean. That location opens up both the entire West Coast of North America, as well as the states bordering the Gulf of Mexico for drug trafficking.

TABLE 11–3

Coast Guard Non-Homeland/Traditional and Homeland Security Missions

Non-Homeland Security Missions	Homeland Security Missions
1. Marine Safety	1. Safeguard and Secure Cyberspace
2. Search and Rescue	2. Prevent Terrorism and Enhance Security
3. Aids to Navigation	3. Secure and Manage Borders
4. Living Marine Resources	4. Enforce and Administer Immigration Laws
5. Marine Environmental Protection	5. Strengthen National Preparedness and Resilience
6. Ice Operations: Ice Patrols and Icebreaking to keep domestic and polar shipping lanes open	6. Other Law Enforcement

(Courtesy U.S. Coast Guard)

FIGURE 11–13

A boarding team from the U.S. Coast Guard Cutter Stratton seizes a self-propelled semi-submersible submarine interdicted in international waters off the coast of Central America. The Stratton's crew recovered more than six tons of cocaine with a street value of $120 million from the 40-foot vessel.

(US Coast Guard Photo/Alamy Stock Photo)

Information Link
For more information regarding the U.S. Coast Guard, visit the website at www.uscg.mil.

Coast Guard Activities

In Fiscal Year (FY) 2017, the USCG had a budget request of $10.3 billion.[112] The USCG had 40,992 active duty, 7,000 reserve duty, 8,577 civilians, and 3,000 volunteers for a total of 87,569 personnel.[113] USCG has 201 aircraft, 243 ships of more than 65 feet in length, ranging from icebreakers to national security cutters, and 1,650 boats of less than 65 feet in length.[114] In a single year, the USCG will respond to 17,801 calls from vessels in distress, use 53,911 hours in doing so, and save 3,768 lives.[115] All vessels in distress may not have lives in imminent danger. They may need equipment such as a replacement pump, have a crew member evacuated because of a serious injury, tow a disabled vessel to port, or land on a cruise ship and take a heart attack victim to an appropriate hospital. At other times, a sailing boat may have been sunk by a rogue wave and people are being tossed around by heavy seas, into which the rescue swimmer leaps to save them.

The USCG's Law Enforcement Detachments (LeDets) accompany foreign governments on actual operations to evaluate their capability and training needs.[116] These and other antiterrorism efforts supporting foreign governments contribute to the expansion of governed space, which deprives terrorists of some safe havens. In another homeland security mission, the USCG made the largest cocaine drug interdiction in American history when two of its cutters stopped the Gatun, a Panamanian flagged ship, and seized 42,845 pounds of cocaine—nearly 20 tons—with a street value of $600 million.[117] The seizure prevented substantial funds flowing to transnational criminal organizations and perhaps some portion of it to support a terrorist movement. Peru's Sendero Luminoso (Shining Path) is described both as a communist/socialist movement as well as being designated as a foreign terrorist organization (FTO).[118] It has played a large role in Peru's cultivation of the coca leaf, from which cocaine is made. By 2013, Peru was the world leader in coca production.[119]

In 2016, as compared to the prior year, the Coast Guard apprehended 60 percent more undocumented Cubans or a total of 7,361 trying to reach the United States. In a few cases, Cubans have reached Puerto Rico and shot themselves to force their evacuation to an American hospital.[120] Unlike other undocumented immigrants who reached United States soil during 1995–2017, Cubans were given special status: They could remain and be on the fast track to citizenship.

Transportation Security Administration (TSA)

The first American airliner was hijacked in 1961, when a passenger demanded that a National Airlines plane take him to Cuba. Following three more hijacking of U.S. flights over the next three months, President Kennedy ordered the creation of armed "sky marshals" to thwart hijackings. Initially there were 18 of them, all U.S. Border Patrol agents. By 9/11 there were only 33 sky marshals and none of those were on hijacked planes that day because they were not being assigned to domestic flights. The number of air marshals is not publicized, but has varied widely. The "descendants" of the sky marshals are now designated as the Federal Air Marshal Service (FAMS) and are part of TSA.

Few hijackings of U.S. airliners have occurred in recent years, 9/11 providing a grotesque exception to this statement. The general absence of hijackings may be due to several factors: (1) a lack of intent or capability by terrorists, (2) marshals may be providing a deterrent, or (3) a shift in tactics by terrorist groups. For example, recent terrorist attacks in Europe suggest a preference for attacks on mass transit systems. On average, attacks against mass transit systems create more than two and a half times the casualties per incident as attacks on aviation targets.[121]

In 1972, a Trans World Airlines Flight 7 (TWA) jet departed from JFK International Airport in New York bound for Los Angeles.[122] Minutes later, an anonymous caller identified only as "Gomez" said there was a bomb on board Flight 7 and it returned to JFK where

Box 11-6
Three Cases on the Road to Airport Security

In 1955, John G. "Jack" Graham put a bomb in his mother's luggage. She was flying on United Airlines from Denver to Portland, Oregon. Eleven minutes after takeoff, the bomb exploded, killing 39 passengers and a crew of 11. Graham, after an exhaustive FBI investigation, was arrested, convicted, and executed two years later. His motive for the bombing was to collect a $37,500 insurance policy on his mother's life.

A man using the name of "Dan Cooper," who has been misidentified in the news media as "D. B. Cooper," hijacked a Northwest Orient Airliner in 1971. It landed in Seattle where he demanded $200,000 in ransom. After receiving the money, Cooper allowed the passengers and some crew members to leave the plane in Seattle and ordered it to take off again. During that night flight, he parachuted into the lower Cascade Mountains. The case was never officially cleared, although a deceased man identified years later is thought to have been the mysterious Cooper.

A Dan Cooper "copycat" hijacking occurred in 1972. A man rode his bicycle onto the airport tarmac in Reno, laid his bike down at the foot of the portable stairs leading to a United Airlines plane, climbed up the stairs, and entered the plane. In preparation for their flight, the attendants and pilots were already onboard. The man put a gun to the head of a flight attendant and demanded $200,000.[123] It was a Friday evening and the banks were closed. The ransom money was gathered from two casinos, receipted by a note on a cocktail napkin, and rushed to the airport. The plane took off on a heading given by the hijacker. Like Dan Cooper, the hijacker put on a parachute and jumped from the lowered tail stairs. The pilot immediately radioed the plane's position and law enforcement officers rushed to that area. They found a car parked in some trees with a license plate reading "Parachute." Thirty minutes later a limping man walked up to the car carrying the ransom money and was arrested.

the passengers were evacuated. Brandy, a bomb-sniffing dog, found the bomb 12 minutes before it exploded. That same day, then-President Richard Nixon ordered the Secretary of Transportation to develop a plan to combat problems cropping up in civil aviation. One result was the Federal Aviation Authority's (FAA) Explosives Detection Canine Team program that placed such units at many airports across the country.

The Airport Transportation Security Act (ATSA) of 1974 required U.S. airport operators to establish weapons-detecting screening of all passengers and carry-on luggage. Many airports elected to contract with private security firms for these tasks. Following the 9/11 attacks, federal legislation in 2001 established the Transportation Security Administration (TSA) and transferred responsibility for civil aviation security from the Federal Aviation Administration (FAA) to TSA. In 2002, the Homeland Security Act (HSA) moved TSA into the Department of Homeland Security (DHS).

TSA Responsibilities

In FY 2017, TSA had 55,608 employees and a budget request of approximately $7.4 billion.[124] Its mission is to maximize transportation security in response to evolving threats while protecting passengers' privacy and facilitating the flow of legal commerce. Although the mere mention of TSA is likely to invoke the image of long screening lines at airports, its responsibilities are much broader than airports.

The TSA has four specific responsibilities:

1. Ensuring effective and efficient screening of 100 percent of air passengers, baggage, and cargo on passenger planes

2. Deploying federal air marshals internationally and domestically to detect, deter, and defeat hostile acts targeting air carriers, airports, passengers, and crews

Quick Facts
What the TSA Protects and Checks Annually

✓ Inspected 3.9 million miles of road

✓ Monitored 10 billion mass transit passengers

✓ Screened 695 million domestic and international air passengers

✓ Inspected 140,000 miles of railroads

✓ Inspected 604,00 bridges over 20 feet long

✓ Inspected 366 highway tunnels longer than 100 meters

✓ Inspected 2.6 million miles of pipelines

✓ Checked 800,000 hazardous waste shipments

✓ Screened 432 million bags

✓ Seized over 117,000 dangerous items, including 2,653 guns, as well as stun grenades, black powder, and swords

FIGURE 11–14
VIPR (Visible Intermodal, Prevention and Response Teams) are deployed to a variety of settings that bring crowds together to monitor mass transportation and other factors. They have been present at Super Bowls, NCAA Basketball Final Fours, cruise ships, and other settings to protect the public and property.

(Transportation Security Administration)

Information Link
To read about TSA Prohibited Items on commercial airlines (No-Fly Items), visit www.tsa.gov/travel/travel-tips/travel-checklist.

3. Managing security risks of the transportation systems (see Figure 11–14) by working with stakeholders, providing support and program direction, and conducting on-site inspections

4. Developing and implementing more efficient, reliable, integrated, and cost-effective screening programs

TSA employs a strategy of focusing resources on known and emerging risks/threats. A key component of this strategy to protect U.S. aviation is using layers of security as shown in Figure 11–15. The TSA uses 94 different factors in its Screening Passengers by Observation Techniques (SPOT) program. A Government Accountability Office study concluded that although TSA spent $900 million on the program, there is no evidence that it works and urged Congress to cut funding.[125] Only 0.59 percent of all passengers screened were arrested and none were charged with terrorism.[126] The ability of SPOT to detect potential threats is only slightly better than random chance.[127] An emerging TSA risk may be pipelines. There are just a handful of incidents where pipelines were discovered to be shot up by protesters, eco advocates, or others. Long miles of isolated pipelines being attacked could force the TSA to reallocate some resources.

TSA has had difficulties with the performance of airport TSA members. In a single year, there were 4,408 cases; 55 percent of them were accounted for by a handful of charges: screening and security lapses, failure to follow instructions, inappropriate conduct or comments, drug and alcohol violations, and neglect of duty.[128]

Despite some problems, TSA has done an excellent job of executing its homeland security mission. A recent innovation that has been well received by the flying public is the "TSA Pre✓™" program, which is based on intelligence and risks. Rather than clinging to a single model of screening aviation passengers, the TSA Pre✓ Program provides expedited screening for low-risk passengers, such as military personnel and people who are part of the "trusted Traveler" program, and frequent travelers nominated by airlines.

U.S. Secret Service (USSS)

Counterfeiting has a long history. During the American Revolution, the British counterfeited Continental currency in such large quantities that it became worthless.[129] During the American Civil War, one-third to one-half of the currency was counterfeit, leading to the establishment in 1865 of the Secret Service to fight this problem.[130] As time passed, the jurisdiction of the Secret Service included other responsibilities.

The U.S. Secret Service has a unique dual mission of protection and investigation.[131] The Secret Service protects:

1. The president, the vice-president, and their families (See 11–16)

2. Former presidents, their spouses, and children under 16 years of age

3. Former vice presidents, their spouses, and children under 16 years of age of a period of not more than six months after leaving office

4. Visiting foreign heads of state or governments and their spouses

5. Distinguished visitors to the United States

6. As directed by the president, official representatives of the United States performing missions abroad

7. Other persons designated by the president

8. National Special Security Events. NSSE is any national or international meeting deemed by DHS as a potential target for terrorism or other criminal activity, such as a specific summit of world leaders (e.g., World Trade Organization—WTO Conference) or any other meeting of foreign leaders in the United States[132]

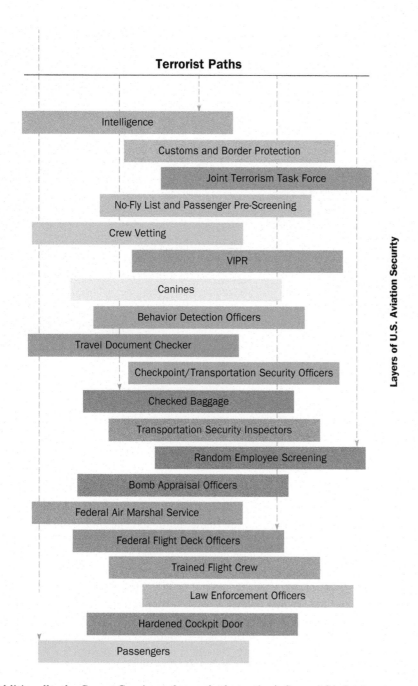

Terrorist Paths

Intelligence

Customs and Border Protection

Joint Terrorism Task Force

No-Fly List and Passenger Pre-Screening

Crew Vetting

VIPR

Canines

Behavior Detection Officers

Travel Document Checker

Checkpoint/Transportation Security Officers

Checked Baggage

Transportation Security Inspectors

Random Employee Screening

Bomb Appraisal Officers

Federal Air Marshal Service

Federal Flight Deck Officers

Trained Flight Crew

Law Enforcement Officers

Hardened Cockpit Door

Passengers

Layers of U.S. Aviation Security

FIGURE 11–15
Layers of Security
Source: Layers of Security, Washington, D.C.: Transportation Security Administration, January 14, 2014), p. 1, www.tsa.gov/about-tsa/layers-security.

Additionally, the Secret Service safeguards the nation's financial infrastructure and payment systems to preserve the integrity of the economy, investigates cyber/electronic crimes, and protects the White House and other designated buildings within the Washington, D.C., area. To meet its responsibilities, the Secret Service has an annual budget of $2.1 billion, 6,300 employees, and operates 114 domestic and 24 foreign investigative offices.[133]

The investigative responsibility of the Secret Service is broad and includes thefts and frauds involving ATMs, debit cards, identity theft, credit cards, computers, passwords, and financial deposits.[134] Secret Service spread around the country protect the integrity of America's financial systems. In a single year, the Secret Service suppressed 188 counterfeiting plants, recovered $58 million in bogus currency, seized $120 million in assets worldwide, and made 6,745 arrests for identity crimes, cyber intrusion, and fraud and related financial crimes over which it has jurisdiction.[135]

In fulfilling its primary protection mission, the Secret Service uses a variety of specialized security operations to eliminate, deter, minimize, and decisively respond to threats, such as its Airspace Security Branch, Counter Sniper Team, Emergency Response Team, Counter Assault Team—CAT Team, Counter Surveillance Team, Hazardous Agent Mitigation and

FIGURE 11–16
U.S. Secret Service agents rush a lone assassin who fired six shots, wounding President Ronald Reagan and two other men on March 31, 1981, outside of the Washington Hilton Hotel in Washington, D.C. Ronald Reagan had been president for only 69 days at the time of this attempt on his life.

(Bettmann/Getty Images)

Medical Emergency Response Team, and the Magnetometer (metal detection) Operations Unit. Other specialized resources provide protection from threats, including chemical, biological, radiological, nuclear, and explosives.[136]

U.S. Immigration and Customs Enforcement (ICE)

ICE was formed in 2003 through a merger of the investigative and interior enforcement elements of the U.S. Customs Service and the Immigration and Naturalization Service.[137] ICE is the principal investigative arm of the Department of Homeland Security and the second largest enforcement agency in the federal government.[138] With a budget of $5.3 billion, ICE deploys its 19,332 employees in all 50 states, the District of Columbia, and 48 foreign countries.[139] ICE promotes homeland security and public safety through broad criminal and civil enforcement of approximately 400 federal laws governing border control, customs, trade, and immigration.[140] Whereas the CBP's Border Patrol focuses on the border areas between ports of entry (POEs) into the United States, ICE enforces applicable laws in the interior of the United States. In FY 2016, DHS apprehended 530,250 individuals with 114,434 being arrested at ports of entry by ICE.[141] A total of 450,954 of those taken into custody were removals, commonly called deported. National security threats, those caught trying to illegal this country, and the most serious categories of convicted criminals, and gang members made up 91 percent of all removals.[142]

Homeland Security Investigations (HSI)

HSI has 6,500 agents who carry out transnational criminal investigations to protect the United States against terrorist and other criminal organizations that threaten public safety and national security and bring to justice those seeking to exploit our customs and immigration laws worldwide.[143] Relying on its legal authority, HSI investigates immigration and customs violations such as export enforcement, human rights violations, narcotics, the smuggling of weapons (see Figure 11–17) and other types of contraband, financial crimes, cybercrimes, human trafficking and smuggling, child exploitation, commercial fraud, such as intellectual property violations, transnational gangs, and identity and immigration benefit fraud.[144] HSI describes itself as the largest investigation unit in DHS. It has a budget of $1.9 billion, 6,200 investigators, enforces 400 federal laws and regulations, and has a presence in 200 cities and 47 countries. In 2014, HIS disrupted or dismantled 520 transnational criminal organizations, made 32,000 arrests, and seized at least 1.3 million pounds of narcotics and 20,000 weapons.[145]

In 2012, the federal Jaime Zapata Border Enforcement Security Task Force (BEST) Act became law. The ACT provides HIS with BEST teams to work jointly with federal, state, local, and foreign law enforcement agencies along America's northern and southern borders, and at major seaports to identify, disrupt, and dismantle criminal organizations that pose significant threats to border security.[146] Two other important organizational units within HSI are the Forensic Laboratory (FL), which has great expertise in several forensic sciences, including questioned document examination, which determines the authenticity of identity, travel, and other documents; and the Law Enforcement Support Center (LESC), which is a single national point of information that provides timely data about immigration status, identity information, and real-time assistance to local, state, and federal law enforcement agencies on aliens suspected, detained, arrested, or convicted of criminal activity.

In addition to these extensive programs, ICE maintains a Counterterrorism and Criminal Exploitation Unit, a Firearms and Explosives Smuggling Unit, a Visa Security Unit, and a National Security Division that concentrates efforts against potential terrorists and assists the FBI in complex terrorist investigations. As important, ICE also maintains a Human Rights Violators and War Crimes Center that actively pursues war criminals from foreign lands, including past dictators and individuals guilty of state terrorism and genocide. For instance, the center has been involved in arresting and deporting former military officers in Central America (e.g., Guatemala, El Salvador) involved in past massacres in their home countries. The Human Rights Violators and War Crimes Center has been in existence for over ten years and marks one of the most important coordination, liaison, and extradition programs in the country. Its work has been instrumental in bringing those that would hide behind the cloak of government to torture and kill their own people to justice in such war-torn areas as Bosnia-Herzegovina, Rwanda, Burma, Guatemala, and El Salvador.

For more information on Immigration and Custom Enforcement (ICE), visit the website at www.ice.gov/index.htm.

FIGURE 11–17
There are 6,700 gun shops along our 2,000-mile border with Mexico. If they were evenly spaced, there would be approximately three gun shops per mile. In contrast, there is one legal gun store in Mexico, used by the police and military. People purchase guns in the United States, smuggle them into Mexico, and are paid the cost of the gun, plus $100. Smuggled arms contribute to the high level of narco terrorism in Mexico. Between 2006 and 2016, it is estimated that 80,000–100,000 of all intentional homicides were related to organized crime, which primarily focuses on drug trafficking.
(Gilles Mingasson/Getty Images)

U.S. Citizenship and Immigration Services (USCIS)

The U.S. Citizenship and Immigration Services (USCIS) has an annual budget of $3.3 billion and 13,151 employees distributed across 240 domestic and foreign offices.[147] In light of the fact that some of the 9/11 attackers entered the United States several times and received flight training here, the work of this agency has become a critical part of preventing future terrorist attacks.

In a single year, USCIS (1) processed 36,000 political asylum applications; and (2) received 21 million E-Verify inquiries.[148] The E-Verify Program requires employers to fill out Form 1-9 on citizens and noncitizens for all potential hires.[149] The Internet-based system returns a confirmation of eligibility or ineligibility within three to five seconds by reviewing select federal records; (3) naturalized 763,690 new citizens, some 9,000 of whom qualified by military service while a non-citizen immigrant.[150] When their enlistment period

Detainer
An immigration detainer or "hold" is a request sent to local and state jails to keep a person of interest in custody 48 hours beyond the time they would otherwise be released. This gives ICE time to investigate the subject's immigration status and assume custody if appropriate. Amnesty jurisdictions do not honor such requests.

Quick Facts
Who Was Jaime Zapata?

Jaime Zapata was an ICE agent working in Mexico. In 2012, as he and another agent were driving back to Monterrey, their armored SUV was forced to the side of the road by two vehicles. Fourteen men surrounded the ICE vehicle and fired shots into it through a cracked window.[151] Zapata was killed and the other agent wounded. A year later, a member of the Zeta drug cartel pleaded guilty to the murder of Zapata.

is over, the veterans and qualified members of their families can apply to become citizens. If killed in action, the deceased's immediate family, spouse, children, and parents get special preference for immigration.[152] Hurdles to non-citizens seeking to enlist include no high school degree, a lack of English proficiency, and an inability to get a security clearance;[153] and (4) interviewed more than 76,750 refugees[154] in 60 countries.[155]

The USCIS is responsible for the delivery of information on citizenship and immigration benefits to applicants in a timely, accurate, consistent, courteous, and professional manner, while also safeguarding our national security.[156] All cases are unique and require attention from experienced USCIS immigration officers. The USCIS is also responsible for enhancing the integrity of America's legal immigration system by deterring, detecting, and pursuing immigration-related fraud.

DHS and Other Homeland Security Units

In support of the U.S. Department of Homeland Security (DHS), there are many homeland security units in state, local, tribal, and territorial governments (SLTT). Forty-nine states, the District of Columbia, and five territories/possessions‡ have their own homeland security organizations. State-level homeland security units are often co-located with fusion centers within the same organizational structure, which may also have an emergency function. Such arrangements end up with a title such as "Department of Homeland Security and Emergency Management," as in the case of Iowa, Alaska, Minnesota, West Virginia, and New Mexico. In other states, the fusion center, emergency management, and homeland security end up in a unit whose title does not include the homeland security tag. Connecticut's Division of Emergency Services and Public Protection illustrates this situation. A common organizational arrangement is to place state homeland security units within a state police, state investigative agency, or a state department of public safety. Additionally, local governments have their own homeland security units.

DHS provides training, guidance, and other resources, including further grants to enhance existing capabilities or add new ones to state, local, tribal, and territorial governments. SLTT and fusion centers excel in gathering human intelligence (HUMINT)[157] because their law enforcement agencies are out in the community and across the state 24/7, giving them many opportunities to see and learn things. Similarly, local fire departments responding to a fire may stumble across bomb-making activity. SLTT programs are also effective at engaging the public and recruiting private sector partners, for example, local aviation. DHS has put $37 billion[158] into creating, staffing, and equipping state, local, tribal, and territorial homeland security units.[159]

---

‡These five territories or possessions of the United States are the Commonwealth of Puerto Rico, Guam, American Samoa, U.S. Virgin Islands, and the Commonwealth of the Northern Mariana Islands. There are also eight largely uninhabited islands that are possessions: Baker, Howland, Kingman Reef, Jarvis, Johnson, Midway, Palmyra, and Wake.

Chapter Summary

SUMMARY BY LEARNING OBJECTIVE

1. **Briefly state why and how the Department of Homeland Security (DHS) was created.**

   The formation of DHS was a direct reaction to the four 9/11 terrorist attacks. DHS was created on November 25, 2002, and it became operational or "opened its doors" on March 1, 2003. All or parts of 22 existing federal agencies became part of DHS.

2. **State the vision statement of DHS**

   A homeland that is safe, secure, and resilient against terrorism and other hazards, where American interests, aspirations, and way of life can thrive.

3. **Explain the purpose of the Quadrennial Homeland Security Review.**

   The QHSR reflects a deep analysis of the evolving strategic environment and outlines the specific changes necessary to keep our Nation secure. The QHSR assessed the threats and challenges DHS faces and is crucial to intelligence gathering, strategic planning, research, programs, performance goals, budgeting, recruitment, training, and operations.

4. **Identify the five DHS core missions.**

   The five security missions are (1) prevent terrorism and enhance security, (2) securing and managing our borders, (3) enforcing and administering our immigration laws, (4) safeguarding and securing our cyberspace, and (5) ensuring resilience to disasters.

5. **Name the steps in the DHS performance management framework.**

   Those elements are: **(1) missions, (2) goals, (3) strategies, (4) mission programs, (5) program performance goals, (6) performance measures, (7) performance targets, and (8) performance results.**

6. **State the broad purpose of Customs and Border Protection (CBP).**

   Broadly, the purpose of CBP is to prevent harmful individuals and substances from entering the United States. This includes terrorists, criminals, illegal immigrants and drugs, weapons, and other contraband, as well as harmful pests and diseases.

REVIEW QUESTIONS

1. If the success of the 9/11 attacks was in part an intelligence failure, why weren't any major intelligence agencies transferred to DHS?
2. In DHS and other organizations, what is the difference between staff and line positions?
3. What are four questions about confronting decentralized terrorism?
4. How does DHS plan to improve its strategic priority of strengthening cybersecurity?
5. What are three new trends in illegal immigration?
6. What is the purpose of the GPRA Modernization Act of 2010?
7. With respect to the U.S. Coast Guard, what are their homeland security missions?

CRITICAL THINKING EXERCISES

1. As mentioned in the chapter, Scotland has a very low incidence on acts of terrorism. Why? Do this alone and then in a group of approximately five to form a consolidated list of possible explanations. How much initial duplication between group members was there as each person read their list?
2. In 2017, the president issued an executive order that would eliminate federal funds to cities, counties, and states that were sanctuaries. Two key U.S. Supreme Court decisions have relevance to the federal District Court's injunction blocking the implementation of the executive order: *South Dakota v. Dole* (1987) and *Printz v. United States* (1997). What relevance do they have?
3. As a class, learn more about the crime of human trafficking. Human trafficking is a major crime investigated by ICE. It is hard to know the exact scope of the problem, as human trafficking is often clouded in an underground activity that thrives on secrecy, seclusion,

and fear, and often begins in foreign countries. The victims are usually illegally transported to large cities and/or vacation and tourist areas, for the purposes of prostitution and child sex slavery. As a class, discuss the following questions:

a. What is bonded and forced labor?
b. Why is human trafficking considered "modern-day slavery"?
c. What do you think of the solution proposed by the International Justice Mission?
d. What new strategies might prevent human trafficking, especially in the United States?

NOTES

1. *One Team, One Response, Securing Our Homeland, U.S. Department of Homeland Security, Strategic Plan Fiscal* (Washington, D.C.: Department of Homeland Security, 2008), p. 3.
2. Charles Perrow, "The Disaster After 9/11: The Department of Homeland Security and the Intelligence Reorganization," *Homeland Security Affairs*, VII, No. 1, April 2006, p. 4, www.hsaj.org/?fullarticle=2.1.3.
3. See Christine A. Henriksen, James M. Bolton, and Jitender Sareen, "The Psychological Impact of Terrorist Attacks: Examining a Dose-Response Relationship Between Exposure to 9/11 and Axis I Mental Disorders," *Depression and Anxiety*, Vol. 27, Issue 11, November 2010, pp. 993–1000.
4. Data on these problems is available at *9/11 Health: What We Know from the Research*, City of New York, www.nyc.gov/html/doh/wtc/html/rescue/know.shtml. This source is undated, but its most recent citation is 2013.
5. See Monica L. P. Robbers and Jonathan Mark Jenkins, "Symptomology of Post-Traumatic Stress Disorder Among First Responders to the Pentagon on 9/11: A Preliminary Analysis of Arlington County Police First Responders," *Police Practice and Research*, Vol. 6, Issue 3, July 2005, pp. 235–249. A 2002 survey of New Yorkers reported 47.5 percent of respondents feared another terrorist attack. See Joseph A. Boscarino, Charles R. Figley, and Richard E. Adams, "Fear of Terrorism in New York After the 9/11 Terrorist Attacks: Implications for Emergency Mental Health and Preparedness," *International Journal of Mental Health*, Vol. 5, Issue 4, 2003, p. 4, www.ncbi.nim.nih.gov/pmc/articles/pmc/articles/pmc26975671.
6. Angie Cannon et al., "Final Words from Flight 93," *U.S. News and World Report*, Vol. 131, Issue 18, October 29, 2001.
7. Derekh Cornwell and Bryan Roberts, "The 9/11 Terrorist Attack and Overseas Travel to the United States: Initial Impacts and Longer-Run Recovery," Department of Homeland Security, Working Paper, March 2010, p. 1.
8. Dov S. Zakheim, "What 9/11 Has Wrought," *Middle East Quarterly*, Vol. 18, Issue 4, Fall 2011, pp. 3–4.
9. Defense Science Board Task Force, "Deployment of Members of the National Guard and Reserve in the Global War on Terrorism," Office of the Under Secretary for Acquisition, Technology, and Logistics, Washington, D.C., September 2007.
10. Zakheim, "What 9/11 Has Wrought," pp. 3–4.
11. Matthew DeLuca, "Report Pulls Back Veil on CIA'S Rendition Program," *NBC News*, February 5, 2013, pp. 1–2, www.usnews.nbcnews.com/_news/2013/02/05/16853156-report-pulls-back-veil-on-cias-rendition-program.
12. This paragraph was prepared from Thomas H. Kean, Chair, *The 9/11 Commission Report* (Washington, D.C., July 22, 2004), pp. 38–39 and "Bush Learns of Attacks on World Trade Center," *This Day in History*, www.history-com/this-day-in-history/bush-learns-of-attack-on-world-trade-center, undated.
13. George W. Bush, Address to the Nation on the Terrorist Attacks on September 11, 2001 (University of California, Santa Barbara, The Presidency Project), www.presidency.ucsb.edu/ws/?pid=58057, undated.
14. Noricks, "Less Than the Sum of Its Parts," p. 1.
15. The budget figure does not include any funds appropriated in supplemental budgets. See Chad C. Haddal, *Homeland Security Department: FY 2011 Appropriations* (Washington, D.C. Congressional Research Service, August 27, 2010), p. 29.

16. Richard A. Clarke, *Your Government Failed You: Breaking the Cycle of National Security Disasters* (New York: HarperCollins Publishing, 2008), p. 204.

17. Darcy Noricks, "Less Than the Sum of Its Parts: Institutional Change, Policy Entrepreneurs, and the Development of the Department of Homeland Security," International Studies Association Annual Meeting, Chicago, Illinois, February 28–March 3, 2007, p. 1.

18. David Wolfe, "Transforming the U.S. Immigration Service After 9/11: The Impact of Organizational Change and Collaboration in the Context of Homeland Security" (Monterey, CA: Master's Thesis, Naval Postgraduate School, December 2008), p. 1.

19. Perrow, "The Disaster After 9/11," p. 6.

20. Andrew D. Grossman, "So Dysfunctional…It's Frightening: The Department of Homeland Security and Public Policy in the Car Bomb Age," American Political Science Association Annual Meeting, Chicago, Illinois, August 30–September 2, 2007.

21. U.S. General Accountability Office, "Homeland Security: Overview of the Department of Homeland Security Management Challenges," April 20, 2005, www.gpo.gov/fdsys/pkg/gaoreports.gao-05-573t/html/gaoreports-gao-05-573t.htm.

22. David W. Chen, "9/11 Aid Requests Returned: FEMA Did not Pay for P.O. Box," *New York Times*, Vol. 152, November 27, 2002.

23. Mike M. Ahlers, "Report: Criticism of FEMA's Katrina Response Deserved," *CNN.com*, April 14, 2006, p. 1, www.cnn.com/2006/politics/04/14/fema.ig.

24. Anna Shoup, "FEMA Faces Intense Scrutiny," *Public Broadcasting System*, September 5, 2005, p. 6, www.pbs.org/newshour/updates/government_programs-july-dec05-fema_09-09.

25. Grossman, "So Dysfunctional…It's Frightening," p. 13. Also see "Chertoff Says He'd Do Things Differently," *USA Today*, February 15, 2006.

26. See, for example, Jena Baker McNeill and Jessica Zuckerman, "Five Reasons Why FEMA Should Stay at DHS," The Heritage Foundation, December 15, 2009, www.heritage.org/research/reports/2009/12/five-reasons-why-fema-should-stay-at-dhs.

27. Veronique de Rugy, "Are We Ready for the Next 9/11?" *Reason*, Vol. 37, Issue 10, March 2006, p. 1.

28. Ibid., pp. 2–3.

29. Office of the Inspector General, "Department of Homeland Security Challenges in Consolidating Terrorist Watch List Information," Department of Homeland Security, August 2004, pp. 3–4.

30. Clarke, *Your Government Failed You*, p. 204.

31. Office of the Inspector General, "Department of Homeland Security Challenges in Consolidating Terrorist Watch List Information," pp. 3–4.

32. Federal Emergency Management Agency, FEMA Strategic Plan 2014–2018, p. ii.

33. No author, The 2014 Homeland Security Quadrennial Review, 2014–2018, p. 1, www.dhs.gov/sites/default/files/publications/qhsr/the-2014-quadrennial-homeland-security-review-overview.pdf, accessed April 25, 2017.

34. The 2014 Homeland Security Quadrennial Review, 2014–2018, p. 1.

35. Jens Manuel Krogstad, Jeffrey S. Passel, and D'Vera Cohn, "5 Facts About Illegal Immigration in the U.S." April 27, 2017, p. 1, www.pewresearch.org/fact-tank/2017/04/27/5-facts-about-illegal-immigration-in-the-u-s/, accessed May 2, 2017.

36. Department of Homeland Security. Our Mission, March 21, 2016, www.dhs.gov/our-mission, accessed April 20, 2017.

37. Senator Tom Coburn, "A Review of the Department of Homeland Security's Missions and Performances, U.S. Senate, 113th Congress, January 2015, pp. 7–14, file:///Users/charles1155/Downloads/Senator%20Coburn%20DHS%20Report%20FINAL%20(1).pdf, accessed April 28, 2017.

38. Ibid., p. 14.

39. See Shawn Reese, Department of Homeland Security Preparedness Grants: A Summary and Issues, October 28, 2016, https://fas.org/sgp/crs/homesec/R44669.pdf, accessed April 28, 2017.

40. Loc. cit.

41. Mark Rockwell, "ACLU Praises DHS Report," FCW, April 18, 2014, https://fcw.com/articles/2014/04/18/dhs-aclu-pii.aspx, accessed April 28, 2017.

42. No author, "GAO Report Praises Federal Efforts to Safeguard Electrical Grid," March 13, 2017, www.securitymagazine.com/articles/87893-gao-report-praises-federal-efforts-to-safeguard-electric-grid, accessed April 28, 2017.

43. Senate Committee of Homeland Security and Governmental Affairs, "Chairman Johnson Applauds DHS Initiative to Help Victims of Illegal Immigrant Crime," April 26, 2017, www.hsgac.senate.gov/media/majority-media/chairman-johnson-applauds-dhs-initiative-to-help-victims-of-illegal-immigrant-crime, accessed April 28, 2017.

44. DHS received approximately $40 billion for spending on identified components of the organization. The balance of the $50 billion was contingency spending for disaster relief and foreign operations.

45. "Budget in Brief Fiscal Year 2014, Homeland Security" (Washington, D.C.: Department of Homeland Security, 2014), p. 5.

46. Nadav Morag, "Customs and Border Patrol Protection: Rooted in Nation's First Congress," Colorado Technical University, p. 1, September 17, 2013, www.coloradotech.edu/resources/blogs/september-2013/customs-border-protection.

47. "Budget in Brief Fiscal Year 2014," p. 110.

48. "Agricultural Fact Sheet," U.S. Customs and Border Patrol, undated, p. 1, www.cbp.gov/linkhandler/cgov/trade/trade_programs/agriculture/agriculture_factsheet.ctt/agriculture_factsheet.pdf.

49. Dean Olson, "Agroterrorism," *FBI Law Enforcement Bulletin*, Vol. 81, Number 2, p. 1.

50. "Agricultural Fact Sheet," p. 1.

51. Olson, "Agroterrorism," p. 1.

52. Loc. cit.

53. "Alexander Hamilton U.S. Custom House, New York, NY" (Washington, D.C.: U.S. General Services Administration, no date), p. 1, www.gsa.gov/portal/ext/html/site/hb/category/25431/actionparameter/explorebybuilding/buildingld/644.

54. "DHS at Work: History of the U.S. Customs Service," undated, p. 1, http://trac.syr.edu/tracus/findings/aboutcus/cushistory.html.

55. "DHS at Work: History of the U.S. Customs Service," p. 1.

56. "Alexander Hamilton U.S. Custom House, New York, NY," p. 1.

57. "Border Patrol History," undated, p. 1, www.cbp.gov/xp/cgov/border-security/border_patrol/border_patrol_ohs/history/history.xml.

58. Loc. cit.

59. Loc. cit.

60. Loc. cit.

61. Ibid., p. 2.

62. Kelly Lytle Hernandez, *Migra!* (Berkeley, California: University of California Press, 2010), p. 2.

63. Ibid., p. 47.

64. "Budget-in-Brief: Fiscal Year 2014, Homeland Security" (Washington, D.C.: Department of Homeland Security, February 2012), p. 109.

65. U.S. Customs and Border Protection, "Snapshot: A Summary of CBP Facts and Figures," February 2017, p. 1, www.cbp.gov/sites/default/files/assets/documents/2017-Mar/CBP-Snapshot-UPDATE-03022017-FY16-Data.pdf, accessed April 26, 2017,

66. Loc. cit.

67. Jerry Markon, "U.S. Illegal Immigrant Population Falls below 11 Million, Continuing Decade-long Decline Report Says," *Washington Post*, January 20, 2016, p. 1, www.washingtonpost.com/news/federal-eye/wp/2016/01/20/u-s-illegal-immigrant-population-falls-below-11-million-continuing-nearly-decade-long-decline-report-says/?utm_term=.d36d2eab7cc5, accessed April 26, 2017.

68. "Snapshots: A Summary of CBP Facts and Figures," 2017, p. 1. Department of Homeland Security, p. 1.

69. Loc. cit.

70. Loc. cit.

71. Associated Press, "U.S. Border Patrol "Tunnel Rats' Plug Underground Passages," March 9, 2017, www.voanews.com/a/us-border-patrol-tunnel-rats-plug-underground-passages/3757636.html, accessed April 25, 2017.

72. Loc. cit.

73. Jason McCammack, "What Lies Beneath," *Frontline Magazine*, September 1, 2015, www.cbp.gov/frontline/print-archive/what-lies-beneath, accessed April 25, 2017.

74. Eric Blum, "Further Reflection," *Frontline Magazine*, June 2, 2015, www.cbp.gov/frontline/frontline-june-az-technology, accessed April 27, 2017.

75. Eric Blum, "Further Reflection," *Frontline Magazine*, June 2, 2015, p. 1, www.cbp.gov/frontline/frontline-june-az-technology, accessed April 27, 2017.

76. Loc. cit.

77. Ibid., p. 2.

78. "History of Federal Disaster Mitigation," *Congressional Digest*, Vol. 84, Issue 9, November 2005, p. 258.

79. Loc. cit.

80. Loc. cit.

81. Fernanda Santos and Rebekah Zemansky, "Arizona Desert Swallows Up Migrants on Riskier Paths," *New York Times*, May 20, 2013.

82. Loc. cit.

83. Loc. cit.

84. Peter Slevin, "In Arizona, 'Los Samaritanos' Leave Water and Food on Trails Used by Immigrants," *Washington Post*, June 6, 2010.

85. Emilie Eaton, "Crimes of the Coyotes," *State Press* (Arizona), October 11, 2010, www.statepress.com/2010/10/11/crimes-of-the-coyotes.

86. Loc. cit.

87. No author, "Deadly Crossing: Death Toll Rises Among Those Desperate for the American Dream," *NBC News*, October 9, 2012, p. 8, http://investigations.nbcnews.com/_news/2012/10/09/14300178-deadly-sing-death-toll-rises-among-those-desperate-for-the-american-dream.

88. Loc. cit.

89. See Tony Payan, *The Three U.S.-Mexico Border Wars* (Westport, CT: Praeger International Press, 2006, revised 2010).

90. Schuyler Kropf, "Angry Words for FEMA," *(Charleston) Post and Courier*, March 22, 2012, p. 1, www.postandcourier.com/article/20090921/pc1602/309219933.

91. Loc. cit.

92. "Federal Emergency Management Agency, "About the Agency," March 31, 2017, www.fema.gov/about-agency, accessed April 27, 2017.

93. Francis X. McCarthy, "Federal Stafford Act Disaster Assistance: Presidential Declarations, Eligible Activities, and Funding" (Washington, D.C.: Congressional Research Service, June 7, 2011), p. 1.

94. Loc. cit.

95. Loc. cit.

96. Ibid., p. 10.

97. Ibid., pp. 1–2.

98. FEMA, "Disaster Declarations by Year," 2017, www.fema.gov/disasters/grid/year, accessed April 27, 2017.

99. FEMA, "The Disaster Declaration Process," April 6, 2017, www.fema.gov/disaster-declaration-process, accessed April 27, 2017.

100. Bruce R. Lindsay and Francis X. McCarthy, "Stafford Act Declarations 1953-2014: Trends, Analyses, and Implications for Congress," Congressional Research Service, July 14, 2015, https://fas.org/sgp/crs/homesec/R42702.pdf, accessed April 27, 2017.

101. Ibid., p. 6.

102. Ibid., p. 17.

103. Email, March 17, 2014, from Emily Skarbek to Charles Swanson, "The Chicago Fire of 1871: A Bottom-Up Approach to Disaster Relief," *Public Choice*, forthcoming.

104. "U.S. Coast Guard Organization and Missions," *Sea Power*, Vol. 55, Issue 1, January 2012, p. 131.

105. Loc. cit.

106. Loc. cit.

107. The 1965–1975 period reflects when the United States had substantial forces in South Vietnam, although advisors were deployed as early as 1954, and other authorities use 1956.

108. See Robert T. Hanley, "Keep the Coast Guard Expeditionary," *U.S. Naval Institute Proceedings*, Vol. 130, Issue 11, November 2004, pp. 64–67.

109. "U.S. Coast Guard Organization and Missions," p. 129.

110. Most sources state the United States has 12,383 miles of coastline. However, "The Coast Guard and Homeland Security," www.uscg.mil/history/uscghist/homeland_security.asp, states USCG patrols 95,000 miles of coastline.

111. "DHS at 10: The U.S. Coast Guard," www.dhs.gov/blog/2013/04/04/dhs-10-us-coast-guard.

112. Department of Homeland Security, "Fiscal Year 2017 Budget-in-Brief Fiscal," p. 49, www.dhs.gov/sites/default/files/publications/FY2017BIB.pdf, accessed May 5, 2017.

113. Information taken from U.S. Coast Guard, site www.overview.uscg.mil, from under tabs on workforce and assets, accessed April 5, 2017.

114. Loc. cit.

115. Loc. cit.

116. Gary R. Bowen, "Coast Guard Law Enforcement Detachments in the War on Terrorism," a monograph submitted to the School of Advanced Military Studies, United States Command and General Staff College, Fort Leavenworth, May 26, 2006, p. 28.

117. Theresa Cook, "U.S. Coast Guard Makes Biggest Cocaine Bust in U.S. History," *ABC News,* www.abcnews.go.com/us/story?id=2799.

118. "Terrorist Organization Profile: Shining Path," National Consortium for the Study of Terrorism and Responses to Terrorism, undated, accessed January 19, 2014. The National Counter Terrorism Center lists it as an FTO by the U.S. Department of State as of January 14, 2014, see "Foreign Terrorist Organizations," www.nctc.gov/site/other/fto.html.

119. "U.S. Ups Anti-Drug Aid as Peru Becomes World Leader in Coca Production," *Fox News Latino*, September 25, 2013, www.latino.foxnews.com/latino/news/2013/09/25/us-ups-anti-drug-aid-as-peru-becomes-world-leader-in-coca-production.

120. Hope Hodge Seck, "Coast Guard Apprehends Most Cuban Migrants in Decade," Military.com, November 29, 2016, pp. 1-2, www.military.com/daily-news/2016/11/29/coast-guard-apprehends-most-cuban-migrants-in-decade.html, accessed May 5, 2017.

121. Daniel B. Prieto, "Written Testimony of Daniel B. Prieto before the Massachusetts Joint Committee on Public Safety and Homeland Security," August 4, 2005, p. 2.

122. "Program History," *Transportation Security Administration*, revised December 16, 2012, www.tsa.gov/about-tsa/program-history.

123. This account is drawn, with restatement and additions, from Howard Putnam, "Through Turbulent Times: The Days of NO Airport Security," undated, www.howardputnam.com/security.php.

124. "Budget in Brief Fiscal Year 2014, Homeland Security" (Washington, D.C.: Department of Homeland Security, 2014), p. 131.

125. Stephen M. Lord, "Airport Security: TSA Should Limit Future Funding for Behavioral Detection Activities" (General Accountability Office, Washington, D.C.: November 14, 2013), p. 1.

126. Michael W. Chapman, "TSA Spent $900 Million on Behavior Detection Officers Who Detected 0 Terrorists," *CNSN News*, November 25, 2013, p. 1, www.cnsn.com/news/article/michael-w-chapman/tsa-spent-900-million-behavior-detection-officers-who-detected-0.

127. Lord, "Airport Security," p. 1.

128. "Transportation Security, TSA Could Strengthen Monitoring of Allegations of Employee Misconduct" (Washington, D.C.: General Accountability Office, July 2013), p. 12.

129. "United States Secret Service, Criminal Investigations," p. 1, undated, but with a 2014 copyright, www.secretservice.gov/criminal.shtml.

130. Loc. cit.

131. The information in this paragraph is taken from "Budget in Brief Fiscal Year 2014, Homeland Security," p. 151.

132. U.S. Secret Service, Annual Report 2014, published 2015, p. 1, www.secretservice.gov/data/press/reports/USSS_FY2014AR.pdf, accessed May 5, 2017. www.ice.gov/news

/releases/dhs-releases-end-fiscal-year-2016-statistics#wcm-survey-target-id, accessed May 5, 2017.

133. Ibid., pp. 150 and 152.

134. "United States Secret Service, Criminal Investigations," p. 1.

135. U.S. Secret Service, Annual Report 2014, published 2015, pp. 2 and 18.

136. Ibid., pp. 53–54.

137. "ICE Overview," undated, p. 1, www.ice.gov/about/overview.

138. "Budget in Brief Fiscal Year 2014, Homeland Security," p. 121.

139. Loc. cit.

140. Loc. cit. and "Written Testimony of ICE Deputy Director Daniel Ragsdale for a House Committee on Appropriations Subcommittee on Homeland Security on ICE's FY 2015 Budget Request," March 13, 2014, p. 1, www.dhs.gov/news/2014/03/13/written-testimony-ice-house-appropriations-subcommittee-homeland-security-hearing.

141. Immigration and Customs Enforcement, "DHS Releases End of Fiscal Year 2016 Statistics," May 5, 2017, p. 1,

142. Loc. cit.

143. Loc. cit.

144. Loc. cit.

145. The profile of HSI was taken from "Name redacted," "Homeland Security Investigations, a Directorate Within U.S. Immigration and Customs Enforcement: In Brief," Congressional Research Service, November 10, 2015, pp. 1, 2, and 4, www.everycrsreport.com/files/20151110_R44269_818e7176c0e468170e572a0cd12424731f3046ae.pdf, accessed April 5, 2017.

146. Ibid., p. 123.

147. "Budget In Brief Fiscal Year 2014, Homeland Security," p. 183.

148. Loc. cit.

149. "What Is E-Verify?" U.S. Citizenship and Immigration Services, undated, www.uscis.gov/e-verify/what-e-verify.

150. "Budget in Brief Fiscal Year 2014, Homeland Security," p. 183.

151. Alberto Cuadra, Laris Karklis, and Bill Webster, "The Killing of Special Agent Jaime Zapata," *Washington Post*, February 15, 2012, www.washingtonpost.com/world/the-killing-of-special-agent-jaime-zapata/2012/02/14/glqalu8qfr_graphic.html.

152. Anita U. Hattiangadi, et al., "Non-Citizens in Today's Military Research Brief," *CNA*, www.cna.org/centers/marine-corps/selectedc-studies/non-citizens-brief.

153. Ibid., pp. 1 and 5.

154. "Budget in Brief Fiscal Year 2014, Homeland Security," p. 183.

155. Ibid., p. 184.

156. Ibid., p. 183.

157. James E. Steiner, "Needed: State Level Integrated Intelligence Enterprises," *Studies in Intelligence*, Vol. 53, No. 3, September 2009, pp. 1–2.

158. "Homeland Security/Law Enforcement: Homeland Security Grants" (Washington, D.C.: Government Accountability Office, undated), p. 1. The data is for fiscal years 2002–2011, www.gao.gov/modules/ereport/handler.php?1=1&path=/ereport/G...er/homeland_security-law_enforcement/17._homeland_security_grants.

159. There has been some debate about whether DHS grants have been allocated to the states on the basis of risk/need or "pork barrel politics." On this subject see Holly Goerdel, "Managing Homeland Security in American States: Politics Versus Risk in State Allocations of Federal Security Grants," Conference Paper, 2009 Annual Meeting of the Midwestern Political Science Association, 2009, Toronto, Canada.

America's Vulnerability to Terrorism

Learning Objectives

After completing this chapter, you should be able to:

1. Explain the all-hazards model in planning for critical infrastructure protection.

2. Describe the role of the Federal Bureau of Investigation (FBI) relating to terrorism.

3. Describe the role of the Federal Emergency Management Agency (FEMA) relating to terrorism.

4. Discuss the National Infrastructure Protection Plan (NIPP) and list the critical infrastructure sectors that make up the plan.

The Three Mile Island nuclear generating station is in Middletown, Pennsylvania. A government study assigns a low probability as to the success of a 9/11-style attack using airplanes to damage the reactor core and causing radioactivity to be released. The study also assigned a low probability that such an attack could cause the release of sufficient radioactivity to harm the public's safety and health.

(Laurence Kesterson/KRT/Newscom)

Introduction

Awake to the startling sounds of the newest Drake song as you roll over and hit the "snooze" button. You desperately try to get a few more winks of sleep, but the new song reminds you of last night's gathering at the local pub. As you embrace yet another day, the shrill siren of an ambulance whizzes by on the busy street below your apartment. You stumble from the bed to turn on the lights and move toward the bathroom, a hot shower, and a little dental hygiene to start the new day. Hmmm, that throat is still a little sore and a cough lingers, probably need to get that checked out at the health clinic today. A bowl of cereal, some fruit ... and the sound of a familiar beep ... a text message from the bank indicating that funds are getting low. Classes start in an hour, just enough time to swing by the ATM and remedy that situation. On the way out the door, send a quick email to mom and wish her a happy birthday. Hop in the car and hope the traffic isn't too bad before your morning meeting with fellow students at the chemistry lab. It's just another day like any other.

This may be a typical day across America for many students. It also is an excellent example of critical infrastructure at work, and the benign attitude that everyday people have regarding the services they receive on a daily basis. Let's take another perspective. Each of the daily activities mentioned above requires critical infrastructure within the country that is generally taken for granted by most people. **Critical infrastructure** is defined as those systems and assets, whether physical or virtual, so vital to the United States that the incapacity or destruction of such systems and assets would have a debilitating impact on national security, national economic security, national public health or safety, or any combination of these matters.[1] Each of the above daily activities requires a properly functioning critical infrastructure at federal as well as local levels. This everyday scenario touches several critical infrastructure sectors. The song on the radio had to travel over the airwaves using equipment from the Communications Sector, the electricity for the lights was carried by transmission lines from the Energy Sector, and the power was most likely generated by the Nuclear Sector or the Dams Sector. The shower water came and went as part of the Water and Wastewater Systems Sector. The soap and shampoo used in the shower contained ingredients created by the Chemical Sector. The original concert where Drake performed his number-one hit was recorded at a New York stadium protected by the Commercial Facilities Sector. And the ambulance racing down the street heading for a nearby health clinic where you need to get your throat and cough "checked out" are all part of the Healthcare and Public Health Sector. Milk, cereal, and fruit fall into the Food and Agriculture Sector, and that low bank account balance is tightly controlled by the Banking and Finance Sector. The car you drove to school was built by the Critical Manufacturing Sector, the fuel used was provided by the Energy Sector, your auto insurance was again, part of the Banking and Finance Sector as well as the ATM you stopped by on your way to school. The freeways you crossed while travelling as well as the roads and bridges you crossed and the traffic lights you stopped at were all part of the Transportation Sector. And, of course, that email you sent to mom as well as all of the other sectors used within this short period of time all relied on the Information Technology Sector.

The loss or disruption of all or part of one of these critical infrastructure sectors would have a devastating impact on this country. The simple fact of the matter is that as our society becomes more advanced and complex, the more we rely on critical infrastructure to support our lifestyle and existence. The simple activities we undertake each day could be interrupted, potentially for an extended period of time, wreaking havoc on our nation. Each critical infrastructure sector relies on the others, just like the example described earlier. A failure in one sector could lead to a cascading failure in others, creating an even bigger problem. Witness the recent impact of forest and grass fires in the West and of hurricanes in the South and East as houses were destroyed or lost power, roads and freeways were impassable due to smoke or flooding, airlines were grounded, Internet providers failed, and, essentially, the nation's economic engine ground to a crawl as people could simply not get to work!

The 9/11 terrorist attacks also highlighted the threat and vulnerability to critical infrastructure. Federal, state, and local government agencies have recognized this

Critical infrastructure
Those systems and assets, whether physical or virtual, so vital to the United States that the incapacity or destruction of such systems and assets would have a debilitating impact on national security.

Information Link
For more information on critical infrastructure, see the definition presented by the U.S. Department of Homeland Security at www.dhs.gov/what-critical-infrastructure.

FIGURE 12–1
On 9/11, the role of police changed forever. In addition to keeping our citizenry safe from crime and maintaining order, police officers must now defend and secure infrastructure resources in the homeland. Members of the Orange County (California) Counter Terrorism Team protect the transportation infrastructure by using a canine to search for bombs.

(Jae C. Hong/AP Images)

vulnerability and the impending threats posed by terrorist organizations, and have taken a number of steps to ensure that a catastrophe of this magnitude is reduced. These measures are known as critical infrastructure protection and were a major part of the USA PATRIOT Act, signed by then-President George W. Bush in 2001.[2]

The Impact of 9/11 and the USA PATRIOT Act

Clearly, the attacks on the World Trade Center and the Pentagon on 9/11 and the ensuing passage of the USA PATRIOT Act in 2001 changed our country forever. The attacks set in motion the development of new roles for federal agencies as well as a national commitment to the prevention of terrorism. Indeed, the role of law enforcement changed dramatically from not only thwarting crime, but also preventing, deterring, and investigating potential acts of terrorism. Nowhere is the nation's commitment to preventing terrorism on the homeland more evident than in the *National Strategy for Counterterrorism* reaffirmed in 2011.[3] Although the focus of the document was on dismantling the al-Qaeda network, the far reaching plan clearly articulates the United States' broad, sustained, and integrated plan to safeguard the homeland[4] (see Figure 12–1). Combined with the USA PATRIOT Act, these two documents not only defined the concept of critical infrastructure and the development of specific critical infrastructure plans, but also set forth specific roles and duties for federal agencies before and during a potential disaster, particularly those that may be caused by man-made or terrorist activities.

The All-Hazards Model

Catastrophe can occur as a result of a natural disaster (e.g., hurricane, flood, earthquake, or tornado) or from a man-made act such as those stemming from a terrorist bombing or intentional forest fire. The coordinated plans and efforts designed to protect critical infrastructure and/or coordinate and manage resources during an emergency are often similar. For instance, target hardening a building or dam assists in deterring a terrorist attack as well as strengthens the physical structure from potential natural disasters. Techniques for safeguarding the general population from disease and dangers stemming from a major earthquake may be similar to those that are undertaken after a significant bombing. Hence, the "**all-hazards model**" recognizes that there are aspects of planning and response that are common in many kinds of catastrophes and disasters regardless of causation. The activities are similar; however, they are not identical. Actual disaster response by federal agencies to acts of terrorism is divided into two distinct responsibilities: crisis management and consequence management.

All-hazards model
The concept that there are similar aspects to planning and responding to a catastrophe or emergency event caused by either natural or man-made origins.

The Role of the Federal Bureau of Investigation (FBI)

Crisis management is handled by law enforcement, principally the Federal Bureau of Investigation (FBI). This includes developing, coordinating, and managing a response to major terrorist events that threaten to harm the national security of the United States. The FBI is also the primary federal agency responsible for investigating crimes conducted by terrorist organizations, and includes investigating the crime (terrorism), evidence collection, scene security, and other law enforcement activities.

Crisis management
Developing, coordinating, and managing an effective response to a major emergency event.

Working closely with a variety of federal, state, and local law enforcement partners, the FBI is the primary agency responsible for protecting the United States from terrorist attacks[5] (see Figure 12–2). In addition to the Joint Terrorism Task Forces discussed in Chapter 9, the FBI manages the nation's domestic effort to detect, investigate, and prevent terrorist strikes through a variety of major programs:

- *National Counterterrorism Center and the Public Internet Tip Line.* As discussed in Chapter 9, the FBI is a major partner in the nation's effort to thwart terrorism through the analysis and sharing of intelligence information.

- *Strategic Information and Operations Center (SIOC).* The SIOC is a state-of-the-art national fusion center located at the FBI Headquarters in Washington, D.C. It acts as a national-level clearinghouse to collect, process, and disseminate intelligence information about terrorist threats and incidents. It provides real-time information to the active JTTFs across the nation. The SIOC also serves as the primary national operations, coordination, and command center dedicated to assisting law enforcement personnel during a national or global crisis or major investigation.[6]

- *The Counterterrorism Fly Team.* The FBI maintains a small, highly trained cadre of terrorism first responders—including field agents, SWAT personnel, intelligence analysts, Middle East experts, bomb technicians, and HAZMAT personnel—readily available to respond to any terrorist incident worldwide.[7] Although their primary mission is to quickly respond to domestic emergencies, most of their deployments have been overseas during the last several years.

- *The Most Wanted Terrorist List.* Historically derived from the FBI's Ten Most Wanted Fugitives, the Most Wanted Terrorist List highlights the ten most wanted terrorists. All individuals on the list have been indicted and/or are wanted on a terrorism-related crime stemming from an international or domestic terrorist event.[8] Usama bin Laden, as well as other al-Qaeda leadership members, have been or were members of this infamous group.

FIGURE 12–2
As part of the FBI's investigation following the Boston Marathon bombing in 2013, agents interviewed Ibrahim Todashev in Orlando because he was believed to be associated with the brothers who were suspects in that crime. The interview suddenly became violent, and Todashev was shot and killed by the FBI. An Orlando officer surrounds the scene with yellow barrier tape. The blue evidence booties of a member of the FBI's Evidence Response Team are seen at the corner of the tent.
(Brian Blanco/EPA/Newscom)

The Role of the Federal Emergency Management Agency (FEMA)

On the other hand, **consequence management** is managed by the Federal Emergency Management Agency (FEMA), and includes search and rescue operations, sheltering and caring for affected persons, debris removal, and mitigating damages *after* an event. **Mitigation** is an effort to reduce loss of life and property by lessening the impact of a terrorist attack or natural disaster. However, according to the Department of Homeland Security, it includes taking action *now*—before the incident—to reduce human and financial consequences later as well responding effectively after the event.[9] Although FEMA is the key federal agency for the emergency management of a terrorist attack or natural disaster site after the event (see Chapter 13), a myriad of other agencies have specific roles in responding to and recovering from a disaster. For instance, the coordination of local relief agencies, food banks, shelters, and the like fall within the FEMA management guidelines, while specific responses to public health issues from open sewage lines, biological agents, or even radiation may be more appropriately handled by another agency such as the Center for Disease Control (CDC), the Environmental Protection Agency (EPA), or the Nuclear Regulatory Commission (NRC).

The Federal Emergency Management Agency (FEMA) was created in response to a series of domestic natural disasters in the 1960s and 1970s, and a number of international

Consequence management
Developing, coordinating, and managing mitigation after an emergency event.

Mitigation
An effort to reduce loss of life and property by lessening the impact of a terrorist attack or natural disaster.

Quick Facts
The National Infrastructure Protection Plan (NIPP)

The National Infrastructure Protection Plan (NIPP) is an actual document produced by the U.S. Department of Homeland Security (DHS). The plan is reviewed and updated every year through a collaborative process involving private sector partners; local, state, and tribal governments; and federal agencies working together to identify weaknesses and continually strengthen those assets, systems, and networks that underpin American society. The 2016 NIPP Security and Resilience Challenge, which updates the 2013 NIPP plan, can be found on the DHS website at: www.dhs.gov/publication/nipp-challenge-fact-sheets; and the NIPP plan can be downloaded for free at www.dhs.gov/sites/default/files/publications/national-infrastructure-protection-plan-2013-508.pdf.

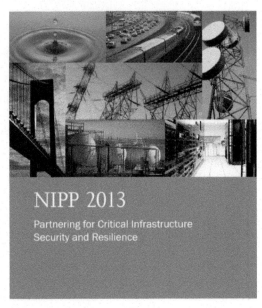

NIPP 2013

Partnering for Critical Infrastructure
Security and Resilience

(Department of Homeland Security)

events in the 1980s.[10] In 1970, then-President Jimmy Carter signed into law Executive Order 12148, charging FEMA with handling "civil emergencies," which included acts of terrorism. In 1988, President Ronald Reagan assigned further responsibility to FEMA to protect "essential resources and facilities" to national security and national welfare at various federal, state, and local levels.[11] Today it is the responsibility of FEMA to protect these "essential resources and facilities" through a systematic plan of identifying, vulnerability assessment, and security preparedness.

The National Infrastructure Protection Plan (NIPP)

National Infrastructure Protection Plan (NIPP)
A formal directive that defines critical infrastructure within the United States and identifies 16 critical infrastructure sectors for protection against man-made (e.g., bombing, terrorist strike, information warfare) as well as natural (e.g., hurricane, flood, tornado, earthquake) disasters.

CI/KRs
Acronym in reference to Critical Infrastructure and Key Resource(s) identified within the National Infrastructure Protection Plan (NIPP).

In 2003, then-President Bush signed Homeland Security Presidential Directive 7, defining a framework for a coordinated approach to identifying and protecting critical infrastructure in the United States.[12] Known as the **National Infrastructure Protection Plan (NIPP)**, the directive originally established 13 critical infrastructure sectors and added a number of key resources that were identified as potential targets from terrorist activities. This included adding agriculture as a critical sector, highlighting dams and nuclear facilities as potential targets, and identifying a number of private commercial facilities (e.g., sports stadiums, entertainment districts like downtown Las Vegas and Disney World, museums, and monuments). The directive also established reference to critical infrastructure and key resources as the acronym **CI/KRs**.

In February 2013, President Barack Obama further extended the NIPP by signing Presidential Policy Directive 21—The Critical Infrastructure and Resilience Directive.[13] This directive consolidated the key resources category into sectors of their own, and produced a total of 16 current critical infrastructure sectors:[14]

- Communications Sector
- Emergency Services Sectors
- Energy Sector
- Dams Sector
- Nuclear Sector
- Water Sector
- Chemical Sector
- Commercial Facilities Sector

- Healthcare and Public Health Sector
- Food and Agriculture Sector
- Critical Manufacturing Sector
- Transportation Sector
- Government Facilities Sector
- Banking and Finance Sector
- Defense Industrial Base Sector
- Information Technology Sector

Each of these sectors has a designated federal agency (or list of related agencies) that serves as the Sector-Specific Agency (SSA) and is charged with coordinating all federal, state, and local entities, both public and private, that ensures that each sector CI/KR is identified, secured, and resilient to a terrorist attack or natural disaster. For instance, the Environmental Protection Agency (EPA) is the SSA for the Chemical Sector. The sector is primarily composed of private chemical companies located throughout the United States, with storage facilities often near major water transportation routes and large urban centers. In addition, each state has an agency with similar duties and functions of the EPA. The National Infrastructure Protection Plan (NIPP) requires the EPA to develop a coordinated plan that identifies potential vulnerabilities within the sector and develop responses to various threat scenarios, coordinating public and private entities at all levels of government. The formalized plan for each of the 16 sectors is then annexed to the NIPP. This is a monumental task that takes considerable resources because the development of these plans is constantly ongoing ... new entities are being built, state and local governmental units change, new threats emerge, and new vulnerabilities are discovered.

Communications Sector

Telecommunications was the first infrastructure to be identified as critical. During the Cuban Missile Crisis, President John F. Kennedy and Soviet Premier Nikita Khrushchev were unable to negotiate directly, and were forced to communicate through written letters. Fax, email, and secure telephones did not exist at the time. As a result, the National Communications System (NCS) was created in 1963 as a planning forum composed of six federal agencies.[15] In 1982, the National Security Telecommunications Advisory Committee (NSTAC), composed of the chief executives of the major telecommunications companies, was established by Executive Order 12382 to advise the president on critical infrastructure protection. The NSTAC was limited to 30 representatives and included companies such as AT&T Communications, General Electric Company, Edison-Bell Telephone Company, American Broadcasting Company-ABC, and the National Broadcasting Company-NBC. In 1984, then-President Ronald Reagan signed Executive Order 12472, which formally made the NCS responsible for the telecommunications infrastructure sector. Today, the NSTAC includes twenty-three member organizations that ensure national security and emergency preparedness telecommunications. The NCTAC represents companies from traditional telephone and broadcasting companies, but also those that are more active in the Internet, cellular telephone, computer, and satellite communication technologies as well, such as Symantec, Microsoft, Intel, Neustar, and Vonage Corporation.[16]

Today the Communications Sector consists of complex systems that incorporate multiple technologies and services, including wireline, wireless, satellite, cable, and broadcasting capabilities, and includes the distribution networks for the Internet and other critical information systems. This sector includes cable, commercial and public broadcasters, information service providers, satellite, undersea cable, telecommunications utility providers, service integrators, equipment vendors, wireless and wireline owners and operators, and the members' respective trade associations. Federal agencies primarily tasked with protecting the Communications Sector include the Department of Commerce, the Federal Communications Commission, and

Quick Facts
The Impact of Major Hurricanes in 2017

The first hurricanes of the 2017 hurricane season in the Atlantic Ocean were Hurricane Harvey and Hurricane Irma. Combined, they represent the most destructive hurricanes to ever make landfall in the United States. In a four-day period (August 24–28), the Hurricane Harvey slammed into the Texas Gulf Coast near Rockport with winds reaching 130 mph (Category 4 Hurricane), and dropped more than 40 inches of rain over the City of Houston, southeast Texas, and southern Louisiana. The rain, particularly in Houston, caused extensive damage and destruction (see Figure 12–3), shutting down roadways, collapsing buildings, disrupting sewer and water treatment, and wiping-out communication pathways like telephone and Internet service for several days. Eighty-nine people in the United States lost their lives to Hurricane Harvey, as it was dubbed the "storm of the century."[17]

However, the impact of Hurricane Harvey was multiplied and intensive by a second, more powerful storm (Hurricane Irma) that quickly developed behind it and also slammed into the United States. Hurricane Irma was an intense storm with some of the highest winds ever recorded in the Atlantic (Category 5 Hurricane with sustained winds of 185 mph) that raged for over 35 hours straight (see Figure 12–4). Nothing like these storms had been observed in the United States since 2005 Hurricanes Wilma and Katrina. Hurricane Irma hit the Florida Keys and the west side of Florida on September 17, less than 20 days after Hurricane Harvey, causing significant flooding and damage throughout Florida and the rest of the southeastern United States.

The combined storms also caused catastrophic damage to many of the island nations of the Caribbean (e.g., Puerto Rico, Cayman Islands, Barbuda, British Virgin Islands, U.S. Virgin Islands, French West Indies, Haiti, and the Dominican Republic as well as the southern states of the continuous U.S. Flooding, high winds and the resulting storm surges of Hurricanes Harvey and Irma taxed the emergency response system of U.S. as well as caused an estimated $200 billion in damages, and the death of at least 250 people throughout the region.

FIGURE 12–3
The city of Houston, Texas bore the brunt of the damage caused by Hurricane Harvey, and the estimated 9 trillion gallons of rain that fell on the region between August 24 and August 28, 2017, causing unprecedented flooding.
(David J. Phillip/AP Images)

FIGURE 12–4
Hurricane Irma's eye (the roughly round dark area at the center of the storm) approaches Florida as it rambles through the Caribbean basin causing catastrophic damages with winds reaching 185 mph.
(NOAA/CIRA)

Department of Justice. These agencies have established information-sharing relationships with state and local jurisdictions and conducted vulnerability assessments of their communications networks. State and local agencies are also involved in Communications Sector protection through state public utility commissions (PUCs), state and local emergency operation centers, and emergency response activities, including first responders and 911 emergency services centers.[18] Unfortunately, even with necessary planning and preparation, communication can be disrupted by violent natural disasters.

Emergency Services Sector

The Emergency Services Sector is the first line of defense in the prevention and mitigation of risk from terrorist attacks, man-made incidents, and natural disasters. This sector includes state and local first responders, composed of law enforcement, fire and emergency services, emergency management agencies, emergency medical services, and public works and utility companies. The Emergency Services Sector represents the primary emergency management agencies and includes a variety of specialized teams, such as Hazardous Materials (HAZMAT), Search and Rescue (SAR), Explosive Ordnance Disposal (EOD), Special Weapons and Tactics and Tactical Operations (SWAT), helicopter and other aviation capabilities, and 911 dispatch centers.[19] Chapter 13 discusses the emergency management function of many of these special units. Unfortunately, as a result of their key role in responding to emergency incidents, terrorists have often targeted first responders by setting secondary explosive devices. For instance, after a bombing, active shooting event, or other criminal act is conducted, **secondary bombs** are hidden and set to detonate when the first responders arrive. The Olympic Park bombing that was perpetrated by Eric Robert Rudolph (July 27, 1996) was the first example of the use of secondary explosive devices in the United States. Rudolph, an active member of the "Army of God," a right-wing, Christian Identity movement, set secondary explosive devices aimed at killing or maiming emergency personnel first arriving at the scene.[20] The phenomenon has also occurred outside the United States in Israel and other countries plagued by terrorist bombings.

Secondary bombs
Hidden bombs often set by terrorists targeting first responders to an emergency event.

Energy Sector

The Energy Sector is divided into three sub sectors: Electricity, Petroleum, and Natural Gas. According to the U.S. Department of Homeland Security, the electrical subsector is huge and vast, containing more than 6,413 power plants producing over 1,075 gigawatts of installed generation per day. This electricity is carried by over 200,000 miles of high-voltage transmission lines and delivered to nearly 200 million customers over an innumerable amount of above and underground lower voltage lines.[21] The electrical subsector is monstrously large and poses a significant vulnerability to the homeland. The system is interconnected and managed by several **electrical power grids**. Each grid serves a specific region of the United States with a secondary grid responsible as a primary or redundant backup. When electric power is interrupted or stopped to a specific area, a **blackout** occurs, and the redundant source immediately transmits power to that area; however, that transmission is often over very long-distance lines. The excessive demand on the redundant grid can be enormous, resulting in a lower transmission to both regional areas that causes a **brownout**, or a drop in voltage to a specific power grid, limiting electrical use and causing lights to glow much dimmer due to the sag in power. The reduction may last for minutes or days, dependent upon restoration of full power to the affected area. Blackouts and brownouts can be the result of a natural disaster, a terrorist attack, or even simple overuse as observed during extreme temperature dips and spikes. New York City has experienced brownouts due to summer heat waves for the past three years, and more are expected as electrical demand for air conditioners often exceeds supply.

Electrical power grid
A system of interconnected electrical processes serving regional areas within the United States.

Blackout
The loss of electrical power in a specific area.

Brownout
A drop in electrical voltage to a specific area.

Quick Facts
Blackout

In July 1977, New York City suffered the longest blackout in history when a simple lightning strike took out two major transmission lines. New York City was without power for nearly two days. Looting, vandalism, and rioting were widespread, in contrast to shorter blackouts suffered in New York in 2003 and 2011.

Box 12–1
Asymmetrical Attacks on the Energy Sector

In 2004, Usama bin Laden stated in an audio recording that "oil prices should be at least $100 a barrel," and called upon radical Islamic groups worldwide to attack oil facilities and pipelines. This was the first documented statement hinting at al-Qaeda's strategy to negatively impact Western economies by disrupting oil supplies and transmission routes. As a result of this threat alone, the price of a barrel of oil skyrocketed by 5 percent the next day. However, bin Laden's strategy was not implemented until spring 2006 when the Abqaiq Oil Refinery in Saudi Arabia was attacked by a suicide truck bomber. The Abqaiq field is one of the largest oil-producing areas in the world and has over 17 billion barrels of oil reserves. In comparison, the entire country of Mexico has only 14.8 billion barrels of reserve; Canada has an estimated 16.8 billion barrels of reserve. Although the attack was averted, the threat was enough to shock the world's oil prices. In just one day, the price of oil increased $3.00, nearly 7 percent per barrel in one day. Just a few short months later in 2007, in an operation known as *Operation Bin Laden Conquest*, an Islamic rebel group based in Nigeria and known as MEND attacked an oil port and pipeline in that nation. These were simultaneous attacks again, aimed at impacting the price of oil on the world economic stage. Bin Laden's statements following these attacks made it clear that al-Qaeda was carrying out attacks against the Western "crusaders and Jews to stop their plundering of Muslim wealth."[22]

How reliant is the American economy on foreign oil? In 2016, 24 percent of the petroleum consumed by the United States was imported from foreign countries. This is the lowest level since 1970; as such, does that change the vulnerability of the Energy Sector to terrorism, both domestically and internationally?

The petroleum subsector of the Energy Sector includes the entire lifecycle of oil from exploration and discovery, extraction from the ground, storage and transportation, to refinement and transmission. It also includes the transmission lines, facilities, and docks used to import foreign crude oil to the country. Today there are more than 525,000 crude oil-producing wells, 30,000 miles of gathering pipeline, and over 51,000 miles of crude oil transmission pipelines in the United States. In addition, there are 150 refineries in operation, 116,000 miles of product pipeline, and 1,400 petroleum terminals.[23] Natural gas is also part of the Energy Sector and is produced from more than nearly 500,000 gas wells and gathered in over 20,000 miles of pipeline. There are more than 500 gas-processing plants and about 320,000 miles of natural gas pipeline throughout the country. Natural gas is stored in over 400 underground storage fields and nearly 110 liquid natural gas (LNG) facilities.[24] Any threat to the Energy Sector not only impacts the physical security of the United States, but also impacts the price of oil on the worldwide market. Threats to this sector can also occur outside the United States in OPEC (Organization of Petroleum Exporting Countries), countries such as Saudi Arabia, Iraq, Venezuela, and Nigeria. See Box 12–1.

Dams Sector

Levees and dams
Dykes, embankments, or walls specifically constructed to regulate water.

Information Link
For more information on dams in the United States, refer to the website by the U.S. Department of the Interior, Bureau of Reclamation at www.usbr.gov/.

Dams in the United States are included in the National Inventory of Dams (NID), maintained by the United States Army Corps of Engineers. Historically, **levees and dams** in the United States were built to protect agricultural operations. Many of these structures are old and were built at a time when good engineering practices were not mandatory. Congress enacted Flood Control Acts in 1928 and 1936 after flooding on the Mississippi and Ohio Rivers. Unlike the National Inventory of Dams, there is not a comprehensive list of levees in the United States, although up to 100,000 miles of levees are estimated. Hurricanes Katrina and Rita, and the resulting flooding throughout the Gulf Coast (Louisiana, Mississippi, Texas, Alabama, and Florida) stemming from the failure of decaying levees and Dams, prompted the National Levee Safety Act of 2007, which required significant remediation of existing levees and dams throughout the United States.[25]

The Department of Homeland Security, Office of Infrastructure Protection is the Sector-Specific Agency responsible for the Dams Sector. Other DHS agencies involved in the Dam Sector include the Federal Emergency Management Agency, U.S. Coast Guard, U.S. Army Corps of Engineers, and the Environmental Protection Agency. Like most critical infrastructure, the majority of dams are privately owned. Private-sector organizations, including the Association of State Dam Safety Officials (ASDSO) and the National Mining Association, among others, are also important partners in securing the Dams Sector.[26] The Dams Sector is also regulated by state, tribal, and territorial governments. Each state has a dam safety regulatory program responsible for the more than 70,000 dams across the United States. Although the Dams Sector is most

---

Box 12-2
Terrorists Are Not the Only Threat to the Dams Sector

In early 2017, after a period of extraordinary drought, heavier-than-usual rains and snow in California caused millions of gallons of water to roar over the Oroville Dam, just north of Sacramento. The high water levels necessitated the use of spillways, which were revealed to have major structural issues. The threat impacted over 188,000 Californians who were evacuated as officials frantically attempted to shore up the spillways. The problem in this case was not a terrorist threat, but an internal one: Dam infrastructure in the United States was recently given a grade of "D" (barely passing) by the American Society of Civil Engineers.[27]

(California DWR/Alamy Stock Photo)

---

vulnerable to natural disasters (hurricanes, tornados, earthquakes), there are an increasing number of terrorist threats made against such structures as well. (See Box 12–2.)

Nuclear Sector

Nuclear power provides approximately 20 percent of the electricity in the United States. This electricity is produced by 99 commercial nuclear reactors located at 61 nuclear power plants.[28] The Nuclear Sector incorporates a variety of related assets aside from the power plants, including non-power nuclear reactors used for research, testing, and training; manufacturers of nuclear reactors or components; radioactive materials used primarily in medical, industrial, and academic settings; nuclear fuel cycle facilities; decommissioned nuclear power reactors; and the transportation, storage, and disposal of nuclear and radioactive waste.[29]

Water Sector

Drinking water and wastewater utilities are included in the Water Sector. Approximately 84 percent of the U.S. population is supplied by 160,000 public drinking water systems and there are more than 16,000 public wastewater treatment systems. More than three-quarters of the country's population has their sewerage treated by these wastewater treatment systems.[30] Bioterrorism or chemical attacks using relatively small quantities of toxic chemicals or biological agents could cause massive contamination, threatening the public health of millions of people in the United States.[31]

Chemical Sector

The Chemical Sector is a major portion of the economy of the United States. There are several hundred thousand facilities that use, store, manufacture, transport, or deliver chemicals throughout the country. The Chemical Sector is a vast industry that employees over a million people and generates nearly $700 billion in revenue, and can be divided into five main segments, based on the end product produced: basic chemicals, specialty chemicals, agricultural chemicals, pharmaceuticals, and consumer products. Like other sectors, the majority of the Chemical Sector is privately owned and includes several functional areas such as manufacturing plants, transport systems, warehouses and storage facilities, and end users.[32]

By its very nature, the Chemical Sector evokes environmental regulation and concern; hence, the primary agency for this sector is the Environmental Protection Agency. The EPA maintains a well-trained and well-equipped **Hazardous Materials (HAZMAT)** team dedicated as a first response to major incidents involving the Chemical Sector (see Chapter 13 on Emergency Management). Individual states, tribal governments, and territories also have occupational safety and health units that may be involved in

Information Link
For more information about the U.S. Department of Homeland Security, Office of Infrastructure Protection, see the website at www.dhs.gov/office-infrastructure-protection.

Hazardous Materials (HAZMAT)
Substances (solid, liquid, or gas) that are dangerous to people, other living organisms, or the environment.

responding to threats and incidents involving the Chemical Sector. Aside from being a target itself, the Chemical Sector is also used by terrorist to procure bomb-making materials, explosives, and other incendiary substances. Several terrorist attacks have unfortunately procured their goods from local chemical plants and/or retail outlets. See Box 12–3 and Box 12–4.

Commercial Facilities Sector

The Commercial Facilities Sector includes large retail centers, hotels, casinos, theme parks, motion picture production studios, office and apartment buildings, convention centers, and sports stadiums. It also includes other sites where large numbers of people congregate to pursue business activities, conduct personal commercial transactions, or enjoy recreational pastimes.[33]

There are eight subsectors in this sector. The Entertainment and Media Subsector includes television and movie media production facilities, print media companies, and broadcast companies. The Gaming Facilities Subsector includes casinos and their accompanying hotels, conference centers, arenas, and shopping centers. The Lodging Subsector consists of non-gaming resorts, hotels and motels, hotel-based conference centers, and bed-and-breakfast establishments. The Outdoor Events Subsector includes amusement parks, fairs, exhibitions, parks, and other outdoor venues. The Public Assembly Subsector encompasses convention centers, auditoriums, stadiums, arenas, movie theaters, cultural properties, and other assets where large numbers of people congregate. The Real Estate Subsector includes office buildings and office parks, apartment buildings, multifamily towers and condominiums, self-storage facilities, and property management companies. The Retail Subsector consists of enclosed malls, shopping centers, strip malls, and free-standing retail establishments. The Sports Leagues Subsector represents the major sports leagues and federations and the ESPN sports broadcasting company[34] (see Figure 12–5).

Healthcare and Public Health Sector

Seventeen percent of the U.S. economy is produced by the Healthcare and Public Health (HPH) Sector, and like many of the other sectors discussed, most of it is privately owned and operated. It consists of hospitals, clinics, and medical research centers located throughout the United States.[35] Aside from the sheer size and economic importance of

---

Box 12-3
The First World Trade Center Terrorist Attack in 1993: Bomb-Making Material Came from Local Chemical Plant

Nidal Ayyad, a naturalized Palestinian, was a distinguished student at Rutgers University who studied chemical engineering and eventually gained a good job at a nearby Morristown, New Jersey, chemical plant. He was well-mannered, quiet, married, and expecting his first child when he first heard a sermon by the radical Islamic cleric, Sheik Omar Abdul Rahman, at his local mosque. Rahman was fighting extradition to Egypt, where he was linked to the political assassination of Anwar Sadat and a variety of terrorist attacks. Rahman expressed rage toward the United States and called on all Muslims to help destroy the American economy. Ayyad became a follower and over the course of his employment stole the chemicals necessary to make the vehicle bomb that was detonated in the first attack of the World Trade Center in 1993. The attack was devastating, causing widespread injury, loss of life, and millions of dollars in damage. It was the worst terrorist attack on American soil to that date. During his trial, information was released that indicated another plan—to use cyanide in combination with the explosives used at the World Trade Center or release massive quantities of cyanide in the ventilation systems of office buildings throughout New York City and Washington, D.C. The cyanide was to be stolen from Ayyad's workplace. The Chemical Sector employs over a million people and the potential threat posed by such workers crosses many critical infrastructure sectors.[36]

▲ This massive crater under the World Trade Center is part of the damage caused by the first attack.
(MARK D. PHILLIPS/Staff/Getty Images)

How would you secure the Chemical Sector in the United States? How would you go about securing private corporations that conduct open commerce of explosives and other dangerous chemicals as part of their business venture?

Box 12-4
The 2013 Boston Marathon Bombing

On April 15, 2013, two bombs exploded during the Boston Marathon, killing three people and wounding another 250 spectators and runners. The bombs were crudely constructed using ordinary pressure cookers as an improvised explosive device (IED) stuffed with explosive material (black powder) and scrap metal (e.g., BBs, nuts, and bolts). A blasting cap was then placed through the cooker cover and attached to a simple timing device or cell phone.

Within two hours after the bombing, a police officer for Massachusetts Institute of Technology (MIT) was killed while confronting two potential suspects, and an ensuing gun battle with police in Watertown, Massachusetts, ensued. One suspect, twenty-seven year old Tamerlan Tsarnaev, was shot and killed during the incident. The other suspect (Tamerlan's brother), twenty-year-old Dzhokhar Tsarnaev, was arrested after he was found hiding in a boat parked in the backyard of a Watertown resident later that same night. During the initial investigation, Dzhokhar alleged

that Tamerlan was the mastermind of the entire bombing and that they had learned how to build the bombs from online instructions hosted by an al-Qaeda affiliate in Yemen. Both Tsarnaev brothers were born in remote areas of the former Soviet Union, near Chechnya, and grew up in Kyrgyzstan. Both were Muslims who became increasingly radicalized by watching Anwar al-Awlaki lectures and other jihadist speakers on the Internet. On April 22, 2015, Dzhokhar Tsarnaev was convicted of using and conspiring to use a weapon of mass destruction (planting bombs) resulting in murder at the Boston Marathon. On May 16, 2015, he was sentenced to death by lethal injection on six of 17 counts of murder He is currently awaiting execution in a federal prison in Colorado.

How vulnerable are we to such attacks? How can the safety and security of players (runners) be improved while still maintaining access for spectators and media? What would you do to improve the security at such events?

A pressure cooker bomb

Investigators say the bombs detonated at the Boston Marathon were made using a pressure cooker; how a common kitchen utensil becomes deadly:

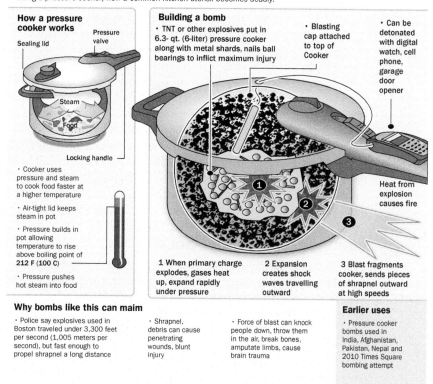

How a pressure cooker works

- Sealing lid
- Pressure valve
- Steam
- Food
- Locking handle

- Cooker uses pressure and steam to cook food faster at a higher temperature
- Air-tight lid keeps steam in pot
- Pressure builds in pot allowing temperature to rise above boiling point of **212 F (100 C)**
- Pressure pushes hot steam into food

Building a bomb

- TNT or other explosives put in 6.3- qt. (6-liter) pressure cooker along with metal shards, nails ball bearings to inflict maximum injury
- Blasting cap attached to top of Cooker
- Can be detonated with digital watch, cell phone, garage door opener

Heat from explosion causes fire

1 When primary charge explodes, gases heat up, expand rapidly under pressure

2 Expansion creates shock waves travelling outward

3 Blast fragments cooker, sends pieces of shrapnel outward at high speeds

Why bombs like this can maim

- Police say explosives used in Boston traveled under 3,300 feet per second (1,005 meters per second), but fast enough to propel shrapnel a long distance
- Shrapnel, debris can cause penetrating wounds, blunt injury
- Force of blast can knock people down, throw them in the air, break bones, amputate limbs, cause brain trauma

Earlier uses

- Pressure cooker bombs used in India, Afghanistan, Pakistan, Nepal and 2010 Times Square bombing attempt

Quick Facts
The Commercial Facilities Sector

The Commercial Facilities Sector is a huge part of the U.S. economy, but most people do not understand the threats to the sector, or their potential impacts. With significant natural disasters, cyber attacks, and terrorist threats on the retail, wholesale, and distribution industry during the last three years, some market experts suggest that disruption may be the new normal in 2018 and beyond.[37] Risks to the sector include natural disasters and extreme weather, armed attackers, pandemics, cyber attacks, explosive devices, mass protests, chemical-biological-radiological attacks, theft, unmanned aircraft attacks (drones), supply chain disruption, and global political and social upheaval.[38]

FIGURE 12–5
The 2017 Super Bowl was held at NRG Stadium in Houston, Texas. More than 100,000 people attended the game, and another 111 million watched the game on the Fox Network. Protecting sports venues where large numbers of people congregate is a major part of securing America's Homeland.
(Andrew Gombert/EPA/REX/ Shutterstock)

Anthrax
Spore-forming bacterium that is often "weaponized" or genetically altered to be more deadly.

Ricin
An easily made and highly toxic poison refined from castor beans.

Ebola Virus Disease (EVD)
Formerly known as Ebola Hemorrhagic Fever, or just Ebola, is a severe and often fatal disease transmitted to people from the fluids of wild animals; and spreads through the human population via direct contact with the bodily fluids of infected people.

Gross domestic product (GDP)
The total value of goods and services produced by a nation during one year.

the sector, it also has a significant role in response, mitigation, and recovery during natural disasters or terrorist events. For instance, during the **anthrax** attack in 2001, following 9/11, five people died and 17 others were sickened. Anthrax is a spore-forming bacterium that is naturally occurring in the United States. Letters containing anthrax spores were mailed to media outlets, news commentators, and government officials. The anthrax contained in these letters was "weaponized," or genetically altered to make it much more deadly. The Healthcare and Public Health Sector quickly responded with plans to distribute antibiotics to a major portion of the population of the United States in the event of a large-scale anthrax attack. In 2013, a similar biological attack occurred when letters containing **ricin** were sent to then-President Obama and members of Congress. Ricin is an easily made and very potent toxin that is refined from castor beans. It was popularized in the hit TV show *Breaking Bad*, as "Mr. White" conjured up the white powder to take care of troublesome business associates. In reality, a lethal dose of ricin for humans is very small, about the size of a grain of salt either injected or inhaled. Although no one was injured during these mail attacks, the HPH Sector was again available with mobile treatment facilities to assist potential victims from a large-scale attack.[39] Unfortunately, there is no known antidote for ricin.

This sector is vulnerable precisely because it is so wide-ranging and interdependent. The HPH Sector responds to natural disasters as well as terrorist attacks, and relies on infrastructure such as phone, power, and Internet to function at full potential. It is also affected by community variables. This makes the HPH response complex, and makes planning for and assessing risks complicated. Emerging threats to this sector include pandemics and health crises, such as the **Ebola Virus Disease (EVD)** breakout in late 2014; natural disasters, extreme weather and climate change; malicious human acts, such as those described above and extending to mass shootings and critical infrastructure attacks; supply chain disruption and corruption, like tainted blood products or contaminated food; cyber attacks on health systems; and more. One interesting consideration is the effect of climate change, which is characterized as a major threat to HPH as it is expected to lead to more extreme weather events that lead to more severe public health emergencies, thus putting a strain on the HPH system.[40]

Food and Agriculture Sector

The Food and Agriculture Sector includes the farming, breeding, production, processing, and delivery systems associated with agricultural and livestock food in the United States. The Sector includes various industry and trade associations, including the American Farm Bureau Federation, National Cattlemen's Beef Association, National Milk Producers Federation, and the National Restaurant Association, among others. The Sector accounts for roughly one-fifth of the economic engine of the United States, with about one-fifth of this production exported to foreign countries. Crop production in the United States alone accounts for nearly $200 billion of **gross domestic product (GDP)**.[41]

Critical Manufacturing Sector

The Critical Manufacturing Sector is another major part of the economic engine of the United States. This sector provides 13 percent of the gross domestic product (GDP) of the United States and employs an estimated 11.7 million people.[42] Primary metal manufacturing, machinery manufacturing, electrical equipment manufacturing (which provides the components that "turn the lights on"), transportation equipment manufacturing, and railroad rolling stock manufacturing are considered major subsectors of the Critical Manufacturing Sector. Any direct attack or disruption of certain elements of the manufacturing industry could easily disrupt essential functions at the national level and across multiple critical infrastructure sectors.[43] A terrorist attack in any of these subsectors with the Critical Manufacturing Sector could have a cascading effect that would limit the ability to move goods, restore electricity, and keep America working.

Quick Facts

The only confirmed Ebola virus cases transmitted in the United States were in late 2014, when a forty-five-year-old Liberian national visited Dallas, Texas, from West Africa. Within two weeks of his visit, two nurses treating the individual were diagnosed with the disease; both recovered. In total, the United States has witnessed eleven cases, however nine of those were, again, contracted outside the United States in Africa and then brought to the United States for treatment. Two of the nine quarantined patients died of the disease. Ebola is a much more devastating disease in Africa, where an estimated 11,500 people have died from the disease. Health-care workers are frequently infected while treating patients; and since there is no licensed Ebola vaccine, fatality rates are usually very high, approaching 90 percent in remote areas.[44]

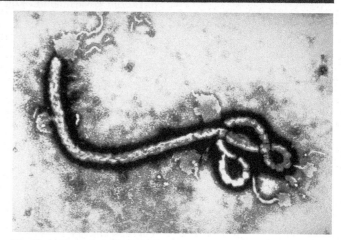

The Ebola Virus magnified 108,000 times
(Charles Smith/Corbis/VCG/Getty Images)

Transportation Sector

People and goods move across the country as part of the Transportation Sector. There are six Sub sectors of the Transportation Sector: Aviation, Highway, Maritime, Mass Transit, Pipeline Transmission, and Rail. The transportation of people and goods is an essential service to maintain the economic efficiency of the country. Most of the raw materials and manufactured products in the United States are transported over the four million miles of freeways and highways that interconnect almost every community in the country. The other primary mode of transporting goods is accomplished by the nearly 1.3 million freight cars that run over nearly 150,000 miles of track.[45] Most of the track is highly vulnerable to terrorist activity. Derailment (either intentionally or by accident) of tank cars commonly transporting chemicals could cause significant harm to populated areas. For instance, in Willard, Ohio, in 2013, the accidental derailment of a tank car carrying styrene monomer, a highly flammable and toxic substance, resulted in over 400 residents being evacuated. Although no deaths or serious injuries occurred, the incident highlighted the vulnerability of dangerous chemicals commonly being transported by both rail and river barges across America every day.

However, when one talks about the Transportation Sector and terrorism, it is the aviation subsector that immediately comes to mind. The skyjacking of four commercial flights and the subsequent use of those fully loaded aircraft as weapons against the World Trade Center and the Pentagon emphasize the impact of terrorism on both the Transportation and Government Facilities Sector. **Skyjacking** is the diversion of a commercial airline flight away from its scheduled flight plan, usually involving violence or the threat of violence against the passengers and/or crew of the aircraft. The events of 9/11 greatly impacted world air travel—from pre-flight records checks to submission of individual persons for physical screening and pat downs, to the target hardening of flight cockpits—air passengers are ever minded of the potential for terrorism. Anyone who has travelled by air in the last decade has certainly been impacted by these changes.

Skyjacking
The diversion of a commercial airline flight away from its scheduled flight plan, usually by violence or threat of violence against passengers and/or crew.

Quick Facts
The First Skyjacking

The first skyjacking of a commercial flight in the United States occurred on May 1, 1961, when a National Airlines flight from Miami to Key West, Florida, was hijacked by a man carrying a knife and gun. He demanded that the plane be diverted to Havana. The incident sparked the beginning of a trend; it was the first of four flights diverted to Cuba that year.[46]

Government Facilities Sector

A wide variety of buildings and structures are owned by federal, state, local, tribal, and territorial governments. For instance, there are nearly 40,000 post offices along, with a myriad of federal and state buildings and monuments. Securing these facilities is a huge challenge. Federal facilities alone cover more than 3 billion square feet and there are another 90,000 municipal governments that maintain their own facilities.[47] Individual government facilities are attractive and strategically important targets for terrorists due to their symbolic value. In 1995, the Alfred P. Murrah Federal Building in Oklahoma City was targeted by two homegrown terrorists (Timothy McVeigh and Terry Nichols). The suspects used a Ryder rental truck loaded with approximately 7,000 pounds of explosives and detonated it in front of the building. The attack killed 168 people; many were the children of federal workers attending day care in the building. The General Services Administration provides physical security for most federal facilities, which have been significantly upgraded since the attack on the Murrah Building.

Banking and Finance Sector

The U.S. Department of Treasury is the Sector-Specific Agency for the Banking and Finance Sector. Federal financial regulators, such as the Board of Governors of the Federal Reserve System (FRB), Federal Deposit Insurance Corporation (FDIC), Federal Housing Finance Agency (FHFA), and Securities and Exchange Commission (SEC) are also heavily involved in this sector. Exchanges, such as the Chicago Mercantile Exchange (CME) and the New York Stock Exchange (NYSE) also play an important role in this sector.

The Banking and Finance Sector is regulated (and categorized) by the various products provided by the sector. These include deposit and payment systems, credit and liquidity products, investment products, and risk transfer documents such as insurance and annuity products. The Banking and Finance Sector accounts for all monetary and fiscal assets of both the government and private enterprise within the country. There are more than 18,800 federally insured depository institutions, thousands of investment product providers, including 18,440 broker-dealers, investment advisers, and investment companies, and millions of risk transfer documents stemming from nearly 10,000 domestic insurers in the United States.[48] It is, by far, the most "valuable" of all sectors within the United States.

Defense Industrial Base Sector

The Department of Defense is the Sector-Specific Agency for the Defense Industrial Base Sector. The sector consists of the various public- and private-sector industrial complexes that support military operations directly, conduct research and development, including the design, production, delivery, and maintenance of military weapons systems, subsystems, and components or parts for the United States military.[49] The private component of this sector is huge and includes hundreds of thousands of domestic and foreign companies, including their manufacturing supply chains.

Information Technology (IT) Sector

As previously mentioned, each of the critical infrastructure sectors are interconnected and rely on one another for functionality, effectiveness, and efficiency. Nowhere is this interdependence more evident than within the Information Technology (IT) Sector. Indeed, all other critical infrastructure and key resources (CI/KRs) are reliant upon the IT Sector to provide data, coordination, and communication during a natural disaster or terrorist event. The IT Sector is basically the "tie that binds" many other assets within critical infrastructure together. As such, it is often the target of terrorists, hackers, social activists, criminals, international organized cartels (see Box 12–5), and state-supported intelligence services that engage in information warfare.

Information warfare (IW) is the concept of using information technology to gain tactical or strategic advantage over an opponent during a conflict. This can be intelligence

Information warfare (IW)
The concept of using information technology to gain tactical or strategic advantage over an opponent.

Box 12-5
Foreign Cyber Threats: Information Warfare as a Threat to Critical U.S. Infrastructure

In early 2013, one of the most significant and controversial security reports regarding cyber threats to U.S. infrastructure emerged from Mandiant, a computer security consulting corporation. The report documented thousands of cyber attacks aimed primarily against public and corporate entities within the United States since 2006 from China, and identified a group known as Advanced Persistent Threat One (APT1) as the primary culprit. APT1 is a single organization of individual operators working within China that have conducted one of the most aggressive and sophisticated cyberespionage campaigns ever uncovered. The sheer amount of activity along with the discovery of various sophisticated tools and tactics used by APT1 led Mandiant to conclude that APT1 is likely a Chinese government-sponsored group with direct ties to the People's Liberation Army (PLA), Unit 61398. Both groups have similar missions, capabilities, and resources and are located in precisely the same building in Shanghai, China.

Mandiant believes that indeed APT1 *is* PLA Unit 61398. APT1's cyber attack information technology is composed of over 1,000 servers within a large organization staffed by hundreds of human operators with direct access to Shanghai communication systems and capabilities. The conclusion that the Chinese

government was not only aware of APT1, but also now actively involved in the direction and management of a group designed primarily to steal digital information and attack Western enterprises, sent shockwaves through the international community. The Mandiant report represents the first conclusive evidence that foreign governments do indeed sponsor military-based, cyber activity designed specifically to steal information and disrupt American critical infrastructure. The Mandiant Report indicates that APT1 poses the single largest threat to American cybersecurity. Since 2006, APT1 has successfully attacked 115 governmental and private-sector infrastructures, some of which represent America's largest banks, corporate and manufacturing entities, defense contractors, and national security agencies. Awareness of this type of threat has provided the stimulus for billions of dollars dedicated to retaining cutting-edge capability in defending infrastructure within the Information Technology Sector.[50]

Information warfare and terrorist attacks sponsored by a nation-state may rise to the level of open conflict and war. How do you think the United States should respond to such attacks? Do you think the United States should also conduct information warfare attacks on other countries, like China, Russia, North Korea, and Iran, in retaliation?

Quick Facts
Russian Hacking Causes Financial Losses, May Have Influenced U.S. Voters

In July 2013, federal prosecutors brought charges against four Russian nationals and one Ukrainian suspect charged with running an organization that hacked the computer networks of more than a dozen corporations, stealing and selling at least 160 million credit and debit card numbers. The scheme had run since 2005 and included, among others, some of the largest credit card corporations, including VISA, Heartland Payment Systems, and J.C. Penney. A separate case involving the NASDAQ stock exchange was also filed against one of the suspects. This "hack" represented the cutting edge of financial fraud and highlights the broader threat that cyber crime poses to a financial system that is almost entirely reliant on networked communications and systems. **Hacking** is the illegal intrusion into a secure data or computer system. The losses from this case alone are staggering, and run in the billions of dollars.[51]

During the 2016 presidential election, emails from the Democratic National Convention and the Hillary Clinton campaign that portrayed potentially unethical and unflattering information were obtained illegally through a directed cyber attack and published. Congress has suggested that while the actual electoral process remained secure, these "hacks" may have influenced U.S. voters as they cast their ballots. An NSA investigation indicated that the cyber attack came from the Russian government, and as a result, Russia was officially sanctioned. In addition, several officials within the Trump Administration and the 2016 campaign are under investigation by the FBI to determine if they coordinated or colluded with Russia to arrange or benefit from the cyber attacks[52].

in the sense of knowing the enemy's capabilities, intentions, and dispositions (deployment), or undermining their capabilities and will to fight. Propaganda, disinformation, counterintelligence, deception, and the disruption of critical infrastructure are all aspects of information warfare.[53] The IT Sector includes physical assets, as well as virtual systems and networks, across the public and private arenas within the United States. Federal agencies involved in the IT Sector include the U.S. Departments of Homeland Security, Commerce, Energy, and Defense; the National Institute of Standards and Technology; and the General Services Administration. Private partners include easily recognizable IT companies, defense contractors, and fiscal entities, such as Apple, Boeing, JP Morgan-Chase, Google, eBay, Raytheon, Cisco, Citibank, Intel, Microsoft, Bank of America, and Lockheed Martin.[54] State and local governments, as well as international partners, are also involved in securing the IT Sector.

Hacking
The illegal intrusion into a secure data or computer system.

Information Link
For more information on the potential for a major cyber attack on our critical infrastructure, and the use of information warfare as both a defensive and offensive weapon of the future, see the U.S. Army Cyber Command (CYBERCOM) website at www.arcyber.army.mil/Pages/ArcyberHome.aspx.

Chapter Summary

1. **Explain the all-hazards model in planning for critical infrastructure protection.**

   The all-hazards model recognizes that there are aspects of planning and response that are common in many kinds of catastrophes and disasters regardless of causation. Therefore, protecting critical infrastructure and responding to and mitigating emergency events are similar in both natural as well as man-made catastrophes.

2. **Describe the role of the Federal Bureau of Investigation (FBI) relating to terrorism.**

   The FBI is the primary agency responsible for crisis management during a terrorist event. The FBI is responsible for developing, coordinating, and managing a response to terrorism as well as conducting and coordinating all aspects of an investigation involving a terrorist event (e.g., crime scene security, interviewing witnesses and victims, collecting evidence, arresting suspects). The FBI works closely with state and local law enforcement agencies and hosts a variety of programs aimed at coordinating investigations and preventing future terrorist strikes. These include the management of the Joint Terrorism Task Forces, the National Counterterrorism Center and the Public Internet Tip Line, the Counterterrorism Fly Team, and the Ten Most Wanted Terrorist List.

3. **Describe the role of the Federal Emergency Management Agency (FEMA) relating to terrorism.**

   The role of FEMA during a terrorist event is consequence management. That is, FEMA is responsible for the emergency management of a major event such as a natural disaster or a terrorist strike. This includes mitigation, or the effort to reduce loss of life and property by lessening the impact of the event. Some of the duties of FEMA at a catastrophe include search and rescue, sheltering and caring for affected persons, managing debris removal, and maintaining safeguards for the general public.

4. **Discuss the National Infrastructure Protection Plan (NIPP) and list the critical infrastructure sectors that make up the plan.**

   The National Infrastructure Protection Plan (NIPP) was developed under President George W. Bush in 2003. It is a formal document that provides a framework for a coordinated approach to identifying and protecting critical infrastructure in the United States. The NIPP establishes an acronym (CI/KR) to refer to critical infrastructure and key resources that are imperative for the broad national security of the United States. The NIPP recognizes 16 critical infrastructure sectors: Communications, Emergency Services, Energy, Dams, Nuclear, Water, Chemical, Commercial Facilities, Healthcare and Public Health, Food and Agriculture, Critical Manufacturing, Transportation, Government Facilities, Banking and Finance, Defense Industrial Base, and Information Technology (IT).

1. What is critical infrastructure, and how does it impact people living in the United States?
2. What is the role of the FBI and FEMA during a terrorist event in the United States?
3. Discuss some of the major programs managed by the FBI to detect, investigate, and prevent terrorist strikes on the homeland.
4. Define the all-hazards model.
5. What is the National Infrastructure Protection Plan (NIPP)? Name some of the identified critical infrastructure sectors identified in the plan.
6. How did Hurricanes Harvey and Irma impact critical infrastructure in the United States?
7. What are anthrax and ricin?
8. Define the term "skyjacking."
9. Relate the activities of hacking and information warfare to threats against the IT Sector.
10. What is APT1?

CRITICAL THINKING EXERCISES

1. **Fire Eye.** Visit the Fire Eye website at www.fireye.com. Check out the "Assess & Prepare," "Detect & Prevent," and "Analyze & Respond" areas to learn more about the use of malware, social engineering, and other tactics and strategies often employed by people attempting to gain illegal access to computer systems. Watch the video entitled *Anatomy of an Attack*. Now, read the M-Trends Report for the year. What new threats lurk in the cyberworld to our infrastructure? Discuss as a class the huge issue of cyber-security and information warfare as a major threat to our infrastructure. Can you think of additional ways to make our country less vulnerable from these types of attack? Think outside the box!

2. **Preparing for Security at this Year's Super Bowl.** Explore the Internet and find articles focused on preparing for this year's Super Bowl. Read the U.S. Department of Justice COPS paper entitled "Planning and Managing Security for Major Special Events" by Edward Connors at: https://hsdl.org/?view&did=482649.

   Now, think about the difficulties in planning for security at the Super Bowl. Where will the event be held? What new arsenal of security initiatives should be enacted for the event? How will parking and public access to the stadium be limited? What agencies will be primarily involved in the security of the event, and more important, what will be the role of those agencies? Identify other areas of the city where the Super Bowl is being held that will also be "on alert." Imagine how much time, energy, and money go into preparing for and providing the security for such an event. Who do you think should pay for the security at the Super Bowl? The host city? The NFL? The people attending the big game? The media networks broadcasting the game? The general public? Now, try to find out by scouring the web. It won't be easy ... try to find out how much security cost for the last Super Bowl.

NOTES

1. The National Infrastructure Protection Plan as defined by the *Critical Infrastructures Protection Act of 2001*, Title 42 USC, Chapter 68, Subchapter IV-B, Subsection 5195c. See also William J. Clinton, Presidential Decision Directive, Critical Infrastructure Protection, May 22, 1998, www.fas.org/irp/offdocs/pdd/pdd-63.pdf.
2. USA PATRIOT ACT, signed on October 26, 2001.
3. See www.whitehouse.gov/blog/2011/06/29/national-strategy-counterterrorism.
4. Ibid.
5. See www.fbi.gov/about-us/investigate/terrorism.
6. See www.fbi.gov/about-us/cirg/sioc.
7. See www.fbi.gov/news/stories/2005/march/flyteam_033005.
8. See www.fbi.gov/wanted/wanted_terrorists.
9. See www.fema.gov/what-mitigation.
10. Federal Emergency Management Agency, "About the Agency," July 22, 2013, www.fema.gov/about-agency.
11. Ted G. Lewis, *Critical Infrastructure Protection in Homeland Security: Defending a Networked Nation* (Hoboken, NJ: Wiley Inter Science, 2006).
12. George W. Bush, Homeland Security Presidential Directive 7, Critical Infrastructure Identification, Prioritization, and Protection. *Code of Federal Regulations*. Title 3, Volume 39, Issue 51 (December 22, 2003) § 1816–1822, www.dhs.gov/homeland-security-presidential-directive-7#1.
13. Barack Obama, Presidential Policy Directive 21, Critical Infrastructure Security and Resilience, February 12, 2013, www.whitehouse.gov/the-press-office/2013/02/12/presidential-policy-directive-critical-infrastructure-security-and-resil.
14. U.S. Department of Homeland Security, "Critical Infrastructure Sectors," no date, www.dhs.gov/critical-infrastructure-sectors.

15. Ted G. Lewis, *Critical Infrastructure Protection in Homeland Security: Defending a Networked Nation* (Hoboken, NJ: Wiley Inter Science, 2006).

16. Refer to membership of the National Security Telecommunications Advisory Committee (NSTAC), as of November 12, 2013, www.dhs.gov/nstac-members.

17. See Robert Miller, "Hurricane Katrina: Communications & Infrastructure Impacts." *National Defense University*, June 2006, www.carlisle.army.mil/DIME/documents/Hurricane%20Katrina%20Communications%20&%20Infrastructure%20Impacts.pdf.

18. U.S. Department of Homeland Security, *Communications Sector-Specific Plan: An Annex to the National Infrastructure Plan*, 2010, www.dhs.gov/xlibrary/assets/nipp-ssp-communications-2010.pdf.

19. U.S. Department of Homeland Security, *Emergency Services Sector-Specific Plan: An Annex to the National Infrastructure Plan*, 2010, www.dhs.gov/xlibrary/assets/nipp-ssp-emergency-services.pdf.

20. U.S. Department of Justice, "Eric Rudolph Charged in Centennial Olympic Park Bombing." *FBI News Release,* October 14, 1998. See also additional information on secondary explosive devices, "FBI Again Warns of Secondary Explosive Devices, Cautions Officer to Watch Surroundings," May 17, 2004, www.policeone.com/terrorism/articles/86852-FBI-Again-Warns-of-Secondary-Explosive-Devices-Cautions-Officers-To-Watch-Surroundings/.

21. U.S. Department of Homeland Security, *Energy Sector-Specific Plan: An Annex to the National Infrastructure Plan*, 2010, www.dhs.gov/xlibrary/assets/nipp-ssp-energy-2010.pdf.

22. For more information on this subject, refer to the sources for this box item: Mordechai Abir, "The Al-Qaeda Threat to Saudi Arabia's Oil Sector," *Journal of Jerusalem Center for Public Affairs*, Vol. 4, No. 13, p. 28. December 2004; and Khalid R. Al-Rodham, "The Impact of the Abqaiq Attack on Saudi Energy Security," *Center for Strategic and International Studies*, February 27, 2006.

23. Ibid.

24. Ibid.

25. U.S. Department of Homeland Security. *Dams Sector-Specific Plan: An Annex to the National Infrastructure Plan*, 2010, www.hsdl.org/?view&did=7980.

26. Ibid.

27. David A. Graham. *How did the Oroville dam crisis get so dire?* February 13, 2017, *Atlantic*. Retrieved from www.theatlantic.com/national/archive/2017/02/how-did-the-oroville-dam-get-so-bad/516429/.

28. U.S. Energy Information Administration. "Frequently Asked Questions." Retrieved from www.eia.gov/tools/faqs/faq.php?id=207&t=3.

29. U.S. Department of Homeland Security, *Nuclear Reactors, Materials, and Waste Sector-Specific Plan: An Annex to the National Infrastructure Plan*, 2010, www.dhs.gov/xlibrary/assets/nipp-ssp-nuclear-2010.pdf; and U.S. Department of Homeland Security, *Nuclear Sector Snapshot*, 2011, www.dhs.gov/xlibrary/assets/nppd/nppd-ip-nuclear-sector-snapshot-2011.pdf.

30. U.S. Department of Homeland Security, *Water Sector-Specific Plan: An Annex to the National Infrastructure Plan*, 2010, www.dhs.gov/xlibrary/assets/nipp-ssp-water-2010.pdf.

31. Claudia Copeland and Betsy Cody, "Terrorism and Security Issues Facing the Water Infrastructure Sector," May 21, 2003, Congressional Research Service. www.cfr.org/targets-for-terrorists/crs-report-terrorism-security-issues-facing-water-infrastructure-sector/p9974.

32. U.S. Department of Homeland Security, *Chemical Sector-Specific Plan: An Annex to the National Infrastructure Plan*, 2010, www.dhs.gov/xlibrary/assets/nppd/nppd-ip-chemical-sector-snapshot-2011.pdf; U.S. Department of Homeland Security, *Chemical Sector Snapshot*, 2011, www.dhs.gov/xlibrary/assets/nppd/nppd-ip-chemical-sector-snapshot-2011.pdf; and U.S. Department of Homeland Security, *Chemical Stockpile Emergency Preparedness Program*, September 30, 2013, www.fema.gov/technological-hazards-division-0/chemical-stockpile-emergency-preparedness-program.

33. U.S. Department of Homeland Security, *Commercial Facilities Sector-Specific Plan: An Annex to the National Infrastructure Plan*, 2010, www.dhs.gov/xlibrary/assets/nipp-ssp -commercial-facilities-2010.pdf.

34. Ibid.

35. U.S. Department of Homeland Security, *Healthcare and Public Health Sector-Specific Plan: An Annex to the National Infrastructure Plan*, 2010, www.dhs.gov/xlibrary/ assets/nipp-ssp-healthcare-and-public-health-2010.pdf.

36. For more information, see the references for this box item: (1) Gebe Martinez and William C. Rempel, "Bombing Suspects: Ties that Bind a Seemingly Odd Pair," *Los Angeles Times*, March 11, 1993; (2) U.S. Congress, Senatorial Records 332–335. See U.S. Congressional Serial Set, Serial No. 15016, 2006; and (3) Eben Kaplan, Council on Foreign Relations, "Targets for Terrorists: Chemical Facilities," December 11, 2006, www.cfr.org/ united-states/targets-terrorists-chemical-facilities/p12207#p8.

37. Rodney R. Sides, "Retail, Wholesale, and Distribution Industry Outlook 2017: An Analysis of Industry Trends," Deloitte Outlooks. See www2.deloitte.com/us/en/pages/consumer -business/articles/retail-distribution-industry-outlook.html.

38. U.S. Department of Homeland Security. *Commercial Facilities Sector-Specific Plan: An Annex to the National Infrastructure Protection Plan*, 2015, www.hsdl .org/?view&did=791103.

39. Brad Bell, "Ricin Scares Reminiscent of Anthrax Attacks for Mail Handlers," *ABC News*, 2013, www.wjla.com/articles/2013/04/ricin-scares-reminiscent-of-anthrax-attacks -for-mail-handlers-87655.html. For more information on the anthrax attacks in 2001, see Council on Foreign Relations, "The Anthrax Letters," January 2006, www.cfr.org/ weapons-of-mass-destruction/anthrax-letters/p9555.

40. U.S. Department of Homeland Security, *Healthcare and Public Health Sector-Specific Plan: An Annex to the National Infrastructure Plan*, 2016, www.dhs.gov/sites/default/ files/publications/nipp-ssp-healthcare-public-health-2015-508.pdf.

41. U.S. Department of Homeland Security, *Food and Agriculture Sector-Specific Plan: An Annex to the National Infrastructure Plan*, 2010, www.dhs.gov/xlibrary/assets/nipp-ssp -food-ag-2010.pdf.

42. U.S. Department of Homeland Security, *Critical Manufacturing Snapshot*, 2011, www.dhs.gov/xlibrary/assets/nppd/nppd-ip-critical-manufacturing-snapshot-2011.pdf.

43. U.S. Department of Homeland Security, *Critical Manufacturing Sector-Specific Plan: An Annex to the National Infrastructure Plan*, 2010, www.dhs.gov/sites/default/files/ publications/nipp-ssp-critical-manufacturing-2010.pdf.

44. World Health Organization, *Fact Sheet on Ebola*, January 2016, at: www.who.int/ mediacentre/factsheets/fs103/en/.

45. U.S. Department of Homeland Security, *Transportation Systems Sector-Specific Plan: An Annex to the National Infrastructure Plan*, 2010, www.dhs.gov/xlibrary/assets/nipp -ssp-transportation-systems-2010.pdf.

46. See Brendan I. Koerner, *The Skies Belong to Us: Love and Terror in the Golden Age of Hijacking* (New York: Random House, 2013).

47. U.S. Department of Homeland Security, *Government Facilities Sector Snapshot*, www.dhs.gov/xlibrary/assets/nipp-ssp-chemical-2010.pdf.

48. U.S. Department of Homeland Security, *Banking and Finance Sector-Specific Plan: An Annex to the National Infrastructure Plan*, 2010, www.dhs.gov/sites/default/files/ publications/nipp-ssp-banking-and-finance-2010.pdf.

49. U.S. Department of Homeland Security, *Defense Industrial Base Sector-Specific Plan: An Annex to the National Infrastructure Plan*, 2010, www.dhs.gov/xlibrary/assets/nipp -ssp-defense-industrial-base-2010.pdf.

50. For more information on this subject, refer to the sources for this box item: Mandiant Corporation, *APT1: Exposing One of China's Cyber Espionage Units* (Alexandria, VA: Mandiant, 2013). For more information regarding Mandiant, refer to its website at www.mandiant.com; and Robert W. Taylor, Eric J. Fritsch, and John Liederbach, *Digital Crime and Digital Terrorism*, 3rd ed. (Upper Saddle River, NJ: Pearson, 2014).

51. See Nathaniel Popper and Somini Sengupta, "U.S. Says Ring Stole 160 Million Credit Card Numbers," *New York Times DealBook*, July 25, 2013, http://dealbook.nytimes .com/2013/07/25/arrests-planned-in-hacking-of-financial-companies/.

52. Kathy Gilsinan and Krishnadev Calamur, "Did Putin Direct Russian Hacking?" *Atlantic,* January 6, 2017, www.theatlantic.com/international/archive/2017/01/ russian-hacking-trump/510689/.

53. Robert W. Taylor, Eric J. Fritsch, and John Liederbach, *Digital Crime and Digital Terrorism*, 3rd ed. (Upper Saddle River, NJ: Pearson, 2014).

54. U.S. Department of Homeland Security, *Information Technology Sector-Specific Plan: An Annex to the National Infrastructure Plan*, 2010, www.dhs.gov/sites/default/files/ publications/IT%20Sector%20Specific%20Plan%202010.pdf.

Emergency Management

A trainer preparing a canine for urban search and rescue directs a dog through heavy rubble. (Blickwinkel/Schmidt-Roeger/Alamy Stock Photo)

Learning Objectives

After completing this chapter, you should be able to:

1. Identify the major categories of threats/hazards and give three examples of each.
2. Summarize the severity continuum.
3. State the five missions communities must plan for when considering threats/hazards.
4. Summarize why FEMA was created and what its performance has been.
5. Briefly describe NIMS and identify its five missions.
6. Explain how the National Preparedness System works within our communities.

Introduction

Historically, disaster relief has suffered from several major issues: (1) The movement toward relief generally was retarded by early American beliefs that were commonly held in colonial times and beyond. Individualism, self-reliance, and the tenets of the protestant ethic—meaning people should work hard, have self-discipline, and be thrifty with what they earned or produced—greatly impacted the idea of giving aid to others, even during an emergency. Many people thought that any kind of aid, even in limited quantities, would make people dependent and was therefore counterproductive. (2) For nearly 130 years, the federal government insisted that local government was the appropriate responder to disasters and gave it little or no assistance. (3) Once established, civil defense had substantial value to the federal government primarily because one of its missions was supporting and protecting the country from foreign enemies by mobilizing public support. However, civil defense had little regard for providing aid and relief. (4) As it emerged, emergency management (EM) did not speak the same "language." The definitions of terms and concepts varied widely from one state to another as well as from one community to another. (5) Until emergency management achieved some standardization of language, approaches, equipment, and capabilities, it had difficulty communicating and operating in a multiagency environment, which often caused confusion during responses. This chapter explores how these and other related issues changed over time, and describes the new emergency management practices that are now at the forefront of hazard and disaster mitigation.

Categories of Threats/Hazards

Emergency management (EM) is the managerial function that creates the framework within which communities reduce their vulnerability to hazards and cope with incidents and disasters.[1] The goals of emergency management are to (1) save lives, (2) prevent injuries, and (3) protect property and the environment.[2] All communities face a variety of threats/hazards, which endanger people, property, and other assets.[3]

There are three categories of threats/hazards (see Figure 13–1):

1. *Natural,* which includes weather conditions as well as animal and human diseases. These threats/hazards are relatively well understood because we learn about many of them from weather and news reports. Examples include tornados, hurricanes, Mad Cow disease, and Ebola. In late 2014, there were several cases of Ebola Virus Disease (EVD, "Ebola") in the United States, creating fears of an epidemic. These fears were compounded when the Centers for Disease Control changed its guidelines for handling Ebola cases, suggesting we were not as well prepared as initially thought. The first American Ebola case resulted from a man being exposed to the disease in a West African nation and traveling to Dallas, Texas, where the symptoms manifested. A health-care worker taking

FIGURE 13–1
Examples of the Three Categories of Threats/ Hazards

From Resolve to Be Ready in 2014. Published by Federal Emergency Management Agency.

Natural	Technological and Accidental	Terrorist/Human Caused
• Animal Disease Breakout	• Aircraft Crash	• Biological
• Avalanche	• Bridge Failure	• Chemical
• Drought	• Building Collapse	• Cyber
• Earthquake	• Dam Failure	• Explosion
• Epidemic/Pandemic	• Hazardous Materials Release/Spill	• Gunfire
• Flood	• Levee Failure	• Nuclear
• Hurricane/Cyclone	• Maritime Accident	• Radiological Dispersion Device (RDD)
• Landslide/Rock Fall	• Mine Accident	• Sabotage
• Lightning	• Power Failure/Blackouts	• Vehicles
• Tornado	• Radiological Release	
• Tropical Storm	• Train Derailment	
• Tsunami	• Urban Fires	
• Volcanic Eruption	• Vehicle Crash	
• Wildfire		
• Winter Storm		

care of the man contracted Ebola, but was quickly treated and recovered. There have also been several other Ebola cases in the United States. Based on what little data we have, the pattern is a health professional or a person visiting a West African nation is exposed to Ebola. Subsequently, the person returns to the United States and at some point is diagnosed as having Ebola. A limited number of health professionals have contracted Ebola treating such patients. The fear of Ebola is so great that staff members at a New York City hospital reportedly took sick days rather than treat the hospital's first Ebola patient.[4] Flooding is the most common type of disaster in the United States.[5]

2. *Technological and accidental*, created by (1) technological failures, such as a collapsed building or a failed dam that causes flooding, and (2) accidents, such as the unintended release of hazardous materials into the environment.

3. *Terrorist and human*, which arise from intentional acts intended to disrupt systems, destroy property, and/or kill people. To illustrate, **sarin** is a nerve agent (loosely, a "poison gas") that acts quickly and causes the nervous system not to function properly. In 1995, five two-man teams entered the Tokyo subway system and released sarin. The attackers from the **Aum Shinrikyo** group quickly took an antidote and fled.

Sarin
A man-made chemical gas that is extremely poisonous; used in a terrorist attack by the Aum Shinrikyo group in the subways of Tokyo, Japan, in 1995.

Aum Shinrikyo
An apocalyptic Christian group in Japan that became the first terrorist organization to use chemical warfare. In 1995, five two-man teams released sarin, a quick-acting nerve agent, in a Tokyo subway system.

Box 13–1
Saddam Hussein and Syria's Use of "Poison Gas"

In 1983, Iraqi dictator Saddam Hussein had used mustard gas against Iranian troops during Iraq's war against them,[6] which constituted a war crime. Mustard gas is a blistering agent/vesicant that severely blisters the eyes, respiratory tract, and skin on contact. Five years later, Hussein used Tabun against Iranian troops. Tabun is a highly poisonous chemical nerve agent that prevents the nervous system from functioning properly.

Starting in 1987, Hussein sought revenge against the Kurds in northern Iraq, some of whom had allied themselves with Iran. He used sarin, mustard gas, and Tabun indiscriminately against the Kurds generally. It is estimated that between 53,000 to 105,000 Kurds were killed. Hundreds of villages were decimated or abandoned.

On April 4, 2017, the rebel-held Syrian town of Khan Sheikhoun was struck by a chemical attack, believed to have been authorized or perpetrated by President Bashar al-Assad's government.

A witness saw a plane drop a single bomb that produced a yellow mushroom cloud. Quickly thereafter, civilians, men, women, and children began having trouble breathing and started dying. In the end, there were at least 86 deaths. American radar tracked two planes taking off from a Syrian airbase; the planes arrived at Khan Sheikhoun minutes before the casualties began. Two independent laboratories confirmed that sarin or a sarin-like nerve gas was used and was the agent producing the casualties. The Russians suggested that a rebel ammo dump containing sarin was hit and the casualties were the fault of the anti-government forces, an explanation dismissed by weapons experts. President Assad dismissed the whole incident as a "fabrication" to justify America's April 7, 2017, launching of 59 cruise missiles on the airbase from which the planes flew the mission. The missiles were intended as a warning to the Assad regime not to use chemical warfare again.

▲ Syrian survivors of the nerve agent gas attack bury their dead. The bodies are passed down to the men working in the burial trench, where others killed by the attack have already been placed.
(Fadi Al-Halabi/Stringer/AFP/Getty Images)

Twelve people were killed and 5,500 injured. It was the first instance of a terrorist group using chemical warfare. Except for a mistake by the group in making the sarin and not using a more effective way of distributing it, fatalities would have been much higher. Although some early arrests were made quickly, it was not until 2012 that the last three attackers were finally brought to justice.[7] Parenthetically, Saddam Hussein's use of poison gas on Kurds living in the north of Iraq beginning in 1987 constituted state terrorism. However, it was undertaken by a government and not a "terrorist group." Therefore, the Aum Shinrikyo action in the Tokyo subway is the first terrorist group attack using "poison gas."

The Severity Continuum

There are many ways to gauge the severity of an incident. Examples of these measures include the number of (1) deaths and injuries, (2) people displaced and evacuated, (3) homes and businesses that have major damage or are destroyed, and (4) financial indicators such as dollar loss and assistance expenditures. In an unusual development, the Federal Emergency Management Agency (FEMA) came up with the idea of the "Waffle House Index" as a measure to gauge severity. FEMA's Waffle House Index is an informal measure. If a Waffle House is up and running, the disaster is green; if it is operating with a backup generator and offering only a limited menu, the disaster is yellow; and if closed, badly damaged, or destroyed, as many were during Hurricane Katrina, the disaster is red.[8]

In contrast, the severity continuum (see Figure 13–3) is a quick "front-end" tool that allows officials to quickly roughly gauge the preliminary answer to the question: "How hard did we get hit?" The threats/hazards listed under terrorist/human caused are the means. The *targets* or *settings* at which they are directed may be civilians walking in a congested area, department stores, major sporting events, schools, government buildings, national monuments, resorts, churches, mass transit systems, and similar entities.

The inclusion of gunfire and vehicles in the "Terrorist/Human Caused" column is illustrated by several examples.[9] In 2016, Omar Mateen, who committed to IS, killed forty-nine people by gunfire in the Orlando, Florida, Pulse nightclub. Vehicles operated by terrorists were used to kill civilians in Nice, France, and Berlin, Germany, during 2016 and London, England, and Stockholm, Sweden, in 2017. The rate of violence in Sweden is extremely low. Nationally, there were 90 murders during 2015.[10] Therefore, the April 7, 2017, attack in Stockholm is simply incomprehensible to Swedish citizens. An unsuccessful asylum seeker from Uzbekistan turned terrorist and used a truck to deliberately run people down.[11] Potentially, there are some "ticking time bombs." A total of 280 people, including thirty-five women, traveled to Syria to join violent extremists groups. Forty were killed there, 125 remain there, and 115 have returned to Sweden.[12]

In 2017, another notable "Terrorist/Human Caused" event was an unprecedented worldwide ransomware attack. Such attacks encrypt your computer data and it is useless unless you pay a fee by a certain time. Heretofore, European casinos may have been the most frequently publicized sites for ransomware demands, although many individuals have paid smaller fees. Attackers used software allegedly stolen from the U.S. National Security Agency. The software used a flaw in Microsoft's Windows to spread ransomware around the world. The ransomware encrypts files, effectively hijacking computer systems, and demands money, in the form of Bitcoin, in exchange for decrypting them.[13] Microsoft quickly issued a fix for the flaw,[14] but it's too late for computers that are already infected by Wannacry. It is estimated that 200,000 victims in 150 countries got hit by Wannacry. Initial evidence points to North Korea as being the source for the malicious software.[15]

Figure 13–3 is the severity continuum. To be useful, the points on a scale must have meaningful definitions so important distinctions can be made. The points on the severity continuum are defined below:

Emergency
A condition of actual danger to the lives of persons and/or the safety of property that requires a response. Emergencies ordinarily are handled locally.

1. An "**emergency**" is a condition of actual danger to the lives of persons and/or the safety of property that requires a response. Emergencies ordinarily are handled

FIGURE 13–2
An outpouring of grief covers Stockholm as people leave flowers to commemorate the five deaths and 15 injured on April 7, 2017. Some people also left written notes asking for prayers for their country.

(Johan Dalstrom/Alamy Stock Photo)

Quick Facts
The Hazards of America's Grain Elevators and Bins

In America's Wheat Belt, which includes such states as Kansas, Iowa, Nebraska, and Oklahoma, grain is often stored in great bins, each of which may hold a million or more bushels. In the process of milling and moving the grain on belts, small particles of grain may begin to float around, suspended in the air. If these particles are coupled with oxygen and an ignition source, small to devastating explosions can occur. Between 1976 and 2011, there were 50 grain elevator explosions with 677 injuries and 188 fatalities.[16] Safety experts from state and U.S. Agriculture departments have operated educational programs about the dangers and they appear to have made an impact. Nationally in 2016, there were five grain dust explosions and three deaths. In contrast, during the previous ten years, there was an average of 9.2 explosions.[17]

locally. One example of a locally handled disaster is a small city in which floodwaters crossed a section of a road and washed it away. The city rebuilt the road at its own expense. However, some emergencies may require limited outside assistance, such as ambulances from a neighboring jurisdiction. There is an exception to this general description. FEMA automatically responds when there is an emergency on federal property. It also responds to local emergencies if: (1) specialized help is requested, such as canine search and rescue teams and (2) when emergency conditions overwhelm the capacity of local agencies to handle them. An example of this is Hurricane Harvey's devastation of Texas and Louisiana in 2017. In six days 51 inches of rain dropped 27 trillion gallons of rain on the coastal portions of those two states. Thirty thousand people needed temporary shelter, and 72,000 people were rescued by volunteers and military units.[18] Estimates of damage reach as high as $115 billion.

2. A "**disaster**" is more severe than an emergency because it causes a serious disruption of the functioning of an entity, such as a community, and produces widespread human, material, economic, and/or environmental losses that exceed the ability of a community to cope with it using just its own resources.[19] For example, hospitals may have been severely damaged by tornados, clean drinking water cannot be provided,

Disaster
A "disaster" is more severe than an emergency because it causes a serious disruption of the functioning of an entity, such as a community, and produces widespread human, material, economic, and/or environmental losses that exceed the ability of a community to cope with it using just its own resources.

Lowest Severity   Highest Severity

Emergency   Disaster   Catastrophe   Extinction Event

FIGURE 13–3
The Severity Continuum

(Federal Emergency Management Agency)

FIGURE 13–4
Substantial rainfall from a weather system that stalled over parts of Colorado produced extensive flooding, a natural disaster. Disaster response groups Hands.org and AmeriCorps joined forces to help muck out homes in Evans.
(Michael Rieger/Federal Emergency Management Agency)

temporary housing for displaced persons is inadequate, power has been knocked out, there are pockets of looting, food supplies urgently need replacement, and few business have continuity of operation (see Figure 13–4).

As a community quickly uses its own resources to respond to a disaster, it will reach a tipping point. Its diminishing resources are no longer sufficient to handle increasing demands and assistance from others becomes essential. The sooner that decision can reliably be made, the faster people in need can be helped (e.g., quickly bringing in temporary housing for displaced people). Under a **mutual aid agreement**, a disaster-stricken community can receive significant assistance from neighboring local governments, and state and federal assistance may be needed as well. If there has been a geographically widespread disaster, for example, from a cluster of tornados or wildfires, neighboring jurisdictions may have their own incidents with which to deal, and mutual aid assistance agreements will be impossible to honor. It is a long-standing principle that federal assistance is intended to supplement state, local, and private assistance, but not to be a substitute for it.[20]

In the city of West, Texas, a fertilizer plant inexplicably exploded and devastated the town, killing 15 people and injuring hundreds more. Aid rushed to the city from nearby communities and the rest of the state of Texas. Previously developed mutual aid

Mutual aid agreement
Mutual aid agreements are agreements between agencies, organizations, and jurisdictions that provide a mechanism to quickly obtain emergency assistance in the form of personnel, equipment, materials, and other associated services. The primary objective is to facilitate rapid, short-term deployment of emergency support prior to, during, and after an incident.

Box 13-2
Mutual Aid Agreements

Mutual aid agreements are agreements between agencies, organizations, and jurisdictions that provide a mechanism to quickly obtain emergency assistance in the form of personnel, equipment, materials, and other associated services.[21] The primary objective is to facilitate rapid, short-term deployment of emergency support prior to, during, and after an incident.[22]

Emergency Management Assistance Compact (EMAC): The Emergency Management Assistance Compact is an interstate mutual aid agreement that allows states to assist one another in responding to all kinds of natural and manmade disasters. It is administered by the National Emergency Management Association (NEMA). EMAC is the law in 50 states, Puerto Rico, Guam, U.S. Virgin Islands, and the District of Columbia.[23]

Model Intrastate Mutual Aid Legislation: This legislation was produced by NEMA in concert with DHS/FEMA and a cross-section of emergency response disciplines to facilitate intrastate mutual aid among participating political subdivisions in a state. The document also contains a list of states that have passed intrastate agreements with links to their legislation, as reference.

Model State-County Mutual Aid Deployment Contract: This is a model intergovernmental contract that allows for the deployment of local emergency responders under the auspices of EMAC.

How useful are these types of agreements are during an emergency, disaster or catastrophe?

FIGURE 13–5
FEMA Urban Search and Rescue
team members search house to
house after a tornado devastated
Moore, Oklahoma, in 2013.
*(Andrea Booher/Federal Emergency
Management Agency).*

agreements allowed neighboring police, fire, and emergency services to work in the city of West. In such disasters, coordination and cooperation are necessary ingredients to mitigate the damages. For instance, in such types of large explosions, there may be missing persons that require the expertise of specially trained search and rescue teams. FEMA's Urban Search and Rescue Task Forces are often combined teams of individuals from local and state agencies, trained together as a federal unit to respond to emergencies anywhere in the United States (see Figure 13–5).

Information Link
To have a better understanding of mutual aid agreements, visit www .google.com/search?q=disaster%2C+h elp+from+mutual+aid+agreement&oq &disaster%2C+help+from+mutual+aid +agreement&aqs=chrome..69i57.197 25j0j7&sourceid=chrome&ie=;UTF-8, which is a multipage template for such agreements.

3. A **catastrophe** is an incident that directly or indirectly affects large portions or all of a country and requires national and sometimes international responses. Early in 2010, a major earthquake struck one of the most impoverished countries in the Western Hemisphere, Haiti, killing 200,000 people and leaving 2.3 million Haitians homeless (see Figure 13–6).[24] Despite massive assistance from the United Nations and a number of countries, Haitian refugees living in temporary camps suffered from deadly outbreaks of cholera later in the year.[25] In the fall, Hurricane Tomas lashed Haiti, creating more misery and deaths, and in 2017 Hurricanes Harvey and Irma again battered the island nation.

Beneath Yellowstone National Park, there are 11,200 cubic miles of red-hot magma, enough to fill the Grand Canyon nearly 14 times.[26] The chances of there being a volcanic eruption of it are 1 in 700,000 annually.[27] An eruption would darken the sky for at least days,[28] cause massive casualties, destroy infrastructure, extensively destroy crops, wipe out entire towns and some local governments, and leave large populations homeless and possibly on their own for a substantial period. Social order would evaporate, and gangs and banditry would flourish. It would be a catastrophe so vast that international assistance would likely be required.

4. An **extinction event** could result or results in the loss of all human life on the planet. In the extreme, there is no effective emergency response to an extinction event. Although these types of apocalyptic events have been historically portrayed in the popular media [e.g., *Planet of the Apes* (1968), *The Last Wave* (1977), *Armageddon* (1998), *Sharing a Friend for the End of the World* (2012), *Transformers: The Age of Extinction* (2013), and *Independence Day* (1996) and *Independence Day: Resurgence* (2016)], the probability of a human extinction event is presently statistically slight. Nonetheless, it is a possibility.

Catastrophe
A catastrophe is an incident that directly or indirectly affects large portions or all of a country and requires national and sometimes international responses.

Extinction event
An extinction event could result or results in the loss of all human life. In the extreme, there is no effective emergency response to an extinction event.

FIGURE 13–6

A portion of the damage caused by the 2010 earthquake damage in Port-au-Prince. More than 250,000 homes and 30,000 businesses were damaged or destroyed. By 2017, many structures had still not been built, when Hurricanes Harvey and Irma hit the island nation again.

(Stocktrek Images, Inc./Alamy Stock Photo)

Pre-Planning and Core Capabilities

Strong pre-planning, and developing as many core capabilities as possible to use in achieving missions, can enhance the pace of progress from a disaster or catastrophe to recovery. The recovery process is a sequence of interdependent and often concurrent activities that progressively move a community toward its planned recovery outcomes. Decisions made and priorities set by a community pre-disaster and early in the recovery process have a cascading effect on the nature, speed, and inclusiveness of recovery.[29] Every community must understand the *plausible* risks it faces. Risks are the possibilities of negative events occurring. The smart way to deal with risks is to understand their consequences and pre-plan to prevent them from happening and mitigating those that do occur.

FEMA's THIRA process (Threat and Hazard Identification and Risk Assessment) helps communities identify capability targets and resource requirements necessary to address anticipated and unanticipated risks (see Figure 13–7).

The four steps in the THIRA Model are summarized as follows:[30]

Step 1: Identify the Threats and Hazards of Concern.
Based on a combination of experience, forecasting, subject matter expertise, and other available resources, identify a list of the threats and hazards of primary concern to the community.

Step 2: Give the Threats and Hazards Context.
Describe the threats and hazards of concern, showing how they may affect the community.

Step 3: Establish Capability Targets.
FEMA has established a list of 32 core capabilities that communities doing risk planning should try to develop (See Figure 13-8). A capability target identifies the core capability the community will try to develop. Core capabilities are further discussed later in this section.

Step 4: Apply the Results.
For each core capability, estimate the resources required to achieve the capability targets with the use of community assets and mutual aid agreements, while also considering preparedness activities, including mitigation opportunities.[31]

Utilizing information gained through the use of the THIRA Model and other sources of data about their jurisdiction, communities plan for five missions:

1. **Prevention:** Prevent, avoid, or stop an imminent, threatened, or actual act of terrorism.

FIGURE 13–7
The THIRA Model

(From Threat and Hazard Identification and Risk Assessment Guide, 2e. Published by United States Department of Homeland Security).

Prevention	Protection	Mitigation	Response	Recovery
Planning				
Public Information and Warning				
Operational Coordination				
Forensics and Attribution	Access Control and Identity Verification	Community Resilience	Critical Transportation	Economic Recovery
Intelligence and Information Sharing	Cybersecurity	Long-term Vulnerability Reduction	Environmental Response/ Health and Safety	Health and Social Services
Interdiction and Disruption	Intelligence and Information Sharing	Risk and Disaster Resilience Assessment	Fatality Management Services	Housing
Screening, Search, and Detection	Interdiction and Disruption	Threats and Hazard Identification	Infrastructure Systems	Infrastructure Systems
	Physical Protective Measures		Mass Care Services	Natural and Cultural Resources
	Risk Management for Protection Programs and Activities		Mass Search and Rescue Operations	
	Screening, Search, and Detection		On-scene Security and Protection	
	Supply Chain Integrity and Security		Operational Communications	
			Public and Private Services and Resources	
			Public Health and Medical Services	
			Situational Assessment	

FIGURE 13–8
Alignment of Five Missions and 32 Core Capabilities

From Threat and Hazard Identification and Risk Assessment Guide, 2e. Published by United States Department of Homeland Security.

2. **Protection:** Protect our citizens, residents, visitors, and assets against the greatest threats and hazards in a manner that allows our interests, aspirations, and way of life to thrive.

3. **Mitigation:** Reduce the loss of life and property by lessening the impact of future disasters.

4. **Response:** Respond quickly to save lives; protect property and the environment; and meet basic human needs in the aftermath of a catastrophic incident.

5. **Recovery:** Recover through a focus on the timely restoration, strengthening, and revitalization of infrastructure, housing, and a sustainable economy, as well as the health, social, cultural, historic, and environmental fabric of communities affected by a catastrophic incident.[32]

To be able to execute each of these five missions, communities need to develop the core capabilities that are related to each separate mission. Although FEMA specifies 32 core capabilities, most communities will only be able to develop some of them and will need assistance to execute the others. The top banner of Figure 13–8 shows the five missions identified immediately above. Under each mission, the relevant core capabilities needed to execute it are identified.

The Recovery Continuum

In our drive to anticipate, plan, and develop other formal elements, we often lose sight of a major asset we neither plan for nor develop, but which is an important part of things from search and rescue all the way to recovery: chaos theory.

When disasters disrupt our everyday routines, things become chaotic. We are in a state of nonequilibrium, out of balance. Many homes are badly damaged or worse. We are fearful of what might happen next and the delivery of social services is disrupted. Getting to medical services may not be possible. Wild and sometimes dangerous animals may be nearby. There's too much speculation and not enough reliable information. The problems facing us are complex and seem insurmountable. Bifurcation is when such conditions also overwhelm agencies. In a disaster, FEMA and Homeland Security and local agencies can't do everything that needs to be done.

FIGURE 13-9
The Recovery Continuum
From National Disaster Recovery Framework, 2e. Published by United States Department of Homeland Security.

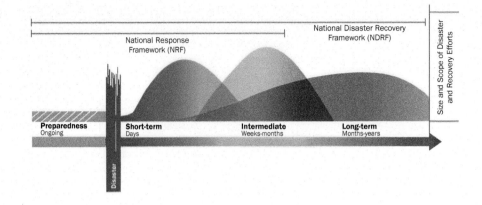

However, chaos theory does not just explain how things spin out of control. Its real value is how order is restored when we are seemingly teetering at the top of a slippery slope. Part of how restoration occurs from the first three words in the preamble to our Constitution: *We the People.*

We the People are individuals, neighbors, ad hoc groups, boaters, volunteers from other communities, civic clubs, and all of the others who rescue people and pets from their rooftops, open their homes to strangers and feed them, set up temporary shelters, locate survivors under the rubble that buries them, open rudimentary medical stations, stand guard, reunite family members, and allow others to use their cellphones. Individual and small group actions create the butterfly effect, which ripples across communities, energizing more people to help. From these accumulated experiences, new community alliances, priorities, and services emerge. Chaos theory explains not only how we the people self-organize; it also teaches us about how we reorganize our lives and move forward toward recovery[33] (see Figure 13-9).

The Evolution of Emergency Management

Self-reliant
In our colonial era, there was already an ingrained belief that people should be self-reliant and responsible for their own lot in life. A corollary of this tradition was that if people were given too much help it would ultimately make them dependent.

During our colonial era, there was an ingrained belief that people should be **self-reliant** and responsible for their own lot in life.[34] For more catastrophic events, people did help each other.[35] If a barn burned down, neighbors pitched in to "raise" (build) a new one; when crop fields were washed away, others shared their bounty. To some degree, that tradition also later translated to towns and cities—for example, volunteers serving as firefighters. A corollary of this tradition was that if people were given too much help it would ultimately make them dependent. American philosophers also praised self-reliance, as did Ralph Waldo Emerson (1803–1882) in an 1841 essay.[36] For these reasons there has donated money that was not distributed to otherwise worthy recipients after the Great Chicago Fire of 1871.

Mutual aid societies
Developed in America during the 1800s and were often faith, country of origin, or ethnicity based. They had several purposes, such as preserving cultural heritage and helping immigrants newly arrived in America to adjust.

As cities grew, private **mutual aid societies** provided some assistance "to their own" when disasters struck. These societies were often based on country of origin, religion, or ethnicity, and their other purposes included helping immigrants make the transition to living in America and preserving cultural heritage. In 1910, there were reportedly 400 Italian mutual aid associations in Chicago.[37] As the United States developed economically, insurance became more available, but many people either didn't know about it or simply could not afford it.[38]

Except for the ad hoc disaster assistance Congress provided starting in 1803, there was little interest in federal or state governments doing more for roughly 130 years. As an example, federal troops were dispatched to the Chicago Fire of 1871 ready to intervene if riots occurred. Founded in 1881, the **American Red Cross** has provided domestic and international relief, although there was often not much to distribute. In 1900, the American Red Cross was given a Congressional charter, giving it the legal status of "a federal instrumentality." The charter recognized the exceptional work of the Red Cross and tasked it to continue its relief work. No other similar American organization has attained this recognition.

American Red Cross
Humanitarian organization originally developed in 1881 by Clara Barton; modeled after the International Red Cross in Europe to provide aid to civilians during emergencies and disasters.

Quick Facts
Clara Barton and The American Red Cross

Clara Barton (1821–1912) was an independent nurse during America's Civil War. She also saw suffering firsthand while working with the International Red Cross in Europe during the Franco-Prussian War in 1869. Out of the experience, she founded the American Red Cross and was its first president. Barton often took personal charge of major relief efforts such as the Great Fire of 1881 and the Johnstown, Pennsylvania, flood in 1889. Starting with President Woodrow Wilson in 1913, American presidents have served as honorary presidents of the American Red Cross.

CLARA BARTON
From portrait taken in Civil War and authorized
by her as the one she wished to be remembered by

▲ Clara Barton *(Centennial Photographic Co./ Library of Congress Prints and Photographs Division Washington, D.C. 20540 USA)*

Despite various piecemeal efforts, the federal government's central position for many decades was that disaster relief was the purview of state and local governments,[39] which should not surprise us. The pervasive ethos of individualism, self-reliance, and the tenets of the protestant work ethic often got in the way of relief. These views help explain why unemployment compensation did not exist in American states until 1932, when Wisconsin became the first state to enact such assistance.

World War I to the 1930s

During World War I (1914–1918), the Germans bombed English cities. Anticipating America's entry into the war, the Council of National Defense (CND) was formed in 1916. German air attacks on the United States were considered unlikely because of the limited abilities of air warfare at that time.[40] Therefore, national defense focused on coordinating war resources, such as manpower, and maintaining high morale among the civilian population.[41] A key tactic in maintaining morale was keeping the public involved. As America fought against Germany in World War I (1917–1918), the CND's Women's Committee had its constituents rolling bandages, selling war bonds, planting Victory Gardens for personal consumption to preserve other food for the war effort, and knitting socks and sweaters for the troops to wear.[42] Nationally, much of the knitting was done under the auspices of the American Red Cross (see Figure 13–10). Following the end of the war, the Council for National Defense was abolished in 1921.

From a national perspective, emergency management ultimately grew out of World War I's modest efforts in civil defense.[43] As civil defense evolved, it ultimately took on a few emergency management–type tasks. However, civil defense had a "dual use" character for most of its existence.[44] Initially, it was a part of the national security effort and much later it began responding to natural disasters.[45]

Two events shaped the 1930s: (1) the crash of the stock market in 1929, which produced a loss of $75 billion[46] and ushered in the Great Depression (see Figures 13–11 and 13–12), the effects of which lasted until roughly 1940 when the economy turned upward

FIGURE 13–10
A 1917 American Red Cross poster exhorting women to support the troops by knitting. Such a program now seems unimaginable.

(Library of Congress Prints and Photographs Division Washington, D.C. 20540 USA)

AMERICAN RED CROSS

OUR BOYS NEED SOX KNIT YOUR BIT

FIGURE 13–11
The stock market began its crash on "Black Tuesday," October 29, 1929. In the Great Depression that followed, many companies and banks failed as well. A bankrupted investor tries to sell his car as quickly as possible, while some people still had money.

(SZ Photo/Scherl/Sueddeutsche Zeitung Photo/Alamy Stock Photo)

as World War II approached; and (2) a drought so severe that it drove many farmers off their land in the heartland of the United States. For instance, in Mississippi alone, 40 percent of the farms went to the auction block.[47] Thirty-seven percent of non-farm workers lost their jobs and most of them their homes.[48] Many Americans left their familiar surroundings in search of a better life. The combination of these events resulted in some cities developing "bum blockades" so unemployed outsiders couldn't come into their communities and use their already strained resources.

Within 100 days of taking office, President Roosevelt and Congress collaborated to produce 15 "New Deal Programs," many of which focused on employment. Most important,

FIGURE 13–12
Migrant workers came to work at a pea-picking camp in California during 1936. The crop failed and the camp broke apart as workers left to find other work. The wife of a picker looks out from under the tent she and her husband just sold to get food for the children. Although only 32 years old, worry is etched in her face.

(Dorothea Lang/Library of Congress Prints and Photographs Division Washington, D.C. 20540 USA)

the New Deal Programs reflected a policy shift away from the federal government's long-standing attachment to the self-reliant philosophy. It was finally recognized that some problems are just too big for communities and states to address, although emergency management still took a long time to emerge.

The Federal Emergency Relief Act of 1933 provided assistance for the unemployed. Illustratively, the Civilian Conservation Corps (CCC) began operation in 1933. It was a public work program that enrolled 2.5 million unmarried men.

The New Deal programs established a major precedent for the federal government to provide assistance to people in distress. Despite the New Deal Programs, millions of other people in great need still received no governmental relief (see Figure 13–12).

The Impact of World War II

The successful Japanese attack on Pearl Harbor in 1941 propelled the United States into World War II (1941–1945). It also raised significant fear of attacks on the mainland. In 1941, the newly created Office of Civilian Defense (OCD) coordinated federal, state, and local defense programs for the protection of civilians during air raids and other emergencies, as well as facilitating civilian participation in war programs.[49] One of these was the volunteer Air Raid Warden Program.[50] The wardens made sure that cities were "blacked out," meaning no lights showed at night so as to deny their use as navigational aids by possible attackers.[51] Civilian volunteers were also trained to be "spotters" and recognize different types of enemy planes and the presence of enemy submarines.

Victory in Europe (V-E Day) was declared on May 8, 1945, and attention turned to ending the war in the Pacific. Following America's dropping of atomic bombs on Hiroshima and Nagasaki, the surrender of the Japanese was announced on Victory over Japan Day (V-J Day) on August 9, 1945. Almost immediately after World War II, Russia began working

Civilian Conservation Corps
A federal program during the 1930s that employed young men in a military-style manner to plant trees and build parks, canals, and other recreational sites throughout America's forests and governmental land.

Works Progress Administration (WPA)
An ancillary organization to the Civilian Conservation Corps during the 1930s; employed over 8.5 million people involved in building bridges, public buildings, and airports throughout the country.

Box 13–3
The Civilian Conservation Corps (CCC)

The primary enrollees in the **Civilian Conservation Corps** were 18- to 25-year-old unmarried men. The CCC planted over three billion trees, built 800 parks, dug canals, stocked fish, and otherwise worked hard. Crime was rampant during the 1930s and the CCC kept its enrollees out of trouble.[52] Most members lived in tents and under a military-style discipline. They were paid $30 monthly, $25 of which they were required to send home.[53] Free evening classes were available and 40,000 young men were given their first opportunities to learn how to read and write.[54] An ancillary organization, the **Works Progress Administration (WPA)**, employed 8.5 million people to build bridges, public buildings, and airports. Even today, you can still occasionally find municipal buildings with a bronze placard on them commemorating their construction by the WPA. The CCC and WPA are what today is called "workfare." Instead of simply receiving benefits, people receive money in exchange for their work efforts on public projects.

If unemployment rises substantially, do you think that a similar program might work today?

▲ A CCC member stands on a scaffold as he helps construct a building to be used as a camp workshop. *(Library of Congress Prints and Photographs Division Washington, D.C. 20540 USA)*

on a nuclear bomb and successfully tested such a device in 1949. The United States and the American public had a new worry ... the Cold War with Russia and the potential for nuclear exchange.

The 1950s and 1960s

The Korean War (1950–1953) heightened the public's anxiety about nuclear war, some of which turned to outright fear. In late 1950, Congress passed a bill creating the Federal Civil Defense Administration (FCDA). Congress had abolished the Office of Civil Defense at the end of World War II, and the creation of the FCDA tacitly acknowledged the public's mood and created a nationwide system of civil defense agencies. Interestingly, most of the responsibility for civil defense was placed on state and local governments with limited federal assistance. One of the Federal Civil Defense Administration's most immediate tasks was developing a national policy to guide state and local civil defense efforts.[55] The FCDA led bomb shelter–building programs, worked to achieve better coordination between federal and state governments, established an attack warning system, and stockpiled supplies.[56] It also conducted thousands of civil defense exercises, sent "Alert America" convoys to eighty-three cities educating over a million people about civil defense, established emergency communication facilities and emergency radio broadcasting capabilities, and educated children in schools.[57]

As far-fetched as it now appears, "Bert the Turtle" was a cartoon character developed by the FCDA to encourage children to "duck and cover" when there was a "bright light" from a nearby nuclear explosion. Teachers actually ran drills, training children to drop under their school desks for cover in the event of a nuclear attack. Some schools even distributed military-style metal "dog tags" so students could be identified after such an attack.[58]

In many regards the FCDA shaped the practice of civil defense for a decade or more. The Disaster Relief Act of 1950 gave the president the authority to issue disaster declarations and authorized federal agencies to provide limited direct assistance to state and local governments in the event of a disaster.

The FCDA's strategy vacillated between planning to evacuate people in the event of nuclear attacks and urging them to stay in place in their personally constructed backyard or public bomb shelters (see Figure 13–13). This vacillation reflected the views expressed by the Congress and various federal leaders. Ultimately, the federal government concluded that given the short warning it might be able to give, there would inevitably be enormous civilian casualties.

Information Link
For more information about the Civilian Conservation Corps, visit http://www.history.com/topics /civilian-conservation-corps, a site that has both information and videos about the CCC.

FIGURE 13–13
One of several models of family-sized underground bunkers designed to protect against nuclear blasts. Notice the lack of a kitchen and a restroom. Homeowners were urged to have two weeks of survival supplies and local and state governments needed to be able to supply such for another four weeks.
(From Annual Report of the Office of Civil and Defense Mobilization for Fiscal Year 1959. Published by U.S. Government Publishing Office.)

Box 13-4
Were 1950s Bomb Shelter Builders the Ancestors of Today's Doomsday Preppers?

Doomsday "**preppers**" believe that a collapse of society is approaching and they are preparing for it. There are numerous reasons given for the impending doom, including asteroids hitting the earth, worldwide epidemics, a biological terrorist attack, hyperinflation, and even the rise of zombies. "Preppers" stock up on all sorts of weapons and supplies to survive the impending doom: guns and ammunition, cross and traditional bows, grains, foodstuffs, medical supplies, fuel, communications gear, clothing, seeds, and other necessities. They may buy tracts of land as a retreat and recruit former military and medical practitioners, such as surgeons and nurses, to join their group. Although once considered a fringe movement, a recent National Geographic poll revealed 28 percent of respondents knew at least one "prepper."[59]

One of the proponents of prepping is James Wesley Rawles, a retired military intelligence officer. He is the author of several novels, including *Survivors: A Novel of the Coming Collapse*, which examines the decisions people make and what happens to them in a collapsed society. Rawls's Internet site can be located at www.survivalblog.com. The site receives 320,000 individual visits weekly.

Why do you think "prepping" has become a movement in the United States? What factors are related to the "prepper" movement?

In 1958, FCDA was merged with the Office of Defense Mobilization (ODM), which had been a powerful independent agency responsible for planning, coordinating, and controlling the mobilization of federal wartime assets, including manpower.[60] The new organization was placed in the Executive Office of the President as the Office of Civil and Defense Mobilization (OCDM).[61]

Throughout the many organizational changes, natural disasters continued to command attention despite the federal government's focus on preparation for war and national security during peacetime. Illustratively, in 1953, a tornado hit Beecher, Michigan, with winds of 261–318 mph, killing hundreds.[62] A powerful earthquake pummeled Alaska in 1964. Hurricane Betsy obliterated eight offshore platforms, hammered New Orleans, and caused seventy-six deaths in 1965.[63] The Army Corps of Engineers was ordered to build flood protection for New Orleans in 1965, only to see it obliterated by Hurricane Katrina in 2005.

In 1961, President Kennedy changed the federal approach to disasters, dividing the Office of Civil Defense and Mobilization (OCDM) into two entities: The Office of Emergency Preparedness (OEP) was created in the Executive Office of the President to respond to natural disasters, and civil defense responsibilities were housed in the Department of Defense.

"Prepper"
Slang word to describe those individuals who are preparing for major apocalyptic events in the future.

The 1970s and the Emergence of FEMA

Building on the federal National Flood Insurance Act of 1968 that encouraged taking mitigation steps to reduce the impact of a disaster, Congress passed the Disaster Relief Act of 1970, setting forth the first major attempt by the federal government to emphasize hazard mitigation as a priority to reduce the impact of future disasters.[64] Further, the Disaster Relief Act of 1974 gave presidents additional authority to declare emergencies and disasters and offer federal funding and assistance. Other federal disaster legislation included the Earthquake Reduction Act of 1977 that was later amended by The National Earthquake Hazards Reduction Program Reauthorization Act of 2004. The later act provided for specific public earthquake education, changes in building codes that called for more earthquake-resistant construction, and development, as far as was practical, of a system to predict earthquakes.

By 1975, nearly 100 federal agencies had some aspect of disaster assistance.[65] Frustrated with this fragmentation, the National Governors Association (NGA) pushed for a single agency to have jurisdiction over natural and environmental disasters.[66] In 1978, President Jimmy Carter responded by issuing Executive Order 12127 creating the **Federal Emergency Management Agency (FEMA)**.[67] Finally, after many historical, legislative, and bureaucratic twists and turns, the apex of modern emergency management arrived.

Federal Emergency Management Agency (FEMA)
Originally developed by Presidential Order in 1978 by President Jimmy Carter, FEMA is the primary federal agency responsible for responding to and mitigating a major disaster within the United States.

The 1980s to Present

Only three hurricanes hit the United States between 1980 and 1984, but the new agency (FEMA) had to deal with a variety of other incidents in its early years. As an example, local residents along the Love Canal area located in Niagara Falls (New York) began suffering from high incidents of cancer, birth defects, and other health problems. According to the Environmental Protection Agency (EPA), the problems were caused by human poisoning from toxic waste dumping in the canal and resulted in over 200 homes being demolished. The EPA was responsible for cleaning the site and FEMA was ordered to assist with residential relocation.

Also in 1980, the eruption of Mount Saint Helens in the State of Washington, near Portland, Oregon, marked the first major natural disaster that introduced FEMA as the primary emergency management agency in the United States. The Mount Saint Helens eruption was a significant event that was preceded by a series of earthquakes and landslides affecting the area. On May 18, 1980, the entire north face of the mountain suddenly exploded, spewing molten lava and steam down its side, as well as expelling gas and ash 80,000 feet into the air.[68] The resulting eruption killed fifty-seven people and caused over $2.8 billion in damages. The impacted area was huge, covering most of the Pacific Northwest and at least eleven other U.S. states that received significant deposits of ash from the eruption. Spokane, Washington, which is located 250 miles due east of Mount Saint Helens, was plunged into darkness for several days.

FEMA's response was lauded as it provided federal funding for cleanup of impacted cities as well as directed the states of Oregon and Washington in a massive reforestation project that continues today. The McKinney-Vento Homeless Assistance Act of 1987 authorized FEMA to help the homeless through the Emergency Food and Shelter Program, adding a new clientele to everyday operations of the agency. Other important challenges also occurred during the late 1980s as Hurricane Hugo slammed into the coast of South Carolina. FEMA's poor performance in responding to Hurricane Hugo resulted in the first major Congressional interest in disbanding FEMA. However, the discussion was abandoned early on, and in 1993, FEMA re-emerged with significant reforms. One of the more crucial changes made it easier for FEMA to redirect civil defense resources made available by the end of the Cold War.[69]

The bombing of Oklahoma City's Alfred P. Murrah Federal Building in 1995 by Timothy McVeigh and his co-conspirators elevated America's awareness about terrorism.[70] The Antiterrorism and Effective Death Penalty Act of 1996 required the Department of Justice (DOJ) and FEMA to train metropolitan firefighters in responding to events caused by weapons of mass destruction. Three years later, the Defense Against Weapons of Mass Destruction Act required training state and local first responders on handling threats and actual weapons of mass destruction incidents. FEMA supported Pennsylvania, Virginia, and New York in responding to the 9/11 attacks in 2001 with thousands of staff and mobile communications gear. In 2003, FEMA was officially moved to the Department of Homeland Security, where it remains today.[71]

In 2005, after severe criticism of FEMA's performance during Hurricane Katrina, the fourth most powerful Gulf of Mexico hurricane ever recorded, Congress passed the Post-Katrina Emergency Management Reform Act of 2006. Among the most important changes developed by the act were (1) FEMA remained a stand-alone agency within the Department of Homeland Security; (2) FEMA was given control over more emergency resources and designated as the primary agency responsible for disaster relief and mitigation; and (3) FEMA's top official became the president's principal advisor on emergencies and disasters regardless of causation.[72] In addition to the laws applicable to FEMA, Presidential Policy Directives (PPDs) have also played a large role in shaping the role of FEMA.

Weapons of Mass Destruction and CBRNE Attacks

Following the 1995 bombing of the Murrah Federal Building in Oklahoma City, President Clinton issued Presidential Decision Directive 39 (PDD-39), "U.S. Policy on Counterterrorism."[73] It required: (1) all federal government units to take actions to reduce vulnerabilities to terrorism at home and abroad and (2) that terrorists and their sponsors would be dealt with vigorously and their actions would not alter American policies. Among other provisions, FEMA became responsible for the development of federal and state response plans associated with a terrorist strike directed at large U.S. populations, especially those utilizing **weapons of mass destruction (WMD)**.

Weapons of mass destruction (WMD)
Weapons designed to cause significant devastation to a population; involves the release of a CBRNE agent.

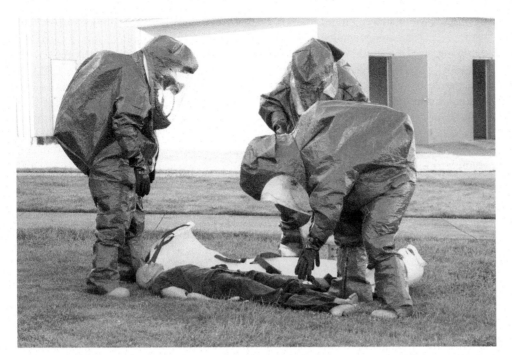

FIGURE 13–14
First responders train at the Center for Domestic Preparedness to be mission ready for actual CBRNE search and rescue operations.
(Center for Domestic Preparedness, Federal Emergency Management Agency)

This directive coincided with previous legislation that established FEMA's **Center for Domestic Preparedness (CDP)** in Anniston, Alabama. The CDP is the only federal chartered center responsible for training state and local agencies on WMD and is the nation's premier **all-hazards** training center that prepares individual agencies to respond to major catastrophic events, often addressing real-world scenarios. In addition, in May 2011, the White House initiated the National Strategy for CBRNE to address attacks that were WMD in nature.[74] The acronym **CBRNE** became the standard to describe these types of attacks of mass destruction:

Chemical
Biological
Radiological
Nuclear
Explosive

The Center for Domestic Preparedness carries out large, multiagency and whole community simulations to prepare for large-scale events (see Figure 13–14). Much of its training focuses on conditions requiring a **HAZMAT** response, which requires first responders to wear **personal protection equipment (PPE)** or a personal protection suit to address the event. In real situations, these types of incidents almost always involve a CBRNE release and are very dangerous for first responders. The CDP provides training for state and local police, as well as fire and medical personnel, who may respond to such incidents. In addition, every FEMA region, as well as most large metropolitan cities, has specially trained units that can respond to HAZMAT events. In most cases, these types of incidents involve overturned trucks carrying chemicals that might spill on the roadway, or accidents that involve train cargo containers that have ruptured and endanger the immediate environment. Remediation and cleanup are key concerns during these types of incidents. However, the use of CBRNE agents during a terrorist attack is one of the most frightening of all scenarios, and one which most endangers first responders.

The U.S. Military and CBRNE Attacks

In addition to the responsibilities assumed by the U.S. Department of Homeland Security and the Federal Emergency Management Agency, several other agencies have a primary or supportive role in case of a CBRNE attack. The U.S. Department of Defense maintains a highly trained, CBRNE rapid response team, using various specialists from all

Center for Domestic Preparedness (CDP)
The primary training facilities in Anniston, Alabama, operated by FEMA to train members of federal, state, and local agencies on all aspects of domestic preparedness; focuses on response training during WMD and CBRNE events.

All-hazards
National preparedness is based on the all-hazards approach. This approach uses a capabilities-based preparedness to prevent, protect against, respond to, and recover from terrorist attacks, major disasters (natural, technological, or human caused), and all other emergencies.

CBRNE
Acronym for Chemical, Biological, Radiological, Nuclear, and Explosive

HAZMAT
Acronym for hazardous and dangerous materials.

Personal protection equipment (PPE)
Used by first responders to protect them against CBRNE agents.

Information Link
For more information on the Center for Domestic Preparedness (CDP), visit the website at https://cdp.dhs.gov/.

branches of the military.[75] In addition, the U.S. Army, 20th Support Command (CBRNE) integrates, coordinates, deploys, and provides trained and ready CBRNE forces capable of addressing any CBRNE contingency globally. The 20th Support Command (CBRNE) has some 5,000 employees spread over nineteen installations in sixteen states. Although their primary purpose is in support of war-fighting operations, the unit also supports federal, state, and local CBRNE assets in support of homeland defense. The concept is that state and local personnel may be overwhelmed should an actual, large-scale CBRNE terrorist attack occur on the homeland. In addition to the 20th Support Command (CBRNE), specific National Guard units have been CBRNE trained and are located in each of ten regions to support FEMA.

The Centers for Disease Control and Prevention (CDC)

The Centers for Disease Control and Prevention (CDC) located in Atlanta, Georgia, has a unique and specific role in securing the country from and during a potential CBRNE attack. The CDC not only responds directly to such attacks, but also prepares first responders and community leaders for these potential hazards. The CDC provides assistance in the design and development of protective gear for first responders as well as information relating to mitigation after an incident, such as cleanup protocols and best practices.

Clearly, the role of the CDC is much more pronounced during real or suspected biologic, nuclear, and radiologic type attacks than during more traditional bombings and shootings that have been the hallmark of terrorist organizations in the past. However, with the higher potential for a CBRNE attack from a sophisticated terrorist group, the CDC's mission has escalated over the last decade. In addition, the 2012 popular hit movie, *Contagion*, highlighted the possibility of a lethal airborne virus that kills within a few days of exposure and sweeps across the globe in a highly connected world.

Pandemic
An epidemic of an infectious disease that involves a large area, usually crossing international boundaries and involving multiple continents.

Although not at the same lethality level, we have already witnessed such a **pandemic** (an epidemic of an infectious disease that involves a large area, usually one that has crossed international boundaries and involves multiple continents) in modern history. The SARS (Severe Acute Respiratory Syndrome) in 2003 and the H1N1 flu pandemic in 2009 spread globally within just a few weeks, and the CDC was instrumental in tracking down the source of the outbreaks and the development of remedial therapies and vaccines used to combat the diseases. More distantly, the Flu Pandemic of 1918 (1918–1920) killed 675,000 Americans and 20 to 50 million people worldwide.[76]

Although the likelihood of a terrorist using a biologic agent is relatively remote because the germ would have to be "weaponized"—meaning highly refined and concentrated, developed under very precise and consistent environmental conditions, and then released over a period of time—such an attack is possible. More likely, any future pandemic would involve accidental human exposure to the myriad of diseases shared with animals. For instance, SARS, HIV, Ebola, Nipah, and various strains of the influenza virus (flu) are just a few of the many diseases humans share with animals. Hence, food markets and food preparation sites are often the pathways for the spread of diseases to humans.

The National Incident Management System

In 2003, President George W. Bush issued Homeland Security Presidential Directive-5 (HSPD-5). The purpose of HSPD-5 was to increase the ability of the United States to respond to domestic emergencies[77] by a system that would prevent, prepare for, respond to, and recover from terrorist attacks, major disasters, and other emergencies. HSPD-5 required DHS to establish a single, comprehensive **National Incident Management System (NIMS)**.

National Incident Management System (NIMS)
The comprehensive, nationwide systematic approach to incident management adopted by FEMA to manage and standardize responses to critical incidents and/or disasters.

Following Hurricane Katrina, the Congress passed the Post-Katrina Emergency Management Reform Act of 2006 and President Obama issued Presidential Protective Directive-8 (PPD-8) to meet requirements in the legislation. PPD-8 also identified the five missions identified in Figure 13–8, which are: (1) prevention, (2) protection, (3) mitigation, (4) response, and (5) recovery.[78] In some documents, the five missions are also referred to as the "National Planning Framework."

NIMS is a system and a proactive approach to guide the actions of national, state, and local units of government, nongovernmental organizations (NGOs), and the private sector.

What NIMS Is:	What NIMS Isn't
• A comprehensive, nationwide, systematic approach to incident management, including the Incident Command System, Multiagency Coordination Systems, and Public Information • A set of preparedness concepts and principles for all hazards • Essential principles for a common operating picture and interoperability of communications and information management • Standardized resource management procedures that enable coordination among different jurisdictions or organizations • Scalable, so it may be used for all incidents (from day-to-day to large-scale) • A dynamic system that promotes ongoing management and maintenance	• A response plan • Only used during large-scale incidents • A communications plan • Only applicable to certain emergency management/incident response personnel • Only the Incident Command System or an organization chart • A static system

FIGURE 13–15
What NIMS Is and Isn't

(From National Incident Management System. Published by United States Department of Homeland Security.)

NIMS allows these varied organizations to work side by side seamlessly because they have all been trained to use the same organizational structures, concepts, and they "speak the same language," so they share a common operating picture, whether handling terrorist attacks, major disasters, or other emergencies. NIMS, regardless of the cause, size, location, or complexity of an incident, reduces the loss of life, damage to property, and harm to the environment. All federal units and agencies are required to use NIMS. For state, tribal, and local units of governments to receive grants from one of several NIMS-related sources, they must elect to use NIMS.

Figure 13–15 summarizes the characteristics of NIMS. It is common knowledge that incidents can range from small to catastrophic. Although disaster incidents are often deadly, they usually are not large scale. They begin locally and are often managed to a relatively quick conclusion at that level,[79] such as an active shooter in a high school. However, if there was an explosion at a nuclear power plant, a large hurricane hitting the entire Gulf Coast, or the eruption of a volcano, successful incident management operations will depend on the involvement of multiple jurisdictions, all levels of government, and private-sector experts.[80] Regardless of the size or severity of an incident, the NIMS template provides a systematic approach to integrating the best processes and methods into a unified national framework.[81] NIMS is valuable because it provides a set of nationally standardized organizational structures and procedures that emergency responders understand. It can be applied to any incident, large or small, allowing different jurisdictions that also use it to quickly work together in a predictable, coordinated manner.[82]

The NIMS Template

The NIMS template consists of a cycle of five components that work together to create a systematic approach to any event or incident. What follows is a synopsis of the five major component of NIMS, as well as a description of how these components work together as a system:[83]

1. **Preparedness.**[84] Effective incident management begins with a host of preparedness activities conducted on a continuing basis (see Figure 13–16), well in advance of any potential incident. Illustrations of the elements making up preparedness include planning, acquisition of appropriate equipment, training, exercises, and personnel qualification established by meeting certification standards. Preparedness can fluctuate, particularly if capabilities are not sustained on an ongoing basis and tested through exercises. Preparedness is not simply a planning exercise, for example, actual capabilities must be established. Preparedness means being ready to respond effectively to real incidents. Three preparedness questions

FIGURE 13–16
The NIMS Preparedness Cycle, which can be applied to other emergency preparedness activities as well.

(Courtesy Federal Emergency Management Agency.)

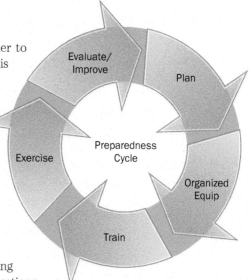

FIGURE 13-17
Resource Management During an Incident

(From National Incident Management System. Published by United States Department of Homeland Security.)

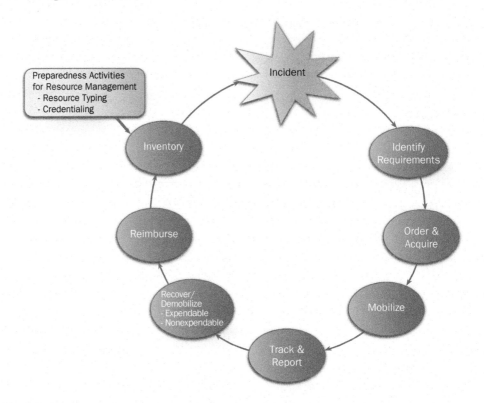

that jurisdictions must be able to answer are: (1) How prepared do we need to be? (2) How prepared are we now? (3.) How do we prioritize efforts to close the gaps?

2. **Communications and Information Management (CIM).** The underlying concepts and principles of this component reinforce the use of a flexible communications and information system in which emergency management/response personnel can maintain a constant flow of information during an incident. These concepts and principles emphasize the need for and maintenance of a common operating picture; interoperability; reliability, scalability, and portability; and resiliency and redundancy of any system and its components.

3. **Resource Management.** NIMS defines standardized mechanisms and establishes requirements for processes to describe, inventory, mobilize, dispatch, track, and recover resources over the life cycle of an incident (see Figure 13–17).

   The right types of resources (e.g., personnel, equipment, and supplies) are needed at the right time, at the right place, in the right quantities. Communications provide fluidity to managing resources so that they can be directed or redirected to rapidly changing incidents. As an illustration, two or three smaller wildfires may quickly merge to form a single large-scale fire when winds gust and change directions. Addressing a disaster or events during a rapidly changing weather environment is particularly challenging, and is often encountered during fire and flood emergencies. Incident commanders must quickly get their new requirements to the resource manager, who must be nimble in responding.

   For this reason, large stockpiles of equipment are pre-positioned near urban areas throughout the United States. In addition, private-public agreements are often pre-developed to be used during an emergency. For instance, the U.S. Coast Guard has existing relationships and agreements with private-sector manufacturers of spill boom (devices placed in water to contain an oil spill) and other oil-absorbent materials. These items can be quickly located through the private sector and delivered to an open water emergency in a matter of hours almost anywhere within the continental United States. Additionally, the U.S. Forest Service has similar agreements with private-sector helicopter and air flight services to provide water and fire retardant quickly to burning areas, as well as their own resources (see Figure 13–18).

4. **Command and Management.** This component of NIMS is designed to enable effective and efficient incident management and coordination by providing a flexible, but standardized incident management structure. The structure is based on three key organizational elements: (1) Incident Command System, (2) Multiagency Coordination Systems, and (3) Public Information System.

4.1 **Incident Command System (ICS).** ICS is standard across emergency response organizations in its operating and other characteristics throughout the lifecycle of an incident. **Most incidents occur within a single jurisdiction and are handled by its own resources.** The majority of responses need go no further. In other instances, incidents that begin with a single response within a single jurisdiction rapidly expand to multidisciplinary, multijurisdictional levels requiring significant additional resources and operational support. ICS provides a flexible core mechanism for coordinated and collaborative incident management, whether for incidents where additional resources are required or are provided from different organizations within a single jurisdiction or outside the jurisdiction, or for complex incidents with national implications (such as an emerging infectious disease or a bioterrorism attack). When a single incident covers a large geographical area, multiple local emergency management and incident response agencies may be required. The responding "agencies" are defined as the governmental agencies, though in certain circumstances nongovernmental organizations (NGOs) and private-sector organizations may be included. Effective cross-jurisdictional coordination using processes and systems is critical in this situation. ICS is of such importance that a subsequent section of this chapter is devoted to it.

4.2 **Multiagency Coordination Systems (MACS).** The primary function of MACS is to coordinate activities above the field level and to prioritize the incident demands for critical or competing resources, thereby assisting the coordination of the operations in the field. MACS consists of a combination of elements: personnel, procedures, protocols, business practices, and communications integrated into a common system. For the purpose of coordinating resources and support between multiple jurisdictions, MACS can be implemented from a fixed facility or virtually if facilities to do so exist. MACS have no direct authority over field operations, but they are a critical support function.

4.3 **Public Information System (PIS).** Public Information refers to processes, procedures, and systems for communicating timely and accurate information to the public during crisis or emergency situations. When Malaysian Airlines Flight 370 disappeared in 2014, both the carrier and the Malaysian government were slow to release information and were soundly criticized by experts and the families of those on the plane. The chief criticisms were that holding back information served no legitimate purpose and doing so placed additional stress on the families. In emergency management, the public information component may literally save lives. Individuals may also be able to get severe weather or other warnings[85] on their mobile devices from Wireless Emergency Alerts (WEAs). WEAs don't require an automated application (app) and originate with an authorized governmental authority. MyWarn is similar, but requires downloading a free app.

5. **Ongoing Management/Maintenance and Supporting Technologies.** The Secretary of Homeland Security is responsible for establishing a mechanism to ensure the ongoing management and maintenance of NIMS. That mechanism is the National Integration Center (NIC). NIC has regular consultations with federal

FIGURE 13–18
A Forest Service air tanker dropping fire retardant. Having the right equipment available in a timely manner at the location of an emergency is often a critical factor in effectively managing the event. The Federal Interagency Fire Center coordinates wildfire-fighting assistance from a number of agencies, including the U.S. Forest Service.

(Keith Crowley/Alamy Stock Photo)

agencies, state, tribal, and local governments, and NGOs, as well as the portions of the private sector that are implementing NIM. Revisions to NIMS and other issues can be proposed by all NIMS users, volunteers, academia, nonprofit organizations, and volunteers. With their feedback and recommendations, as well as information from other sources, NIC provides strategic oversight of NIMS. Additionally, the NIC administers NIMS compliance requirements, facilitates the development of guidance standards for typing and credentialing, supports NIMS training and exercises, and manages the publication of various NIMS-related materials.

The ongoing development of science and technology is crucial to the continual improvement and refinement of NIMS. Strategic research and development (R&D) programs ensure that this development takes place. NIMS also relies on scientifically based technical standards that support incident management. Maintaining a focus on appropriate science and technology solutions requires a long-term collaborative effort among NIMS and its partners. To ensure the effective development of incident-management science and technology solutions, the NIC works in coordination with the DHS Under Secretary for Science and Technology to assess the needs of emergency management/response personnel and their affiliated organizations

In another development that followed FEMA's performance during Hurricane Katrina, the Congress mandated the federal Emergency Communications Preparedness Center (ECPC) to foster better communications and coordination between fourteen federal agencies. The basic goal in ECPC is to provide a communication and information management system that affords interoperability and standardization for all jurisdictions and entities responding to an emergency or catastrophic event, thereby

Quick Facts
The U.S. Coast Guard National Strike Force

The U.S. Coast Guard National Strike Force responds to any hazard, any place, at any time involving oil or any dangerous substance that threatens to pollute the marine environment. The team consists of over 200 active-duty civilian, reserve, and auxiliary personnel and includes the National Strike Force Coordination Center. The team has responded during every

major hurricane and such high-profile events as the Exxon Valdez spill in Prince William Sound, Alaska (1989), the 9/11 terrorist attacks (2001), the Space Shuttle Columbia recovery (2003), and British Petroleum's (BPs) Deep Water Horizon explosion and oil spill (2010), which did $17.2 billion in damages to natural resources[86] (see Figure 13–19).

FIGURE 13–19

BP's Deepwater Horizon oil rig was located in the Gulf of Mexico, 45 miles from Louisiana. Multiple Coast Guard helicopters, planes, and cutters searched for the 126 crew staffing the oil rig, while firefighting boats attempted to bring the blaze under control. A total of 115 were rescued and 11 were not found.

(US Coast Guard)

enhancing coordination of effort and the effective use of all resources. WEBEOC is a privately developed, secure, real-time, Internet-based emergency operations communication system with 10-year history. It is in its eighth edition of software and has users in twenty-five countries. Some twenty-five federal agencies use it and over 600 state and local agencies use it as well.

The Incident Command System (ICS)

ICS was developed following a series of wildfires in California during the 1970s.[87] Property damage ran into the millions and many people died or were injured. A surprising finding came out of studies of each of those fires: Rarely was a "bad" outcome the result of a lack of equipment or a failure of tactics. Instead, the single greatest contributor to "bad" outcomes was inadequate management.[88] Factors hindering effective management included poor communication capabilities and therefore the inability to direct and influence operations. These findings led to the development of ICS.

The Incident Command System (ICS) is a vital part of NIMS and represents a standardized, on-scene, all-hazards incident management approach that allows for the integration of facilities, equipment, personnel, procedures, and communications operating within a common organizational structure.[89] ICS also enables a coordinated response among various jurisdictions, both public and private, as well as establishes a common process for planning and managing diverse resources from multiple venues. The ICS includes the use of a temporary organizational structure in the field that is established as close as safety permits to the scene of an incident—the Incident Command Center (ICC). That structure is "retired" after each incident. Beyond actual incidents, the Incident Command Center is also activated during readiness exercises. The staffing of the structure will vary depending on the complexity of the incident. The Incident Command System is used by all levels of government, as well as many nongovernmental organizations and the private sector. For instance, almost every hospital utilizes ICS during an emergency to create a triage system and provide specialty expertise, equipment, and resources to various trauma centers throughout a specific region during a crisis. This type of information sharing, coordination of services, and use of valuable resources is vastly enhanced through ICS. The Incident Command System can be used with any type or size of event. By using it in smaller incidents, valuable experience can be gained, which will be useful in dealing with larger incidents later.[90] More specifically, ICS is a standardized, on-scene, all-hazards management structure and process that:[91]

1. Allows for integration of facilities, equipment, personnel, procedures operating within a single organizational structure (see Figure 13–20) and using a common terminology.
2. Enables a coordinated response among the various responders to incidents.
3. Establishes common processes for planning and managing resources. For example, most incident communication is not based on dispatch codes; everything is

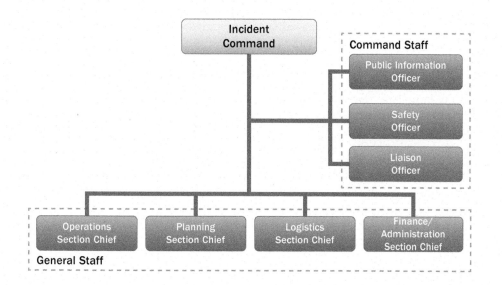

FIGURE 13–20
The ICS Command and General Staff Structure
Depending on the type and severity of an incident the general staff structure may be less or more specialized (e.g., air support, decontamination centers, and the presence of NGOs such as the American Red Cross).

(From National Incident Management System. Published by United States Department of Homeland Security.)

Unified Command

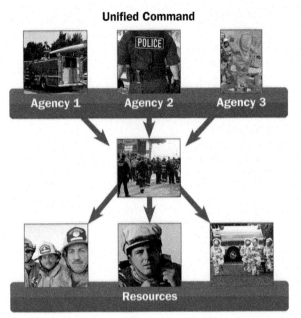

FIGURE 13–21

The unified command organization consists of incident commanders from various agencies working together to form a single command structure in the field.

(Left to Right [top]: Mike Brake/ Shutterstock, sirtravelalot/ Shutterstock, TFoxFoto/Shutterstock, Center: Christopher Penler/Alamy Stock Photo; Left to Right [bottom]: sirtravelalot/Shutterstock, MC Images/Alamy Stock Photo, Ben Carlson/Shutterstock)

Incident commander
The most senior commander first arriving at the scene of an incident from a specific first responder agency, such as from police, fire, or emergency services.

Unified command
The primary command organization for the Incident Command System in the field; incident commanders from different agencies combine to form a single unified command structure.

communicated in plain English. However, an encryption system is also needed for incidents such as an ongoing terrorist attack or active shooter situation.

4. Communicates and coordinates with its Emergency Operations Center (EOC), which is normally activated if the ICS commander requests additional support and resources. State statutes may provide other ways a local EOC can be activated, such as by the sheriff, the county judge, the emergency center director, or some other arrangement. City/County EOCs have a policy/executive board composed of key local officials, such as the sheriff, mayors, and chairs of county commissions, who may be present in the EOC during an incident.

The first arriving emergency responder to an incident automatically becomes the **incident commander** and remains in that role until (1) a more senior person arrives and takes command; (2) he/she needs rest or is injured and the EOC director appoints a replacement; or (3) he/she is replaced for cause or other reason and the EOC director designates a new incident commander. One of the most important elements of the Incident Command System is the development of a **unified command**. The unified command is a structure that combines all incident commanders from all major organizations or responding agencies involved in an incident under one umbrella. The idea is to link all organizations together and provide a forum for all agencies to coordinate a specific response to an incident based on the combined expertise of the agencies responding. Under the unified command, decisions are made by consensus of those leaders who are actually on the scene so that an integrated and efficient response can occur (see Figure 13–21).

The Emergency Operation Center (EOC)[92]

An Emergency Operation Center (EOC) is a concept used by many jurisdictions and is mandated by NIMS. When activated, its primary purpose is to provide support to the incident commander. An EOC has levels of activation, such as:

1. A standby/warning alert to the EOC staff that activation may occur (for instance, due to a hurricane that is 72 hours from making landfall in the area),

2. Partial activation (for instance, the interstate that runs through the city/county is blocked by tornado debris and there are some medical emergencies, requiring a limited level of EOC services), and

3. Full activation (for instance, a violent lightning storm with winds gusting to 65 miles an hour with softball-sized hail causes a series of ongoing fires; signs and some roofs are torn off in the business district, along with broken windows, which led to looting in that area; and a school bus has been overturned with an unknown number of injuries to middle school students).

Some states require all EOC activations to be reported to their regional and federal coordinators. Other states have a list that identifies the mandatory incident reporting to the state. In Indiana, that list includes incidents involving weapons of mass destruction, sniper activity, severe flooding, suspected or actual acts of terrorism, catastrophic failure of buildings, and injury or death to members of the legislature, the executive branch, and judiciary. A number of EOCs have an alternate or back-up location in case the primary site is damaged or destroyed. For instance, the Emergency Operations Center for the City of Dallas (Texas) is located in the basement of city hall, while the back-up EOC is the existing fusion center within the Dallas Police Department, located several miles away. Personnel within the EOC often work 12-hour shifts during an emergency and stay on-site versus going home. The need to have personnel working on an extended basis often requires the EOC to have lodging capabilities, food services, and showers and restroom accommodations in the likely event that staff coming and going will not be feasible during an incident.

The EOC's broader role is to provide support such as incident coordination, resource allocation, and information collection, analysis, and dissemination. Most states have an EOC, as do many local jurisdictions, and some states require cities of a certain size to have one or to join a multi-jurisdictional emergency operations center. EOCs are usually housed in a permanent location and may be "hardened" to protect them from severe weather or other threats. They are not routinely staffed unless their anticipated workload justifies it or a major incident occurs. An EOC is staffed from emergency "disciplines," such as the police, fire, health, and public works departments, and geographic information support (GIS) and mutual aid personnel. Key elected officials in the EOC do not have authority over the incident commander, who is on the scene and responsible for all tactical decisions, although key officials are empowered to issue disaster declarations. The types of emergency management disciplines represented at an EOC may change as the incident passes to a different phase, that is, from response to recovery, and produces new needs that must be met.

The National Preparedness System: How It All Fits Together

Every day, we take steps to keep our nation safe and ensure that we thrive after disasters occur. Whether we face risks related to earthquakes, cyber attacks, or chemical spills, our goal is shared: safety and resilience. The National Preparedness System outlines an organized process for everyone in the whole community to move forward with their preparedness activities and achieve the National Preparedness Goal. The National Preparedness System has six parts:[93]

1. **Identifying and Assessing Risk.** This part involves collecting historical and recent data on existing, potential, and perceived threats and hazards. The results of these risk assessments form the basis for the remaining steps.

2. **Estimating Capability Requirements.** Next, you can determine the specific capabilities and activities to best address those risks. Some capabilities may already exist and some may need to be built or improved. FEMA provides a list of core capabilities related to protection, prevention, mitigation, response and recovery, the five mission areas of preparedness.

3. **Building and Sustaining Capabilities.** This involves figuring out the best way to use limited resources to build capabilities. You can use the risk assessment to prioritize resources to address the highest probability or highest consequence threats.

4. **Planning to Deliver Capabilities.** Because preparedness efforts involve and affect the whole community, it's important that you coordinate your plans with other organizations. This includes all parts of the whole community: individuals, businesses, nonprofits, community and faith-based groups, and all levels of government.

5. **Validating Capabilities.** Now it's time to see if your activities are working as intended. Participating in exercises, simulations, or other activities helps you identify gaps in your plans and capabilities. It also helps you see progress toward meeting preparedness goals. Please visit the National Exercise Division for more information.

6. **Reviewing and Updating.** It is important to regularly review and update all capabilities, resources, and plans. Risks and resources evolve—and so should your preparedness efforts.

The National Preparedness Goal

The National Preparedness Goal defines what it means to be prepared for all types of disasters and emergencies:

> "A secure and resilient nation with the capabilities required across the whole community to prevent, protect against, mitigate, respond to, and recover from the threats and hazards that pose the greatest risk."[94]

National Preparedness Goal
Released in September 2011, the National Preparedness Goal defined national preparedness as: *"A secure and resilient nation with the capabilities required across the whole community to prevent, protect against, mitigate, respond to, and recover from the threats and hazards that pose the greatest risk."*

Enable Response:
- Situational Assessment
- Public Messaging
- Command, Control, and Coordination
- Critical Communications
- Environmental Health and Safety Critical Transportation

Survivor Needs:
- On-Scene Security and Protection
- Mass Search and Rescue Operations
- Health and Medical Treatment
- Mass Care Services
- Public and Private Services and Resources
- Stabilize and Repair Essential Infrastructure
- Fatality Management Services

Restoration:
- Essential Service Facilities
- Utilities
- Transportation Routes
- Schools
- Neighborhood Retail Businesses
- Offices and Other Workplaces

FIGURE 13–22
Targeted Core Capabilities for the Stabilization and Restoration Mission of FEMA
(Courtesy Federal Emergency Management Agency.)

"Whole community"
A concept within the National Preparedness Goal referring to all federal, state, and local government agencies, as well as the nongovernmental organizations, private sector, schools, families, and individuals focused on national preparedness.

When a community knows the threats/hazards it realistically faces, it will establish goals to deal with each threat/hazard. To achieve each goal, the community must develop different competencies or proficiencies called core capabilities. For example, if goal is to rescue survivors of an earthquake within 72 hours of its occurrence, the community will have to buy and train rescue dogs and recruit the people who will be working them. While this is going on, they are at the *capability target* stage. They know what they want to be able to do, but are not yet able. When search and rescue teams are fully proficient, the community no longer has a capability target; it has a core competency, which provides a means of achieving their goal. There are thirty-two activities that constitute core capabilities. Many jurisdiction will only be able to develop some of them. The rest will have to be provided through mutual aid agreements or other arrangements. The high risks communities face are where they should start developing their core capabilities. In the Midwest, the frequency of tornados will dictate one approach, while states bordering the Atlantic Ocean or the Gulf of Mexico will give careful attention to hurricanes and flooding. The Federal Emergency Management Agency (FEMA) has its own core capabilities to develop (see Figure 13–22). The first 72 hours in a disaster are critical, for example, if it takes too long to rescue people and get them to a hospital, some of them will die.

The National Preparedness Report

The last step of the National Preparedness model presented by President Obama in Presidential Policy Directive #8 is the National Preparedness Report (NPR). The NPR is an annual assessment of national progress toward delivering the core capabilities outlined in the National Preparedness Goal (NPG). The report focuses on the progress made by the **whole community** partners—including all levels of government, private and nonprofit sectors, faith-based organizations, communities, and individuals—in the previous year. The report identifies strengths and progress, as well as weaknesses and gaps that still remain.

Chapter Summary

SUMMARY BY LEARNING OBJECTIVE

1. **Identify the major categories of threats/hazards and give three examples of each.**

   Table 13-1 contains the answer to this question. The top line identifies the major categories and the examples are under each column below them. You may also wish to learn specific illustrations of the examples in the columns. To illustrate, under "Natural," you may want to think "What is an example of animal disease breakout?" After considering it, you may have come up with Mad Cow disease or rabies. For "Technological and Accidental," you may want to do a little research to see how many dams actually fail annually in the United States, under what circumstances, and with what consequences. And, for "Terrorist/Human Caused," you may want to explore the number of deaths caused by gunfire versus explosion. Thinking out-of-the-box provide a means to identify the myriad of potential threats and hazards that exist in our world today.

2. **Summarize the severity continuum.**

   The severity continuum is a guide to categorizing events so that important distinctions can be made between them. It is composed of four points: (1) An "*emergency*" is marked by actual danger to the lives of persons and/or the safety of property that requires a response (emergencies ordinarily are handled locally). (2) A "*disaster*" is more severe than an emergency because it causes a serious disruption of the functioning of an entity, such as a community, and produces widespread human, material, economic, and/or environmental losses that exceed the ability of a community to cope with it using just its own resources. (3) A "*catastrophe*"

TABLE 13–1

Natural	Technological and Accidental	Terrorist/Human Caused
• Animal Disease Breakout	• Aircraft Crash	• Biological
• Avalanche	• Bridge Failure	• Chemical
• Drought	• Building Collapse	• Cyber
• Earthquake	• Dam Failure	• Explosion
• Epidemic/Pandemic	• Hazardous Materials Release/Spill	• Gunfire
• Flood	• Levee Failure	• Nuclear
• Hurricane/Cyclone	• Maritime Accident	• Radiological Dispersion Device (RDD)
• Landslide/Rock Fall	• Mine Accident	• Sabotage
• Lightning	• Power Failure/Blackouts	• Vehicles
• Tornado	• Radiological Release	
• Tropical Storm	• Train Derailment	
• Tsunami	• Urban Fires	
• Volcanic Eruption	• Vehicle Crash	
• Wildfire		
• Winter Storm		

is an incident that directly or indirectly affects large portions or all of an entire country and requires national and sometimes international responses. (4) An "*extinction event*" is the final event in human history, resulting in the loss of all human life on the planet. The probability of a human extinction event is presently very slight.

3. **State the five missions communities must plan for when considering threats/hazards.**

Those five missions are prevent, protect, mitigate, respond, and recover.

4. **Summarize why FEMA was created and what its performance has been.**

By 1975, nearly 100 federal agencies had some aspect of disaster assistance. Frustrated with this fragmentation, the National Governor's Association (NGA) pushed President Carter for a single agency to have jurisdiction over natural and environmental disasters. In 1978, President Carter issued an executive order creating FEMA. From 1980 until 2003, when it was transferred to DHS. During the pre-DHS days, it dealt with a variety of issues, such as the homeless, birth defects caused by toxic in Love Canal, the eruption of Mount Saint Helens, and the Oklahoma City bombing by Timothy McVeigh. FEMA's first major criticism by Congress was its inept handling of Hurricane Hugo, which hit South Carolina hard in the late 1980s. Congressional dissatisfaction with the handling of Hugo was high and there was some sentiment to disband it. By 1993, FEMA had made some significant reforms. Congressional criticism after Hurricane Katrina in 2005 was again high after FEMA's poor showing. Congress passed the Post-Katrina Emergency Management Reform Act of 2006 and it has made headway since then.

5. **Briefly describe NIMS and identify its five missions.**

The National Incident Management System (NIMS) was established to create a single, comprehensive system which would prevent, prepare for, respond to, and recover from terrorist attacks, major disasters, and other emergencies.

The five NIMS missions are: (1) prevention, (2) protection, (3) mitigation, (4) response, and (5) recovery. In some documents, the five missions are also referred to as the "National Planning Framework."

6. **Explain how the National Preparedness System works within our communities.**

The National Preparedness Goal defines what it means for the entire community to be prepared for all types of disasters and emergencies: "A secure and resilient nation with the capabilities required across the whole community to prevent, protect against, mitigate, respond to, and recover from the threats and hazards that pose the greatest risk."

When a community knows the threats/hazards it realistically faces, it will establish goals to deal with each threat/hazard. To achieve each goal, the community must develop different competencies or proficiencies called core capabilities. For example, if goal is to rescue survivors of an earthquake within 72 hour of its occurrence, the community will have to buy and train rescue dogs and recruit the people that will be working them. While this is going on they are at the *capability target* stage. They know what they want to be able to do, but are not yet able. When search and rescue teams are fully proficient, the community no longer has a capability target, it has a core competency, which provides a means of achieving their goal. There are thirty-two activities that constitute core capabilities. Many jurisdiction will only be able to develop some of them. The rest will have to be provided through mutual aid agreements or other arrangements. The high risks communities face are where they should start developing their core capabilities. In the Midwest, the frequency of tornados will dictate one approach, while states bordering the Atlantic Ocean or the Gulf of Mexico will give careful attention to hurricanes and flooding. The Federal Emergency Management Agency (FEMA) also has its own core capabilities to develop. The first 72 hours in a disaster are critical, e.g., if it takes too long to rescue people and get them to a hospital, some of them will die.

The National Preparedness System has six parts:

1. **Identifying and Assessing Risk.** This part involves collecting historical and recent data on existing, potential and perceived threats and hazards. The results of these risk assessments form the basis for the remaining steps.

2. **Estimating Capability Requirements.** Next, you can determine the specific capabilities and activities to best address those risks. Some capabilities may already exist and some may need to be built or improved. FEMA provides a list of core capabilities related to protection, prevention, mitigation, response and recovery, the five mission areas of preparedness.

3. **Building and Sustaining Capabilities.** This involves figuring out the best way to use limited resources to build capabilities. You can use the risk assessment to prioritize resources to address the highest probability or highest consequence threats.

4. **Planning to Deliver Capabilities.** Because preparedness efforts involve and affect the whole community, it's important that you coordinate your plans with other organizations. This includes all parts of the whole community: individuals, businesses, nonprofits, community and faith-based groups, and all levels of government.

5. **Validating Capabilities.** Now it's time to see if your activities are working as intended. Participating in exercises, simulations or other activities helps you identify gaps in your plans and capabilities. It also helps you see progress toward meeting preparedness goals. Please visit the National Exercise Division for more information.

6. **Reviewing and Updating.** It is important to regularly review and update all capabilities, resources, and plans. Risks and resources evolve—and so should your preparedness efforts.

REVIEW QUESTIONS

1. During the colonial era in what was to become the United States, what belief held back disaster relief?
2. What are the four steps in the THIRA model?
3. How is chaos theory an asset in disasters?
4. After a series of wildfires in California during the 1970s, what was found to be the single most important factor in "bad" outcomes? Why?
5. What is an EOC and what is its primary purpose?
6. What is the difference between a capability target and a core capability?
7. What was the first major natural disaster that introduced FEMA as the primary emergency management agency in the United States?
8. What are three examples of poor performance in FEMA's early years?
9. The final step in the National Preparedness System is the National Preparedness Report (NPR). What does the NPR cover?

CRITICAL THINKING EXERCISES

1. Compare the population density of California with Alaska and then do the same for the largest city in each of those states. What does population density suggest about the consequences of natural disasters and preparedness?

2. Visit and explore the website of the CDC at www.cdc.gov/. Under the tab labeled "Emergency Preparedness," explore the recent "outbreaks and incidents" that have occurred around the world. What has been the role of the CDC during these incidents? Discuss the importance of this agency in responding to a terrorist strike using CBRNE agents.

3. Discuss the possibility of a disaster in your community. What is the most likely type of disaster—natural, technological, man-made—and what do you think is the probability that an act will occur in the next two years? Five years? Ten years? How severe do you think this event will be, what agencies will respond, and what plans are already in place to address such an event? Ask an appropriate local official to discuss emergency management in your area.

NOTES

1. *Principles of Emergency Management Supplement*, September 11, 2007, p. 1, www .ndsu.edu/fileadmin/principlesofemergencymanagement.pdf.

2. *Fundamentals of Emergency Management* (Washington, D.C.: Federal Emergency Management Agency, January 14, 2010), p. 217.

3. Loc. cit.

4. "Bellevue Hospital Staffers Reportedly Take Sick Days Rather Than Treat New York's First Ebola Patient," *Fox News*, October 25, 2014, www.foxnews.com/health/2014/10/25 /hospital-staffers-reportedly-take-sick-day-rather-than-treat-new-yorks-first.

5. *How Flood Smart Are You?* (Washington, D.C.: Federal Emergency Management Agency, undated), p. 1, www.floodsmart.gov/floodsmart/pages/media_resources/fact_floodfacts.jsp.

6. This information is taken in part from "Saddam's Iraq, Chemical Warfare 1983–1988," *BBC News*, undated, http://news.bbc.co.uk/2/shared/spl/hi/middle_east/02/iraq_events /html/chemical_warfare.stm; and "Chemical Agents," *Centers for Disease Control and Prevention*, April 18, 2013, http://emergency.cdc.gov/agent/agentlistchem-category.asp.

7. Holly Fletcher, "Aum Shinrikyo," Council on Foreign Relations, June 19, 2012, pp. 1–3, www.cfr.org/japan/aum-shinrikyo/p9238.

8. FEMA Administrator Craig Fugate came up with the idea of a Waffle House Index. See Ewen MacAskill, "FEMA Uses 'Waffle House Index' to Take Stock of Oklahoma Tornado Disaster," *Guardian*, May 21, 2013, p. 1, www.theguardian.com/world/2013/may/21 /fema-waffle-house-index-oklahoma.

9. Department of Homeland Security, "Threats and Hazards Identification and Risk Assessment Guide," 2nd ed., August 2013, p. 6, www.fema.gov/media-library-data/8ca0a9e 54dc8b037a55b402b2a269e94/CPG201_htirag_2nd_edition.pdf, accessed May 13, 2017.

10. U.S. Department of State, OSAC, Sweden 2016 Crime and Safety Report, May 13, 2016, p.6, www.fema.gov/media-library-data/8ca0a9e54dc8b037a55b402b2a269e94/CPG201_ htirag_2nd_edition.pdf, accessed May 15, 2017.

11. Martin Evans, "Everything We Know So Far About the Stockholm Attack," *Telegraph* (England), April 9, 2017, www.telegraph.co.uk/news/2017/04/07/everything-know-far-stockholm-terror-attack/, accessed May 15, 2017.

12. Sweden 2016 Crime and Safety Report, p. 5.

13. WSJ Staff, "What We Know About the Global Ransomware Attack," *Wall Street Journal*, May 14, 2017, p. 1, www.wsj.com/articles/what-we-know-about-the-global-ransomware-attack-1494684034, accessed May 15, 2017.

14. Loc. cit.

15. Mark Thompson and Jethro Mullen, "World's Biggest Cyberattack Sends Countries into Disaster Recovery Mode," CNN.com, May 14, 2017, p. 1, http://money.cnn.com/2017/05/14 /technology/ransomware-attack-threat-escalating, accessed May 16, 2017.

16. "Grain Elevator Explosion Chart," Occupational Safety and Health Administration, www .osha.gov/sltc/grainhandling/explosion%20chart.html.

17. Jessica Merzdorf, "Fewer Grain Dust Explosions Reported Nationwide in 2016," Purdue University College of Agriculture, February 13, 2017, p. 1, www.purdue.edu/newsroom /releases/2017/Q1/fewer-grain-dust-explosions-reported-nationwide-in-2016.html, accessed May 9, 2017.

18. The numbers were taken from Brandon Griggs, "Harvey's Devastating Impact by the Numbers," CNN News, September 1, 2017, http://www.cnn.com/2017/08/27/us/harvey-impact-by-the-numbers-trnd/index.html, accessed September 3, 2017.

19. B. Wayne Blanchard, "Guide to Emergency Management and Related Terms, Definitions, Concepts, Acronyms, Organizations, Programs, Guidance, Executive Orders, and Legislation," October 22, 2008, pp. 284–285, www.training.fema.gov/emiweb/docs/terms%20and%20definitions.pdf.

20. In 1952, President Truman issued Executive Order 10427, which emphasized this point.

21. The information in this Quick Facts box is drawn from *Preparedness* (Washington, D.C.: Federal Emergency Management Agency, July 24, 2014), p. 1.

22. Loc. cit.

23. Nationally Adopted Interstate Mutual Aid Agreement, April 10, 2014, p. 1, www.emacweb.org.

24. "Haiti Earthquake," January 13, 2014, Thomson Reuters Foundation, www.trust.org/spotlight/Haiti-earthquake-2010.

25. Loc. cit.

26. Sarah Zielinski, "Giant New Magma Reservoir Found Beneath Yellowstone," Smithsonian.com, April 23, 2015, p. 1, www.smithsonianmag.com/science-nature/giant-new-magma-reservoir-found-beneath-yellowstone-180955086, accessed May 10, 2017.

27. Loc. cit.

28. Loc. cit.

29. Department of Homeland Security, National Disaster Recovery Framework, 2nd ed., June 2016, p. 4, www.fema.gov/media-library-data/1466014998123-4bec8550930f774269e0c596 8b120ba2/National_Disaster_Recovery_Framework2nd.pdf, accessed May 12, 2017.

30. "Threats and Hazards Identification," 2nd ed., pp. 1–3.

31. Department of Homeland Security, "Threat and Risk Assessment Guide," 2nd ed. 2013, pp. 1–2), www.fema.gov/media-library-data/8ca0a9e54dc8b037a55b402b2a269e94/CPG201_htirag_2nd_edition.pdf, accessed May 10 2017.

32. Ibid., pp. 2–3.

33. The material on chaos theory is taken from Charles R. Swanson, Leonard Territo, and Robert W. Taylor, *Police Administration: Structures, Processes, and Behavior* (Boston: Pearson, 2017), p. 167.

34. Richard Sylves, *Disaster Policy and Politics* (Washington, D.C.: CQ Press, 2008), p. 3.

35. Some of the structure on self-reliance is drawn from Claire B. Rubin, "Local Emergency Management," pp. 26–17 in William L. Waugh, Jr. and Kathleen Tierney, *Emergency Management* (Washington, D.C.: International City/County Management Association, 2007).

36. Ralph Waldo Emerson, "Self Reliance," in *Essays*, originally published in 1841. See www.emersoncentral.com/selfreliance.htm.

37. Thomas Sowell, *Ethnic America* (New York: Basic Books, 1983), p. 117.

38. Richard Sylves, *Disaster Policy and Politics* (Los Angeles: Sage, 2008), p. 3.

39. Rubin, "Local Emergency Management," p. 27.

40. *Civil Defense and Homeland Security: A Short History of National Preparedness Efforts* (Washington, D.C.: Federal Emergency Management Agency, September 2006), p. 5.

41. Loc. cit.

42. Jennifer D. Keene, *World War I* (Westport, Connecticut: Greenwood Publishing Group, January 1, 2006), p. 114.

43. Sylves, *Disaster Policy and Politics*, p. 5.

44. Loc. cit.

45. Loc. cit.

46. "The New Deal," The Roosevelt Institute, undated, p. 1, http://rooseveltinstitute.org/policy-and-ideasroosevelt-historyfdr/new-deal.

47. "The Great Depression," The George Washington University Eleanor Roosevelt Papers Project, undated, p. 1, www.gwu.edu/~erpapers/teachinger/glossary/great-depression.cfm.

48. Gene Smiley, "Great Depression," *Library of Economic and Liberty*, undated, p. 1, www.econlib.org/library/Enc/GreatDepression.html.

49. Records of the Office of Civilian Defense, National Archives, Record Group 171, 171.1, Administrative History, undated, p. 1, www.archives.gov/research/guide-fed-records/groups/171.html#171.1.

50. For more information on this program, see *A Handbook for Air Raid Wardens* (Washington, D.C.: Office of Civilian Defense, April 1942).

51. Library of Congress Prints and Photographs Online Catalog, from 1943 photograph caption, www.loc.gov/pictures/item/oem2002008497/pp.

52. "Introduction: The Civilian Conservation Corps," *PBS*, undated, p. 1, www.pbs.org/wgbh/americanexperience/features/introduction/ccc-introduction.

53. Loc. cit.

54. Loc. cit.

55. Thomas J. Kerr, *Civil Defense in the U.S.* (Boulder, Colorado: Westview Press, 1983), pp. 27–28.

56. Andrew D. Grossman, *Neither Dead Nor Red* (New York: Routledge Press, 2001), pp. 41–42.

57. No author, Annual Report for 1952, Federal Civil Defense Administration (Washington, D.C.: Federal Civil Defense Administration, 1952), pp. 1–2.

58. *Duck and Cover* (York, Nebraska: Wessels, undated), p. 1, www.livinghistoryfarm.org/farminginthe1950s/life_04.html.

59. "For Preppers, Every Day Could Be Doomsday," *USA Today*, November 13, 2012, p. 1, www.usatoday.com/story/news/nation/2012/11/12/for-preppers-every-day-could-be-doomsday/1701151.

60. *Annual Report of the Office of Civil and Defense Mobilization for Fiscal Year 1959* (Washington, D.C.: Government Printing Office, 1960), p. 1, http://training.fema.gov/EMIWeb/edu/docs/HistoricalInterest/Office%20of%20Civil%20and%20Defense%20Mobilization%20-%201959%20-%20Annual%20Rep.pdf.

61. Loc. cit.

62. "Beecher 50th Anniversary Commemoration," *National Oceanic and Atmospheric Administration*, undated, p. 1, www.crh.noaa.gov/dtx/1953beecher/facts.php.

63. See Joseph A. Pratt, *The Challenge of Remaining Innovative in the Twentieth Century* (Redwood, CA: Stanford University Press, 2009), p. 10.

64. Loc. cit.

65. "Origins of U.S. Emergency Management," Anna Maria College, undated, p. 1, http://online.annamaria.edu/emergencymanagementhistory.asp.

66. Ibid., p. 7.

67. Among other agencies, FEMA absorbed the Federal Insurance Administration, the National Fire Prevention and Control Administration, the National Weather Service Community Preparedness Program, the Federal Preparedness Agency of the General Services Administration, the Federal Disaster Assistance Administration activities from HUD, and Civil Defense responsibilities from the Defense Department's Defense Civil Preparedness Agency.

68. Blaine Harden, "Explosive Lessons of 25 Years Ago," *Washington Post*, May 18, 2005. p. A3.

69. The Federal Emergency Management Agency, "About the Agency," August 14, 2014, www.fema.gov/about-agency.

70. Ibid., pp. 9–10.

71. Ibid., p. 10.

72. Ibid., p. 12.

73. White House Memorandum, President Clinton to 14 Key Administrative Officials, U.S. Policy on Counterterrorism, June 21, 1995, Unclassified January 24, 1997 (or possibly 1999, handwriting is difficult to read) with redactions.

74. See www.whitehouse.gov/sites/default/files/microsites/ostp/chns_cbrne_standards_final_24_aug_11.pdf.

75. Al Mauroni, "Homeland Insecurity: Thinking About CBRN Terrorism," *Homeland Security Affairs Journal*, Volume VI, No. 3, September 2000, www.hsaj.org/?fullarticle=6.3.3.

76. No author, "1918 Flu Pandemic," History, undated, p. 1, www.history.com/topics/1918-flu-pandemic, accessed May 13, 2017.

77. Homeland Security Presidential Directive/HSPD-5.

78. Federal Emergency Management Agency, "Presidential Policy Directive 8/PPD-8," 2013, p. 1.

79. Homeland Security Presidential Directive/HSPD-5.

80. Loc. cit.

81. Loc. cit.

82. Ibid., p. 6.

83. Department of Homeland Security, National Incident Management System (NIMS), December 2008, pp. 1–3, www.fema.gov/pdf/emergency/nims/NIMS_core.pdf, accessed May 15, 2017.

84. Federal Management Emergency Agency, "NIMS: Frequently Asked Questions (Washington, D.C.: September 17, 2017), pp. 1-3.

85. The Amber Alert broadcasts details about specific child abduction cases, making each recipient an extra set of eyes looking for that child. The system operates as a collaboration between local law enforcement and the National Center for Missing and Exploited Children (NCMEC) and is broadcast to mobile devices, Facebook, and other outlets.

86. Virginia Polytechnic University, "BP Oil Spill Did $17.2 Billion to Natural Resources, Scientists Find," *Science Daily*, April 20, 2017, p. 1, www.sciencedaily.com /releases/2017/04/170420141825.htm, accessed May 15, 2017.

87. Department of Homeland Security, Incident Command System, May 2008, p. 1, https:// training.fema.gov/emiweb/is/icsresource/assets/reviewmaterials.pdf, accessed May 15, 2017.

88. Loc. cit.

89. See www.fema.gov/incident-command-system.

90. *Incident Command System (ICS) Overview* (Washington, D.C.: Federal Emergency Management Agency, April 22, 2014), www.fema.gov/incident-management-system.

91. Ibid., p. 3.

92. The information in this box was influenced by reading a number of EOC plans and procedures. For example, see *Support Staff Procedures for EOC/Command Postoperative* (San Joaquin County, California: Department of Emergency Operation, February 2009), www.sjgov.org/oes/getplan/EOC-Staff%20procedures.pdf; and *Emergency Operations Center (EOC) Operations Guide* (Lewis and Clark County, Montana, Disaster and Emergency Services, May 11, 2011), www.lccountymt.gov/disaster-and-emergency-services.html.

93. Department of Homeland Security, "National Preparedness System," (Washington, D.C.: Federal Emergency Management Agency, March 30, 2016, pp. 1-6.

94. Department of Homeland Security, "National Preparedness Goal," July 5, 2016, p. 1, www.fema.gov/national-preparedness-goal, accessed May 15, 2016.

Combatting Terrorism

CHARLES SWANSON AND JOHN MATTHEW SWANSON

CHAPTER

14

Learning Objectives

After completing this chapter, you should be able to:

1. Explain what national security policy and national security strategy are and how they are related.

2. Contrast anti-terrorism and counterterrorism efforts.

3. Explain the role of each anti-terrorism organization.

4. Identify the five forms of military action associated with counterterrorism.

5. Identify the mission and subcommands of USSOCOM.

6. Explain the role of each domestic counterterrorism organization.

7. Describe SAS, GSG9, and Mista'arvim.

U.S. Navy SEALs discovered a vast al Qaeda network of caves and tunnels in Eastern Afghanistan and destroyed munitions, arms, and other goods. *(U.S. Navy, www.navy.mil)*

Introduction

The purposes of this chapter are to: (1) briefly explain the difference between national security policy and national security strategy and (2) introduce the concepts of anti-terrorism and counterterrorism. Comprehending these concepts is central to understanding the role of the military in combating terrorism worldwide.

Listen to the radio, read a blog, watch television, scan a newspaper, or overhear a conversation while waiting in line at your favorite coffee shop and you are likely to hear varied opinions about topics that involve politics, freedom, individual rights, and protests. That we can also have such discussions openly without looking around to see who is listening or recording them is in and of itself astonishing. The United States is among a small number of nations that from their founding documents forward have cherished freedom and liberty. We resolved the question of slavery by feat of arms and people of all races were involved in the civil rights movement. In two world wars, we freed countries that had been controlled by dictators and then helped rebuild the very countries we had defeated. The Vietnam War was accompanied by massive anti-war demonstrations in our cities. Reaching America after a tour in Vietnam, veterans were sometimes reviled, spit on and worse. In 1977, to help heal a divided nation, President Carter gave unconditional pardons to hundreds of thousands "draft dodgers" who left the country to avoid military service during that war. We are not a perfect nation, but certainly a decent one, reaching forward to grapple with tough questions, sometimes making mistakes. Despite these mistakes, we realize democracy is the still the best form of government, ever striving to balance the security of our nation with the individual freedoms guaranteed within our Constitution.

The discussion that follows provides a broad overview of how the United States and our allies combat terrorism. Our nation's terrorism and strategy positions will, and should be, subject to vigorous debate among friends, places of learning, town halls, Congress, the federal executive branch, in our courts, and elsewhere . . . for the concept of "We the people" is tantamount in our form of government.

National Security Policy and Strategy

"Policy" and "strategy" are often used synonymously, but they are not. Our national security policy represents the *goals* the United States intends to accomplish, while our national security strategy is the *actions* we will take to ensure that our national security policies are achieved. Our national security policies and strategies have faced unusually strong challenges in recent decades. As illustrations, North Korea and Iran have nuclear ambitions; Russia makes smaller eastern European countries nervous; China with a far flung modern naval fleet is asserting its presence on the world stage; and lone wolves and terrorist organizations threaten our sense of security.

National Security Policy

Within the executive branch of government, Presidents of the United States are responsible for protecting this country, they determine national security policy and approve national security strategy. In both cases, presidents provide direction and guidance through such means as Presidential Policy Directives (PPDs) and executive orders.[1] The National Security Council (NSC) is the president's primary organizational forum for discussing, formulating, establishing, and executing our foreign policy and national security measures.

NSC membership includes senior advisors, some cabinet officials, such as the secretaries of defense and state, as well as representatives of other agencies. In 2009, then-President Barack Obama merged the White House staff supporting the Homeland Security Council (HSC) and the National Security Council into one National Security Staff (NSS).[2]

National Security Strategy Formulation

Like policy, strategy formulation is part art and somewhat scientific in that it follows certain patterns that require an understanding of terminology, adherence to certain principles, and thought processes that must simultaneously be creative and disciplined.[3] Strategy

Strategy Formulation Framework

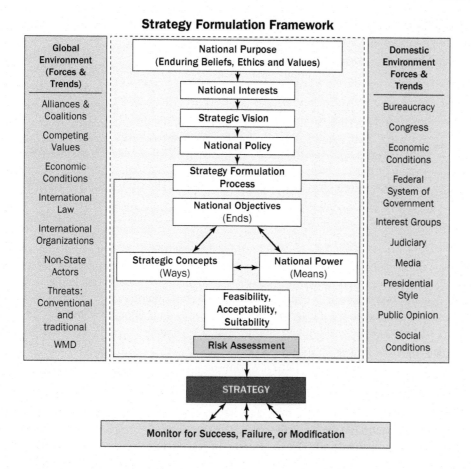

FIGURE 14–1
Strategy Formulation Framework
Source: Colonel Robert E. Hamilton,
et. al., *National Security Policy
and Strategy,* Appendix 1 (Carlisle,
Pennsylvania: United States War
College, Department of National
Security and Strategy, Academic
Year 2017), p. 87.

formulation models don't work like formulas because life's situations vary according to time, place, and other variables.[4] Nevertheless, strategy formulation models provide a means to managing the complexities of situations.

Figure 14–1 summarizes a strategy formulation framework that can be used to determine how we combat terrorism, as well as other purposes. Elements in the model[5] are described as:

1. *The National Purpose:* The enduring values and beliefs embodied in our national purpose represent the legal, philosophical and moral basis for our country. From the nation's purpose, the United States derives its enduring core national interests.

2. *Our Enduring National Interests:* There are four generally agreed upon core U.S. national interests: (a) physical security, defined as protection against attacks on the homeland and people of the United States to ensure survival with our fundamental values and institutions intact; (b) promotion of our values on the world stage; (c) stable international order; and (d) economic prosperity. These interests have changed little over the course of U.S. history.

3. *Our Strategic Vision:* At the highest strategic level, the ways and means to achieve U.S. core national interests are based on the national leadership's strategic vision of what America's role in the world should be to safeguard these national interests. Presidents establish different strategic visions of America's role in the world, often causing them to emphasize certain national interests over others. These views have ranged from isolationism, a non-interventionist stance, to global engagement. Since 9/11, combatting terrorism has been part of our strategic vision.

4. *National Policy,* such as combatting terrorism, is conveyed in many iterative and cumulative forms ranging from formal national security directives and pronouncements in presidential and cabinet-level speeches to presidential replies to press queries and cabinet-level appearances on current affairs television shows. Leaders must work constantly to understand, interpret, and infuse their agencies or institutions with national policy.

5. *The Strategy Formulation Process* is summarized in the lower portion of Figure 14–1 and it consists of the following elements:

   a) *Strategic Concepts ("The Ways")*

   Concurrent with conditions in states like Somalia, Yemen, Iraq, Syria, and Libya, violent extremist organizations, such as al Qaida, Boko Haram, Shining Path, Abu Sayyaf Group, Hezbollah, Hamas, al-Shabaab, and the self-proclaimed Islamic State (IS), are working to undermine transregional security, especially in the Middle East and North Africa. In this complex strategic security environment, the U.S. military does not have the luxury of focusing on one challenge to the exclusion of others. It must provide a full range of military options for addressing failing states and those whose current leadership is hostile to the United States and/or friendly to violent extremist organizations.[6]

   From our enduring national interests, the U.S. military has derived National Security Interests to prioritize its missions. These are: the survival of the nation; the prevention of catastrophic attack against the U.S. homeland; the security of the global economic system; the security, confidence, and reliability of our allies; the protection of American citizens abroad; and the preservation and extension of universal values. The National Security Interests guide military leaders in providing recommendations on when and where our nation should use military force, the type and degree of force to employ, and at what cost.[7]

   b) *National Power ("The Means")*

   The United States maintains a worldwide approach to countering violent extremists and terrorist threats using a combination of economic, diplomatic, intelligence, law enforcement, research and development, and military tools. For instance, the federal government and military cybersecurity team continues working with the Department of Homeland Security (DHS) to improve critical infrastructure cybersecurity, and with the Federal Bureau of Investigation to support law enforcement activities. The federal government assists civilian law enforcement agencies in preventing attacks by homegrown violent extremists as well as other groups that may threaten the homeland.[8]

6. *Feasibility and Acceptability*: Before a strategy can be articulated, it must pass the tests of being feasible and acceptable under the standards of our government. It must be acceptable within the framework of our system, and suitable for accomplishing the objectives.

7. *Risk Assessment*: A strategy is not immutable to change; it must be constantly monitored for what it accomplishes or fails to achieve and is subject to modification for its shortcomings. Modifications represent changes in the risk assessment variable and may also drive strategy changes. As an example, if terrorists deployed weapons of mass destruction in our homeland, our entire strategy may well dramatically change.

A Military Subordinate to Civil Authority

Americans view liberty and freedom, not as abstract ideals, but as entitlements to free speech, peaceable assembly, worship, the right to vote, petition of elected officials, and to be secure in their "house, papers and effects" from unreasonable searches and seizures, to name a few. Globally, national police forces are the rule and not the exception. However, in the United States, we render the military independent from civil authority. Combatting terrorism domestically is primarily a civil law enforcement function, and not a military responsibility. As a reminder, the National Guard can act in a law enforcement capacity within its own state only if they have not been activated by their respective state governor. Hence, the governors of each state (civilians) are the commanders-in-chief of their Guard units.

The bottom line is that while we may not agree with deploying members of our armed services on one combat mission or another—or for that matter, any such mission—a great deal of effort has gone into making the decision. Such a decision may be made swiftly because of the forethought and contingency planning that has already been completed.

Anti-Terrorism and Counterterrorism

Over the past two decades, the United States has improved its capabilities to address domestic and transnational terrorism, including protecting U.S. interests abroad.[9] Two short definitions of important elements of fighting terrorism are: (1) **anti-terrorism**, which is defensive in nature, and (2) **counterterrorism**, which is offensive in nature, "taking the fight to the enemy" (see Figure 14–2).

Many, but not all, anti-terrorism activities are carried out by units of local and state governments, as well as nonmilitary organizations of the federal government and private contractors. Local and state governments often have units with "counterterrorism" in their titles, but they usually perform anti-terrorism duties. This may happen for two reasons: (1) precise definitions sometimes don't survive their encounter with reality, and (2) local and state law enforcement leaders know the difference between anti and counterterrorism, but they may reason that their citizens may feel safer with a more aggressive sounding "counterterrorism" unit, and, therefore, it may be easier to get appropriations for a unit titled "counterterrorism."

Unless their National Guard or Air National Guard has been called to federal duty, the governors of the respective states are the commanders-in-chief of such units. Governors may deploy those units for law enforcement duties within their states as an exception to the Posse Comitatus Act.

The governor of Texas has done so multiple times to assist with maintaining the security of his state's border with Mexico. In 2014, there was a major surge in unaccompanied minors trying to cross into the United States, which has since declined. Then Governor Perry assigned the National Guard to assist with that surge. Since that time, the Texas National Guard has helped install hundreds of remote cameras to monitor the border, and that state's legislature approved $800 million to assist with border control.[10]

The military, and to a smaller degree, the Central Intelligence Agency, execute the majority of all counterterrorism efforts, but they may also have some anti-terrorism responsibilities. Housed within the U.S. Department of Defense, the **U.S. Special Operations Command** (USSOCOM or SOCOM) is the organization responsible for many counterterrorism actions by the military. America's allies, such as Great Britain, Australia, Canada, France, Italy, Denmark, and Poland also participate in the global war on terrorism. Others, closer to regions where there is ground combat, including Jordan and Pakistan, are also helping.

Special operations require unique modes of employment, tactics, techniques, procedures, and equipment. They are often conducted in hostile, denied, or politically and/or diplomatically sensitive environments, and are characterized by one or more of the following: time-sensitivity, clandestine or covert nature, low visibility, work with or through indigenous forces, greater requirements for regional orientation and cultural expertise, and a higher degree of risk.[11]

After IS became a military threat to Tunisia during 2015–2016, that country has cooperated much more closely with the alliance against terrorism. In combating terrorism, nations participate in ways that reflect their capabilities and their political choices. One nation may not commit combat troops, but it shares intelligence or provides critical geographical space for bases and/or listening posts.

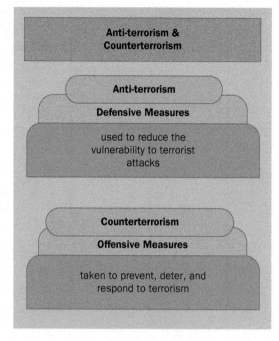

FIGURE 14–2
A basic version of the anti-terrorism and counterterrorism concepts.

Anti-terrorism
Defensive actions taken to reduce the vulnerability of people and property to terrorist acts, including rapid containment by local military and civilian forces.

Counterterrorism
Offensive actions (usually military or paramilitary) taken to prevent, deter, or respond to terrorist threats or attacks.

U.S. Special Operations Command
(USSOCOM or SOCOM) The organization responsible for many counterterrorism actions by the military.

Quick Facts
The Bardo Museum and the Other IS Attacks That Followed

Tunisia is closer to the West than at any time in the past three decades due to IS attacks and are actively involved in fighting terrorism. On March 18, 2015, twenty people, mostly Western tourists, were killed by three terrorists at the Bardo Museum. Two of the gunmen were killed and one is still at large. An IS gunman killed 38 tourists at Sousse, a popular beach resort on June 26, 2015. Just months later, twelve members of the Presidential Guard were killed when their bus was hit by an apparent suicide bomber. The town of Ben Guerdane came under heavy attack on March 6, 2016, with forty terrorists killed, mostly Tunisians who were trained in Libya and returned for the attack.

There is a logic to these attacks: Those on tourist destinations were intended to help destabilize the country by reducing the influx of tourist spending. The bus attack communicated that no target is beyond our reach and finally, the attack on the town was a signal: Your government can't protect you.

FIGURE 14–3
In addition to ATAP, other U.S. entities provide training to foreign governments. Here, Special Forces "Green Berets" work with Mali troops, training them in counter ambush tactics.

(Alfred de Montesquiou/AP Images)

Overview of Anti-Terrorism

A complete definition of anti-terrorism is the defensive actions taken to reduce the vulnerability of people and property to terrorist acts, to include rapid containment by local military and civilian forces.[12] Note that anti-terrorism programs have a proactive component of engaging in activities that are intended to prevent an attack or reduce the losses caused by one and a reactive component of managing the aftermath of an attack.[13] Many countries have anti-terrorism programs; South Korea and Israel have particularly robust anti-terrorism programs, largely because they both have borders with countries opposed to their existence. Referring back to Chapter 13, many actions taken as part of emergency preparedness, for example "hardening" of emergency operations centers and the National Infrastructure Protection Plan, are anti-terrorism measures.

America's anti-terrorism program has been characterized as being geographically limited to the United States. However, this is not accurate. The U.S. Department of State's Anti-Terrorism Assistance Program (ATAP) trains personnel in friendly foreign countries in such topics as protecting critical infrastructures, cybersecurity, dignitary protection, terrorist interdiction, countering violent extremism, and handling improvised explosive devices (IEDs). In any typical year, the Anti-Terrorism Assistance Program (ATAP) provides over 500 courses in over fifty countries (see Figure 14–3).[14] Some of the countries served include the Philippines, Colombia, Kenya, Bahrain, Mexico, Peru, and countries in the Caribbean.

Anti-Terrorism Organizations and Activities

This section provides a discussion of American anti-terrorism organizations and what they do. For each agency identified, one or more examples of its anti-terrorism activities are covered. The agencies selected are intended to convey a sense of the broadness of anti-terrorism efforts. Coverage of all American anti-terrorism efforts is beyond the scope of this chapter. The basic concepts of antiterrorism programs is shown in Figure 14-4.

U.S. Department of Treasury

The U.S. Department of Treasury's Office for Terrorism and Financial Intelligence is led by an undersecretary. This unit is responsible for the department's twin goals of safeguarding the financial system against illicit use and combating rogue nations, terrorist facilitators, weapons of mass destruction (WMD) proliferators, money launderers, drug kingpins, and other national security threats.[15] The intelligence and enforcement functions are executed

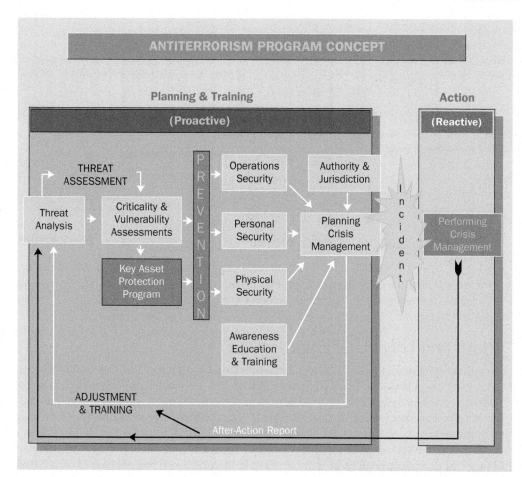

FIGURE 14–4
This figure summarizes the key activities of antiterrorism programs. The "Action" column on the right hand side of the image refers to reactive actions taken in the aftermath of an attack, as distinguished from the direct action taken in counterterrorism efforts, such as the military.

(Courtesy Joint Tactics, Techniques, and Procedures for Anti-Terrorism, Joint Chiefs of Staff)

by several units, including the Financial Crimes Enforcement Network (FinCen) and the Executive Office for Asset Forfeiture.

An example of the Department of Treasury's anti-terrorism work is the investigations conducted into potential criminal cases involving charitable giving. At least seven "charities" with Muslim affiliations have shut down.[16] These "charities" revealed a practice of diverting contributions to al Qaeda and Hamas[17] or otherwise supporting terrorism. As a result, new guidelines were put in place and monitoring of other potential sources of funding to terrorist organization increased.

Federal Bureau of Investigation (FBI)

The FBI's mission statement is "To protect the American people and uphold the Constitution of the United States."[18] The FBI is the lead agency for the Foreign Terrorist Tracking Task Force (FTTTF), which was created by Homeland Security Presidential Directive-2 in 2001. It directed federal agencies to cooperate in an effort to (1) deny entry of aliens into the United States associated with, suspected of being engaged in, or supporting terrorist activity; and (2) locate, detain, prosecute, and deport any such aliens already present in the United States (see Figure 14–5).[19] The Department of Justice's Office of the Inspector General conducted an audit of the Foreign Terrorist Tracking Task Force (FTTTF), which was released in 2013 and concluded that it was of "significant value."[20]

Immigration and Customs Enforcement (ICE)

In the Department of Homeland Security, the Immigration and Customs Enforcement (ICE) has a Terrorist Tracking and Pursuit Group that identifies nonimmigrants who have overstayed the terms of their admission and who may pose a potential risk or threat to national security.[21] "The "terms of their admission" is defined as admissions to the United

FIGURE 14–5
This flow chart depicts what happens after the FTTTF identifies a person considered a national security threat.[22]

(Courtesy The Federal Bureau of Investigation's Foreign Terrorist Tracking Task Force, Department of Justice, Office of the Inspector General, March 2013, p. 5.)

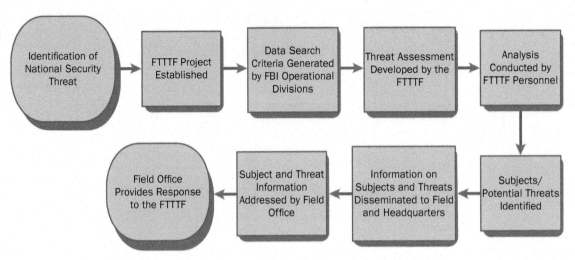

States for business or pleasure, academic or vocational study, temporary employment, or to act as a representative of a foreign government or international organization.[23] Refer back to Chapter 11, "Homeland Security," for more detailed information on ICE.

State and Local Law Enforcement

American state and local law enforcement agencies have an important role to play in anti-terrorism. Local law enforcement has been cast as the "eyes and ears" on the front lines of anti-terrorism and counterterrorism efforts. States and large cities are ordinarily members of Joint Terrorism Task Forces, but also have their own "counterterrorism" units, which actually perform more defensive anti-terrorism tasks as opposed to executing offensive operations.

New York City, several times a target of terrorist attacks, has made the largest American municipal commitment to combating terrorism with more than 1,000 officers assigned to various specialized "counterterrorism" units, some of whom are assigned abroad. The New York Police Department's counterterrorism program is sophisticated. Its Transit Order Maintenance Sweep illustrates a defensive tactic, with many New York Police Department officers randomly appearing at different commuter train cars and going through all suspicious packages and checking all suspicious people. The NYPD's Intelligence Division and Counterterrorism Bureau is resource intensive, but far less expensive than the consequences of a major terrorist attack. Despite the Bureau's vigilance, a terrorist attack or attempt is still made. For instance, a Pakistani-born, naturalized American citizen, Faisal Shahzad, parked a bomb-filled car in Times Square.[24] The ignition system failed and immediately attracted police. Shahzad, who received training from the Taliban, subsequently pleaded guilty to bombing-related charges and was sentenced to life in prison. And in November 2017, an Uzbeki immigrant and Islamic State supporter, Mokhammadzokir Kadirov, drove a rented truck down a bicycle lane in crowded Manhattan, killing eight people and injuring another dozen.

U.S. Attorney's Office

Across the country, every United States Attorney's Office has substantial responsibility for combating domestic and international terrorism. One way that responsibility gets expressed is through an Anti-Terrorism Advisory Council, each headed by a U.S. Attorney and with

Quick Facts
Anti-Terrorism Phone Applications (Apps)

The Pennsylvania State Police distributes an anti-terrorism phone application (app), "See Something, Say Something," which is free to iPhone and Android users. The app allows citizens to quickly report suspicious activity or even send an accompanying photo. The Delaware State Police, the Los Angeles Police Department, and the Dallas Police Department are examples of other jurisdictions that have also released apps with the same capabilities. In fact, the Dallas PD app allows citizens to take a photograph of suspicious activity and send it directly to the local fusion center for review and potential investigation.

wide-ranging membership, including the National Guard and state, local, and federal law enforcement agencies. The Anti-Terrorist Advisory Councils seek to deter, detect, and prevent future attacks within the United States by creating partnerships that (1) coordinate anti-terrorism initiatives, (2) initiate and support anti-terror training programs, and (3) facilitate information sharing across all levels of government.

Transportation Security Administration (TSA)

Covered in some detail in Chapter 11, "Homeland Security," only a brief statement is needed here about the Transportation Security Administration (TSA). As part of the U.S. Department of Homeland Security, the TSA is responsible for security of America's transportation systems and freedom of movement for people and commerce. One of TSA's enforcement arms is the federal air marshals, responsible for primarily securing aviation transportation assets (e.g., commercial airliners) domestically and internationally. The exact number of air marshals is not public information for security purposes.

U.S. Department of Energy

Under the Atomic Energy Act, the Federal Bureau of Investigation is responsible for investigating illegal activities involving the use of nuclear materials within the United States, including terrorist threats concerning the use of nuclear materials. A series of executive orders authorizes the Department of Energy's National Nuclear Security Administration to provide technical assistance to the FBI. The National Nuclear Security Administration has a number of assets related to a potential nuclear incident. In a terrorist situation, Nuclear Emergency Support Teams (NESTs) can search for and identify nuclear materials, assess potential nuclear devices, render such devices safe, and package them for transportation to a place of final disposition. NESTS consist of five to several dozen specialists depending on the situation. Terrorism involving a nuclear device is both a public concern and a focus of the federal government.

U.S. Northern Command (NORTHCOM)

The **U.S. Northern Command (NORTHCOM)** has much wider responsibilities than anti-terrorism, such as directing the entire North American Aerospace Defense Command, but those other important responsibilities are not relevant here. Established in 2002, NORTHCOM area of responsibility[25] for securing the United States includes land, air, and sea approaches to all forty-eight continental states, Alaska, Hawaii, Canada, and Mexico.[26]

NORTHCOM directs the U.S. Department of Defense's homeland security efforts and the planning, organizing, and execution of military support to civil authorities.[27] An easy way of thinking about the relationship between NORTHCOM and civilian authorities is that NORTHCOM is responsible for accurately identifying and quickly deploying to civilian agencies the right mix of Department of Defense assets to address natural and manmade disasters. Such assistance does not violate the federal Posse Comitatus Act because NORTHCOM is not directly involved in law enforcement activities.

NORTHCOM established Joint Task Force North in 2004 to assist local, state, and federal law enforcement agencies protecting the border between Mexico and the United States,[28] reasoning that reducing the number of illegal border crossers diminishes the opportunity for terrorists and weapons of mass destruction to enter the country. In 2010, NORTHCOM worked closely with the Canadian government to protect athletes and visitors to the 2010 Vancouver Winter Olympics, which was beneficial to the protection of both countries from terrorist attacks. In the last several years, NORTHCOM has made progress with Mexican authorities on matters of mutual interest, including drug smuggling. NORTHCOM, like some other federal agencies, focuses on the relationship between terrorist groups and sophisticated criminal organizations.[29]

NORTHCOM sets the level (Alpha, Bravo, Charlie, and the highest, Delta) of force protection at Department of Defense installations, facilities, and units within its area of responsibility. Force protection is an anti-terrorism effort defined as the preventative measures taken to mitigate hostile actions against Department of Defense personnel and family members, resources, facilities, and critical information.[30] In turn, military commanders are responsible for ensuring those standards are

U.S. Northern Command (NORTHCOM)
Directs the U.S. Department of Defense's homeland security efforts and the planning, organizing, and execution of military support to civil authorities during emergencies, disasters, and/or terrorist attacks.

Information Link
For more information on the Inspector General's audit of the FBI's Foreign Terrorist Tracking Task Force (FTTTF), visit https://oig.justice.gov/reports/2013/a1318r.pdf.

Box 14–1
NORTHCOM Civil Support Following Hurricane Katrina

Although these NORTHCOM responses are not anti-terrorism efforts, they do serve as an indicator that it has the capability to respond quickly to a major terrorist attack, or even if several of them occur simultaneously. In 2005, Hurricane Katrina did $100 billion in damage and was one of America's five deadliest natural disasters.[31] About 22 percent of all New Orleans residents did not have cars.[32] When the levees protecting New Orleans and other Southern cities collapsed, massive flooding occurred. In some cities, a portion of the residents were able to flee, but in New Orleans, roughly one in five people had no place to go but their roofs.

In response to Hurricane Katrina, NORTHCOM forces deployed more than 22,000 personnel from every branch of military service,[33] including the Coast Guard, which alone rescued 34,000 people. NORTHCOM personnel in the New Orleans area provided a wide range of essential services, including search and rescue; evacuation; recovery of deceased persons; health and medical support; debris removal; restoration of infrastructure; logistics, including distribution of food, water, and ice; temporary shelter; housing of FEMA officials and relief workers; and provision of geospatial products and evaluations, including monitoring changing conditions and providing a high level of situational awareness.

Other illustrations of NORTHCOM civil support include responding to wildfires in Western states, spring flooding in the central United States, and to Haiti's devastating earthquake in 2010 and its devastation following Hurricane Matthew in 2016.

How well do you think NORTHCOM will be able to respond to a major terrorist incident? What if there were three simultaneous major attacks, each with 200,000 total casualties?

---

met or exceeded. NORTHCOM, as do other federal agencies, focuses on dealing with the consequences of cyber, chemical, biological, radiological, and nuclear attacks.

Some information about the U.S. Department of Defense's anti-terrorism and counterterrorism programs is available, but details are sometimes sparse for security reasons. To illustrate, the **Joint Special Operations Command (JSOC)** at Fort Bragg, North Carolina, is a joint services headquarters responsible for studying operational requirements and techniques, ensuring the interoperability and standardization of equipment, planning and conducting special operations exercises and training, and developing joint special operations tactics.[34] Information about these responsibilities and operations is closely held. The existence of JSOC illustrates another important feature of anti-terrorism and counterterrorism: It is often a cooperative, interdependent undertaking supported by multiple partners from different branches of the armed forces, which is why "Joint" is part of JSOC designation.

Joint Special Operations Command (JSOC)

In addition to the responsibilities already mentioned, JSOC is one of the five components reporting to SOCOM. As a joint command, JSOC has a number or units under its "umbrella," such as Seal Team 6, Delta Force, 24th Special Tactics Squadron, and the Intelligence Support Activity.

U.S. Marine Corps

Among the U.S. Marine Corps' anti-terrorism units is the Chemical, Biological, Immediate Response Force (CBIRF), a battalion-sized unit (usually over 500 soldiers) that can be deployed to a terrorist incident anywhere in the world within 24 hours.[35] The unit is stationed at the Naval Support Facility, Indian Head, Maryland. CBIRF consist of Marines and Navy sailors representing over 40 different specialties. CBIRF will assist local, state, and federal agencies and military commanders when there is a credible threat of or an actual incident involving chemical, biological, radiological, nuclear, or high-yield explosives (CBRNE). CBIRF capabilities include agent detection and identification, casualty search and rescue, personnel decontamination, emergency medical care, stabilization of contaminated personnel, and consequent management. Depending on the fact situation of an incident, CBIRF could come under the command of NORTHCOM.

Overview of Counterterrorism

Counterterrorism includes a constellation of strategies, such as denying the rationale for terrorism and promoting other more attractive ideas, such as reducing the flow of recruits by providing them with alternative futures, strengthening the economies of failing nations to eliminate terrorists sanctuaries, interdicting materials (supplies and weapons) intended for use by terrorists, impounding funds in transit to terrorists, implementing civil action programs, and direct military action (see Figure 14–6). While many of these activities have been discussed in earlier chapters, this chapter focuses on combating terrorism through

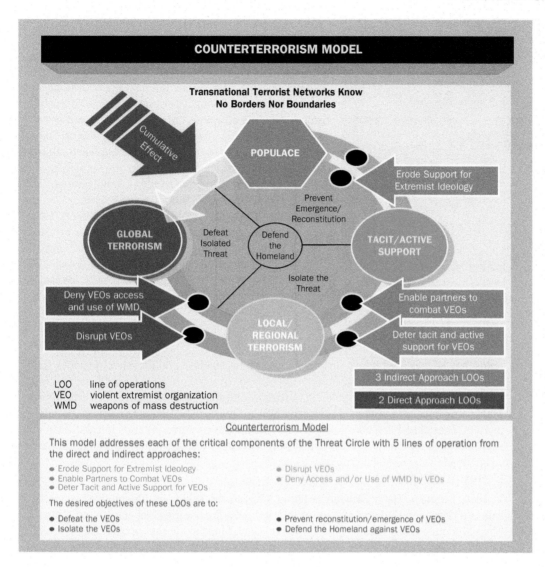

FIGURE 14–6
The counterterrorism model depicts a variety of actions, including eroding support for violent extremist organizations, disrupting their plans, and countering support for them.

(Courtesy Counterterrorism, Joint Publication 3-26, Joint Chiefs of Staff)

the use of specially trained military and law enforcement counterterrorism units, many of which are under the umbrella of the Joint Special Operations Command within SOCOM, discussed later in this section.

Counterterrorism and Forms of Military Action

In contrast to anti-terrorism, a counterterrorism program is characterized by direct actions (usually military) that prevent, deter, and respond to terrorists.[36] A key component of counterterrorism is identifying, locating, and taking action against high-value human targets. This action disrupts terrorists' intentions, capabilities, and operations. Counterterrorism military operations are frequently, but not exclusively, carried out by military units.

Open Warfare

Examples of open warfare include the actions of the United States and its allies in Iraq during the First Gulf War (1991), triggered by Iraq's invasion of Kuwait. As a preemptive action, discussed more fully below, the United States and its allies returned to Iraq (2003–2011) to conduct open warfare, although special operations units were also active (e.g., searching for the deposed dictator Saddam Hussein). After gaining control of the country, the United States spent billions of dollars training and equipping the Iraqi police

FIGURE 14–7
American troops patrol through an Afghanistan village. Notice the troops are well trained, each looking at the areas of their responsibility. An axiom is that is your gun muzzle goes where your eyes do. While the muzzles are pointed downward, they are in line with their vision and can be swung up immediately if needed.

(U.S. Army)

and military to foster a stable government. Fostering a stable government is often a difficult and time-consuming task. In 2014, the terrorist group Islamic State exploited long-standing conflicts between the Sunni and Shia populations in Iraq and began military operations against the government of Iraq,[37] raising questions of whether America and its allies left Iraq too soon. The answer was soon apparent as IS quickly became a dominant power on the battlefield in Iraq and Syria and launched multiple attacks against the civilian population of several European countries, as well as in Tunisia, Egypt, and Lebanon.

Moreover, in early 2017, it was clear that the Afghanistan Army and contingent of U.S. military forces left in-country had reached a stalemate with al Qaeda (See Figure 14-7), newly arrived IS fighters, and the Taliban. The Commander of U.S. forces requested 2,500 more troops. As mentioned in Chapter 1, President Trump authorized up to 3,900 more troops, noting that future conditions may require additional military deployments.

Raids

Raids may be executed to take prisoners, gather intelligence, and for other purposes. Raids may also be punitive in reaction to terrorist acts for which there is no peaceful redress (e.g., the United States bombed Tripoli and Benghazi, Libya, in 1986 because of that nation's role in the bombing of a nightclub in Berlin that was frequented by American soldiers). Similarly, in 1998, President Bill Clinton ordered missile strikes on terrorist sites in the Sudan and Afghanistan in reaction to the bombings of American Embassies in Kenya and Tanzania.[38]

Preemptive Strikes

In 1950, President Harry Truman declared, "We do not believe in preemptive war. Such a war is the weapon of dictators, not of free democratic countries like the United States."[39] The sixteenth-century Italian scholar Alberico Gentili held a different opinion, "No one ought to wait to be struck unless he is a fool."[40] These contrasting views fundamentally undergird the debate about preemptive strikes and wars, which is often tied to the moral question "Is preemptive military action moral?" **Preemptive military action** is defined as striking a target in advance of a reasonably anticipated attack to circumvent its occurrence and to avoid suffering its effects.

During the Cold War Era, roughly 1947–1991, the Russians and Americans did not fight a "hot war," but they were ideologically opposed, which played itself out in situations like the Soviet isolation of East Berlin and their support of regimes opposed to the United States and its allies. Because both Russia and the United States had numerous nuclear missiles, warfare did not erupt because **mutually assured destruction (MAD)** would be the result. Transnational terrorism has no equivalent to mutually assured destruction: Terrorists have no nation or citizens to defend.[41] As a result, then President George W. Bush announced a

Preemptive military action
Striking a target in advance of a reasonably anticipated attack to circumvent its occurrence and to avoid suffering its effects.

Mutually assured destruction (MAD)
A military doctrine prevalent during the Cold War between the United States and the former Soviet Union, postulating that an all-out nuclear war would effectively destroy both entities (the attacker and the defender)

Quick Facts
The Seal Team 6 Yemen Raid

In early 2017, President Trump ordered the execution of a raid in Yemen by Seal Team 6. The action was also approved by the previous administration. The military wanted a moonless night to launch, the next of which was after President Obama left office. One SEAL was killed, several others wounded, and a $75 million aircraft crashed and had to be destroyed. Some women and children were killed during the firefight, as well as fourteen terrorists.

The eight-year-old daughter of the deceased terrorist Anwar Awlaki was among the dead. The purpose of the raid was to seize cellphones and computers for intelligence analysis. Criticisms were made that the raid was launched with insufficient intelligence. The al Qaeda base was heavily defended with unexpectedly high numbers of defenders.[42]

major shift in American foreign policy—the right to take preemptive military action to protect the United States, its citizens, and interests.

In 2001, preemption was used to justify the American attack on Afghanistan, which had been harboring al Qaeda terrorists and Usama bin Laden before and after 9/11. The ultra conservative Islamic Taliban had seized control of most of the country by 1996, and in the wake of the 9/11 attacks refused to deliver bin Laden to the United States. Anticipating further attacks on the homeland, the United States and its allies softened Afghanistan's defenses with missile and air strikes before executing a ground invasion. The Second Gulf War (2003–2011) was also a preemptive action in the mistaken belief, that Iraq's Saddam Hussein had weapons of mass destruction and would use them against the United States or arm terrorists with them for such an attack.

Direct Action

The United States has used direct action to eliminate leaders of terrorist organizations in order to disrupt their plans and operations. Two examples from 2011 illustrate this point: (1) A drone attacked a convoy in Yemen and killed American-born Anwar al-Awlaki, an important al Qaeda figure. Coincidentally, Samir Khan, a naturalized American citizen who operated the *Jihadi Internet Magazine*, was also killed; and (2) Usama bin Laden was killed at his compound in Abbottabad, Pakistan, by Navy SEALS. It is not publically known if his death was a tactical necessity. Arguably, if captured he may have divulged significant intelligence, but if put on trial, bin Laden would have had a commanding venue from which to justify al Qaeda's actions.

Hostage Rescue

Historically, there are a number of incidences where highly trained military units attempted to or did rescue hostages. The rescue of Captain Richard Phillips (see Figure 14–8) from Somali pirates illustrates this point. In 2009, Somali pirates hijacked the cargo ship *Maersk Alabama* in the Indian Ocean.[44] The pirates held an American, Captain Richard Phillips, hostage in a covered lifeboat and threatened to kill him unless they were given $2 million. The FBI Crisis Negotiation Unit maintained communication with the pirates to reduce volatility. Hostage and crisis negotiation teams perform a variety of tasks during a terrorist incident such as this (See Box 14-2).

A Navy SEAL team parachuted into the ocean "over the horizon" and moved to a Navy ship without the pirates noticing. The captain as well as three pirates were in an 18-foot, hard-covered lifeboat, in the open sea, bobbing up and down. When it seemed that Captain Phillips was in imminent danger of being killed, the SEAL Team snipers were given the "green light" to shoot. All three pirates in the lifeboat were killed and Captain Phillips was rescued unharmed (see Figure 14–8). A fourth pirate, Abduwali Muse, was being treated for injuries and negotiating for Captain Phillips' release aboard the USS *Bainbridge* when the SEALs fired. He later pleaded guilty to piracy charges and received a sentence of 33 years. Two private security contractors were found dead on the Maersk Alabama. The 2013 movie, *Captain Phillips*, tells the story of this incident.

FIGURE 14–8

The USS *Bainbridge* (L) tows the orange lifeboat in which Captain Phillips was held to the USS *Boxer* (C) where it was processed for evidence.

(Megan E. Sindelar/U.S. Navy)

Quick Facts
The Term "Operator"

Within the U.S. special military operations community, an "operator" is any soldier who has completed selection and graduates from an Operator's Training Course (OTC). Although the origin of the word is most likely from U.S. Army Delta Force, all other special operational forces such as Navy SEALs, Army Rangers, and CIA Special Activities Division personnel often refer to themselves as "operators" or "special operators" versus the conventional concept of soldier.[45]

Box 14–2
Hostage and Crisis Negotiations ... and Terrorism

By: Douglas M. Whitten and Robert W. Taylor

Doug Whitten is a retired agent and lead hostage negotiator for the Federal Bureau of Investigation, and Dr. Taylor is an early student and graduate of hostage negotiations training taught by Dr. Harvey Schlossberg and Captain Frank Bolz, Jr. (NYPD) in the early 1970s.

The civil unrest and activism of the 1960s gave rise to a series of dramatic social and cultural changes. Crime quickly became a focus of national media attention. Popular television shows, like Jack Webb's *Dragnet*, reflected a law enforcement philosophy that modern criminologists associate with the "Professional Era" of policing. The "Watergate Scandal," and President Nixon's corruption, rocked the nation. Suddenly, "the cop" replaced the cowboy in television shows, and movies like Clint Eastwood's *Dirty Harry* ruled at the box office. It appears that many, if not most, Americans just wanted a return to stability and the "rule of law." Amazingly, it was this world of dishonest politicians, flower children, and morally ambiguous police lieutenants, with really big guns, that gave birth to the concept of contemporary crisis and hostage negotiations.

Prior to 1971, there was no standard police response to "crisis situations" involving hostages and/or barricaded persons and the law enforcement reaction depended upon a multitude of factors.[46] In most cases, the law enforcement response was fairly simple, "either you come out or we'll come in and get you." Indeed, this response was not only reflected in the popular media, but also the reality of local police as then-Chief of Police Darryl Gates in Los Angeles built the concept of a paramilitary and highly trained team of officers in special weapons and tactics (SWAT) to enter dangerous situations and apprehend suspects. Unfortunately, these types of police encounters more often than not resulted in the use of deadly force in which either the hostage, the hostage-taker, a police officer, or a combination of all three were killed.

In 1972, the Black September Organization (BSO) invaded the Olympic compound during the summer games in Munich, Germany, and seized eleven Israeli hostages. By all accounts, the German authorities handled the situation poorly, and during an ill-fated rescue attempt, all the hostages and several members of the BSO were killed. The incident proved to be a catalyst for change on several fronts. Most important, it prompted one major police department in the United States, the New York Police Department (NYPD), to reevaluate its historical position on the use of coercive physical force, especially in hostage situations.[47] Experts in the field have referred to this event as the "defining incident," and it is believed to represent the birth of what has evolved into the "modern crisis and hostage negotiations model."[48] Specifically, when NYPD officers reviewed the Munich incident, they concluded that the options available to the German authorities were very limited. Essentially, the authorities in Munich could (1) launch a direct assault; (2) use selective sniper fire; (3) deploy chemical agents; or (4) contain the terrorists and negotiate. Of the four available options, three involved direct assault and were almost certain to precipitate additional violence.[49] The fourth option, "contain and negotiate," involved no immediate violence and offered the opportunity for potentially beneficial things to occur. More important, this approach was consistent with a growing position within the courts that police and federal agent had an affirmative duty to attempt to negotiate with hostage-takers and barricaded persons before using force options.[50] It is interesting and a worthy note, that "crisis negotiations" as a field of study had its origins in a terrorist attack.

At first, hostage negotiation strategies and tactics were simple, and yet, surprisingly, they were often successful. Time became the primary ally of the negotiator ... the passage of time had its own value. First, the concept of "crisis" and high emotion quickly dissolved as time passed and nothing really happened except the opening of dialogue with a non threatening police negotiator. Second, time allowed for better planning, and hence better and safer responses by tactical teams if an assault was required. Third, intelligence information stemming from the negotiation as well as direct observation by other officers dramatically increased. For instance, exactly how many hostages had been taken, what are they wearing and where are they being kept, how many suspects are there and how are they armed, are there any explosive devices being employed, and the like were critical questions to be answered for better and safer police responses. Finally, while discussion continued, an interesting and powerful psychological transference occurred between the negotiator and the hostage negotiator called "the Stockholm Syndrome."[51] Hostages and captors became allied to the fulfillment of a peaceful end to the crisis. Each considered the other to be locked in a mutual fate that highlighted the surrender of the captor and the freeing of the hostages ... everyone wins. Hence, the first hostage negotiation approaches were relatively simple, stall for time, increase the interaction between the hostages and the captors, maybe catch a break, and something good might happen. As experience grew with success, new approaches evolved from the collaboration of mental health counselors, psychologists, and police negotiators. The application of new approaches based on inherent power differentials, and frequently employed in the world of business negotiations, was introduced with success; and each innovation in the study of negotiations brought more and more violent incidents to peaceful resolutions.[52]

However, since the 9/11 attacks, the central issue regarding the art of hostage and crisis negotiation has been: Will hostage negotiation tactics work within the context of contemporary terrorism? Can we use hostage and crisis negotiation strategies with ideologically motivated individuals (like radical Islamic terrorists) who are willing to die for their cause and/or use suicide attacks indiscriminately to cause mass carnage? The questions are more dramatically emphasized as the Islamic State continues to expand throughout the world, and the fractionalization of radicalized Islamic groups appears to have fostered an increase in the number of "homegrown" and "lone wolf" terrorist attacks.

Numerous studies stemming from hostage incidents involving terrorist groups as well as the disaster at the grade school in Beslan, North Ossetia, Russia, in September 2004 reveal that crisis and hostage negotiation skills can be effective, even when dealing with terrorists (See Figure 14–9).[53] For instance, Yotam Dagan, a noted expert from the Israeli Defense Forces Hostage Negotiation Unit, discussed the results of a study, conducted by members of his unit.[54] In this study, a researcher went into Israeli prisons and interviewed "suicide bombers" who had been arrested and incarcerated, either because the explosive device they were wearing failed to detonate or because they somehow miraculously survived the blast. In contrast to what has been written in some scholarly articles by Hoffman and McCormick,[55] the IDF research found that "suicide bombers" were very much like other suicidal individuals. A significant number suffered from psychological issues, and in many cases, they were social outcasts who saw martyrdom as a way to redeem themselves in the eyes of their peers. Dagan noted that the women in particular had often either been accused of sexual infidelity during marriage or of sexual promiscuity before marriage, and that in the Islamic culture, this essentially has the effect of rendering a woman untouchable; meaning that she lives in disgrace and that no one in her community will marry her.

Dagan doesn't disagree with Hoffman and McCormick central premise[56] regarding the motivations of terrorist leaders. Clearly, "suicide" attacks are designed to garner media attention, while emotionally destabilizing the victims and their communities by showing the absolute commitment of the terrorists to their cause. Rather, Dagan simply takes the position that suicide bombers tend to have the same psychological vulnerabilities typical of all people who commit suicide, and that this condition makes it possible for them to be weaponized and deployed by their terrorist leaders or indoctrination.

Notwithstanding the above, the essential point of Dagan's lecture was that terrorists are, first and foremost, human beings. They display the same range of psychological attributes (defense mechanisms, ego needs, mental illness, etc.) that crisis and hostage negotiators have now been observing and dealing with for more than four and half decades. In view of this information, the most important step that crisis negotiators must take when dealing with a terrorist, in a "crisis situation," is put aside any and all preconceptions about the terrorist, and deal with the suspect as an individual just as they would in any other crisis situation.

Crisis and hostage negotiation transcends the concept of terrorism, because it reflects a growing understanding of fundamental human behavior. Simply put, one person may be emotionally compromised because of the loss of a child, while another is emotionally compromised because he or she believes they are losing their ethnic identity, religious culture, or personal values. Nevertheless, in both cases, the proven psychological mechanisms for dealing with emotionally compromised people remain the same. Clearly, additional research is needed in this area to confirm the applicability of modern and contemporary crisis negotiation procedures during terrorist incidents. Sadly however, the academic community has conducted very little empirical psychological research on terrorist behavior.[57] Therefore, assuming the general applicability of contemporary hostage and crisis negotiation strategies, and the fact that the fundamental principles of human psychology appear to transcend racial, cultural, and ethnic differences, successfully employing such a strategy requires a deep and profound understanding of the different perspectives, values, and beliefs associated with various, racial, cultural, and ethnic backgrounds.

To be successful, the hostage and crisis negotiator must be able to establish "rapport." To do this, the negotiator must be able to relate to, empathize with, and understand the hostage taker's perspective, be the hostage-taker a terrorist or otherwise. To facilitate this kind of understanding, every crisis and hostage negotiator should be trained in the broad aspects of understanding the historical roots of violence, hate, and terrorism, as well as the rise of radical Islamic fundamentalism. This type of training will simply be for background information for the negotiator. In every terrorism incident that calls for negotiations, a team of experts, including those specializing in right-wing hate, various nationalist movements around the globe, and particularly on the Middle East and radical Islamic philosophies, must be available for consultation with the negotiator or negotiation team.

Understanding the psychological, emotional, and intellectual motivations of the hostage taker or the terrorist is critical for a potentially successful and peaceful resolution to the crisis. However, trained negotiators should also be the first to detect the impossibility of a peaceful resolution and the deterioration of the situation. If such a condition arises, forceful assault by well-trained tactical teams may be the last and, unfortunately, the only alternative.

Do you think that hostage and crisis negotiations should be a strategy to effectively deal with a terrorist incident?

FIGURE 14–9
Emergency workers removing casualties at the Beslan, Russia grade school attacked by Chechen terrorists.
The massacre of 330 hostages, including 186 children in Beslan, Russia, in 2004 still remains the worst hostage crisis situation gone wrong. Chechen militants had taken the school with children and teachers as hostage and had booby-trapped the building with explosives. After three days of intensive negotiations, the militants began detonating bombs among the children, thus forcing Russian military troops to storm the building. The situation quickly deteriorated into a battle claiming the lives of children, teachers, military personnel, and terrorists. The incident sparked discussion on whether or not hostage and crisis negotiation should be an acceptable strategy during terrorist incidents.

(ZUMA Press, Inc./Alamy Stock Photo)

Counterterrorism Organizations and Activities

Much of the war on terrorism is fought by special military operational units, as opposed to conventional forces. When they were first formed in the early 1950s, soon after World War II, the conventional army at that time, and for some years thereafter, was suspicious and somewhat resentful of specialized tactical units. There was a concern that a tour of duty in such a unit might make a soldier unsuitable for service in the conventional military. Some conventional commanders thought just the existence of special military units deprived them of outstanding soldiers. Presently, service in a special operations command is where many career-minded soldiers in the armed forces want to be.

The actions taken by special operations forces are newsworthy, if known about, and action movies featuring them are popular. The reality is that such units are only the "tip of the spear." Behind them are small armies of data collection experts, analysts using **metrics**, experience, and their best judgment, communications arrays, and a variety of transportation systems to deliver and recover specially trained operators from the field.

Metrics
Standard measures taken periodically to determine the level of performance in a given field. For instance, a metric used during the Vietnam War was enemy body count. Terrorism metrics can be an indication of how we are doing in the global war on terrorism if carefully selected, defined, and measured.

This section is a sampler of American counterterrorism units, including two non-military organizations, the Central Intelligence Agency-Special Activities Division and the FBI's Hostage Rescue Team. The military units covered are the U.S. Special Operations Command, the Joint Special Operations Command, U.S. Army Special Forces (Green Berets), U.S. Army Delta Force, U.S. Navy SEAL Teams, and the U.S. Army 75th Ranger Regiment. Federal law dictates which units have a primary counterterrorism mission. All of the above units have a counterterrorism mission, except the 75th Ranger Regiment. However, it often conducts counterterrorism operations or augments units that do have that primary mission. Therefore, the 75th Ranger Regiment was included in this discussion.

Central Intelligence Agency—Special Activities Division

The Central Intelligence Agency (CIA) was established by the National Security Act of 1947.[58] Fundamentally, the Act directed the CIA to collect, analyze, and disseminate intelligence.[59] Although conducting covert operations was not specifically authorized, the language of the Act was sufficiently elastic that the CIA soon began such operations. America's Office of Strategic Service (OSS) had been quickly disbanded following the end of World War II. However, the federal government substantially preserved OSS Secret Intelligence and Counter Espionage branches, which later joined the newly minted CIA, giving the agency a wealth of **covert activity** experience from its very inception.[60]

Covert activity
An action of the U.S. government intended to influence politics, economic, or military conditions abroad, where it is intended that the role of the government will not be apparent or acknowledged publicly.

The Special Activities Division (SAD) is a group of paramilitary officers within the Central Intelligence Agency. Their exact number is not publically known. Many of them were recruited from highly experienced military units. They conduct clandestine military operations in foreign countries, including counterterrorism and capture or kill missions. During 1967, in one of SAD's best-known actions, they collaborated with U.S. and Bolivian Special Forces in the capture of Che Guevara, who was executed by the Bolivians in the field.

Following the 1979 invasion of Afghanistan by the USSR, SAD aided the Muslim Mujahedeen in fighting the Soviets with training and weapons.[61] When the Soviets left the country in 1989, Afghanistan factions fought for control and the Taliban seized power. Under its protection, al Qaeda trained, operated, and prepared for its attacks on America.[62] Following the 9/11 attacks, the Taliban refused to surrender Usama bin Laden to the United States. President George W. Bush told the Taliban to "... act immediately ... or share their (al Qaeda's) fate."[63] The Taliban made a counterproposal, to try bin Laden before an Islamic court. The U.S. response to this unsatisfactory proposal was to quickly deploy cutting-edge military technology and precision weapons, making it possible to use a smaller sized ground force[64] against the Taliban and al Qaeda.

Within two weeks, SAD personnel, later augmented by approximately 300 special operations personnel (Delta and SEALs), had infiltrated into Afghanistan and were working with Taliban opposition forces, many of them from the so-called indigenous Northern Alliance.[65] The ensuing barrage of missile, drone, and precision air strikes, guided by ground forces, drove the Taliban out of their cities and al Qaeda into Pakistan.[66] Only a small coalition of military forces, led by the United States, remains in Afghanistan. CIA operators there and elsewhere continue their secret and largely unheralded fight against terrorism.

Federal Bureau of Investigation—Hostage Rescue Team

As discussed in Chapter 9, the FBI is the lead agency in more than 119 Joint Terrorism Task Forces spread across the country. Their membership consists of federal agencies, such as Customs and Border Protection and Immigration and Customs Enforcement from the Department of Homeland Security, as well as state and local law enforcement agencies. The mission of Joint Terrorism Task Forces is to investigate, detect, interdict, prosecute, and remove terrorists and dismantle their organizations.[67] Less well known is the FBI's involvement in military counterterrorism raids in foreign countries.

In 2014, Ahmed Abu Khatallah was arrested in Libya by a combined unit consisting of Delta operators and FBI agents on outstanding felony warrants for his role in the 2012 attack on the American Consulate compound in Benghazi, Libya[68] (see Figure 14–10). He is the alleged mastermind of the attack.[69] Libya claimed their sovereignty was violated by the United States, which maintains it was a preemptive action because of intelligence information revealing that Abu Khatallah was planning further attacks against America.[70] Abu Khatallah was transported to the United States on a U.S. Navy vessel and interrogated by civilian law enforcement (FBI) personnel. The FBI was embedded in Delta because of the law enforcement knowledge required to potentially convict Abu Khatallah in federal court. These include expertise in evidence identification, collection, and preservation, skills and knowledge not normally the concern of special operations units. The trial for Abu Khatallah began in early October 2017. If convicted in federal district court, Abu Khatallah could receive the death penalty.

The FBI team also provides expertise in hostage and crisis negotiations as observed in the Somali pirate incident involving Captain Phillips and the *Maersk Alabama* discussed earlier in this chapter.

FIGURE 14–10
A Libyan man examines the inside of a portion of the U.S. Consulate in Benghazi. The attack killed four men, including Ambassador Chris Stevens, on the night of September 11, 2012. Among the criticisms made were why wasn't the consulate better defended and why weren't military reaction forces rushed to the scene.

(Mohammad Hannon/AP Images)

U.S. Special Operations Command (USSOCOM)

The Special Operations Command (USSOCOM or simply SOCOM) was formed in 1987 and is headquartered at MacDill Air Force Base in Tampa, Florida. Its mission is to provide fully capable Special Operations Forces to defend the United States and its interests and to synchronize global military operations against terrorist networks.[71] Essentially, SOCOM is the "parent" organization for the special operations community. It is composed of special warfare elements from various branches of the military (see Figure 14–11). It is important to remember that the Joint Special Operations Command (JSOC) is a subordinate command of SOCOM.

FIGURE 14–11
Organizational Chart for SOCOM (USSOCOM)

(United States Special Operations Command)

Box 14-3
Operation Eagle Claw: Anatomy of a Disaster

Reducing the plan to bare bones, Operation Eagle Claw's elements included: (1) the infiltration of U.S. agents into Tehran to gather intelligence; (2) the rendezvous of three EC-130 refueling planes and eight helicopters at a secret location (Desert 1) in the Iranian desert; (3) Delta's seizure of the American Embassy and freeing the hostages; (4) Delta escorting the hostages to a soccer stadium; (5) Army Rangers controlling a nearby airfield; (6) helicopters transferring Delta and hostages to the seized airport; (7) a C-14 landing and flying the hostages to safety; and (8) other mission forces egressing from Iran.[72]

A post-mission analysis revealed problems: (1) the plan was too complex; (2) intelligence was limited and collected more slowly than anticipated; (3) weather intelligence did not predict the severe dust storms ("haboobs") that caused the helicopter flight separation and eliminated one of the needed helicopters; (4) a weather reconnaissance C-130 should have been incorporated into the plan; (5) although there were more qualified Air Force helicopters pilots, Marine Corp pilots were used; (6) the Marine pilots did not train on the actual type of helicopters that were used; (7) unanticipated traffic passing Desert 1 resulted in 44 bus riders being taken prisoner and a fuel tanker stopped with an anti-tank weapon, creating a fireball that could be seen for miles in the night; (8) in flight, one helicopter had an automated warning of an impending rotor blade failure, landed and checked it out, and had to abandon the aircraft; (9) a third helicopter had damaged hydraulics and couldn't be used; (10) the loss of three helicopters reduced the number available to

five, one fewer than the mission required; (11) there should have been more helicopters; (12) the mission was scrubbed and a maneuvering helicopter hit one of the fuel EC-130s, killing eight servicemen and destroying both aircraft; and (13) for operational security, all of the different services involved in the mission trained separately and there were no thoroughly integrated mission rehearsals.[73]

Mission planning tried to limit the aircraft at Desert 1 to avoid detection, but the post-mission analysis called for more of them. More helicopters may also have required a fourth EC-130 fueling plane, further increasing the possibility of being detected. Change the fact situation just a little and one post-mission problem identified would be that the footprint was too large, leading to detection, and the mission being scrubbed.

Planning for a second rescue attempt was cancelled when intelligence learned that the hostages had been dispersed to different locations, realistically eliminating any further rescue attempts.

The hostages were taken on November 4, 1979, and released on January 20, 1981. President Carter's inability to rescue or otherwise affect the release of the hostages made him an ineffective figure. On the same day Ronald Reagan made his inaugural address, the hostages were released after 444 days of captivity[74].

What should have America learned from this incident as it looked to the future?

Operation Eagle Claw
Failed U.S. military attempt to rescue hostages held by Iran in 1980.

Before the establishment of SOCOM in 1980, the United States executed **Operation Eagle Claw** to rescue sixty-six hostages seized in late 1979 at the American Embassy in Tehran, Iran, by radical Muslims.[75] The success of the final plan depended on a near-perfect execution of all of its phases during the mission's 40-hour timetable. Instead, a confluence of mistakes resulted in a badly failed mission (See Box 14-3).[76]

Albeit at a terrible price, positive things ultimately resulted from Operation Eagle Claw's failure. It stimulated interest in the U.S. Department of Defense to reform the entire special operations community. By 1983, there was also a small but growing sense in Congress for the need for military reform.[77] Adding impetus to these developments were two events that happened during that same year: (1) the terrorist bombing of the U.S. Marine Barracks in Lebanon, and (2) the continuing failure of command and coordination special operations revealed during the invasion of Grenada by the United States and its allies in order to reestablish order and protect the lives of American students in that island nation. Legislative hearings were held during 1986 on bills to create a special operations command.[78] By most accounts, retired army Major General Richard A. Scholtes gave the most compelling reason for creating such a command: Leaders of conventional forces did not understand how to use special operations personnel or to take advantage of their unique abilities, which led to avoidable casualties during the Grenada Invasion.[79] Arguably, special operations needed its own major command structure to protect it from commanders of conventional forces.

The FBI and Joint Special Operations Command (JSOC)

The FBI and the Joint Special Operations Command (JSOC) have an alliance that benefits both parties and has moved the FBI deeper into counterterrorism operations in Iraq, Afghanistan, and other countries.[80] FBI agents have participated in hundreds of such operations.[81] JSOC enjoys access to FBI expertise in civilian law enforcement, such as criminal investigation techniques, analyzing digital material and codes, interrogation, and safeguarding the chain of evidence for prosecution;[82] that expertise helps to identify insurgents and terrorists; to detect terrorist plots, including those against the United States; and most important, to convict those individuals in civilian courts of law.[83]

U.S. Army Special Forces—"Green Berets"

At the end of World War II in 1945, Colonels Aaron Banks and Russell Volckmann returned to the Army from the soon to be disbanded Office of Strategic Services (OSS). They believed the world was changing and that a new type of military force would be needed for unconventional warfare.[84] As a result of their efforts, U.S. Army Special Forces was created in 1952 at Fort Bragg, North Carolina. Colonel Banks became its first commander, and he is regarded as the father of Special Forces. Some 2,300 positions[85] were allocated to the incipient unit; they came from the deactivation of Ranger companies deemed no longer needed after the war.[86] These slots were also filled with former OSS members and experienced soldiers from the war. Although the unit was poorly funded and not well supported within the traditional military establishment, it had a unique and vital role to play in the Cold War. In the event of a Russian invasion of Europe, Special Forces were to stay behind enemy lines, recruit and arm partisans, and wage war against the Russians,[87] severing supply lines and eliminating communications centers. To some degree, Special Forces assumed the mission of World War II commandos.

FIGURE 14–12
Every year, Special Forces commemorate President Kennedy's death by having a delegation go to his gravesite in Arlington National Cemetery. They honor him as the man who gave them their namesake Green Berets.

(Jeremy D. Crisp/United States Army)

The initial volunteers were fluent in two languages, held the rank of Sergeant or higher, and were well trained in airborne and infantry skills.[88] The federal Lodge Act (1950) allowed for 2,500 alien males to gain citizenship in return for five years, service in the U.S. Army.[89] Many of those taking advantage of the Lodge Act came from Eastern European countries, were staunchly anti-communist, and had significant military and combat experience. These immigrants tended to gravitate to Special Forces, which used those experiences in the burgeoning Cold War with Russia.[90]

OSS personnel who joined Special Forces often wore berets of the foreign military units with which they operated,[91] and Europeans joining Special Forces came from a culture where many men wore berets. Consequently, it was not surprising that Special Forces began wearing a green beret informally. In 1954, the Special Forces command authorized wearing of the green beret, although the U.S. Department of the Army did not recognize it as official headwear. In 1957, the Fort Bragg, North Carolina, Post Commander banned it, although Special Forces soldiers continued wearing it in the field. In 1961, President John F. Kennedy visited Fort Bragg and was impressed with the Special Forces training and activities. By no coincidence, several months later the U.S. Department of Army suddenly reversed itself and authorized the beret. President Kennedy called the Green Beret "a symbol of excellence, a badge of courage, a mark of distinction in the fight for freedom."[92] Since that time, Special Forces members have been known as "Green Berets." When President Kennedy was assassinated in 1963, Special Forces sent a forty-eight-man delegation to Washington, D.C., and they placed their "mark of distinction" on the President's grave. On each anniversary of President Kennedy's death they send a delegation to honor him (see Figure 14–12).

In 1967, the communist revolutionary Che Guevara was captured by Bolivian soldiers who had been trained and equipped by Special Forces and other U.S. special operations personnel.[93] American Special Forces were with the Bolivians when Guevara was wounded and captured. He was executed by the Bolivians in the field shortly after his capture. During the 1960s, Special Forces were heavily involved in the Vietnam War, often building "camps" astride routes used by the North Vietnamese Army (NVA) to infiltrate troops and supplies into South Vietnam. The camps provided vital intelligence for air and missile strikes, and soon became major targets for the NVA. Defended by paramilitary indigenous troops recruited and trained by Green Berets, the camps were often defended successfully. More recently, during the Persian Gulf War (1991), Iraq's Saddam Hussein shot missiles into Israel, Saudi Arabia, and Bahrain, as well as launched an all-out attack on Kuwait. Special Forces and other special operations units were deployed into the desert to gather intelligence on Hussein's army, and to find and destroy military targets. Special Forces were among the earliest American units on the ground in Iraq, and continued their counterterrorism activities in Afghanistan as well (see Figure 14–13).

FIGURE 14–13
Members of the 3rd Special Forces Group (Airborne) recon Afghanistan's remote Shok Valley. Previously, accompanied by Afghan troops, they had fought a six-hour battle with terrorists in a village in that valley.

(David N. Gunn/United States Army)

Delta Force
"Delta Force" has used a variety of names, including 1st Special Forces Operational Detachment-D (1st SFOD-D), Combat Applications Group (CAG), and Army Compartmentalized Elements (ACE). It is believed there are five active duty Special Forces Groups and two National Guard Groups. The strength of each Group is in its four battalions. The number of people in an SF battalion is classified. Each SF Group has limited counterterrorism mission and capability.

U.S. Army—Delta Force

Lieutenant Charles Beckwith saw combat during the Korean War (1952–1953).[94] Upon returning to the United States, he completed Ranger training and joined Special Forces. In 1960, then-Captain Beckwith and other Special Forces "Green Berets" were sent to Laos to train local forces in special warfare.[95] During 1961–1962, he served with the elite British Air Service (SAS) and fought communist insurgents in Malaya. The "SAS way" left him confused because there was little emphasis on rank, things seemingly were done casually, and yet its accomplishments could not be denied.[96] Beckwith lamented, "I couldn't make heads or tails of it … everything I'd been taught about soldiering, been trained to believe, was turned upside down."[97]

Upon his return, he submitted several concept papers to senior commanders to form an SAS-type unit, but the papers were brushed aside. Intermittently over the next 14 years he made additional attempts, to no avail. As terrorism became more prominent during the 1970s, the Army concluded it needed a counterterrorism unit. In 1977, Lieutenant Colonel Beckwith was given two years to create and make the new "**Delta Force**" mission-ready. Most of the personnel for this new unit came from Special Forces.[98] In 1980, Delta participated in Operation Eagle Claw. In the wake of its failure, now-Colonel Beckwith saw the need for more special operations training.

The secrecy surrounding Delta[99] is such that the U.S. government routinely denies its existence.[100] Still, a limited number of missions assigned to Delta by the U.S. Special Operations Command have become public. One such incident involves activities in Somalia in 1993.

Although the Battle of Mogadishu, Somalia, did not involve terrorism, Delta operators participated in it to assist in capturing Warlord Mohamed Farrah Aidid. Somalia dictator and strongman Siad Barre seized power in Somalia during 1969.[101] Barre showed increasing ferocity to those who opposed him, and ultimately the Somalia army and the people turned against him. He fled the country in 1991 and the country quickly descended into clan warfare in the absence of a functional national government. Drought and famine brought starvation that private and voluntary relief could not control because warlords hijacked the food to sell for weapons or to feed their clan to ensure loyalty. United Nation humanitarian efforts fared no better and ultimately an international coalition sent military forces to quell the fighting and ensure the distribution of food. Warlord Mohamed Farrah Aidid opposed this move and his irregular militia began using improvised explosive devices (IEDs) to kill American servicemen.

Aidid was a major obstacle to restoring Somalia's national government, and thus had to be removed. As part of that process, a raid was planned to seize two of Aidid's lieutenants. That raid by American forces was supposed to last an hour, but actually ended more than a day later. During the operation, two American helicopters were shot down and a long battle ensued between Aidid's irregulars and a force of Army Rangers and Special Forces and Delta operators. Two Delta members, Master Sergeant Gary Gordon and Sergeant First Class Randy Shughart, were inserted into the heart of the firefights to protect the downed aircraft crews. Help failed to reach them in time and eventually both were killed. Both received the Medal of Honor for their actions. The 2001 movie *Blackhawk Down* covers the raid and subsequent battle.

U.S. Navy—SEAL Teams

Navy SEALs evolved out of four separate World War II organizations. Like other elite special operations units, members volunteer and then pass one of the most rigorous selection courses in the armed forces of the world. Those in the selection course for the 75th Ranger Regiment say "On a slab or with the tab;" meaning that they will either die trying or earn the slender gold and black Ranger tab. For aspiring SEALs, it's "The only easy day was yesterday."

The four World War II legacy units comprising today's Navy SEALs were (1) The Amphibious Scouts and Raiders, which conducted amphibious reconnaissance and raids in

Quick Facts
Ghillie Suits

Ghillie suits are often used by Special Forces and other snipers. They are made by weaving local fresh foliage into a net that is worn as camouflage. The suits originated with Scottish gamekeepers during the eighteenth century who were hired by landowners to protect stock and game animals from predators and poachers. The ghillie allowed a gamekeeper to "hide in plain sight," making them more efficient. During World War I, ghillies were used by a British sniper unit and soon picked up by other military units.

◀ Snipers practicing their stalking and marksmanship skills.
(United States Army (http://usarmy.vo.llnwd .net/e2/rv5_images/yearinphotos/2010 /photos/october/full/army_2010_1014.jpg)

Europe and the South Pacific; (2) The Naval Combat Demolition Units, which trained exclusively for clearing beach obstacles on D-Day, June 6, 1944; (3) The Underwater Demolition Teams (UDT), which conducted hydrographic reconnaissance and obstacle demolitions for beach landings in the Pacific; and (4) The Office of Strategic Service (OSS) maritime operators.[102] OSS used the maritime operators for covert operations from the sea, including infiltrating agents, supplying resistance groups, engaging in maritime sabotage, and developing special equipment for their needs.[103]

The end of World War II meant that millions of men and women in the armed forces were released to restart their lives as civilians. It also meant the end of many units essential to the war effort, but not to a peacetime military. The rapid demobilization eliminated thousands of servicemen from the legacy units. From these units, only two Underwater Demolition Teams (UDTs) survived, each with seven officers and forty-five enlisted men. One UDT unit was stationed on the East Coast and the other on the West coast.[104]

The sudden attack by the North Korean army on South Korea in June 1950 rapidly propelled Allied forces into the shrinking and defensive "Pusan Pocket" in Southern Korea. South Korea's army was not well equipped to resist the invasion and stationed U.S. forces were not well-honed combat troops. Instead, they were fundamentally peacetime garrison troops. However, U.S. General Douglas MacArthur conceived a surprise amphibious landing at Inchon, South Korea, that completely changed the tactical situation of the war, and the North Korean aggressors were steadily driven back from that point.

Prior to the amphibious landing at the port city of Inchon, UDT units provided detailed information for the operation (e.g., information about defenses, tides, channels, and the like) and cleared mines from the bay, essentially preparing the way for landing craft to reach the beachhead.[105] During the balance of the Korean War (1950–1953), the UDT units were used throughout the Korean peninsula because of their familiarity with the use of explosives.[106] They were assigned to blow up tunnels, bridges, and other targets.[107] This enlargement of the use of the UDT units onto land was a crucial part of their evolution into today's SEAL teams.

As President John F. Kennedy assumed office in 1961, Russian Premier Nikita Khrushchev gave a speech "establishing the legitimacy" of "wars of national liberation."[108]

FIGURE 14–14
Although SEALs can infiltrate by
sea, air, or land, they must also be
able to do so under extreme conditions. SEALs performed Advanced
Cold Weather training in Kodiak,
Alaska, to experience the physical
stress of the environment as well
as test how their equipment would
operate and perform under such
conditions.

(Eric S. Logsdon/U.S. Navy)

This resulted in Russia supporting movements, with training and arms, that were often anti-American and an indirect challenge to the United States. President Kennedy envisioned a new type of military capability—one that was required to fight guerrilla and unconventional wars in foreign lands. He championed that agenda in the military as well as in Congress for additional funding.

The Army's Special Forces ("Green Berets") had been established in 1952; however, the unit was given few resources with which to build and expand. President Kennedy rebadged the UDT teams as U.S. Navy SEALs (**SE**a–**A**ir–**L**and) in 1962 and gave them a much wider mandate than underwater demolition. The Vietnam War resulted in plentiful resources flowing to Special Forces and SEALs because they had important roles. Today, the most visible SEAL contributions have been in Iraq and more recently Afghanistan,[109] as well as in isolated incidents involving hostages such as the Captain Phillips rescue previously mentioned. SEAL Team 6 represents the apex of a counterterrorism unit. It received considerable, but unwanted, attention for the 2011 raid on Abbottabad, Pakistan, that resulted in the death of Usama bin Laden. Most Americans associate SEAL Team 6 with all SEAL teams. In reality, SEAL Team 6 is a specific team, often referred to as the U.S. Naval Special Warfare Development Group (DEVGRU). DEVGRU is SEAL Team 6, whose primary mission is counterterrorism. Most information regarding DEVGRU is classified and details regarding its existence and mission are difficult to obtain. DEVGRU (SEAL Team 6) and their Army counterpart, Delta Force, are the U.S. military's primary direct action counterterrorism units.

There are approximately 2,200 members of SEAL Teams (divided into nine active-duty teams, including SEAL Team 6) and perhaps 600 in the Special Boat Squadrons that transport each team.[110] All SEAL teams are required to be ready to deploy within 18 hours after notification. Their assigned missions include (1) direct warfare action, (2) special reconnaissance, (3) unconventional warfare (i.e., training, leading, and equipping guerilla forces behind enemy lines), (4) foreign defense strengthening (i.e., training and advising military, paramilitary, and law enforcement personnel of allied nations, normally in a noncombat environment), and (5) counterterrorism operations.[111] As with all special military operators, training is constant within the SEAL teams when not deployed in order to learn new skills (see Figure 14–14).

U.S. Army—75th Ranger Regiment

Rangers have a long and distinguished military history. In New England during 1675–1678, Captain Church led a company of rangers to fight against Native Americans led by "King Philip," as he was called by the colonists.[112] During the French and Indian War (1754–1763), Major Rogers's rangers scouted ahead to find routes for regular British troops, conducted reconnaissance missions, and attacked distance targets. Major Rogers wrote a set of rules for his rangers that are still used by Rangers today. A Corps of Rangers, led by Francis Marion (1732–1795, the "Swamp Fox"), fought for colonists in the Revolutionary War. Marion is considered the American father of military guerilla tactics. During America's Civil War (1861–1865), Union troops were baffled by the Confederate's John Mosby (1833–1916), the "Grey Ghost" who led lightning-quick cavalry raids and would then disappear.

Rangers reappeared during World War II, referred to as Darby's Rangers after their leader, Colonel William Darby. On D-Day on the Normandy Beach of France, Rangers received their motto, "Rangers lead the way." In the Philippines, the 6th Ranger Battalion was the force that liberated and evacuated 500 Allied prisoners held by the Japanese at Cabanatuan in 1945 (see Figure 14–15). Another popular movie, *The Great Raid* (2005), depicted this event.

The Korean War (1950–1953) again signaled the need for Rangers. Fifteen Ranger Companies were formed to do reconnoitering work: scouting, patrolling, raids, ambushes, and spearheading assaults. Small units in the Army, for example, Long Range Reconnaissance Patrols ("LRRPS"), were highly effective during the Vietnam War in providing operational and strategic intelligence. The 75th Ranger Regiment was reorganized in 1969 (at the height of the Vietnam conflict) to consolidate many of these units. However, it was deactivated in 1973 as combat commands returned to the United States.

In 1974, ranger battalions were again created and the 75th Ranger Regiment with three battalions was designated in 1986. Elements of the 1st Ranger Battalion participated in Operation Eagle Claw in 1980, and in Operation Urgent Fury, Rangers parachuted from low altitudes to seize Grenada's Salines Airfield and rescue students at the medical school. Rangers have played key roles in action in Panama, Kosovo, Somalia, Afghanistan, and Iraq. The 75th Ranger Regiment has taken part in every major combat operation since their initial development during the Vietnam War.[113]

FIGURE 14–15
Some of the members of the 6th Ranger Battalion who freed American and Filipino prisoners of war (POWs) held at Cabanatuan. Many of the POWs were captured in 1942.

(Bettmann/Contributor/Getty Images)

Today's 75th Ranger Regiment consists of the 1st Battalion (Hunter Army Airfield, Georgia), 2nd Battalion (Fort Lewis, Washington), and the 3rd Battalion and the Regimental Special Troops Battalion (Fort Benning, Georgia).[114] The 1st, 2nd, and 3rd Battalions each have approximately 600 rangers. The Regimental Special Troops Battalion (RSTB) provides the Ranger Regiment and Special Operations Forces with increased operational capabilities to sustain combat operations. The RSTB conducts command and control communications, computers, intelligence, surveillance, and reconnaissance functions in support of the Regiment and other special operations task forces.

The 75th Ranger Regiment has six primary missions: (1) direct action, seize, destroy, or capture enemy facilities and materials; (2) airport seizure for use by follow-on forces; (3) special reconnaissance, locate hostile forces for future operations; (4) personnel recovery, including evacuation or rescue of civilians and POWS in enemy territory or hostile terrain; (5) clandestine insertion to surprise the opponent, seize the initiative, and instill confusion in hostile forces; and (6) sensitive site exploitation, collect and analyze information gained on missions to conduct rapid follow-on operations.

It is fair to say that Rangers lack a primary counterterrorism mission. Rangers may be called on to perform counterterrorism operations on their own or augment other premier direct action units, such as Delta Force and SEAL Team 6. Nonetheless, the Rangers' counterterrorism operations are important contributions to the global war on terrorism. More than 70 percent of current Rangers have multiple deployments in support of America's war against terrorists.[115] That experience is valuable in the special operations community.

Rangers, all of whom are volunteers, are highly trained, and a battalion can be deployed anywhere in the world within 18 hours, infiltrating by land, sea, or air. Because of this flexibility and their capabilities, the 75th Ranger Regiment is often formally used to augment other units in joint counterterrorism operations.

Foreign Counterterrorism Organizations

Across the world the challenge of confronting terrorism has resulted in many governments creating special units. Military action against terrorists is referred to as **low intensity conflict** because it is somewhere between the diplomatic or economic tensions that flare up between countries and open/conventional warfare between them. However, there is nothing "low intensity" for people who are killed by terrorists or have to risk their lives fighting against them.

This section covers foreign counterterrorist organizations from three Allied nations: (1) The British Special Air Service (SAS) is included because it became

Low intensity conflict
A level of military action that falls short of a full-scale conventional war; includes peacekeeping, anti-terrorism programs, assistance to foreign militaries and police organizations, fulfillment of international treaty obligations, as well as subversive and counterterrorism actions.

Information Link
For more information on the Special Air Service (SAS) Selection Process, visit the website at www.eliteukforces .info/special-air-service/sas-selection/.

a model for so many other countries, including the U.S. "Delta" counterterrorism unit; (2) the rationale for covering Germany's GSG9 is that the necessity for it arose out of one of history's most heinous terrorist attacks—the murder of members of Israel's delegation to the 1972 Olympics in Munich; and (3) Israel's Sayeret Matkal, Shayetet-13, and Mistaravim are included in this discussion because in the modern world, Israel may have more experience dealing with terrorism than any other nation. Other foreign counterterrorism units with substantial capabilities include France's National Gendarmerie Intervention Group (GIGN), Austria's Einsatzkommando Cobra (EKO Cobra), Turkey's unique motorcycle teams called the Yunuslar (or Dolphins), Mexico's Force Marines (FEAM), and the Russian Alpha Group.[116]

Great Britain—22nd Special Air Service (SAS) Regiment

The British SAS is responsible for counterterrorism, intelligence gathering, forward air control, behind enemy lines sabotage, close protection (in America often called dignitary protection), and training foreign militaries. SAS was originally formed as "L Detachment" Special Air Service Brigade and initially conducted raids on airfields behind German lines in Africa during 1941–1942.[117] Beginning in 1943, SAS's missions became more varied, striking behind enemy lines to rescue prisoners of war, gathering intelligence, disrupting enemy forces, arming and training partisan groups, and severing rail and communications lines.[118] On D-Day, June 6, 1944, Allied forces landed on the coast of France. To prevent German supplies and reinforcements being quickly brought to the front, SAS cut rail lines in Southern France.[119] For the rest of the war, SAS specialized in intelligence collection and unconventional warfare against the Germans. Thought to be unnecessary after the war, the British government disbanded SAS, only to reconstitute it two years later.[120] The selection course for SAS is very demanding (see Figure 14–16).

During the years that followed, SAS successfully fought insurgents in Malaysia during the 1950s and 1960s, and in Oman in the 1970s. In 1980, desperate to create their own homeland, six Iranians seized their country's Embassy in London. When their demands for a new homeland and the release of prisoners were rebuffed, the incident turned into a siege. After a daring raid, the SAS successfully freed twenty-four of twenty-five hostages and killed five of six terrorists, without loss of a single soldier. During the First Gulf War (1990–1991), the SAS ran deep reconnaissance behind Iraqi lines. The SAS has made a concerted effort to learn about terrorist threats from events in other countries. For instance, in 1993, at least one SAS officer was observed at the Branch Davidian Compound siege in Waco, Texas. It is also believed that one or more SAS representatives were also present in the 1996/1997 hostage taking incident at the Japanese Ambassador's residence in Lima, Peru, by the Marxist Tupac Amaru Revolutionary Movement. This type of activity represents a forward-thinking perspective of gathering intelligence information on tactics used by terrorists from a global perspective. Today, informal arrangements between friendly country intelligence and counterterrorism forces allow "observers" at protracted conflict or terrorist events.

In Iraq during 2005–2008, SAS reportedly joined forces with operators from the U.S. Army's 1st Special Forces Operational Detachment-Delta (1st SFOD-D, "Delta").

The low-profile unit had several different names, including "Task Force Black" (TFB). Over a period of 18 months, the unit took 3,500 insurgents "off the street," most of which were captured.[121] The primary targets were persons involved with suicide bombings in Baghdad, which substantially declined due to "Task Force Black's" development of a network of spies and informers to identify potential targets.[122] "Task Force Black" also killed between 350 and 400 people, most of whom were senior Islamic militants with ties directly

FIGURE 14–16
The SAS selection course is the most demanding test in the British Armed Forces, with a pass rate of only 10 percent. It is a test of endurance, strength, and resolve. The endurance phase culminates with a 40-mile "walk" over mountain terrain that must be completed in 24 hours while carrying a 55-pound Bergen (Rucksack).

(Andrew Chittock/Alamy Stock Photo)

to al Qaeda.[123] American General David Petraeus, then-commander of American forces in Iraq, had high praise for SAS: "They have exceptional initiative, exceptional skill, exceptional courage and savvy. I can't say enough about how impressive they are in thinking on their feet."[124] In Afghanistan during 2009–2010, SAS operations were credited with "completely destroying the Taliban's middle management."[125] British SAS has been the model for a number of other nations who formed special units of the same name, including Australia, Canada, New Zealand, and Rhodesia.

Germany—GSG9 (Grenzschutzgruppe 9)

At the 1972 Olympics in Munich Germany, members of the Palestinian terrorist group Black September entered the Olympic compound. As they tried to enter the Israeli quarters, Yossef Gutfreund, a wrestling referee, held the door against them. Although he was killed, he gave others time to escape. At various points Moshe Weinberg and Yossef Romano also fought their captors and although killed, their valor allowed one more Jewish hostage to escape. The terrorists demanded the release of Palestinian prisoners held by Israel, helicopters to fly them and eight Israeli hostages to an airbase, and a jet airline to eventually fly them all on to Egypt. As the helicopters were being boarded, a rescue attempt failed badly and the hostages and terrorists all died.[126]

Recognizing that existing German military units were not trained for hostage rescue and counterterrorism, GSG9 was formed six months later. Like other leading counterterrorism units, its training is demanding and 80 percent of GSG9 candidates cannot meet standards.[127] If attempting to join GSG9 from a military unit, candidates must give up their rank and enter training as a private. GSG9 has become one of the elite counterterrorism forces in the world (see Figure 14–17). It specializes in hostage rescue, particularly in regard to aviation terrorism.[128] In an early operation in 1977, GSG9 was active in combating the Red Army Faction. The unit freed German hostages held on a plane in Somalia by Palestinian terrorists by entering the plane at multiple points, and killing or capturing all the terrorists.[129] None of the hostages nor any of the GSG9 group were killed. In another incident, during 2011–2012, GSG9 arrested four members of a terrorist cell planning to conduct attacks on German transit systems.[130]

Israel—Sayeret Matkal, Shayetet-13, and Mista'arvim

Sayeret Matkal may be Israel's most respected counterterrorism unit and its most secretive.[131] Since the founding of Israel as a modern nation in 1948, Sayeret Matkal has participated in practically every major Israeli counterterrorism operation,[132] including the rescue of hostages held by terrorists at Entebbe, Uganda. It was founded in 1957 and patterned after the British SAS. Sayeret Matkal also has responsibility for hostage rescue within the country, and during war, deep reconnaissance behind enemy lines to develop strategic intelligence.[133] Sayeret Matkal is comparable to America's Delta Force.

Since the terrorist attack in 2000 on the USS *Cole* while docked in a Yemeni port, "maritime security" has become a much greater concern.[134] Although maritime terrorism has only accounted for 2 percent of all terrorist incidents since 1969, maritime security continues to be a major concern.[135] Israel was forward thinking about maritime security, creating a special unit within the Israeli Defense Forces in 1948 called Shayetet-13. Although its existence was not made public until 1960,[136] it has been very active in combating maritime terrorism and is comparable to the U.S. Navy SEALs.

FIGURE 14–17

GSG9 members practicing a fast rope insertion. Two snipers are on the roof and an officer in a ghillie suit is in front of the door. On the near side of the road, note the operator has a bipod on his weapon. It may be an automatic weapon, although it seems small for that purpose, suggesting he has a sniper rifle.

(Guido Ohlenbostel/Newscom)

Israel has a coastline on the Mediterranean Sea that is approximately 170 miles long, and traditional terrorist enemies such as the Palestinian Liberation Front, Hamas, Palestinian Islamic Jihad, and Lebanese Hezbollah all have maritime capabilities.[137] Israel has suffered 80 maritime attacks over the past decades, most of which were foiled.[138] Maritime terrorism in Israel may present itself as a single point attack or simultaneous attacks at multiple points from a "mothership."[139] Maritime terrorists have raided beachfront hotels for hostages, planted mines on coastal roads, and filled speedboats and fishing vessels with explosives for suicide drivers. Both al Qaeda and Hezbollah have launched rockets toward ships in Israeli ports.

Mista'arvim is a secretive undercover counterterrorism unit attached to the Israeli Border Guard (Magav).[140] However, it reports to the Israel Security Agency, better known as Shin Bet, which is responsible for internal security and counterterrorism. Members of Mista'arvim are substantially drawn from minority Arabs, such as the Druze, who have become more assimilated to Israel than other Arab people living there. Mista'arvim operators work undercover in disguise to locate and take direct action against suicide bombers, and capture or kill wanted terrorists. Mista'arvim operates with a great deal of secrecy. In addition to other requirements, recruits must speak Arabic fluently and be able to pass as an Arab in an undercover operation. The extensive training course spends months teaching recruits the smallest details of Arab life, Islam, and the Arabic language. Members of the Mista'arvim are also required to live and pass as an Arab to gather intelligence and discover plots against Israel.

Chapter Summary

SUMMARY BY LEARNING OBJECTIVE

1. **Explain what national security policy and national security strategy are and how they are related.**

   Our national security policy is what the United States intends to accomplish, while our national security strategy is the actions we will take to ensure that our national security policies are achieved.

2. **Contrast anti-terrorism and counterterrorism efforts.**

   Fundamentally, anti-terrorism efforts are defensive in nature. Anti-terrorism efforts are defensive actions taken to reduce the vulnerability of people and property to terrorist acts, including rapid containment by local military and civilian forces. On the other hand, counterterrorism efforts are offensive in nature, and usually involve military or paramilitary actions taken to prevent, deter, or respond to terrorist threats or attacks.

3. **Explain the role of each anti-terrorism organization.**

   The U.S Department of State's Anti-Terrorism Assistance Program (ATAP) trains personnel in friendly foreign countries in such subjects as protecting critical infrastructures, cybersecurity, dignitary protection, terrorist interdiction, countering violent extremism, and handling improvised explosive devices (IEDs).

   The U.S. Department of Treasury's Office for Terrorism and Financial Intelligence is responsible for safeguarding the financial system against illicit use and combating rogue nations, terrorist facilitators, weapons of mass destruction (WMD) proliferators, money launderers, drug kingpins, and other national security threats. The intelligence and enforcement functions are the Financial Crimes Enforcement Network (FinCen) and the Executive Office for Asset Forfeiture. An example of the Department of Treasury's anti-terrorism work is investigation into potential criminal cases involving charitable giving. At least seven charities have been shut down for collecting charitable donations and then sending them to Hamas and al Qaeda or otherwise supporting terrorism.

   The Federal Bureau of Investigation (FBI) has both anti-terrorism and counterterrorism missions. The FBI is the lead agency for the Foreign Terrorist Tracking Task Force (FTTTF), which was created by Homeland Security Presidential Directive-2 in 2001. The FBI is the lead federal agency (LFA) of federal agencies cooperating in the effort to (1) deny entry of aliens into the United States if they are associated with, suspected of being engaged in, or support terrorist activity; and (2) locating, detaining, prosecuting, and deporting any such aliens already present in the United States.

In the Department of Homeland Security, Immigration and Customs Enforcement (ICE) has a Terrorist Tracking and Pursuit Group that identifies non-immigrants who have over-stayed the terms of their admission and who may pose a potential risk or threat to national security.

American state and local law enforcement agencies have an important role to play in anti-terrorism. Local law enforcement is cast as the "eyes and ears" on the front lines of anti-terrorism and counterterrorism efforts. State and large counties and cities are ordinarily members of federal Joint Terrorism Task Forces (JTTF), but also have their own "counter-terrorism" units, which actually perform more defensive anti-terrorism tasks as opposed to executing offensive operations. New York City is the most notable example of a municipality having both anti-terrorism and robust counterterrorism responsibilities.

All U.S. Attorney's Offices have substantial responsibility for combating domestic and international terrorism. One way that responsibility gets expressed is through an Anti-Terrorism Advisory Council, each headed by a U.S. Attorney and with wide-ranging membership, including the National Guard and state, local, and federal law enforcement agencies. The Anti-Terrorist Advisory Councils seek to deter, detect, and prevent future attacks within the United States by creating partnerships that (1) coordinate anti-terrorism initiatives, (2) initiate and support anti-terror training programs, and (3) facilitate information sharing across all levels of government.

The Transportation Security Administration (TSA) is responsible for security of America's transportation systems and freedom of movement for people and commerce. One of TSA's enforcement arms is the federal air marshals, responsible for primarily securing aviation transportation assets (e.g., commercial airliners) domestically and internationally. The exact number of air marshals is not public information for security purposes.

Under the Atomic Energy Act, the Federal Bureau of Investigation is responsible for investigating illegal activities involving the use of nuclear materials within the United States, including terrorist threats involving the use of nuclear materials. The Department of Energy's National Nuclear Security Administration provides technical assistance to the FBI. The National Nuclear Security Administration has assets related to a potential nuclear incident. In a terrorist situation, Nuclear Emergency Support Teams (NESTs) can search for and identify nuclear materials, assess potential nuclear devices, render such devices safe, and package them for transportation to a place of final disposition. NESTs consist of five to several dozen specialists depending on the situation. Terrorism involving a nuclear device is both a public concern and a focus of the federal government.

Established in 2002, the U.S. Northern Command (NORTHCOM) has wider responsibilities than anti-terrorism, e.g., directing the entire North American Aerospace Defense Command, but those other important responsibilities are not relevant here. However, note that NORTHCOM area of responsibility for protecting the United States includes land, air, and sea approaches to all forty-eight continental states, Alaska, Hawaii, Canada, and Mexico. Although not an anti-terrorism activity, NORTHCOM has a civil support mission, e.g. the Department of Homeland Security by accurately identifying the right mix of Department of Defense assets and quickly deploying them to counter the effects of natural and manmade disasters. NORTHCOM formed Joint Task Force North in 2004 to assist local, state, and federal law enforcement agencies protecting the border between Mexico and the United States reasoning that reducing the number of illegal border crossers reduces the opportunity for terrorists and weapons of mass destruction to enter the country. It has worked with Mexico to reduce drug smuggling and with Canada in protecting the 2010 winter Olympics in Vancouver. NORTHCOM sets the level (Alpha, Bravo, Charlie, and the highest, Delta) of force protection at Department of Defense installations, facilities, and units within its area of responsibility. Force protection is an anti-terrorism effort defined as the preventative measures taken to mitigate hostile actions against Department of Defense personnel and family members, resources, facilities, and critical information.

The Joint Special Operations Command (JSOC) is located at Fort Bragg, North Carolina. It comprised of special operations personnel from different branches of the service, including as Seal Team 6, Delta Force, 24th Special Tactics Squadron, and the Intelligence Support Activity. Although JSOC has a primary counterterrorism mission, some units may have work with indigenous people of different countries in a limited civil affairs mode, winning their "hearts and minds" by providing medical care or other assistance which at its core is anti-terrorism.

Among the U.S. Marine Corps' anti-terrorism units is the Chemical, Biological, Immediate Response Force (CBIRF), a battalion-sized unit (usually over 500 soldiers) that can be deployed to a terrorist incident anywhere in the world within 24 hours.

4. Identify the five forms of military action associated with counterterrorism.

The five types of military action associated with counterterrorism are (1) open warfare, (2) raids, (3) preemptive strikes, (4) direct action, and (5) hostage rescue.

5. Identify the mission and subcommands of USSOCOM.

The U.S. Special Operations Command (USSOCOM or simply SOCOM) was formed in 1987 and is headquartered at MacDill Air Force Base in Tampa, Florida. Its mission is to provide fully capable Special Operations Forces to defend the United States and its interests and to synchronize global military operations against terrorist networks. USSOCOM is the "parent" organization for the special operations community, and is composed of the five major special operations or special warfare commands from each military branch. They are U.S. Army Special Operations Command, Naval Special Warfare Command, Air Force Special Operations Command, U.S. Marine Corps Special Operations Command, and Joint Special Operations Command. The last command, Joint Special Operations Command (JSOC), commands the special military operational units like Army Delta, Army Special Forces, and Navy SEAL Teams that are often used for counterterrorism missions.

6. Explain the role of each domestic counterterrorism organization.

JSOC is a shadowy unit based at Fort Bragg, North Carolina. It has regular units assigned to it from several branches of our military service. It can obtain additional expertise for missions, which become part of JSOC for the duration of an operation. JSOC has four subunits: Delta Force, Seal Team 6, the 24th Special Tactics Squadron, and the Intelligence Support Activity. Although clearly a CT function, some units in it may engage in activities, such as providing medical care, to "win the hearts and minds" of indigenous people. JSOC is a subordinate command of SOCOM.

SOCOM was created in 1987, following the failed Operation Eagle Claw, which was intended to free hostages seized in Iran. SOCOM's mission is to provide fully capable Special Operations Forces to defend the United States and its interests and to synchronize global military operations against terrorist networks. Essentially, SOCOM is the "parent" organization for the special operations community and their use in counterterrorism. It is composed of special warfare elements from various branches of the military: (1) the U.S. Army Special Operations Command (USASOC), (2) Naval Special Warfare Command (NAVSPECWARCOM), (3) JSOC, (4) the Air Force Special Operations Command (AFSOC), and the U.S. Marine Corps Special Operations Command (MARSOC).

The Special Activities Division (SAD) is a group of paramilitary officers within the Central Intelligence Agency. Their exact number is not publically known. Many of them were recruited from highly experienced military units. They conduct clandestine military operations in foreign countries, including counterterrorism and capture or kill missions. During 1967, in one of SAD's publicized actions, they collaborated with U.S. and Bolivian Special Forces in the capture of Che Guevara, who was executed by the Bolivians in the field.

Federal Bureau of Investigation—Hostage Rescue Team, When the mastermind of the 2014 Benghazi attack in Libya was located, Delta was assigned the mission of capturing him. The successful raid into Libya was conducted with collaboration between the FBI and Delta. The FBI was embedded in Delta because of the law enforcement knowledge required to potentially convict mastermind Abu Khatallah in federal court. These include expertise in evidence identification, collection, and preservation, hostage and crisis negotiation skills and knowledge not normally the concern of special operations units.

U.S. Army Special Forces (SF)—"Green Berets," at the end of World War II, it was clear going forward there was a need for special operations units to fight unconventional. Many of the initial members of SF came from the soon to be disbanded Office of Strategic Service (OSS). Many of the OSS members were from foreign countries, spoke several languages, had substantial behind the lines combat experience, and could earn U.S. citizenship. Only 2,500 positions or "slots" were allocated to SF. It was under budgeted and lacked cutting edge equipment, which changed as their demonstrated value grew.

In their own countries, many men wore berets and those selected for SF did so, although the green beret was not recognized as official headwear. In 1961, President Kennedy spoke approvingly about the green berets and the military establishment quickly approved the green beret as official headwear. There are five active duty SF groups, the 1st, 3rd, 5th, 7th, and 10th, and two National Guard groups, the 19th and the 20th. Each group has a geographical area in which they specialize. Among the missions of SF are counterterrorism, direct action, and foreign internal defense.

U.S. Army—Delta Force is a counterterrorism unit under the command of JSOC. It is the brainchild of Captain Charlie Beckwith who saw combat during the Korean War and subsequently spent a tour of duty with the British SAS fighting rebels in Malaya with the elite British Special Air Service (SAS). SAS conducted operations with little emphasis on rank and things were seemingly done casually, but the accomplishments could not be denied.

Over the next 14 years, Beckwith submitted a series of papers calling for the creation of a unit modeled after SAS. Based on acts of terrorism being committed, the Army decided it needed a counterterrorism unit and in 1977 gave Beckwith two years to get it up and running. Initially, most recruits to Delta came from Special Forces. It participated in the ill-fated Operation Eagle Claw in Iran, which drove Beckwith to increase training.

Delta Force, Seal Team 6, and the 24th Special Tactics Squadron units are a national asset. They are the most secretive units, the existence of some, like Delta and Seal Team 6, is not even acknowledged by the military. They draw the toughest assignments, which are often clandestine, have the best equipment, and have an easier time getting support from other units. Membership is strictly by invitation.

Elite special mission units (SMUs) include the Rangers, Seals, Marine Recon, and Green Berets. Their operators tend to be younger because several of them allow enlistment in the service with a contract to attend the preparatory/indoctrination screening. All SMUs have participated in counterterrorism operations.

U.S. Navy—SEAL Teams, SEAL Teams history starts with World War II with units such as those that blew up beach obstacles which would have slowed landing craft and expose then to prolonged enemy firepower and after covert landings infiltrated agents, supplied resistance groups, and engaged in maritime sabotage.

After the war, only two Underwater Demolition Teams (UDTs) survived demobilization, each with seven officers and forty-five personnel. With Vietnam looming on the horizon, President Kennedy rebadged the UDTs as SEALs and resources began flowing to them. In Vietnam, SEALs clandestinely infiltrated Viet Cong and North Vietnam controlled areas to capture prisoners, gather intelligence, and execute ambushes. The VCs and NVAs called them "The men with green faces" because of the camouflage paint they wore. The VCs and NVAs called them "The men with green faces" because of the camouflage paint they wore.

SEALs were deployed to Iraq and Afghanistan, while presently they are present in a number of countries, helping to build internal capacity to fight terrorists. They have also conducted recent direct actions in other countries, including Syria, Nigeria, and Somalia. They have also been involved in some hostage rescues. Many people confuse SEAL Team 6 with all SEAL teams. However, SEAL Team 6 is a specific team in JSOC.

U.S. Army—75th Ranger Regiment has a distinguished lineage. Rangers existed in colonial America, the Revolution War, the Civil War, and then reappeared during World War II. On June 6, 1944, on the stalled beachhead of Normandy Rangers earned their motto, "Rangers lead the way." In the Pacific during 1945, Rangers freed 500 American and Filipino prisoners from the Japanese prisoner of war (POW) camp at Cabanatuan, some of whom were captured in 1942. Ranger companies were formed during the Korean War to conduct raids, and ambushes, reconnaissance, scouting, patrolling, and spearheading assaults. The use of special operations units to spearhead assaults is today widely regarded as a misuse of highly trained personnel. Long Range Reconnaissance Patrols ("LRRPS") were highly effective during the Vietnam War in providing operational and strategic intelligence. The 75th Ranger Regiment was reorganized in 1969, at the height of the Vietnam conflict, to consolidate many of these units. The 75th was deactivated in 1973, but reappeared the next year. In 1986, the 75th Ranger Regiment was formed with three battalions.

The 75th Ranger Regiment has six primary missions: (1) direct action, seize, destroy, or capture enemy facilities and materials; (2) airport seizure for use by follow-on forces; (3) special reconnaissance, locate hostile forces for future operations; (4) personnel recovery, including evacuation or rescue of civilians and POWS in enemy territory or hostile terrain; (5) clandestine insertion to surprise the opponent, seize the initiative, and instill confusion in hostile forces; and (6) sensitive site exploitation, collect and analyze information gained on missions to conduct rapid follow-on operations.

It is fair to say that Rangers lack a primary counterterrorism mission. Rangers may be called on to perform counterterrorism operations on their own or augment other units, such as Delta Force and SEAL Team 6. Nonetheless, the Rangers' counterterrorism operations are important contributions to the global war on terrorism. More than 70 percent of current Rangers have multiple deployments in support of America's war against terrorism.

7. Describe SAS, GSG9, and Mista'arvim.

These forerunners of Great Britain's Special Air Service (SAS) were operational during World War II and by war's end were running intelligence collection and unconventional warfare operations. Disbanded at the end of that war, SAS was reconstituted two years later and fought communists in Malaysia and Oman in the 1960s and 1970s.

SAS ran deep reconnaissance during the first Gulf War in Iraq and during 2005 worked with Delta to eliminate people associated with suicide bombers and to eliminate terrorists associated with al Qaeda. SAS and Delta also developed a network of informers and spies. Delta was developed using SAS as a model, as were similar units in Canada, New Zealand, Rhodesia, and Australia.

Germany's GSG9 is also one of the elite counterterrorism groups in the world. It was created following Germany's poor performance in trying to rescue the Israeli hostages taken by Black September at the 1972 Olympics in Munich. Recognizing its need for an anti-terrorist and hostage rescue force, Germany formed GSG9, which is particularly skilled in aviation hostage rescue operations. Soldiers who want to become a GSG9 member must give up all of their military rank to become a candidate.

Mista'arvim is an Israeli secret undercover unit whose members work in disguise and must speak Arabic fluently. Their job is to work against suicide bombers and capture or kill wanted terrorists.

REVIEW QUESTIONS

1. What is the relationship between ways, ends, and means and strategy? The relationship of ends, ways, and means forms strategy.
2. Counterterrorism is often thought of as just being military actions, although it is a constellation of activities. Can you name some counterterrorism activities other than military?
3. Why is it important for South Korea and Israel to have robust anti-terrorism programs?
4. Assume Usama bin Laden was captured instead of killed. What drawbacks could arise from his capture?
5. After Operation Eagle Claw failed in 1980, there were no more attempts to rescue the American hostages. Why?
6. What are the most compelling reasons for creating a special operations command?
7. What are NESTs and what services do they provide?
8. What are the five forms of military action associated with counterterrorism?

CRITICAL THINKING EXERCISES

1. In 2011, U.S. Army Ranger Sergeant Kristoffer B. Domeij (75th Ranger Regiment) was killed in Afghanistan on his 14th combat deployment—after four tours in Iraq and ten in Afghanistan. He and two other soldiers were killed by an IED (improvised explosive device) in Kandahar province. Sgt. Domeij was 29 years old. Should there be a policy on limiting combat tours? If so, what should it be? Would America and Sgt. Domeij family (wife and two children) have been better served by taking his vast experience and assigning him to another task, such as training and preparing others for combat, intelligence analysis, or the like? Is it possible Sgt. Domeij is a "natural warrior" and would have left the military if assigned to a stateside job?
2. Does the protection of the U.S. Constitution apply to American citizens at all times? Anwar al-Awlaki was targeted and killed by a drone strike in Yemen without a trial or any of the protections normally associated with a trial.
3. Is all speech in places of worship within the United States protected by the First Amendment regardless of its content?
4. What criteria do you advocate for a terror attack to be considered a crime against humanity?
5. Are there any similarities and/or differences of U.S. policy on containing communism in Vietnam, violent extremist organizations (VEOs), and the War on Drugs?

NOTES

1. David E. Sanger, Eric Schmitt, and Peter Baker, "Turmoil at the National Security Council, From the Top Down," *New York Times*, February 12, 2017, pp. 1–3, www.nytimes.com/2017/02/12/us/politics/national-security-council-turmoil.html, accessed May 11, 2017.

2. Helene Cooper, "In Security Shuffle, White House Merges Staffs," *New York Times*, May 26, 2009, www.nytimes.com/2009/05/27/us/27homeland.html?ref=us, accessed May 11, 2017.

3. Colonel Robert E. Hamilton, et. al., *National Security Policy and Strategy*, Appendix 1 (Carlisle, Pennsylvania: United States War College, Department of National Security and Strategy, Academic Year 2017), p. 87. Also see Alan G. Whittaker, et. al, *The National Security Policy Process: The National Security Council and Interagency system* (Washington, D.C.: The White House, August 15, 2011).

4. "National Security Policy and Strategy," p. 87.

5. Ibid., pp. 88–89, with restatement.

6. See The National Military Strategy of the United States of America 2015, p. 3.

7. The National Military Strategy of the United States of America 2015, p. 5.

8. Defense Security Review and the Quadrennial Defense Review, 2014, p. 33.

9. A. Hunsicker, *Understanding International Counter Terrorism* (Boca Raton, Florida: Universal Publishers, 2006), p. 58. Hunsicker's statement was the "last decade." To account for a publication date of 2006 and our own knowledge of what has happened since, the authors changed the statement to "Over the past two decades."

10. David McSwane and Tom Benning, "Gov. Abbott Extends National Guard on the Border in Response to Unaccompanied Minors," *Dallas Morning News*, December 15, 2015, p. 1, www.dallasnews.com/news/politics/2015/12/15/gov-abbott-extends-national-guard-on-the-border-in-response-to-unaccompanied-minors, accessed May 7, 2017.

11. Joint Chiefs of Staff, Joint Publication 3-05, Special Operations (Washington, D.C.: Joint Chiefs of Staff), p. ix, http://www.dtic.mil/doctrine/new_pubs/jp3_05.pdf.

12. *Counterterrorism*, Joint Publication 3-26, p. GL-4.

13. Loc. cit.

14. *Annual Report on Assistance Related to International Terrorism* (Washington, D.C.: U.S. Department of State, Office for the Coordination for Counter Terrorism, February 11, 2014), p. 1, www.state.gov/j/ct/rls/other/rpt/221544.htm.

15. *Terrorism and Financial Intelligence* (Washington, D.C.: Department of the Treasury, June 28, 2013), p. 1, www.treasury.gov/about/organizational-structure/offices/Pages/Office-of-Terrorism-and-Financial-Intelligence.aspx.

16. Nathaniel J. Turner, *U.S. Muslim Charities and the War on Terror* (Washington, D.C.: Charity and Security Network, December 2011), p. 3.

17. *Anti-Terrorist Financing Guidelines* (Washington, D.C.: Department of the Treasury, undated), p. 1, www.treasury.gov/resource-center/terrorist-illicit-finance/Pages/-protecting-charities-intro.aspx.

18. Federal Bureau of Investigation, "Missions and Priorities," p. 1, undated, https://www.fbi.gov/about/mission.

19. *Homeland Security Presidential Directive-2* (Washington, D.C.: Office of the President, October 29, 2001), p. 1, http://georgewbush-whitehouse.archives.gov/news/-releases/2001/10/20011030-2.html.

20. *The Federal Bureau of Investigation's Foreign Terrorist Tracking Task Force* (Washington, D.C.: U.S. Department of Justice, Office of the Inspector General, March 2013), p. i.

21. *Counterterrorism and Criminal Exploitation Unit* (Washington, D.C.: Immigration and Customs Enforcement, undated, but the likely date is 2012 because it is reporting 2011 program data), p. 1, www.ice.gov/counterterrorism-criminal-exploitation/.

22. Ibid., p. 5.

23. Randall Monger, *Nonimmigrant Admission to the United States* (Washington, D.C.: Immigration and Customs Enforcement, undated), p. 1, www.dhs.gov/xlibrary/assets/statistics/publications/ni_fr_2011.pdf.

24. This account is drawn with restatement from Aaron Katersky and Richard Esposito, "Faisal Shahzad: "War With Muslims Has Just Begun," *ABC News*, October 5, 2010, pp. 1–3, abcnews.go.com/Blotter/times-square-bomber-faisal-shahzad-sentenced-life /story?id=11802740.

25. NORTHCOM Anti-Terrorism Operations Order (U) 05-01, July 9, 2009, contains a more extensive description of its area of responsibility (AOR).

26. Loc. cit.

27. Loc. cit.

28. William Knight, *Homeland Security Roles and Missions for United States Northern Command* (Washington, D.C.: Congressional Research Service, June 3, 2008), p. CRS-4.

29. Cheryl Pellerin, "NORTHCOM Prioritizes Homeland Defense, Cyber Partners," March 13, 2012, DoD Armed Forces Press Service, www.defense.gov/news/newsarticle .aspx?id=67535.

30. *Protection*, ADRP 3-37 (Washington, D.C.: Headquarters, Department of the Army, August 2012), p. v.

31. No author, "Hurricane Katrina" History Vault, undated, p. 1, www.history.com/topics /hurricane-katrina, accessed May 7, 2017.

32. Loc. cit.

33. *A Short History of the United States Northern Command* (Peterson Air Force Base, Colorado: Northern Command, December 31, 2012), p. 7.

34. United States Marine Corps, "Chemical Biological Response Team," http://www.cbirf .marines.mil/About-CBIRF/History, undated, accessed November 12, 2017.

35. The description of CBIRF is taken from *Marine Expeditionary Force: Chemical, Biological Incident Response Force*, undated, p. 1, www.cbirf.marines.mil/About /History.aspx.

36. *Dictionary of Military and Associated Terms*, Department of Defense, August 15, 2014, p. 130, www.dtic.mil/doctrine/dod_dictionary.

37. Terrence McCoy, "ISIS, Beheadings and the Success of Horrifying Violence," *Washington Post*, June 13, 2014.

38. The account of this incident is taken with restatement from James Bennett, "U.S. Cruise Missiles Strike Sudan and Afghanistan, Targets Tied to Terrorist Network," *New York Times* (International Edition), August 21, 1998.

39. Henry Shue and David Rodin, *Preemption: Military War and Moral Justification* (Oxford, New York: Oxford University Press, 2007), p. 1.

40. Loc. cit.

41. Brigitte L. Nacos, *Terrorism and Counterterrorism* (Glenview, Illinois: Pearson, 4th ed., 2012), p. 181.

42. Eris Schmitt and David E. Sanger, "Raid in Yemen" Risky from the Start and Costly in the End", *New York Times*, February 1, 2017, pp. 1–2, www.nytimes.com/2017/02/01 /world/middleeast/donald-trump-yemen-commando-raid-questions.html, accessed May 8, 2017.

43. Jeff Thompson, "Crisis of Hostage Negotiation? The Distinction Between Two Important Terms," *FBI Law Enforcement Bulletin*, March 2014, no page number, http://leb.fbi.gov /2014/march/crisis-or-hostage-negotiation-the-distinction-between-two-important-terms.

44. The description of this incident is taken with restatement from Robert D. McFadden, "In Rescue of Captain, Navy Kills 3 Pirates," *New York Times*, April 12, 2009.

45. See U.S. Army Intelligence Support Activity at www.oafnation.com/united-states-army/.

46. See Robert W. Taylor, "Hostage and Crisis Negotiation Procedures: Assessing Police Liability," *TRIAL Magazine*, Vol. 19, No. 3, March 1983, pp. 6–15.

47. Michael J. McMains and Wayman C. Mullins, *Crisis Negotiation*, 5th ed. (Cincinnati, OH: Anderson Publishing, 2014).

48. Ibid.

49. Frank Bolz, Jr., and Edward Hershey, *Hostage Cop* (New York: Macmillan Publishing, 1979) and Harvey Schlossberg, *Psychologist with a Gun* (New York: Cowan, McCann & Geoghegan, 1974).

50. See Downs v. United States, 3382 F. Supp. 752 (1971) and Thomas Strentz, *Psychological Aspects of Negotiation* (Boca Raton, FL: Taylor & Francis, 2006).

51. Named after the unique relationship that developed between hostages and a suspect during a bank robbery in Stockholm, Sweden, in August 1973. See: Abraham H. Miller, *Terrorism and Hostage Negotiations* (Boulder, CO: Westview Press, 1980), pp. 37–59 and Thomas Strentz, "Law Enforcement Policy and Ego Defenses of the Hostage," *FBI Law Enforcement Bulletin* (April 1979), pp. 2–12.

52. Clint Van Zandt and Daniel Paisner, *Facing Down Evil: Life on the Edges as an FBI Hostage Negotiator* (New York: G. P. Putnam, 2006).

53. See Adam Dolnik and Keith Fitzgerald, "Negotiating Hostage Crises with the New Terrorists," *Studies in Conflict and Terrorism*, Vol. 34, No. 2, April 2011; and "Successful Police Negotiation Strategies in Terrorism Motivated Hostage Situations," in *Understanding and Responding to the Terrorism Phenomenon,* by Ozgur Nikbay and Suleyman Hancerli (Amsterdam, Netherlands: IOS Press, June 2007).

54. Yotam Dagan, Director of Community Programming and Outreach, NATAL, Israel and the International Institute for Counter-Terrorism. Much of this material was presented at the "World Summit Conference on Counter Terrorism," in Herzliya, Israel, in September 2012, "Expressive Terrorism: Lessons Learned from Crisis Negotiators," as well as the Texas Association of Hostage Negotiators Conference in San Antonio, Texas, November, 2008.

55. Bruce Hoffman and Gordon H. McCormick, "Terrorism, Signaling, and Suicide Attack," *Studies in Conflict and Terrorism*, Vol. 27, No. 4, pp. 243–281.

56. Ibid.

57. John G. Horgan, "Psychology of Terrorism: Introduction to the Special Issue," *American Psychologist*, Vol. 72, No. 3, (2017), pp. 199–204.

58. Richard A. Best Jr. and Andrew Feickert, *Special Operations Forces (SOF) and Paramilitary Operations: Issues for Congress* (Washington, D.C.: Congressional Research Service, August 3, 2009), p. 1.

59. Loc. cit.

60. *An End and a Beginning* (Washington, D.C.: Central Intelligence Service, March 15, 2007), p. 2, www.cia.gov/library/center-for-the-study-of-intelligence/csi-publications/books-and-monographs/oss/art10.htm.

61. Steve Bowman and Catherine Dale, *War in Afghanistan: Strategy, Military Operations, and Issues for Congress* (Washington, D.C.: Congressional Research Service, December 3, 2009), p. 6.

62. Ibid., p. 7.

63. Loc. cit.

64. Ibid., p. 8.

65. Loc. cit.

66. Loc. cit.

67. *Joint Terrorism Task Forces* (Washington, D.C. Immigration and Customs Enforcement, undated, but containing dates through 2010), p. 1, www.ice.gov/jttf/.

68. Michael Martinez, Evan Perez, and Barbra Starr, "Sources: Benghazi 'Mastermind' Captured without a Single Shot Fired," *CNN World News*, June 17, 2014, pp. 1–2, http://www.google.com/webhp?sourceid=chrome-instant&ion=1&espv=2&ie=UTF-8#q=martinez%2C%20benghazi%20mastermind%20captured.

69. Michael Zennie and James Nye, "Libyan Government Demands U.S. Return Benghazi Mastermind and Calls Delta Force Raid That Captured Him an Attack on Our Sovereignty," June 18, 2014, p. 1, http://www.google.com/webhp?sourceid=chrome-instant&ion=1&espv=2&ie=UTF-,8#q=michael+zennie,+Libyan+Government+DEmands+U.S.+Returns&tbm=nws.

70. Ibid., pp. 1, 4.

71. *Mission of U.S. Special Operations Command*, undated, p. 1, www.socom.mil/Pages/Mission.aspx.

72. Dr. Christine Coker, "Planning in Hostage Rescue Missions, U.S. Operation Eagle Claw and U.K. Operation Barras," *Military Technology*, Vol. 30, Issue 9, 2006, details taken and restated from p. 66.

73. Ibid., with restated facts from pp. 66 and 67; Statement of Admiral J. L. Holloway (Retired), "Iran Hostage Rescue Mission Report," *Report of the Special Operations Review Group to the Joint Chiefs of Staff, Admiral Holloway Chair, August 1980*, pp. 20, 23, 29, 33, and 40, www.history.navy.mil/library/online/hollowayrpt.htm; and Otto Kreisher, "Desert One," *Air Force Magazine*, Vol. 82, No. 1, January 1999, p. 1, www.airforcemag.com/MagazineArchive/Pages/1999/January%201999/0199desertone.aspx.

74. Susan Chun, ""Six Things You Didn't Know the Iran Hostage Crisis," CNN News, July 26, 2015, http://www.cnn.com/2014/10/27/world/ac-six-things-you-didnt-know-about-the-iran-hostage-crisis/index.html, accessed November 13, 2017.

75. Forrest L. Marion, "Air Force Combat Controllers at Desert One: April 24–25, 1980," *Air Power History*, Vol. 56, Issue 1, Spring 2009, p. 48.

76. Loc. cit.

77. Loc. cit.

78. Ibid., p. 6.

79. Loc. cit.

80. Adam Goldman and Julie Tate, "Inside the FBI's Secret Relationship with the Military's Special Operations," *Washington Post*, April 10, 2014, p. 2, http://www.google.com/webhp?sourceid=chrome-instant&ion=1amp;espv=2&ie=UTF-8#q=fbi+works+with+delta+force&start=0.

81. Loc. cit.

82. Loc. cit.

83. Loc. cit.

84. Fred J. Pushies, et al., *U.S. Counter Terrorist Forces* (St. Paul, Minnesota: MBI Publishing Company, 2002), p. 22.

85. At the end of 1952, SF had filled 1,700 of those positions, 10th SFG (A) History, U.S. Special Operations Command, undated, p. 1, www.soc.mil/USASFC/Groups/10th/history.html.

86. John M. Glenn, "Father of the Green Berets," *Military History*, Vol. 13, Issue 6, February 1998, 7 pp., unnumbered manuscript.

87. 10th SFG (A) History, U.S. Special Operations Command, p. 1.

88. Pushies et al., *U.S. Counter Terrorist Forces*, pp. 23–24.

89. Public Law 597 (1950).

90. Charles K. Dalgleish, "A New Lodge Act for the U.S. Army–A Strategic Tool for the Global War on Terrorism," *National War College*, undated, p. 1.

91. "History of the Green Beret," *Military.com*, 2014, p. 1, www.military.com/special-operations/army-special-forces-missions-and-history.html.

92. "Green Berets," John F. Kennedy Presidential Library and Museum, 2014, p. 1, www.jfklibrary.org/JFK/JFK-in-History/Green-Berets.aspx.

93. Peter Kornbluh, "The Death of Che Guevara: Declassified," *National Security Archive Electronic Briefing Book 5*, 2011, p. 1, www2.gwu.edu/~nsarchiv/NSAEBB/NSAEBB5/#chron.

94. "Charging Charlie" Beckwith attended the University of Georgia where he enrolled in the ROTC program and played left guard on the university's football team. He turned down an offer to play for the Green Bay Packers to accept an Army commission as a Second Lieutenant. Beckwith retired as a Colonel and a much-decorated combat veteran.

95. David Morrison, Lewis Grizzard, and Jim Stewart, "Charging Charlie Beckwith—The Green Berets One-Man Gang," *Lakeland (Florida) Ledger*, May 25, 1980 (Obituary), http://news.google.com/newspapers?nid=1346&dat=19800525&id=buhMAAAAIBAJ&sjid=IfsDAAAAIBAJ&pg=7142,3955873.

96. Tony Geraghty, *Black Ops: The Rise of Special Forces in the C.I.A., the S.A.S. and Mossad* (New York: Pegasus Books, 2010), p. Xlii.

97. Loc. cit.

98. John C. Fredriksen, *Fighting Elites: A History of U.S. Special Forces* (Santa Barbara, California: ABC-CLIO, 2011), p. 154.

99. Delta has had a number of names, including Special Forces Operational Detachment D (SFOD-Delta), Combat Applications Group (CAG), and Army Compartmented Element

(ACE). Given its secrecy, we don't know what it is called and will therefore continue to use "Delta" as a convenience.

100. Jack Kelley, "Commando Force Poised to Track and Kill Saddam," *USA Today*, March 18, 2003.

101. Many of the details in this account of the Battle of Mogadishu are drawn with restatement from *United States Forces, Somalia After Action Report and Historical Overview, 1992–1994* (Washington, D.C.: Center for Military History, 2003).

102. Tom Hawkins, "U.S. L Teams: Origins and Evolution 1942–1962," *Defense Media Network*, December 26, 2013, p. 2, www.defensemedianetwork.com/stories/origins-and-evolution-of-u-s-navy-seal-teams-1942-1962/, with restatement.

103. Ibid., p. 7.

104. "Navy SEALs: Background and Brief History," undated, p. 1, www.military.com/special-operations/about-the-navy-seals.html.

105. Hans Halberstadt, *U.S. Navy SEALs* (Minneapolis, Minnesota: Zenith Press, 2011), p. 27.

106. Loc. cit.

107. Loc. cit.

108. J. Paul de B. Taillon, *The Evolution of Special Forces in Counter Terrorism* (Westport, CT: Praeger Publishers, 2001), p. 72.

109. Ronald O'Rourke, *Navy Irregular Warfare and Counter Terrorism Operations: Background and Issues for Congress* (Washington, D.C.: Congressional Research Service, October 18, 2012), p. 2.

110. Halberstadt, *U.S. Navy SEALs*, pp. 7 and 11.

111. Ibid., pp. 15–16.

112. The Ranger history is taken from "75th Ranger Regiment History," May 6, 2014, pp. 1–2, www.benning.army.mil/tenant/75thRanger/history.htm; and "75th Ranger Regiment History," undated, pp. 1–2, www.soc.mil/Rangers/history.html, with restatement and reorganization.

113. "75th Ranger Regiment," p. 1, 2012, www.baseops.net/militarybooks/Armyranger.html.

114. "Army Rangers: The 75th Ranger Regiment," p. 1, 2014, www.military.com/special-operations/army-rangers-75th-regiment.html.

115. Loc. cit.

116. Henry Plater-Zyberk, *Russia's Special Forces* (Shrivenham, England: Conflict Studies Research Centre, September 2005), p. 3.

117. "Chronology of Major SAS Operations," 2002, p. 1, www.sasspecialairservice.com/sas-history-timeline-operations-list.html.

118. For information about special operations units during World War II, see Chris Burton, "The Eureka-Rebecca Compromises: Another Look at Special Operations Security During World War II," *Air Power History*, Vol. 52, Issue 4, Winter 2005, pp. 23–37.

119. Ibid., p. 2.

120. "SAS Regiment," History of the SAS Regiment, 2012, p. 1, www.sasregiment.org.uk.

121. Sean Rayment, "SAS Kills Hundreds of Terrorists in Secret War Against al Qaeda in Iraq," *Telegraph* (England), August 30, 2008, p. 1.

122. Loc. cit.

123. Jason Burke, "Task Force Black by Mark Urban," *Guardian* (England), February 27, 2010, p. 1.

124. Rayment, "SAS Kills Hundreds of Terrorists in Secret War Against al Qaeda in Iraq," p. 2.

125. Ben Endley, "If the SAS Leave Afghanistan the Taliban Will Take Over Say Top U.S. Generals," *Daily Mirror* (England), April 26, 2014.

126. This account is drawn from Terry Martin, "Munich Massacre Remembered," *Europe*, October 1, 2001, p. 43; and "Munich Olympic Massacre: Background and Overview," *Jewish Virtual Library*, undated, but the most recent source cited in this article was 2012, www.jewishvirtuallibrary.org/jsource/Terrorism/munich.html.

127. Cindy C. Combs and Martin Slann, "Grenzschutzgruppe 9 (GSG9)," *Encyclopedia of Terrorism*, 2007, New York, Facts on File Inc., p. 2, www.fofweb.com/History/MainPrintPage.asp?iPin=TER0126&DataType=WorldHistory&WinType=Free.

128. *GSG9 (Grenzschutzgruppe 9)* (St. Andrews, Scotland: University of St. Andrews, undated), p. 1, www.terrorism.com/gsg9.

129. Loc. cit.

130. Loc. cit.

131. David B. Green, "The Different Faces of Ehud Barak," *New Leader*, Vol. 82, Issue 8, July 12, 199, p. 5,

132. "Israel Defense Forces: Commando and Special Forces," *Jewish Virtual Library*, 2014, p. 3, www.jewishvirtuallibrary.org/jsource/society_and_culture/forcestoc.html.

133. Loc. cit.

134. Akiva Lorenz, *The Threat of Maritime Terrorism to Israel* (Herzliya, Israel: International Center for Counter-Terrorism, September 24, 2009), p. 1.

135. Loc. cit.

136. No author, "Israel's Special Forces—Shayetet 13," *Armed Forces History Museum*, undated, p. 1, http://armedforcesmuseum.com/israels-special-forces-shayetet-13.

137. Loc. cit.

138. Loc. cit.

139. Ibid., p. 12.

140. Mathieu Deflem, "Yehida Mishtaritit Mista'arvim (YAMAS) (Israel)," in Frank G. Shanty, editor, *Counter Terrorism: From the Cold War to the War on Terror*, Volume 2 (Santa Barbara, CA: Praeger/ABC-CLIO, 2012), pp. 71–72.

Terrorism, Intelligence, and Homeland Security: The Future

Learning Objectives

After completing this chapter, you should be able to:

1. Describe broad trends in terrorism, including general statistics about frequency, location, and targets of attacks.

2. Elaborate on the rise of homegrown and lone wolf terrorists and their weapons usage.

3. Discuss how al-Qaeda has been splintered and what the effects of that phenomenon might be.

4. Identify targets currently favored by terrorists, as well as future means of attack.

5. Discuss the role of modern media in terrorism.

6. Describe policies and strategies that might be implemented in counterterrorism in the future.

Many terrorist groups ensure their future by grooming children to accept their same intolerant beliefs. In Nashville, Tennessee, children are seen with familiar symbols of hate.

(Zuma Press/Newscom)

Introduction

At this point in any text on modern terrorism, some variation of the phrase "after the events of September 11, 2001" has been used countless times throughout the pages. Nearly two decades later, that terrible day still figures so strongly in this country that it continues to inform foreign relations, domestic policy, law enforcement, and everyday life—including travel, Internet privacy, and more. It's led to wars that continue, to suspicions that linger, and even to petty personal annoyances that persist (such as airport security checkpoints). And it's something that happened in the past—yet still manages to shape perceptions about what the future of terrorism looks like. Many citizens of this country—and many policy makers, as well—continue to see terrorism as something that may be best prevented by increased security measures and traditional methodologies, such as "target hardening" of specific locations, use of new technology to bolster airport security, targeting radical Muslims both home and abroad for surveillance, and focusing intelligence on the same networks of informants, couriers, and organizations that have been major players in the past two decade.

However, just as policy and intelligence related to terrorism have evolved, so too have the terrorists themselves. Today, known al-Qaeda sympathizers use YouTube and Twitter as a means of recruitment and communication—establishing an audience that reaches far beyond training facilities in remote areas of Afghanistan. Radicalization is increasingly an individual pursuit, cultured in the glow of a computer screen as opposed to in secretive meetings in mosques. The availability and affordability of weapons or elements used to assemble weapons have made them accessible to just about anyone who really wants to obtain them, further widening the pool of potential terrorists. Furthermore, intelligence methods that many consider to have been effective at uncovering terror plots have met with an uproar from human rights and/or privacy advocates in recent years, limiting how information can be obtained—and according to some, the ability to secure our country against certain kinds of attacks. These are just a few examples of how perceptions of terrorism and related intelligence have evolved over the past decade; this chapter will touch on several others, as well.

Trends in Terrorist Activities

In January 2013, a study by the National Consortium for the Study of Terrorism and Responses to Terrorism (START) detailed trends in terrorist activity for the United States. The data they examined indicated that in the span of time between 2001 and 2011, there had been a total of 207 attacks that were classified as terrorist in nature, 21 of which were fatal. From 2001 until 2011, the number of terrorist attacks in this country had declined from a peak of 40 attacks in that first year to 9 in the last. These numbers include serious attacks that were attempted (i.e., bombs that didn't detonate or shootings that didn't meet their target) but ultimately not successful. In 2011, this measure accounted for four out of the nine total reported incidents.[1] The study also included a broad definition of terror attacks, encompassing murders of abortion clinic personnel and a shooting (in 2009) of a guard at the National Holocaust Museum.

The START study will be updated at the end of 2017; however, at this writing, the latest available data from the Global Terrorism Database indicates 305 attacks classified as terrorist in nature on the United States between 2001 and 2015, 50 of which were fatal. While 2001 shows a peak of 41 incidents, the number plummets to fewer than 20 for many of the intervening years between then and 2015—rising in 2014 and 2015 to 26 instances and 28 instances per year, respectively.[2]

The data from 2001 to 2015 indicates that businesses are still the primary targets with 76 attacks, followed closely by private citizens and property (73 attacks), and governmental targets with 55 attacks. Most attacks were carried out via an incendiary means (e.g., fire, arson), with 156 attacks attributed to that means, followed by 64 incidents facilitated by explosives or bombs and then 62 episodes involving firearms.[3]

Interestingly, Islamic State (IS) attacks do not figure into statistics for the 2001 to 2015 era, despite dominating the current U.S. narrative on terror. Most of the attacks for that time period in the United States were actually carried out by the Earth Liberation Front, followed by 36 attacks by another single-issue terrorist associate, the Animal Liberation Front. As reported earlier in Chapter 7, the ALF and ELF attacks did not include any fatalities. Al-Qaeda registers with four attacks, though those were obviously the deadliest attacks in recent history (i.e., 09/11/2001 attacks on the World Trade Center in New York and the Pentagon in Washington, D.C.). The vast majority of the remaining terrorist incidents found in the database are attributed to unaffiliated individuals or persons/groups with unknown affiliations.[4] This data set classified the mass shooting in San Bernardino in December of 2015 as an attack by unaffiliated individuals; despite the fact that the perpetrators were apparently supporters of the Islamic State, no direct links to the terrorist organization were found. It remains to be seen how the Orlando nightclub shooting in 2016 will be classified in such datasets; since the gunman pledged allegiance to the Islamic State, and the group claimed responsibility—but there is no proof that IS was directly involved in the shooting. It will likely end up as attributed to an unaffiliated individual. Half of all plots with an IS connection are conducted by those with no direct contact to the group.[5]

Unfortunately, data shows preliminarily that domestic extremism is on the rise since 2015: the Anti-Defamation League attributes sixty-five deaths in 2015 to just four domestic movements, including white supremacists, anti-government extremists, domestic Islamist extremists, and anti-abortion extremists. In 2016, that number increased to 69, primarily due to the Orlando attack on the Pulse Nightclub—and it also included deaths of police officers in Dallas, Texas, and Baton Rouge, Louisiana, attributed to a fifth group: black nationalists.[6] It should be noted that the Anti-Defamation League report includes broader classification than terrorism: Individual hate crimes are included, as well.

Globally speaking, the data is very clear: Terrorism is rapidly changing and evolving. In 2014, the number of deaths from terrorism increased by 80 percent when compared to the previous year. And between 2000 and 2014, there was a ninefold increase in the number of deaths attributed to terrorism. The majority of this activity occurred in just five countries: Iraq, Nigeria, Afghanistan, Pakistan, and Syria. However, there were an additional six countries with more than 500 deaths each, including Somalia, Ukraine, Yemen, the Central African Republic, South Sudan, and Cameroon.[7] See Figure 15–1.

Overall, the vast majority of deaths from terrorism do not occur in the Western world, though the Islamic State advocates for such operations and has begun to increase its transnational attacks, particularly in Europe and throughout the Middle East. Attacks in the Western world increased by 650 percent between 2014 and 2015.[8] Yet, if the grim statistics generated by the 9/11 attacks are removed, Western terrorist incidents only represent a small percentage of deaths attributed to terrorism. Western terrorism, however, was overwhelmingly committed by lone wolf attacks, which account for about 70 percent of all terrorist deaths. Notably, 80 percent of those deaths can be ascribed to perpetrators linked to right-wing extremism, nationalism, anti-government sentiment, and other types of political or racial domestic extremism. But regardless of who commits the act of terror or where it occurs, one thing the data makes obvious is that the targets have changed. Terrorism that targets the lives of private citizens increased 172 percent between 2013 and 2014, indicating a shift in strategy for terrorists—who used to favor symbolic, governmental, or property-based targets.[9] Clearly, the goal is mass carnage on targeted innocent civilians.

The implications here are fairly clear: a mix of state-based conflict in the Middle East and African regions, coupled with sectarian and religious clashes, continues to drive terrorism in those areas. Unrest in Syria and Nigeria have emboldened groups such as Boko Haram and the Islamic State,

FIGURE 15–1

Countries with the Highest Number of Deaths by Terrorism, 2015

Five countries (Iraq, Nigeria, Afghanistan, Pakistan, and Syria) account for almost 75 percent of global terrorism.

Source: http://visionofhumanity.org/app/uploads/2017/02/Global-Terrorism-Index-2016.pdf

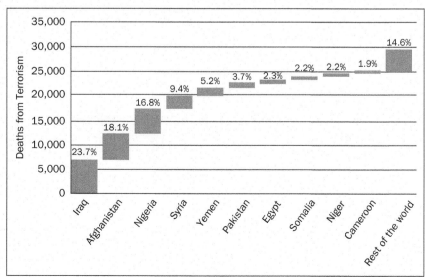

Box 15-1
Predicting Terror Attacks

Policies, laws, intelligence, and our fear level are all related to terrorism and can be based on a single attack. However, a specific attack by a specific group or individual is largely unpredictable in nature. While certain clues were overlooked in the months before 9/11, it's still difficult (if not impossible) to say with any certainty that the events of that day could have been predicted. Furthermore, the current trends in terrorism mean smaller-scale attacks perpetrated by individuals who are rarely the subject of previous law enforcement scrutiny; hence, there is no historical data on these individuals.

Surprisingly, however, terror attacks may not occur as randomly as we once thought they did. That's the conclusion reached by Aaron Clauset, a thirty-five-year-old data scientist in Denver, Colorado, who examined complex information related to terrorist attacks and identified statistical patterns behind the frequency and severity of terrorist attacks across the globe. What Clauset noticed about terror attacks is that they seemed to mirror earthquakes in some ways, following a power-law distribution. Earthquakes tend to occur in groups of really small quakes, followed by a handful of stronger medium-sized quakes, and then one or two really massive, devastating quakes. Clauset found that terror attacks followed the same pattern; for example, there had been scores of small terror attacks, a couple of medium-intensity attacks (like the Oklahoma City Bombing and the Lockerbie airline explosions), and then the massive 9/11 attack that killed 3,000 people. This is useful for law enforcement, security, and policymakers because the frequency and severity of "small" terrorist attacks may help to determine the likelihood of another "big one"; events like the attacks on Oklahoma City or Lockerbie should have suggested the potential for something much worse in the future.

Despite its seeming applicability to homeland security, Clauset's conclusions have not been utilized by the U.S. government. The methodology is complex, and perhaps beyond the capabilities of many of the agencies that would need to be involved in its use. Interestingly, Clauset points out the following implications for his findings:

> If we believe the power-law is a fundamental property of terrorism—and it appears to be so in a very robust way—it's reasonable to conclude that there may be a really big terrorist attack coming ... involving chemical, biological, or radiological attacks. And almost surely, the probability of these kinds of events is much higher than people might expect. If we don't have some people thinking about this in the long term, we are going to be very surprised. We are going to be unprepared.[10]

(From How Aaron Clauset Discovered a Pattern Behind Terrorist Attacks?.?.?.? And What It Told Him by Joel Warner. Published by Denver Westword LLC, © 2013.)

How effective and accurate do you think these types of prediction models are to police and security agencies?

---

which—combined with the Taliban and Al Qaeda—are responsible for 74 percent of all deaths from terrorism in 2015.[11] In these countries, terrorism is driven by armed conflict, political instability, human rights violations, corruption, and weak economic environments. This type of terror drives refugee and humanitarian crises, as well. In the West, terrorism is driven largely by socioeconomic factors like unemployment, drug crime, and immigration attitudes—though radical Islamic Jihadist doctrine plays a role, as well. Political turmoil in the Western world, including in Great Britain, the United States, and France, coupled with continued conflict and unsettled populations in the Middle East and parts of Africa, have experts warning of increased and deadlier terror attacks occurring globally in the near future. However, predicting terrorist attacks is often fraught with difficulty. See Box 15–1.

The above data gives a good overview of basic trends in terrorism, while also offering hints at broader paradigms in the field of study—such as the increase of individuals as opposed to groups carrying out attacks, as well as the fractionalization of terror groups in foreign countries. Identifying trends and predicting terrorist attacks is a tricky endeavor, fraught with an unlimited number of variables and a high degree of association between terrorist attacks and seemingly unrelated activities and incidents.

Information Link
For more information on the National Consortium for the Study of Terrorism and Responses to Terrorism (START), visit the website at the University of Maryland, www.start.umd .edu/. Browse the site and notice the emphasis placed on research, publication, and education focused on terrorism.

Quick Facts
Terrorism and the United States

Although terrorism is something of an ever-present specter in the American consciousness post-9/11, the United States is actually a relatively safe country compared to other places around the world. The United States ranks 36th in the world on measures of the impact of terrorism, which includes considerations of property damage, loss of life, injury, and other socioeconomic indicators. The United States also ranks safer than the United Kingdom, which sits at 34th on the list and France, which at number twenty-nine ranks the highest of any European country.

(Data from Institute for Economics and Peace. "Global Terrorism Index 2016." http://visionofhumanity.org/app/uploads/2017/02/Global-Terrorism-Index-2016.pdf.)

Homegrown and Lone Wolf Terrorists

In the United States, this trend has been relatively easy to spot. The last few major attacks that have occurred in the United States were carried out by so-called homegrown terrorists using lone wolf terrorist tactics. See Chapters 1 and 5 for a more thorough discussion of homegrown and lone wolf terrorism. The term *homegrown terrorist* refers to extremists who are legal U.S. residents or even citizens, and who are linked to or inspired by a specific, often intolerant ideology. This ideology may be motivated by political or religious sources and may be centered in domestic or foreign movements. Indeed, some of them have made connections with well-known, international terror groups, such as al-Qaeda or associated movements.[12] These individuals may receive ideological encouragement, but not financial or material support, making them ancillary to the primary group and very difficult to detect by intelligence and law enforcement services. For instance, Major Nidal Hasan, perpetrator of the 2009 Fort Hood shootings that killed thirteen people and wounded more than 30 others, is a prime example of this type of terrorist—a man who was radicalized due to a belief that American wars in Iraq and Afghanistan were wars against the Muslim faith. Hasan had expressed his opposition to these wars, despite his position as a psychiatrist in the United States Army, and carried out his attack about a month before he was to be deployed to Afghanistan. Hasan had been in contact with radical Muslim cleric and suspected al-Qaeda officer Anwar al-Awlaki via a series of emails before his attack.

In other cases, terrorist groups target first-generation foreign nationals living in the United States to join their ranks. The perpetrators of the Boston Marathon bombings in 2013 are good examples of this activity and are considered homegrown terrorists. Tamerlan Tsarnaev, who apparently masterminded the attack with the help of his younger brother Dzhokhar, was another young Muslim who had been radicalized by his anger over perceived injustices against the Muslim faith by the United States. Though no direct connections between the two Chechens and any specific terrorist group have ever been identified, the two did view al-Qaeda training videos on the Internet, and espoused doctrine that is common among al-Qaeda and Islamic State sympathizers.[13]

Other attacks considered as "homegrown" terrorism include the San Bernardino shooting in 2015 by Syed Rizwan Farook and Tashfeen Malik that killed 14 and the Orlando nightclub shooting that killed forty-nine people in 2016 by Omar Mateen. The killing of five police officers in Dallas, Texas, in July of 2016 by Micah Xavier Johnson has also been described as an act of lone wolf terrorism motivated by a hatred of police for officer-involved shootings of black men in the United States. Dylann Roof, who shot and killed nine churchgoers in a racially motivated attack in 2016, has also been described as a lone wolf terrorist, though he was charged and convicted of federal hate crimes as opposed to terrorism.

Why are some Muslim Americans identifying with terror groups? The first reason has already been discussed. They believe that the American presence in Iraq and Afghanistan is an affront to Islam and a direct attack on Muslim nations and people. For instance, a small population of Somali Muslims (mainly teenagers) in Minnesota believe that the U.S. backing of an Ethiopian invasion in their home country was an attack on Islam, resulting in a number of them connecting with **al Shabaab**, an extremist organization affiliated with al-Qaeda in Somalia.[14] (See Figure 15–2.) The second reason is that they have access to such groups via increased connectivity. The Internet and various social media platforms have allowed U.S. residents to reach out to or be recruited by extremists around the globe, gaining access to ideologies, philosophies, propaganda, and even their methods of violence (see Box 15–2). Access to training and operational support, although not as simple as a Google search, can be found online for those seeking it.

Al Shabaab
A radical Islamic group affiliated with al-Qaeda operating in the country of Somalia.

FIGURE 15–2
There are strong Somali communities in Minneapolis and Cedar Riverside, Minnesota, from which the terrorist group al Shabaab recruits. Since 2006, an estimated 25 to 50 young Somali men have gone to fight with al Shabaab throughout the Middle East and Africa.

(Jonathan Alpeyrie/Polaris/Newscom)

Box 15-2
Social Media and Jihad

In fact, the Islamic State (IS) is incredibly, and dangerously, adept at the use of social media. The Islamic State uses platforms like Twitter and Facebook extensively to spread propaganda, using decentralized and autonomous units across the globe to log on and send out memes and messages. Interestingly, and in direct contrast to many of their primary recruitment and propaganda videos, the group does not focus on the grisly images of executions and sadistic torture that many assume is their main output; instead, their feeds are a mix of photos and descriptions of accomplishments like public works projects, economic achievements, and inspiring religious quotes. Their outreach has been, by any standard, extremely successful—recruiting somewhere in the area of 30,000 people to travel and join their ranks and inspiring others to take up arms and commit acts of terror in their home countries on behalf of IS. This type of branding has never before been seen among terrorist organizations—allowing people with only slight ideological ties to the group to find something appealing in their narrative.[15]

IS excels at using technology—including drones and GoPros to create slick, high-quality videos of carnage—and using "freelance" jihadists to post exclusive content on visible social networks that inspires real-world action. Social networks and law enforcement try to root out users that trade in radical Islamic Jihadist imagery and verbiage, but content can be spread very quickly, and even if one account is shut down, the user can often start a new profile almost immediately.

(Amer Ghazzal/Alamy Stock Photo)

Should social media websites restrict access to individuals and groups that express violent or anti-American philosophies? Should law enforcement and intelligence services monitor social media websites?

In the United States, such homegrown terrorists have largely flown beneath the radar—many have no criminal records, and while their European counterparts tend to be more socially marginalized, it's more likely that American-grown extremists come from a broad variety of educational and socioeconomic statuses. Consider that Major Nidal Hasan had completed medical school; Tamerlan Tsarnaev had gone to college for a time to pursue engineering; and his brother, Dzhokhar, was enrolled in university at the time of the attacks.

The future of homegrown terrorism is one that will see shifts in the composition of participants, as well as in the networking that they engage in with al-Qaeda and other affiliated movements. As the United States continues to see successes in dismantling the major arteries of these terrorist organizations, homegrown terrorists will seek new ways to interact with them. In the past, some had physically attended training camps or, as in the case of Hasan, communicated directly with terror operatives. As surveillance has intensified and travel has become more scrutinized, those who seek out these radically inclined connections will retreat further into the Internet, particularly the "**deep web**," utilizing gaming sites that appear innocuous on the outside but allow encrypted conversations using their platforms, social media sites, and chat rooms to communicate.[16] The deep web is a vast part of the World Wide Web, not accessible through regular Internet browsing or search engines. Most of the information in the deep web is hidden, accessible from dynamic websites requiring the use of an application called *Tor*. The **Tor network** is synonymous for the deep web. This secretive online world remains mostly untraceable and difficult to access for the regular Internet user and even law enforcement and intelligence operatives. This subsequently allows a large criminal domain to thrive and a hidden venue for secret communications between terrorists, particularly astute worldwide terrorists sharing a jihadi Salafist philosophy.[17]

Crude Devices and Non-Sophisticated Weapons

Another result of the effects of splintering terror cells and increased intelligence is that homegrown terrorists are now largely forced to use crude devices or easily obtained weapons (such as firearms) to carry out their attacks. The bombs used in the Boston Marathon attacks were basically pressure cookers, found in any large retailer, filled with nails and ball bearings. They were reportedly made using instructions found online. Major Nidal Hasan

Deep web
A secret part of the World Wide Web, not accessible through regular Internet browsing or search engines; accessible from dynamic websites requiring the use of an application program called *Tor* that allows encrypted conversations.

Tor network
Synonymous for the deep web; see deep web. Acronym for a previous software program that allows complete anonymity on the web, called, **T**he **O**nion **R**outer.

used legally obtained firearms. Other terror attacks in the past few years have utilized vehicles as weapons, as well as a litany of homemade explosives. Purchasing materials to make more complex weaponry is made more difficult by policy changes restricting certain hazardous or biologic materials—or, if not restricting them outright, triggering a level of scrutiny that would-be terrorists might avoid.[18]

It's for these reasons that former Attorney General Eric Holder stated that these were the types of potential attacks that keep him up at night; he singled out the homegrown, lone wolf terrorist, stating that he was "very concerned about individuals who get radicalized in a variety of ways ... sometimes self-radicalized."[19] As we learned in Chapter 5, lone wolves include homegrown terrorists, but the term also encompasses those who identify with ideologies other than radical Islam; lone wolves can be right-wing extremists, anti-abortion radicals, and leftist environmentalists. They typically operate the same way that homegrown terrorists do—by networking online, seeking out their own information, and utilizing easily made or easily obtained weaponry for their attacks, though they may have more of a tendency than their radical Muslim counterparts to broadcast their intentions in some way.[20] They generally act on their own accord, in the name of some deeply held ideological belief system. As for their prevalence, a 2012 study by Ramon Spaaij found that lone wolf terror attacks were on the rise—increasing at a rate of about 45 percent between the 1970s and the 2000s.[21]

Al-Qaeda, Islamic State, Fractionalization, and the Rest of the World

Once the "big bad" of global terror, al-Qaeda's threat today is much harder to assess than it was even five years ago. At one point, this enemy was a large organization, headquartered for the most part in one major geographic location and fronted by a figurehead (Osama bin Laden) with undeniable power and reach. Today, this is not the case. The organization has become almost completely unrecognizable, with command and control dismantled through the death of prominent leaders, and remnant soldiers joining the ranks of the Islamic State. The centralized and powerful al-Qaeda organization of old is no longer a single entity, but has diffused throughout the Middle East and beyond—maintaining a presence in at least sixteen different countries.[22] For example, what was once the core of the organization in Pakistan has been largely decimated as part of the U.S. military involvement in Afghanistan and Iraq. Further, CIA drone strikes in Pakistan, which have killed approximately 33 senior al-Qaeda operatives since 2008, have left only a handful of former leaders in that country.[23] Similar activities in Somalia and Yemen have neutralized al-Qaeda threats in those areas.

Although this was, in theory, the goal of the U.S. military offensive against al-Qaeda, it has had the unintended consequence of allowing the organization to reformulate and still flourish as a decentralized, heavily networked and transnational movement, freed from the bureaucracy of its earlier iterations and able to move about more covertly as a result. The "brand" of al-Qaeda is an enduring one; as discussed previously in relation to homegrown and lone wolf operatives, the message that the United States and other Western powers are waging a war on Islam is one that continues to resonate with an audience throughout the world. This has allowed them to shift their strategy somewhat—encouraging these lone wolf attacks in the United States, and also taking advantage of an extremely unstable situation in the Middle East to launch attacks against Western interests in those areas.

The events of the Arab Spring have also created a new opportunity for al-Qaeda splinter groups to strengthen, allowing groups that were operating in just eight areas of the Middle East (Afghanistan, Indonesia, Iraq, Lebanon, Nigeria, Pakistan, the Philippines, and Somalia) to establish new footholds in just a few short years in Algeria, Libya, Mali, Mauritania, Sudan, Syria, Tunisia, and Lebanon. Large quantities of weapons, used as part of the civil unrest in many of these areas, have made their way into the hands of al-Qaeda spin-offs, and prison breaks due to regional unrest have allowed former al-Qaeda operatives to make their way back into the network.[24]

The al-Qaeda cells that have popped up in the past few years have largely focused on domestic targets—for example, al-Qaeda in Iraq (AQI) has focused on attacking Shia Muslim populations within that country (though al-Qaeda proper has distanced itself from that

Boko Haram
A radical Islamic group linked to al-Qaeda in the Islamic Maghreb (AQIM) in North Africa; active in Nigeria.

particular sect), and **Boko Haram**, with ties to al-Qaeda in the Islamic Maghreb in Nigeria, has led a campaign of kidnappings and killings in that country.[25] Indeed, in early January 2015, Boko Haram conducted a series of raids on the Nigerian village of Baga, near the border with Chad, resulting in a bloody massacre leaving over 2,000 innocent civilians killed.

There have been some attacks against Western interests perpetrated by those groups—most notably the attacks on the American diplomatic mission and CIA annex in Benghazi, Libya, in September 2012. That particular attack claimed the lives of three Americans and injured ten more. Another group of al-Qaeda-affiliated jihadists from Algeria attacked a British Petroleum facility in January of 2013 in Amenas, Algeria, leaving 37 hostages dead.[26] These remain the exception, rather than the rule, but also illustrate quite clearly the capabilities these groups have to attack Western targets throughout the region.

The continued and current unrest in the Middle East is yet another factor in promoting the successful diffusion of al-Qaeda organizations and philosophy. In late April 2014, al-Qaeda chief Ayman al-Zawahiri (see Figure 15–3) made that clear in an audio recording where he expressed support for the Muslim Brotherhood in the midst of a violent crackdown by the army-backed government in Egypt; he also urged unity among rebels in the fight against Syrian President Bashar al-Assad.[27] He characterized both conflicts as a fight for marginalized Muslims across the globe, stating, "the duty of every Muslim is to deter the aggressor by any means, and especially the oppressed Muslims of the Middle East."[28] Syria in particular has drawn jihadist sympathizers from across the globe to assist in the fight against al-Assad. The fear is that these fighters may become even further radicalized by their experiences and training in Syria, and that al-Qaeda–affiliated jihadists may have access to the large quantities of arms flowing into the country, intended for the rebels.[29] This certainly appears to be the case as the Islamic State became a much more prominent group in 2014. And, on January 7, 2015, terrorist gunmen armed with automatic weapons and having prior military training and experience in Syria and Yemen, attacked the offices of a French satirical newspaper, *Charlie Hebdo,* in Paris. The massacre left twelve people dead, including the editor and cartoonists associated with the newspaper, as well as 11 others injured. The attack was in response to cartoons that radical Muslims believed insulted the Prophet Mohammad published by the magazine over three years prior to the attack. The ensuing manhunt for the terrorists, all French citizens of Middle Eastern descent (Cherif Kouachi, Said Kouachi, and Amedy Coulibaly) over the next two days resulted in a series of bloody encounters with the French police, again resulting in numerous deaths of civilians and police officers as well as the terrorists themselves. The bloody attack shocked the world and marked a significant departure in radical Islamic terrorist tactics from random, suicide attacks aimed at inflicting significant human carnage as observed in the past by al-Qaeda and Hamas operatives, to much more sophisticated, militarily planned attacks with specific targets conducted by trained individuals.

FIGURE 15–3
The late Usama bin Laden (L), head of al-Qaeda, and his then-deputy Ayman al-Zawahiri meeting at an undisclosed location in Afghanistan on November 8, 2001. Now the leader of al-Qaeda, al-Zawahiri was previously involved with directing the affairs of al-Qaeda for nearly a decade. Recently, he sent video messages aimed at changing the tactical practices of the group.

(Ausaf Newspapar/EPA/Newscom)

In addition, in the same recording in which he called for jihadist support in Syria and Egypt, al-Zawahiri also introduced a relatively new terrorist tactic in that region, that of kidnapping and extortion, particularly of Americans. Al-Zawahiri stated that this type of activity should be a primary focus of al-Qaeda affiliates, as they may be useful tools in obtaining money to further the jihadi philosophy and the release of jailed al-Qaeda members in the United States: "I ask Allah the Glorious to help us set free Sheik Omar Abdel-Rahman and the rest of the captive Muslims, and I ask Allah to help us capture from among the Americans and the Westerners to enable us to exchange them for our captives."[30] Sheik Abdul Rahman is the blind Egyptian cleric currently serving a life sentence in the United States from charges stemming from the first bombing attack on the World Trade Center in 1993.

Three parts of eastern Spain were simultaneously hit by radical Islamic terrorist on August 17, 2017: Las Ramblas Boulevard in Barcelona, the resort city of Cambrils on the Mediterranean, and the southern Catalonian town of Alcanar. Each attack was based on the same methodology of either ramming a van into a crowd of people, or detonating a van loaded with explosives. The unsophisticated attacks were definitely planned by a group of individuals to occur at roughly the same time, causing mass carnage. In Barcelona, sixteen people were killed and more than 130 injured; in Cambrils, five men drove a car down a walkway along the beach and plowed into pedestrians, then got out of the car and stabbed other individuals on the walkway. The five suspects, armed with knives and axes were killed by police, and had an association with former al-Qaeda associates in Morocco. However, the Islamic State took responsibility for the attack, revealing again the linkage between individuals with the two radical Islamic movements. And in Alcanar, a house was devastated as police believe that jihadist terrorists were making bombs in the house when they accidently exploded, killing one resident inside.

Sources: Stephen Burgen, Kim Willsher, and Ian Cobain, "Viable Suicide Vest Found in Rubble of Spain Attackers' Bomb Factory," *The Guardian* (August 13, 2017).
Bill Chappell, "What We Know: Multiple Terrorist Attacks Hit Spain," *NPR* (August 18, 2017).
SITE Intel Group, "Amaq News Agency Reported ISIS Responsibility for Barcelona Attack (August 17, 2017). See: https://twitter.com/siteintelgroup/status/898263784833163264/photo/1

This call for increased kidnappings of Westerners certainly signals a new tactical emphasis for the extremists and should be expected to spur increased activity—kidnappings are a relatively easy task for splinter groups to accomplish, requiring few resources compared to large-scale attacks and generating much publicity. Thus far, however, the United States has expressed an unwillingness to negotiate with terrorist organizations in kidnapping situations.

Transportation Hubs and Other Terrorist Targets

Since 2001, much of the attention on the potential for terror attacks has focused on transportation hubs. It is not a problem peculiar to America (see Figure 15–4). Aviation travel in particular has been an emphasis for policy and practice related to terror prevention. Toughened security standards around the globe have been largely successful—commercial aviation is a front-loaded access system, and screenings and security checkpoints have been difficult for would-be terrorists to overcome in the past decade and a half. That's not to say that the system is impenetrable, however. In 2014, a California teenager scaled the fences at San Jose International Airport and climbed into the wheel well of an awaiting jet destined for Hawaii. The fact that he was able to access a commercial jetliner fully undetected raises questions about perimeter security of airports, and suggests that physical access from airport perimeters may be a vulnerability that terrorists might attempt to take advantage of in the future. Airport perimeters generally are the jurisdiction of both local and airport police, but the areas are sprawling; even the relatively small San Jose airport contains nearly six miles of perimeter fencing.[31] Aviation targets have continued to be attractive to terrorists since 9/11, resulting in around 1,104 total deaths, a number that is tragic but does emphasize that airline travel remains a mostly safe endeavor.[32]

Ground transportation targeting by terrorists in the same time period, however, remained a point of easy access for terrorists. Buses and trains were struck 1,800 times between 2001 and 2012, killing just under 4,000 people. Such modes of transportation are notoriously difficult to secure—there are far too many access points along bus routes and in train stations. And while closed caption television security has

FIGURE 15–4
Airport security is not just a domestic concern. Here, a counterterrorism unit practices "taking down" an airplane at the Minsk National Airport in Belarus. The exercise was part of security preparations for the 2014 World Hockey Championship in Minsk.

(Tatyana Zenkovich/Newscom)

proven to be somewhat effective in deterring certain types of attacks, suicide bombers are inherently unconcerned with having their actions traced on camera. Intelligence and security awareness among the general public seem to be the most important factors in deterring such an event.[33]

Another concern for future terror attacks is that of school shootings. While America has certainly seen far too many of those in the recent past, they are not classified as terrorism, per se, largely because they don't seem to spring from any sort of strongly held political or religious ideology. But an attack in Norway in 2011 showed how devastating such an event could be. In that case, right-wing extremist **Anders Behring Breivik** bombed two buildings in Oslo, killing eight people. He then travelled to an island summer camp for youth affiliated with a Norwegian political party and opened fire on teenagers and staff, killing 69, mainly children and teenagers. Another school attack, this one in Toulouse, France, was carried out by an alleged al-Qaeda sympathizer, Mohamed Merah, earlier in 2012. After shooting and killing three French soldiers at close range, he proceeded to a Jewish grade school and killed three children and a rabbi.[34] Both of these attacks illustrate (as does the Newtown school shooting in December 2013) just how easily lone wolf–style attackers can infiltrate schools (or other educational and recreational facilities). Fortunately, these types of **soft targets** have not been utilized extensively by terrorists in the United States. Most of those occurring in the United States have been attributed to individuals with mental and emotional disturbances rather than political or terrorist motivations.

Attacks on random targets also appear to be a new methodology by terrorist individuals and organizations. Though the act of terror itself cannot be considered random, as it is designed to achieve some sort of political or ideological aim, the targets themselves might be unconnected to those ideologies—or might be happened upon by chance. Such is the case with the murder of British soldier Lee Rigby. Rigby was on his way to his barracks after a shift at the Tower of London had ended when he was suddenly hit by a car. The men driving then exited the vehicle and began stabbing and hacking at Rigby in full view of a horrified neighborhood. As cell phone video cameras rolled, Michael Adebolajo and Michael Adebowale attempted to decapitate their victim, then paused to make statements to those with cameras. Adebolajo ranted that the killing was justified as many Muslims had been killed at the hands of British soldiers. The act was extremely violent, mostly captured on video, and the image of Adebolajo standing in front a camera, covered in blood, is particularly unnerving—not only to the public at large, but also to police and security agencies. Britain's intelligence service (MI-5) had long feared an attack such as the one on Rigby: an attack on a victim chosen at random, due only to his affiliation with the military, by lone wolf terrorists using easily obtained and relatively crude weapons, and a sympathy toward al-Qaeda minus all the bureaucracy that comes with actually being an affiliate of that organization.[35] Such an attack is extremely difficult if not impossible to predict, much less prevent. Although British soldiers were encouraged shortly afterward to wear their uniforms only while on-duty, it was an impractical suggestion that quickly faded as the months passed. Even in this country, American soldiers are often seen travelling in airports while in uniform, or congregating at a restaurant for lunch or dinner, seemingly unaware of their potential as victims of an attack.

Another random target for a terror attack was the Westgate shopping mall in Kenya, which was the site of a mass shooting in September 2013. Well-organized members of Somalia's al Shabaab entered the shopping center and began shooting randomly at victims, encouraging Muslims to identify themselves and get out of harm's way. Sixty-three victims were claimed in the attack, at a site that wasn't particularly symbolic or strategic, except that it was located in Kenya—a country that had invaded Somalia in 2011. The barbaric killings of small children and families going about their shopping on a Sunday morning speaks even further to the ruthlessness of modern terrorist groups affiliated with al-Qaeda. No longer concerned about answering to a larger organizational structure or centralized command, new jihadi groups are now free to target whomever they choose, including those innocent individuals who enjoy the embodiments of modern social life, like shopping malls, markets, restaurants, schools, and office centers. Clearly, the new modality of terror now targets people for sheer carnage versus the more common political or social statement of the past.

Anders Behring Breivik
Norwegian ultra-right-wing perpetrator of the July 22, 2011, attacks killing eight people in Oslo, and another 69 more on the island of Utoya, in one of the deadliest mass shootings in history.

Soft target
A military term to describe a non-defended or innocent target—usually refers to innocent civilians; versus a *hard target* that represents armed soldiers, operators, or well-defended locations.

Quick Facts
Low-Tech Terrorist Attacks

Low-tech terrorist attacks appear to be an increasingly popular method for terrorists. These types of attacks allow suspects to fly "under-the-radar" of monitoring federal law enforcement agencies, as no sophisticated supplies or contraband are required for the attack. Further, planning and communication require minimal involvement between actors. Listed below are significant and relatively recent, low-tech attacks:

Stockholm, Sweden, April 7, 2017: Four people were killed when a stolen truck was driven by Rakhmat Akilov into a busy sidewalk fronting a department store.

London, England, March 22, 2017: Khalid Masood rams a rental car into pedestrians on Westminster Bridge, killing four before he shot and killed a policeman on UK Parliament grounds.

Berlin, Germany, December 19, 2016: A stolen truck is used to ram pedestrians at a Christmas market, killing 12.

Nice, France, July 14, 2016: Mohamed Lahouaiej Bouhlel plowed into Bastille Day festivities using a rented 20-ton truck, killing 84 people.

Barcelona, Spain, August 17, 2017: Two simultaneous attacks: One in Barcelona when a jihadist driver drove a van into a crowd on popular Las Ramblas Boulevard killing 16 and injuring 130 more, and in Cambrils, five radical Islamic suspects drove a van down a walkway along the beach, running over civilians and then stabbing them with knives and axes. All five suspects, as well as the driver in the Barcelona attack were killed by police.

Future Attacks on Critical Infrastructure

As discussed in Chapter 12, America is vulnerable to a variety of attacks; however, none is more concerning than a cyber attack on our critical infrastructure. Much of our national infrastructure—including water systems, power grids, gas pipelines, nuclear power functions, and financial and communication networks—was built long before the specter of terrorism was a consideration and contains less-than-desirable defenses against potential attacks by terrorists. There has been much hand-wringing over the possibilities of such assaults, yet relatively few security measures have been taken in regard to these vulnerabilities. In fact, in 2015, the U.S. Department of Homeland Security reported that there had been 295 separate attacks on infrastructure, representing an increase of 20 percent from the previous year.[36] A number of these attacks rose to the level that they could facilitate remote operations—and these are just the attacks that were reported. Many private companies choose not to disclose their attacks in an attempt to limit their vulnerabilities and to maintain their public image.

Many infrastructure companies have been identified with weaknesses such as easy online access to critical operations systems, unsecure or easily guessed passwords (such as 1234) for major controls, and weak credentialing standards. However, experts warn that many industries have become complacent when it comes to the potential for cyber attacks. Better security protocols and isolated (or offline) control systems should be far more common than they currently are—and many believe that it may take a massive breach into U.S. critical infrastructure to spur action.[37] Rather than focusing on attacks that might stem from weapons of mass destruction (WMD), it might be more prudent to assume that the next terrorist attack may be cyber in nature (see Box 15–3).

> **Information Link**
> For more information on predicting the future of terrorism, visit the CNN World website at www.cnn.com/WORLD/. Search the site for articles by correspondent Fareed Zakaria. His GPS podcasts and in-depth analysis of events in the Middle East often provide an excellent analysis of current events and their impact on future terrorist strikes. Read his article entitled, "The Future of the Terrorist Threat to America."

> **Dirty bomb**
> A device or bomb that combines radioactive material with conventional explosives; usually crudely made with the purpose of contaminating a specific area.

Box 15–3
Has the Potential for Weapons of Mass Destruction Been Exaggerated?

In the dialogue that surrounds our discussion and understanding of the potential for future terrorist attacks, weapons of mass destruction figure prominently. Foreign policy has been preoccupied with access to such types of weaponry, including nuclear, chemical, radiological, or biological agents that could be employed to cause mass chaos, death, and destruction. Funding for homeland security projects has been heavily weighted toward preparation for these types of events. Quite understandably so, even a small devices, like a **"dirty bomb"** composed of nuclear waste from an X-ray machine attached to an explosive device like a stick of dynamite or a "pressure

cooker bomb" like the one used in the Boston Marathon incident could have a massive impact on our society. Even though the initial explosion from such a device may not be very deadly, the impending psychological impact on society would be huge, and the immediate area surrounding the blast may be uninhabitable for years.

A recent report from the Bipartisan Policy Center reveals that since September 11, 2001, no domestic Islamic terror organization or individual has gained access to or used any type of weapon of mass destruction (WMD). Foreign governments, such as the regimes in Syria and Iraq, may have used chemical weaponry against its citizens, but such events have not translated to a transnational or international terror attack. That doesn't mean that preparations for such an attack should be abandoned—just that the main focus of homeland security should not be on such an event. For example, the same report from the Bipartisan Policy Center also noted that smaller terrorist attacks are becoming more deadly. As such, perhaps resources should be funneled more proportionately toward identifying and rooting out small terror cells or lone wolf terrorists increasingly capable of death and destruction with fewer resources than would be required for a WMD attack.

WMD preparations, then, should be focused into two areas: Public health preparedness to deal with the fallout from any one of these types of attacks, and in strengthening the nation's critical infrastructure to both eliminate weaknesses that could be exploited by WMD-style attacks and to increase resiliency in case of a catastrophic terrorist event.[38]

▲ It's a worst-case scenario: A smoke plume rises over a computer-generated image of a city where a dirty bomb explodes.

(National Geographic Channel)

How prepared do you really think the United States is for a major terrorist attack involving a "dirty bomb" that might contain chemical, biological, or radiological elements?

The Role of Modern Media in Terrorism

Terrorism would not exist without the media. In each of the above examples of terrorist attacks and trends, the media transmitted the images from the attacks almost immediately—sending images that were horrific in nature around the globe and frightening audiences the world over. Such is the intent of terrorism—to cause terror on a global scale, and to intimidate or coerce a population. None of these things can be accomplished without the help of the media—populations cannot be intimidated if the news of the event meant to intimidate them does not reach them. As such, modern terrorism is essentially a media phenomenon—both transmitting the news of such events to the public and influencing the behavior of the terrorists themselves. For example, al-Qaeda literally had a media advisor: American-born Adam Gadahn. Gadahn advised the organization on strategies to maximize media exposure, including timing releases of videos strategically after elections and how to exploit the coverage of the ten-year anniversary of September 11 in 2011. He also offered Usama Bin Laden analysis of the various news networks in the United States, criticizing Fox News and mentioning the perceived neutrality of MSNBC.[39]

The news media has also stoked feelings of fear and apprehension after terrorist attacks. On the one hand, it's what audiences demand, to a certain extent; on the other hand, it plays directly into the goals of the terrorist, serving as a mouthpiece for groups looking to instill fear into consumers of media. President Juan Manuel Santos of Colombia said in 2012, "I'm not saying, and be careful not to misinterpret me, that terrorism is the media's fault. No. But terrorism thrives on generating terror."[40] As longtime news anchor and reporter Dan Rather stated, it's not that President Santos expected the media to turn its back on a major story. Rather gave the example of how newspapers in Mexico frequently printed photographs of decapitated and dismembered victims of drug cartels on the front page of its newspapers, effectively turning them into a propaganda tool designed to scare a population into submission.[41] Additionally, the news media can affect individual terrorist behavior, giving them tactical information in ongoing situations. In one case, during an airline hijacking, the BBC reported that they thought the standoff was about to be resolved, due to the "slackening will of the terrorists." The hijackers, hearing this, actually killed the pilot of the airline they had overtaken and threw his body onto the tarmac in full view of the cameras to send a message that, indeed, their will was not "slackening."[42]

As a result, Dan Rather recommends that news organizations tread carefully and emphasize the human elements of any terror attack—for instance, focusing less on the gruesome details and more on the small acts that prove resiliency of the population under attack, like the four-year-old in the Westgate Mall attack in Nigeria who stood up to terrorists who injured his mother, or the scores of volunteers at the Boston Marathon in 2013 who rushed to the aid of the injured, saving lives with their quick response.

Rather also cautions that news organizations fill their reporting on terror attacks with context as they make editorial decisions about what images should or should not be shown.[43] For example, in the killing of Lee Rigby, many British media outlets showed unedited video footage of the savage attacks—giving the two perpetrators exactly what they had hoped for: a global audience for their message of jihad. Thousands of viewers and media watchdogs complained: Was it necessary to show a near-beheading of a man live on television? Perhaps the networks could have taken a more intellectual approach to the awful attack; editing their images, asking if everything they showed was a critical part of their reporting, and giving historical perspectives, carefully checking facts, and again—reporting on the information that serves the public, as opposed to unwittingly aiding the terrorists' cause.

The events of the Boston Marathon highlighted not how the media can be manipulated by the terrorists, but rather how the media can mislead the public. In the hours after that attack, many news outlets pulled their information from Twitter, taking information that ordinary citizens tweeted from what they heard on police scanners or from what they thought they saw or heard. The problem with this scenario is that police scanners rely on tips from the general public or investigational leads from law enforcement that are in the middle of an investigation—in other words, bits and pieces of information that are not confirmed and based on unreliable sources and partial facts. Nonetheless, in the fight to be the first to share information about the Boston Marathon bombing, many news agencies ran with unverified information—with some outlets erroneously reporting the capture of a suspect long before that was the case, as well as an additional bombing at a nearby library that never happened, the discovery of five more bombs that didn't exist at the site of the attack, and that cell phone service had been shut down in the immediate area around the bombing site, when, in fact, it had not.[44] These errors prompted President Barack Obama to make a strong statement aimed at the media following the arrest of Dzhokhar Tsarnaev: "In this age of instant reporting and tweets and blogs, there's a temptation to latch on to any bit of information, sometimes to jump to conclusions. But when a tragedy like this happens ... it's important that we do this right."[45] This will be a continuing challenge for all media in the future: covering terrorist attacks intelligently and factually, serving the needs of the public as opposed to those of the terrorists, and sifting through social media to uncover facts rather than headlines. (See Figure 15–5.)

FIGURE 15–5
The media's role should be to report the news, accurately and fairly, especially during terrorist events. Recently, however, the media has been criticized for being too sensational during such events. For instance, in their rush to grab headlines during the 2013 Boston Marathon bombing, the media all too often reported on the victim's injuries and the "gore" of the event versus accurately reporting the facts of the case to the public.
(Charles Krupa/AP Images)

Strategy, Policy, and Beyond

Given the history of terrorism, the current paradigm of Middle East unrest, and the always volatile, fluid nature of the issues and players at stake, it stands to reason that there is no one-size-fits-all approach to terrorism prevention. Attacking and destroying the command, control, and communications functions of al-Qaeda have certainly stemmed their capability to implement a large-scale attack, but has splintered the group geographically, allowing for the growth of ruthless Islamic State groups and hard-to-detect lone wolf operatives. U.S. counterterrorism success requires that a long-term strategy must be employed to address threats posed by future generations of terrorists. Based on our current understanding of the issues surrounding terrorism, the United States has much work to do beyond its current counterterror efforts.

Reevaluate intelligence programs that collect mass amounts of data. Much time and energy is expended by the National Security Agency on the collection of phone records and other types of mass data. However, a report released in early 2014 shows that this type of data analysis "has had no discernible impact on preventing acts of terrorism" and that more traditional law enforcement and investigative methods have been more effective at foiling terror plots.[46]

Ensure that investigations, interrogations, and operations are in line with current human rights practices. Drone strikes that kill innocent bystanders, Guantanamo refugees who have been long cleared for repatriation to their home countries, and allegations of torture during interrogation further stoke the flames of extremist hatred toward the United States. American counterterrorism policy should recognize that drone usage should be overseen carefully, with a centralized program that can be independently evaluated regularly. Guantanamo detainees who are being held indefinitely should be tried in court and handled per the outcome of their cases; to continue to hold suspected terrorists without legal standing is problematic for the United States, a democratic nation that prides itself on the concepts of fundamental fairness, innocent until proven guilty, and justice.

Continue to refine emergency response plans to adapt to smaller-scale incidents. Although the response to the Boston Marathon bombings looked to be well coordinated, the closure of Boston Logan Airport and the downtown areas led to absolute paralysis within the city. The response may have shown future terrorists that even a relatively small—though tragic—attack has a major impact. Emergency plans should consider that inducing complete paralysis in a city is perhaps overreaction, and that a culture of resilience—even during the investigation and apprehension of subjects—should be emphasized.[47] As important, the media must report terrorist incidents honestly and without their often weak and politically biased analysis. Accurately reporting the scale of an attack as well as the response by local, state and federal authorities often provides calm midst a disastrous situation. So-called "fake news" has no place in the reporting of terrorist incidents. (See Box 15–4.)

The Middle East should be carefully and continuously monitored, especially the problematic countries like Iran and Syria. The United States should constantly evaluate the leadership and stability within Middle East nations. In particular, the tenor of leadership within Syria and Iran are of immediate importance. Both countries have historically "meddled" in the politics of their neighbors, causing disruptions and civil wars. Further, the leadership in Iran has been especially aggressive against U.S. interests in the area. Iran's movement toward nuclear power, and hence weapons of mass destruction, poses a serious threat to long-term stability in the region. In Syria, the flow of arms into this volatile country poses additional problems for the future. Many of these weapons could easily fall into the hands of jihadi fighters previously in Iraq and Afghanistan. Care must be taken to identify and track foreign jihadi fighters who have travelled to Syria to assist rebel factions. Historically, the backbone of al-Qaeda emerged in the 1980s as similar warriors who had fought in Afghanistan and Bosnia returned to their home countries in the Middle East.[48] The stage is now set in Syria for the emergence of a similar situation with Islamic State fighters.

Box 15-4
Fake News, the Media, and Terrorism

By Jennifer Davis-Lamm

(Amer Ghazzal/Alamy Stock Photo)

The term "fake news" became something of a sensation in early 2017, thanks to U.S. President Donald Trump's regular use of the phrase. But beyond political talking points and comedy jabs, the phrase is actually relevant when it comes to some very serious issues—including terrorism. Inaccurate reporting, bold claims, and incorrect tweets by public figures can have profound effects during times of crisis.

Anti-immigration rhetoric is one area that can be fueled by erroneous information or "fake news." For instance, in February of 2017, President Trump suggested at a rally in Florida that Sweden's openness to immigration led to a terror attack in the country the night before. In fact, such an attack had not occurred. Pundits accused Trump's speech of inflaming anti-immigrant and anti-Muslim views in the United States that many believe are linked to a rise in anti-Muslim hate crimes in the country.[49].

However, an attack in Sweden in April 2017 (just four months after President Trump's statements) that killed four people, was indeed, carried out by a foreign alien and asylum seeker.

In the London attacks that targeted pedestrians on the Westminster Bridge in 2017, "fake news" that was picked up by a reputable news source and distributed as part of their reporting, named the wrong suspect in the attack. The same thing happened in Dallas, Texas, when five police officers were killed in July of 2016. The Dallas Police Department erroneously named a "person of interest" and distributed his photo, which was immediately further distributed in the local media. Given the intensity and emotion behind the shooting, the named "person of interest" could have been harmed as a result of the mistake—despite the fact that he had no links to the attack.

Additionally, "fake news" can be used for propaganda purposes by terrorist groups. During the 2017 London attacks, Fox News claimed that "one man can shut down a city," which is a potentially valuable recruiting statement for a terrorist organization. However, London generally carried on as usual that day, with only one tube (underground subway) station closed and aboveground street closures remaining localized to the actual incident.

"Fake news" has influenced elections, political opinions, and social media timelines—but the ways that it may mislead the public during terror events erodes trust in sources of information vital to public safety, and unfortunately, at times supports and informs terrorist propaganda. As a result, "fake news" remains a concern for media outlets, law enforcement, government, and private citizens.

What role do you think "fake news" might play in facilitating terrorism?

Focus on individuals, as well as known terrorist groups. The United States should focus on the pace and trajectory of the radicalization and recruitment of terrorists who may act as lone wolves, directing intelligence resources and identifying at-risk individuals using law enforcement data and other known risk factors.

Engage the public. Complacency has again become common since the September 11, 2001, attacks. A nation once on high alert has settled into routine, trudging through airport security without much thought about why such measures are necessary. However, the Boston Marathon attack brought to light a number of missed opportunities for friends and family of the perpetrators to report on suspicious behavior and potentially prevent the attacks that left three people dead and injured nearly 300 others. Smartphone applications that make "if you see something, say something" programs easy for users have been developed and should be adopted and promoted in major metropolitan areas.

Evaluate U.S. progress in counterterrorism strategies in the years since September 11, 2001. The United States should hold public congressional hearings that address the following questions:

- Do the various components of U.S. counterterrorism strategy match the shape of the threat today, and are we monitoring threats both domestically and internationally to our nation?

- Are all of these components being implemented? And with what success, or is government bureaucracy and fractionalization between agencies at various governmental levels thwarting coordination of effort?

- Is the nation absorbing the institutional lessons learned since 2001, or are our intelligence failures particularly continuing today?

- Is the government spending money in the right places and getting the most "bang for its buck" in developing an infrastructure that is capable of preventing and responding to terrorism, or are we continuing to throw money at programs that yield very little in terms of effectiveness?

- Are we continually thinking about the future? What is missing from our counterterrorism strategy and can we be flexible and nimble enough to address new threats, new groups, and new types of attacks, particularly those that might be less traditional in nature, like cyber attacks and the use of "dirty bombs"?[50]

Reflecting on the earlier chapters of this book, we learned that terrorism attacks the very fabric of our society, destroying the mutual trust, respect, and security on which we all rely on to communicate with each other, conduct commerce and business, and most important, understand and respect cultural, social, and religious differences. Terrorism is emotive as well; it forces each of us to experience our own frailty ... to not only preserve our basic instinct for survival and security, but also to cluster around those who share our own beliefs, culture, and religion. Fear is the most primal and powerful of human emotions. Indeed, the very word "terrorism" evokes fear and the emotional response to protect our own, to fight for our own culture, religion, and personal identity. When we react in such a manner, we see things only through our own "rose-colored glasses"; we become **ethnocentric**, believing that our own culture is superior to all others. The most troubling perspective associated with terrorism is not the next attack, but rather how we as a nation and a society react to the next major incident. Will we be more willing to give up those individual liberties and personal safeguards that define our way of life in the folly of additional security? Will our fear be so gripping that we will no longer venture outside the confines of our own homes and cities? Will we be so afraid as to not congregate in mass for fear of another bombing? Or will we be strong enough to embrace those tenets of our nation that have endured the test of time? Remembering that terrorism often targets innocent civilians in an overt attempt to create fear and change governmental policy, it will be the manner in which we cope with the next major attack that will define whether or not terrorism succeeds. Historically, terrorism is a relatively minor "blip" on the litany of incidents that have killed, maimed, and injured mankind across our globe. We stand not on the precipice of crisis and disaster, but rather on the rock of democracy that yields diplomacy and rationality, and most important, the enduring hope of freedom, respect, and human dignity for all mankind. We recall the words of President Franklin Delano Roosevelt facing such a dilemma years ago: "The only thing that we have to fear is fear itself—nameless, unreasoning, unjustified terror which paralyzes needed efforts to convert retreat into advance."[51]

Ethnocentric
The belief that one's own culture is superior to all others; often contributes to fear of other people from other cultures.

Chapter Summary

SUMMARY BY LEARNING OBJECTIVE

1. **Describe broad trends in terrorism, including general statistics about frequency, location, and targets of attacks.**

   The number of terrorist attacks in the United States has declined since 2001, though fatal attacks have increased slightly since 2008; explosive devices remained the main types of weapons used, and over half of attacks were aimed at damaging property. Attacks perpetrated by individuals are also on the rise.

2. **Elaborate on the rise of homegrown and lone wolf terrorists and their weapons usage.**

   Homegrown terrorists are American citizens or legal residents who have become radicalized either on their own or through some form of recruitment by the Islamic State. Increasingly, they act as "lone wolves," allowing them to operate under the radar. Such terrorists are more likely to use crude or easily obtained weaponry and may communicate with terrorist organizations online or simply view materials of interest that have been posted by terrorist cells.

3. **Discuss how al-Qaeda has been splintered and what the effects of that phenomenon might be.**

   U.S. campaigns against al-Qaeda have been successful in killing much of the leadership; however, this has had the unintended effect of decentralizing the groups and allowing them to operate free of bureaucracy, and in some cases, free of any type of rigid operational codes or accountability. This has allowed for militant groups to pop up in areas where conflict is rife and is also responsible for the expansion of the "lone wolf" phenomenon.

4. **Identify targets currently favored by terrorists, as well as future means of attack.**

Terrorists still target transportation hubs, including both air and ground travel. Some newer trends, however, include school shootings, seemingly random targeting, and attacks on critical infrastructure.

5. **Discuss the role of modern media in terrorism.**

The media must tread a thin line between unwittingly assisting the terrorists in their propaganda efforts and informing the public. Careful fact-checking plus emphasis on the human element and broad context should outweigh the impulse for media outlets to show graphic images and publish unverified information.

6. **Describe policies and strategies that might be implemented in counterterrorism in the future.**

Evaluate intelligence programs that collect mass data, line up with globally accepted human rights practices, refine emergency response plans so that they are appropriate for smaller-scale attacks, monitor the situation in Syria carefully, focus on individuals; engage the public in counterterrorism efforts; and evaluate the United States' progress as relevant to counterterrorism.

REVIEW QUESTIONS

1. What do the trends in terrorist activities tell us?
2. What is so dangerous about lone wolf operatives?
3. Describe how fractionalization of al-Qaeda will impact counterterror activities in the future.
4. How has Middle East unrest energized jihadist groups in the past several years?
5. What type of terrorist targets do you think will be most prevalent in the future?
6. Explain the thin line that media organizations must walk when reporting on terrorism.
7. What additional counterterrorism policies or strategies should be adopted to address new issues and paradigms in terrorism?

CRITICAL THINKING EXERCISES

1. **Interactive Terrorism Map.** Visit the website at www.globalincidentmap.com and view the global incident map. Click on one of the flashing items in the Middle East. How many of the incidents represent threats to critical infrastructure (oil and gas wells or pipelines) in the area? How many involve threats from radical Islamic groups? Now click on one of the flashing points in the United States or Europe. Discuss the above questions for the new area. Finally, notice that the entire map is delivered in real-time for subscribers. As a free user, the map is time-delayed 24 to 48 hours. Notice how many of the incidents are "hoaxes," or threats that never materialized. As a class, discuss the value of having real-time access to such a map for response measures, deployment of personnel, identifying trend activity, analytic examination of specific threats, research, and the like.

2. **What is a "dirty bomb?"** Visit the BBC News documentary and in-depth report on dirty bombs at http://news.bbc.co.uk/2/shared/spl/hi/in_depth/dirty_bomb/html/1.stm. Review the blast scenarios and discuss the potential of such an event occurring within the homeland of the United States. What can be done to predict and prevent such an event from occurring? Discuss the social and economic impact of such an event as well as the long-term effect on the psyche of the American public. Now, visit the National Geographic site on Naked Science: Dirty Bomb Attack at http://channel.nationalgeographic.com/galleries/episode-dirty-bomb-attack/at/4252_naked_science_dirty_bomb_attack-09_04700300-4934/. If a worst-nightmare scenario ever occurred, do you think that the U.S. government and public would continue to support individual freedoms as defined in the

Constitution, or would there be calls to abandon the 200-year-old document in favor of one that is more realistic in a nuclear age threatened by radical terrorists? Discuss this question as a class.

NOTES

1. National Consortium for the Study of Terrorism and Responses to Terrorism (START). *Integrated United States Security Database (IUSSD): Data on the Terrorist Attacks in the United States Homeland, 1970 to 2011.* December 2012, www.start.umd.edu/sites/default/files/files/publications/START_IUSSDDataTerroristAttacksUS_1970-2011.pdf.

2. National Consortium for the Study of Terrorism and Response to Terrorism. Global Terrorism Database, retrieved April 3, 2017 from www.start.umd.edu/gtd/search/Results.aspx?page=12&casualties_type=b&casualties_max=&start_yearonly=2001&end_yearonly=2015&dtp2=all&country=217&expanded=no&charttype=line&chart=overtime&ob=City&od=asc#results-table.

3. Ibid.

4. Ibid.

5. Institute for Economics and Peace, "Global Terrorism Index 2016," http://visionofhumanity.org/app/uploads/2017/02/Global-Terrorism-Index-2016.pdf.

6. Anti-Defamation League, "Murder and Extremism in the United States in 2016: An Anti-Defamation League Report," 2017, retrieved April 21, 2017 from www.adl.org/sites/default/files/documents/MurderAndExtremismInUS2016.pdf.

7. Institute for Economics and Peace, "Global Terrorism Index 2015," "Global Terrorism Index 2015," http://economicsandpeace.org/wp-content/uploads/2015/11/Global-Terrorism-Index-2015.pdf.

8. Institute for Economics and Peace.

9. Institute for Economics and Peace, "Global Terrorism Index 2015," http://economicsandpeace.org/wp-content/uploads/2015/11/Global-Terrorism-Index-2015.pdf.

10. For more information, refer to the source for this box. See Joel Warner, "How Aaron Clauset Discovered a Pattern Behind Terrorist Attacks ... And What It Told Him," *Denver Westword News*, July 4, 2013, www.westword.com/2013-07-04/news/adam-clauset-terrorism-formula/full/.

11. Institute for Economics and Peace, "Global Terrorism Index 2016," http://visionofhumanity.org/app/uploads/2017/02/Global-Terrorism-Index-2016.pdf.

12. Ally Pregulman and Emily Burke, "Homegrown Terrorism," *AQAM Futures Project Case Studies Series,* April 2012, http://csis.org/files/publication/120425_Pregulman_AQAMCaseStudy7_web.pdf.

13. Katherine Q. Seelye, "Bombing Suspect Cites Islamic Extremist Beliefs as Motive," *New York Times*, April 23, 2013, www.nytimes.com/2013/04/24/us/boston-marathon-bombing-developments.html?hp&pagewanted=all&_r=1&.

14. Pregulman and Burke, "Homegrown Terrorism."

15. Brendan I. Koerner, "Why ISIS Is Winning the Social Media War," April 2016, *Wired Magazine*, www.wired.com/2016/03/isis-winning-social-media-war-heres-beat/.

16. Frank Gardner, "How Do Terrorists Communicate?" *British Broadcasting Company*, November 2, 2013, www.bbc.com/news/world-24784756.

17. Robert W. Taylor, Eric J. Fritsch, and John Liederbach, *Digital Crime and Digital Terrorism* (Upper Saddle River, NJ: Pearson, 2014).

18. Pregulman and Burke, "Homegrown Terrorism."

19. Evan Perez and LeeAnn Caldwell, "Holder Fears 'Lone Wolf' Terrorist Attack, Doesn't Want TSA Armed," *CNN*, November 5, 2014, www.cnn.com/2013/11/05/politics/holder-terror-snowden-interview/.

20. Sarah Teich, "Trends and Developments in Lone Wolf Terrorism in the Western World: An Analysis of Terrorist Attacks and Attempted Attacks by Islamic Extremists," *International Institute for Counterterrorism*, October 2013, www.ict.org.il/LinkClick.aspx?fileticket=qAv1zIPJlGE%3D&tabid=66.

21. Ramon Spaaij, *Understanding Lone Wolf Terrorism: Global Patterns, Motivations and Prevention* (Heidelberg, London, New York: Springer, 2012).

22. National Security Program, "Jihadist Terrorism: A Threat Assessment," *Homeland Security Project*, Bipartisan Policy Center, September 2013, http://bipartisanpolicy.org/ sites/default/files/Jihadist%20Terrorism-A%20Threat%20Assesment_0.pdf.

23. New America Foundation, National Security Studies Program, "Pakistan Strikes: Leaders Killed," July 2, 2013, http://natsec.newamerica.net/drones/pakistan/leaders-killed.

24. National Security Program, "Jihadist Terrorism."

25. Carl Ungerer, "Beyond Bin Laden: Future Trends in Terrorism," *Australian Strategic Policy Institute*, December 2011, www.aspi.org.au/publications/ beyond-bin-laden-future-trends-in-terrorism/Beyond_bin_Laden_v2.pdf.

26. Sri Jegarajah, "Experts Had Warned of Attack in Amenas Gas Plant," *CNBC*, January 27, 2013, www.cnbc.com/id/100410586.

27. Reuters, "Al-Qaeda Leader Urges Muslims to Kidnap Westerners," *New York Daily News* April 26, 2014, www.nydailynews.com/news/world/al-qaeda-chief-urges-muslims-kidnap -westerners-americans-article-1.1769947#ixzz30axT084k.

28. Reuters, "Al-Qaeda Chief Ayman Al-Zawahiri Calls For More Kidnappings In Interview Tape," *Huffington Post*, April 25, 2014, www.huffingtonpost.com/2014/04/26/ayman-al -zawahiri-tape_n_5217738.html.

29. National Security Program, "Jihadist Terrorism."

30. Ibid.

31. Holly Yann, "Teen Stowaway Raises Questions about Airport Security," *CNN* April 22, 2014,www.cnn.com/2014/04/22/travel/plane-stowaway-security/.

32. Institute for Economics and Peace, "Global Terrorism Index 2015," http://economicsand- peace .org/wp-content/uploads/2015/11/Global-Terrorism-Index-2015.pdf.

33. Matthew Hardwood, "Trends in Terrorism Targets," *International Centre for Crowd Management and Security Studies*, August 9, 2012, www.iccmss.co.uk/2012/08/ surface-transport-vulnerabilities/.

34. Edward Cody, "Mohammed Merah: Face of the New Terrorism," *Washington Post*, March 22, 2013, www.washingtonpost.com/world/europe/mohammed-merah-face-of-the -new-terrorism/2012/03/22/gIQA2kL4TS_story.html.

35. Tom Whitehead, "Woolwich Killing: The Random Attack Has Always Been MI5's Greatest Fear," *Telegraph* (London), May 22, 2013, www.telegraph.co.uk/news/uknews/terrorism -in-the-uk/10074658/Woolwich-killing-the-random-attack-has-always-been-MI5s-greatest -fear.html.

36. Eduard Kovacs, "Critical Infrastructure Incidents Increased in 2015: ICS- CERT," January 20, 2016, *Security Week*, www.securityweek.com/ critical-infrastructure-incidents-increased-2015-ics-cert.

37. David Goldman, "Hacker Hits on U.S. Power and Nuclear Targets Spiked in 2012," *CNN Money*, January 9, 2013, http://money.cnn.com/2013/01/09/technology/security/ infrastructure-cyberattacks/.

38. For more information on this subject, refer to the sources of this box item: National Security Program, "Jihadist Terrorism: A Threat Assessment," *Homeland Security Project, Bipartisan Policy Center*, September 2013, http://bipartisanpolicy.org/ sites/default/files/Jihadist%20Terrorism-A%20Threat%20Assesment_0.pdf; and Rachel Oswald, "Expert Report: Talk of WMD Terror Threat to U.S. Has Been 'Overheated,'" *Global Security Newswire*, September 9, 2013, www.nti.org/gsn/article/ new-expert-report-says-talk-wmd-terror-threat-us-has-been-overheated/.

39. David Ignatius, "How al-Qaeda Tried to Control the Media," *Washington Post*, March 20, 2013, www.washingtonpost.com/opinions/al-qaedas-attempts-to-control-the -media/2012/03/20/gIQAbu0EQS_story.html.

40. Dan Rather, "Media's Balancing Act with Terrorism," *CNN*, September 11, 2012, www.cnn.com/2012/09/11/opinion/rather-media-and-terrorism/index.html.

41. Ibid.

42. Anna North, "How Media Coverage Influences Terrorism," *BuzzFeed*, April 19, 2013, www.buzzfeed.com/annanorth/how-media-coverage-influences-terrorism.

43. Dan Rather, "Media's Balancing Act with Terrorism."

44. Sabrina Siddiqui, "Boston Bombings Reveal Media Full Of Mistakes, False Reports," *Huffington Post*, April 22, 2013, www.huffingtonpost.com/2013/04/22/boston-bombings -media-mistakes_n_3135105.html.

45. Ibid.

46. Ellen Nakashima, "NSA Phone Record Collection Does Little to Prevent Terrorist Attacks, Group Says," *Washington Post*, January 12, 2014, www.washingtonpost.com/world/ national-security/nsa-phone-record-collection-does-little-to-prevent-terrorist-attacks -group-says/2014/01/12/8aa860aa-77dd-11e3-8963-b4b654bcc9b2_story.html.

47. National Security Program, "Jihadist Terrorism."

48. Ibid.

49. Claire Foran, "Donald Trump and the Rise of Anti-Muslim Violence," *Atlantic*, September 22, 2016, www.theatlantic.com/politics/archive/2016/09/ trump-muslims-islamophobia-hate-crime/500840/.

50. Ibid.

51. Franklin Delano Roosevelt, *First Inaugural Speech*, Washington, D.C., March 4, 1933.

Glossary

442nd Regimental Combat Team A Japanese-American unit that served in the European Theater, consistently serving with valor. Members of the 442nd were Japanese-American volunteers from Hawaii and the internment camps. The 442nd became the most heavily decorated unit of its size in military history. See Japanese-American internment camps.

Abu Bakr The first Caliph or ruler of Arabia and the leader of the Muslim community after the death of the Prophet Muhammad.

Abu Bakr al-Baghdadi The current leader of the Islamic State; while his true identity is unknown, his code name is Abu Bakr al-Bghdadi.

Abu Sayaff Abu Sayaff is the most violent of the separatist groups operating in the Philippines. They use terror as fundraising tool and to promote their jihadist movement. Their most common money-producing tactic may be kidnapping and collecting ransom.

Accelerator sanctions For certain types of crimes, such as hate-based and terrorism, the law provides more severe sentences for persons convicted of them. It is how society demonstrates its revulsion about such crimes.

Active supporters Participate in fund-raising and other activities, such as providing safe houses, medical care, and transportation. They are fully aware of their relationship with the terrorist organization. They may or may not be known to those outside of the terrorist organization.

Ad hoc A Latin phrase meaning "for this." Ad hoc generally means a process, decision, or solution that applies only to "this" particular situation and does not have a wider/general application.

Agro-terrorism Malicious acts directed at the agricultural or food supply system in the United States.

Ahmad Shuqayri The first head of the Palestinian Congress in 1964.

Al Shabaab A radical Islamic group affiliated with al-Qaeda operating in the country of Somalia.

Al-Aqsa Martyrs Brigade One of the first Palestinian terrorist groups to move from a secular to a radical Islamic ideology.

al-Qaeda Arabic, "The Base." Foreign terrorist organization (FTO) led by Usama bin Laden until his death in 2011; currently led by Ayman al-Zawahiri. He avows continued jihad against Crusader America and its supporters.

Al-Qaeda in Iraq (AQI) The primary precursor entity that became the current Islamic State

Alien A foreign national living in the United States.

All-hazards model The concept that there are similar aspects to planning and responding to a catastrophe or emergency event caused by either natural or man-made origins.

All-hazards National preparedness is based on the all-hazards approach. This approach uses a capabilities-based preparedness to prevent, protect against, respond to, and recover from terrorist attacks, major disasters (natural, technological, or human caused), and all other emergencies.

Allah u Akbar Arabic, Allah (God) is great or Allah is the greatest.

Allah Arabic, literally "The God"; the Islamic God.

American Civil Liberties Union (ACLU) A national organization (primarily composed of attorneys and legal scholars) focused on defending and preserving the rights and liberties guaranteed to individuals within the United States Constitution.

American Red Cross Humanitarian organization originally developed in 1881 by Clara Barton; modeled after the International Red Cross in Europe to provide aid to civilians during emergencies and disasters.

Anarchist An anarchist believes in the political theory of anarchy. Pure anarchy is characterized by the absence of a central government and strong cooperation among members of a society. Anarchists seek to overthrow rulers and governments. Practical anarchists recognize the impossibility of actually achieving pure anarchy. Consequentially, they are willing to settle for a weak government that is minimally intrusive in the lives of its citizens.

Anarchist wave Roughly 1880–1920, anti-authoritarian and revolutionary concept that in pure form exists as a society without any government.

Anders Behring Breivik Norwegian ultra-right-wing perpetrator of the July 22, 2011, attacks killing eight people in Oslo, and another 69 more on the island of Utoya, in one of the deadliest mass shootings in history.

Andrew MacDonald See Dr. William L. Pierce.

Animal Liberation Front (ALF) ALF rejects the institutional position that animals are property and can be used as test subjects by corporations. ALF members or sympathizers may "liberate" animals and find "good homes" for them or return them to the wild and damage or destroy associated research facilities.

Anthrax Spore-forming bacterium that is often "weaponized" or genetically altered to be more deadly.

Anti-colonial wave Prevalent during 1920s–1960s. Colonies sought independence from major powers controlling them.

Anti-terrorism Defensive actions taken to reduce the vulnerability of people and property to terrorist acts, including rapid containment by local military and civilian forces.

Anwar al-Awlaki Born in New Mexico to Yemeni parents. Became radicalized Islamic cleric linked to 19 terrorist operations. Killed in Yemen by drone in 2011.

Arab Spring Refers to a series of recent revolutions beginning in December 2010 in Tunisia aimed at increasing individual rights and freedoms for the people living in Middle Eastern countries.

Arab Spring The Arab Spring began in December 2010, when people in Tunisia demonstrated in cities across their country for social, political, and economic reforms. They also demanded the resignation of their president, which he did in January 2011. The example excited people in countries in that region, and soon demonstrations seemed to be occurring everywhere. In Syria, it led to open warfare to remove the president and implement reforms.

Army of God Anti-abortion group, underground Christians, who produced manual on how to attack clinics.

Asymmetrical Warfare In warfare, it is the attempt to circumvent or undermine an opposing force's superior strengths while exploiting its weaknesses. Asymmetrical warfare often has a major psychological impact, such as shock or fear and often involves the use of nontraditional strategy, tactics, and weapons. Examples include the use of guerilla tactics against a powerful conventional army or flying hijacked planes into buildings.

Aum Shinrikyo An apocalyptic Christian group in Japan that became the first terrorist organization to use chemical warfare. In 1995, five two-man teams released sarin, a quick-acting nerve agent, in a Tokyo subway system.

Balfour Declaration A formal letter from British Foreign Secretary Alfred Balfour in 1917 signaling British support for the development of a new, sovereign Jewish state in the Middle East.

Bekaa Valley Located in Lebanon, it has perhaps the longest continuous history as an operational space for terrorist groups.

Bermuda Triangle of Terrorism The hundreds of competing definitions of terrorism.

Bill of Rights   The collective name for the first ten amendments of the U.S. Constitution, explicitly enumerating such freedoms of religion, speech, a free press, freedom to assemble, the right to bear arms, freedom from unreasonable searches and seizures, security and privacy of personal effects, freedom from warrantless searches not based on probable cause, guarantee of a speedy trial and judgment by an impartial jury, prohibition of cruel and unusual punishments including torture, prohibition of double jeopardy, and the guarantee to live without unnecessary governmental intrusion.

Bitcoin   It is a new currency that was invented in 2009 by someone using the alias of Satoshi Nakamoto. It is a digital coin that doesn't rely on a central bank. You can buy and sell bitcoins at exchanges on the Internet.

Black September Organization   The Palestinian nationalist group that massacred members of the Israeli delegation at the 1972 Summer Olympics in Munich, Germany.

Black Swan events   Black Swan events are so unique, so far from the norm, and so different from all other events and patterns that analysts will be unable to forecast them.

Blackout   The loss of electrical power in a specific area.

Blind pigs   In modern use, unlicensed bars that sell alcohol to patrons after legal bars have closed. Gambling and prostitution are activities in some blind pigs.

Boko Haram   A radical Islamic group linked to al-Qaeda in the Islamic Maghreb (AQIM) in North Africa; active in Nigeria.

Boston Tea Party   December 16, 1773, tax protest when colonists, disguised as Indians, threw tea from ships into Boston Harbor.

Boundless Informant   A real-time global surveillance software tracker used by the NSA that details and maps the metadata it received from computers, phone systems, and the Internet.

Bourgeoisie   The wealthy upper class, those who were property owners.

Brownout   A drop in electrical voltage to a specific area.

CBRNE   Acronym for Chemical, Biological, Radiological, Nuclear, and Explosive.

CI/KRs   Acronym in reference to Critical Infrastructure and Key Resource(s) identified within the National Infrastructure Protection Plan (NIPP).

Cadre   A cadre is a group of core members that form a dependable nucleus within a terrorist organization.

Caliph   The political leader or head of a caliphate or Muslim state; a successor to the Prophet Muhammad.

Caliphate   An Islamic state where the political and religious leader are the same.

Capitalism   Economies that focus on competition in a free market enterprise, valuing the ownership of private property to determine wealth.

Carlos Marighella   A Brazilian revolutionary who expressed the concept of guerrilla movements stemming from urban areas. His book, The *Minimanual of the Urban Guerrilla,* was very influential in Latin American leftist movements.

Catastrophe   A catastrophe is an incident that directly or indirectly affects large portions or all of a country and requires national and sometimes international responses.

Category 4 hurricane   Hurricanes are characterized as being one of five categories. Category 1 is the least severe and has winds from 74 to 95 MPH and other descriptors also apply, such as damage to unanchored mobile homes. The most severe hurricane is Category 5, with winds of 156 MPH or greater and descriptors such as complete roof failures of many buildings and massive evacuations may be required.

Cell   A cell is multiple terrorists working cooperatively toward achieving a particular goal, such as raising funds, gathering intelligence, or executing an attack. Alternatively, a cell may not be specialized and all of these functions may be performed within a single cell.

Center for Domestic Preparedness (CDP)   The primary training facilities in Anniston, Alabama, operated by FEMA to train members of federal, state, and local agencies on all aspects of domestic preparedness; focuses on response training during WMD and CBRNE events.

Center of gravity   The primary source of strength, power, and resistance for a nation or organization and that of an adversary.

Chain of command   The chain of command is a clear and unbroken line of authority and responsibility from the top to the bottom of the organization, which makes it possible to establish accountability.

Christian Identity Movement   The CI movement in its most extreme form postulates that the Jews were not God's chosen people, but instead are the spawn of the devil, the mating of Eve and the Serpent in the Garden. Different strands of CI believe it is wrong to mix with other races, interracial marriage is a sin, the Jews are the natural enemies of the Aryan race, racial treason is the greatest crime, and homosexuality should be punished by death. See Counterfeit Christians.

Civilian Conservation Corps   A federal program during the 1930s that employed young men in a military-style manner to plant trees and build parks, canals, and other recreational sites throughout America's forests and governmental land.

Collapsed state   The most extreme example of a failed state. See Ungoverned space and safe haven.

Colonialism   A practice of domination, involving political and economic control of a territory.

Command and control cells   C2 cells make all of the final decisions about the execution of an attack and other matters pertaining to the activities of a cell.

Communism   The ideal utopian state as proposed by Karl Marx, characterized by the total elimination of privately held property and government.

Compartmentalized information   Information to which access is restricted to those with a need to know.

Consequence management   Developing, coordinating, and managing mitigation after an emergency event.

Constitutional monarchies   A form of government commonly observed in the Middle East when a country has a ruling family or kingdom versus a democratically elected republic or dictatorship.

Contras   Nicaraguan counter revolutionary group battling the Sandinistas for control of the country (see Sandinistas).

Counterfeit Christians   Sometimes used to refer to Christian Identity adherents.

Counterintelligence (CI)   Activities intended to prevent adversaries from acquiring accurate information about another organization's capabilities.

Counterterrorism   Offensive actions (usually military or paramilitary) taken to prevent, deter, or respond to terrorist threats or attacks.

Coup d'état   The sudden and quick illegal seizure of a government by a small group of existing governmental people, usually a group from within the existing military.

Covert activity   An action of the U.S. government intended to influence politics, economic, or military conditions abroad, where it is intended that the role of the government will not be apparent or acknowledged publicly.

Crisis management   Developing, coordinating, and managing an effective response to a major emergency event.

Critical infrastructure   Those systems and assets, whether physical or virtual, so vital to the United States that the incapacity or destruction of such systems and assets would have a debilitating impact on national security.

Culture   Culture is the shared beliefs, experiences, and behaviors, such as language, values, customs, history, law, and religion, that cause its members to substantially interpret things in a similar manner and distinguish them from other cultures.

Cyberterrorism (or digital terrorism)   The premeditated, politically, or ideologically motivated attack against information networks, computer systems, computer programs, and/or data that can result in violence against civilian targets.

DHS Inspector General (IG)   The DHS IG was created by Congress to ensure integrity and efficiency in the DHS. The office conducts or supervises studies and research to improve DHS administration and operations.

Daesh   The Arabic acronym for the Islamic State comes from the root of the ISIS-ISIL inconsistency in the Arabic work "al-Sham," meaning "the Levant" or the "Greater Syria." Hence, the acronym is short for al-Dawla al Islamiya al Iraq al Sham.

Data fusion   The exchange of information from different sources, with analysis, that results in meaningful and actionable intelligence.

David Koresh   Leader of the Branch Davidians. Died at their compound in Waco, Texas.

De-Baathafication   A term used to signify the elimination and subsequent banning of all members of the Ba'ath Party of Saddam Hussein from future Iraqi politics after the Second Gulf War (2003).

Dead drop   A dead drop is a secret place where one courier hides documents, often encrypted, for the next courier to pick up.

Deep web   A secret part of the World Wide Web, not accessible through regular Internet browsing or search engines; accessible from dynamic websites requiring the use of an application program called Tor that allows encrypted conversations.

Delta Force   "Delta Force" has used a variety of names, including 1st Special Forces Operational Detachment-D (1st SFOD-D), Combat Applications Group (CAG), and Army Compartmentalized Elements (ACE). It is believed there are five active duty Special Forces Groups and two National Guard Groups. The strength of each Group is in its four battalions. The number of people in an SF battalion is classified. Each SF Group has limited counterterrorism mission and capability.

Desaparecidos   From roughly the early 1970s to the early 1980s, a military junta (group) ruled Argentina. The junta labeled anyone who opposed them as communists or subversives. When the junta came to power, it had a "kill list" of perhaps 30,000 people who were abducted and placed in concentration camps. Most often they were killed. Their bodies were thrown from aircraft into the ocean or other large bodies of water and the deceased were never found. Therefore, they were called the disappeared. Children born to women in the camps were given to families the junta thought were "reliable." Children were also abducted for the same purpose.

Detainer   An immigration detainer or "hold" is a request sent to local and state jails to keep a person of interest in custody 48 hours beyond the time they would otherwise be released. This gives ICE time to investigate the subject's immigration status and assume custody if appropriate. Amnesty jurisdictions do not honor such requests.

Diaspora   The scattering or dispersion of people from their native homeland, often to a different, smaller, or less desirable geographic area.

Dirty bomb   A device or bomb that combines radioactive material with conventional explosives; usually crudely made with the purpose of contaminating a specific area.

Disaster   A "disaster" is more severe than an emergency because it causes a serious disruption of the functioning of an entity, such as a community, and produces widespread human, material, economic, and/or environmental losses that exceed the ability of a community to cope with it using just its own resources.

Domestic terrorism   As provided by federal law, domestic terrorism involves violations of federal or state law that appear to intimidate or coerce a civilian population or affect the policy of a government by intimidation or coercion, or affect the conduct of a government by mass destruction, assassination, or kidnapping and occur primarily with the territorial jurisdiction of the United States. See the federal legal definition in Table 1–1.

Dr. William Luther Pierce   As Andrew MacDonald authored *The Turner Diaries,* still considered one of the right wing's most influential publications. He also wrote *Hunter,* which did not receive nearly the acclaim that *The Turner Diaries* did.

Drones   Unmanned aircraft that can navigate autonomously.

Earth Liberation Front (ELF)   ELF's mission is to cause as much economic loss to persons and other entities whose selfish greed and desire for profits result in the destruction of the natural environment and life. By doing so, ELF members and/or sympathizers hope to compel them to discontinue their destructive practices.

Ebola Virus Disease (EVD)   Formerly known as Ebola Hemorrhagic Fever, or just Ebola, is a severe and often fatal disease transmitted to people from the fluids of wild animals; and spreads through the human population via direct contact with the bodily fluids of infected people.

Ecotage   Earth Liberation Front (ELF) corruption of eco (pertaining to the environment) and sabotage; used synonymously with monkey wrenching. See monkey wrenching.

Egalitarian democracy   The political concept that all humans are equal in fundamental political, economic, and social worth; hence, social economic divisions or classes of people as well as centralized power should be diminished.

Electrical power grid   A system of interconnected electrical processes serving regional areas within the United States.

Emergency   A condition of actual danger to the lives of persons and/or the safety of property that requires a response. Emergencies ordinarily are handled locally.

Enemy combatant   A special designation of an individual who has engaged in hostilities against the United States or its coalition partners.

English Defence League   The EDL represents a growing phenomenon in Europe: right-wing groups that are not simply racist, but profoundly hostile toward Islam and their immigration into

Western Europe. The EDL and other anti jihad movements are united in their belief that Islam and Muslims are a fundamental threat to the resources, identities, and survival of Western nations.

Ernesto "Che" Guevara   An iconic, revolutionary figure in Latin America during the 1950s and 60s; he symbolized discontent with capitalism and colonization in the world, and believed that revolution was sparked by those most oppressed in a country—poor farmers living in rural areas.

Eschatology   A part of religion that focuses on the last days, or ultimate destruction, of the world.

Ethnocentric   The belief that one's own culture is superior to all others; often contributes to fear of other people from other cultures.

European Union   The EU is a political and economic union founded in 1993 with 28 member nations that are primarily located in Europe.

Extinction event   An extinction event could result or results in the loss of all human life. In the extreme, there is no effective emergency response to an extinction event.

Extraordinary rendition   The apprehension, detention, and extrajudicial transfer of a person from one country to another, outside the confinements and jurisdiction of the United States.

Failed states   States that cannot govern their own territory. Their governments may be unstable, corrupt, cannot provide basic services, their citizens resent the government, and the government cannot guarantee the security of any weapons of mass destruction in its possession. See Collapsed state and Ungoverned space.

Federal Emergency Management Agency (FEMA)   Originally developed by Presidential Order in 1978 by President Jimmy Carter, FEMA is the primary federal agency responsible for responding to and mitigating a major disaster within the United States.

Force multiplier   A military term that means a capability that when added to, and employed by, a combat unit significantly enhances its combat potential and increases the likelihood of a successful mission.

Foreign Intelligence Surveillance Act of 1978 (FISA)   Passed by Congress in 1978, the law was intended to increase counterintelligence capabilities and established procedures for the judicial authorization of foreign intelligence surveillance and established the Foreign Intelligence Surveillance Court.

Foreign Intelligence Surveillance Court (FISC)   Secret federal court created by the Foreign Intelligence Surveillance Act in 1978. The court authorizes wiretaps and other forms of electronic surveillance and authorizes searches involving suspected terrorists and spies by U.S. intelligence agencies.

Foreign terrorist organization (FTO)   The U.S. Department of State lists an organization as a "foreign terrorist organization" if it engages in terrorist activity or has retained the capacity or intention to do so and it threatens U.S. nationals or America's national security.

Four waves of terrorism   Typology developed by David Rapoport to better understand terrorism: anarchist, anti-colonial, new left, and religious.

Frankenfood   Term developed by anti-genetically modified organism (GMO) groups to describe genetically altered agricultural plants, such as wheat and potatoes.

Fund-raising cells   FRCs almost exclusively commit illegal acts to raise funds for their terrorist organization or to be used in support of a particular attack.

Fundamentalism   A strategy in which beleaguered believers attempt to preserve their distinctive identity as a people or group.

Fusion center   A "clearinghouse" or information "hub" that blends the power of information technology with terrorism prevention and crime fighting.

Gaza Strip   Administered by the Palestinian Authority, 25 miles long and from 3.5 to 7 miles wide. Situated on Eastern Mediterranean, bounded by Egypt to the south and Israel to its east and north.

Genocide   The systematic killing of all or part of a racial, ethnic, religious, or national group within a specific country or area; often linked to totalitarian regimes.

George Habash   A Christian Marxist physician who led the Popular Front for the Liberation of Palestine (PFLP).

George Lincoln Rockwell   Founder of the American Nazi Party who ran for president to change the U.S. Constitution and laws to align with the racist perspectives of the Nazi Party.

Geospatial intelligence (GEOINT)   Intelligence information derived from maps, imagery, charts, and/or satellite data.

German-American Bund   In the 1930s, the GAB emerged in this country as a pro-Nazi movement that sang the praises of Hitler and the Third Reich, encouraged Americans to stay out of the war in Europe, and was anti-Semitic. Its members were largely drawn from German Americans. Unlike the wholesale internment of Japanese-Americans, only a small number of the GAB were incarcerated after it was outlawed.

Gilmore Commission   Congressionally sponsored inquiry after 9/11 to assess the domestic response of federal law enforcement and intelligence agencies against terrorism.

Going postal   The phrase "going postal," means becoming uncontrollably mad. It originated at the Edmond, Oklahoma, Post Office. In 1986, a disgruntled postal worker went on a murderous rampage and then committed suicide.

Gross domestic product (GDP)   The total value of goods and services produced by a nation during one year.

Hacking   The illegal intrusion into a secure data or computer system.

Hacktivists   Single-issue/unique cause extremists who use the Internet to attack hate or other sites and disclose personal information about their members.

Hadith   A collection of the words and deeds of the Prophet Muhammad, his closest companions, and the views of luminary Islamic scholars and religious figures within the Islamic faith.

Hamas   Arabic, "zeal," fundamentalist foreign terrorist organization (FTO) that provides extensive social services. It also has a well-armed militia/paramilitary arm. Opposed to the existence of Israel, Hamas has a strong presence in Palestine and Israel.

Hammerskin Nation   The Hammerskin Nation is a leaderless Dallas-based movement that advocates a "White power skinhead" lifestyle and whose goal is "We must secure the existence of our people and a future for White children." At its earliest, leaderless resistance consisted of one or several people who formed cells to promote white supremacy and resist the oppressive government.

Hardcore leadership   The hardcore leadership of a terrorist movement may have helped to establish the terrorist organization or been promoted multiple times. It has a vision of what the movement wants to achieve, establishes policies, rules of administration and conduct, articulates goals, and approves operations. Finally, it ensures that the targeting and violence support the vision and goals.

Hawala   An Asian-based alternative remittance system that is based on trust and which allows users to remain unknown and escape contact with banking and other officials.

Hazardous Materials (HAZMAT)   Substances (solid, liquid, or gas) that are dangerous to people, other living organisms, or the environment.

Hezbollah   "The Party of God (Allah)"; the largest Shi'a terrorist group in the world, led by Hassan Nasrallah and headquartered in Lebanon.

Hezbollah   Arabic, "Party of Allahu." Fundamentalist Islamic FTO, supported by Iran and Syria, originally Lebanon-based, now present in many other locations.

HAZMAT   Acronym for hazardous and dangerous materials.

Holy or Noble Qur'an   The central book of Islam consisting of 114 chapters developed through the visits of the Archangel Gabriel to the Prophet Muhammad. Simply, the Qur'an or Koran in Western nations.

Homegrown jihadist cell   A group of homegrown jihadists working collectively make up a homegrown jihadist cell.

Homegrown jihadist   A homegrown terrorist is a self-directed citizen or legal resident who attacks his/her country using radicalized Islam as the ideological basis for doing so.

Homegrown terrorists   Although it may send encouraging messages, homegrown terrorists have no real support from a terrorist movement. There may be a psychological identification with one, or homegrown terrorists may act on their own special interests, for example, "government spying" or protecting the whales.

Homegrown violent extremist (HVE)   A person of any citizenship who mostly lives in the United States and who commits terrorist activity to advance an ideology when that person is influenced by a foreign terrorist organization (FTO), but acts alone.

Homeland Security Data Network (HSDN)   A classified information network that allows the federal government to move information and intelligence to state and local jurisdictions at the "secret" level.

Homophobic   Describes a range of negative attitudes and feelings toward people who are gay, lesbian, bisexual, transgender, or queer (GLBTQ).

Hubs   In terrorist network language, "hubs" are "chiefs," from local operational commanders to ideological leaders. The lines between nodes in a cell are called links or edges and represent a communication channel.

Hunter   See Dr. William L. Pierce.

Imam   Local spiritual leader of the Islamic faith, similar to a priest, rabbi, or pastor in other religions.

Incident commander   The most senior commander first arriving at the scene of an incident from a specific first responder agency, such as from police, fire, or emergency services.

Individual perspective   A particular way of thinking about something, reduced to a simple image: On which side of the street do you stand?

Information warfare (IW)   The concept of using information technology to gain tactical or strategic advantage over an opponent.

Insurgency   A type of irregular warfare characterized by subversion, armed conflict, and occasional terrorism to overthrow the legally constituted government of a country.

Intel cells   ICs collect data, make recommendations, may select targets, and provide information about the best routes for ingressing to and egressing from targets.

Intel-driven organization   An organization that combines investigation and intelligence operations to be more predictive and preventative in nature.

Intelligence community (IC)   Sixteen federal agencies representing various governmental groups reporting to the Office of the Director of National Intelligence.

Intelligence-led policing (ILP)   A new style of policing that integrates intelligence, with an emphasis on predictive analysis derived from the discovery of hard facts, information, patterns, and traditional crime analysis.

Intelligence   An information process and product derived from systematic and thoughtful examination (analysis).

International terrorism   As provided for by federal law, international terrorism involves violent acts or acts dangerous to human life that violate federal or state laws if committed within the jurisdiction of the United States or any state, which appear to be intended to intimidate or coerce a civilian population, influence the policy of government by mass destruction, assassination, or kidnapping, and occur primarily outside of the territorial jurisdiction of the United States or transcend national boundaries by the means by which they are accomplished, the persons they appear to intimidate or coerce, or the locale in which the perpetrators operate or seek asylum. See the federal definition in Table 1–1.

Internet Service Providers (ISPs)   An organization or private corporation that provides services for accessing, using, or participating on the Internet (e.g., AOL, NetZero, Comcast, Microsoft Network, EarthLink, Verizon, Google Prodigy, Sprint, and local telephone companies).

Iran-Contra Affair   Reports of human rights violations/atrocities by the Contras caused Congress to prohibit further U.S. funding for them. To secure the release of hostages taken during Iran's 1979 Islamic Revolution, American illegally sold them arms. The profits were then secretly used to fund the Contras. This became known as the "Iran-Contra Affair" and brought significant Congressional criticism of President Reagan's administration.

Irish Republican Army   Ireland's military arm during the Anglo-Irish War of 1919–1921.

Islam   The religion of Muslims, referred to earlier in history as Moslems, who believe there is no God but Allah and Muhammad is his prophet. It is Allah that founded Islam through Muhammad. Islam's religious book is the Qur'an (Anglicized as the Koran).

Islamaphobic   An unfounded hostility toward Muslims resulting in a fear or dislike of all or most Muslims. Coined in 1991, the term was developed in the context of Muslims in the United Kingdom in particular and Europe in general.

Islamic State   A terrorist organization and movement that has evolved to become a major international threat in 2014. Previously known as the Islamic State in Syria (ISIS) and the Islamic State in the Levant (ISIL). IS is an evolution of radical Islamic thought beginning with al Qaeda in Iraq (AQI) and al-Qaeda in the Arabian Peninsula (AQAP); both groups are presently in conflict against coalition forces in Iraq as well as Syria.

Islamic State   The primary radical Islamic movement active in Iraq, Syria, and the rest of the Middle East; claims to be the new Islamic Caliphate in the world today. Previous names associated with this movement have been al-Qaeda in Iraq (AQI), Islamic State is Iraq and Syria (ISIS) and Islamic State in Iraq and the Levant (ISIL). Also known as its Arabic language acronym, Daesh.

Islamic: of, or pertaining to Islam   Practices or persons that adhere to the beliefs of Islam. See Islam.

Israeli Mossad   The intelligence and secret service unit of the country of Israel; responsible for carrying out extensive covert operations throughout the Middle East and the rest of the world.

Jabat Fatah al Sham (JFS)   Al-Nusra was created by al-Qaeda in Iraq (AQI) and sent to Syria in support of President Bashar al-Assad's government. With on-going fighting there AQI thought some advantage might be gained from doing so. In 2016, al Nusra, now renamed as Jabhat Fateh al-Sham (The Front for the Conquest of the Levant), separated from al Qaeda and also remains separate from IS.

James Earl Ray   He assassinated civil rights champion Reverend Martin Luther King in Memphis, Tennessee, in 1968.

Japanese-American internment camps   At the outbreak of World War II, Japanese-Americans were placed in internment camps for "national security." Some volunteered to serve in the 442nd Regimental Combat Team to demonstrate their loyalty. In 1988, the Congress recognized the "grave injustice" done to those interred and awarded each surviving camp member $20,000; each reparation paid was accompanied by a letter of apology from President Reagan.

Jihad   Derived from the Holy Qur'an, the word jihad represents an internal struggle to overcome adversity and difficulty in submitting to the will of Allah (God). Perverted historically by Islamic fundamentalists to mean "holy war."

Jihadist Salafism   The ideology of al-Qaeda; a second generation of Islamic Salafism that justifies violence and revolution as the means to an end.

Joint Special Operations Command (JSOC)   In addition to the responsibilities already mentioned, JSOC is one of the five components reporting to SOCOM. As a joint command, JSOC has a number or units under its "umbrella," such as Seal Team 6, Delta Force, 24th Special Tactics Squadron, and the Intelligence Support Activity.

Joint Terrorism Task Forces (JTTFs)   A group of highly trained federal, state, and local law enforcement officers and agents focusing on terrorism-related intelligence and investigations.

Kaaba   According to Islam, the altar of Abraham (built by Abraham and his son Ishmael) and the focus of Hajj, or the pilgrimage to Mecca.

Khmer Rouge   "Red Cambodians," communists who came to power by overthrowing the existing government. See Zero year.

Khomeinism   A Shi'a ideology that embraces Islamic worldwide revolution as well as Islamic unity and strict adherence to Sharia; based on the teachings of Ayatollah Ruhollah Khomeini.

Klaverns   Local chapters of the KKK.

Kurdistan Workers Party (PKK)   An ethnic Kurdish terrorist organization fighting to create a homeland for ethnic Kurds in Northern Iraq and Southeastern Turkey; responsible for significant deaths of Turkish civilians (over 20,000) during the past two decades.

Kurds   A Middle East ethnic minority that does not have a homeland. Kurds live in parts of Iraq, Turkey, Syria, and Iran.

Leaderless resistance cell   This type of cell is characterized by no leaders and equality of members who share the leadership functions.

Left-wing   A political designation that encompasses ideologies more radical in nature, including anarchism and Marxism.

Levees and dams   Dikes, embankments, or walls specifically constructed to regulate water.

Links or edges   In terrorist network language, the lines between nodes in a cell are called links or edges and represent a communication channel between nodes and/or hubs.

Logistics cells   LCs provide supplies and various types of support to other cells.

Lone wolf attack   A violent attack by a single perpetrator, acting alone, without any direction or assistance from an organization or another person.

Low intensity conflict   A level of military action that falls short of a full-scale conventional war; includes peacekeeping, anti-terrorism programs, assistance to foreign militaries and police organizations, fulfillment of international treaty obligations, as well as subversive and counter terrorism actions.

Mandate system   The system of colonization after World War I dividing areas in the Middle East, primarily between Great Britain, France, and Italy.

Manifest Destiny   In 1845, as Americans pushed westward, newspaper editor John O'Sullivan coined the term "manifest destiny," meaning the United States had a divine obligation to push its boundaries everforward. At the heart of manifest destiny was the pervasive belief in American cultural and racial superiority.

Marxism   The economic and sociological theories of Karl Marx and Friedrich Engels that encompassed a revolutionary view of social change.

Material support   Defined by the PATRIOT Act as "training," "expert advice or assistance," "service," and "personnel" given to terrorist organizations.

Mecca   The holiest city in the religion of Islam, located in southwest Saudi Arabia near the Red Sea. The birthplace of the Prophet Muhammad and the focus of the Hajj or Pilgrimage to Mecca.

Metadata   Data that describes other data; for example, telephone metadata records the number called, what time the call was made, and how long it lasted.

Metrics   Standard measures taken periodically to determine the level of performance in a given field. For instance, a metric used during the Vietnam War was enemy body count. Terrorism metrics can be an indication of how we are doing in the global war on terrorism if carefully selected, defined, and measured.

Michael Collins   Commander of the Irish Republican Army (IRA) and advocate of selective terrorism.

Military Commissions Act of 2006 (MCA)   An act of Congress signed by President George W. Bush in 2006 to authorize trial by military commission for violations of the law of war and for other purposes. It prohibited detainees who had been classified as enemy combatants or were awaiting hearings on their status from using "Habeas corpus" to petition federal courts in challenges to their detention.

Military junta   A government led by a group or committee of military leaders in a specific country; a military dictatorship.

Mitigation   An effort to reduce loss of life and property by lessening the impact of a terrorist attack or natural disaster.

Modernity   An epoch of time, usually referring to post-traditional and post-agrarian (feudal) states toward capitalism, industrialization, secularization, and technological innovation.

Monkey wrenching   Earth Liberation Front (ELF) term for economic sabotage. Involves acts of destruction and obstruction. See ecotage.

Monotheistic   The belief in one God expressed by three major religions in the world: Judaism, Christianity, and Islam.

Mosque   A holy place of worship in Islam.

Muhammad   Born in 570 A.D. in Mecca, the Prophet Muhammad was believed to be the final messenger of God and the founder of the Islam religion.

Muslim Brotherhood (MB)   An Islamic fundamental movement stemming from the writings of the radical Islamic scholars Hassan al-Banna and Sayyid Qutb in twentieth-century Egypt. See Chapter 4.

Muslim Brotherhood   An Islamic fundamental movement stemming from the writings of Hassan al-Banna and Sayyid Qutb in twentieth century Egypt.

Muslim   From the Arabic root word for Islam, literally one who submits to the will of God; westernized to "Moslem" or "Muslim."

Muslim   One who adheres to the Islamic faith. See Islamic.

Mutual aid agreement   Mutual aid agreements are agreements between agencies, organizations, and jurisdictions that provide a mechanism to quickly obtain emergency assistance in the form of personnel, equipment, materials, and other associated services. The primary objective is to facilitate rapid, short-term deployment of emergency support prior to, during, and after an incident.

Mutual aid societies   Developed in America during the 1800s and were often faith, country of origin, or ethnicity based. They had several purposes, such as preserving cultural heritage and helping immigrants newly arrived in America to adjust.

Mutually assured destruction (MAD)   A military doctrine prevalent during the Cold War between the United States and the former Soviet Union, postulating that an all-out nuclear war would effectively destroy both entities (the attacker and the defender).

National Clandestine Service   The operational wing of the CIA that carries out covert paramilitary operations against terrorist groups and cells outside the United States.

National Criminal Intelligence Sharing Plan (NCISP)   A national effort that combines public partnerships with problem-solving tactics aimed at enhancing police efficiency in preventing terrorist attacks through effective communication and coordination.

National Fusion Center Association (NFCA)   A formal group that represents the interests of state and major urban area fusion centers nationally.

National Incident Management System (NIMS)   The comprehensive, nationwide systematic approach to incident management adopted by FEMA to manage and standardize responses to critical incidents and/or disasters.

National Infrastructure Protection Plan (NIPP)   A formal directive that defines critical infrastructure within the United States and identifies 16 critical infrastructure sectors for protection against man-made (e.g., bombing, terrorist strike, information warfare) as well as natural (e.g., hurricane, flood, tornado, earthquake) disasters.

National Intelligence Program (NIP)   The primary funding budget for the strengthening the nation's intelligence agencies.

National Preparedness Goal   Released in September 2011, the National Preparedness Goal defined national preparedness as: "A secure and resilient nation with the capabilities required across the whole community to prevent, protect against, mitigate, respond to, and recover from the threats and hazards that pose the greatest risk."

National Security Act of 1947   The Act reorganized the military and foreign policy elements of the federal government, including the creation of the Central Intelligence Agency (CIA). Illustratively, it also combined the War and Navy departments into the Department of Defense.

National Socialist Movement (NSM)   Formed in 1974. Roots in the American Nazi Party. Self-billed as the "premier while civil rights organization."

Nativism   The right wing rests on nativism, the ultra preference for the traditional culture of a homeland to the exclusion of immigrants and their alien ways, as well as opposition to foreign ideas and influences. Nativism also rejects those in the homeland who champion immigrants, "alien" ways, and nontraditional ways of looking at the world.

Network models   Network models include the chain, hub or star, spoke or wheel, and all channel structures.

New left wave   Concluded that terrorism was the way to reform governments.

New terrorism   Most commonly, a religious belief undergirds the violence. New terrorism is more transnational than the old and, unlike the old, it deliberately targets civilians/non-combatants to create fear. Many groups are autonomous or loosely affiliated with another group. Inspires lone wolf attacks. The new terrorism is nimble, quick to learn, technologically savvy, and operationally competent.

Nisaab   Arabic for "portion," the threshold after which a person is obliged to pay zakat; varies throughout the Middle East.

Nodes   In terrorist network language, "nodes" are more expendable members, such as fighters, whose loss is less critical to the terrorist movement.

Office of the Director of National Intelligence (ODNI)   The national office created to centralize all intelligence information functions from all federal, state, and local agencies.

Old terrorism   Generally, it had specific political, social, and economic goals. Because the goals were limited, some could ultimately be resolved by negotiation.

Omar Hammami   An American who went to Somalia and joined the clan-based Islamic terrorist movement al-Shabaab, which later killed him. Because Hammami was murdered by the movement he joined, Americans aspiring to be part of a foreign terrorist organization may have second thoughts about doing so.

Operation Eagle Claw   Failed U.S. military attempt to rescue hostages held by Iran in 1980.

Operational security   A process to deny potential adversaries information about capabilities and/or intentions by identifying, controlling, and protecting unclassified information that gives evidence of the planning and execution of sensitive activities, such as future operations (OPSEC).

Operational space   This term means having a sanctuary or safe haven where attacks can be safely planned, trained for, and rehearsed.

Oslo Accords   In 1993, the negotiation of a bilateral peace agreement between the Palestinian Liberation Organization (PLO) represented by Yassir Arafat and Israel represented by Prime Minister Yitzhak Rabin, moderated by President Bill Clinton.

Palestinian Islamic Jihad (PIJ)   One of the early terrorist groups to adopt a radical Islamic ideology that justified violence and suicide bombing as a means to liberate Palestine.

Palestinian Islamic Resistance Movement (Hamas)   The largest and most politically powerful group expressing radical Islamic ideologies to justify the liberation of Palestine and the destruction of Israel.

Palestinians   People of Arab descent tracing their cultural heritage to an area known as Palestine, now occupied by the country of Israel.

Pan Am Flight 103   Blown up in 1988 by a Libyan intelligence officer killing 259 people on board, as well as some people on the ground in Scotland, over which the plane exploded. Believed to have been ordered by Libya's dictator Muammar Gaddafi in retaliation for the United States bombing his country in 1986.

Pandemic   An epidemic of an infectious disease that involves a large area, usually crossing international boundaries and involving multiple continents.

Parsley Massacre   In 1937, Dominican Republic dictator Trujillo ordered the military to kill all people immediately who could not pronounce the Spanish word for parsley with the proper Spanish trill on the "r," on the suspicion they were Haitians who had illegally entered the country.

Passive supporters   These types of supporters are sympathetic to the goals of the terrorist organization, but not committed enough to take an active role. They may assist a front for the terrorist organization and not be fully aware of their relationship to the terrorist organization.

Pen register   Provides law enforcement agency access to the numbers dialed from a subject's phone.

Personal protection equipment (PPE)   Used by first responders to protect them against CBRNE agents.

Pierre-Joseph Proudhon   French philosopher who was the first person to declare himself an anarchist; instrumental in sparking French revolutionary activities in 1848.

Point of Entry (POE)   A specific location where one may lawfully enter the United States; typically where passports and visa are inspected (e.g., international airports, seaports).

Political ideology   The set of beliefs about the proper order of society and how that order can be achieved.

Political terrorism   A symbolic act designed to influence political behavior based on extranormal means, entailing the use or threat of violence.

Posse Comitatus   The Latin phrase translates to the "power of the county." It refers to a right-wing movement that opposes the federal government and holds that local authority trumps federal authority. It was founded by William Potter Gale in 1970, but did not gain momentum until he incorporated Christian Identity (CI). The group was substantially defunct by 1990, several years after Gale's death.

Posse comitatus   Common law term meaning literally "power of the county"; refers to the military's role in enforcing state or civilian law.

Post-Traumatic Stress Disorder   Classically, some people involved in a terrifying, life-threatening event develop the anxiety disorder PTSD. They may relive the event frequently, have angry outbursts, dramatic bad dreams and frightening thoughts, be easily startled, or constantly seem "on edge."

Preemptive military action   Striking a target in advance of a reasonably anticipated attack to circumvent its occurrence and to avoid suffering its effects.

"Prepper"   Slang word to describe those individuals who are preparing for major apocalyptic events in the future.

Principle of hierarchy   This principle dictates that each lower organizational unit is under the direct control and supervision of a superior organizational unit. This produces a pyramid-shaped form.

Proletariat   A Marxist concept that describes the working class, peasants, or oppressed people.

Propaganda by the deed   An ideology that advocates acts of violence as a principal means of revolution.

Provisional Irish Republican Army (PIRA)   The Provisional Irish Republican Army was the first and primary movement in Ireland to use terrorism as a means to justify its revolt against Great Britain and gain world status as a separate nation (Ireland). The group officially ended its campaign against Great Britain for a unified and separate Ireland in 2005, and now continues in political dialogue for the same goal.

Radicalization   The processing of acquiring and holding extremist beliefs. See violent extremism.

Real Irish Republican Army (RIRA)   The Real Irish Republican Army in Northern Ireland uses terrorist tactics to support its ideology of a unified Ireland; RIRA is a successor to the original PIRA.

Red Laces   Worn in the boots of skinheads, they denote the wearer has shed blood for the skinhead movement.

Redundant leader protocol   If the leader of a cell is captured, killed, or otherwise not available, a designated member of the cell will assume the leadership role.

Reign of Terror   Particularly violent period during the French Revolution (1793–1794) when the guillotine was used to behead over 16,000 people including Robespierre. See Robespierre.

Religious Wave   Began in 1979 with Iran's Islamic Revolution and continues.

Rendition   Rendition is the "handing over" or transfer of a person from one legal jurisdiction to another. Some apprehended terrorists have immediately been handed over to foreign countries to be able to use more harsh interrogation methods. Captured terrorists were placed on planes in the countries in which they were captured and taken to friendly countries where they could be interrogated using methods beyond those allowed by both U.S. military and Constitutional guidelines.

Ricin   An easily made and highly toxic poison refined from castor beans.

Robespierre   A Frenchman and key architect of the reign of terror. He believed terror was the speedy, severe, and inflexible administration of justice from which virtue flowed. Seemingly, terror and virtue became synonymous to him.

Ruby Ridge (Idaho)   Federal agents went to Randy Weaver's rural home to arrest him on weapons charges. A standoff ensued and eventually gunfire was exchanged, killing Weaver's wife and son. The incident added fuel to the patriot, militia, and right-wing movements.

Sabri al-Banna   A highly entrepreneurial revolutionary and mercenary who headed the Abu Nidal Organization (ANO).

Safe havens   A place or situation that allows terrorists and other types of criminals to operate with relative impunity because the state is unable or lacks the political will to expel them.

Safe havens   Places or situations that allow illicit actors, including criminals, smugglers, and terrorists, to operate with relative impunity.

Salafism   A broad intellectual movement spawned by the writings of Egyptian scholars such as Muhammad Abdul, Jamal al-Afghani, and Rashid Rida, focusing on the adoption of modernity and technology within Islam; soon became corrupted and blended with Wahhabism.

Sandinistas   Left-wing revolutionary group that overthrew the government of Nicaragua in 1979.

Sarin   A man-made chemical gas that is extremely poisonous; used in a terrorist attack by the Aum Shinrikyo group in the subways of Tokyo, Japan, in 1995.

Search Warrant   Legal document that authorizes police to search a specific area for a specific person or item of interest. Must be based on probable cause and signed by a judge.

Secondary bombs   Hidden bombs often set by terrorists targeting first responders to an emergency event.

Secular   Separation of church (religion) and state or government.

Secularism   The separation of church and state; the form of government where persons mandated to represent the state are not members of religious institutions nor are religious dignitaries.

Selective terrorism   Tactic advocated by Michael Collins, Commander of the Irish Republian Army (IRA). Instead of using unfocused, indiscriminate violence that killed many people, Collins used selective violence to focus on the people and institutions that supported continued British subjugation of Ireland. See Michael Collins and Irish Republican Army.

Self-reliant   In our colonial era, there was already an ingrained belief that people should be self-reliant and responsible for their own lot in life. A corollary of this tradition was that if people were given too much help it would ultimately make them dependent.

Shahid   A Muslim "martyr" who dies in defense of their faith; often inappropriately associated with those who conduct suicide bombings. Originates from the Qur'anic Arabic word for "witness."

Sharia   Islamic law; the moral and religious code of Islam as prescribed by the Prophet Muhammad.

Shi'a or Shiite   One of the two primary Muslim traditions stemming from the "Shi'at Ali" or "The Party of Ali." Followers of the Shi'a tradition believe that Ali was given a divine right of successorship to lead the Muslim community after the death of the Prophet Muhammad.

Single-issue/special-issue extremists   As a rule of thumb, typically attack property as opposed to persons. Most common form of violent political extremism in the United States. May be members of, or loosely affiliated with, extreme group, may never have contacted group, but has an affinity for it, may have their own unique cause. Typically espouse a single issue or narrow range of issues.

Skinbyrd   A female skinhead.

Skinhead   A member of or affiliated with the white power or white nationalist movement commonly called the Hammerskin Nation.

Skinhead   A white supremacist group that originated in London, England, among working class youths in the 1960s. Eventually becoming associated with a much larger subculture named for their shaved or close-cropped heads, military-style clothing, including Nazi-type "jack" boots and hard rock, punk-style music. Often heavily tattooed.

Skyjacking   The diversion of a commercial airline flight away from its scheduled flight plan, usually by violence or threat of violence against passengers and/or crew.

Slave patrols   The first formal racist organization in America.

Sleeper cells   Members of sleeper cells lead normal lives and call no attention to themselves. The jobs they select may facilitate future terrorist activities. Illustratively, a taxi driver will learn a great deal about a city's geography and can identify potential targets and move terrorists around. A sleeper cell may receive a signal that "awakens" it for a specific purpose, such as sabotage or an assassination.

Socialism   A Marxist perspective of a transitory and revolutionary period between capitalism and communism wherein the ruling class is "purged" from the land, all people are equal, and the government owns everything; the period is marked by violence and terrorism.

Soft target   A military term to describe a non-defended or innocent target—usually refers to innocent civilians; versus a hard target that represents armed soldiers, operators, or well-defended locations.

Sovereign Citizen movement   Anti-government extremists who believe they are separate or sovereign from the federal government. Referring to themselves as freemen, or free patriots, the people associated with this movement do not pay taxes or recognize any federal or state authority, including the courts, motor vehicle departments, or law enforcement agencies.

Speakeasies   Unlicensed bars operating during the prohibition era gained the name of speakeasies because patrons desiring to enter were allegedly told to knock and softly say (speak easy) the password.

State terrorism   Terrorism committed by a national government, inside of its national borders and directed at its own citizens and sometimes visitors.

State-enabled terrorism   A state that tolerates the presence of terrorists in the country so long as they only attack other states and citizens of other states.

State-perpetrated/state international terrorism   A state uses its own internal security forces to commit acts of terrorism in another country to promote its own international policy objectives.

State-sponsored terrorism   A relatively recent development. States use terrorist groups as proxies to further their agenda in international affairs.

Sunni   The "True Path of Allah" and the largest of the two primary Muslim traditions within Islam.

Sykes-Picot Agreement of 1916   An agreement between Great Britain and France as to the development of colonies resulting from the impending collapse of the Ottoman Empire after World War I.

System disruption   System disruption attacks are called the New War. Instead of concentrating on attacks that produce mass casualties, system disruption attacks focus on the systems that are essential to our daily lives, such as mass transit, electrical grids, and water.

Tactical operations cells   TAC-OPS cells execute attacks under the guidance of C2 cells.

Taliban   Pashto, "student." The Taliban largely consists of members of the Pashtun tribes occupying parts of the border between Afghanistan and Pakistan. It is a fundamental-

ist Islamic movement that insists on strict enforcement of Sharia law.

Taqiyya   Taqiyya absolves Islamic fighters from religious condemnation for shaving off their required beards, not praying five times a day, and adopting a Western lifestyle as part of OPSEC.

Tawhid   The Islamic concept of the oneness of God (Allah). There is but one God (Allah).

Taxonomies   Categories that are formed by empirically studying observable and measureable characteristics.

Terrorism (General/Working definition)   The deliberate and unlawful use of threats or actual violence to inculcate fear, intended to intimidate or coerce individuals, groups, or governments to change their political, social, or religious basis.

Texas Rangers   In 1823, when Texas was still part of Mexico, Stephen Austin gained permission to employ ten men to range over the territory and scout for Indian threats. These men were the first of the Texas Rangers.

The Revolutionary Armed Forces of Colombia People's Army (FARC)   FARC has waged an insurgency against Colombia's national government for over 50 years. Growing out of the communist party, it has socialist ideas. In late 2016, FARC and the national government signed a treaty that presumably ended the hostilities.

The Turner Diaries   See Dr. William L. Pierce.

Theodore Kaczynski   Nicknamed the "Unabomber," Kaczynski was a mathematician and murderer who carried out a nationwide bombing campaign against people associated with industrialization and modern technology in the United States. Most of his bombs were crude, homemade bombs that were mailed to his victims.

Tonton Macoute   A long-standing private force answering only to the president of Haiti. Hacked and shot to death opposition leaders and reformists in extra-judicial executions.

Tor network   Synonymous for the deep web; see deep web. Acronym for a previous software program that allows complete anonymity on the web, called, The Onion Router.

Trap and trace   Provides law enforcement agency access to incoming numbers on a subject's phone.

Typologies   Rationally group related concepts and other things into categories.

U.S. Government Accountability Office   The U.S. "Government" Accountability Office (GAO) is an independent, nonpartisan agency that works for Congress. Often called the "Congressional watchdog," the GAO investigates matters of concern to the Congress.

U.S. Northern Command (NORTHCOM)   Directs the U.S. Department of Defense's homeland security efforts and the planning, organizing, and execution of military support to civil authorities during emergencies, disasters, and/or terrorist attacks.

U.S. Special Operations Command (USSOCOM or SOCOM) The organization responsible for many counterterrorism actions by the military.

USA PATRIOT Act   Act of Congress that was signed into law by President George W. Bush on October 26, 2001. The title stands for Uniting and Strengthening America by Providing Appropriate Tools Required to Intercept and Obstruct Terrorism Act.

USS Cole   Successfully attacked in 2000 by al-Qaeda in the Port of Aden, Yemen, by a suicide "bomber" piloting a launch loaded with explosives.

Ummah   The worldwide community of the Islamic faithful.

Unabomber   See Theodore Kaczynski

Ungoverned space   A government that cannot control its borders usually ends with space it cannot govern, "ungoverned space." The term also includes space that is ungoverned, under-governed, and where governance is contested. See Failed state and Collapsed state.

Unified command   The primary command organization for the Incident Command System in the field; incident commanders from different agencies combine to form a single unified command structure.

Uniform Code of Military Justice (UCMJ)   The UCMJ was established by the Congress and is the basis for military law in the United States.

Usama bin Laden   Saudi Arabian-born American ally who supported Afghanistan mujahedeen's resistance against the Soviets. When the Soviets left, he turned against the Americans and masterminded the 9/11 attacks. Head of al-Qaeda until his death in a 2011 raid on his compound in Pakistan by U.S. troops (Seal Team 6).

Vanguard   A concept that advocates a method of arousing a level of political consciousness among proletariats in order to foster the belief among them that revolution and any changes it brings are far preferable to the status quo.

Violent extremism   Violent action taken on the basis of extremist beliefs.

Virtual terrorist organization   A virtual terrorist organization exists in cyberspace. Its members can be dispersed geographically, but work together exploiting information technology to achieve their common goals by sharing their skills and knowledge collaboratively.

Wade Page   Failed in the Army, where some believe he may have become a white supremacist neo-Nazi, and later played in a band that spouted lyrics of hatred. He may have attacked the Sikhs thinking they were Muslims or because they were simply what he called "dirt people."

Wadi Haddad   A Christian Marxist physician who directed the military and guerrilla actions of the Popular Front for the Liberation of Palestine (PFLP); credited for developing the modern-day hijacking of airliners as a methodology and tactic of terrorism.

Wahhabism   A fundamentalist interpretation of Islam stemming from the teachings of Ibn al-Wahhab in the late 1700s; widely adopted throughout the Arabian Peninsula expressing the radicalization of Islam and the alternative meaning of "jihad" as "holy war" against those that do not accept strict adherence to Sharia.

Weapons of mass destruction (WMD)   Weapons designed to cause significant devastation to a population; involves the release of a CBRNE agent.

Weapons of mass destruction   There are at least 50 official definitions of WMDs in the United States and other national governments, as well as international organizations such as the United Nations. A common thread in these definitions approximates the following: WMDs are nuclear, biological, chemical, radiological, and high explosive weapons capable of producing major destruction, mass casualties, and/or significant infrastructure damage.

Weather Underground   Originally called the Weathermen, this group broke away from the Students for a Democratic Society (SDS) in the late 1960s. It issued a "state of war" against the United States and was strongly opposed to the war in Vietnam, calling it an example of American imperialism in Southeast Asia. The group committed bombings of government buildings and banks; however, it was not responsible for anyone's death. The group disbanded in 1977.

"Whole community"   A concept within the National Preparedness Goal referring to all federal, state, and local government agencies, as well as the nongovernmental organizations, private sector, schools, families, and individuals focused on national preparedness.

WikiLeaks   A nonprofit international organization dedicated to publishing classified documents in the name of transparency.

Wiretaps   Surreptitious eavesdropping on a third-party conversation by wire, oral, or electronic communication.

Wolf pack   A group of lone wolves that form a cell are sometimes called a "wolf pack."

Works Progress Administration (WPA)   An ancillary organization to the Civilian Conservation Corps during the 1930s; employed over 8.5 million people involved in building bridges, public buildings, and airports throughout the country.

Xenophobia   An irrational fear, hatred, and hostility toward people who are "different," including not only immigrants but also those with different lifestyles or sexual preferences, and "strange" ideas.

Xenophobic   A person who manifests xenophobia. See xenophobia.

Yasser Arafat   The leader of the al-Fatah Palestinian group and later head of the Palestinian Liberation Organization (PLO).

Zakat   An annual humanitarian giving by Muslims.

Zero year   Pol Pot, leader of the Khmer Rouge, wanted to "turn the clock back" to "zero year." This "required" emptying the cities and returning to an agrarian society. In doing so 1.7 million Cambodians were killed, often beaten to death because they were Catholics or some other religion, businessmen, intellectuals, and others.

Zionist Occupied Government   A right-wing term sometimes used to refer to the U.S. government.

Zionists   People sympathetic to the creation of a Jewish state in the Middle Eastern area of Palestine.

Zoot suit   A men's fashion that moved from the African American jazz movement into Chicano style. The exaggerated style was offensive to World War II American servicemen who saw the style as wasteful and subversive. The result were some violent clashes between the Chicano "zoot suiters" and servicemen.

Index

Note: The letters 'f', 'n' and 't' following locators refer to figures, notes and tables respectively

bin Laden, Usama (UBL), 14, 15
  anti-American sentiments by, 63, 71
  background and profile, 75
  declining support for, 73
  Jihadist Salafism and, 106
  September 11, 2001 and, 69n86
Biological attacks. *See* CBRNE attacks
BitCoin, 171
Black and Tans, 236
Blackouts, 341
Black Panther Party, 10–11, 231
Black September Organization (BSO),
  60–61, 183, 400
Black Swan events, 7, 11
Bledsoe, Carlos. *See* Muhammad,
  Abdulhakim
Blind pigs, 312
BMG. *See* Baader-Meinhof Group
Boko Haram, 430
Bolshevik Party, 43–44
Border Patrol Officer, 314
Boston Marathon bombing, 345, 427,
  428, 435
Boston Tea Party, 14, 15
Boundless Informant, 288–289
Bourgeoisie, 41
Branch Davidian cult, 82, 92, 229
Breivik, Anders Behring, 432
Bremer, L. Paul, 186
Brown, John, 9
Brownouts, 341
BSO. *See* Black September Organization
Bureau of Intelligence and Research
  (INR), 258
Butler, Richard, 92, 229–230
Byrd, James, Jr., 25

C

C2 cells. *See* Command and control cells
Cadre, 121
Caliph, 78–79
Caliphate, 78–79
Cambodia, 191
Capitalism, 42
Cartels, 171, 315
Carter, Jimmy, 22
Cartoons, 160
Castro, Fidel, 44
Catastrophe incident, 361
Category 4 hurricane, 316
CBIRF. *See* Chemical, Biological,
  Immediate Response Force
CBP. *See* Customs and Border Protection
CBRNE attacks, 371–372
CCC. *See* Civilian Conservation Corps
CCP. *See* Chinese Communist Party
CDC. *See* Centers for Disease Control and
  Prevention
CDP. *See* Center for Domestic
  Preparedness
Cell models, 130–132

Center for Domestic Preparedness
  (CDP), 371
Center of gravity, 137
Centers for Disease Control and
  Prevention (CDC), 372
Central Intelligence Agency (CIA),
  251–253, 251t
  SAD, 402
Chain network, 132f
Chain of command, 133–134
Charismatic leadership, 92–93, 159
Charities, 173–174
Chechnya, 22–23
Chemical attacks. *See* CBRNE attacks
Chemical, Biological, Immediate
  Response Force (CBIRF), 396
Chemical Sector, 343–344
Cherif Kouachi, 430
Chesimard, Joann, 196, 197f
Children
  Amber Alert, 386n85
  recruitment of, 160
  "The Disappeared," 192
Chinese bandit gangs, 123
Chinese Communist Party (CCP), 190
Chinese immigration, 220
Chinese separatists, 233
The Christian Identity Movement, 219,
  229–230
Christianity, 76, 78
  Counterfeit Christians, 223
Christian Patriot Movement (CPM), 214,
  227–229
Church, Frank, 253
CI. *See* Counterintelligence
CIA. *See* Central Intelligence Agency
CI/KRs. *See* Critical Infrastructure and
  Key Resources
CIMS. *See* Communication and
  Information Management
Citizenship, 325–326
Civilian Conservation Corps
  (CCC), 367, 368
Civil Rights Movement, 7
Class struggle, 42–43
Clauset, Aaron, 426
Clinton, Hillary, 288
Cold War, 398
Collapsed states, 194
Collins, Michael, 13, 14
Colonialism, 96
  anti-colonial wave, 182
  Arab resistance and, 52
  Balfour Declaration, 51
  definition of, 50
  French resistance and, 52
  mandate system and, 50–52
  Ottoman Empire and, 50
  Sykes-Picot Agreement, 1916, 50–51
Columbia, 46, 158
Combatting terrorism. *See also*
  Counterterrorism

anti-terrorism, 392–395, 393f
  introduction to, 391
  JSOC, 159, 396, 404
  on license plates, 392
  USSOCOM, 391, 403–404, 403
Command and control (C2) cells,
  131–132, 164
Commercial Facilities Sector, 344
Communication and Information
  Management (CIMS), 374
Communications Sector, 339–341
Communism
  CCP, 190
  definition of, 42
  Vietnam and, 44
Community, 380. *See also* Intelligence
  community
Compartmentalized information, 132
Connor, Jeffrey, 126
Consequence management, 337
Constituencies, 123
Constitutional monarchies, 94
Constitutional rights
  ACLU on, 272
  Bill of Rights, 272, 274
  Fifth Amendment, 277
  First Amendment, 272–274
  Fourth Amendment, 274–277
  material support clause, 272–273
  Sixth Amendment, 277
  USA PATRIOT Act relating to, 272–278
Contras, 198
Control structure, 120
Convergence, 174
Cooper, D. B., 321
Core capability
  capability targets, 362
  and pre-planning, 362
  results, 362
  suicide bombings and, 138
  threats and hazards concern, 362
  threats and hazards context, 362
Counterfeit Christians, 223
Counterfeiting, 173
Counterintelligence (CI), 169
  defining, 248
  NCTC, 250–251, 337
Counterterrorism
  and criminal exploitation unit, 324
  definition of, 391
  foreign organizations in, 410–411
  governmental focus, 3
  metrics, 402
  military action relating to, 397–402
  model, 397f
  NCTC, 250–251, 337
  organizations and activities, 402–409
  overview of, 396–397
  progress evaluation, 437–438
Counter Terrorism Committee (CTC), 3
Counterterrorism Fly Team, 337
Coup d'état, 73